P9-DGP-881

ILLUSTRATED DICTIONARY OF

BIBLE LIFE & TIMES

ILLUSTRATED DICTIONARY OF

BIBLE LIFE & TIMES

The Reader's Digest Association, Inc.
Pleasantville, New York • Montreal

ILLUSTRATED DICTIONARY OF

BIBLE LIFE & TIMES

Address any comments about ILLUSTRATED DICTIONARY OF BIBLE LIFE & TIMES to Editor, U.S. General Books, c/o Customer Service, Reader's Digest, Pleasantville, NY 10570.

To order additional copies of ILLUSTRATED DICTIONARY OF BIBLE LIFE & TIMES, call 1-800-846-2100.

You can also visit us on the World Wide Web at http://www.readersdigest.com

The credits and acknowledgments that appear on pages 404–407 are hereby made a part of this copyright page.

CONTRIBUTORS

CONSULTANTS

Michael D. Coogan, Ph.D.
Professor of Religious Studies
Stonehill College
North Easton, MA

David F. Graf, Ph.D.
Professor of History
University of Miami
Coral Gables, FL

Pamela Kladzyk, Ph.D.
Professor of Architecture and Environmental Design
Parsons School of Design
New York

David Marcus, Ph.D.
Professor of Bible
Jewish Theological Seminary of America
New York

John R. McRay, Ph.D.
Professor of New Testament and Archaeology
Wheaton College Graduate School,
Wheaton, IL

Robert R. Stieglitz, Ph.D.
Professor of Archaeology
Rutgers University
Newark, NJ

Thomas L. Robinson, Ph.D.
Former Professor of Biblical Studies
Union Theological Seminary
New York

WRITERS

Marjorie Flory
Charles Flowers
Robert P. Kiener
Peter R. Limburg
Donna M. Lucey
Stephen M. Miller
Polly A. Morrice
John S. Tompkins
Carol Weeg
Henry Wiencek

ART PRODUCTION ASSOCIATE

Patrizia Bove

PICTURE RESEARCH EDITOR

Yvonne Silver

COPY EDITOR

Susan Converse Winslow

INDEXER

Marion Lerner-Levine

ENGRAVER

Applied Graphics Technologies
Carlstadt, NJ

Library of Congress Cataloging in Publication Data
Illustrated Dictionary of Bible Life & Times
p. cm.
Includes Index
ISBN 0-89577-987-0
1. Bible—Antiquities—Dictionaries. I. Reader's Digest Association.
BS622.I45 1997
220.9'5' 003—dc21 97-5429

Printed in the United States of America

About This Book

The Old and New Testaments present contemporary readers with a host of unfamiliar terms for things once considered commonplace by biblical peoples, such as *ephod, greaves,* and *sherd.* Conversely, the meanings of many familiar words, such as *apron, lattice,* and *village,* have changed dramatically over the course of time. The passage of some 2,000 years similarly has obscured the significance of many of the customs and practices, trades and activities, cited in the Bible. Reader's Digest ILLUSTRATED DICTIONARY OF BIBLE LIFE & TIMES sheds light on such scriptural references in a beautifully illustrated A-to-Z guide to daily life in biblical times. From Aaron's rod to Zion, accursed ones to Ziv, more than 1,500 entries explain the meanings of everyday objects, beliefs, occupations, pastimes, and religious rituals that comprised the fabric of civilization in the period of the Old and New Testaments. More than 500 full-color photographs, artifacts, and specially commissioned illustrations bring this material vividly to life.

Designed for ease of use, the main section of this handsome reference work presents major dictionary entries, each with a chapter and verse citation to show how the word is used in the Bible. In some cases, the detailed text accompanying each entry contains a cross-reference in small capital letters to a related entry in the book. An extensive glossary provides additional biblical terms, each with a succinct definition and biblical citation to place the word in context. A comprehensive index follows to guide the reader quickly to further information.

By bringing into focus the details of daily life in the times of the patriarchs and prophets, pharaohs and Pharisees, this companion guide to the Bible illuminates as well the timeless truths embodied in the greatest book ever written.

–The Editors

Contents

TIMELINE OF THE BIBLE

	2000 BC- 1700 BC	1700 BC- 1200 BC	1200 BC- 1000 BC	1000 BC- 800BC	800 BC- 700 BC
BIBLE WORLD EVENTS	**2000 BC** THE EPIC OF GILGAMESH, about a legendary Sumerian king, is written in cuneiform on clay tablets. **2000 BC** DESTRUCTION OF UR ends Sumerian domination. **1792–1750 BC** HAMMURABI promulgates a set of laws, known as the Code of Hammurabi, in Babylon. **1786 BC** EGYPTIAN Middle Kingdom ends. **1750 BC** HITTITES begin to exert power in Middle East.	**1554–1070 BC** EGYPTIAN New Kingdom flourishes. **1500 BC** CANAANITES invent first alphabet. **1500 BC** LATE BRONZE AGE begins. **1350–1200 BC** HITTITES become a leading power in Near East. **1347–1339 BC** TUTANKHAMEN reigns as pharaoh of Egypt. **1290–1224 BC** RAMSES II reigns as pharaoh of Egypt. **1250 BC** CITY OF TROY is sacked.	**1200 BC** HITTITES decline in power. **1200 BC** IRON AGE begins. **1190 BC** PHILISTINES, along with other Sea Peoples, invade the eastern Mediterranean. **1100 BC** PHOENICIANS rise to power in cities on coast of Lebanon. 	**850 BC** ASSYRIANS extend their power to Phoenician cities. **950 BC** GEZER CALENDAR is written. *A Hittite armor-bearer*	 *The Forum in Rome* **776 BC** OLYMPIC GAMES take place in Athens for the first time. **753 BC** ROME is founded, according to tradition. **747–727 BC** ASSYRIAN EMPIRE begins its period of greatest domination, under King Tiglath-pileser III.
BIBLE EVENTS	 *Ten commandments delivered to Moses on Mt. Sinai* **2000–1700 BC** AGE OF THE PATRIARCHS is dominated by Abraham, Isaac, and Jacob. **1700–1550 BC** ISRAELITES settle in Egypt to escape famine.	**1280 BC** MOSES leads exodus of Israelites from Egypt. **1240–1200 BC** ISRAELITES, led by Joshua, invade Canaan.	**1200–1020 BC** JUDGES rule Israel. **1020 BC** SAUL is named king of Israel.  *Samuel anointing Saul*	**1000–961 BC** DAVID unites Judah and Israel. **961–922 BC** SOLOMON rules united Israel. **950 BC** FIRST TEMPLE is completed by Solomon. **922 BC** DIVIDED MONARCHY begins. **842 BC** JEHU leads revolt and becomes ruler of northern kingdom of Israel.	**786–746 BC** JEROBOAM II rules Israel. **722 BC** ASSYRIANS conquer northern kingdom of Israel. **715–687 BC** HEZEKIAH rules Judah; religious reforms are instituted. **701 BC** SENNACHERIB, king of Assyria, captures Lachish and besieges Jerusalem.
BIBLE BOOKS	*The chronology of the Bible books reflects the time described by the books rather than the time when they were written.* **4000–1650 BC** GENESIS  *God, the creator, depicted on a throne*	**1700 BC** JOB **1325–1280 BC** EXODUS **1280 BC** LEVITICUS **1279 BC–1240 BC** NUMBERS **1240 BC** DEUTERONOMY **1240–1200 BC** JOSHUA	**1200–1050 BC** JUDGES **1090–1000 BC** 1 SAMUEL **1075–1050 BC** RUTH	**1000–961 BC** 1 CHRONICLES **1000–970 BC** 2 SAMUEL **1000–500 BC** PSALMS, PSALM 151 **970–850 BC** 1 KINGS **970–560 BC** 2 CHRONICLES **961–500 BC** PROVERBS **930 BC** ECCLESIASTES, SONG OF SOLOMON, WISDOM OF SOLOMON **850–560 BC** 2 KINGS	**760–750 BC** AMOS **755–725 BC** HOSEA **750 BC** JONAH **740–700 BC** MICAH **738–520 BC** ISAIAH **722–650 BC** TOBIT 

Tobit burying the dead

Dates given below are approximate.

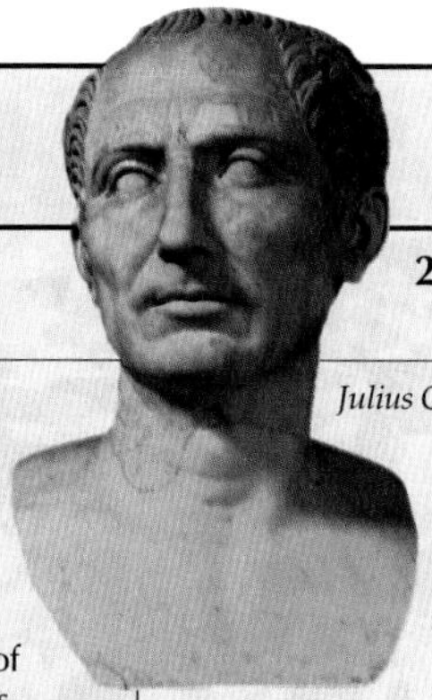

700 BC- 600 BC	600 BC- 500 BC	500 BC- 200 BC	200 BC- 1 BC	1 BC- AD 100
681–669 BC ASSYRIAN EMPIRE conquers Egypt and reaches its greatest extent, during the reign of Esarhaddon. **650 BC** FIRST COINS are minted in Lydia. **614–612 BC** ASSYRIAN EMPIRE ends when its capital city, Nineveh, is captured by Babylonians. **605 BC** BABYLONIAN pre-eminence is established at the Battle of Carchemish. Nebuchadnezzar defeats Egyptians.	**539 BC** PERSIAN EMPIRE begins; King Cyrus defeats Babylonians at the Battle of Opis. **509 BC** ROMAN REPUBLIC is founded. *Return of the Jews to Jerusalem from Babylonian exile* 	**447–432 BC** PARTHENON is built in Athens. **332 BC** ALEXANDER THE GREAT conquers Egypt; founds city of Alexandria; spreads Greek culture and language throughout Near East. **323 BC** ALEXANDER DIES. His empire is divided. **264–146 BC** ROMAN EMPIRE becomes dominant political force in the Mediterranean.	*Julius Caesar* **63 BC** ROME conquers all of Syria and Judea. **50 BC** GLASSBLOWING is invented by Phoenicians. **44 BC** JULIUS CAESAR, dictator of Rome, is assassinated. **27 BC** AUGUSTUS becomes first Roman emperor.	**AD 14–37** EMPEROR TIBERIUS rules; expels Jews from Rome. **AD 64** ROME is partially destroyed by fire. Nero blames Christians and persecutes them. **AD 79** POMPEII and Herculeum are buried in the eruption of Mt. Vesuvius. **AD 80** ROMAN COLOSSEUM is dedicated. **AD 100** ROMAN EMPIRE reaches the height of its power.
622 BC JOSIAH, king of Judah, establishes sweeping religious reforms; Assyrian power wanes. **609 BC** BATTLE OF MEGIDDO takes place; Josiah is killed.	**597 BC** JEHOIAKIM, king of Judah, surrenders to Nebuchadnezzar, king of Babylon; first deportation of Jews occurs. **587 BC** JERUSALEM and first temple are destroyed by Babylonians. **538 BC** EDICT OF CYRUS permits Jews to return to Holy Land. **515 BC** SECOND TEMPLE is dedicated.	**445 BC** NEHEMIAH rebuilds walls of Jerusalem. **440 BC** EZRA brings law from Babylon. **332 BC** ALEXANDER THE GREAT occupies Israel. **301 BC** HOLY LAND comes under control of Alexander's successor, Ptolemy I. **250 BC–70 AD** DEAD SEA SCROLLS are written.	**175–164 BC** ANTIOCHUS IV, Seleucid king of Syria, desecrates Jerusalem temple by erecting image of Zeus. **167–164 BC** MACCABEAN REVOLT takes place; temple is rededicated. **104–63 BC** HASMONEANS rule Judea. **37–4 BC** HEROD THE GREAT rules Judea; rebuilds temple. **7 BC** JESUS is born.	**AD 26–36** PONTIUS PILATE is governor of Judea. **AD 29** JESUS is crucified and resurrected. **AD 44** PAUL begins missionary journeys. **AD 66–73** FIRST JEWISH REVOLT against Rome occurs. **AD 70** THIRD TEMPLE is destroyed by Romans.
675 BC PRAYER OF MANASSEH **639 BC** ZEPHANIAH **626–580 BC** JEREMIAH, LETTER OF JEREMIAH **625–618 BC** NAHUM **622 BC** HABUKKUK **620–430 BC** 1 ESDRAS **606–536 BC** DANIEL, PRAYER OF AZARIAH, SUSANNA, BEL AND THE DRAGON	**600–571 BC** EZEKIEL **593–587 BC** JUDITH **581 BC** BARUCH **580 BC** LAMENTAIONS **560 BC** OBADIAH **538–435 BC** EZRA **520 BC** ZECHARIAH **520 BC** HAGGAI	**480 BC** ESTHER, ADDITIONS TO ESTHER **460 BC** MALACHI **450 BC** 2 ESDRAS **445–433 BC** NEHEMIAH **375 BC** JOEL **333–104 BC** 1 MACCABEES **217–203 BC** 3 MACCABEES	 *Jesus preaching in a synagogue* **180–163 BC** 4 MACCABEES **180–124 BC** 2 MACCABEES **180 BC** ECCLESIASTICUS	**7BC–AD 29** MATTHEW, LUKE **AD 25–29** MARK, JOHN **AD 30–62** ACTS OF THE APOSTLES **AD 50–100** NEW TESTAMENT LETTERS **AD 95** REVELATION

ARAMAIC, *which is closely related to Hebrew, was the Near East's most widely used language in biblical times. The Aramaic text of this fragment of a ninth-century* BC *monument from northern Israel mentions the House of David. It is the only known reference outside the Bible to King David's dynasty.*

Aaron's Rod

In [the Holy of Holies] stood the golden altar of incense and the ark of the covenant . . . and Aaron's rod that budded . . . .–Hebrews 9:4

Moses' brother Aaron carried a rod, or staff, that showed his authority. To convince Pharaoh of God's power, Aaron threw down his rod and it turned into a snake (Ex 7:10). Pharaoh ordered his magicians to do the same, and their staffs also turned into snakes. Unimpressed, Pharaoh refused to allow the Israelites to leave Egypt. Aaron waved his rod and sent frogs swarming over the countryside—a feat again duplicated by Pharaoh's magicians (Ex 8:5–7). When God later told Moses to place the staffs of the leaders of Israel's 12 tribes in the tabernacle, Aaron's rod blossomed overnight and bore ripe almonds. God had chosen him to be chief PRIEST, and his heirs—"your sons and your ancestral house" (Num 18:1)—were to retain that sacred office.

Abba

When we cry, "Abba! Father!" it is that very Spirit bearing witness with our spirit that we are children of God . . . .–Romans 8:15–16

In biblical times, children called their fathers Abba. This Aramaic word for "dear father" or "my father" conveyed filial piety and a warm, personal feeling in the same way as "daddy" and "papa" might today. When Jesus called God "Abba" in prayer (Mk 14:36), he affirmed the intimacy of their relationship. Early Christians used the term to express their belief that they were all children of God—"and if children, then heirs, heirs of God and joint heirs with Christ" (Rom 8:17).

Abraham, the "Abba" of all Israel, leads his clan out of Haran (Gen 12) in a 19th-century painting.

Abib

Observe the month of Abib by keeping the passover for the LORD your God . . . .–Deuteronomy 16:1

The first month of the ancient Hebrew calendar, Abib, began at the first new moon after the spring equinox and spanned a period that today falls in the months of March and April. For herdsmen and farmers, Abib (or Nisan, as it was called after the Babylonian exile) was a time when sheep gave birth and grain ripened. (In fact, *Abib* probably means "ears of grain.")

For the Israelites, Abib was important as the month in which God led their ancestors out of slavery in Egypt, an event commemorated by the feast of Passover. "You shall observe the festival of unleavened bread . . . in the month of Abib, for in it you came out of Egypt" (Ex 23:15). It was also the time of spring rituals that merged religion with agriculture and sheep herding, as in sacrificing a lamb to God. The month became significant for Christians because Jesus' crucifixion occurred at that time.

Abomination

Lying lips are an abomination to the LORD . . . .–Proverbs 12:22

In many English-language Bibles, any practice considered detestable is described as an "abomination"—a translation of several Hebrew words that refer to something rotten, stinking, or disgusting. The term usually applies to something that God hates to see, such as idolatry, child sacrifice, or injustice. Daniel prophesies a coming "abomination that makes desolate" (Dan 11:31). He may have been referring to the statue of Zeus that the invading Syrians put in the Jerusalem temple about 167 BC, but Jesus later alluded to this passage in what was apparently a prophecy of Rome's destruction of the temple in AD 70 (Mt 24:15–16).

Abstinence

... "Should I mourn and practice abstinence in the fifth month, as I have done for so many years?"–Zechariah 7:3

Abstinence, the refusal to indulge in something, was often a spiritual discipline. The Israelites were not to eat animals deemed ritually unclean, such as pork or shellfish. Christians were to "abstain from the desires of the flesh that wage war against the soul" (1 Pet 2:11).

Some forms of abstinence were temporary. On the DAY OF ATONEMENT, when the high priest offered sacrifices for the sins of Israel, the entire nation fasted and gave full attention to the importance of the day. Men or women could observe "the vow of a nazirite," as Samson did, "to separate themselves to the LORD" (Num 6:2). Those who took this vow were supposed to abstain from grapes, wine, and vinegar, from cutting their hair, and from going near a corpse. This separation dramatized Israel's separation from neigboring societies. The vow was usually taken for a limited time only, but as in Samson's case, it could be lifelong.

Abstinence sometimes accompanied requests made to God. King David refused to rise from the ground or eat any food for seven days while his son by Bathsheba lay dying. David stopped fasting the day the child died, explaining, "I fasted and wept; for I said, 'Who knows? The LORD may be gracious to me, and the child may live.' But now he is dead; why should I fast?" (2 Sam 12:22–23).

Although Jesus occasionally fasted, he did not demand it of his disciples, saying, "The days will come when the bridegroom will be taken away from them, and then they will fast" (Lk 5:35).

The acacia's distinctive silhouette was familiar to travelers in the Sinai, where it was the most common tree, as well as the tallest, rising 15 to 25 feet above the desert floor.

Abyss

They begged him not to order them to go back into the abyss. –Luke 8:31

Derived from a Greek word that means "bottomless"—which originally referred to the underworld or the ocean beneath the earth—*abyss* is frequently translated in the book of Revelation with the phrase "bottomless pit." It is the place of the dead (Rom 10:7) and the dark abode of legions of devils (Lk 8:31). Home to the antichrist—the murderous beast that will menace the world at the end of time (Rev 11:7)—the abyss is also said to be ruled over by an angel called Abaddon or Apollyon, meaning respectively "Destruction" and "Destroyer" (Rev 9:11).

Acacia Wood

They shall make an ark of acacia wood .... –Exodus 25:10

Thorny but wide-branching and bearing yellow or white blossoms, acacias were among the few hardwood trees growing in the Sinai desert near the mountain where Moses received the ten commandments. Thus it was natural for him to use acacia wood to build the ARK OF THE COVENANT—overlaying it with gold, as God instructed—and the long poles used to carry it (Ex 25:10–14).

God further directed the Israelites to construct "a sanctuary, so that I may dwell among them" (Ex 25:8). This tabernacle, or tent, in which the sacred ark resided, was also built in accordance with God's instructions. It was supported by a framework of pillars and beams, and among its ceremonial furnishings were a table for the bread of the Presence and altars for incense and burnt offerings—all made of strong acacia wood, dazzlingly overlaid with gold (Ex 25:23–26:32).

Peter's accent belies his attempts to deny knowing Jesus. As a cock crows, he recalls Jesus' prediction that "this very night, before the cock crows, you will deny me three times" (Mt 26:34). The scene is depicted in Peter's Denial, *by Carl Heinrich Bloch.*

Accent

. . . "Certainly you are also one of them, for your accent betrays you."–Matthew 26:73

Jesus and his Galilean disciples spoke ARAMAIC with a distinctive accent. There is no record of the actual differences in pronunciation, but Jerusalem's residents tended to view Galileans as illiterate country folk, belittling their speech as unrefined. When Peter was waiting in the high priest's courtyard, a servant girl came up and said, "You also were with Jesus the Galilean" (Mt 26:69). Three times he denied any association with Jesus, prompting skeptical bystanders to jeer that his accent gave him away. Peter's Aramaic, however it sounded, was one of many versions that could be heard; it had long been the language of commerce across the Babylonian and Persian empires.

Acts of the Apostles

". . . you will be my witnesses . . . to the ends of the earth." –Acts of the Apostles 1:8

The fifth book in the New Testament, Acts of the Apostles, provides a narrative sequel to the Gospel of Luke. Since the second century AD, authorship of both books has been ascribed to "Luke, the beloved physician" (Col 4:14). Acts of the Apostles preserves scenes from the church's first three decades, beginning with Jesus' resurrection appearances. Its initial focus is on events in and around Jerusalem, but the dramatic conversion of Paul (Acts 9:1–20) marks a turning point. Attention thereafter shifts to Paul's journeys outside Palestine and the issues they raised among church leaders in Jerusalem. The book ends with Paul's two years of preaching from prison in Rome.

Adoption

He destined us for adoption as his children through Jesus Christ . . . . –Ephesians 1:5

In the ancient Near East, adoption in one form or another was a common practice and an accepted way to maintain a family line. For a childless couple, adoption ensured that someone would care for them in their old age, give them a proper burial, and mourn them after they died. The adopted child, in exchange, would inherit the family property as well as the other benefits and obligations that a child by birth would have otherwise assumed. If, however, a child should later be born to that couple, it would be considered the principal heir, and the adopted child would have secondary status.

Often the adopted child was already a relative. The book of Esther records that Mordecai brought up his cousin Esther after her father and mother died and that he "adopted her as his own daughter" (Esth 2:7). In some cases an adoption took place strictly for the purpose of inheritance. Jacob adopted two grandchildren—Joseph's sons Ephraim and Manasseh—as his own sons (Gen 48:5), each of whom founded one of the tribes of Israel and inherited part of the land apportioned in Canaan.

Occasionally people adopted foundlings. When Moses' mother was forced to abandon him, the baby was found among the bulrushes, and "Pharaoh's daughter adopted him and brought him up as her own son" (Acts 7:21).

A CONCUBINE sometimes acted as a surrogate mother for a woman who could not have children of her own. The childless Rachel gave her maid, Bilhah, to Jacob as a concubine. When a child was born, Rachel signaled her intent to adopt him by saying, "God has . . . given me a son" (Gen 30:6). She also wanted Bilhah to "bear upon my knees" (Gen 30:3), a phrase that scholars believe refers to an adoption ceremony.

In the New Testament, Paul uses the term *adoption* to describe God's relationship to members of the church. It is not the unique relationship God has with his "only Son" (Jn 1:18), Jesus, but it is nevertheless a bond of special intimacy. Paul wrote to one congregation that "you have received a spirit of adoption" (Rom 8:15). He told another, "God sent his Son . . . in order to redeem those who were under the law, so that we might receive adoption as children" (Gal 4:4–5). Believers, Paul asserted, enjoy the privileges and shoulder the responsibilities of children who are actually born to their parents, and they have the right to inherit eternal life from God.

ADULTERY

YOU SHALL NOT COMMIT ADULTERY.
–EXODUS 20:14

From the time Moses received God's commandments, Israel's law prohibited adultery, which was considered treachery of the worst sort. Adultery was defined in the Old Testament as voluntary sexual relations between a married or betrothed woman and a man other than her husband. A married man was allowed to have more than one sexual partner. He might have other wives, as well as concubines; however, he was not to have sexual relations with another man's wife or fiancée. A married woman could have only one partner. This was probably to ensure that any children a woman bore would be her husband's, so as to keep the family line intact.

King David's adulterous liaison with Bathsheba (2 Sam 11) is portrayed in an illumination from a 13th-century French psalter.

Adultery was so serious an offense that the penalty for the woman and her partner was death (Lev 20:10), usually by stoning but sometimes by burning. This severity reflects how grave a threat infidelity posed to marriage and the entire community. "He who commits adultery has no sense . . . jealousy arouses a husband's fury, and he shows no restraint when he takes revenge" (Prov 6:32–34).

By the first century, adultery had become grounds for DIVORCE and thus was no longer always punished by extreme sentences. If a husband suspected his wife of adultery but had no proof, he would take her to a priest who would make her take an oath and drink bitter water, which placed her under a curse. It was believed that if she was innocent, she would not be harmed, but if guilty, "her womb shall discharge, her uterus drop" (Num 5:27).

The law of Mesopotamia allowed the injured husband to pardon the transgression or accept payment to mitigate it. But Israelite law granted the husband no such powers, viewing adultery as a sin against the Lord as well as a crime against the community. Prophets in the Old Testament drew a close parallel between adultery and unfaithfulness to God. Those who worshiped false idols or performed other pagan rites were viewed as having "forsaken the LORD to devote themselves to whoredom" (Hos 4:10–11). Jeremiah speaks of "all the adulteries of that faithless one, Israel" (Jer 3:8).

In the New Testament, Jesus expanded the definition of adultery to include a husband's infidelity to his wife. Jesus said to the Pharisees, "Anyone who divorces his wife and marries another commits adultery, and whoever marries a woman divorced from her husband commits adultery" (Lk 16:18). He condemned not just adultery but adulterous thoughts: "I say to you that everyone who looks at a woman with lust has already committed adultery with her in his heart" (Mt 5:28). Adulterers were threatened with a penalty even worse than death: they would not inherit the kingdom of God (1 Cor 6:9). Yet punishment was still tempered by compassion. When the scribes and Pharisees brought a woman accused of adultery before Jesus, he refused to condemn her, telling her only, "Go your way, and from now on do not sin again" (Jn 8:11). Indeed, adulterers who repented were counted among God's flock.

ADVERSARY

"HE HAS TORN ME IN HIS WRATH . . .
HE HAS GNASHED HIS TEETH AT ME;
MY ADVERSARY SHARPENS HIS EYES
AGAINST ME."–JOB 16:9

To the Bible's authors, any person or thing opposing the will of God or his people was an adversary. An adversary might be encountered on the field of battle (Num 10:9) or on the street—the angel of the Lord blocked Balaam's path, saying, "I have come out as an adversary, because your way is perverse before me" (Num 22:32).

One of the Hebrew words for adversary is *Satan;* it was Satan who tormented Job to test his piety (Job 1:6–2:10). In the New Testament, Satan was seen as evil incarnate, the ultimate adversary: "Like a roaring lion your adversary the devil prowls around, looking for someone to devour" (1 Pet 5:8).

Agate

They set in it four rows of stones. . . . the third row, a jacinth, an agate, and an amethyst . . . . –Exodus 39:10–12

Agate, a whitish or brown quartz with bands of color, was among the Hebrews' favorite semiprecious stones. They wore it on secular as well as religious occasions. Unlike gold and silver, it was probably available locally in Israel, where many pieces of agate jewelry have been found. Agate and other gemstones were also polished and incised for use as personal seals.

An agate seal, right, dated about 700 BC, belonged to "Gedalyahu son of Samakh." His name, cut into its face, was impressed on sealing clay, left.

In the splendid ceremonial breastplate designed for the high priest's use in the TABERNACLE, the agate and 11 other stones were engraved with the names of the tribes of Israel (Ex 28:19). According to Revelation, agates were also to be set in the foundation walls of the new Jerusalem (Rev 21:19).

Age

Do not cast me off in the time of old age; do not forsake me when my strength is spent.–Psalm 71:9

Although some patriarchs before the flood attained great age—Methuselah lived to 969 years—the Bible refers to a lifespan equal to the modern one: "The days of our life are seventy years, or perhaps eighty, if we are strong" (Ps 90:10). The Israelites looked upon 60 as the threshold of old age. Advancing years brought a variety of infirmities, which the Bible describes: "Ahijah could not see, for his eyes were dim because of his age" (1 Kings 14:4). But the aged were not despised; indeed, they were esteemed for the wisdom and grace earned by years: "The glory of youths is their strength, but the beauty of the aged is their gray hair" (Prov 20:29). Nevertheless, it was thought that older men should step aside and yield responsibilities and pleasures to the younger. Invited by David to Jerusalem, Barzillai advised the king to select a younger man instead: "Today I am eighty years old; can I discern what is pleasant and what is not?" (2 Sam 19:35).

Described as the "King of the ages" (1 Tim 1:17), God is not limited by time: "with the Lord one day is like a thousand years, and a thousand years are like one day" (2 Pet 3:8). The earth itself, with its "eternal mountains" and "everlasting hills" (Gen 49:26), is the oldest measure of time comprehensible to man. Human time began with the creation, but God existed before time: "Before the mountains were brought forth, or ever you had formed the earth and the world, from everlasting to everlasting you are God" (Ps 90:2). Paul referred to the secret and divine wisdom "which God decreed before the ages" (1 Cor 2:7). Jesus, looking to the future, warned the skeptical Pharisees that "whoever speaks against the Holy Spirit will not be forgiven, either in this age or in the age to come" (Mt 12:32).

Agreement

. . . you have said, "We have made a covenant with death, and with Sheol we have an agreement . . . ." –Isaiah 28:14–15

The concept of agreement as a means of defining mutual relationships operated on many levels in the biblical world. Political relations were formalized in written agreements, including treaties, alliances, and pacts. Israel's COVENANT with God (Ex 19–24) in many ways paralleled treaties between nations. Less formal agreements were the glue that held communities together, as Paul

An important agreement reached by two men was commemorated in a Syrian limestone relief of the 14th century BC.

reminded the church in Corinth: "I appeal to you . . . that all of you be in agreement and that there be no divisions among you" (1 Cor 1:10). Ecclesiasticus lists three things "beautiful in the sight of God," the first of which is "agreement among brothers and sisters" (Sir 25:1).

AIR

THE MAN GAVE NAMES TO ALL CATTLE, AND TO THE BIRDS OF THE AIR . . . . –GENESIS 2:20

For the ancient Hebrews, the air was the place where birds fly—an open space between the earth and the "dome of the sky" (Gen 1:20). But that open space could harbor harm: "Moses threw [soot] in the air, and it caused festering boils" (Ex 9:10). For early Christians it was also the realm of SATAN, "ruler of the power of the air" (Eph 2:2). Those who fought this evil with their faith would be rewarded at the time of Christ's return: "Then we who are alive . . . will be caught up in the clouds together with them to meet the Lord in the air" (1 Thess 4:17).

ALABASTER

. . . A WOMAN CAME TO HIM WITH AN ALABASTER JAR OF VERY COSTLY OINTMENT . . . . –MATTHEW 26:7

The alabaster of the Bible was a whitish, translucent form of calcium carbonate soft enough to be carved into vases or flasks for perfumes. Matthew's mention of an alabaster jar is repeated by Mark (Mk 14:3), and Luke also tells of a woman anointing Jesus' feet with ointment from an alabaster jar (Lk 7:37). Such jars were common and similar containers made of any material became known as alabasters. They were probably shaped like teardrops, with thin necks that were broken to pour out the contents. The word *alabaster* is used to poetic effect in Song of Solomon's description of the woman's beloved: "His legs are alabaster columns, set upon bases of gold" (Song of S 5:15).

Alabaster carving has an ancient history in the Holy Land; the vase above, with a handle shaped like a monkey, was made about 1800 BC.

ALARM

. . . YOU SHALL SOUND AN ALARM WITH THE TRUMPETS, SO THAT YOU MAY BE REMEMBERED BEFORE THE LORD YOUR GOD . . . . –NUMBERS 10:9

Because history in the ancient Near East was filled with desert wandering, invasion, siege, exile, and conquest, it was inevitable that easily recognizable alarm signals were devised. The distinctive warning call sounded on trumpets has not been passed down, but it alerted the Israelites in Sinai to begin the day's march or prepare for battle against the enemy. In later times, trumpets blared as great armies of rival empires approached.

The Hebrew word for alarm also means "shout," as when the people roared before the walls of Jericho, which came tumbling down (Jos 6:20). At religious jubilees, shouts and blasts of the ram's horn proclaimed a different message, uniting the nation in joy.

In ancient times the sound of the shofar, or ram's horn, was an alarm calling the people to war. It is still heard today on Rosh Hashana.

ALGUM

"SEND ME ALSO CEDAR, CYPRESS, AND ALGUM TIMBER FROM LEBANON . . . ." –2 CHRONICLES 2:8

Algum was an exotic wood that Solomon ordered from Lebanon for the construction of his temple. Scholars disagree as to whether it was a kind of fir or juniper, or whether algum was simply an alternative name for the almug (probably red sandalwood) that was imported along with gold and other luxuries from the mysterious land of Ophir (1 Kings 10:11).

Solomon used algum (or almug) wood to build the temple steps and to make musical instruments of exceptional beauty: "From the algum wood, the king made . . . lyres also and harps for the singers; there never was seen the like of them before in the land of Judah" (2 Chr 9:11).

Alien

You shall not oppress a resident alien; you know the heart of an alien, for you were aliens in the land of Egypt.–Exodus 23:9

The term *alien* in biblical times might have been applied broadly to any stranger visiting temporarily. More significant in Israelite life was the resident alien, an outsider living more or less permanently in a community, with no relatives or blood ties—a status indicated in some Bible translations by the word *sojourner.*

Abraham, Isaac, and Jacob had once lived as aliens in Canaan; the entire nation of Israel had done so in Egypt. Thus, although foreigners were potentially disruptive to the social order, they were accorded special recognition in Israelite law and custom: Israelite men were not to marry foreign wives, aliens were barred from participation in certain religious activities, and they could be charged interest on loans. However, they were permitted to worship God and observe the SABBATH, and special laws made provision to feed and clothe them. In sum, the alien was not to be oppressed, but rather to be loved (Lev 19:33–34; Deut 24:17).

In the New Testament, God's covenant with Israel was extended to all who accepted Jesus' message. As Paul wrote to the Ephesians, "you are no longer strangers and aliens, but you are citizens with the saints and also members of the household of God" (Eph 2:19). Yet the early Christians, a tiny minority in a vast and often hostile world, could not ignore their status as outsiders. Peter exhorted, "I urge you as aliens and exiles to . . . conduct yourselves honorably among the Gentiles, so that . . . they may see your honorable deeds and glorify God when he comes to judge" (1 Pet 2:11–12).

As an alien from the land of Moab, Ruth expected little in Israel but won the heart of Boaz. Here, Boaz looks on as Ruth gleans wheat in his fields.

Allegory

O mortal, propound a riddle, and speak an allegory to the house of Israel.–Ezekiel 17:2

The "allegory" related by Ezekiel ("parable" in some translations) includes two eagles, a cedar, and other images, each symbolizing one of the story's real subjects—the rulers of Babylon and Egypt symbolized by the eagles, the Davidic dynasty by the cedar, and so on. Parables and allegories both used metaphors to teach moral truths, the parable usually making its point with one metaphor, the allegory combining several in complex, sometimes ambiguous ways.

By New Testament times, many Jewish scholars were re-reading Scripture allegorically, looking for hidden spiritual meanings. Paul used this method to interpret the story of Hagar and Sarah as "an allegory: these women are two covenants" (Gal 4:24), equating Ishmael with enslavement to Mosaic law and Isaac with liberation through Christ.

Alliance

Solomon made a marriage alliance with Pharaoh king of Egypt . . . . –1 Kings 3:1

From ancient Hittite and Assyrian writings, it is clear that Near Eastern nations had a long tradition of detailed agreements between allies, often involving payments for privileges. Defying God's warnings about entering into binding relationships with foreigners, Israel sought several treaties. Pacts might be enacted between equal allies such as David and the Phoenician King Hiram of Tyre (1 Kings 5:12), or a vassal treaty could be contracted between a strong nation and a weaker one, as when the Gibeonites appealed for aid as "servants" of the Israelites (Josh 10:6). All alliances were made under oath with pagan gods or God looking on, and punishment for noncompliance was likely to be severe.

Allegory is used several times in the Bible, as when Paul compared muzzling oxen with not paying disciples for their services (1 Cor 9:9). Paul was alluding to the law that forbids muzzling an ox "while it is treading out the grain" (Deut 25:4) because it should be able to eat as it works.

ALLOTMENT

SO JOSHUA . . . GAVE [THE LAND] FOR AN INHERITANCE TO ISRAEL ACCORDING TO THEIR TRIBAL ALLOTMENTS.–JOSHUA 11:23

The allocation of land in Canaan among the Israelites was guided by God's decree that Moses take a census in order that each tribe be given an area proportionate to its size (Num 26). Joshua then cast LOTS (hence *allotment*) to learn which area God had chosen for each tribe (see map). The Levites inherited no land of their own—only towns in the lands of other tribes—but the division of Joseph's heirs into the tribes of Manasseh and Ephraim produced 12 tribal allotments (Josh 13–19).

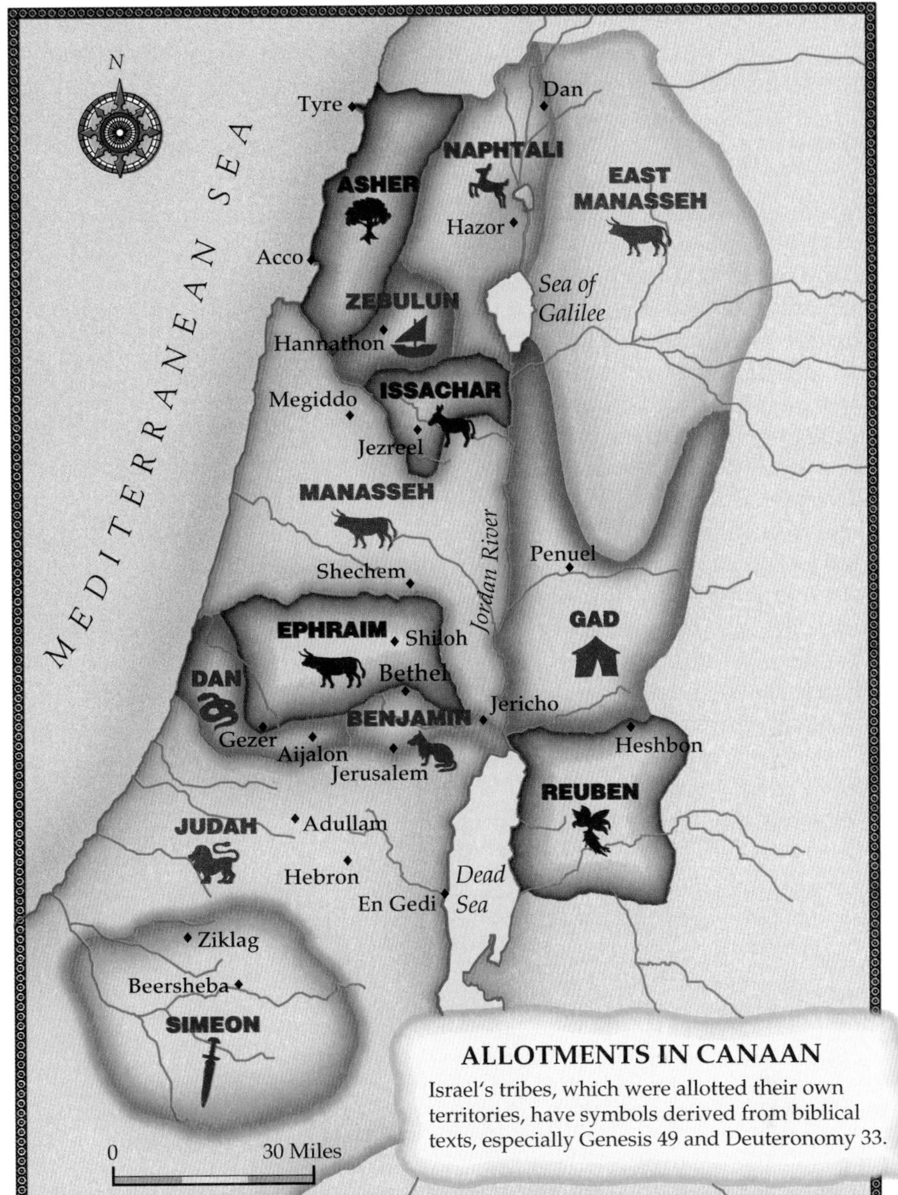

ALLOTMENTS IN CANAAN
Israel's tribes, which were allotted their own territories, have symbols derived from biblical texts, especially Genesis 49 and Deuteronomy 33.

ALLOWANCE

. . . THE PRIESTS HAD A FIXED ALLOWANCE FROM PHARAOH . . . .–GENESIS 47:22

Rulers in the Near East gave select subjects a food allowance. All biblical references to allowances specify food rather than money or any other commodity. Jeremiah, who urged his people not to resist the Babylonians, was treated favorably by his captors, who "gave him an allowance of food and a present, and let him go" (Jer 40:5). After 36 years of exile, King Jehoiachin of Judah was released from prison and given "a regular allowance . . . a portion every day, as long as he lived" (2 Kings 25:30).

ALMOND

ON THE LAMPSTAND ITSELF THERE WERE FOUR CUPS SHAPED LIKE ALMOND BLOSSOMS, EACH WITH ITS CALYXES AND PETALS.–EXODUS 37:20

Almonds were prized in biblical times, adding flavor and variety to meals and providing a source of oil. They were considered suitable diplomatic offerings, as in the account of Jacob's gifts to Joseph (Gen 43:11), and could even signify divine favor: Aaron's staff miraculously bore blossoms and ripe almonds, designating him Israel's chief priest (Num 17:8).

Almond blossoms regularly appeared in January, before those of any other fruit tree. Their white or pinkish color brightened the winter landscape, and their graceful shape was chosen to decorate ceremonial objects, including the lampstand designed for the sacred tabernacle (Ex 25:33).

ALMS

AND A MAN LAME FROM BIRTH . . . ASKED THEM FOR ALMS. –ACTS OF THE APOSTLES 3:2–3

Giving aid, or alms, to the needy is encouraged throughout the Bible. In Old Testament times, farmers let the poor glean what remained after they harvested their crops, and every third year they were to bring the TITHE of their produce to town so that priests, travelers, orphans, and widows could "eat their fill" (Deut 14:29). God commanded, "Open your hand to the poor and needy neighbor in your land" (Deut 15:11) and "give liberally and be ungrudging when you do so" (Deut 15:10).

Tobit 12:9 encouraged almsgiving as a central part of religious life in the third century BC: "For almsgiving saves from death and purges away every sin. Those who give alms will enjoy a full life" (see illustration). By New Testament times, people brought alms to the temple and synagogues. Some called attention to their act of piety, causing Jesus to warn, "Whenever you give alms, do not sound a trumpet before you, as the hypocrites do" (Mt 6:2). Jesus also lauded the spirit of giving over the actual amount of the gift.

Early Christians in Jerusalem sold some of their possessions and donated the money to the apostles for distribution among the poorer members of the church. As a result, "There was not a needy person among them" (Acts 4:34). During his missionary journeys, Paul took up a collection for the poor, instructing Christians: "On the first day of every week, each of you is to put aside and save whatever extra you earn" (1 Cor 16:2).

ALOES

". . . HOW FAIR ARE YOUR TENTS, O JACOB . . . LIKE ALOES THAT THE LORD HAS PLANTED . . . ."
–NUMBERS 24:5–6

The aloes of the Old Testament are not the succulent plants we know; rather, the Oriental trees were probably eaglewood or sandalwood. Their beauty and fragrance apparently inspired the prophet Balaam to include them in his blessing on Israel (Num 2:6). Aloes yielded perfumes sometimes applied to clothes or bedding: one psalm describes a king's wedding robes as "all fragrant with myrrh and aloes and cassia" (Ps 45:8). Elsewhere a temptress says, "I have perfumed my bed with myrrh, aloes, and cinnamon" (Prov 7:17).

A different aloe plant, often used for embalming, may have been involved in preparing Jesus' body for burial: "Nicodemus . . . also came, bringing a mixture of myrrh and aloes, weighing about a hundred pounds" (Jn 19:39). But many scholars identify it with the Old Testament PERFUME, perhaps intended to scent the linen that wrapped the body.

Almsgiving was a religious duty, which temple officials fulfilled by distributing either money or food to the poor.

Alpha and Omega

"I am the Alpha and the Omega, the first and the last, the beginning and the end."
–Revelation 22:13

Alpha and *Omega*—the first and last letters in the Greek alphabet—appear three times in the book of Revelation, which, like the rest of the New Testament, is written in Greek. The passage cited above (Rev 22:13) is attributed to Jesus. In Revelation 1:8 and 21:6 the words are from the Father: "'I am the Alpha and the Omega,' says the Lord God, who is and who was and who is to come, the Almighty" (Rev 1:8). The union of first and last in one entity can be taken to mean that God is all-encompassing and infinite. Some interpreters explain that God and Christ were present at the creation of the world and will be at the end.

The letters Alpha *and* Omega *often signify God in Christian art.*

Altar

Then Noah built an altar to the LORD . . . and offered burnt offerings . . . .–Genesis 8:20

On raised platforms often made of dirt, rocks, or single blocks of cut stone, the people of Israel burned sacrificial offerings to atone for their sins or to give thanks to God. Though Cain and Abel offered the first sacrifices in the Bible and may have built altars, the first mention of an altar is of the one that Noah built after the time of the FLOOD.

The word *altar,* in Hebrew, means "place of slaughter." Yet animals were not always killed on the altar but nearby. Then cut pieces of the animals were put on the altar to be consumed by fire. There were exceptions, however. As Abraham prepared to sacrifice Isaac, he "laid him on the altar . . . reached out his hand and took the knife to kill his son" (Gen 22:9–10).

Incense altars flank the steps leading to the Holy of Holies at the temple of Arad in southern Israel. They were cut from limestone possibly as early as the 10th century BC.

Before the tabernacle and the later temple became focal points of sacrificial worship, Hebrews often constructed altars of simple materials. "You need make for me only an altar of earth," God said, "and sacrifice on it your burnt offerings and your offerings of well-being, your sheep and your oxen" (Ex 20:24).

Altars of piled rocks were also common; many have been discovered in Israel. Elijah built one from 12 stones, representing the 12 tribes of Israel, in a religious duel with the prophets of Baal on Mount Carmel. In addition, horned altars cut from solid blocks of stone have been unearthed at worship sites in Beersheba and Arad. The "horns" projected a few inches up from the four corners. Scholars speculate that a metal grating rested on the horns, while the wood burned beneath.

The tabernacle and temple each had two altars, one inside for burning incense and a horned altar in the courtyard for burning sacrifices of animals or produce. The tabernacle's courtyard altar, made of wood and plated with bronze, was 7½ feet square and more than 4 feet high. On top rested a bronze grating, and nearby sat bronze pots and shovels to remove the ashes. Solomon's altar was more than triple that size, standing 15 feet high and 30 feet square.

More than a place of sacrifice, altars also offered sanctuary, like churches in later times. When Adonijah learned that his half-brother, Solomon, had been chosen to succeed David, he "laid hold of the horns of the altar, saying, 'Let King Solomon swear to me first that he will not kill his servant with the sword'" (1 Kings 1:51).

After the death of Jesus, Christians began to teach that the altar was obsolete and no longer the place to give a life and receive atonement. Jesus had become both the SACRIFICE and the altar. "We have an altar. . . . Let us then go to him" (Heb 13:10, 13). About 40 years after the crucifixion, the altar became obsolete for Jews as well. Romans destroyed the temple. It has never been rebuilt nor has the sacrificial system been reinstated.

AMBASSADOR

SO WE ARE AMBASSADORS FOR CHRIST, SINCE GOD IS MAKING HIS APPEAL THROUGH US . . . . –2 CORINTHIANS 5:20

Official representatives were sent from one nation to another to deliver messages, offer congratulations or condolences, seek alliances, and register complaints. Such ambassadors were expected to be treated with dignity; if not, dire consequences might result. When David's envoys to the Ammonites were humiliated—their clothes partially stripped off and half their beards shaved off—it led to war. Paul considered himself an envoy for Christ's message of salvation; even while imprisoned, he declared himself "an ambassador in chains" (Eph 6:20).

Elamite ambassadors, dressed in elaborate headbands and robes, below right, formally greet their Urartian counterparts in this seventh-century BC stone relief.

AMBER

. . . I SAW SOMETHING LIKE GLEAMING AMBER . . . AND THERE WAS A SPLENDOR ALL AROUND.–EZEKIEL 1:27

The Bible mentions amber only in the prophet Ezekiel's often enigmatic visions. "As I looked," he said, "a stormy wind came out of the north: a great cloud with brightness around it and fire flashing forth continually, and in the middle of the fire, something like gleaming amber" (Ezek 1:4). Some scholars believe that he was referring not to what is known today as amber but to electrum, a brightly shining alloy of gold and silver.

Amber itself, a hard yellowish or brownish substance produced from tree resin, is found around the world. It can be highly polished and has been used for beads and decorative objects since ancient times. It would have been a splendid adornment for the heavenly beings glimpsed by Ezekiel.

AMBUSH

". . . YOU SHALL RISE UP FROM THE AMBUSH AND SEIZE THE CITY . . . ."–JOSHUA 8:7

The tactic of lying in wait to attack an unwitting enemy was only one of many techniques of warfare practiced widely in biblical times. From Mesopotamia to Egypt, warrior-kings and their generals also learned how to mount surprise attacks, move their forces with unexpected speed, and maneuver infantry and chariots for maximum effect. Typically, battles were fought face to face and hand to hand. But some stunning victories were won by defying precedent: Gideon's small band of 300 defeated the powerful Midianite camel cavalry in a surprise night attack (Judg 7). Ultimately, however, Israel's fortunes were in God's hands. When Joshua lured the defenders of Ai out of the city, then ambushed and slaughtered them, God had already promised that outcome (Josh 8).

AMEN

ALL THE PEOPLE SHALL SAY, "AMEN!"–DEUTERONOMY 27:16

The Hebrew word *amen* was spoken in unison by Israelites and, later, Christians at the end of hymns of praise and prayer. Often Jesus introduced his statements with *amen* in order to indicate their trustworthiness. The word connotes certainty, truthfulness, faithfulness, and absence of doubt. When used to describe God, for example, the word *amen* is translated "the God of faithfulness" (Isa 65:16). Similarly, in the book of Revelation, Jesus is called simply "the Amen" (Rev 3:14) because his witness is sure. In English-language Bibles, Jesus' prefatory amens are usually rendered as "I tell you the truth" or "truly," as in Matthew 5:18.

AMETHYST

THE FOUNDATIONS OF THE WALL OF THE CITY ARE ADORNED WITH EVERY JEWEL; THE FIRST WAS JASPER . . . THE TWELFTH AMETHYST. –REVELATION 21:19–20

The transparent, purplish gemstone known as amethyst is a form of quartz, although some scholars think the stone referred to in the Bible was a different crystalline substance chemically identified as aluminum oxide. Amethyst was appreciated in Israel and throughout the ancient world. More than being merely beautiful it was said to protect its wearer from drunkenness; its name in Greek means "not intoxicated."

Long before its mention in Revelation, amethyst had religious significance for Jews. It and most of the other jewels adorning the wall of the new Jerusalem in Revelation were the same kinds as those set in the BREASTPIECE worn by the high priest in the tabernacle (Ex 28:19).

AMOS, BOOK OF

". . . THE LORD SAID TO ME,
'GO, PROPHESY TO MY PEOPLE ISRAEL.'"
–AMOS 7:14–15

Amos was the earliest of the classical prophets to whom books are ascribed. Called by God in the mid-eighth century BC, Amos wrote down his pronouncements of God's judgment on the northern tribes of Israel, who "rejected the law of the LORD . . . who trample the head of the poor into the dust" (Am 2:4, 7). He foresaw EXILE for the Israelites if they did not "let justice roll down like waters, and righteousness like an ever-flowing stream" (Am 5:24). Israel ignored the prophet's message, and the nation was taken captive by Assyria 40 years later.

AMULET

. . . THE LORD WILL TAKE AWAY
THE FINERY OF THE ANKLETS, THE
HEADBANDS, AND THE CRESCENTS . . .
THE SASHES, THE PERFUME
BOXES, AND THE AMULETS . . . .
ISAIAH 3:18–20

Magic charms were extremely common in Near Eastern cultures, as shown by the profusion of them unearthed by archaeologists. Often pierced and hung around the neck on a cord, they were thought to ward off evil or confer the protection of a benign power. Those who wore them believed that amulets derived their potency from having touched a sacred person or object. Despite attempts to root them out, amulets were widely used by the Hebrews. When Jacob disposed of the idols in his household, he buried not only the idols but also earrings, which were probably worn as charms (Gen 35:4). The crescents described in Isaiah as abhorrent were symbols of a moon deity (Isa 3:18). Amulets took the form of seals, rings, metal plaques, emblems, semiprecious stones, and beads. Many found in biblical lands are Egyptian in style, depicting gods such as Osiris and Isis, flowers such as the lotus, and exotic animals, such as the baboon. Pendants in the shape of limbs were most likely worn to effect cures of crippled arms or legs.

ANCESTOR

". . . YOU SHALL BE THE ANCESTOR
OF A MULTITUDE OF NATIONS."
–GENESIS 17:4

Ancestors were exceedingly important in the ancient Near East, as reflected in the number of genealogies in the Bible. A family consisted not only of the living members but also of generations going back to the familial PATRIARCH. A person's ancestry helped to determine his social rank and claim to property. Since all priests had to be descendants of Aaron, genealogies also determined who served in the temple.

Genesis is the narrative of Israel's ancestors: the fathers Abraham, Isaac, and Jacob, and the mothers Sarah, Rebekah, Leah, Rachel, Bilhah, and Zilpah. God's actions are often depicted as being motivated by promises that he made to ancestors, such as when he tells the Israelites to "go in and take possession of the land that I swore to your ancestors" (Deut 1:8). But the sins of the ancestors could bring down vengeance on their children, and God threatens those who worship false gods that he will punish "children for the iniquity of parents, to the third and the fourth generation" (Ex 20:5).

The tree—or "stump"—of Jesse, depicted in a 13th-century illumination, traced Jesus' ancestry back to Jesse, father of David, from whom it was long believed the Messiah would be descended (Isa 11:1).

In Israel there were some instances of ancestor worship, although the practice of deifying an ancestor was strictly forbidden. More common was the cult of the dead, which involved not only worshiping dead ancestors but using them as a link to the spiritual world. But God warned the Israelites not to consult dead ancestors for advice, for those who do "will have no dawn" (Isa 8:20).

A gold amulet dating from about 1400 BC bears an image of the Egyptian fertility goddess Hathor, also called Ishtar or Astarte.

The Sea Peoples, who invaded ancient Canaan from Greece, improved the stone anchor, above right, by adding wooden flukes, which dug into the sea floor.

Anchor

Fearing that we might run on the rocks, they let down four anchors from the stern and prayed for day to come.–Acts of the Apostles 27:29

In New Testament times, seagoing ships often carried three or more anchors, generally wooden shafts with heavy lead or iron crosspieces. Except in severe storms, like the one that led to the apostle Paul's shipwreck off the island of Malta, they were usually dropped from the bow, with the stern secured to the shore by cables.

The word *anchor* was also used figuratively to represent God's promise of unfailing spiritual help: "We have this hope, a sure and steadfast anchor of the soul" (Heb 6:19). Such a nautical image, rare in Jewish writings, may show the influence of the Greeks and Romans, to whom seafaring was more familiar.

Angel

Are not all angels spirits in the divine service, sent to serve for the sake of those who are to inherit salvation? –Hebrews 1:14

Angels are divine beings in the service of God. In the Old and New Testaments, they appear as God's messengers and attendants to his throne. In a few instances, they serve as soldiers in his army, the HOST OF HEAVEN, thus making him the "Lord of hosts."

References to cherubim, seraphim, and especially archangels, such as Michael (Jude 1:9) and Jeremiel (2 Esd 4:36), lend support to the idea of an angelic hierarchy. Gabriel says, "I stand in the presence of God" (Lk 1:19). In Tobit, Raphael refers to himself as "one of the seven angels who stand ready and enter before the glory of the Lord" (Tob 12:15). This group is thought to consist of archangels.

Although angels are often pictured as having wings, the Bible portrays only the cherubim and seraphim viewed by the prophets Ezekiel and Isaiah, respectively, as winged beings. Relatively little is actually said about angels' appearance. Sometimes these mysterious creatures look like human beings, but they are also described as being of great and even blinding beauty. Angels in the New Testament frequently appear cloaked in a brilliant white light.

In their role as divine messengers, angels may foretell an imminent manifestation of God's will, deliver God's judgment on the fallen, punish Israel's enemies and aid its allies, inform a prophet of his mission, or comfort the afflicted. An appearance of the "angel of the Lord" invariably heralds a portentous occurrence. In the Old Testament, the angel of the Lord is sometimes indistinguishable from God and speaks as if the Lord were speaking.

Although they are spiritual rather than corporeal beings, angels can succumb to temptation. SATAN and his minions are traditionally described as fallen angels. Yet despite their evil nature, they are of a higher order than humans.

The popular concept of the guardian angel may derive mainly from Jesus' command to his disciples concerning children: "Take care that you do not despise one of these little ones; for, I tell you, in heaven their angels continually see the face of my Father in heaven" (Mt 18:10). In the Old Testament, the archangel Michael is said to watch over Israel (Dan 12:1).

The angel Gabriel appeared to Daniel, Zechariah, and Mary. This illumination is from a medieval English prayer book.

Animals

God made the wild animals . . . and the cattle . . . and everything that creeps upon the ground of every kind.–Genesis 1:25

The Bible distinguishes between domesticated and wild animals: "all animals and . . . all wild creatures" (Gen 3:14). Domestic animals were seen as a measure of a family's wealth because they provided meat, milk, hides, wool, and transportation. Wild animals, by contrast, were often sources of danger and disease.

The Bible also makes a distinction between animals that are CLEAN AND UNCLEAN. A clean animal is considered fit to eat; an unclean animal is not. The rules are spelled out in Leviticus and Deuteronomy: If a mammal both chews its cud and has cloven hooves, it is clean; otherwise, it is not. An animal that fits one criterion but not the other, such as the pig, is unclean. Birds that are carnivorous or scavengers are unclean. Of marine creatures, only fish with scales and fins are clean. Flying insects, except for locusts, are unclean. Dead bodies are also considered unclean; thus a clean animal that dies a natural death becomes unfit to eat. The rules eliminated animals and birds that were unfamiliar, ate carrion, might cause disease, or were linked with pagan cults.

Noah took "seven pairs of all clean animals" (Gen 7:2) into the ark, not only for food but also eventually for sacrifice to God. Usually cattle, goats, or sheep taken from the herd were offered as sacrifice before being eaten, and all firstborn male animals were sacrificed at an annual feast.

At Passover a lamb was sacrificed and eaten in commemoration of the exodus. Jesus was called "the Lamb of God who takes away the sin of the world!" (Jn 1:29).

Samuel poured oil on David's head and named him king of Israel. A 19th-century engraving captures the anointing of the young man as he returned from the fields.

Anointing

Then Samuel took the horn of oil, and anointed him . . . and the spirit of the LORD came mightily upon David . . . . –1 Samuel 16:13

Anointing someone with oil might mean nothing more than applying a cosmetic or nothing less than invoking the power of God. In the dry land of the Near East, people applied oil to their skin as a moisturizer, often after bathing. They also anointed themselves with scented oils on such occasions as weddings. Before Esther or any other woman from the harem could spend the night with the Persian king Ahasuerus, she had to complete a year of beautifying treatments, including "six months with oil of myrrh" (Esth 2:12).

Anointing with OIL was also a symbol, used in dedicating someone or something to God's service. Priests and kings were anointed with oil, as were the tabernacle and its altar. This ritual of anointing was so sacred that anyone who used it improperly was "cut off from the people" (Ex 30:33).

Israel's first king, Saul, was identified as "the Lord's anointed" (1 Sam 24:6) —literally MESSIAH — which was translated into Greek as *Christos,* from which the word *Christ* is derived.

The sick and the dead were also anointed. The apostles "anointed with oil many who were sick and cured them" (Mk 6:13). When a woman poured expensive ointment over Jesus' head, he said, "She has done what she could; she has anointed my body beforehand for its burial" (Mk 14:8).

After the resurrection of Jesus, Peter preached about "how God anointed Jesus of Nazareth with the Holy Spirit" (Acts 10:38). The apostles in general taught that the prophesied age of the new covenant had dawned. No longer did God's people need to look to others for spiritual leadership, for all believers had been "anointed by the Holy One" (1 Jn 2:20).

Antelope

Your children . . . lie at the head of every street like an antelope in a net; they are full of the wrath of the LORD . . . .–Isaiah 51:20

The Israelites knew two kinds of antelope: the GAZELLE, which is still present in Israel today, and the Arabian oryx, a white antelope that has black marks on its legs and face, long straight horns, and a black tuft of hair below its neck. A fleet-footed animal that could survive without water for long periods of time, the oryx lived in the Arabian desert. There the practice of hunting it with nets, referred to by Isaiah, continued until the 20th century. The oryx is now believed to be extinct in the wild. In Mosaic law, both types of antelope were considered clean—"animals you may eat" (Deut 14:4–5).

ANTICHRIST

THIS IS THE ANTICHRIST, THE ONE WHO DENIES THE FATHER AND THE SON.–1 JOHN 2:22

The term *antichrist* appears only in the letters of John. Written at a time when the early church was under attack, the letters portray the antichrist as both a single individual and as all "those who do not confess that Jesus Christ has come in the flesh" (2 Jn 1:7). Thus, these enemies of Christ are not necessarily individuals who present themselves as the Christ, or Messiah.

Related terms occur in other New Testament books. In a letter to the Thessalonians, for example, Paul warns the early Christians about "the lawless one" (2 Thess 2:3). The antichrist has also been associated with the beast of the book of Revelation.

ANTIMONY

. . . I AM ABOUT TO SET YOUR STONES IN ANTIMONY, AND LAY YOUR FOUNDATIONS WITH SAPPHIRES.–ISAIAH 54:11

Combined with other substances, antimony can produce strong metal alloys or medically useful compounds. In biblical times, powder made from minerals containing antimony was used as eye shadow. Apparently it also served as a mortar for setting mosaic stones, as in Isaiah's prophecy about the building of a new Jerusalem.

Before coins were widely used, antimony, like other metals, sometimes took the place of MONEY. The Black Obelisk, found at the site of the ancient city of Calah (modern Nimrud in Iraq), tells of blocks of antimony paid as part of a tribute to an Assyrian ruler by the Hebrew king Jehu in the ninth century BC. Antimony was one of the precious materials David provided to build Solomon's temple (1 Chr 29:2).

The "apes" in the Bible were probably monkeys, like the one on this bronze weight (shown from both sides).

APE

ONCE EVERY THREE YEARS THE FLEET OF SHIPS OF TARSHISH USED TO COME BRINGING GOLD, SILVER, IVORY, APES, AND PEACOCKS.–1 KINGS 10:22

As the above quotation implies, the "apes" mentioned in the Bible were not native to the Holy Land. Even though the Hebrew word is translated "ape," baboons or vervet monkeys are believed to have been the actual cargo, imported into Egypt via the Red Sea.

People kept monkeys as pets, and Solomon's trading vessels brought the animals back along with other exotic products. Scholars do not know where Tarshish was, but the phrase "ship of Tarshish" indicates a vessel made for long voyages. Speculation has placed Tarshish in Spain, the Sudan, India, and elsewhere.

APOSTLE

AND HE APPOINTED TWELVE, WHOM HE ALSO NAMED APOSTLES, TO BE WITH HIM, AND TO BE SENT OUT . . . .–MARK 3:14

The idea of an apostle, the Greek word for emissary, may be related to the Jewish custom of dispatching messengers in pairs. Such secular officials, however, were appointed only to carry out a specific function for a set period of time. The apostles who served Jesus were spiritual emissaries for the rest of their lives.

The precise usage of the word *apostle,* which occurs 79 times in the New Testament, has been debated but is generally accepted to include Jesus' inner circle of 12 disciples as well as Matthias and Paul. The original group, perhaps symbolizing Israel's tribes, knew Jesus and witnessed his resurrection. They were distinguished from the many other disciples and from the select group of 70 that Jesus commissioned to proclaim his arrival and to heal the sick (Lk 10:1).

The 12 apostles are listed four times in the New Testament, with Peter, or Simon, always at the head of the group. His brother Andrew and possibly Peter himself had earlier been disciples of John the Baptist. According to John's Gospel, Andrew followed Jesus after John the Baptist proclaimed Jesus the "LAMB OF GOD" (Jn 1:35). However, Matthew's and Mark's accounts suggest that Andrew and Peter first saw Jesus while fishing in the Sea of Galilee: "And he said to them, 'Follow me, and I will make you fish for people'" (Mt 4:19).

The Bible does not tell how each of the apostles first encountered Jesus, but James son of Zebedee and his brother John were called by Jesus while they mended nets in their boats, and Matthew was called as he was collecting taxes at his booth. The names of the apostles vary somewhat in the biblical accounts. For example, Judas son of James is alternately called Thaddaeus; similarly, Nathanael and Bartholomew may be the same person or two different people. All the accounts mention John, Philip, James, Thomas, James son of Alphaeus, Simon the Cananaean or Zealot, and Judas Iscariot

Jesus gave all of the apostles the task of carrying on the mission of spreading the gospel. They were to act as his envoys in imitation of his work. The Gospel of Matthew indi-

The apostles John and Peter rush to Jesus' tomb, in this realistic French painting, after Mary Magdalene tells them that the body is no longer there (Jn 20:2–4).

cates that Jesus singled out Peter for recognizing him as the Messiah: "You are Peter, and on this rock I will build my church . . . I will give you the keys of the kingdom of HEAVEN, and whatever you bind on earth will be bound in heaven, and whatever you loose on earth will be loosed in heaven" (Mt 16:18–19).

When Judas, one of the inner circle, killed himself after the crucifixion, Peter called together the believers in Jesus, who proposed two of their group to replace him. They cast lots, and a disciple named Matthias became the new twelfth apostle (Acts 1:15–26). Later Paul, formerly called Saul, was granted an apostolic mission through the grace of a direct revelation from Jesus (Gal 1:1, 15–16).

Acts of the Apostles portrays the apostles as leaders of the church in Jerusalem during the church's first decade. James son of Zebedee was the first apostle to be martyred. It is unknown when most of the apostles left Jerusalem, but by AD 49 the church was under the leadership of James the brother of Jesus. Many legends developed in later years about the missionary journeys of the various apostles.

Paul insisted on his right as a Roman citizen to appeal his case to the emperor. A stained-glass window shows Paul being held in chains.

APPEAL

BUT WHEN THE JEWS OBJECTED, I WAS COMPELLED TO APPEAL TO THE EMPEROR . . . . –ACTS OF THE APOSTLES 28:19

Roman citizens enjoyed the privilege of an "appeal to Caesar"—the right to transfer a case from the provincial court where it was first heard to final disposition before the emperor in Rome. The appeal could be invoked only in cases that fell outside the written statute law, and the emperor could delegate his authority to hear the matter to a lesser official. In Caesarea, the governor acknowledged Paul's right to appeal (Acts 25:12).

APPLE

SUSTAIN ME WITH RAISINS, REFRESH ME WITH APPLES; FOR I AM FAINT WITH LOVE.–SONG OF SOLOMON 2:5

In several instances, the Bible mentions apples, alluding to their pleasing taste and scent. Yet many scholars wonder if common apples grew in the hot climate of ancient Palestine. Some identify the biblical fruit with apricots, which were also tasty and fragrant. The "apples of gold" in Proverbs were probably apricots (Prov 25:11).

Others believe, however, that the ancient Hebrews may well have cultivated apples, as nearby peoples did, according to Babylonian texts. Still unidentified is the fruit that Adam and Eve ate in the Garden of Eden. Though traditionally considered an apple, it is called in Genesis simply the fruit of "the tree of the knowledge of good and evil" (Gen 2:9).

APRON

. . . WHEN THE HANDKERCHEIFS OR APRONS THAT HAD TOUCHED [PAUL'S] SKIN WERE BROUGHT TO THE SICK, THEIR DISEASES LEFT THEM, AND THE EVIL SPIRITS CAME OUT OF THEM.–ACTS OF THE APOSTLES 19:12

The word *apron* appears only twice in the New Revised Standard Version of the Bible: in the quotation above and in Luke. Scholars suggest that "apron" is a translation of a Hebrew word that means "girdle" or "loincloth." For instance, when Adam and Eve ate the forbidden fruit, they became aware of their nakedness and used fig leaves as a loincloth (Gen 3:7). Some versions of the Bible call this makeshift garment an apron.

In the New Testament reference, an apron is probably a sash tied around a tunic at the waist. Paul's aprons have restorative powers because God has chosen to perform "extraordinary miracles through Paul" (Acts 19:11).

In Luke, Jesus talks about a slave putting on his apron to serve the master while he eats and drinks (Lk 17:8), bringing to mind the modern sense of the word.

Aramaic

. . . "Please speak to your servants in Aramaic, for we understand it; do not speak to us in the language of Judah . . . ."–Isaiah 36:11

Aramaic was an ancient Semitic language that originated among the Aramaeans, desert nomads who eventually settled in Syria during the second millennium BC. By the eighth century BC, Aramaic was the main language of business and diplomacy in the Near East.

When the Hebrews were exiled in Babylon, they spoke Aramaic but retained Hebrew as their sacred written language. Large parts of the books of Daniel and Ezra were written in Aramaic, and some New Testament words, such as *Golgotha,* came from Aramaic. Jesus probably spoke one of the language's dialects. Aramaic dialects continue to be spoken today.

An Aramaic commemoration of a king's victories over his enemies was inscribed on this monument, which was unearthed in the ancient city of Dan. Dots separate the words.

Archer

Let not the archer bend his bow, and let him not array himself in his coat of mail.–Jeremiah 51:3

Archers made up one of the four main subdivisions of infantry in ancient armies, along with spearmen, slingers, and auxiliaries. Archers used either a triangular bow or a bi-concave one, which was curved at each end and could shoot up to a distance of 400 yards.

Because they could not swiftly aim their flights of arrows and reload while carrying shields, the strategically important companies of archers were protected in the field by assigned shield bearers. When defending cities, archers tried to cover all possible approaches of attack, and concentrated their fire upon combatants who employed the lethally effective BATTERING RAM.

Canaanite archers used the arrowheads shown above during the late second or early first millennium BC. Below, a detail from a relief depicts a kneeling Assyrian archer attacking the Judean stronghold of Lachish in 701 BC.

Archives

Then King Darius made a decree, and they searched the archives where the documents were stored in Babylon.–Ezra 6:1

Official royal documents, often written on rolls of PAPYRUS or leather, were stored in the archives, or "house of the rolls." The Assyrians and Babylonians wrote on clay tablets, which became their archival documents. Genealogical records may also have been stored in archives. A fifth-century BC letter to Artaxerxes I, king of Persia, urged him to look "in the annals of your ancestors" (Ezra 4:15).

Royal treasury offices sometimes doubled as archives. The nation of Israel may have stored records in the temple, for it was in the temple in 621 BC that the priest Hilkiah discovered an old book of laws, which was probably a version of Deuteronomy.

Ark

And God said to Noah, ". . . make yourself an ark . . . ." –Genesis 6:13–14

In the Old Testament there are two Hebrew words for what most English-language Bibles render as *ark.* Both Hebrew words can be translated as "chest" or "box."

The first of these words, *tebah,* literally means "box" or "chest" and is used for both Noah's ark (see reconstruction, pp. 26–27) and the papyrus basket in which the infant Moses floated among the bulrushes on the Nile (Ex 2:3–5). Both of these structures, so different in size, were thought of as containers for something precious rather than as waterborne vessels or boats.

The other Hebrew word for ark is *aron,* meaning "chest." It is used mainly for the ark of the covenant, but it is also used to describe the

Archives that date from the 23rd century BC *were discovered by archaeologists in the ruins of a palace in Syria in 1975. More than 15,000 tablets and fragments, including treaties and commercial records, revealed the importance of the city of Ebla in the ancient world.*

coffin in which Joseph was buried (Gen 50:26).

Both Hebrew words convey the idea of containers. However, the contents of two of the containers have given the word *ark* a special significance. Noah's ark, by carrying at least two of "every living thing," made it possible for life on earth to continue (Gen 6:19). The ark of the covenant carried the tablets of the TEN COMMANDMENTS.

ARK OF THE COVENANT

THEN THE PRIESTS BROUGHT THE ARK OF THE COVENANT OF THE LORD TO . . . THE MOST HOLY PLACE, UNDERNEATH THE WINGS OF THE CHERUBIM.–1 KINGS 8:6.

The most sacred object in Jewish history, the ark of the covenant was a portable chest that held the stone tablets on which God had inscribed the ten commandments, the basic laws that lay at the heart of his covenant with Israel.

The ark was a chest of acacia wood about 4 feet long and 2 feet deep and wide. Gold plates covered it, inside and out. To carry the ark, gilded wooden poles were placed into gold rings that were attached near the chest's corners. The ark's lid was pure gold and was decorated with two cherubim (probably in the form of winged bullocks) facing each other. The lid was called the mercy seat because it represented the earthly throne of God. "From between the two cherubim that are on the ark of the covenant," God told Moses, "I will deliver to you all my commands for the Israelites" (Ex 25:22).

The ark led the Hebrews' march through the wilderness to the Promised Land. When priests carrying the ark waded into the Jordan River, the water stopped flowing, and the people entered Canaan on dry land, just as they had crossed the Red Sea.

The ark was sometimes brought into battle to symbolize God fighting for Israel. On one such occasion, the Philistines captured it. Seven months later, when the ark had caused the Philistines disaster, they put it on an unmanned oxcart and pointed the animals toward Israel. After the ark arrived in Beth-shemesh, 70 men died—either because they looked inside or because they did not rejoice (Bible translations differ). The community sent the ark to nearby Kiriath-jearim, where a priest kept it for 20 years. King Saul occasionally took the ark to war, but it generally remained in obscurity until David, amid rejoicing and dancing, took it to Jerusalem and provided a tent in which to house it. In Solomon's temple, the ark was placed in the Holy of Holies. Once a year the high priest entered the room to atone for Israel's sins by sprinkling onto the mercy seat the blood of sacrificial animals.

The Babylonians apparently stole the ark when they captured Jerusalem in 587 BC. However, a Jewish legend from the second century BC said that Jeremiah, released by the Babylonians, hid the ark in a cave on the mountain where Moses died (2 Macc 2:4–8). Earlier, Jeremiah had prophesied a day would come when the ark "shall not come to mind, or be remembered, or missed; nor shall another one be made. At that time Jerusalem shall be called the throne of the LORD" (Jer 3:16–17).

Noah's Ark

"This is how you are to make it: the length of the ark three hundred cubits, its width fifty cubits, and its height thirty cubits." – Genesis 6:15

Noah's ark was a colossal barge or houseboat that was shaped more like a gigantic shoebox than a seaworthy ship. The vessel may have been constructed of some kind of cypress, a wood used by the ancients to build ships because of its durability. The boat's three decks were divided into rooms; a single doorway, located in the side of the vessel, provided the only access. According to the Bible, God commanded Noah to cover the vessel with a roof, which overhung an 18-inch-high opening that provided light and ventilation. The ark was covered inside and out with pitch to waterproof it. The size of the ark given in cubits in Genesis translates in modern terms to about 450 feet long, 75 feet wide, and 45 feet high—roughly the size of the American liberty ships that served in World War II. The ark's design would have provided an interior space of approximately 1,500,000 cubic feet. Its cargo included eight humans, thousands of different kinds of animals, and enough supplies to last the full time they remained on board, which was about a year.

Armor

Put on the whole armor of God, so that you may be able to stand against the wiles of the devil. –*Ephesians 6:11*

History's first protective military attire was probably the metal-studded leather vests worn by Sumerian infantrymen as early as 3000 BC. These Mesopotamian warriors also wore pointed metal helmets and carried large, rectangular wood-and-leather shields.

Little more is known about the earliest armor in the ancient Near East. About 1,500 years later, leather body armor, covered with oblong bronze scales, was invented to ward off the blades of battle-axes and the arrows shot from composite bows. Made of as many as 600 scales apiece, these heavy coats of mail were worn by archers, charioteers, and horses. Though vulnerable, especially at the collar and sleeve joints (1 Kings 22:34), the scale mail made it possible to use smaller shields. Head coverings varied widely, from the round Canaanite helmet to the tasseled, pointed Hittite helmet, which included neck and ear shields. The Philistines decorated their helmets with feather crests. Goliath's celebrated armor—a metal coat weighing 5,000 bronze shekels, a bronze helmet, and bronze greaves protecting his legs—typified other Philistine innovations. Their scale mail was formed by laying strips of metal at angles, producing a surface of V shapes. By the time of the kingdom of Israel, virtually all armies used the same type of armor: a short-sleeved, sack-shaped coat of mail. Each soldier was also issued a helmet and a kind of mail scarf to connect it to the collar of the armor. Sometimes one man acted as an armor bearer for another, as David did for Saul (1 Sam 16:21).

Protected by armor, Assyrian warriors scale an Egyptian wall. This is a detail from a seventh-century BC bas-relief that commemorates Assyria's conquest of Egypt.

Arms

. . . the Jews had grown strong from the arms . . . that they had taken from the armies they had cut down . . . . –*1 Maccabees 6:6*

The same basic weapons were used from pre-biblical times on through the biblical period, but they became steadily more deadly as the civilizations of the ancient Near East grew in wealth and technological achievement. In addition to the bow and arrow, soldiers relied on the spear for hand-to-hand fighting and the lighter, smaller javelin for hurling from a distance. When armies met on the battlefield, they lunged at each other with swords or daggers, heavy clubs, and battle-axes.

Some 5,000 years ago, swords were only about 10 inches long because of the limitations of metalworking. The crescent-shaped battle-ax developed gradually until it was long and strong enough to gash through metal helmets, making it often a better close-combat weapon than the sword. Battle-ax blades became sharper and tougher, and the shaft and its connection to the blade were strengthened. Each advance in weaponry caused a corresponding improvement in body armor.

By about 1500 BC, innovations in metalworking made it possible to cast a sword's blade, hilt, and handle as one piece, giving the whole weapon added strength. A sickle shape was used until the invading Sea Peoples introduced a long, straight iron sword capable of both stabbing and cutting. Battle-axes eventually disappeared. Swords became double-edged, with handles designed to conform to the hand; they fit into sheaths hooked to belts. Several nations, including the Israelites, used the leather SLING, which lethally propelled baseball-size stones a long distance. Soldiers who could wield the sling with either hand were prized.

Army

Though an army encamp against me, my heart shall not fear . . . . –*Psalm 27:3*

When cities began to rise throughout the lands of the Bible some 5,000 years ago, it became necessary to raise and train armies to defend the cities, as well as to conquer them. Increasingly, the great empires massed their forces in pursuit of conquest. The Assyrians perfected a military organization that became the standard for its time: they split their troops into infantry, cavalry, and chariots. The infantry was further broken down into archers, spearmen, slingers, and auxiliaries, with each division performing a specific function on the battlefield or during a siege. Military leaders were well versed

Joshua's army storms Jericho, whose walls have fallen, in a painting by James Tissot. The taking of Jericho was attributed to divine intervention as well as military prowess.

in strategy, knew that military discipline was critical to success, and could adapt their tactics to the changing conditions of battle.

In the Bible, images of warfare often refer to the ongoing conflict between God and his enemies or the pagan enemies of Israel. Hebrew soldiers in early Old Testament books participated in the army as a sacred activity that was encouraged and protected by Yahweh, requiring spiritual purity of the participants.

Saul created Israel's first tribal militia. David established the nation's first professional army, part of which was made up of Cherethites and Pelethites, foreign mercenaries who were fiercely loyal to David. Solomon, in his reign, added a CAVALRY. Using information supplied by spies, ancient armies were extremely reliant upon the tactic of surprise attacks. The Israelites were especially skillful at splitting their forces into two or more bands in order to disguise their primary objective.

ARROW

JEHU DREW HIS BOW WITH ALL HIS STRENGTH, AND SHOT JORAM BETWEEN THE SHOULDERS, SO THAT THE ARROW PIERCED HIS HEART . . . .–2 KINGS 9:24

Flint-tipped arrows and simple wooden bows were used as far back as prehistoric times in the Near East, but they became more sophisticated as artisans gained skill in working with metal, treating wood, and joining the two.

By perhaps 3000 BC, arrows with hollow-reed shafts had triangular metal heads with protruding spines. A millennium later, large armies began relying upon the powerful composite BOW, which probably combined birch wood with animal horn and sinew. It was the universal weapon by the time of the judges of Israel, when arrowheads were smoothed flat and sometimes inscribed with their owner's name.

ARTISAN

SO NOW SEND ME AN ARTISAN SKILLED TO WORK IN GOLD, SILVER, BRONZE, AND IRON, AND IN PURPLE, CRIMSON, AND BLUE FABRICS . . . .
–2 CHRONICLES 2:7

The first artisan, or craftsman, described in the Bible is Cain's descendant Tubal-cain, "who made all kinds of bronze and iron tools" (Gen 4:22). During the exodus, God imbued a man named Bezalel, of the tribe of Judah, with superior skills so that he could build the tabernacle: "I have filled him with divine spirit, with ability . . . and knowledge in every kind of craft, to devise artistic designs, to work . . . in cutting stones . . . and in carving wood" (Ex 31:3–5).

Though Bezalel's work was elaborate, Solomon's temple, built about 960 BC, was far grander. Solomon decreed that the temple be decorated with elaborate carvings and metalwork of the highest order: "He covered the two doors of olivewood with carvings of cherubim, palm trees, and open flowers; he overlaid them with gold, and spread gold on the cherubim and on the palm trees" (1 Kings 6:32). He even brought in foreign artisans, such as Hiram from Tyre. Trained by his father, Hiram made bronze pillars with capitals, bronze stands with wheels, and "the molten sea" (1 Kings 7:23), a huge bronze basin, supported by bronze oxen, used for purification rites.

Artisans abounded in biblical times: metalsmiths in gold, silver, copper, and BRONZE; stonemasons and potters; and tanners, weavers, and fullers, who washed fabrics. Still others dyed yarns purple, crimson, and yellow—a skill learned from the Phoenicians. These specialized workers tended to group together according to craft. Isaiah refers to the Fuller's Field (Isa 7:3) and Nehemiah refers to "the valley of artisans" (Neh 11:35). Although they had shops, the workers often plied their trades out of doors.

Artisans also formed guilds. Chronicles refers to "the guild of linen workers" (1 Chr 4:21). The silversmiths who rioted against Paul in Epheseus were obviously organized (Acts 19:23–29). Jesus is thought by many to have been a simple carpenter, but he himself never mentioned his craft.

As Elisha watches, "a chariot of fire" pulled by "horses of fire" appears (2 Kings 2:11), and Elijah ascends to heaven.

ASCENSION

"NO ONE HAS ASCENDED INTO HEAVEN EXCEPT THE ONE WHO DESCENDED FROM HEAVEN, THE SON OF MAN."—JOHN 3:13

In the two works attributed to Luke, he offers two accounts of Jesus' ascension into heaven. In his Gospel, Luke notes three appearances of Jesus on the day of his resurrection and describes how Jesus then led his disciples from Jerusalem to Bethany, blessed them, and "was carried up into heaven" (Lk 24:51). This event Luke clearly dates to the evening after the resurrection.

In Acts of the Apostles, he describes Jesus ascending into heaven some 40 days after the resurrection. During that time, Luke tells us, Jesus appeared to his disciples to prepare them for the formidable task that lay before them of witnessing to him.

In the second account of the ascension, witnesses see Jesus ascend into a cloud—perhaps a parallel to the transfiguration and to Old Testament imagery, such as Elijah's ascending into heaven "in a whirlwind" (2 Kings 2:11). To clarify the event, two men in white robes appear and reveal that Jesus, "who has been taken up from you into heaven, will come in the same way as you saw him go into heaven" (Acts 1:11).

ASHERAH

THE ISRAELITES DID WHAT WAS EVIL IN THE SIGHT OF THE LORD, FORGETTING THE LORD THEIR GOD, AND WORSHIPING THE BAALS AND THE ASHERAHS.—JUDGES 3:7

Asherah, or Ashtaroth in the King James Version of the Bible, was a fertility goddess venerated in various ancient Near Eastern cultures. In Ugaritic mythology Asherah was the wife of El and the mother of the pantheon. In the Old Testament she was associated with the god Baal. The Phoenician princess Jezebel married King Ahab of Israel and promoted the worship of both Baal and Asherah among the Israelites. Some Israelites may even have worshiped Asherah as the consort of Yahweh. The word *Asherah* referred to both the goddess herself and the cultic symbols that represented her, such as a "sacred pole" that might be a carving or a specially planted TREE (Judg 6:25; Deut 16:21).

ASHES

. . . CRY OUT; ROLL IN ASHES . . . FOR THE DAYS OF YOUR SLAUGHTER HAVE COME . . . .—JEREMIAH 25:34

Ashes, the remnant of a consuming fire, symbolized destruction. In times of mourning, repentance, and humiliation, people put ashes on their heads or sat in ash heaps. Ashes also symbolized insignificance. When speaking to God, Abraham referred to himself as "but dust and ashes" (Gen 18:27). In a similar metaphor, Job defended himself against his accusing guests by charging: "Your maxims are proverbs of ashes" (Job 13:12).

Priests sometimes added water to the ashes left from a burned animal sacrifice; they then sprinkled the mixture on people or objects ritually to purify them.

Ashes used for ceremonial purposes were probably handled with these iron shovels, found near an altar in the biblical city of Dan.

ASSASSINS

"Then you are not the Egyptian who recently stirred up a revolt and led the four thousand assassins out into the wilderness?"
–Acts of the Apostles 21:38

Concealing daggers within their robes, the Assassins, a militant Jewish political group, used the cover of crowds to protect themselves as they stabbed their victims. These revolutionaries were known as *Sicarii*, a Latin term meaning "dagger-men." Their enemies were Jewish high priests and others who supported Roman rule of Israel. Paul was arrested when he was mistaken for an Egyptian who planned to lead several thousand of the Assassins in a rebellion against the Romans (Acts 21:38).

ATHLETE

Athletes exercise self-control in all things; they do it to receive a perishable wreath, but we an imperishable one.
–1 Corinthians 9:25

Biblical references to athletes occur only in 4 Maccabees and in two letters written by the apostle Paul. During New Testament times, organized Greek GAMES dominated the world of sports. Paul found metaphorical significance in these athletic events and wrote to Timothy: "I have fought the good fight, I have finished the race, I have kept the faith. From now on there is reserved for me the crown of righteousness" (2 Tim 4:7–8).

While ordinary athletes race for prizes of laurel wreaths to wear as crowns, Christians "run" for a spiritual crown. Peter also referred to the race that ends in God: "And when the chief shepherd appears, you will win the crown of glory that never fades away" (1 Pet 5:4).

The Old Testament also mentions races and runners, as in Ecclesiastes: "I saw that under the sun the race is not to the swift" (Eccl 9:11). In those earlier times, running, throwing, and wrestling, though not described in detail, were quite possibly popular activities among the Hebrews.

ATONEMENT

For on this day atonement shall be made for you, to cleanse you; from all your sins you shall be clean before the LORD.
–Leviticus 16:30

Atonement wiped clean the record of offenses a person had committed against God. An individual who had sinned but was repentant went to the priest, taking an animal to be killed and burned on an altar. This blood sacrifice provided a dramatic visual reminder of the seriousness of sin. But it also became the occasion for God to extend mercy and forgiveness to the penitent.

Every autumn on the Day of Atonement, known in Hebrew as *Yom Kippur*, the high priest offered sacrifices for the Israelites. On this most solemn day of the year, the people fasted as the priest performed the sacrifices. On this day alone the priest was permitted to enter the temple's holiest room, which held the ark of the covenant. There he sprinkled blood from the sacrifices onto the ark.

For Christians the death of Jesus became the atoning sacrifice that fulfilled the words of the prophet Isaiah, who foresaw that "he was wounded for our transgressions . . . like a lamb that is led to the slaughter" (Isa 53:5, 7). His death became the sacrifice to end all sacrifices. Hebrews 10:10 explains that "we have been sanctified through the offering of the body of Jesus Christ once for all." Atonement for the repentant was available through Jesus, and animal sacrifice was no longer necessary. Jews stopped offering sacrifices when the Romans destroyed the temple in AD 70, but they continued to observe Yom Kippur as a day of confession.

An athlete who won an event in the ancient Athenian games, which occurred every four years, received a prize jar that depicted his competition—here a footrace.

When Abner killed David's soldier Asahel, he marked himself for death at the hands of Joab, Asahel's brother and avenger.

Avenger

. . . then the elders of the killer's city shall send to have the culprit taken from there and handed over to the avenger of blood to be put to death. –Deuteronomy 19:12

Hebrew law recognized the concept of vengeance, particularly in retaliation for murder. The law designated someone responsible—the avenger, or avenger of blood—for seeking justice on behalf of the person killed. According to Numbers, "The avenger of blood is the one who shall put the murderer to death; when they meet, the avenger of blood shall execute the sentence" (Num 35:19). Usually the avenger was the victim's next of kin. However, this type of retribution could not be exacted unrestrictedly; under certain circumstances it was not permissible. For example, an avenger of blood was not allowed to harm a person who had killed unintentionally and had escaped to a CITY OF REFUGE.

In both the Old and New Testaments, the Bible speaks of God as an avenger on behalf of his people. In Deuteronomy, Moses asserts that God "will avenge the blood of his children" (Deut 32:43). Centuries later, Paul also advised leaving vengeance in the hands of God: "Beloved, never avenge yourselves, but leave room for the wrath of God" (Rom 12:19).

Awl

He shall be brought to the door . . . and his master shall pierce his ear with an awl; and he shall serve him for life.–Exodus 21:6

An awl is a small tool having a rounded wooden handle that fits in the palm of the hand. From the handle a thin metal piece extends three or four inches. It narrows to a very sharp point, which can pierce holes in leather or other thick materials so that separate pieces can be joined. In biblical times, the icepick-like blade might have been made of bone, stone, or flint.

Use of the awl was linked to slavery, a practice the Hebrews permitted. A Hebrew slave could be kept six years but in the seventh had to be granted freedom. If the slave chose not to leave because he had been well treated, the owner was to "take an awl and thrust it through his earlobe into the door, and he shall be your slave forever" (Deut 15:17). It may be that the slave then wore an identifying earring or other item in the hole.

Ax

Abimelech took an ax in his hand, cut down a bundle of brushwood, and took it up and laid it on his shoulder.–Judges 9:48

An ax usually consisted of a metal head and a wooden handle, the two pieces held tightly together by leather strips. It was employed for various jobs, including cutting stone and felling trees. Iron axes were used in working timber and stone for Solomon's temple. In an emergency, the Israelites could turn their axes into weapons of war (1 Sam 13:20).

The ax head was always in danger of coming loose from its handle (Deut 19:5). In one account, the head of a borrowed ax fell into the river, and the prophet Elisha recovered it by miraculously causing the ax head to float (2 Kings 6:4–7). Isaiah, in speaking of a vengeful God, finds metaphorical significance in chopping down trees with an ax: "He will hack down the thickets of the forest with an ax, and Lebanon with its majestic trees will fall" (Isa 10:34).

Azariah, Prayer of

But the angel of the LORD came down into the furnace to be with Azariah and his companions . . . . –Prayer of Azariah 26

The Prayer of Azariah and the Song of the Three Jews, a section of the Apocrypha, was part of the ancient Greek version of the book of Daniel. It takes up the story of the three Jews thrown into the FURNACE by Nebuchadnezzar. In the Greek text, Abednego retains his original name, Azariah. Azariah's prayer for deliverance summons forth an angel of the Lord. After the angel drives the flames from the furnace, the three men sing praise to God.

BURIAL *could take place more than once in the ancient world. This stone tablet marked the place, now unknown, where the remains of Uzziah, a king of Judah in the eighth century* BC, *were brought centuries after his death. The Aramaic inscription ends with a warning: "Do not open!"*

BABBLER

SOME SAID, "WHAT DOES THIS BABBLER WANT TO SAY?" OTHERS SAID, "HE SEEMS TO BE A PROCLAIMER OF FOREIGN DIVINITIES." –ACTS OF THE APOSTLES 17:18

The Greek word for babbler literally means "seed picker," a reference to birds who scavenge for food. It was also used to describe both people who survived by stealing food and phrase-droppers who used the words and ideas of others without fully comprehending them. Some Stoic and Epicurean philosophers in Athens dismissed Paul as a babbler because they believed he did not understand what he was saying when he preached about the resurrection of Jesus (Acts 17:18).

Babbling could refer to idle chatter, and according to PROVERBS, those who indulge in it should be avoided: "A gossip reveals secrets; therefore do not associate with a babbler" (Prov 20:19). Babbling was also associated in the Old Testament with madness (2 Kings 9:11).

BADGER

. . . THE BADGERS ARE A PEOPLE WITHOUT POWER, YET THEY MAKE THEIR HOMES IN THE ROCKS . . . . –PROVERBS 30:26

The true badger, a burrowing animal belonging to the weasel family, usually keeps itself hidden from human sight. The "badger" or "rock badger" of the Bible probably instead refers to the Syrian coney, or rock hyrax. This creature, a sure-footed inhabitant of rocky terrain, has a size and color that are similar to a rabbit's. The book of Proverbs uses the animal's habits to teach that power is not necessary for survival and that wisdom does not depend on size and strength.

The rock badger was considered unclean because, although it chewed the cud, it did not have divided hooves (Lev 11:5; Deut 14:7). The coney is actually not a ruminant; however, its sideward jaw action and its habit of chewing food twice resemble closely the cud-chewing of ruminants.

BAG

HE ORDERED THEM TO TAKE NOTHING FOR THEIR JOURNEY EXCEPT A STAFF; NO BREAD, NO BAG, NO MONEY IN THEIR BELTS . . . . –MARK 6:8

In the Old Testament, a bag was typically an animal-skin sack that shepherds or travelers would sling over a shoulder to carry necessities. These might include fruit, spices, grain, weights, money, and CLOTHING. The young shepherd David placed in his bag five smooth stones, one of which he used in his slingshot to kill Goliath, his towering opponent (1 Sam 17:40).

As related in the Gospels, in giving a lesson in charity Jesus used a bag as an example of worldly necessities. When Jesus sent his apostles to spread the Word, he told them not to take a bag of provisions. God would provide for them if they gave freely to those who accepted his teachings.

The bags used in biblical times were similar to the goat skin container being cleaned by this Bedouin girl in the Nile River.

BAGGAGE

YOU SHALL BRING OUT YOUR BAGGAGE BY DAY IN THEIR SIGHT . . . AS THOSE DO WHO GO INTO EXILE.
–EZEKIEL 12:4

As a seminomadic people, the Israelites moved frequently. Typically they would pack their belongings—clothing, utensils, and tents—in baggage transported by donkey or, in later times, CAMEL. Their removal to Babylon inspired Ezekiel to speak of his "baggage for exile" (Ezek 12:7).

Perhaps the most famous reference to baggage concerns Saul, who was chosen by the Lord to be king of Israel. Ill at ease with people and having no political aspirations, Saul was an unlikely choice. When Samuel brought the Israelites to find him, he was missing. They asked God, "'Did the man come here?' and the LORD said, 'See, he has hidden himself among the baggage'" (1 Sam 10:22).

The baggage of Israelite captives goes with them into exile in an Assyrian relief commemorating the fall of Lachish in 701 BC.

BAKING

. . . SHE TOOK FLOUR, KNEADED IT, AND BAKED UNLEAVENED CAKES.
–1 SAMUEL 28:24

From prehistoric times, bread was one of the basic foods of biblical life, and baking one of the essential skills (see box). When three men appeared near the oaks of Mamre, Abraham greeted them and said to Sarah, "Make ready quickly three measures of choice flour, knead it, and make cakes" (Gen 18:6).

Baking remained primarily a household activity, but Jerusalem also had a street on which professional bakers made and sold their wares. These were the bakers instructed to give Jeremiah bread each day (Jer 37:21). In New Testament times, bakeries sold sour-

baking bread

Few people in the Holy Land could afford to eat meat on a regular basis, but as the prayer taught by Jesus implied, one staple shared by people everywhere was their "daily bread" (Mt 6:11). Making that bread was almost always a woman's chore. The job began in the morning, with the grinding of flour from grain; the rich usually baked with wheat and the less affluent used barley. The process ended many hours later, when the family's oven, which was typically made of clay lined with stones and situated just outside the house, yielded the last of that day's loaves.

1. Two women grind grain for the family's meals. The one at left feeds grain from a basket into a hand-operated mill. The circular mill stone on top is moved to and fro over the lower stone, crushing the kernels until they are ground into flour, and the flour emerging from between the stones is collected in a bowl.

dough starters and kneaded dough ready for baking at home, as well as loaves of fresh bread.

Balances

Honest balances and scales are the Lord's; all the weights in the bag are his work.
–Proverbs 16:11

Balance scales have been in use since perhaps 5000 BC, as recorded in Egyptian drawings. They were used to measure precious metals such as gold, silver, and COPPER, as well as grains and other products. The material to be weighed was placed in a pan hanging from one end of a balancing bar. At the other end was a pan holding stone or ceramic weights used for measurement, each with its weight chiseled on the side. Some merchants reportedly cheated customers by using slightly heavier weights when buying and lighter ones when selling.

Fragments of 3,000-year-old bronze balances have been uncovered in Israel. Some were found at the city gate, where the Bible says business was often conducted.

Baldness

. . . I will bring sackcloth on all loins, and baldness on every head . . . .–Amos 8:10

When a crowd of young boys taunted Elisha with the words, "Go away, baldhead! Go away, baldhead!" (2 Kings 2:23), their disrespect to the prophet brought swift consequences. Two bears appeared and mauled 42 of the boys. Indeed, for women baldness was considered so grave a defect that it gave Isaiah a metaphor to warn Jerusalem of God's coming punishment: "Instead of perfume there will be a stench . . . instead of well-set hair, baldness . . . instead of beauty, shame" (Isa 3:24).

Shaving the head was a traditional sign of GRIEF and repentance (Isa 22:12). In some texts, however, Israelites were forbidden to make such a display (Deut 14:1), possibly because it might appear to emulate a heathen funeral custom. Canaanite mourners ritually shaved off their hair and buried it with the deceased, believing that it would be a source of power in the after-

2. After mixing the flour with water and salt and adding yeast-filled dough from the previous day's baking to leaven it, one of the women kneads the mixture into dough. Meanwhile, the other woman shapes the dough into loaves that are thin enough to cook quickly, thus saving fuel.

3. One of the women uses a long-handled baker's palette to slide the loaves into the oven, where they bake in a compartment built above the fire. In other types of ovens, she might either sweep the coals to one side and put the loaves on the stones lining the bottom, or else stick the loaves directly against the sides of the oven to bake.

life. Similarly, cutting Samson's hair broke the NAZIRITE vow that endowed him with superhuman strength (Judg 16:17).

BALL

HE WILL SEIZE FIRM HOLD ON YOU, WHIRL YOU ROUND AND ROUND, AND THROW YOU LIKE A BALL INTO A WIDE LAND . . . .–ISAIAH 22:17–18

The word *ball* appears just once in the New Revised Standard Version of the Bible, in Isaiah's prophecy that God would seize King Hezekiah's arrogant steward, Shebnah, and hurl him like a ball into a far land. Isaiah gave no hint of the games played with balls. But archaeologists tell us that balls of leather or painted fabric were among the toys of children in Egypt—toys no doubt popular across the biblical world. Egyptian children had marbles, too, which they used to knock down wooden sticks. They may also have used larger balls and sticks in a game akin to bowling. Another ancient sport, juggling, probably used balls of various kinds.

BALLAD

THEREFORE THE BALLAD SINGERS SAY, "COME TO HESHBON, LET IT BE BUILT; LET THE CITY OF SHIHON BE ESTABLISHED."–NUMBERS 21:27

Stories set to MUSIC became an important part of the Israelites' form of worship and a way of helping them to remember what God had done for them. The Bible's first ballad was sung after Pharaoh's army sank in the Red Sea: "The floods covered them; they went down into the depths like a stone" (Ex 15:5). Many ballads were probably in the lost Book of the Wars of the LORD (Num 21:14); the Song of Deborah (Judg 5) is an example that has survived.

Valuable balms and perfumes were kept in containers like this fine glass bottle from Syria, dating from the first century AD.

BALM

IS THERE NO BALM IN GILEAD? IS THERE NO PHYSICIAN THERE? –JEREMIAH 8:22

The sap of a fragrant plant yielded an all-purpose salve, or balm, that physicians used for such things as treating cuts and reducing the swelling of hemorrhoids. Scholars disagree about which plant it was, though most argue in favor of a tree or a shrub. Apparently produced in Gilead (in modern Jordan), the valuable commodity was exported by caravans like the one that carried Joseph to slavery in Egypt (Gen 37:25–28).

BALSAM TREES

WHEN YOU HEAR THE SOUND OF MARCHING IN THE TOPS OF THE BALSAM TREES, THEN BE ON THE ALERT . . . . –2 SAMUEL 5:24

Scholars are unsure about what kind of trees are meant in the Old Testament account of King David's battle against the Philistines. Rather than evergreens related to the balsam fir, which are unlikely to have grown near Jerusalem, they may have been poplars, whose rustling leaves could sound like marching feet. (The sound alerted David that the Philistine forces were on the move and that the Israelites should attack them from the rear.) Some experts believe the passage may refer to mulberry trees or aspens. Others speculate that the Hebrew word translated as "balsam trees" may be the name of a place near Jerusalem where the decisive battle occurred.

BANK

"'WHY THEN DID YOU NOT PUT MY MONEY INTO THE BANK? . . . WHEN I RETURNED, I COULD HAVE COLLECTED IT WITH INTEREST.'"–LUKE 19:23

The biblical world, which gauged wealth more by land or livestock than by money, had no banks as they exist today. Even so, taxes for the support of the sanctuary had been levied since early times (Ex 30:11–16), and in practice the temple long served as a bank. Because only "shekels of the sanctuary" could be used to buy sacrificial animals, visitors had to exchange their currency with the temple money changers, who were expelled by Jesus (Mt 21:12–13).

Mosaic law prohibited requring interest on loans to fellow Israelites but not on those to foreigners, and in the parable of the talents Jesus affirmed that profiting from some investments was not only legitimate but imperative (Mt 25:14–30).

BANNER

MAY WE SHOUT FOR JOY OVER YOUR VICTORY, AND IN THE NAME OF OUR GOD SET UP OUR BANNERS. –PSALM 20:5

The Israelites used various types of banners as easily recognizable rallying points during military operations, encampments, and actions that required coordination. Basically there were two types of banners: flags made of cloth and wooden or metal emblems in the shapes of animals—devices used also by the Egyptians, Assyrians, and other powers of the region.

When the Israelites began their march out of Sinai, they proceeded from camp under tribal banners (Num 10:11–25). An army on the march with banners fluttering was an overpowering sight; Song of Solomon compares a woman of great beauty with "an army with banners" (Song of S 6:4).

BANQUET

THEN ESTHER SAID, "IF IT PLEASES THE KING, LET THE KING AND HAMAN COME TODAY TO A BANQUET THAT I HAVE PREPARED . . . ."
–ESTHER 5:4

Elaborate formal banquets or feasts fulfilled many important functions in the societies of the ancient Near East. They were staged to celebrate weddings, victorious battles, and other private or public events. They showed hospitality to strangers, sealed friendships, and accompanied religious rituals.

Even when an occasion in the Bible was not overtly religious, the description of feasting and drinking often conveyed a spiritual message. At Belshazzar's feast, mysterious writing appeared on the wall, and the prophet Daniel interpreted it as warning that the tyrannical Babylonian king would be destroyed because he had been "weighed on the scales and found wanting" (Dan 5:13–27) in humility and reverence for God.

Jesus' first miracle occurred at the wedding feast at Cana (Jn 2:1–11). Banquets also figured in several of Jesus' parables, including that of the prodigal son, whose repentance was rewarded when his father ordered his servants to "get the fatted calf and kill it . . . for this son of mine was dead and is alive again; he was lost and is found" (Lk 15:23–24).

Killing the fatted calf, which would have been specially fed in preparation, was a luxury usually reserved for extraordinary occasions. More often, banquet fare featured fish, bread, cheese, honey, and assorted fruits and vegetables. WINE, sometimes brought by guests, was considered an essential accompaniment, although drunken carousing was condemned. There might also be music and dancing. Guests did not sit down to eat but, as in Greece and Rome, reclined on long couches. Women were generally not invited as guests; unless the household had servants, they instead waited on the male diners.

BAPTISM

"GO THEREFORE AND MAKE DISCIPLES OF ALL NATIONS, BAPTIZING THEM IN THE NAME OF THE FATHER AND OF THE SON AND OF THE HOLY SPIRIT . . . ."–MATTHEW 28:19

From a Greek word meaning "to immerse" or "cleanse with water," the term *baptism* is found only in the New Testament. Ceremonial uses of water, however, were long established in Mosaic law. Ritual PURIFICATION was required after recovering from skin diseases, (Lev 14:8–9), and Aaronite priests had to cleanse themselves before performing their offices (Ex 40:12–15). In the New Testament era, such ceremonial practices had become part of Jewish life. At the

John the Baptist drew Jews from all over Palestine to the Jordan River to be dipped in its waters as a sign of their repentance and preparation for God's judgment.

wedding at Cana, Jesus' first miracle involved water jars kept in many households for "the Jewish rites of purification" (Jn 2:6). Ritual bathing was also important to the Essenes, the religious sect located at Qumran that produced the Dead Sea Scrolls.

The Judean ministry of John the Baptist marked the beginning of what became Christian baptism. The rites of immersion he performed in the Jordan River symbolically washed away the sins of those who repented. John made it clear, however, that he was only a forerunner and not the expected Messiah: "I baptize you with WATER for repentance, but one who is more powerful than I is coming after me. . . . He will baptize you with the Holy Spirit and fire" (Mt 3:11). When John subsequently baptized Jesus, the ceremony was followed by the descent of the Holy Spirit, in the form of a dove that alighted on Jesus, and the voice of God proclaiming Jesus to be his Son (Mt 3:13–17).

Thereafter, baptism became a proclamation of faith, sealed by the bestowal of grace by means of "the Holy Spirit and fire" (Lk 3:16). Although outwardly similar to various Jewish purification rites, Christian baptism involved the attainment of eternal salvation: "Peter said to them, 'Repent, and be baptized every one of you in the name of Jesus Christ so that your sins may be forgiven; and you will receive the gift of the Holy Spirit. For the promise is for you, for your children, and for all who are far away'" (Acts 2:38–39).

Jesus did not perform baptisms himself (Jn 4:2), but his disciples did so in his name. In time, baptism became a formal rite of initiation into the Christian community: "As many of you as were baptized into Christ have clothed yourselves with Christ . . . all of you are one in Christ Jesus" (Gal 3:27–28).

BARBARIAN

I AM A DEBTOR BOTH TO GREEKS AND TO BARBARIANS, BOTH TO THE WISE AND TO THE FOOLISH . . . . –ROMANS 1:14

Of Greek derivation, the word *barbarian* originally meant "foreigner," specifically someone whose incomprehensible speech seemed to sound like the nonsense syllables "bar-bar." Later the word came to denote all non-Greeks.

The fifth-century BC Greek historian Herodotus referred to the Egyptians, who were a highly cultivated people, as barbarians. Just as the Jews thought of the world's peoples as being either Jew or Gentile, the Greeks saw the world as divided into Greeks and barbarians. But all such differences, wrote Paul, were erased by Christianity, as "there is no longer Greek and Jew, circumcised and uncircumcised, barbarian, Scythian, slave and free; but Christ is all and in all!" (Col 3:11).

BARLEY

THEN SHE BEAT OUT WHAT SHE HAD GLEANED, AND IT WAS ABOUT AN EPHAH OF BARLEY. –RUTH 2:17

Barley was an important crop in biblical times, used for bread and animal feed. Ripening several weeks earlier than the more highly valued WHEAT, it was harvested in April and May.

Still a staple crop, barley flourishes in the warm, arid climate of Israel.

A barley harvest figures prominently in the story of Ruth. After returning to Bethlehem—her late husband's home—with her impoverished mother-in-law, Naomi, Ruth went to the barley fields to glean behind the landowners' workers. By law, harvesters in ancient Israel never reaped all the grain, but rather let poor people gather their leavings. There Ruth attracted the attention of Boaz, whose favors included giving her six measures of barley (Ruth 3:17). In the New Testament, Jesus' miracle of the loaves and fishes involved barley loaves (Jn 6:9, 13).

BARN

. . . THEN YOUR BARNS WILL BE FILLED WITH PLENTY, AND YOUR VATS WILL BE BURSTING WITH WINE. –PROVERBS 3:10

The barns mentioned in the Bible were storage places for grain or seeds—what might be called silos or granaries today. They were often underground depositories in which wheat or barley could be preserved for years. A full barn figuratively represented abundance and the rewards of a godly life, while an empty one meant disaster and poverty. The book of Proverbs promises full barns to all who honor the Lord with their produce; Joel grimly prophesies that Israel's barns will be depleted by a plague of locusts, which he sees as punishment from God: "The seed shrivels under the clods, the storehouses are desolate; the granaries are ruined because the grain has failed" (Joel 1:17).

In the New Testament, Jesus refers to a barn in the parable of weeds among the wheat, when "'at harvest time I will tell the reapers, Collect the weeds first and bind them in bundles to be burned, but gather the wheat into my barn'" (Mt 13:30).

Barrenness

You shall be the most blessed of peoples, with neither sterility nor barrenness among you . . . .–Deuteronomy 7:14

In biblical times, childlessness was thought to be not only a great tragedy but also a curse on a woman. Sarah said to Abraham, "You see that the LORD has prevented me from bearing children" (Gen 16:2). CHILDREN were deemed essential to the long-term stability of society, carrying on the family name as well as caring for aged parents and seeing to it that they were buried properly after they died. Thus women who bore no children were pitied, and sometimes scorned as well. Rachel said to her husband, Jacob, "Give me children, or I shall die!" (Gen 30:1). Sarah, Rebekah, and Rachel were all barren until God intervened and made them the mothers of the Israelite nation. When Rachel finally gave birth to Joseph, she said, "God has taken away my reproach" (Gen 30:23). During his ministry, Jesus foretold the terrible fate that awaited Jerusalem when he said, "For the days are surely coming when they will say, 'Blessed are the barren'" (Lk 23:29).

Baruch, Book of

. . . Baruch took the vessels of the house of the Lord . . . and brought them to Babylon.–Baruch 1:8–9

The book of Baruch was purportedly written during the Jewish exile in Babylon by the secretary of the prophet Jeremiah, although Jeremiah said that he and Baruch escaped exile and "came into the land of Egypt" (Jer 43:7). The book features a prayer of confession for Jews in Jerusalem and assurance that God will bring the exiles home. Most scholars agree that it was written no earlier than 200 BC, some 300 years after the exile. Treated as part of the Apocrypha in Protestant Bibles, the book of Baruch is accepted as canonical by Roman Catholic and Eastern Orthodox authorities.

Basket

The LORD showed me two baskets of figs placed before the temple of the LORD.–Jeremiah 24:1

The Bible names several different kinds of baskets. One was a common household utensil most often used to carry and store food. Another was used in harvesting grain, and a third to trap birds. A fourth one was sturdy enough to haul clay for bricks. It was in this kind of basket that the severed heads of Ahab's sons were carried (2 Kings 10:7). Another term is used in Greek for the 12 baskets in which leftover bread was gathered after Jesus fed a multitude of people (Mt 14:20). Still another Greek term refers to the large hamper in which the apostle Paul was lowered through an opening in the Damascus wall (Acts 9:25).

This 14th-century BC Egyptian basket was made of papyrus reeds, like those used by Moses' mother (Ex 2:3).

Bat

On that day people will throw away to the moles and to the bats their idols of silver and their idols of gold . . . .–Isaiah 2:20

Since earliest times, the limestone caves of biblical lands were a hiding place for valuables as well as a home for bats. So it was that Isaiah foresaw the people of Israel frantically trying to hide their idols in the bat-filled caves on the day when the Lord "rises to terrify the earth" (Isa 2:21).

Bats are common across the Near East, roosting in the region's many caves and clustering together in other dark places. The Bible lists bats among the unclean birds that are not to be eaten (Lev 11:13–19). Although they are actually mammals, the logic is clear enough: bats feed on INSECTS, and most insects are forbidden as food (Lev 11:20–23).

Her barrenness miraculously cured, Elizabeth feels the infant in her womb—John the Baptist—leap "for joy" when Mary greets her (Lk 1:44).

BATH

FOR TEN ACRES OF VINEYARD SHALL YIELD BUT ONE BATH, AND A HOMER OF SEED SHALL YIELD A MERE EPHAH.–ISAIAH 5:10

A bath was a standard liquid measure, equal to about $5^{1}/_{2}$ gallons, that was used for oil, wine, and water. It was equivalent to the dry measures of one ephah or one-tenth of a homer.

In the book of 1 Kings, the measure is used to convey the vastness of the molten sea, a bronze tank in Solomon's temple, which held 2,000 baths, or approximately 11,000 gallons, of water (1 Kings 7:26). To entice the king of Tyre to send wood for the temple, Solomon promised, "I will provide for . . . those who cut the timber . . . twenty thousand baths of wine, and twenty thousand baths of oil" (2 Chr 2:10). See also chart for MEASURES.

BATHING

THE DAUGHTER OF PHARAOH CAME DOWN TO BATHE AT THE RIVER . . . .–EXODUS 2:5

In the arid climate of the Near East, water was so scarce that bathing by full immersion was very unusual. The Old Testament contains only a handful of references to such bathing. In one of them, the Syrian army commander Naaman, following the instructions of the prophet Elisha, immersed himself seven times in the Jordan River and was cured of leprosy (2 Kings 5:14). The practice of washing outdoors made it possible for King David, walking on his roof, to catch sight of Bathsheba bathing (2 Sam 11:2).

In Leviticus bathing often means the use of the mikvah, a bath or bathing place for removing ritual uncleanliness of various kinds by washing or immersion in clean water. Elaborate ritual washing was required of priests, and the temple complex had large containers of water for this purpose.

The Bible frequently mentions the washing of feet. The dust of the roads was extreme, and a host's first duty was to see to the washing of a guest's feet. When the Lord appeared to Abraham with two angels, he took them for human visitors and immediately said, "Let a little water be brought, and wash your feet" (Gen 18:4).

Some Egyptian palaces had bathrooms; however, in Exodus Pharaoh's daughter bathes in the Nile. Public baths, though common in Greek cities, were unknown in biblical lands until the Roman conquest. Herod the Great, a lover of things Roman, had elaborate bathing facilities built at his palace on Masada and in his winter palace.

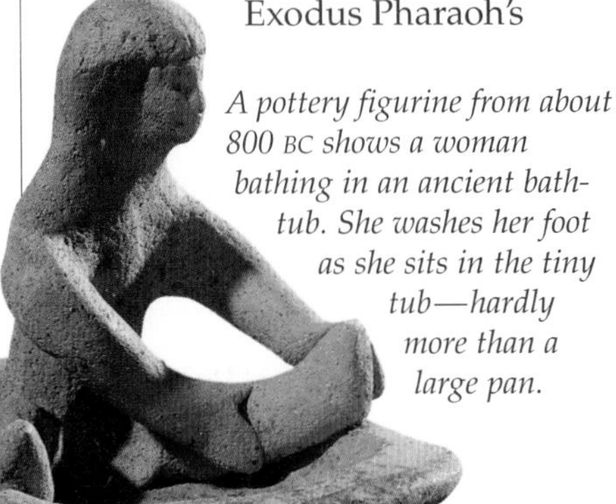

A pottery figurine from about 800 BC shows a woman bathing in an ancient bathtub. She washes her foot as she sits in the tiny tub—hardly more than a large pan.

BATTERING RAM

HE SHALL DIRECT THE SHOCK OF HIS BATTERING RAMS AGAINST YOUR WALLS . . . .–EZEKIEL 26:9

About 2000 BC, armies began using heavy wooden poles to breach walls, running with them toward their targets. Over the centuries, battering rams developed into powerful machines, often mobile and with the pole suspended on ropes from a tower. Warriors inside a hut pushed the pole, which gained force as it swung back and forth. Assyrian six-wheeled devices, protected by metal and leather coverings, carried archers, as well as a soldier to douse torches thrown by defenders. The tips of battering instruments, frequently metal, were either pointed to crack the wall or blunt to break whole sections of it.

BEAM

THE SHAFT OF [GOLIATH'S] SPEAR WAS LIKE A WEAVER'S BEAM . . . .–1 SAMUEL 17:7

In the Bible, a beam is a long piece of wood, usually cedar, used in a loom or construction. A weaver's beam is the horizontal cross-bar on a loom, around which the warp is wound. The likening of Goliath's spear to a weaver's beam suggests the giant's enormous size.

In constructions, wooden beams were used to support walls and ceilings. The Bible contains several references to house beams. In one, the author of the book of Ezra says that as a punishment, a beam from a perpetrator's own house should be used to impale him (Ezra 6:11). Beams might also be parts of gates, such as those of the temple fortress and Jerusalem's Fish Gate and Old Gate (Neh 2:8; 3:3, 6), where sometimes they acted as the pivots and sometimes as the bolts. See also BUILDING.

BEANS

. . . TAKE WHEAT AND BARLEY, BEANS AND LENTILS, MILLET AND SPELT; PUT THEM INTO ONE VESSEL, AND MAKE BREAD FOR YOURSELF. –EZEKIEL 4:9

The beans in the Bible were probably a flat-podded variety called broad beans, or horsebeans. Farmers sowed them in the fall and harvested them in early spring. Beans

The Bible speaks of growling, charging, and enraged bears, which were often females whose cubs had been stolen. This sixth-century mosaic formed part of a church floor.

were cooked and eaten fresh or dried. Dried beans were threshed and winnowed like grain. Since meat was a luxury for most Israelites, beans and other legumes were an important source of protein. When food was scarce, people mixed beans with grains and lentils to make bread, as Ezekiel was warned to do in a vision before the siege of Jerusalem.

Beans were among the foods that were offered to King David's troops when they were "hungry and weary and thirsty in the wilderness" (2 Sam 17:29).

BEAR

"... WHENEVER A LION OR A BEAR CAME, AND TOOK A LAMB FROM THE FLOCK, I WENT AFTER IT AND STRUCK IT DOWN, RESCUING THE LAMB FROM ITS MOUTH ...." –1 SAMUEL 17:34–35

David convinced King Saul that a youth brave enough to protect his sheep from lions and bears could win a battle against the Philistine giant, Goliath. The type of bear he was referring to was the huge, brown, shaggy Syrian bear, which was notorious for raiding vineyards and attacking sheep when foraging for food. Its great strength and unpredictable behavior made it even more fearful than the lion.

The bear's ferocity was also used to convey the importance of respect. When small boys jeered at the prophet Elisha, he cursed them and "two she-bears came out of the woods and mauled forty-two of the boys" (2 Kings 2:24).

BEARD

IT IS LIKE THE PRECIOUS OIL ON THE HEAD, RUNNING DOWN UPON THE BEARD, ON THE BEARD OF AARON ....–PSALM 133:2

An important aspect of a man's appearance in biblical times, a full beard was considered handsome. In Leviticus, God orders the Israelites not to "round off the hair on your temples or mar the edges of your beard" (Lev 19:27). Priests, such as Aaron, must be especially careful not to shave off those edges (Lev 21:5).

A black beard is a prominent feature of this painted terracotta mask, found in a Phoenician cemetery.

Altering another man's beard was sometimes done to cause humiliation (2 Sam 10:4–5). Shaving one's own beard could be part of the mourning ritual (Jer 41:5). It could also be a prediction of doom, as when the prophet Ezekiel is instructed by the Lord to "take a sharp sword; use it as a barber's razor and run it over your head and your beard" (Ezek 5:1). This radical action symbolized the coming destruction of Jerusalem.

BEAST

AND THE BEAST WAS CAPTURED, AND WITH IT THE FALSE PROPHET . . . THESE TWO WERE THROWN ALIVE INTO THE LAKE OF FIRE . . . . –REVELATION 19:20

The word *beast* has several meanings in the Bible. It is a general term for an animal, as in "every beast of the earth" (Gen 1:30). It is used for wild and dangerous animals, as in "that which was torn by wild beasts" (Gen 31:39), and as a metaphorical reference to people, as in "I was like a brute beast toward you" (Ps 73:22).

In modern translations, "beast" is used largely as a word for a symbolic creature, especially as found in the books of DANIEL and Revelation. Daniel symbolizes four kingdoms of the Near East by picturing four beasts: a lion with eagle's wings, a bear with three tusks, a leopard with four wings and four heads, and a beast with iron teeth and 10 horns (Dan 7:2–7). In Revelation there are two beasts. The beast "rising out of the sea" (Rev 13:1) represents the Roman state and is a mix of the four beasts from Daniel. The second beast, "out of the earth" (Rev 13:11), is called the false prophet and seems to represent the emperor and emperor worship. Both are defeated in the cosmic battles described in Revelation.

Bed

Upon my bed at night,
I sought him whom my soul loves . . . .
–Song of Solomon 3:1

The very poor used a straw mat on the ground as a bed and garments as blankets. Those a bit more fortunate had a one-room mud-brick house, where they could lay a mat on the ground or on a mud-brick bench. Only the very wealthy few, who lived in large, many-roomed houses, had separate bedchambers. These rooms often had elaborately decorated beds that were off the ground. Some bed frames were covered with gold or silver or inlaid with IVORY. The Assyrian general Holofernes had a bed with a canopy "woven with purple and gold, emeralds and other precious stones" (Jdt 10:21).

People used beds for sleeping and resting and sometimes as cots or stretchers for the sick and pallets for the dead. In the Greco–Roman period, the rich often reclined on couches or beds while eating or applying cosmetics.

Isaiah 28:20 says, "For the bed is too short to stretch oneself on it, and the covering too narrow to wrap oneself in it"—a proverb indicating an impossible situation. The Bible also warns that the marriage bed should be kept undefiled (Heb 13:4).

This Sumerian terra-cotta sculpture, only about four inches long, is modeled after a bed from about the 18th century BC.

Bee

. . . There was a swarm of bees
in the body of the lion, and honey.
He scraped it out . . . and went on,
eating as he went.–Judges 14:8–9

The honeybee provided HONEY, an important food that was used for sweetening. Samson obtained honey from a most unusual source: a lion's carcass. He then invented a riddle to test the Philistines: "Out of the eater came something to eat. Out of the strong came something sweet" (Judg 14:14). Normally people obtained honey from wild bees living in hives in natural hollows or from domesticated bees nesting in baskets or earthenware.

Bees, which were plentiful in biblical lands, were associated with antagonism, and honey was thought to provide courage. Armies might be compared to swarms of bees: "The Amorites . . . came out against you and chased you as bees do" (Deut 1:44).

This bee is a hieroglyphic character in a chronological list of Egyptian kings, found in the temple of Ramses II.

Beggar

Do not become a beggar by feasting
with borrowed money . . . .
–Ecclesiasticus 18:33

Beggars were despised in biblical times, even when they were forced into begging by ill health, blindness, or other disabilities. In the book of Psalms, the poverty that leads to beggary is part of a terrible curse hurled against the family of an enemy: "May his children wander about and beg" (Ps 109:10). The apocryphal book of Sirach goes so far as to say that "it is better to die than to beg" (Sir 40:28).

Jesus, who restored the sight of the "blind beggar" Bartimaeus (Mk 10:46), commanded compassion toward beggars. One of his most famous parables concerned the beggar Lazarus, who was afflicted with sores and yearning for crumbs from a rich man's table. At his death Lazarus found comfort in the bosom of Abraham, but the rich man who denied him was cast into hell (Lk 16:19–31).

Behemoth

"Look at Behemoth . . .
It is the first of the great acts
of God . . . ."–Job 40:15, 19

Behemoth is a mighty beast that serves as a lesson to Job of the power of God. Its description sounds most like a hippopotamus: it has enormous strength, eats grass "like an ox," and lives "in the covert of the reeds and in the marsh" (Job 40:15, 21).

In Egyptian myth the forces of chaos in the forms of the hippopotamus and crocodile fight the god Horus. This reinforces identifying Behemoth with a hippo-like creature, since the Bible also paints Behemoth as a monster that came out of chaos. Whatever the fearful beast may be, it is still a creature of God and subject to his power.

Bel and the Dragon

. . . "The king has become a Jew; he has destroyed Bel, and killed the dragon . . . ."–Bel and the Dragon 28

This short story in the Apocrypha concluded the book of Daniel in the Greek translation of Scripture used in Jesus' day. In it Daniel proved that Bel, the primary god of the Babylonians, was not a "living god" who could eat and drink: Daniel scattered ashes on the temple floor, and the next day he showed King Cyrus the footprints left by the priests, who sneaked in through a hidden passage to eat the food left for Bel. Daniel also destroyed the "great dragon" revered by the Babylonians by feeding it cakes of tar, fat, and hair: after eating, the dragon burst. Enraged at the king, the Babylonians insisted that he hand Daniel over to them. They threw Daniel into the lions' den, but with God's help he survived unscathed. This miracle convinced the king to believe only in Daniel's God.

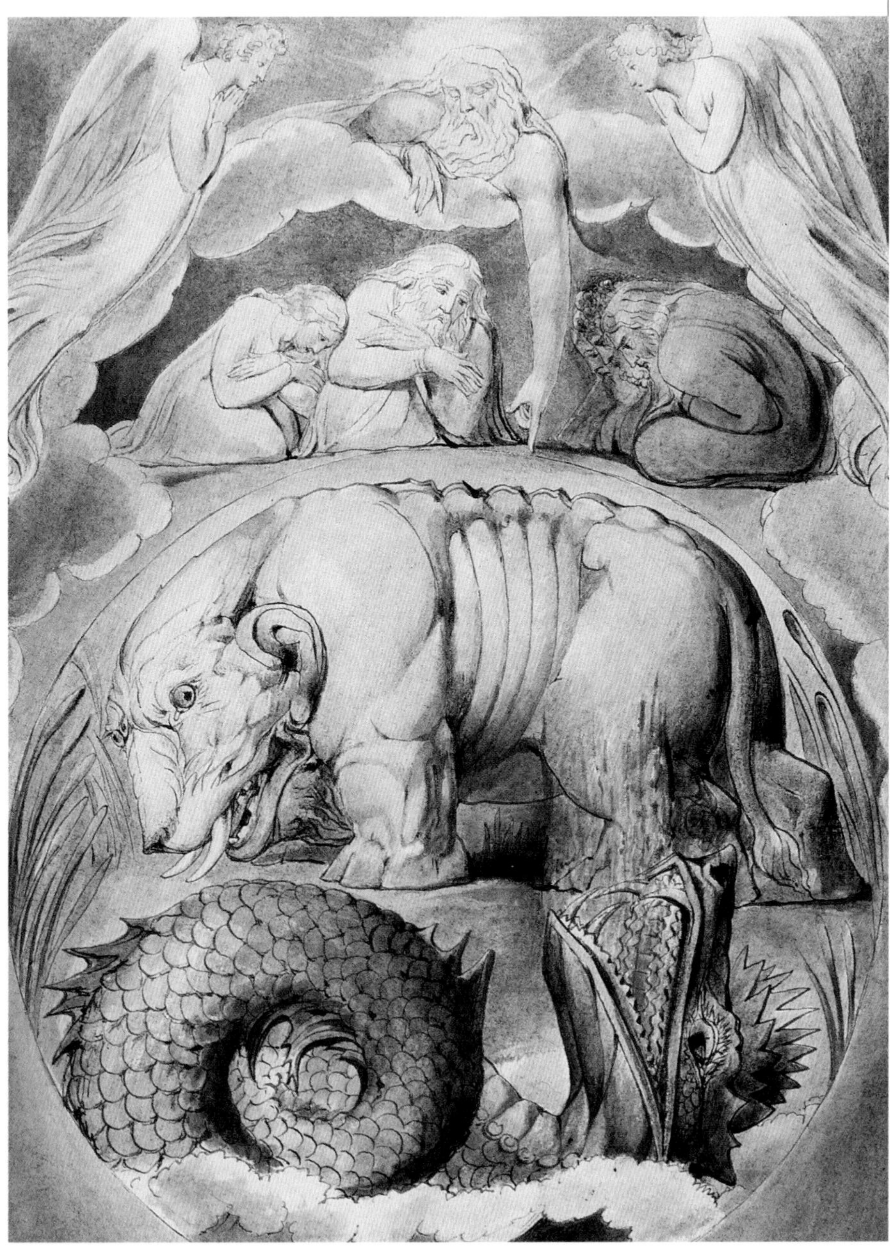

English artist William Blake illustrated the book of Job during the 1820s, rendering the creatures Behemoth and Leviathan as frightening monsters ruled over by God in heaven.

Bells

On the lower hem of the robe they made . . . bells of pure gold . . . .–Exodus 39:24–25

The high priest wore golden bells, which were attached to the bottom of his robe. The sound of the bells let the crowd outside the temple follow the high priest's movements as he walked about, ministering on their behalf. Inside the temple, he burned incense offerings to create a cloud that protected him from the glory of God, who had proclaimed that "no one shall see me and live" (Ex 33:20).

Most bells found by archaeologists are from one to two inches high, suggesting that they were worn instead of held. The book of Zechariah indicates that bells were also worn by horses (Zech 14:20). Assyrian illustrations confirm this practice.

Belly

The righteous have enough to satisfy their appetite, but the belly of the wicked is empty.–Proverbs 13:25

To punish the serpent for deceiving Eve, God decreed that serpents must forever crawl upon their bellies (Gen 3:14). Later Leviticus classified creatures that travel on their bellies as ritually impure and "detestable" (Lev 11:42).

Elsewhere in the Bible, the belly, or stomach, is seen in its central role in physical life, either as the organ of sustenance or as a vulnerable target for an enemy's sword. The Hebrew word for navel was used to indicate the center of the earth—Jerusalem (Ezek 38:12). Perhaps the most famous biblical belly belongs to the fish that swallowed Jonah and vomited him up on dry land, symbolizing a divine rescue from SHEOL, the underworld.

Belt

Now John wore clothing of camel's hair with a leather belt around his waist . . . . –Matthew 3:4

In biblical times a belt, usually made of leather, or a cloth sash was tied around a person's tunic at the waist. The tunic, of woolen or linen cloth, extended from the neck to the knees or ankles. The belt gathered and secured the cloth.

In an early ritual, a belt was specially tied around the waist of a new priest. When Moses ordained Aaron, for example, "he put the tunic on him, [and] fastened the sash around him" (Lev 8:7).

Paul used "belt" in exhorting the church at Ephesus: "Stand therefore, and fasten the belt of truth around your waist, and put on the breastplate of righteousness" (Eph 6:14).

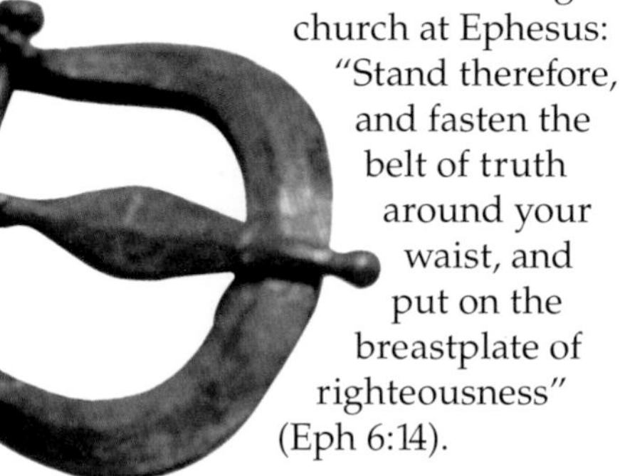

Belt buckles were rare until late in the biblical era; this one, from Masada, was probably worn by a Roman soldier.

Benefactor

But he said to them, "The kings of the Gentiles lord it over them; and those in authority over them are called benefactors."–Luke 22:25

The honorific title *benefactor* was used by some of the Hellenistic kings of Egypt and Syria. The Greek term is *euergetes*, and it was imprinted on their coins. The title was also bestowed upon those who performed great public service. Yet the conspicuous kind of work necessary to attract such acclaim would not stand one in good stead in the kingdom of God.

During the Last Supper, the apostles debated among themselves as to which one of them would be considered the greatest. Jesus rebuked them, saying that a title such as *benefactor* was hardly honorable, but "rather the greatest among you must become like the youngest, and the leader like one who serves" (Lk 22:26).

Beryl

. . . every precious stone was your covering, carnelian, chrysolite, and moonstone, beryl, onyx, and jasper . . . .–Ezekiel 28:13

Beryl, a usually green mineral, comes in several varieties. Emeralds are a form of beryl, although apparently distinct from that called beryl in the Bible. In fact, some scholars think the Old Testament's "beryl" was actually Spanish topaz. Like many gemstones, beryl was often sewn onto royal or priestly garments. The prophet Ezekiel cited beryl among the lavish adornments worn by the king of Tyre—emblems of sinful pride punishable by expulsion from a latter-day garden of Eden. Yet beryl was also among the stones set into the high priest's breastpiece (Ex 28:20). Both beryl and emeralds were to embellish the new Jerusalem promised in the book of Revelation (Rev 21:19–20).

Bier

Then David said to Joab . . . "Tear your clothes, and put on sackcloth, and mourn over Abner." And King David followed the bier.–2 Samuel 3:31

A bier was a litter, probably a wooden board, that was used to move a corpse. A deceased young man from Nain was being carried outside the walls of the town for burial when Jesus encountered the funeral procession. Touching the bier was a dramatic thing to do because it violated Jewish purity laws about contact with a dead body. The bier of royalty, such as that of King Asa, would have been an elaborately decorated COUCH: "They laid him on a bier that had been filled with various kinds of spices" (2 Chr 16:14). It was probably left in the tomb.

Birds

By the streams the birds of the air have their habitation; they sing among the branches. –Psalm 104:12

The Holy Land has a variety of habitats suitable for different species of birds, and the avian migration route between Europe and Africa runs its length. Not surprisingly, birds are mentioned about 300 times in the Bible.

Sarah's body is carried on a bier to her burial site in the cave at Machpelah as Abraham walks mournfully by her side.

In Old Testament times the bird population was divided into "screamers" and "twitterers." The former group includes birds of prey and owls; the latter, sparrows and similar birds. Twenty unclean birds are listed, including the eagle, the vulture, the raven, the sea gull, the hawk, the great owl, and the heron (Lev 11:13–19). Probably these birds were taboo because they were thought to be carnivorous, meaning they ate dead meat. All other birds are clean, including the pigeon, partridge, and QUAIL, which were used for food.

Birds are integral to many Bible stories, beginning with that of Noah, who released a raven to see if the flood waters had receded. The raven was a logical choice because it could fly long distances and, being at home on rocky heights, would seek out mountaintops. When the raven did not return, Noah released a dove, which "came back to him in the evening, and there in its beak was a freshly plucked olive leaf" (Gen 8:11).

God provided food for the Israelites during the exodus when "quails came up and covered the camp" (Ex 16:13). The migration route of the flock, which probably headed north after wintering in Africa, would have crossed the Israelites' path in the wilderness.

In the story of Peter's denial of Jesus, Peter was warned by Jesus, "Truly I tell you, this day, this very night, before the cock crows twice, you will deny me three times" (Mk 14:30).

The dove is famous for being the form that the Holy Spirit took after the baptism of Jesus: "And when Jesus had been baptized, just as he came up from the water, suddenly the heavens were opened to him and he saw the Spirit of God descending like a dove. . . . And a voice from heaven said, 'This is my Son . . . with whom I am well pleased'" (Mt 3:16–17).

The ordeal of giving birth in ancient times—exhausting, painful, and often perilous—is preserved in this limestone relief of a Roman woman in labor, seated on a birth stool and aided by two midwives.

BIRTH

SHE WAS PREGNANT AND WAS CRYING OUT IN BIRTH PANGS, IN THE AGONY OF GIVING BIRTH.
–REVELATION 12:2

The Bible regards childbirth as an agonizing experience. God punished Eve for disobeying him by saying, "I will greatly increase your pangs in childbearing; in pain you shall bring forth children" (Gen 3:16). Nonetheless, childbirth was a joyful occasion—especially the birth of a son—and a child was usually named right away.

Women often gave birth under unsanitary conditions, and the mortality rate for both infants and mothers was high. Women in labor commonly sat on a birth stool made of two stones or bricks. They were usually attended by midwives, who would cut the umbilical cord, rub the baby's skin with salt to toughen it, and wrap the baby in swaddling cloths—a practice thought to make the bones strong. Apparently the mother of Jesus had no midwife to help her during childbirth. After Jesus was born, Mary herself "wrapped him in bands of cloth, and laid him in a manger" (Lk 2:7).

Biblical writers used birth pains as a metaphor for the coming of the Lord. According to Isaiah: "Pangs and agony will seize them; they will be in anguish like a woman in labor" (Isa 13:8).

BIRTHRIGHT

SEE TO IT THAT NO ONE BECOMES LIKE ESAU . . . WHO SOLD HIS BIRTHRIGHT FOR A SINGLE MEAL.
–HEBREWS 12:16

The birthright was the highly valued set of privileges to which the oldest son of a family was entitled, "since he is the first issue of his [father's] virility" (Deut 21:17). The most important of these privileges was a double share of his father's estate. This custom was common throughout the ancient Near East and replaced an earlier practice evidenced in the 18th-century BC Code of Hammurabi, in which all male heirs received an equal portion of an INHERITANCE.

The father's special blessing usually went to the oldest son, through whom the family line was continued. He became the head of the family, with responsibility for his younger brothers, his unmarried sisters, and his father's widow or widows. When there were no sons, the birthright belonged to the oldest daughter.

The birthright, or primogeniture, was protected in the Bible. Mosaic law states that a man cannot play favorites but must give his inheritance to his firstborn son even if the firstborn is the son of a wife he dislikes (Deut 21:15–16). The sons of concubines and slaves were not usually considered equal to the sons of wives when it came to inheriting, although they could be so considered if the father wished it. A birthright could be traded or sold within a family. The best-known example is the starving Esau selling his birthright to his brother Jacob in exchange for some stew. Esau reasoned, "I am about to die; of what use is a birthright to me?" (Gen 25:32). A son's birthright could also be forfeited because of a serious transgression. Reuben lost his birthright by sleeping with his father's concubine, Bilhah.

There are many examples in the Bible of a father or grandfather preferring a younger son to an older one. Abraham passed over Ishmael in favor of his younger brother, Isaac. When Jacob blessed Joseph's sons, he put his right hand on the head of Ephraim instead of on that of Manasseh, thus giving the younger son the greater blessing. Although Joseph tried to stop him, Jacob insisted, saying, "[Manasseh] also shall become a people, and he also shall be great. Nevertheless his younger brother shall be greater than he" (Gen 48:19). The prophet Samuel selected David to succeed to the throne of Israel, even though he was the youngest of his brothers.

Bishop

For a bishop, as God's steward, must be blameless . . . a lover of goodness, prudent, upright, devout, and self-controlled.
–Titus 1:7–8

The English word *bishop* comes from the Greek word *episkopos,* meaning "watchman" or "overseer." In the New Testament, it refers to an official of the early church. In his letter to the Philippians, Paul links the bishops with the deacons as leaders of the congregation. In writing to Titus and to Timothy, the apostle spells out not only what a bishop must be but also what he must not be: arrogant, quarrelsome, alcoholic, violent, or greedy. The position required "a firm grasp" of Christian teachings so as to facilitate both preaching and debate (Titus 1:9). In older churches the bishops may have been elders, such as those at Ephesus to whom Paul says, "Keep watch over . . . all the flock, of which the Holy Spirit has made you overseers, to shepherd the church of God" (Acts 20:28).

Bit

Do not be like a horse or a mule, without understanding, whose temper must be curbed with bit and bridle . . . .–Psalm 32:9

The most important part of a horse bridle, the bit is a metal bar placed between the horse's teeth and connnected to reins at either end. Using this simple device, a rider can with one hand control an animal vastly superior in size and strength. The image of bit and bridle in a psalm of thanksgiving asserts God's ability to control those who stray (Ps 32:9). When the Assyrian king Sennacherib laid siege to Jerusalem, God promised that he would not let the enemy prevail, telling Sennacherib: "I will put . . . my bit in your mouth; [and] turn you back on the way . . . you came" (Isa 37:29).

This finely crafted bronze bit was cast about 700 BC in Iran, an early center of horsemanship.

Bitter Herbs

They shall eat the lamb . . . with unleavened bread and bitter herbs.–Exodus 12:8

Bitter herbs were part of the Passover feast, evidently a reminder of the Israelites' bitter enslavement in Egypt. The Babylonian exile evoked similar harsh memories, poetically described in the book of Lamentations: "He has filled me with bitterness, he has sated me with WORMWOOD" (Lam 3:15). The herbs might also have simply represented a salad, hastily prepared during the exodus.

The Bible does not name the herbs involved. Among the possibilities scholars have suggested are chicory, endive, chervil, and dandelion. Later rabbinical teachings prescribed horseradish and certain other European herbs for Passover seders. Although the ancient Israelites may not have had access to them, they did have other bitter plants, including wormwood.

Bitumen

And they said to one another, "Come, let us make bricks, and burn them thoroughly." And they had brick for stone, and bitumen for mortar.
–Genesis 11:3

Bitumen is a naturally occurring black, tarry substance that is actually an asphalt or mineral pitch. Tar pits such as those in the Valley of Siddim trapped the kings of the East as they fled the destruction of Sodom and Gomorrah (Gen 14:10). Bitumen can also be produced as a byproduct of heating coal or wood.

Bitumen had many practical uses in biblical times. It was an excellent mortar for holding bricks together, a fact that enabled Noah's descendants to build the tower of Babel (Gen

In the marshes of the lower Tigris and Euphrates rivers a canoe is repaired with bitumen, the same tarry substance used to waterproof leaky boats since the days of the patriarchs.

11:3). It could also hold flint knife blades in a wooden handle. Bitumen's stickiness made it an effective waterproofing agent, as Moses' mother knew when she prepared his small papyrus basket to float safely on the Nile (Ex 2:3).

Blasphemy

The Jews answered, "It is not for a good work that we are going to stone you, but for blasphemy . . . ."–John 10:33

Misusing the holy name of God—*Yahweh*—was considered to be blasphemy, a capital offense. When a young man during the exodus abused God's name in a curse, the people "took the blasphemer outside the camp, and stoned him to death" (Lev 24:23). When Jesus stood before the Jewish court on the eve of his crucifixion and claimed to be the Son of God, he was charged with blasphemy: "All of them condemned him as deserving death" (Mk 14:64). Stephen was later stoned to death after he claimed to have seen "the SON OF MAN standing at the right hand of God" (Acts 7:56).

Jesus said that every sin could be forgiven except the sin of "blasphemy against the Spirit" (Mt 12:31), a phrase he used after religious leaders attributed his healing power to Satan. Some scholars believe the phrase means to credit evil with something that is clearly of God. Others say it means to reject all work of the Spirit, including forgiveness, without which a person cannot be saved.

Blemish

. . . you shall offer a bull without blemish . . . .–Ezekiel 43:23

Animal sacrifices and the priests who offered them had to be free of any obvious physical defect. Disqualified animals included those that were blind, lame, or suffered from a rash, a draining wound, or a scab. Priests were also disqualified for these reasons, as well as for being "a hunchback, or a DWARF" (Lev 21:20). These rules apparently emphasized the respect due to God. They were also later interpreted as foreshadowing the sacrifice of Jesus, "a lamb without defect or blemish" (1 Pet 1:19).

Blessing

. . . the LORD blessed the Egyptian's house for Joseph's sake; the blessing of the LORD was on all that he had, in house and field.–Genesis 39:5

Blessings can be either spiritual or material. The "blessed" person is in a state of happiness, enjoying health, prosperity, long life, and numerous offspring. The presence of such blessings is a sign not only of God's favor on an individual but also of God's actual presence in the world and of the reality of his relationship with his people.

God's covenant with Abraham explicitly included a promise of blessings: "I will make of you a great nation, and I will bless you, and make your name great, so that you will be a blessing" (Gen 12:2). The relationship between God and his people is a reciprocal one, for not only does God bless his people, but they also bless him in prayer, song, and expressions of thanks.

The Israelites also took every opportunity to call down God's blessings on one another. In greeting and bidding farewell, Israelites used expressions of blessing. When Laban and Bethuel sent their sister Rebekah from Haran to become the wife of Isaac, they "blessed Rebekah and said to her, 'May you, our sister, become thousands of myriads; may your offspring gain possession of the gates of their foes'" (Gen 24:60). Mortals, however, do not actually

The high priest Eli gives his blessing to Samuel, brought to the sanctuary at Shiloh by his mother, Hannah (1 Sam 1:24–25).

possess the power to confer blessings, so they must call upon God for them. Sometimes the call is indirect or implicit, as when the passive "be blessed" is used. Even those people who are materially poor and seemingly pitiable may possess spiritual blessings far greater than anyone can imagine. Jesus articulated this paradox in the Beatitudes, in which he proclaimed, "Blessed are you who are poor, for yours is the kingdom of God" (Lk 6:20).

Blight

The LORD will afflict you . . . with fiery heat and drought, and with blight and mildew . . . . –Deuteronomy 28:22

Blight, a plant disease, is caused in many areas by insects or bacteria. But in ancient Palestine it generally resulted from an east or south wind that could blow for days, bringing hot, dry air and leaving crops shriveled in its wake. The devastation was considered punishment for disobedience to God. The righteous might be spared by prayer. They might also recall Joseph's practical approach to the problem in Egypt. After correctly interpreting Pharaoh's dream about seven ears of corn "blighted by the east wind" as warning of a seven-year famine, Joseph recommended accumulating reserves of GRAIN during years of plenty. The strategy proved life-saving for the region (Gen 41:25–57).

Blindness

. . . Elisha prayed to the LORD, and said, "Strike this people . . . with blindness."–2 Kings 6:18

The only natural causes of blindness mentioned in the Bible are birth defects and old age, but leprosy and various infections made the affliction quite common in the ancient Near East. Painful trachoma, caused by bacteria and chronically contagious, may have been the most prevalent eye disease. In the Old Testament, God is credited with causing blindness and restoring sight, occasionally defending his people by blinding their enemies. Blind animals were not deemed appropriate for sacrifice (Deut 15:21), and blind priests were barred from the altar (Lev 21:18). It was widely believed that blindness and other afflictions were punishments for sin. Even so, according to many experts, the Israelites did not literally exact the famous punishment of an "eye for eye" (Ex 21:24).

The Scriptures warn against exploiting the helplessness of blind people, such as giving them false directions or making them stumble (Deut 27:18; Lev 19:14), but otherwise the law considered them normal citizens. Ointments and crude surgical operations were tried in order to cure blindness. Their lack of effectiveness assured that the afflicted eagerly hoped for miraculous cures of the kind prophesied by Isaiah: "On that day the deaf shall hear . . . and out of their gloom and darkness the eyes of the blind shall see" (Isa 29:18).

Jesus often healed the blind. Once, when asked what sin had caused a man's blindness, he said sin was not the reason; rather, "he was born blind so that God's works might be revealed in him" (Jn 9:3). Of greater concern to Jesus, however, was spiritual blindness: "I came into this world for judgment so that those who do not see may see, and those who do see may become blind" (Jn 9:39).

Blood

For the life of the flesh is in the blood; and I have given it to you for making atonement for your lives on the altar . . . .–Leviticus 17:11

For the Israelites, blood was understood not just as a bodily fluid somehow necessary to life but as the location of life itself. Thus it is stressed repeatedly in the Old Testament that "the blood is the life" (Deut 12:23) and "the life of the flesh is in the blood" (Lev 17:11). Blood was not to be consumed; spilling it—that is, taking a life—was punishable by death. At the same time, the blood of an animal constituted the highest element of ritual sacrifice in Israelite worship. Only the priest, himself consecrated by blood (Ex 29:19–21), could apply the blood to the altar (Lev 1:5), where it served as an offering for atonement for sin—"for, as life, it is the blood that makes atonement" (Lev 17:11). Similarly, in perhaps one of the most dramatic episodes of the Old Testament, it was the blood of a lamb or kid, smeared on the door frame, that provided a signal to the angel to pass over the houses of the Israelites in Egypt and spare their FIRSTBORN (Ex 12:12–13). The Lord's covenant with Israel at Sinai was likewise sealed by Moses with a blood sacrifice of oxen (Ex 24).

Ultimately, Jesus offered himself as "a lamb without . . . blemish" (1 Pet 1:19), giving up his own life as the blood sacrifice of a new covenant between God and humankind (Mt 26:28; Mk 14:24).

Bloodguilt

. . . THE BLOOD OF AN INNOCENT PERSON MAY NOT BE SHED IN THE LAND . . . THEREBY BRINGING BLOODGUILT UPON YOU. –*DEUTERONOMY 19:10*

Mosaic law found the taking of a life to be justified in some cases, as in an act of war or self-defense. But an unjustified homicide was murder and incurred the stigma of bloodguilt; this crime tainted not just the killer but the land itself and it could be expiated only with the killer's own blood (Num 35:33). The victim's closest male relative became "the avenger of blood" and was responsible for executing the murderer if guilt was established (Num 35:19, 30).

Blue

THIS IS THE OFFERING THAT YOU SHALL RECEIVE FROM THEM: GOLD, SILVER, AND BRONZE, BLUE, PURPLE, AND CRIMSON YARNS AND FINE LINEN . . . .–*EXODUS 25:3-4*

The color blue was a popular one in the Bible. Although not as precious as purple, it was prized in its own right as one of the colors of royalty (Esth 8:15). Blue was extracted from mollusks gathered from the Mediterranean Sea. Yarn was dyed various shades of blue and used in embroidery that embellished the tabernacle, as decreed by God (Ex 26:31, 36). Blue was again prominent in the temple built by Solomon, whose assistance from the king of Tyre included "an artisan skilled to work in . . . purple, crimson, and blue fabrics" (2 Chr. 2:7)—colors that also appeared in the priestly vestments of Aaron and his sons (Ex 28:5).

Boat

A GREAT WINDSTORM AROSE, AND THE WAVES BEAT INTO THE BOAT, SO THAT THE BOAT WAS ALREADY BEING SWAMPED. –*MARK 4:37*

The ancient Israelites were not seafarers; they rarely had direct access to good Mediterranean harbors, and their rivers were not easily navigable. But they frequently used boats on the Sea of Galilee, which was a freshwater lake. The kind of boat Jesus and his disciples were traveling on during the storm (Mt 8:23–24), propelled by oars or a single sail, was essential to the lake's thriving fishing industry. A first-century BC example was recently found by archaeologists.

Although the Old Testament rarely mentions sailing, some of the Israelites' neighbors had been operating crude boats since before 4000 BC. The Egyptians, lacking lumber, first ventured onto the Nile in rafts and boats made of reeds that were probably papyrus, like those used for the basket in which Moses was left by the river (Ex 2:3). Imported WOOD, chiefly cedar from Lebanon, later enabled them to build larger boats that were rowed by 40 or more oarsmen.

The Philistines, and especially the Phoenicians, were expert mariners. To transport the timber he needed for his temple, King Solomon called on his valued trading partner, Hiram, king of Tyre, a major Phoenician seaport. Hiram reassured him: "My servants shall bring it down to the sea from the Lebanon; I will make it into rafts to go by sea to the place you indicate [and] have them broken up there for you to take away" (1 Kings 5:9). An Assyrian relief from the eighth century BC shows high-prowed Phoenician boats, equipped with paddles, shepherding rafts of logs like those described by Hiram.

In 1986 the remains of a 2,000-year-old fishing boat, left, were discovered in the Sea of Galilee after having been exposed by a two-year drought. Clay from the seabed had helped to preserve the ancient wood; the boat has since been specially treated. A model, above, shows the boat as it would have looked originally.

Body

"Do not fear those who kill the body but cannot kill the soul. . . ."–Matthew 10:28

Although the Old Testament does at times distinguish between the human body and the SOUL, the Israelites did not make as rigid a separation between them as did some later cultures, especially the Greeks. For biblical writers, the body was not to be praised in itself but to be appreciated as God's creation, because it was a divine act that "formed man from the dust of the ground" (Gen 2:7).

The Old Testament holds no clear indication that humans can exist without their bodies. Integrated with the individual soul, the body is the vehicle through which a human being interacts with the physical world and serves God. Moreover, the body ultimately belongs to God. As the apostle Paul writes in the New Testament: "Or do you not know that your body is a temple of the Holy Spirit within you, which you have from God, and that you are not your own?" (1 Cor 6:19).

By contrast, many Greek philosophers during the days of the early church argued that the body is worth little, functioning only as a resting place for the soul; in other words, the body is mortal and the soul immortal. In the Scriptures, the soul unites with the body even in death. Paul takes special care in his letters to explain more than once that the resurrection of Jesus paves the way for the resurrection of all believers: "For since death came through a human being, the resurrection of the dead has also come through a human being" (1 Cor 15:21). The transformation of the earthly body into the resurrected body is an act of the Holy Spirit, a mystery that cannot be understood until the body's actual redemption.

The "boils" of Job 2:7 in older Bible translations have become "loathsome sores" in some newer translations. This scene appears on a capital from a Spanish cathedral.

Body of Christ

Now you are the body of Christ and individually members of it.–1 Corinthians 12:27

The body of Christ served as a metaphor for the unity of the early church, as explained by Paul. "For in the one Spirit," he wrote to the Corinthians, "we were all baptized into one body" (1 Cor 12:13). Paul emphasized that as each member affects the whole body, so each Christian affects the entire church and is responsible for "building up the body of Christ" (Eph 4:12). Paul also used the phrase when asking rhetorically whether the bread eaten communally during the LORD'S SUPPER was not "a sharing in the body of Christ?" (1 Cor 10:16).

Bodyguard

Achish said to David, "Very well, I will make you my bodyguard for life."–1 Samuel 28:2

The Hebrew word for bodyguard originally meant "slaughterer," suggesting that men were chosen for this duty on the basis of their ferocity. King David had a special bodyguard of foreign troops who were loyal to him and immune to the influence of Israelite factions. A small corps of Levite guards made sure that no unauthorized person entered the temple. Pharaoh had bodyguards (Gen 37:36), as did King Nebuchadnezzar of Babylon. The latter royal guard was an elite force charged with special military tasks, such as when it was sent to destroy the temple, palace, and houses of Jerusalem in 586 BC (2 Kings 25:8–12). In the Bible, the terms *bodyguard* and *guard* are sometimes interchangeable.

Boil

The magicians could not stand before Moses because of the boils, for the boils afflicted the magicians as well as all the Egyptians.–Exodus 9:11

The disabling boils of God's sixth plague upon the Egyptians afflicted animals as well as humans, suggesting to some scholars that these excruciating sores were a symptom of anthrax. Usually fatal to sheep and cattle, this bacterial disease affects humans only by producing pus-filled eruptions on the skin.

Other boils mentioned in the Bible, such as in Leviticus 13, could indicate furunculosis, an infection that causes a swelling of pus at the site of a hair follicle. Skin diseases, which are sometimes associated with general ill health, were commonplace in the ancient Near East.

Bond

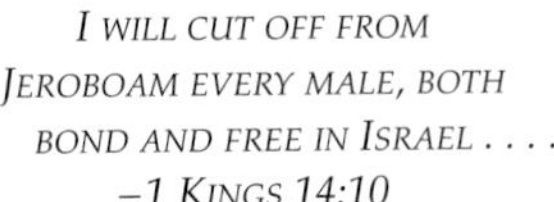

I will cut off from Jeroboam every male, both bond and free in Israel . . . .
–1 Kings 14:10

The word *bond* has both a literal and a figurative meaning in the Bible. Used in the plural, it often refers to cords, ropes, or chains used to bind prisoners. In one of the most powerful scenes in the Old Testament, the Israelites bound Samson in "new ropes" and delivered him over to the Philistines for punishment. Then the spirit of God rushed over Samson and his bonds melted away, allowing him to seize a weapon and slay a thousand Philistines (Judg 15:13–15).

Figurative bonds include evil, affliction, oaths, royal authority, and the covenant bond with the Lord. In the Old Testament, *bond* also refers to SLAVERY.

Bones

. . . there was a noise, a rattling, and the bones came together, bone to its bone.–Ezekiel 37:7

Bones are often used as images of deep feeling in the Scriptures, perhaps because they outlast every other part of the body. The Psalms describe misery as bones that "burn like a furnace" (Ps102:3), and Job says that fear "made all my bones shake" (Job 4:14). In Ezekiel's vision of the dry bones that God restores to vivid, fleshly life, the dryness represents the despair of the Jews in Babylonian exile (Ezek 37:1–10). Human bones were to be treated with respect and given a decent BURIAL. Even an enemy's bones were not to be burned. Ezekiel noted that it would take seven months to bury properly the bones of a defeated army (Ezek 39:12). In the Roman period, the bones of the dead were held in small stone chests called ossuaries.

Book

Go now, write it before them on a tablet, and inscribe it in a book, so that it may be . . . as a witness forever.–Isaiah 30:8

Books in the form used today, with stacked sheets bound between covers, were not known until the second century AD. Such a book, called a codex, consisted of single or folded sheets, usually of vellum or parchment, sewn together along one side. However, written records, which the Bible at times refers to as books (see chart, p. 52), had been kept for millennia in a variety of other forms. Writing was preserved on metal plaques; on wax, clay, or stone tablets; and on papyrus, leather, or parchment scrolls.

The Bible mentions a number of books that have not survived. Some of these were used as sources for the biblical text, and scholars can discern evidence of them in certain passages. For example, the laws contained in Exodus 20:22–23:33 are thought to be from the "book of the covenant" (Ex 24:7). Jeremiah dictated a book to his scribe Baruch (Jer 36:4). In Joshua, two books are mentioned—one about the covenant and the other about the Israelites taking possession of Canaan. Royal scribes wrote the "Book of the Acts of Solomon" (1 Kings 11:41) and compiled the "Book of the Annals of the Kings of Israel" (1 Kings 14:19), drawing upon records in the royal archives of the northern kingdom. Similarly, scribes of the southern kingdom compiled the "Book of the Annals of the Kings of Judah" (1 Kings 14:29). These works may have been sources for 1 and 2 Chronicles. Chronicles also refers to several books and commentaries concerning kings—although some experts believe they are all the same work—as well as the records of prophets. King Josiah launched religious reforms based on "the book of the law" (2 Kings 22:11) discovered in the temple, which was probably a copy of Deuteronomy, also called "the book of Moses" (2 Chr 25:4). Two volumes that were most likely poetry, the "Book of the Wars of the LORD" (Num 21:14) and the "Book of Jashar" (Josh 10:13), are quoted in the Old Testament.

In the New Testament, the author of the Acts of the Apostles refers to the "book of the prophets" (Acts 7:42) when quoting Amos; the writings of the 12 Minor Prophets were considered a unit.

The Apocrypha contains two references to libraries. One was a royal library, or archive (Add Esth 2:23), and one belonged to Nehemiah after the Babylonian exile (2 Macc 2:13).

Book of Life

. . . and anyone whose name was not found written in the book of life was thrown into the lake of fire.–Revelation 20:15

The concept that God keeps a book in which he records the names of individuals who are good appears in various guises in the Old Testament. Usually, the idea is linked with the belief that God will erase the names of those who sin (Ex 32:32). A less dire note is sounded in the book of Daniel, when God reveals that "everyone who is found written in the book" will "shine like the brightness of the sky" (Dan 12:1, 3). Daniel also refers to the "book of truth" (Dan

Books of the Bible

The Bible consists of many books, written by numerous authors. The order of the books shown in this chart is that used by Protestants; other denominations order the books differently. Some denominations do not recognize the apocryphal books as part of the Scripture.

Old Testament

Also called the Hebrew Bible

Pentateuch

- Genesis
- Exodus
- Leviticus
- Numbers
- Deuteronomy

Historical Narratives

- Joshua
- Judges
- Ruth
- 1 Samuel
- 2 Samuel
- 1 Kings
- 2 Kings
- 1 Chronicles
- 2 Chronicles
- Ezra
- Nehemiah
- Esther

Wisdom Literature

- Job
- Psalms
- Proverbs
- Ecclesiastes
- Song of Solomon

The Prophets

- Isaiah
- Jeremiah
- Lamentations
- Ezekiel
- Daniel
- Hosea
- Joel
- Amos
- Obadiah
- Jonah
- Micah
- Nahum
- Habakkuk
- Zephaniah
- Haggai
- Zechariah
- Malachi

Apocryphal Books

Also called the Deuterocanonical Books

- Tobit
- Judith
- Esther (Additions)
- Wisdom of Solomon
- Ecclesiasticus (Sirach)
- Baruch
- Letter of Jeremiah
- Daniel (Additions)
  - Prayer of Azariah and the Song of the Three Jews
  - Susanna
  - Bel and the Dragon
- 1 Maccabees
- 2 Maccabees
- 1 Esdras
- Prayer of Manasseh
- Psalm 151
- 3 Maccabees
- 2 Esdras
- 4 Maccabees

New Testament

Gospels

- Matthew
- Mark
- Luke
- John

History

- Acts of the Apostles

Letters

- Romans
- 1 Corinthians
- 2 Corinthians
- Galatians
- Ephesians
- Philippians
- Colossians
- 1 Thessalonians
- 2 Thessalonians
- 1 Timothy
- 2 Timothy
- Titus
- Philemon
- Hebrews
- James
- 1 Peter
- 2 Peter
- 1 John
- 2 John
- 3 John
- Jude

Apocalypse

- Revelation

10:21), probably another name for the book of life. Similarly, Malachi speaks of the "book of remembrance" (Mal 3:16). The Old Testament contains references to other record books written by God. These include the Lord's design for each human (Ps 139:16) and an account of human travails (Ps 56:8).

Revelation mentions the book of life several times. One passage alludes to the final judgment: "Another book was opened, the book of life. And the dead were judged according to their works, as recorded in the books" (Rev 20:12).

Dating from the first century BC, *a stone marker shows the boundary of Gezer. The inscription, in both Hebrew and Greek, includes what is probably the name of the city's governor.*

Booths

. . . "GO OUT INTO THE HILLS AND BRING BRANCHES OF OLIVE, WILD OLIVE, MYRTLE, PALM, AND OTHER LEAFY TREES TO MAKE BOOTHS . . . ."
–NEHEMIAH 8:15

Booths—temporary shelters made of leafy branches or twigs—were often built to keep cattle from straying, to protect farm workers from the sun, or to provide refuges for soldiers. The Israelites lived in such shelters during their wanderings after fleeing from Egypt. Their booths came to symbolize God's protection during times that were perilous.

This living arrangement was prescribed during the FESTIVAL OF BOOTHS, or Tabernacles, called *Succoth* in Hebrew. A joyful seven-day event, the festival celebrated the autumn harvest.

Borrower

THE RICH RULE OVER THE POOR, AND THE BORROWER IS THE SLAVE OF THE LENDER.
–PROVERBS 22:7

The Bible does not mention commercial loans. A borrower was usually someone desperately in need of money to sustain life, especially someone reduced to poverty by a crop failure or other disaster. Biblical law banned charging interest to fellow Israelites, although not to Gentiles (Deut 23:19–20). In spite of the law, the charging of interest was a recurring problem.

Jesus taught that generosity to the needy should have no bounds, with unselfish concern for the borrower coming before a person's own interests: "Lend, expecting nothing in return. Your reward will be great" (Lk 6:35).

Bottle

HE GATHERED THE WATERS OF THE SEA AS IN A BOTTLE . . . .
–PSALM 33:7

The Hebrew word translated as "bottle" was actually a general term for a container of liquids. Glass was a luxury, and glass bottles were chiefly used to hold costly perfumes and unguents. Bottles were more often made of pottery or goatskin, sewn up so as to be watertight. For this reason, some Bible translations say "old wineskins"—instead of the "old bottles" to which the King James Version refers (Mk 2:22)—are unsuitable to hold new wine.

This water bottle is made of leather, a popular material in biblical times because of its durability. Animal skins were also much less costly than glass.

Boundary

"CURSED BE ANYONE WHO MOVES A NEIGHBOR'S BOUNDARY MARKER."
–DEUTERONOMY 27:17

Land ownership began for the Israelites with tribal property allotments, which were decreed by God. Families or clans then received plots within their tribe's designated area. Landmarks delineated boundaries. They could be natural, such as rivers, or erected, such as cairns or stone pillars. Since the land was God-given, its ownership was considered an inalienable right. Laws forbade the removal of boundary markers, which might be inscribed with the owner's name. Markers were also used to indicate borders between nations. See also LAND.

Bow

HE TRAINS MY HANDS FOR WAR, SO THAT MY ARMS CAN BEND A BOW OF BRONZE.–2 SAMUEL 22:35

David's description of what God did to make him strong against his enemies emphasized the importance of the bow and arrow in ancient warfare. They were long-range weapons that could kill from 400 yards away. Bows were made of strong, resilient wood, and bowstrings were made from the intestines of bulls or camels. Sometimes bows were reinforced with bands of bronze, which added range but made them harder to wield.

Widely used for hunting, the bow was a symbol of strength. Breaking a man's bow figuratively destroyed his power.

Bowels

. . . falling headlong, [Judas] burst open in the middle and all his bowels gushed out.
–Acts of the Apostles 1:18

In biblical times, the intestines, stomach, and reproductive system were all described as bowels. Matthew 27:5 says that Judas, after his betrayal of Jesus, hanged himself. This account seems to conflict with the description of his death that appears in Acts of the Apostles. Some scholars assume that the rope broke, causing Judas to fall and rupture his abdomen.

The Greek word translated as "bowels" was also a metaphor for strong emotions, such as love. Thus the King James Version of the Bible uses such expressions as "bowels of mercies" (Col 3:12).

Bowl

. . . he wrung enough dew from the fleece to fill a bowl with water.–Judges 6:38

Bowls were common and indispensable utensils of daily life in all social classes. They were used to hold food and drink at mealtimes. At the Last Supper, Jesus identified his betrayer as "one who is dipping bread into the bowl with me" (Mk 14:20). This act refers to a bowl, used communally, containing sauce. Bowls were usually made of pottery, but wealthy people owned bowls of precious metals, alabaster, or glass.

Bowls were used in the temple for offerings. Large bowls, or basins, held the blood of sacrificial animals. Basins were also used for washing hands and feet. Jesus used a basin to wash his disciples' feet (Jn 13:5). See also KNEADING BOWL.

Bracelet

"And we have brought the Lord's offering . . . articles of gold, armlets and bracelets . . . ."
–Numbers 31:50

Both men and women wore bracelets on their wrists and forearms. These pieces of jewelry were treasured adornments and a portable form of wealth before the invention of coins. Bracelets were made mostly of bronze or precious metals. Often the spoils of war, gold bracelets were part of the gift to God after the Israelites defeated the Midianites. In Genesis 24:22, Rebekah receives two bracelets weighing 10 gold shekels. Armlets were similar to bracelets but worn around the upper arm.

Bramble

"Figs are not gathered from thorns, nor are grapes picked from a bramble bush."
–Luke 6:44

Several kinds of thorny bushes grow in biblical lands. Some reach as high as 25 feet and form a tangled thicket bristling with thorns that pierce skin and hurt animals. Brambles grow mainly on uncultivated land and are often hard to remove except by burning. Because they catch fire easily, they were sometimes used for fuel. The bramble bush has flowers and black berries often eaten by birds. Jesus referred to it figuratively in telling his listeners that behavior reveals the innermost secrets of the heart.

Branch

"I am the vine, you are the branches. Those who abide in me and I in them bear much fruit . . . ."–John 15:5

The Bible often uses the branch as a symbol. It likens God's people to branches, with the nation of Israel being the tree or vine. Similarly, Jesus applies the term to his disciples. The branch was also Isaiah's prophetic symbol for David's descendant who would be the messianic king of Israel.

The golden menorah, or lampstand, used in the tabernacle had six branches. A welcoming crowd greeted Jesus with branches of palm trees as he rode into Jerusalem on a donkey (Jn 12:13).

Brazier

. . . there was a fire burning in the brazier before him.
–Jeremiah 36:22

A portable space heater of ancient times, the brazier was a wide, shallow pan made of metal, pottery, or stone that held burning charcoal or other fuel. It was set upon legs to raise it a few inches off the ground. This arrangement allowed for better air circulation and distribution of heat.

Because of their relatively small size, braziers could easily be moved from room to room, and they did not need much fuel. Charcoal was the fuel of choice because it burned with a steady heat instead of flaring up and dying down like a wood fire.

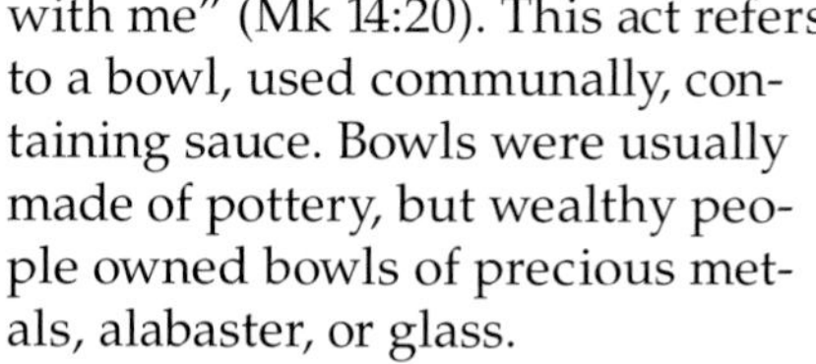

Bowls varied both in material and use. The spouted bronze bowl, far left, from about the eighth century BC, acted as a dipping ladle. The glass bowl, left, from about the first century BC, held a drink.

The 12 loaves of the bread of the Presence were an offering to God. In this detail from painted metal and wood doors in a synagogue, two loaves are missing.

Bread

"Come, eat of my bread and drink of the wine I have mixed."–Proverbs 9:5

Bread was the staff of life in the ancient world. Without bread, no meal was complete. The father of the house gave thanks, tore or broke the loaf, and passed pieces around before anyone could start eating. Bread was so basic to life that it became an idiom for every necessity. When Jesus taught the disciples how to pray, he told them to provide for their needs by petitioning the Lord: "Give us this day our daily bread" (Mt 6:11).

Women made bread every day from wheat or barley flour, salt, water, and leavening—usually a bit of old dough to make the new dough rise. Unleavened bread was eaten during the seven days of Passover to remind the Israelites that their ancestors had had no time to leaven their bread when they left Egypt. Baked on hot stones or in an oven, bread typically emerged as a round flat loaf about half an inch thick and up to a foot in diameter. See also box for BAKING.

Bread of the Presence

And you shall set the bread of the Presence on the table before me always.
–Exodus 25:30

After God instructed Moses as to how to make various implements for worship inside the temple, he told him always to keep bread set on a table of acacia wood, overlaid with gold, before the Holy of Holies. This bread of the Presence, called shewbread or showbread in some Bible translations, consisted of a dozen loaves of unleavened bread. These were laid out in two rows of six, along with frankincense. The priests later ate the bread within the sanctuary. The high priest was to make a new offering of bread each sabbath.

Breast

Yet it was you who took me from the womb; you kept me safe on my mother's breast.
–Psalm 22:9

In the Bible the word *breast* or *bosom* often refers to a woman's breast or breasts. In Song of Solomon, a man poetically praises the beauty of his bride's breasts (Song of S 4:5). A mother's breast symbolizes the comfort, peace, and joy that a baby feels when nursing (Isa 66:11). *Breast* or *bosom* can also mean the chest, especially as the seat of feelings. A person might express pain or sorrow by beating the breast—or chest—with a fist, as the tax collector does in one of Jesus' parables (Lk 18:13).

The breast is also an important portion of a sacrificial animal, such as a ram (Ex 29:26).

Breastpiece

He placed the breastpiece on him, and in the breastpiece he put the Urim and the Thummim.–Leviticus 8:8

An elaborately woven pouch about nine inches square, the breastpiece was worn by the high priest as he carried out ceremonies in the temple or tabernacle. It was made with gold, blue, purple, and scarlet wool yarn as well as linen. Gold cords and rings attached it to the EPHOD. The breastpiece was set with 12 gemstones engraved with the names of the 12 tribes of Israel. Because only the high priest was allowed within the Holy of Holies, the stones symbolized all of Israel worshiping with him. Inside the pouch were two sacred stones called the Urim and Thummim, which the priest used to cast lots in order to procure a divine response to a yes-or-no question.

The glittering breastpiece indicates the rank of high priest. In a detail from a 17th-century painting, Jehoiada wears it as part of his sacred vestments.

Breastplate

Stand therefore, and fasten the belt of truth around your waist, and put on the breastplate of righteousness.
–Ephesians 6:14

Worn into combat by soldiers of biblical times, a breastplate was a chest guard made of leather covered with metal scales, chain mail, or solid metal designed to offer some protection against sword strokes, spear thrusts, and stabs of daggers. The breastplate was usually part of a set of ARMOR covering the soldier's back and sometimes the shoulders and arms.

In his letter to the Ephesians, the apostle Paul figuratively urged Christians to put on the "whole armor" of God as warriors in the battle against the devil's crafty plots and the forces of evil.

A layered metal breastplate with hinged shoulder guards was worn by Roman troops of the first century AD.

Bribe

The wicked accept a concealed bribe to pervert the ways of justice.
–Proverbs 17:23

Taking a bribe was specifically condemned in the Old Testament. In setting out God's covenant with Israel, Moses emphasized the absolute justice of "the great God, mighty and awesome, who is not partial and takes no bribe" (Deut 10:17). Bribery was prohibited because it corrupted justice, which was sacred: "Cursed be anyone who takes a bribe to shed innocent blood" (Deut 27:25). Yet bribery often occurred to gain a legal hearing or an advantage, as Isaiah suggested with his accusation: "Everyone loves a bribe and runs after gifts" (Isa 1:23).

Brick

"You shall no longer give the people straw to make bricks as before; let them go and gather straw for themselves."–Exodus 5:7

One of the chief building materials in the Near East, bricks were made by mixing clay with water and chopped straw, pressing the compound into wooden molds, and letting the bricks dry in the sun (see box). Brick making was repetitive and exhausting labor—a task for slaves like the Israelites in Egypt (Ex 5:7–19) or for conquered foes like the Ammonites sent by King David to the brickworks (2 Sam 12:31).

The powerful societies of Mesopotamia often used kiln-fired bricks, which were stronger than those dried in the sun. The tower of Babel was built with this kind of brick: "Come, let us make bricks, and burn them thoroughly" (Gen 11:3). The fiery furnace into which Nebuchadnezzar ordered Shadrach, Meshach, and Abednego to be thrown (Dan 3:19–23) was probably a brick kiln.

In Israel, the high cost of FUEL made fired bricks a rarity before Roman times. But sun-dried bricks proved durable enough to meet most needs. They were used for fortifications in Solomon's kingdom and at times had to withstand the onslaught of a besieging army: "Draw water for the siege, strengthen your forts; trample the clay, tread the mortar, take hold of the brick mold!" (Nah 3:14).

Bride

. . . as the bridegroom rejoices over the bride, so shall your God rejoice over you.–Isaiah 62:5

A bride and bridegroom had special significance in the Old Testament. In addition to their roles in society, they symbolized God's relationship with Israel—the bride representing the people of Israel and the bridegroom representing God. However, the relationship was not always smooth, and the prophets repeatedly denounced the nation of Israel as an adulterous bride—someone who must suffer punishment for her waywardness before she could be reconciled with her husband.

Song of Solomon contains the best-known biblical references to brides. Probably originating as a collection of secular love poems, it was interpreted allegorically to justify its inclusion in the Bible. The imagery of bride and bridegroom was carried further in the New Testament, where the role of bride was assigned to the church and that of bridegroom to Christ.

Brier

The house of Israel shall no longer find a pricking brier or a piercing thorn among all their neighbors . . . .–Ezekiel 28:24

Of the many thorny plants in the desert, the brier was notably unpleasant. Its sharp spines made the land where it grew worthless. The prophet Micah described corrupt judges as "like a brier" (Mic 7:4). Isaiah foresaw the destruction of Judah and used the image of fertile land reduced to "a waste . . . overgrown with briers and thorns" (Isa 5:6) to evoke the impending desolation. After the exile, by contrast, Isaiah promised that "instead of the brier shall come up the myrtle" (Isa 55:13).

1. Workers chop the straw they have gathered from fields and threshing floors into small pieces. A vital ingredient in the production of bricks, straw physically reinforced the muddy mixture, making it easier to handle. Acids released from the straw as it decomposed chemically strengthened the bricks as well, preventing warping and cracking.

Brick Making

From Egypt to Mesopotamia, bricks were literally the building blocks with which early societies created the towns and cities that marked the rise of civilization. As opposed to wood or stone, which might not be readily available as building material, the mud and straw needed to make bricks were always in abundant supply. The process of brick making was relatively simple, if labor-intensive, and a good brick building would last for years in the arid climate of the ancient Near East.

2. Adding water and straw to a mass of fresh mud, the workers laboriously trample the dense mixture underfoot until it is properly blended, sometimes using a crude hoe to help with the job.

3. The mud is pressed into wooden molds that vary in size according to the intended use. Then, with the molds removed, the bricks are laid out in the sun to dry, and in about three weeks they are ready.

Bronze

"Is my strength the strength of stones, or is my flesh bronze?"
–Job 6:12

About 3200 BC, metalworkers in Mesopotamia discovered that nine parts of copper mixed with one part of tin produced the durable alloy bronze. By the Middle Bronze Age (2000–1550 BC), bronze was replacing copper as the metal of choice for weapons, ornaments, and utensils because it was a harder substance. The Old Testament contains many references to bronze objects, such as temple basins. Biblical writers also invoked the metal to symbolize hardness, as Job does in his agonized question above.

A bronze Egyptian figurine from the fourth century BC shows a man whose prayerful posture suggests he may have been a priest.

Brook

. . . I will let them walk by brooks of water, in a straight path in which they shall not stumble . . . .
–Jeremiah 31:9

The Bible uses the words *brook* and *wadi* interchangeably to describe either a flowing stream or a dry riverbed that fills during rainy seasons. Brooks and wadis not only provided precious water but also marked geographical and symbolic boundaries. The Israelites entering Canaan crossed the "the Wadi Zered" (Deut 2:13). In Isaiah the same streambed is called "the Wadi of the Willows" (Isa 15:7), a reference to its lush cover of oleanders and other vegetation.

Broom Tree

Then [Elijah] lay down under the broom tree and fell asleep.
–1 Kings 19:5

Although the leaves of a broom tree are quite sparse, the Bible mentions that the prophet Elijah, after a day's wandering in the wilderness south of Judah, sought shade under one. The account seems otherwise plausible: more akin to a shrub than a tree, the broom was one of the few sizeable plants that were hardy enough to thrive in the desert. In spring its white flowers garnished the landscape around the Dead Sea.

Found almost everywhere, the broom tree offered more than shade to travelers. Its roots were bitter but could be eaten when roasted. The roots also served as fuel, giving off intense heat (Job 30:4); it was said that the embers kept burning inside even after the fire was put out.

Brother

As he went from there, he saw two other brothers, James son of Zebedee and his brother John . . . .
–Matthew 4:21

In biblical times, the word *brother* meant first of all a sibling, but it was often extended metaphorically to cover blood relatives, fellow CLAN members, close friends, and political allies. In the Old Testament, it was also used in the sense of "fellow countryman" to denote all Israelites. In the New Testament, Paul referred to the Christian community as brothers.

Brothers were expected to support one another in disputes with outsiders and to help one another within the family. However, there are many examples in the Bible of fraternal rivals who did their best to undermine each other, as Jacob did to Esau, or killed each other, as Cain did Abel.

The dense, upright branches of the broom, a shrub erroneously called a juniper in some translations, were familiar to desert travelers across the Near East. The plant's extremely long roots could supply it with ground water in even the driest years.

Brother-In-Law

. . . "Go in to your brother's wife and perform the duty of a brother-in-law to her; raise up offspring for your brother."
–Genesis 38:8

Among the ancient Israelites, levirate law (from the Latin *levir,* meaning "brother-in-law") commanded that if a married man died without a son, his brother should marry the widow and have a male child by her. The firstborn male of such a union was to be credited to the dead brother, carrying on his name and the family line, and the living brother was responsible for the child's support. The custom promoted social stability and kept property in the family, but it was not always gladly accepted, as the

story of Onan illustrates (Gen 38:8–10). Under Mosaic law, a man who shirked his levirate responsibility was subject to public humiliation by the widow (Deut 25:5–10).

Bucket

"Water shall flow from his buckets, and his seed shall have abundant water . . . ."
–Numbers 24:7

Although the word *bucket* appears only four times in the Bible, this humble container played an important part in the life of the biblical world. The common English expression "a drop in the bucket," meaning something insignificant, can be traced back as far as the prophet Isaiah (Isa 40:15). Often buckets were goatskin bags held open at the mouth by crossed sticks and were used mainly for lifting water from a WELL. Made of leather, they were lighter and much sturdier than pottery jars.

Building

A wooden beam firmly bonded into a building is not loosened by an earthquake . . . .
–Ecclesiasticus 22:16

Early biblical references to building include Cain's construction of the city of Enoch (Gen 4:17) and the story of the tower of Babel. The latter mentions that the people had "brick for stone, and bitumen for mortar" (Gen 11:3).

During both Old and New Testament times, many of the poorer people lived in houses made of unbaked mud bricks, sometimes with foundations of stone. The walls of some houses were made of stone, too, but they were built of rubble (unshaped stones) with clay mortar to make them lie more or less evenly and hold them in place. The clay chinking also made the walls fairly weathertight, and the mud bricks were often plastered. These houses had from one to four rooms and often a small COURTYARD. Courtyards were sometimes partly roofed over to provide shelter for animals and implements that were stored there.

Houses were dark inside. A single door let in most of the light. Windows, if there were any, were frequently simply open slits. Doors and windows faced north whenever possible to avoid the fierce summer sun. Roofs were flat. The roof was used as a kind of extra, outdoor room. Here people could sleep during the hot, dry seasons, dry laundry and do other household tasks, and gossip with their village neighbors. The roof was constructed of horizontal log beams covered with brushwood and topped off with a layer of packed clay. A parapet surrounded the roof to keep anyone on it—especially small children—from falling off. So important was this safety feature that the Israelites were commanded to build them by law (Deut 22:8).

More prosperous families built larger houses, often with second stories. In such residences the inside of the walls was usually evened off and given a coating of plaster, and the corners were built with squared-off stones. The richest had houses built entirely of dressed (squared and smoothed) stones, a luxurious practice denounced by the prophet Amos (Am 5:11).

Styles of building changed little in biblical times. Many houses of Jesus' day looked much like this clay model from Syria, which dates from the third millennium BC.

Although most ordinary people probably built their houses themselves with the aid of family members or neighbors, professional carpenters and masons were mentioned as early as the book of Samuel, about 1000 BC. For his temple in Jerusalem, Solomon imported skilled craftsmen and architects from the neighboring Phoenician states of Tyre and Sidon. The massive stones for the temple were shaped and smoothed at the quarry, because iron tools were forbidden at the holy site. Costly imported cedar from the mountains of Lebanon was used for the beams and planks of the roof. Columns decorated and supported the splendid structure.

Builders of ancient times used linen cords to lay out straight lines and to measure length. Sturdy reeds cut to a standard length of 10 feet were also used as measuring rods. Plumb lines—cords with a weight at one end—were used for vertical alignment. The Bible does not tell how the huge stones used for temples and palaces and the fortified walls of cities were moved. It is likely that they were dragged to the building site on wooden sledges by teams of oxen, then levered into place by gangs of men—sometimes prisoners of war, often Israelites conscripted for varying periods of FORCED LABOR.

The Greeks, who entered the region beginning in the late fourth century BC after the conquests of Alexander the Great, brought new architectural styles. The Romans, who occupied the land in the first century BC, introduced the revolutionary use of concrete.

Although the Greeks and Romans built imposing limestone and marble buildings, grand structures that included Mesopotamian temples and palaces, Egyptian pyramids, and Solomon's palace-temple complex already existed since much earlier times in biblical lands. Public building projects over the years also had created silos for grain storage, stables for military horses, storehouses for wine and oil, and fortresses to guard strategic locations, as well as a network of roads connecting them all.

BULL

THE BULL SHALL BE SLAUGHTERED BEFORE THE LORD; AND AARON'S SONS THE PRIESTS SHALL OFFER THE BLOOD . . . AT THE ENTRANCE OF THE TENT OF MEETING. —*LEVITICUS 1:5*

The bull was of great importance in ancient Israel as a sacrificial animal. The book of Leviticus details the standards to be met for a bull to be acceptable as an offering: it must not be injured or maimed, blind, crippled, castrated, or suffering from a skin disease (Lev 22:21–25). Such flaws would clearly be fatal to this symbol of strength and potency: "A firstborn bull—majesty is his! His horns are the horns of a wild ox" (Deut 33:17).

The bull was revered in much of the ancient world. This clay vessel from Cyprus dates from the 14th century BC.

Bulls were also sacrificed in religious rites of the Canaanites and others. In the dramatic contest between Elijah and the prophets of Baal, who were worshiping openly in Israel under Ahab and Jezebel, Elijah proposed that each side prepare a bull as a burnt offering but with no fire beneath: "Then you call on the name of your god and I will call on the name of the LORD; the god who answers by fire is indeed God" (1 Kings 18:24).

BURDEN

YOUR NEW MOONS AND YOUR APPOINTED FESTIVALS . . . HAVE BECOME A BURDEN TO ME . . . . —*ISAIAH 1:14*

In biblical times most physical burdens were carried on the backs of animals or humans, usually slaves. *Burden* also figuratively meant anything hard to bear, ranging from the oppressive—"They shall soon writhe under the burden of kings" (Hos 8:10)—to the trivial: "A fool's chatter is like a burden on a journey" (Sir 21:16). One Hebrew term for burden also carried the meaning of "ORACLE," giving rise to wordplays in which Jeremiah castigated prophets and priests who claimed to have a burden (oracular revelation) from the Lord but were actually a burden (bothersome load) to the Lord (Jer 23:33–40).

BURIAL

LAY OUT THE BODY WITH DUE CEREMONY, AND DO NOT NEGLECT THE BURIAL. —*ECCLESIASTICUS 38:16*

Because of the warm climate, the lack of embalming, and the widespread belief that a corpse was ritually unclean, burial or entombment in biblical times was done without delay, usually within 24 hours after death. Even a criminal who had been executed was buried quickly; Deuteronomy stipulated that "his corpse must not remain all night upon the tree; you shall bury him that same day" (Deut 21:23). To die unburied was a horrible fate. The prophet Jeremiah commanded that King Jehoiakim, for his crimes against God, be buried "with the burial of a donkey . . . dragged off and thrown out beyond the gates of Jerusalem" (Jer 22:19).

Wealthy people were often placed in tombs outside towns in family caves or sepulchers cut out of rock. Usually the bodies were washed, clothed, wrapped in a shroud, sprinkled with aromatic herbs, and laid on a stone platform inside the sepulcher, near the bones of their ancestors. Tombs were sealed with a hinged door or a heavy wheel-shaped stone. Unlike the Egyptians, the ancient Israelites favored simple, unostentatious tombs. They did not use movable stones or terra-cotta sepulchers, which only became common in New Testament times. Most ordinary people, whose families could not afford an elaborate sepulcher, were wrapped in cloth and buried in the earth.

Mourning was a key element in every burial. In addition to family, friends, and servants, who made up funeral processions, some families hired professional mourners who were skilled at singing dirges, as noted by Jeremiah, "so that our eyes may run down with tears" (Jer 9:18). Seven days was the traditional period of mourning.

Burning Bush

There the angel of the LORD appeared to him in a flame of fire out of a bush . . . .—Exodus 3:2

While tending the sheep belonging to his father-in-law, Jethro, near Mount Horeb, Moses was startled to see a bush that was burning but not being consumed. He was even more amazed when he heard the voice of God speaking to him from within the flames and instructing him to deliver the Israelites from slavery: "So come, I will send you to Pharaoh to bring my people, the Israelites, out of Egypt" (Ex 3:10). Fire is used frequently in the Scriptures to symbolize the presence of God. Because of God's presence, Moses was standing on "holy ground" (Ex 3:5).

This Jewish burial hall, reflecting the pervasive Greek culture of the third and second centuries BC, was one of several carved into caves under the Judean city of Mareshah.

In a 13th-century French manuscript illumination, Gideon's burnt offering is ignited by God's angel (Judg 6:21).

Burnt Offering

. . . it is a burnt offering, an offering by fire of pleasing odor to the LORD.—Leviticus 1:17

To express thanks, penitence, or devotion to God, people from the earliest times killed and burnt animals as sacrifices, as Noah did after the great flood (Gen 8:20). The Israelites began and ended each day and marked special days such as the sabbath and festivals with the sacrifice of an animal in the temple.

The Pentateuch set out strict requirements for these burnt offerings. Animals sacrificed—young bulls, lambs, goats, turtledoves—had to be without blemish and, with the exception of birds, male. A person would bring the animal to the sanctuary; after purification it would be killed, cut up, and skinned. The priest would sprinkle its blood on the ALTAR and lay it on top of the altar. The animal was then usually burnt as a sacrifice to God. The only part preserved was the hide, which the priest received. In some sacrifices, such as that of "well-being," parts of the animal were saved from burning and given to the worshipers to eat.

Unearthed in the citadel at Arad on the Judean border, this early sixth-century BC CLAY fragment bore a message to Elyashib (probably the citadel's commander) that includes what may be the earliest written reference outside the Bible to the Jerusalem temple.

CALF

THEN THE LORD SENT A PLAGUE ON THE PEOPLE, BECAUSE THEY MADE THE CALF—THE ONE THAT AARON MADE.
–EXODUS 32:35

Across the ancient Near East, young cattle had particular value for both practical and spiritual reasons. Israelite custom dictated that calves be killed for food on special occasions and as sin offerings to God. Young bulls were also revered as symbols of deity in many places. This tradition led to the episode during which, in Moses' absence, the Israelites persuaded Aaron to make a golden calf for them to worship. Moses was enraged by this blatant idolatry when he returned from Mount Sinai: "He took the calf that they had made, burned it with fire, ground it to powder, scattered it on the water, and made the Israelites drink it" (Ex 32:20).

When Israel separated from Judah after Solomon's death, Jeroboam felt that the northern kingdom should have its own centers of worship to lessen Jerusalem's dominance. He installed golden calves at the ancient sanctuaries of Bethel and Dan (1 Kings 12:29). Although probably inspired more by political than religious motives, Jeroboam's "calf of Samaria" was reviled by Hosea as an abomination for which the northern kingdom felt God's fury (Hos 8:5–6).

CAMEL

"AGAIN I TELL YOU, IT IS EASIER FOR A CAMEL TO GO THROUGH THE EYE OF A NEEDLE THAN FOR SOMEONE WHO IS RICH TO ENTER THE KINGDOM OF GOD."
–MATTHEW 19:24

Few things had a greater impact on life in the ancient Near East than the domestication of camels, whose speed, stamina, and ability to endure days without water made long-distance desert travel possible. Camels entered Israelite history during the 12th and 11th centuries BC (references to them in Genesis are usually considered anachronistic), when Israelite settlers in Canaan were attacked by camel-mounted Midianites and Amalekites (Judg 7:12).

Recognizing the animals' value, the Israelites seized them as booty after battles, used them to build trade networks under David and Solomon, and counted them as a measure of personal WEALTH. The queen of Sheba "came to Jerusalem with a very great retinue, with camels bearing spices, and very much gold, and precious stones" (1 Kings 10:2). The camel was ritually unfit for eating or sacrifice, but it remained a fixture of everyday life throughout the New Testament and provided the basis for two of Jesus' most memorable sayings (Mt 19:24; 23:24).

Camel's Hair

Now John was clothed with camel's hair, with a leather belt around his waist . . . .
–Mark 1:6

The dramatic appearance of John the Baptist in the Judean wilderness would have reminded many who saw him of the traditional rough garment—the "hairy mantle"—worn by Israelite prophets in earlier times (Zech 13:4). A different sort of CLOTH, supple and very expensive, could be woven from the fine hairs around the camel's belly. But what John undoubtedly wore was either a camel's skin with the hair still on it or a garment woven from the coarse hair on the camel's back. Both were thick, rough materials used for tents and heavy cloaks—a pointed contrast to the "soft robes" worn by those living in palaces (Mt 11:8).

Camp

Because the LORD your God travels along with your camp, to save you and to hand over your enemies . . . your camp must be holy . . . .
–Deuteronomy 23:14

Wandering was so much a part of the Israelites' early history that the idea of a temporary dwelling place, or camp, became entwined with their identity as a people. Each of the tribes had its own section within the camp, which was required to be properly laid out (Num 2) and kept ritually clean (Deut 23:9–14). This arrangement of tribal areas, always in the same location relative to the tabernacle and to one another, reflected both the political structure of the Israelites and the presence of God in their midst (see illustration).

Tribal affiliation was inevitably subordinated to national unity in times of WAR. During a crucial encounter with the Philistines, for example, "When the ark of the covenant . . . came into the camp, all Israel gave a mighty shout" (1 Sam 4:5)—a situation in which the people and their camp had effectively become one.

At a camp in the Sinai during the exodus, two priests blow trumpets of hammered silver to summon Israel's tribes to assemble, as God commanded, "at the entrance of the tent of meeting," in which the sacred ark was kept (Num 10:1–3).

CANE

Of what use to me is frankincense that comes from Sheba, or sweet cane from a distant land? –Jeremiah 6:20

A sweet-scented grass or reed, cane was one of several aromatic plants imported into Israel for use in burnt offerings and other rites. God chastised Israel through Isaiah for disregarding its religious obligations: "You have not bought me sweet cane . . . or satisfied me with the fat of your sacrifices" (Isa 43:24). Among those obligations was the preparation of holy anointing oil, made by combining olive oil with four exotic spices: "liquid myrrh," "sweet-smelling cinnamon," "aromatic cane" (sometimes called calamus), and "cassia" (Ex 30:23–24). However, ritual offerings alone did not guarantee God's forgiveness—a point resoundingly made by both Isaiah and Jeremiah (Isa 1:11–13; Jer 6:20).

CANOPY

Blow the trumpet in Zion . . . gather the people. . . . Let the bridegroom leave his room, and the bride her canopy. –Joel 2:15–16

The word *canopy* meant different things in the Bible, depending on context. Most familiar was the marriage canopy, a curtain hung over a couple indicating the sanctity of their marriage. Israel's ultimate place of sanctity, Solomon's temple, had "a porch in front with pillars, and a canopy in front of them" (1 Kings 7:6). Ezekiel's vision of the restored temple included "a canopy of wood in front of the vestibule" (Ezek 41:25). Another prophet foresaw divine protection in its purest form on the final day, when "over all the glory there will be a canopy" (Isa 4:5).

A canopied structure, possibly used by the king for public audiences, rested on a stone foundation, above, outside the main gate of the city of Dan. The illustration at left suggests how it may have looked.

CAPTAIN

So they said to one another, "Let us choose a captain, and go back to Egypt." –Numbers 14:4

The term translated as "captain" in the Bible is usually a military designation, but it might apply to someone as important as Potiphar, Pharaoh's captain of the guard (Gen 37:36), or merely to a captain of 50 men. An Assyrian commander predicted that Jerusalem could not repel "a single captain among the least of my master's servants" (Isa 36:9). Yet a captain might be marked for greatness: "Everyone who was in distress . . . gathered to [David]; and he became captain over them" (1 Sam 22:2). The captain of the temple in Jerusalem answered only to the high priest; it was his police who arrested and flogged the apostles for preaching there (Acts 4:1; 5:24–40).

CARAVAN

. . . They saw a caravan of Ishmaelites coming from Gilead . . . carrying gum, balm, and resin, on their way to carry it down to Egypt. – Genesis 37:25

From the age of the patriarchs, the caravan traffic that crisscrossed the Near East bearing valuable merchandise to distant markets played a continuous role in Israel's life and fortunes. The epochal journey of Abraham and Sarah (Gen 11:31; 12:5) took them along a caravan route that extended from the Persian Gulf up through the Euphrates valley to Haran; from there they would have turned southwest to the teeming crossroads of Damascus, where caravans bound for Canaan and Egypt were outfitted.

Vital trade routes linking Asia Minor and Mesopotamia with Egypt ran through Palestine, and struggles for control of the routes had a direct impact on commerce and the prosperity it created. During the turbulent era of the Judges, "caravans ceased and travelers kept to the byways" (Judg 5:6), a stark contrast to luxury-laden caravans arriving from Arabia with the legendary Queen of Sheba in better times (1 Kings 10:2).

Trade routes needed stopping places where there was water for the animals and lodging for tired caravaneers. One such inn, or caravansary, is mentioned in Luke's telling of the story of Jesus' birth. When Joseph and Mary arrived in Bethlehem for the census decreed by Rome, they discovered that "there was no place for them in the inn" (Luke 2:7). See also JOURNEY.

Carpenter

The carpenter stretches a line, marks it out with a stylus, fashions it with planes, and marks it with a compass . . . . –Isaiah 44:13

The identification of Jesus in the Gospels as a carpenter (Mk 6:3) or a carpenter's son (Mt 13:55) established the modest status of his family; men of rank did not practice such a trade. Nevertheless, the skills possessed by a good carpenter clearly were in high demand among the people of ancient Israel (see reconstruction, pp. 66–67).

Trees were scarce in the Holy Land, and wood was expensive. Apart from farm tools and furniture, the use of wood was restricted largely to windows, doors, and decorative trim in public buildings and large houses. Much of a carpenter's work on public buildings involved intricate carving, a craft the early Israelites had little opportunity to master. For that reason it was necessary to import carpenters—as well as lumber—from Tyre when David built his palace and Solomon his temple in Jerusalem. That lack of expertise had evidently been corrected by the ninth century BC, when carpenters repaired the temple during the reign of Joash, king of Judah (2 Kings 12:11). Carpenters were likely to have been among the artisans whose skills helped to rebuild Jerusalem and its temple when they returned from Babylon (Jer 24:1; 29:2).

The TOOLS and techniques of a master carpenter were detailed in Isaiah 44:13–17. A passage in Proverbs relates that during the creation of the world, "when he drew a circle on the face of the deep . . . when he marked out the foundations of the earth, then I was beside him, like a master worker" (Prov 8:27–30).

Cart

Take the ark of the LORD and place it on the cart . . . . and let it go its way. –1 Samuel 6:8

Wooden carts in the Bible had a variety of forms—two-wheeled or four, open or covered, pulled by one or more animals—and functions. They were most common as farm vehicles, used to haul produce (Am 2:13) or to crush grain under their wheels for bread (Isa 28:28). They also carried more precious cargo. The Philistines returned the ark on a new cart pulled by "two milch cows that have never borne a yoke" (1 Sam 6:7), as required for ritual purity (Deut 21:3), and the Israelites joyously broke up the cart and offered the cows as a burnt offering (1 Sam 6:14). David also used a new cart to bring the ark triumphantly to Jerusalem (2 Sam 6:3).

Cassia

Therefore God . . . has anointed you with the oil of gladness . . . your robes are all fragrant with myrrh and aloes and cassia.–Psalm 45:7–8

Imported from the Far East by way of merchants in Tyre—"wrought iron, cassia, and sweet cane were bartered for your merchandise" (Ezek 27:19)—the sweet-smelling bark, leaves, and other parts of the cassia tree were as coveted as they were costly. A species of CINNAMON, cassia was an ingredient priests used to make the "sacred anointing oil" (Ex 30:23–25).

Used by the rich to scent their clothing before festive occasions, as the psalmist suggests (Ps 45:7–8), cassia seemed to epitomize everything that was fine and rare. "In all the land there were no women so beautiful as Job's daughters" (Job 42:15)—one of whom had the lovely name *Keziah*, which means "cassia."

Caravans were the mainstay of trade in biblical times, and no animal was better suited for caravan duty than the camel, able to carry a rider and 400 pounds of cargo across hot, shifting sand for a week or more without food or water.

Carpenter's Shop

"Is not this the carpenter's son? Is not his mother called Mary?"–Matthew 13:55

A busy carpenter's shop in Jesus' time would have looked much like this one, where an obviously impatient farmer with fields to plant has a broken plow that needs mending as soon as possible. However, the proprietor and his two apprentices already have their hands full; in sizeable towns this was usually the case. Carpenters made or repaired furniture and housewares of all kinds—including tables, chairs, beds, and stools—as well as plows, carts, yokes, and other heavy farm equipment. Among the woodworking tools seen here are the chief carpenter's mallet, an adze used by his older apprentice, a bow-drill with which the boy is cutting through a board, and an array of saws, chisels, awls, and other implements on the wall behind them.

CATAPULT

[LYSIAS] SET UP SIEGE TOWERS, ENGINES OF WAR TO THROW FIRE AND STONES, MACHINES TO SHOOT ARROWS, AND CATAPULTS.
—1 MACCABEES 6:51

One of the oldest forms of warfare, the SIEGE played an important part in Israel's military history from the conquest of Canaan (Josh 10:31–34) onward. By the Hellenistic period (fourth to first centuries BC), the arsenal of siege warfare had come to include catapults. These massive wood-framed weapons used the same principle as the sling: a rock was placed in a holder at the end of a wooden arm, which was cranked back by ropes wound steadily tighter around a drum, then released—snapping forward with tremendous force. Boulders thus launched could weaken even the thickest city walls, an image that was awesome enough to convey the power of God's judgment, when "hailstones full of wrath will be hurled as from a catapult" (Wis 5:22).

CATERPILLAR

HE GAVE THEIR CROPS TO THE CATERPILLAR, AND THE FRUIT OF THEIR LABOR TO THE LOCUST.
—PSALM 78:46

Across the biblical world, caterpillars and locusts were the voracious enemies of every farmer, appearing suddenly in a field to destroy crops like a plundering army: "Spoil was gathered as the caterpillar gathers; as locusts leap, they leaped upon it" (Isa 33:4). Their arrival raised the specter of famine and the fear that God's wrath had been kindled—a wrath that the Israelites could only pray would be tempered by mercy: "If there is famine in the land, if there is plague, blight, mildew, locust, or caterpillar . . . then hear in heaven your dwelling place, forgive, act, and render to all whose hearts you know" (1 Kings 8:37, 39).

CATTLE

BLESSED SHALL BE . . . THE FRUIT OF YOUR LIVESTOCK, BOTH THE INCREASE OF YOUR CATTLE AND THE ISSUE OF YOUR FLOCK.—DEUTERONOMY 28:4

In biblical usage, the word *cattle* refers generally to larger animals—oxen or asses—as distinct from sheep or goats. Such large animals had great value in the ancient Near East. The Israelites were herders to whom livestock represented tangible wealth, which could be taken as spoils of war (1 Sam 30:20). Cattle, like people, were entitled to rest on the sabbath (Ex 20:10). They could be sacrificed if found to be without blemish (Lev 22:19) and were eaten on special occasions; royalty could eat meat on a daily basis (1 Kings 4:23). Cattle were also evoked in a prophetic lament for all that Israel had lost; then "the lowing of cattle is not heard . . . the animals have fled and are gone" (Jer 9:10).

From a set of painted wooden figures discovered in the tomb of Meketre, Egypt's chancellor about 2000 BC, a herder prods cattle onward.

CAVALRY

AT THE NOISE OF CAVALRY, WHEELS, AND CHARIOTS YOUR VERY WALLS SHALL SHAKE, WHEN [NEBUCHADNEZZAR] ENTERS YOUR GATES . . . .
—EZEKIEL 26:10

The term *cavalry* occurs several times in the Scriptures, but in most cases it signifies chariot forces rather than soldiers on horseback. The Israelites faced enemy chariots during the exodus and in Canaan (Ex 14:9; Judg 4:3), and David kept horses and chariots captured from the Arameans (2 Sam 8:4). Under Solomon thousands of horses, chariots, and horsemen were garrisoned in cities across the kingdom (1 Kings 4:26; 9:19). However, references to cavalry and horsemen probably meant the various personnel attached to CHARIOT units, not men on horseback. Mules were ridden during this period (2 Sam 13:29; 1 Kings 1:33), but the Israelites evidently did not make mounted troops part of their military system. The Assyrian army of King Sen-

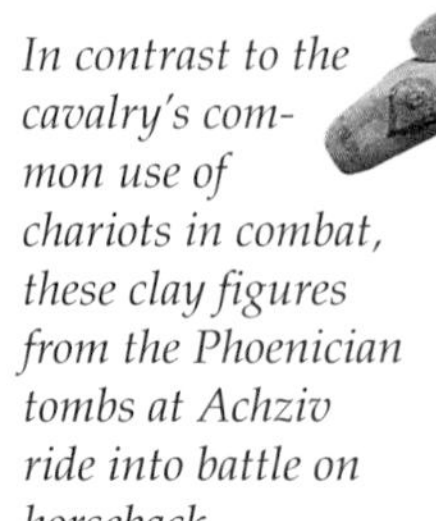

In contrast to the cavalry's common use of chariots in combat, these clay figures from the Phoenician tombs at Achziv ride into battle on horseback.

nacherib had forces on horseback when it invaded Judah in 701 BC, and Assyria's commander taunted the Judeans for their shortage of trained riders (2 Kings 18:23–24). However, Isaiah cautioned against misplaced faith in such prowess: "Alas for those who . . . rely on horses, who trust . . . in horsemen because they are very strong, but do not look to the Holy One of Israel" (Isa 31:1).

Cave

. . . the Israelites provided for themselves hiding places in the mountains, caves and strongholds.–Judges 6:2

Limestone regions produce more and larger caves than other areas, as evidenced by the limestone hills and cliffs of Palestine and Syria. Several Hebrew words in the Scriptures denote caves, holes, and fissures—one is translated in the New Revised Standard Version of the Bible as "cavern" (Isa 2:21)—and some of those places were prominent in Israel's history. From earliest times, people of the region used them as homes. Lot "lived in a cave with his two daughters" after fleeing the destruction of Sodom and Gomorrah (Gen 19:30). Caves also made natural burial sites. Abraham purchased the cave of Machpelah near Hebron as a tomb for Sarah (Gen 23:11–16) and was later buried there with her. Centuries later, a cave in Bethany was the grave site from which Jesus raised Lazarus (Jn 11:38).

Caves are also mentioned in the Bible as hiding places. During the conquest, five defeated Amorite kings tried to hide in a cave at Makkedah, only to be discovered and executed by Joshua, who placed their bodies in the cave and sealed it off (Josh 10:16–27). David and his men hid from King Saul in the cave of Adullam, near Bethlehem (1 Sam 22:1–2), and later in "the innermost parts of the cave" at En-gedi, where David stealthily cut off a corner of Saul's cloak (1 Sam 24:3–4). In Samaria, "when Jezebel was killing off the prophets of the LORD," Elijah's friend Obadiah hid 100 of them, "fifty to a cave" (1 Kings 18:4). A Roman invasion in AD 68 led the Essenes to hide their priceless scrolls in caves around the Dead Sea, where they were recovered in the 20th century.

The cedar tree, valued in the Holy Land for its durable red wood, once blanketed the mountains of Lebanon.

Cedar

The righteous flourish like the palm tree, and grow like a cedar in Lebanon.–Psalm 92:12

Majestic, deep-rooted, and long-lived, the renowned cedar tree in biblical times was a symbol of enduring strength and beauty and produced lumber worthy of its reputation. Harvested on the mountainsides of Lebanon, the coveted wood was exported to cities of ancient Mesopotamia and elsewhere to build royal palaces and shrines. It figures prominently in accounts of the building projects carried out by David and Solomon in Jerusalem. Pillars, beams, and planks were cut from cedar (1 Kings 6:9, 7:2), idols were hewn (Isa 44:14–15), and masts were made for ships (Ezek 27:5). The wood was known for its fragrance (Song of S 4:11) and used in purification rites (Lev 14:4).

It was also true, however, that this mighty tree created at God's command—"the cedars of Lebanon that he planted" (Ps 104:16)—was as fragile as a twig before his anger: "The voice of the LORD breaks the cedars" (Ps 29:5).

Censer

"Take your censer, put fire on it from the altar and lay incense on it . . . ."–Numbers 16:46

A long-handled container for hot coals over which INCENSE was sprinkled (Lev 16:12), the censer was used to make offerings before the Lord. Bronze censers were employed in priestly ceremonies (Num 16:39); in the temple they were made of gold and called firepans (1 Kings 7:50). Aaron's sons Nadab and Abihu filled their censers without authority and "offered unholy fire before the Lord" (Lev 10:1), an offense for which they perished in flames. Misfortune awaited anyone other than an Aaronic priest who used a censer in the temple (2 Chr 26:16–21). Censers remained important ritual objects throughout the biblical era; in Revelation an angel holding a golden censer appears after the seventh seal is opened (Rev 8:3–5).

Only about a foot long, this sixth- to fifth-century BC bronze censer, with a long slender neck and finely crafted duck-headed handle, may have been used to offer incense on the altar of the temple.

CENSUS

. . . "GO THROUGH ALL THE TRIBES OF ISRAEL . . . AND TAKE A CENSUS OF THE PEOPLE, SO THAT I MAY KNOW HOW MANY THERE ARE." –2 SAMUEL 24:2

In the ancient world a census of the population was usually held for purposes of taxation or military service. The earliest in biblical records was Moses' registration of the Israelites at Sinai (Ex 38:25–26); to forestall God's anger, those registered had to pay TAXES to support the sanctuary—"a ransom . . . so that no plague may come upon them" (Ex 30:12). The same census excluded Levites from military duty, designating them instead for priestly service (Num 1:49–53). A second generation was enrolled decades later, as Israel approached the Promised Land (Num 26).

A census may have been thought sinful because it implied a secular society governed by humans, not a tribal confederation that entrusted its fate to God. Reprisals followed the census ordered by King David (2 Sam 24), when a plague ravaged the land, stopping just north of Jerusalem's city wall—the site on which David erected an altar and Solomon later built the temple.

In the fifth century BC a census was taken to count those returned to Judah from Babylonian exile (Ezra 2:1–65). In the New Testament, Gamaliel mentions an uprising by Judas the Galilean "at the time of the census" (Acts 5:37), possibly one conducted in AD 6 to prepare a new tax levy. A census based on Caesar's decree that "all the world should be registered" (Lk 2:1) required that Joseph travel to his ancestral home in Bethlehem; thus Jesus was born in the city of David, where it had been prophesied that the Messiah would be born (Mic 5:2).

CENTURION

AND TO THE CENTURION JESUS SAID, "GO; LET IT BE DONE FOR YOU ACCORDING TO YOUR FAITH."–MATTHEW 8:13

Nominally in command of 100 soldiers (a century), a centurion was a figure of respect in Rome's legions, and two such officers are mentioned by name in the New Testament. The conversion of Cornelius at Caesarea made it clear that Gentiles as well as Jews could become Christians, a key event in the early history of the church (Acts 10). The centurion Julius, who conducted Paul and other prisoners to Rome, treated Paul kindly and later saved his life (Acts 27:1, 3, 43). Two other centurions became believers: one, at Capernaum, asked Jesus to cure his ailing servant (Mt 8:5–13); the other was in charge of Jesus' crucifixion and exclaimed, "Truly this man was God's Son!" (Mt 27:54).

Immortalized in bronze, this legionary, a soldier in the Roman army, was under the command of a centurion.

CHAIN

. . . PHARAOH . . . ARRAYED HIM IN GARMENTS OF FINE LINEN, AND PUT A GOLD CHAIN AROUND HIS NECK.–GENESIS 41:42

After Pharaoh appointed Joseph to a position of leadership in Egypt, Joseph wore a gold chain as a sign of his royal favor and high office. Chains, or necklaces, sometimes set with precious stones, were worn as personal JEWELRY (Ezek 16:11). Gold chains were part of the elaborately adorned breastpiece worn by a high priest (Ex 28:22). They were also used to decorate temple walls: in 1 Kings 6:21, Solomon created a partition with chains of gold linked together and drew it across the inner sanctuary of his temple.

A different kind of metal chain leashed Roman prisoners to their guards, wrist to wrist, to prevent escape (Acts 12:6).

CHAMBER

AND YOUNG WOMEN WHO HAD JUST ENTERED THE BRIDAL CHAMBER TO SHARE MARRIED LIFE EXCHANGED JOY FOR WAILING . . . . –3 MACCABEES 4:6

In the Bible, the word *chamber* is used to translate a number of Hebrew words referring to rooms within a building. These include sleeping quarters, bathrooms, private inner rooms, and storage rooms. Chambers were also built on the roofs of houses for coolness, a desirable feature in lands with long, hot summers (Judg 3:20). King David retreats to a private chamber over the city gate to mourn the death of his rebellious son Absalom (2 Sam 18:33). The side chambers in Ezekiel's temple were probably storerooms (Ezek 41:6), and the priest's chambers facing the temple court functioned as sacristies (Ezek 41:1).

A clay model of an ancient two-wheeled chariot that would have been drawn by horses is manned by a driver and archer.

CHARIOT

SOME TAKE PRIDE IN CHARIOTS, AND SOME IN HORSES, BUT OUR PRIDE IS IN THE NAME OF THE LORD OUR GOD.
–PSALM 20:7

By about 2000 BC, the horse-drawn chariot was in use in Egypt, Syria, and Palestine. The Egyptian chariots that pursued Moses and the fleeing Israelites (Ex 14:8–9) were lightweight, two-wheeled vehicles constructed of wood and leather, with a small amount of bronze or iron used for fittings. Pulled by two swift horses that were yoked together, and manned by a chariot driver and an ARCHER, Pharaoh's chariots were highly effective for plains warfare. But they were no match for the rising waters of the Red Sea, which "covered the chariots and the chariot drivers, the entire army of Pharaoh . . . not one of them remained" (Ex 14:28).

The Israelites first settled the hill country of Palestine, where the mountainous terrain was unsuitable for chariots. David, who had fought against chariots in his campaigns against the Philistines (2 Sam 8:4), probably first introduced chariots into the Israelite army. But it was not until King Solomon's reign that chariots became an essential part of the army. Solomon built "cities for his chariots" (1 Kings 9:19) and established himself as a trader in fine horses and superior chariots, which were manufactured in Egypt (1 Kings 10:29).

Biblical chariots can signify the power of God as well as kings: the prophet Elijah is spirited into heaven by a "chariot of fire and horse of fire" (2 Kings 2:11).

CHERUBIM

I LOOKED, AND THERE WERE FOUR WHEELS BESIDE THE CHERUBIM, ONE BESIDE EACH CHERUB . . . .–EZEKIEL 10:9

Although there are dozens of references to cherubim (the plural of cherub) in the Bible, these celestial beings are never precisely described. The Scriptures depict them variously as winged creatures with one, two, or four faces representing beasts and humans (Ezek 10:14). They often act as guardians: fierce, sword-bearing cherubim prevented Adam and Eve from returning to the garden of Eden (Gen 3:24). Cherubim also flanked the mercy seat atop the ark of the covenant (Ex 25:17–22). The biblical bestial cherubim have no relation to the angelic winged infants called cherubs that are often depicted in later Western art.

CHEST

THEN THE PRIEST JEHOIADA TOOK A CHEST, MADE A HOLE IN ITS LID, AND SET IT BESIDE THE ALTAR . . . .
–2 KINGS 12:9

Treasure chests were first placed inside the temple by Joash (also called Jehoash), the ninth king of Judah, to increase donations made by worshipers for its upkeep and repair. When the chests were full, the high priest collected the money and used it to pay carpenters and masons. The Wise Men used chests to carry their gifts of gold, frankincense, and myrrh to the infant Jesus (Mt 2:11).

CHIEF

AND WHEN THE CHIEF SHEPHERD APPEARS, YOU WILL WIN THE CROWN OF GLORY THAT NEVER FADES AWAY.
–1 PETER 5:4

The Hebrew of the Old Testament has more than a dozen words for a military, religious, or political leader, which occasionally are translated into English as "chief." *Chief* is frequently combined with another word, as in chief baker, chief jailor, and chief officer; the title *chief priest* was used to designate a high religious official (Mt 26:3). Daniel, summoned as a diviner to interpret the dreams of King Nebuchadnezzar, was hailed as "chief of the magicians" (Dan 4:9). Heads of tribes were at times called chieftains (Jdt 7:8).

CHILDREN

. . . SHE SAID TO JACOB, "GIVE ME CHILDREN, OR I SHALL DIE!"
–GENESIS 30:1

In ancient Israel, children, particularly sons, were valued as blessings from God (Ps 127:3) and a fulfillment of God's promise to Israel's ancestors (Gen 15:4–5). Children had economic value as a source of labor; more important, they perpetuated the FAMILY. Childlessness was a terrible fate and was believed to be a punishment from God.

According to Mosaic law, children were to honor their father and mother (Ex 20:12). In practice, this meant that children were to obey their parents, behave deferentially,

The good shepherd, the fish, and the anchor—Christian symbols for Jesus Christ—were engraved on the sarcophagus of Livia Primitiva, left, in the third century BC.

and support them in old age. In patriarchal societies, sons had certain rights above daughters. For example, daughters could not inherit from their fathers unless there were no sons (Num 27:8). Parents were expected to provide for daughters until they married or came of age. Girls came of age at about 12, boys at about 13.

Parents were responsible for their children's religious education. Moses charged the Israelites with teaching about the rite of Passover: "And when your children ask you, 'What do you mean by this observance?' you shall say, 'It is the passover sacrifice to the LORD'" (Ex 12:26–27).

The Israelites were called "children of Israel" (1 Kings 6:13) because they were descendents of Jacob (also called Israel). In the New Testament, Paul addressed a fledgling Christian community as "children of God" (Rom 9:8).

CHRISTIAN

. . . AND IT WAS IN ANTIOCH THAT THE DISCIPLES WERE FIRST CALLED "CHRISTIANS."
–ACTS OF THE APOSTLES 11:26

Jesus' followers described themselves as "brothers," "saints," "disciples," or "the Way." It is believed that they were first called Christians in order to distinguish them from Jews; the title probably also carried an element of scorn or ridicule. Coined in the Greco-Roman city of Antioch, the term combines the Greek word *Christos* with the Latin ending *-ianus* to form a name meaning "belonging to Christ." It is unlikely that Jews used the word, because *Christ* means "the Messiah"; rather, they referred to this breakaway group as "the sect of the Nazarenes" (Acts 24:5).

Roman officials in Antioch may have first used the term *Christian* to differentiate the Antioch Christians from the Jews there. The word appears only three times in the New Testament. Despite its origins outside the church, Christians adopted the term as their own. Roman prejudice against Christians was quick to develop. By the second century AD, a person could be summarily executed for being a Christian. As the apostle Peter wrote in his letter to those who feared persecution, "Yet if any of you suffers as a Christian, do not consider it a disgrace, but glorify God because you bear this name" (1 Pet 4:16).

CHRONICLES, 1 & 2

"THE LORD, THE GOD OF HEAVEN . . . HAS CHARGED ME TO BUILD HIM A HOUSE AT JERUSALEM, WHICH IS IN JUDAH."
–2 CHRONICLES 36:23

The history of Israel from the time of Adam up to the return from exile is told in 1 and 2 Chronicles. They also recount the story of the Davidic dynasty. Most scholars believe that the two books were originally one work, perhaps written in the fourth century BC by a Jewish historian and theologian known only as the Chronicler. Tradition has attributed these books, as well as Ezra and Nehemiah, to the priest and SCRIBE Ezra. Whatever its authorship, Chronicles is more than a simple recounting of events. It interprets Israel's history through the lens of faith and seeks to inspire the people in their worship and devotion to God's law.

CHURCH

AND [GOD] HAS PUT ALL THINGS UNDER [CHRIST'S] FEET AND MADE HIM THE HEAD OVER ALL THINGS FOR THE CHURCH, WHICH IS HIS BODY . . . .–EPHESIANS 1:22–23

Today the word *church* means primarily a building or a denomination. In New Testament times *church* simply referred to any size gathering or assembly of Christian people, from all Christians in general to those who came together to worship in a particular house.

After breaking away from Jewish synagogues, the earliest Christians met and worshiped at one another's homes because they had no formal places of worship. For example, Paul sent greetings to the Corinthians from "Aquila and Prisca, together with the church in their house" (1 Cor 16:19). Such house churches were widespread and had a strong impact on the development of Christianity.

The first Christians considered themselves to be a family—"members of the household of God" (Eph 2:19)—and they rejected class or racial distinctions. As Paul wrote to the Galatians: "There is no longer JEW or Greek . . . slave or free . . . male or female; for all of you are one in Christ Jesus" (Gal 3:28). Members of this family turned to one another for help in both spiritual and material matters. When, for example, it was discovered that widows were going hungry, they appointed leaders to make sure the women received food. In the early days of the church, members also shared their possessions (Acts 2:44–45).

Christians thought of the church as "the body of Christ" (1 Cor 12:27) and were unified by their shared commitment to Jesus Christ as Lord. Converts became a part of this body of Christ by belief in Jesus as God's Messiah, public proclamation of their faith, and baptism (Acts 2:38–39). At the center of Christian worship was the "Lord's supper" (1 Cor 11:23–26), a religious meal that linked Christians to Jesus' crucifixion and allowed them to share in the body of Christ (1 Cor 10:16). Services were held on the first day of the week and included preaching and reading Scriptures and letters from church leaders (Col 4:16).

The first Christians were a tightly knit group. Although in the beginning they were not officially persecuted, they were at times regarded with suspicion and even hatred. Because their religion forced them to abstain from pagan worship, they were looked on with disdain by their fellow citizens.

Every church member had a role to play in fulfilling Christ's ministry. Some members were appointed to be ELDERS, who were sometimes called overseers or bishops (Acts 14:23). There was, however, no rigid organization. Rather, the early church had a loosely developed structure that allowed it to evolve as it grew.

The remains of the bema, or judgment seat, in Corinth's marketplace mark where Paul preached in the first century AD. The upper city of Acrocorinth rises in the background.

CINNAMON

I HAVE PERFUMED MY BED WITH MYRRH, ALOES, AND CINNAMON.
–PROVERBS 7:17

Cinnamon was a valued aromatic spice used to make perfumed oils and incense and to flavor food. From a tree native to what is now Sri Lanka, cinnamon came over ancient land and sea trade routes to the Holy Land, where it fetched high prices.

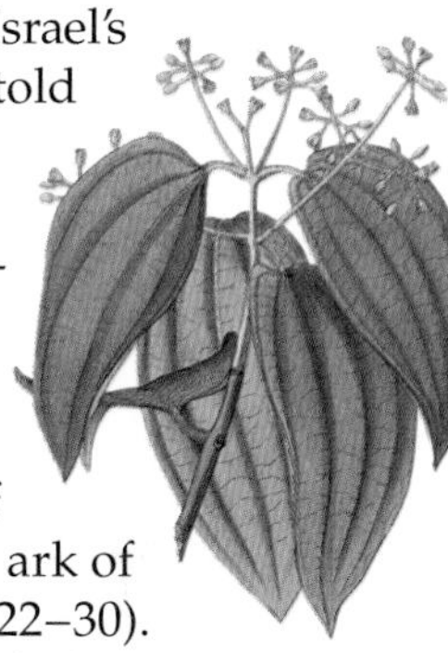

As part of his elaborate instructions for setting up Israel's sanctuary, the Lord told Moses to use 250 shekels worth of "sweet-smelling cinnamon" in making a sacred oil to anoint the priests, as well as the tent of the meeting and the ark of the covenant (Ex 30:22–30). In Proverbs its scent helps an adulteress to seduce a young man.

CIRCUIT

[SAMUEL] WENT ON A CIRCUIT YEAR BY YEAR TO BETHEL, GILGAL, AND MIZPAH; AND HE JUDGED ISRAEL IN ALL THESE PLACES.
–1 SAMUEL 7:15–16

As used in 1 Samuel, the word *circuit* means a circular path or route that leads around and back to its starting point. Thus Samuel was a kind of circuit judge, traveling throughout the country to the same cities each year to dispense justice. The territory on the outskirts of Jerusalem was described as forming a circuit around the city walls (Neh 12:28). In Ecclesiastes, *circuit* means repetitive, meaningless motion, like that of a restless wind: "The wind blows to the south, and goes around to the north; round and round goes the wind, and on its circuits the wind returns" (Eccl 1:6).

CIRCUMCISION

"YOU SHALL CIRCUMCISE THE FLESH OF YOUR FORESKINS, AND IT SHALL BE A SIGN OF THE COVENANT BETWEEN ME AND YOU."
–GENESIS 17:11

After God commanded Abraham to circumcise (cut the foreskin of) every male descendant eight days after birth, circumcision became a physical, external SIGN of the covenant between God and his chosen people (Gen 17:14). Though the ritual of circumcision was not practiced during the 40 years Israel wandered in the wilderness, it was reinstated when the Israelites invaded Canaan (Josh 5:2–7). Circumcision was known variously as the "sign of the covenant," "covenant in the flesh," and the "covenant of circumcision."

Not only the descendants of Abraham but also servants, aliens, and converts were expected to be circumcised. Initially the rite was carried out by the child's father, using a flint knife, but in time, specialists performed the ceremony. Being circumcised came to represent being clean and pure; being uncircumcised connoted uncleanliness and something forbidden. Only those who were circumcised were allowed to eat the Passover meal (Ex 12:43–49).

Although most neighboring peoples—including the Ammonites, Moabites, Arabs, and Egyptians—practiced circumcision, the Israelites looked on the rite as a sign of their distinctive relationship with God. Of Israel's immediate neighbors, only the Philistines did not practice circumcision: in 1 Samuel 17:26, David referred to Goliath with distain as "this uncircumcised Philistine." Even the circumcised did not escape contempt: Jeremiah denounced Israel's neighbors as "circumcised only in the foreskin" (Jer 9:25), meaning that their condition had no religious significance. When Jeremiah told his people, "Circumcise yourselves to the LORD, remove the foreskin of your hearts" (Jer 4:4), he used the symbol of circumcision to remind them to devote themselves to God.

As parents and witnesses stand by, a newly born child bravely submits to a ritual circumcision performed by an attending priest, as depicted in this detail from a 15th- to 16th-century Italian painting from the studio of Giovanni Bellini.

In New Testament times circumcision was the cause of the first major controversy within the fledgling church. As Greeks and other non-Jews heard the message about Jesus and believed, some Jewish Christian leaders told them, "'Unless you are circumcised according to the custom of Moses, you cannot be saved'" (Acts 15:11). Paul argued adamantly that the gospel message required that Gentiles be accepted without converting to Judaism. As he noted, "Circumcision is nothing, and uncircumcision is nothing; but obeying the commandments of God is everything" (1 Cor 7:19).

The issue was sufficiently important that leaders of the church met in Jerusalem to decide the matter. Though some Christian groups argued that circumcision was required by God, the apostles and elders determined that circumcision was not required of Gentiles (Acts 15:19).

CISTERN

"'. . . EVERYONE OF YOU WILL EAT FROM YOUR OWN VINE AND YOUR OWN FIG TREE AND DRINK WATER FROM YOUR OWN CISTERN . . . .'"
–ISAIAH 36:16

To survive a yearly dry season that stretches from May to October, people of the Holy Land dug and maintained cisterns, man-made reservoirs supplied with water from the runoff of rainfalls (Jdt 8:31). Often cisterns had covers to keep out debris and prevent accidents. Bottle-shaped cisterns were hewn from native limestone, then plastered inside to keep the water from seeping out. In the Bible, empty cisterns were occasionally used as disposal pits for corpses (Jer 41:9) and as prison cells: Jeremiah was held captive in an empty, muddy cistern belonging to Malchiah, son of King Zedekiah (Jer 38:6).

Rising out of the Negeb Desert, the ancient citadel at Arat, refortified during Solomon's reign about 1000 BC, was strategically situated to control one of the major trade routes in biblical times. In the distance, the lower city of Arat dates from about 3000 BC.

CITADEL

WITHIN ITS CITADELS GOD HAS SHOWN HIMSELF A SURE DEFENSE.
–PSALM 48:3

A citadel was a stronghold or fortified area built to protect places of importance, such as cities, palaces, and temples. Citadels also served as places of refuge from, and the last defense against, the invading enemy. Jerusalem boasted outer walls, or ramparts, and inner walls studded with stone towers (Ps 48:12–13). Inside, several citadel strongholds promised tough resistance. When Judas Maccabeus revolted against Jerusalem's Syrian rulers in 165 BC, his army found that "aliens held the citadel" (1 Macc 3:45). The foreign forces within Jerusalem's citadel were so well protected that some 20 years passed before they could be dislodged (1 Macc 13:49–50).

CITIZEN

". . . JUDGE RIGHTLY BETWEEN ONE PERSON AND ANOTHER, WHETHER CITIZEN OR RESIDENT ALIEN."
–DEUTERONOMY 1:16

In The Old Testament, the word *citizen* is almost exclusively used to mean "native born," as contrasted with ALIEN. The book of Leviticus recounts the story of a "blasphemer" of God's name, who, because of his father's Egyptian nationality, is considered an alien, yet he is punished as harshly as if he were a full citizen of Israel. His fate reflected God's decree that citizens and noncitizens were to be judged equally (Lev 24:22).

When the Romans conquered the Holy Land in the first century BC, they brought with them a legal system that gave Roman citizens distinct rights above everyone else. Among these were the privilege of voting and owning property. In the New Testament Paul, a Roman citizen by birth, declares his citizenship in order to gain respite from corporal punishment (Acts 22:25) and ultimately to "appeal to the emperor" (Acts 25:11) and claim his right to a trial in Rome.

CITY

THEN THEY SAID, "COME, LET US BUILD OURSELVES A CITY . . . OTHERWISE WE SHALL BE SCATTERED ABROAD UPON THE FACE OF THE WHOLE EARTH."
–GENESIS 11:4

The modern notion of a city as a great population center covering a large area does not apply to the cities of ancient Palestine. In the Old Testament, the word *city* signifies a walled settlement (2 Chr 14:7); a VILLAGE is a group of houses without a fortification or citadel (1 Sam 6:18). The earliest walled city known is Jericho, whose impressive defenses date from between 8000 BC and 7000 BC. Yet ancient Jericho comprised an area of less than 10 acres.

For centuries Palestine's cities remained small. King Solomon made Jerusalem a center for international trade and built a magnificent temple there (1 Kings 6:1), but during his reign, from about 971 BC to 931 BC, the city covered only 33 acres and had perhaps 6,500 inhabitants. In contrast to the Israelites' cities, those in Mesopotamia were vast metropolises. At its height in the seventh century BC, Nineveh, the capital of Assyria, was "an exceedingly large city, a three days' walk across" (Jon 3:3). Scholars estimate that Nineveh was at least 50 times larger than Jerusalem.

The Palestinian cities of the Old Testament had many features in common—evidence that the art of city planning was well advanced. In earliest times, cities were surrounded by a wall, usually made of stone and mud brick. After the invention of the battering ram, the walls were thickened and enclosed in a massive sloping embankment, up to 250 feet wide at the base, to repel invaders.

Cities required an adequate water supply, accessible in time of siege. For this reason, cities were generally constructed near a spring, from which sometimes very elaborate tunnel systems were dug to convey the water inside the city walls. Perhaps the most impressive is the Siloam tunnel, built during the reign of Hezekiah, to supply water to Jerusalem (2 Kings 20:20). Many houses also had private cisterns.

Cities served as protectors of the local small villages. In times of war, people fled to the walled cities from surrounding villages and farming areas. When the city fell to invaders, so did its villages (2 Chr 13:19). The point of entry to a city was its gate, which was the place of justice (2 Sam 15: 2–6) and commerce as well as the weakest point in the city's defenses. City gates were heavily fortified, with stout wooden doors that could be shut and braced by bars. Both outside and inside the gate lay open squares, which the people used as marketplaces.

The market square just inside the gate narrowed on the left and right into a ROAD that often circled the city's perimeter; smaller roads led from this circular path into the center of the city. These narrow, winding inner roads were frequently unpaved: Jerusalem's streets, for instance, remained unpaved until the time of Herod (37–4 BC). Situated at the city's highest point was the acropolis, where royalty lived in palaces and a temple often stood.

During the Hellenistic, Roman, and Byzantine periods, the face of Palestine was transformed as new and elegant cities arose. Herod rebuilt Jerusalem in Greco-Roman style, complete with a new temple, amphitheater, and aqueducts. It was not until Herod's reign—at the time of Jesus' birth—that Jerusalem reached a population of more than 40,000 people. Later rulers constructed the broad, paved thoroughfares typical of Roman cities: the *cardo*, running north and south, and the *decuman*, running east and west.

The ancient city of Beth-shan once sat upon the hill above. After Saul's defeat at the hands of the Philistines, they fastened his body and the bodies of his sons to the city walls.

City of Refuge

. . . YOU SHALL DESIGNATE THREE CITIES BEYOND THE JORDAN, AND THREE CITIES IN THE LAND OF CANAAN, TO BE CITIES OF REFUGE.
–NUMBERS 35:14

In ancient Israel, a person who killed another accidentally could flee to one of the six cities of refuge, which could be easily reached from most parts of the country. There the fugitive was safe from "the avenger of blood" (Num 35:19–21)—the nearest male relative of the victim, who was permitted to slay the killer of his kinsman if he could catch him. However, if a trial determined that the homicide had, in fact, been deliberate, the murderer would be handed over to the avenger. If the verdict found the accused innocent of willful manslaughter, he was sheltered from the avenger so long as he stayed within "the bounds of the original city of refuge" (Num 35:26–27). Not until the death of the high priest could the slayer leave the city of refuge and return home without fear of retribution (Num 35:28; Josh 20:6). It was believed that the death of the priest was a symbolic atonement for the original killing.

Clan

"NOW THEREFORE PRESENT YOURSELVES BEFORE THE LORD BY YOUR TRIBES AND BY YOUR CLANS."
–1 SAMUEL 10:19

In the ancient Near East a clan was a family grouping between a TRIBE and an ancestral house, all based on descent from a common patriarch. A tribe was made up of several clans, and each clan had several ancestral houses. In the family-oriented world of that time, people took their identity from their clan and tribe. Thus, the

Messengers bestow God's seal of protection on Israel's clans in this illumination.

descendants of Reuben—the eldest of Jacob's 12 sons—belonged to the tribe of Reuben and in turn took their clan affiliation from one of Reuben's four sons: Hanoch, Pallu, Hezron, or Carmi (Gen 46:8–9). As the Israelites trekked with Moses through the Sinai, they camped at night "by clans, according to ancestral houses" (Num 2:34). When beset by enemies, each clan was expected to supply its quota of troops to the tribal levy. After settling in the Promised Land, clan members tended to stick together, often living in the same villages.

CLAY

JUST LIKE THE CLAY IN THE POTTER'S HAND, SO ARE YOU IN MY HAND, O HOUSE OF ISRAEL. –JEREMIAH 18:6

Clay was so important to the Israelites that they used five words to distinguish the varieties. Artisans collected the finest clay from natural sources, such as river banks, and used it to make pottery, figurines, toys, and molds for bronze objects in Solomon's temple (1 Kings 7:46).

A lesser grade of clay was manufactured by mixing soil and water with bits of vegetation as a binding agent. Builders used this material to make BRICK for houses, to plaster walls and ceilings, and to provide flooring. Firing clay in a kiln made the object durable and waterproof. In the Bible, the word *clay* is also used to illustrate man's pliability in God's hands (Isa 64:8).

CLEAN AND UNCLEAN

YOU ARE TO DISTINGUISH BETWEEN THE HOLY AND THE COMMON, AND BETWEEN THE UNCLEAN AND THE CLEAN . . . . –LEVITICUS 10:10

Many ancient peoples, including the people of Israel, followed laws of ritual cleanliness. The division between clean and unclean, as found in the Old Testament, was fundamental to the Israelite religion. From the time of Moses, God enjoined his people to protect themselves from any form of physical, moral, or ritual contamination. Sources of impurity included dead humans, animal carcasses (Lev 11:24–40), skin diseases such as leprosy (Lev 13:6), certain bodily discharges, and the eating of forbidden animals (Lev 11:26–27).

The dietary laws given in the Pentateuch declared all beasts of prey to be unclean and therefore unfit for consumption. Only cud-chewing animals with cloven hooves, such as cows, were permissible to eat (Lev 11:3–7). Of seafood, only fish with scales and fins could be eaten.

Because some forms of uncleanliness were considered to be contagious, each defilement required immediate ritual purification, which was usually a period of isolation followed by cleansing with water, and perhaps an animal sacrifice (Lev 14:19). In some cases, priests were called in to make an inspection and perform the ceremony (Lev 14:48). After all rites were observed, the unclean person was again clean in the eyes of God.

Ancient potters kept clay submerged in pools of water, as in the photograph above, to achieve the right consistency and filter out impurities. Clay fashioned into vessels was then set in the sun to dry. Pots from Qumran, left, were fired in kilns for durability.

In New Testament times, less emphasis was placed on the external rituals of cleanliness. Jesus taught that impurity came not from outside forces but from within the human heart (Mk 7:22–23). He declared the old dietary laws obsolete (Mk 7:18–20), along with most purification rituals. The apostle John proclaimed that "the blood of Jesus . . . cleanses us from all sin" (1 Jn 1:7), meaning that the blood of Jesus was the last sacrifice for the purification of all people.

CLOTH

A certain woman named Lydia, a worshiper of God, was listening to us; she was from the city of Thyatira and a dealer in purple cloth.
–Acts of the Apostles 16:14

In biblical times, the Israelites were well known for making wool into cloth, especially in Judah. The wool was spun from fleece and woven into lengths of fabric that were sewn together to make garments.

The Egyptians wove natural FLAX fibers into fine linen cloth that was used to make clothing and sails for boats (Ezek 27:7). In Mesopotamia, cotton, which grew well in the humid climate of the south, was valued for the soft, brightly colored, durable cloth it produced. The Sumerians considered wool clothing to be very fashionable. In biblical lands, tent makers often used a coarse cloth made from the hair of animals such as goats and camels. The people of Israel were admonished by the Lord neither to sow with two kinds of seed, "nor shall you put on a garment made of two different materials" (Lev 19:19).

To make cloth more beautiful, patterns were sometimes used in the weave, and cloth was frequently dyed. In the first century AD, silk, linen, and wool cloth and clothing were traded among the Roman Empire and China and India. Royalty and other people of great wealth treasured silk that was imported from China or India.

A large number of woolen cloth fragments have been recovered from the ruins of the ancient fortress Masada, comprising the oldest and most extensive textile collection from the Roman period discovered to date. These swatches are thought to be from a man's cloak or blanket, worn about the first century BC.

CLOTHING

. . . your clothing was of fine linen, rich fabric, and embroidered cloth.
–Ezekiel 16:13

The Bible first mentions clothing in the story of Adam and Eve, who covered themselves with leaves. Their descendants wore animal skins and then cloth. After cloth came into use, women began to wear somewhat different clothing from men. Indeed, the Bible forbade women to wear men's clothing and vice versa, "for whoever does such things is abhorrent to the LORD your God" (Deut 22:5).

Men typically wore a loincloth made of linen, wool, or leather that went from the waist to the knees. Over that hung a loose tunic from the neck to the knees or lower. Jesus wore such a tunic; after he was crucified, the soldiers "took his tunic. . . . the tunic was seamless, woven in one piece from the top" (Jn 19:23). They then cast lots to see who would get it. Women wore tunics that reached to their ankles. The tunics of the poor were made of coarse wool, but the rich could afford fine imported linen and silk. Both men and women belted or sashed their tunics and wore over them loose, ankle-length robes, which could also serve as blankets on cold nights. When it was warm, little children often wore no clothing.

The rich wore garments colored with DYE made from plants and insects. Women's clothes were often more colorful than men's. Robes might also be fringed and embroidered, the hems being especially ornate: those of the high priests' robes were hung with golden bells and appliquéd with pomegranates (Ex 28:33).

Everyone who could afford them wore sandals, which were generally made of leather. Priests, however, may have gone barefoot in the temple as a sign of reverence. As protection against the sun or rain, both men and women covered their heads with cloths. Men often wrapped them around their head to form turbans. Women also occasionally wore turbans (Isa 3:23), and women of rank wore long flowing veils.

A Semitic dignitary, left, clothed in elaborate robe and sash, is shown with his servant, right, on a painted ceramic tile.

Special occasions usually called for special clothes. For feasts and weddings, both men and women dressed in costly garments; people in mourning wore dull, coarse sackcloth.

In the Bible, tearing or removing one's clothing was often a symbolic act, in some instances indicating a state of mourning or despair, as when David learned of Saul's death (2 Sam 1: 11–12). When Isaiah walked the land barefoot and naked—that is, as a prisoner would—it was to foretell the captivity that awaited Egypt and Ethiopia (Isa 20:3–4).

CLOUD

AT THE SEVENTH TIME HE SAID, "LOOK, A LITTLE CLOUD NO BIGGER THAN A PERSON'S HAND IS RISING OUT OF THE SEA. . . . ."–1 KINGS 18:44

A cloud rising from the Mediterranean in the west was a sign of approaching rain for the Israelites. Especially welcome were "clouds that bring the spring rain" (Prov 16:15). In contrast, high cirrus clouds in the east foretold hot desert winds and disastrous dust storms.

The Bible usually mentions clouds symbolically rather than meteorologically. Disappearing clouds represent fleeting fortunes. Job complains that "my prosperity has passed away like a cloud" (Job 30:15). They can also signify forgiveness. God reassures Israel: "I have swept away your transgressions like a cloud" (Isa 44:22). Clouds also demonstrate divine power. God "loads the thick cloud with moisture . . . they turn round and round by his guidance" (Job 37:11–12). In the New Testament, a voice from a cloud identifies Jesus as the Son of God (Mt 17:5).

COCK

JESUS SAID TO HIM, ". . . BEFORE THE COCK CROWS, YOU WILL DENY ME THREE TIMES."–MATTHEW 26:34

Israelite seals from hundreds of years before Jesus' birth portray cocks, indicating that chickens were already present in biblical

With its mirror impression in clay at left, an ancient seal, right, is engraved with cocks and the name of the prophet Haggai.

lands at that time. In Jesus' day the sound of a crowing rooster was so commonplace and predictable—the birds probably crowed about midnight and 3 AM—that the Romans used it to signal the changing of the guard. It was their custom to divide the night into four watches: evening (9 PM), midnight, "cockcrow" (3 AM), and dawn (6 AM). The cry of the rooster punctuated Peter's final denial that he knew Jesus. Overcome with remorse, Peter "went out and wept bitterly" (Mt 26:75).

COHORT

THEN THE SOLDIERS LED HIM INTO THE COURTYARD OF THE PALACE (THAT IS, THE GOVERNOR'S HEADQUARTERS); AND THEY CALLED TOGETHER THE WHOLE COHORT. –MARK 15:16

A military cohort was one-tenth of a Roman legion. It could include as many as 1,000 men but was typically smaller, perhaps comprised of six centuries, or subdivisions, of 70 to 100 soldiers each, who were usually infantry. Auxiliary cohorts were composed of freed slaves and other non-Romans (excluding Jews), who might earn citizenship after serving for 25 years. Cornelius was a CENTURION in charge of 100 soldiers in such a division, called the Italian Cohort, in Caesarea (Acts 10:1). The Augustan Cohort that guarded Paul when he was transferred to Rome (Acts 27:1) probably earned its prestigious title for valorous service.

COIN

"... 'REJOICE WITH ME,
FOR I HAVE FOUND THE COIN
THAT I HAD LOST.'"
–LUKE 15:9

The earliest coined money, dated about 650 BC, was apparently issued by King Croesus in Lydia (modern Turkey). About a century later, a Greek coin inscribed with an owl became the first metal currency used in the Holy Land, to be followed there by Phoenician, Egyptian, and Persian coinage, including the gold DARIC.

For centuries before coinage, the trading of the Near East took place by barter, which often involved prized and easily movable cattle, and by the exchange of precious metals, such as the silver SHEKEL. A shekel was a weight of about one-third of an ounce; it came in various shapes. Most references to shekels probably mean silver, the Near East's most widespread precious metal. In the days of the kingdoms of Israel and Judah, the gold or silver talent, with a weight of about 66 pounds, was frequently used in large transactions. Gold was especially important in deals between countries, but it was relatively rare and had to be obtained from Anatolia or Egypt.

About 400 BC, some Judean governors were given permission by their Persian overlords to strike small silver coins. The design, borrowed from Greek coins, included the Aramaic word *Yehud,* meaning "Judah." The Jews minted their own state currency in the Hasmonean period, beginning under John Hyrcanus I (135–104 BC). Most of these coins were bronze. In keeping with the second commandment, Hasmonean currency never depicted living beings, whether human or animal. The money was instead decorated with inanimate objects, such as wreaths, stars, palm branches, cornucopias, and menorahs. Not until the reign of Alexander Jannaeus (103–76 BC) did Jewish coins include dates.

Most New Testament references to coinage cite the Roman silver DENARIUS, which was roughly a day's wages for a laborer; it was equivalent to the Greek silver drachma. However, the temple tax of Matthew 17:24 was a half-shekel, and biblical experts infer that Judas' blood money consisted of shekels. By this time a shekel had become a silver coin weighing approximately half an ounce. Also in the New Testament are the coins that Jesus sees a poor widow give to the temple: two lepta, the least valuable Greek copper coins. The two were equal to one *quadrans,* the smallest Roman copper coin, called a penny in Mark 12:42. By contrast, the talents mentioned in two of Jesus' parables were apparently quite valuable, worth many thousands of dollars each today. The money changers that Jesus routed from the temple reflect the cosmopolitan nature of Jerusalem, which attracted pilgrims carrying different currencies. See also chart for MONEY.

Connected coins, below, came from stone molds, left. Those minting the coins poured a molten precious metal, such as silver, into the mold. After the strings of coins hardened, they were cut apart.

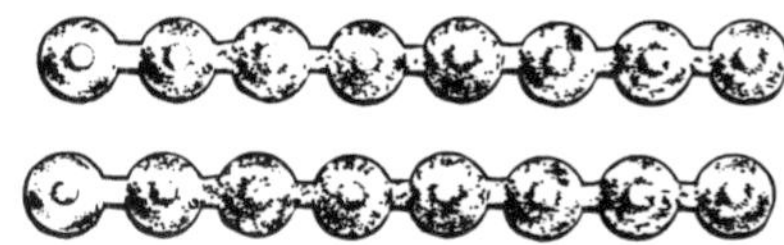

COLLAR

"WITH VIOLENCE HE SEIZES MY
GARMENT; HE GRASPS MY BY THE COLLAR
OF MY TUNIC."–JOB 30:18

"Collar" is the translation of several Hebrew words with different meanings. One type of collar was an iron shackle that was put around a prisoner's neck. Another was a pillory or stocks used to keep someone confined. A collar could also be the open space in a garment for the head. The blue robe of the high priest had "a woven binding around the opening, like the opening in a coat of mail" (Ex 28:32). The word *collar* was also used for the ornamental necklaces worn by the camels of the Midianite kings (Judg 8:26).

COLLECTION

NOW CONCERNING THE COLLECTION
FOR THE SAINTS: YOU SHOULD FOLLOW
THE DIRECTIONS I GAVE TO THE CHURCHES
OF GALATIA.–1 CORINTHIANS 16:1

Religious leaders collected money by imposing taxes and by soliciting voluntary contributions. When the temple needed repair, King Johash ordered the priests to go to all the cities and collect a tax that Moses had apparently established for the upkeep of the tabernacle. The priests, reluctant to become tax collectors, compromised by setting up a CHEST at the temple entrance and taking a voluntary collection; the people responded generously. Later King Hezekiah ordered the nation to support the priests by bringing harvest offerings of grain, wine, oil, and honey.

Paul took up voluntary collections for two projects. While working with the church in Antioch, he collected famine relief funds for Judea. Later, during his missionary travels, he again raised money for needy Christians in Jerusalem. Paul apparently hoped that this offering, collected from Gentile Christians and donated to Jewish Christians, would help unite these two branches of Christianity that were arguing over whether Gentiles should obey Jewish laws. Unfortunately, after Paul arrived in Jerusalem with the collection, he was arrested by Roman soldiers.

In Colossians 4:13, Paul mentions Hierapolis, the ruins of which are shown above. Both Colossae and Hierapolis, neighboring cities in Asia Minor, had Christian communities.

COLOR

. . . THE RIDERS WORE BREASTPLATES THE COLOR OF FIRE AND OF SAPPHIRE AND OF SULFUR . . . .
–REVELATION 9:17

The Israelites were generally more interested in an object's material than its hue. But they made colors from plants, minerals, and other substances (see box), as did the Assyrians, Egyptians, and Babylonians. The colors were used to dye fabrics, color glass and glazed pottery, and paint wood, pottery, and walls. When building a ziggurat, or temple tower, the Babylonians used a different color of enamel bricks for each story.

When mentioned in the Bible, colors are often symbolic. Purple was the most highly prized color, indicating luxury or royalty. Priests' garments were made of purple or blue fabric. Blue, the color of the sky, was associated with God and was used in the tabernacle. White symbolized joy or victory. Black stood for pestilence or decay, and red could represent lifeblood or sin. A greenish gray color signified death, as in Revelation: "I looked and there was a pale green horse! Its rider's name was Death, and Hades followed with him" (Rev 6:8).

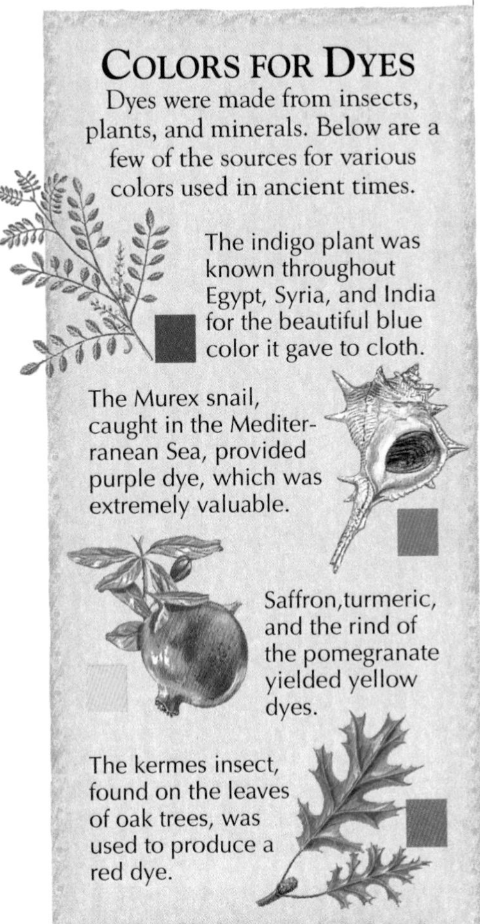

COLORS FOR DYES

Dyes were made from insects, plants, and minerals. Below are a few of the sources for various colors used in ancient times.

The indigo plant was known throughout Egypt, Syria, and India for the beautiful blue color it gave to cloth.

The Murex snail, caught in the Mediterranean Sea, provided purple dye, which was extremely valuable.

Saffron,turmeric, and the rind of the pomegranate yielded yellow dyes.

The kermes insect, found on the leaves of oak trees, was used to produce a red dye.

COLOSSIANS, LETTER OF PAUL TO THE

SO IF YOU HAVE BEEN RAISED WITH CHRIST, SEEK THE THINGS THAT ARE ABOVE, WHERE CHRIST IS . . . .
–COLOSSIANS 3:1

Paul wrote his letter to the Colossians, the inhabitants of the town of Colossae in Asia Minor in about AD 60. His main purpose was to combat some kind of false teaching that had sprung up there. The precise nature of the teaching is not known, but it included belief in the worship of angels as divine intermediaries. Paul forcefully restated the primacy of Christ as the agent of salvation.

The authenticity of the LETTER has been questioned by some historians, but at many points it closely parallels Paul's letter to the Ephesians. It also shows the extent of Paul's influence, even in a church he never visited.

COLT

LO, YOUR KING COMES TO YOU . . . HUMBLE AND RIDING . . . ON A COLT, THE FOAL OF A DONKEY.
–ZECHARIAH 9:9

Young camels and donkeys were both referred to as colts in the Old Testament (Gen 32:15; 49:11). Zechariah predicted the arrival of Jerusalem's triumphant but humble king on a young donkey. Jesus' entry into the city on a donkey (Jn 12:14) had rich symbolism for the onlookers, since the animal was used for transport not only by the average person but also by the kings of the ancient Near East. Jesus arrived in Jerusalem as the prophesied king amid great exultation, but he chose, in accordance with Scripture, to come on the back of a young donkey, a figure of peace, rather than a HORSE, a figure of power and war.

COMMANDMENT

". . . I WILL GIVE YOU THE TABLETS OF STONE, WITH THE LAW AND THE COMMANDMENT, WHICH I HAVE WRITTEN FOR THEIR INSTRUCTION."
–EXODUS 24:12

A commandment is an order. When the term is used in the Old Testament, it almost always refers to God's instructions to the Israelites as laid down in the Pentateuch, the first five books of the Bible. Most of the commandments that God gave to Moses on Mount Sinai reflect case law, as in "Whoever strikes father or mother shall be put to death" (Ex 21:15). The ten commandments, however, are examples of categorical law. Rather than listing specific crimes and punishments, they establish social values that are essential to God's covenant.

COMMISSION

". . . TAKE JOSHUA . . . LAY YOUR HAND UPON HIM; HAVE HIM STAND BEFORE ELEAZAR THE PRIEST AND ALL THE CONGREGATION, AND COMMISSION HIM IN THEIR SIGHT."
–NUMBERS 27:18–19

Commissioning someone meant entrusting that person with the responsibility to act on behalf of God or someone in authority. When Moses was about to die, God told him to commission Joshua to lead Israel in his place. When Paul, before his conversion, set off for Damascus to hunt Christians, he did so "with the authority and commission of the chief priests" (Acts 26:12).

Commanded by an angel, Hagar, concubine of Abraham, returns to his household in a 17th-century painting by Pietro da Cortona. Abraham's wife, Sarah, is seen in the background.

In what is known as the "great commission," Jesus told his followers to "make disciples of all nations" (Mt 28:19). Paul extended this charge to all Christians.

COMPANY

IN JEZREEL, THE SENTINEL STANDING ON THE TOWER SPIED THE COMPANY OF JEHU ARRIVING . . . .–2 KINGS 9:17

When the Bible speaks of companies, it is often referring to military units, such as those that Moses set up within the 12 tribes of Israel (Num 1:3). But a company can mean other groups as well—usually large assemblies. Joseph leads "a very great company" to Canaan to bury his father (Gen 50:9). In the book of Numbers, a company of 250 men and their households are swallowed up by the earth after they resist Moses' leadership (Num 16). The Bible also mentions "the company of the prophets," perhaps an organized group led by Samuel (1 Sam 19:20).

CONCUBINE

HIS CONCUBINE WHO WAS IN SHECHEM ALSO BORE HIM A SON, AND HE NAMED HIM ABIMELECH.
–JUDGES 8:31

In the ancient Near East, a concubine was a woman bought from a poor family or taken captive in battle to be a man's unmarried companion. Generally only wealthy men could afford to keep them. Abraham had concubines, as did David, but for sheer numbers, Solomon topped them all: "Among his wives were seven hundred princesses and three hundred concubines" (1 Kings 11:3). The book of Deuteronomy was probably referring to Solomon when it said that the king "must not acquire many wives for himself, or else his heart will turn away" (Deut 17:17).

A concubine bore children and was responsible for taking care of some portion of the household. A man was expected to assume the obligations of a husband to his concubine, whom he was not allowed to sell. However, she did not have the same rights as his legal wife. Childless wives, such as Sarah and Rachel, sometimes gave their handmaidens to their husbands as concubines to bear children for them. A concubine's sons could have the same right to inheritance as the sons of wives, which often created tension between the two groups.

To have sexual relations with a ruler's concubines was an act of treason. When Absalom, at the time of his revolt against David, "went in to his father's concubines in the sight of all Israel" (2 Sam 16:22), it was an act to usurp the king's authority.

Confession

"Now make confession to the LORD the God of your ancestors, and do his will . . . ."–Ezra 10:11

Israel's faith called for confessing sins to God. Some sins also required restitution or a sacrifice. The Israelites believed that once the sin was confessed and the stipulations of the law were fulfilled, God would grant forgiveness. Some people, however, merely went through the motions of confession: they offered the sacrifice and admitted their sin, but they felt no sorrow. The psalmist expressed God's displeasure with this absence of remorse: "The sacrifice acceptable to God is a broken spirit; a broken and contrite heart, O God, you will not despise" (Ps 51:17).

On occasion, religious leaders confessed the sin of the entire nation. The high priest did this on the Day of Atonement, and Daniel did so while in exile (Dan 9:20).

Like the Old Testament, the New Testament teaches that God forgives the penitent sinner. Christians were urged to "confess your sins to one another, and pray for one another" (Jas 5:16).

Sometimes when the Bible speaks of confession, the word has nothing to do with sin. Instead, it refers to a declaration of faith in God or Christ. Paul says in his letter to the Romans that "if you confess with your lips that Jesus is Lord and believe in your heart that God raised him from the dead, you will be saved" (Rom 10:9). John's first letter states, "God abides in those who confess that Jesus is the Son of God" (1 Jn 4:15).

Congregation

Then the whole congregation of the Israelites assembled at Shiloh, and set up the tent of meeting there.–Joshua 18:1

When the members of the nation of Israel came together for any reason—to worship God, fight a battle, anoint a king—they did so as a congregation of people united by their covenant with the Lord.

A clay dish, found in the Sinai Desert, depicts the Israelites gathered together as a congregation to listen to Moses preach.

When the law required them to arrive in a state of ritual purity, such as when they gathered to observe a religious holiday, the people became a "solemn assembly" (Lev 23:36), according to Old Testament writers.

The Old Testament most commonly identifies Israel as a congregation when recounting the story of the exodus. The New Testament echoes this meaning when it describes Moses as "the one who was in the congregation in the wilderness" (Acts 7:38). Other New Testament uses of the word *congregation* refer to local Christian communities, such as Antioch, a city in ancient Syria (Acts 15:30).

Conscience

"Therefore I do my best always to have a clear conscience toward God and all people."–Acts of the Apostles 24:16

The inner voice that a person hears can condemn or praise. David avoided "pangs of conscience" when Abigail convinced him not to seek revenge on her husband (1 Sam 25:31). Paul's clear conscience enabled him to declare his innocence to critics. However, following one's conscience in the early church was not always a simple matter. For example, some thought that eating meat from animals offered to idols amounted to worshiping false gods. Others, confident in the knowledge of one God, disagreed. Paul advised not eating such food so as not to tempt those who were less enlightened into doing something they felt was wrong (1 Cor 8:1–13).

Consecration

He shall not go outside the sanctuary and thus profane the sanctuary . . . for the consecration of the anointing oil of his God is upon him . . . .–Leviticus 21:12

God commanded that people who performed a sacred office as well as objects used in worship be consecrated, or rendered holy, through specific rituals. When Moses built the tabernacle and Solomon built the temple, priests consecrated the structures and their furnishings by touching each object with oil. New houses and crop offerings were also consecrated. Sometimes the entire nation of Israel was consecrated for special events, such as when the people washed their clothes and abstained from sexual relations before Moses climbed Mount Sinai to receive the ten commandments (Ex 19:14–15). See also NAZIRITE.

CONSTELLATION

SHE IS MORE BEAUTIFUL THAN THE SUN, AND EXCELS EVERY CONSTELLATION OF THE STARS.
–WISDOM OF SOLOMON 7:29

Three constellations familiar to modern astronomers are named in the Old Testament: the Bear (Ursa Major), Orion (the Hunter), and the Pleiades, which is actually a cluster of stars in Taurus. The book of Job refers to all three and also to a mysterious heavenly configuration called Mazzaroth—either an unidentified constellation or a term for all 12 signs of the zodiac. Equally obscure is Job's reference to the "chambers of the south" (Job 9:9), perhaps a very bright section of the southern skies. Some think that the star of Bethlehem appeared in the constellation Pisces, with the convergence of the planets Jupiter and Saturn in 7 BC.

CONSUMPTION

. . . I WILL BRING TERROR ON YOU; CONSUMPTION AND FEVER THAT WASTE THE EYES AND CAUSE LIFE TO PINE AWAY.–LEVITICUS 26:16

Most often identified by scholars as pulmonary tuberculosis, the wasting disease known as consumption in the Bible may also refer to the emaciating side effects of malaria or to cancer. Severe pulmonary tuberculosis, a contagious bacterial disease that infects the lungs and thrives in unsanitary conditions, is characterized by loss of appetite, coughing, spitting of blood, fever, night sweating, and weight loss. In the Old Testament, the malady is named in divine curses of retribution for disobeying the law (Deut 28:22).

CONVERSION

. . . THEY REPORTED THE CONVERSION OF THE GENTILES, AND BROUGHT GREAT JOY TO ALL THE BELIEVERS.
–ACTS OF THE APOSTLES 15:3

Conversion means turning away from faithlessness or other religions to God. The Old Testament talks mostly about conversions of nations, such as Israel "returning to the LORD" (1 Sam. 7:3). But there are cases of individual conversions: Ruth, a Moabite and ancestor of David, tells Naomi that "your God [shall be] my God" (Ruth 1:16).

The New Testament focuses on Christian conversion, which involves the acknowledgment of Jesus as the Son of God. However, early Jewish Christians continued to attend synagogues, keep the Mosaic law, and observe traditional customs (Acts 9:2; 21:20–21). For them, conversion meant turning to Christ, but it did not entail—as it did for the Gentiles—completely changing religions.

COOKING

ONCE WHEN JACOB WAS COOKING A STEW, ESAU CAME IN FROM THE FIELD, AND HE WAS FAMISHED.
–GENESIS 25:29

Boiling and baking were the most common cooking methods in biblical times. The lentil stew for

A 15th-century painting shows Paul's conversion, including the light from heaven that blinds the apostle. Jesus asks him, "Why do you persecute me?"

which Esau sold his birthright to his younger brother, Jacob, was probably boiled in an earthenware pot over a fire fueled with sticks, thistles, or dung. Fires were usually made outdoors, although in winter, cooking might be done inside the house on a charcoal brazier that also provided a source of heat for the family.

The Israelites added onions, garlic, and other vegetables to the peas and beans commonly boiled in their pots. Herbs included cummin and dill. Dietary laws forbade the eating of blood because it was identified with life (Gen 9:4; Deut 12:23). After the blood was drained from a slaughtered animal, however, it was acceptable to roast it on a spit or cook it in pieces. Meat was generally cut up and stewed; fish was usually grilled.

Bread, the staple of the Near Eastern diet, was regularly baked at home. Olive oil and vinegar were used in food preparation. Salt, often from the Dead Sea, was essential for preserving foods and also provided flavoring.

Fruits were sometimes stewed or dried. Grape juice could be boiled to make a thick syrup. Some scholars believe this syrup was the "honey" reported to flow in abundance in the Promised Land according to Exodus 3:8. Milk, often from goats, was used in cooking, although a law prohibited stewing a kid in its mother's milk (Ex 23:19). See also box for BAKING.

COPPER

FOR THE LORD YOUR GOD IS BRINGING YOU INTO A GOOD LAND . . . FROM WHOSE HILLS YOU MAY MINE COPPER.–DEUTERONOMY 8:7, 9

Copper was processed at several sites in biblical lands. Job explained: "Copper is smelted from ore. Miners . . . search out to the farthest bound the ore in gloom and deep darkness. They open shafts in a valley away from human habitation" (Job 28:2–4).

Copper was often cast in the "ox-hide" shape, above, which made it easier to carry. These ingots, from 1200 BC, were part of a ship's cargo.

Copper was used to make many things, including weapons and tools; however, by about 2000 BC, it was usually alloyed with tin to form bronze. Copper had far less monetary value than gold or silver: the poor widow's temple offering of two copper coins that drew Jesus' praise (Mk 12:43–44) represented only a minuscule fraction of a day laborer's pay.

Corroded copper could symbolize evil: "Never trust your enemy, for like corrosion in copper, so is his wickedness" (Sir 12:10).

CORAL

. . . THEY EXCHANGED FOR YOUR WARES TURQUOISE, PURPLE, EMBROIDERED WORK, FINE LINEN, CORAL, AND RUBIES.–EZEKIEL 27:16

For centuries, coral was thought to be wood because it resembles tree branches. It was only at the beginning of the 18th century that it was recognized as the skeletal deposits of marine polyps. In biblical times red—or precious—coral, found in the Mediterranean and Red seas, was used to make beads and other types of jewelry. It was also an important trade item between Israel and Edom.

The Bible refers to "bodies . . . more ruddy than coral" (Lam 4:7). In Job 28:12–18, coral is listed with other precious items, such as gold, silver, sapphires, and pearls, but wisdom is judged more valuable than all of them.

CORBAN

". . . 'WHATEVER SUPPORT YOU MIGHT HAVE HAD FROM ME IS CORBAN' (THAT IS, AN OFFERING TO GOD) . . . ."–MARK 7:11

Tradition allowed the Israelites to make a VOW dedicating their property to God in an offering called Corban. Since the person retained the use of his assets as a caretaker until death, this was not necessarily a sacrifice; if someone did not want to help his relatives financially, however, it provided him with a ready excuse not to use his assets for their support. Jesus criticized this practice as a loophole through which people could crawl to escape God's commandment to honor one's parents, noting that "you no longer permit doing anything for a father or mother, thus making void the word of God through your tradition" (Mk 7:12–13).

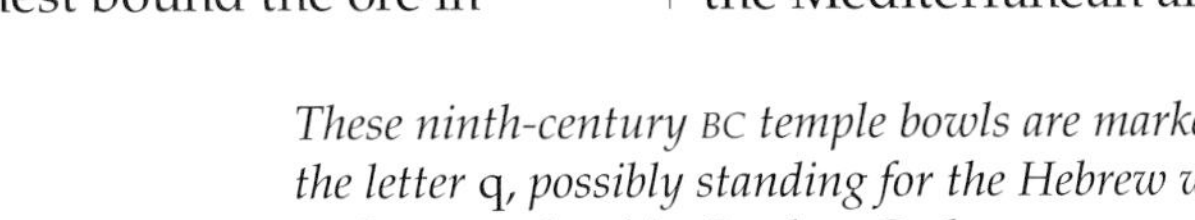

These ninth-century BC temple bowls are marked with the letter q, *possibly standing for the Hebrew word* qorbān, *rendered in Greek as Corban.*

The use of cosmetics was an important part of many women's morning rituals in biblical times. Above, three servants help a wealthy Roman matron prepare for her day. The woman checks herself in a mirror of polished silver after one servant, using a jar of powder and a moistened spatula, has applied her makeup. Another fixes her hair with an ivory comb. A third waits with a stole, which will go on over her tunic.

Cord

. . . [David] measured two lengths of cord for those who were to be put to death, and one length for those who were to be spared.
–2 Samuel 8:2

A cord was made of twisted or braided leather, string, pieces of cloth, goat or camel hair, papyrus, or other strong substances. Cords had many uses in everyday life. They could be used as a mooring line or a belt, to tie a prisoner or lead an animal, to erect and secure tents and the tabernacle, or to pull a cart. Jesus used a whip made of cords to clear the temple (John 2:15). The gold chains of the high priest's ephod, or sacred garment, were also referred to as "twisted like cords" (Ex 28:22).

Corinthians, 1 & 2

And now faith, hope, and love abide, these three; and the greatest of these is love.
–1 Corinthians 13:13

Paul's letters to the Corinthians are among the most valuable sources of information about the growth of the CHURCH in the first century and about the apostle himself. Paul had established the congregation in Corinth, spending 18 months there during his second missionary journey. But controversies subsequently erupted over questions of morality, worship, and other matters. Paul wrote the letter known as 1 Corinthians to respond to those issues. Later, newly arrived Christian missionaries preached ideas that directly opposed many of Paul's teachings, and Paul himself came under personal criticism. Paul wrote a second letter, 2 Corinthians, which combined arguments, encouragement, and stern warnings to the Corinthians, who responded by accepting his leadership and teachings.

CORNERSTONE

"HAVE YOU NOT READ THIS SCRIPTURE: 'THE STONE THAT THE BUILDERS REJECTED HAS BECOME THE CORNERSTONE . . .'?"
–MARK 12:10

When masons erected walls on a foundation, one of the first stones laid was the cornerstone, linking two walls at what was usually the most visible corner. Because it was so important to the structural integrity of the building, it was chosen with great care. Most biblical references to cornerstones are symbolic, however. In Job 38:6 the term refers to the stability of the earth that God created. In Zechariah 10:4 it may refer to a coming leader, perhaps the Messiah. New Testament writers portray Jesus as a cornerstone rejected by his own people but selected by God as the pivotal building block in the Lord's temple (Eph 2:20).

CORRUPTION

. . . REMEMBER CORRUPTION AND DEATH, AND BE TRUE TO THE COMMANDMENTS.
–ECCLESIASTICUS 28:6

The ancients believed that the material world was in a constant state of flux and change and that all within it was in "bondage to decay" (Rom 8:21). The body itself was subject to death, followed by physical decay and corruption. In contrast, Jesus, whose body was raised from the dead, "experienced no corruption" (Acts 13:37). By accepting his message, believers "may escape from the corruption that is in the world . . . and may become participants of the divine nature" (2 Pet 1:4) and find eternal life. In the Bible, corruption refers mainly to the physical decay of the body and the material world, but it also applies to moral decay, which makes human beings "slaves of corruption" (2 Pet 2:19).

COSMETICS

. . . THIS WAS THE REGULAR PERIOD OF THEIR COSMETIC TREATMENT, SIX MONTHS WITH OIL OF MYRRH AND SIX MONTHS WITH PERFUMES AND COSMETICS . . . .
–ESTHER 2:12

In the ancient Near East, men and women used a wide range of preparations to enhance beauty and soothe skin parched by the hot, dry climate. Men rubbed oil onto their skin, hair, and beard. The oil was extracted from almonds, olives, and fish and animal fat and was perfumed with fragrances such as saffron, balsam, and cinnamon. Oils offered some protection from the sun and masked body odor in a time when bathing was infrequent.

Women used body oil, as well as eye paint, rouge, powder, and perfume. Minerals were often crushed and mixed with gum or water to create kohl or ANTIMONY, and the eyes might be heavily outlined with this paint. Egyptians painted the upper eyelid black and applied a green paste made from ground turquoise or malachite to the lower lid. Mesopotamian women used red and yellow paints. Eye paint not only accentuated the eyes but also protected against the glare of the sun and insects. The Bible sometimes associates painting the eyes with women of ill repute, such as when the wicked queen Jezebel "painted her eyes, and adorned her head" (2 Kings 9:30) before taunting Jehu.

Lips and possibly cheeks were colored with red ocher, and crushed henna leaves made a reddish dye that was used on hair and nails. Sumerian women used yellow ochre as face powder, known as "face bloom." Cosmetics were kept in small stone or pottery jars—the rich had finely crafted glass and ivory containers—and were applied by fingertips or tiny bone spatulas (see illustration.)

A figure reclines on a couch in an Egyptian funeral monument from the third century BC.

COUCH

. . . EVERY NIGHT I FLOOD MY BED WITH TEARS; I DRENCH MY COUCH WITH MY WEEPING.
–PSALM 6:6

Chairs were rare in biblical times, and a bed often served as a couch as well. Rich people of the Near East possessed couches inlaid with ivory and decorated with motifs in gold leaf and GLASS. Amos decried their decadence and warned of the coming judgment when he prophesied, "Alas for those who lie on beds of ivory, and lounge on their couches" (Am 6:4).

In the Roman era, a U-shaped couch around a low table was used by banqueters, who reclined as they ate—a custom reflected in the account of the Last Supper: "One of his disciples . . . was reclining next to him" (Jn 13:23).

COUNCIL

". . . IF YOU INSULT A BROTHER OR SISTER, YOU WILL BE LIABLE TO THE COUNCIL . . . ."–MATTHEW 5:22

Although political authority in Near Eastern societies flowed from the king, councils played a major role at many levels in government, the military, law, and religion.

An informal council of leaders that met on the Areopagus, foreground, a sacred hill facing the Acropolis in Athens, asked Paul to speak during his second journey (Acts 17:19).

Israel's village councils, called Sanhedrin in some versions of the New Testament, had judicial authority and were thought by early Christians to be a source of persecution. Israel's king had his own high council, as did the Persian king Darius, who summoned all his nobles, satraps, governors, generals, and prefects to a council chamber to decide a contest (1 Esd 3:14–15). In Athens, Paul preached to a gathering of philosophers on the Areopagus, a meeting place of Athenian ruling councils. This institution was believed to have a parallel in a council of the heavenly hosts, over which God presided. Its members did not advise God but only heard his decrees (Ps 89:5–7).

COUNSELOR

. . . AUTHORITY RESTS UPON
HIS SHOULDERS; AND HE IS NAMED
WONDERFUL COUNSELOR . . . .
–ISAIAH 9:6

Rulers and commoners alike valued wise advice, to such a degree that counselors at court may have held authority just below that of the king himself. The book of Proverbs warns against taking advice from the wicked and proclaims, "Where there is no guidance, a nation falls" (Prov 11:14). The king of Persia had seven counselors, and at the court of David the adviser Ahithophel was highly esteemed because his counsel "was as if one consulted the oracle of God" (2 Sam 16:23). Job took pride that people valued his advice, "and kept silence for my counsel" (Job 29:21). The joyous names bestowed on the Messiah in Isaiah 9:6 reveal how exalted the counselor's role could be: "Wonderful Counselor, Mighty God, Everlasting Father, Prince of Peace."

COUNTRY

MOSES . . . SAID TO THEM,
"GO UP . . . INTO THE HILL COUNTRY,
AND SEE WHAT THE LAND IS LIKE . . . ."
–NUMBERS 13:17–18

The spies that Moses sent to explore the land of Canaan returned to report that it "flows with milk and honey" (Num 13:27); it was soon identified as the Promised Land that God had described to Moses (Ex 3:8). Much of the territory was hill country—chiefly the low hills bordering the Jordan River from the Dead Sea north to Galilee and west to the coastal plain.

Elsewhere in the Old Testament, the country was often contrasted with the CITY. Villages without walls were considered country in matters of property ownership. Mosaic laws related to murder and adultery had special conditions if the crime occurred in open country where the criminal was unknown and the victim could not call for help.

In the New Testament, the country was sometimes a refuge for Jesus. He told a leper he had cured not to reveal the miracle but rather to present himself to the priest and make the ritual offering required for such a cleansing. Instead the astonished man "spread the word, so that Jesus could no longer go into a town openly, but stayed out in the country" (Mk 1:45).

COURIER

SO THE COURIERS WENT
FROM CITY TO CITY
THROUGH THE COUNTRY . . . .
–2 CHRONICLES 30:10

When the king wished to disseminate news or commands throughout his realm, he would dispatch couriers, who were sometimes members of the royal guard. Couriers may have had elite status because they could read—a rare ability in Israel or any other society of ancient times. They were handed letters at court and traveled through the country, reading aloud from the documents to public gatherings in the fashion of town criers. In Persia, couriers riding the fastest horses—specially bred from the king's own herd—carried copies of royal edicts, which they posted in public places.

Court

The court sat in judgment, and the books were opened. –Daniel 7:10

In the ancient Near East, legal disputes could be settled at several different levels. The family head usually judged disputes within a family. When an accusation or complaint was made against someone from another family, the case was taken to the town elders, who sat in judgment at the town gate. As the heads of that town's clans, they had the authority to decide guilt or innocence and to punish the guilty.

In the ninth century BC, King Jehoshaphat of Judah established courts of law in the larger cities and appointed judges to them. He also created a court of appeals in Jerusalem made up of "certain Levites and priests and heads of families of Israel" (2 Chr 19:8). The courts had sufficient authority to interpret the LAW.

During the time when the Romans ruled Palestine, the Sanhedrin was the highest court of the Jews in Jerusalem. The power of the Sanhedrin is disputed, but most historians believe that it addressed a variety of legal and religious matters. Paul insisted that disputes between church members should not be taken to Roman courts to be argued "before the unrighteous" (1 Cor 6:1).

In the Bible the word *court* also refers to the courtyard of a house, palace, or temple. The court of the tabernacle was formed by a rectangular fence that measured 150 feet by 75 feet and was made from linen curtains hung from erect poles. Sacrifices were made in the court, in which there was a bronze wash basin and an altar. The "royal court" refers to a king's often sizable entourage, from bodyguards to secretaries, priests, and prophets.

Courtyard

. . . he went with Jesus into the courtyard of the high priest, but Peter was standing outside at the gate.–John 18:15–16

A courtyard was the entrance to the house; it was also found in gardens, palaces, and temples. The city homes of poorer Israelites usually consisted of one room and an enclosed courtyard, although the wealthy would build a number of rooms around three sides of a rectangular courtyard. On the fourth side was a wall and door to the street. A courtyard typically had grain silos, a cistern for the household's water supply, grinding stones, and an oven where the cooking was done. The courtyard was usually uncovered, but it might be partially roofed to provide shelter for the family's livestock.

Covenant

. . . the LORD your God . . . maintains covenant loyalty with those who love him and keep his commandments . . . . –Deuteronomy 7:9

A covenant is a binding contract between two parties that usually involves promises and obligations. In the Bible, the word *covenant* is used most often to describe an agreement between God and his people, but it can also refer to a treaty. In the ancient Near East, covenants were common and could exist between individuals or states. Abraham established a covenant with King Abimelech, giving the king seven ewe lambs for a disputed well in Beer-sheba (Gen 21:25–32).

Covenants between greater and lesser powers followed a basic structure established by the Hittites: the document introduced the powerful king and outlined the history of his generosity toward the vassal state. Then the king's demands—usually for loyalty—were stated, in exchange for which the vassal received protection or special favors. The vassal was required to store the treaty in the temple and read it periodically. To make a covenant binding, it was celebrated with a special feast or blood sacrifice.

This was the pattern followed by God's covenant with the Israelites at Sinai. The demands God made upon his people consisted of the ten commandments, as well as laws concerning WORSHIP and justice. His favor rested upon the Israelites' obedience to these edicts. When God established a covenant with Abraham, promising that his offspring would multiply and have possession of the Promised Land, the fulfillment of his word was contingent upon the circumcision of all male offspring (Gen 17:9–14). Similarly, God's promise to David that "your throne shall be established forever" (2 Sam 7:16) was subject to David's keeping the covenant.

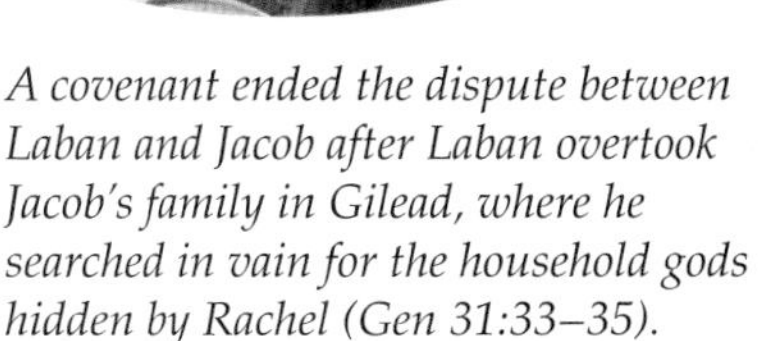

A covenant ended the dispute between Laban and Jacob after Laban overtook Jacob's family in Gilead, where he searched in vain for the household gods hidden by Rachel (Gen 31:33–35).

To invalidate a written covenant, the tablets on which it was inscribed were broken. When Moses descended from the mountain to find the Israelites worshiping a golden calf, he shattered the tablets inscribed with the ten commandments to show the people that they had broken their covenant with God. Still, this act did not sever God's relationship with Israel. Moses went up to Mount Sinai and rewrote the tablets with the ten commandments, as God instructed him (Ex 34).

Eventually God established a new covenant with Israel: "I will put my laws in their minds, and write them on their hearts" (Heb 8:10). Thus, if the covenant became an integral part of man's nature, it would less likely be broken. In the New Testament, Jesus' followers are viewed as members of this new covenant (2 Cor 3:6).

Covetousness

Because of their wicked covetousness I was angry; I struck them . . . but they kept turning back to their own ways. —*Isaiah 57:17*

People of the ancient Near East were certainly familiar with the human impulse to covet and expropriate property belonging to others. The tenth commandment forbids covetousness (Ex 20:17), which involves not just desiring but actually plotting to obtain the property or wife of one's neighbor. Later commentators held covetousness to be a heinous sin because it led to many forms of social injustice, including lying, trouble in the home, ROBBERY, and murder. Indeed, biblical law tried rigorously to counteract covetousness with a host of regulations that ranged from obligations toward servants and the poor to stipulations concerning usury and pledges.

Cow

Their bull breeds without fail; their cow calves and never miscarries. —*Job 21:10*

Wealth in biblical times was often calculated by the size of one's flocks and herds. When Jacob was trying to appease the wrath of his brother Esau, he sent him a gift of livestock, including 40 cows (Gen 32:15). Cows were valued because they produced and nurtured calves, the firstborn of which were offered in Old Testament sacrifice to God (Num 18:17).

The prophet Amos castigated the wealthy women of Samaria, the capital city of the northern kingdom of Israel, for their overtly imperious and greedy ways, and he referred to them scornfully as "cows of Bashan" (Am 4:1)—Bashan being an area east of the Jordan River noted for its fertile plains and its well-fed livestock. See also CALF.

Creation

. . . since the creation of the world his eternal power and divine nature . . . have been understood and seen through the things he has made. —*Romans 1:20*

Creation is the act of God making an ordered universe filled with life and beauty. There are two accounts of the creation in Genesis. In the first account (Gen 1:1–2:4), God created light on the first day, making night and day. On the second day, he brought forth the firmament separating the waters of earth and heaven. On the third he created dry land and vegetation. On the fourth day, he brought forth the sun, the moon, and the stars. The fifth day he created all the birds that fly through the air and creatures that swim in the seas. On the sixth day he created animals and human beings, and on the seventh day, he "rested from all the work that he had done" (Gen 2:3). The second—and probably older—account, in Genesis 2:4–25, seems to reverse the order, with human beings made first and the plants and animals appearing later: "the Lord God formed every animal of the field and every bird of the air, and brought them to the man to see what he would call them; and whatever the man called every living creature, that was its name" (Gen 2:19).

In a miniature from an English psalter fragment dating from the early 14th century, animals look on as God places the sun and moon in the sky in a scene adapted from the creation narrative in Genesis 1–2.

Two of the creeping things with which the earth was populated—a snake, above, and a rat or mouse, top—were cast in bronze about the sixth century BC *in Egypt.*

CREEPING THING

. . . "LET THE EARTH BRING FORTH LIVING CREATURES OF EVERY KIND: CATTLE AND CREEPING THINGS AND WILD ANIMALS . . . ."
–GENESIS 1:24

In the opening chapter of Genesis, God commanded the earth to "bring forth" the various animals that would roam the earth's surface, including large domesticated and wild beasts and "creeping things"—reptiles, insects, worms, and other small creatures that crawl along the ground (Gen 1:24). Humankind would have dominion over all wildlife, including "every creeping thing that creeps upon the earth" (Gen 1:26). These lowly animals would join flying birds and the rest of creation in praising God (Ps 148:10). Yet sinister associations remained. "Crawling things" could refer to venomous snakes (Mic 7:17), and Ezekiel's vision of "vile abominations" portrayed on the walls of the temple included "all kinds of creeping things, and loathsome animals, and all the idols of the house of Israel" (Ezek 8:10).

CRIME

A SINGLE WITNESS SHALL NOT SUFFICE TO CONVICT A PERSON OF ANY CRIME . . . .
–DEUTERONOMY 19:15

Because the ancient Israelites considered their laws to have come from God, breaking a law was not only a crime against man and state but also against God. Despite this perception, Israel's laws concerning crime were not always as harsh as those of its neighbors. Unlike other cultures, Israel did not punish crimes against property with a death sentence but rather with corporal punishment or a fine. The law of Israel allowed for retaliation—"eye for eye, tooth for tooth" (Ex 21:24)—but it was restricted to the person charged. In Babylon, the earlier Code of Hammurabi sometimes permitted family members of the accused to be punished in his place.

In contrast to its neighbors, Israel punished crimes more or less equally across class lines, excluding slaves and foreigners. This equality did not extend to women, however, who could be charged with offenses regarding matrimonial or sexual matters that were not considered crimes for men. In other countries, sacrifices could sometimes be substituted for punishment for intentional crimes, but in Israel, they were allowed only for unintentional sins.

The Bible often refers to a criminal being "cut off" from Israel. Although some historians interpret this phrase as excommunication, many understand it to mean the death penalty, as in "everyone who profanes [the sabbath] shall be put to death; whoever does any work on it shall be cut off from among the people" (Ex 31:14). Other crimes that warranted capital punishment were intentional MURDER or serious negligence, kidnapping someone for slavery, and offenses against one's parents. Many sexual offenses also merited a death sentence, as did some sins against God, such as blasphemy and violation of sacred property.

There was a category of lesser crimes for which one could be arrested, such as intentionally injuring someone. Corporal punishment was the penalty in such a case. A fine could compensate for other crimes, such as causing a miscarriage, seducing a virgin, raping a female slave who was betrothed, or falsely accusing one's bride of not being a virgin. A thief could be fined up to five times the value of the stolen property as restitution, and someone who unintentionally injured a person had to pay for the cost of the victim's recovery and loss of income.

In the New Testament, Jesus asked his disciples who had been wronged to forego retaliation: "But if anyone strikes you on the right cheek," he told them, "turn the other also" (Mt 5:39).

CRIMSON

THE SHIELDS OF HIS WARRIORS ARE RED; HIS SOLDIERS ARE CLOTHED IN CRIMSON.
–NAHUM 2:3

The brilliant red color of crimson was highly valued as a dye for the high priest's garments and for the tabernacle curtains, into which were woven "blue, purple, and crimson yarns" (Ex 26:1). The pigment was extracted from the bodies of kermes, or cochineal insects. Along with purple, crimson and scarlet were the colors most often associated with royalty. In Isaiah 1:18, however, they became vivid symbols of Israel's wickedness in God's eyes, glaringly contrasted against the whiteness of purity—"though your sins are like scarlet, they shall be like snow; though they are red like crimson, they shall become like wool."

Crocus

. . . THE DESERT SHALL REJOICE AND BLOSSOM; LIKE THE CROCUS IT SHALL BLOSSOM ABUNDANTLY . . . .
–ISAIAH 35:1–2

After the winter rains fell in the Holy Land, a colorful display of blossoms would burst forth, announcing springtime—a welcome respite before the searing heat of summer parched the landscape once again. Myriad varieties of spring wildflowers grew on the plains and craggy hillsides. Scholars disagree over the precise identification of the flower called a crocus in the book of Isaiah, but many think it is the autumn crocus, also called meadow saffron. Other possibilities are the asphodel or the narcissus, which grows on the Plain of Sharon. The "rose of Sharon," used to describe the bride in Song of Solomon 2:1, is probably not a rose; it may be the same flower as Isaiah's crocus.

Crown

TAKE THE SILVER AND GOLD AND MAKE A CROWN . . . .–ZECHARIAH 6:11

Although chiefly associated with kings, crowns were also worn by high priests and other honored individuals. Crowns varied widely in type and ornamentation. Archaeologists have discovered a number of circlets and plates in biblical lands, one of them a very plain strip of gold decorated with dots. The royal crown of the Ammonites, which David stripped from the defeated king's head, was a heavy golden circlet, set with "a precious stone" (2 Sam 12:30). The crown of the Israelite high priest is described as a gold diadem inscribed with the words "Holy to the LORD" (Ex 39:30). This diadem was attached to the priest's turban at his ceremonial investiture.

A royal Israelite coronation included the laying on of the crown by the chief priest and the anointing of the new KING. As the ritual concluded, the onlookers "clapped their hands and shouted, 'Long live the king!'" (2 Kings 11:12).

Crown of Thorns

AND THE SOLDIERS WOVE A CROWN OF THORNS AND PUT IT ON HIS HEAD . . . .–JOHN 19:2

Thrust contemptuously on Jesus' head by Roman soldiers mocking him as the "King of the Jews" (Jn 19:3), the crown of thorns was either a circlet or helmet-like in form. Although the Greek word translated as "thorn" is a general term, some experts believe that the crown was made from the jujube. This plant, found near Jerusalem, is a member of the buckthorn family; it has both curved and straight spines.

The Roman soldiers added a purple robe, another symbol of royalty, to ridicule Jesus further. Ironically, their cruel joke anticipated the Christian belief that Jesus is truly the king of all.

Birds and other ornaments top this crown, which dates from the fourth millennium BC. The crown and other copper items were found in the Cave of Treasure in the Judean desert.

Angels reverently hold Jesus' crown of thorns in an illumination from a medieval prayerbook, made for a French queen.

Crucifixion

AND THEY CRUCIFIED HIM, AND DIVIDED HIS CLOTHES AMONG THEM . . . .–MARK 15:24

Crucifixion was the most painful and humiliating form of capital punishment. Originally it was considered too barbarous to be inflicted on anyone other than enemies of the state. In the Roman Empire, crucifixion was also used for slaves and criminals of the lowest classes. In the rare instance that it was used for a citizen, Caesar had to give a direct order. By the time of Jesus' death, crucifixion was used regularly to deter criminal activity.

Crucifixion originally meant tying a dead body to a stake or, in the case of the Assyrians, executing someone by impaling the person on a stake. According to Israelite law, the corpses of executed criminals tied onto trees had to be removed before sundown.

In Jesus' time, the victim was first scourged until he bled. This cruel practice had a humane side, since it sped up the dying process. Then the prisoner carried the crossbeam to the execution site, where it was affixed to a pole already in place. Crosses could be in the shape of a T or an X. A wooden peg on the cross supported the weight of the body, and the victim was tied or nailed to the cross at the wrists and feet. Although tying the victim seems less barbaric, it actually prolonged the agonizing suffering, which could last for two or three days. Death finally came from starvation, dehydration, and the loss of circulation. Breaking a victim's legs caused the body to sag, leading to a quick death by suffocation. The corpse was sometimes left hanging for days as a grim warning to other criminals.

The crucifixion of Jesus followed Roman custom. Convicted of treason for claiming to be a king, Jesus was flogged and made to carry the crossbeam to Golgotha (meaning "skull"), his execution site. The placement of the cross on a hill meant that the Romans wanted to make a very public display of him. He refused the executioner's offer of wine mixed with myrrh or gall—a drink intended to dull the pain. After six hours on the cross, Jesus "bowed his head and gave up his spirit" (Jn 19:30).

Crucifixion was outlawed in the fourth century AD by Constantine the Great, a Roman emperor who converted to Christianity. It was also during Constantine's time that the cross became a sacred symbol of Christianity.

CRYSTAL

THEN THE ANGEL SHOWED ME THE RIVER OF THE WATER OF LIFE, BRIGHT AS CRYSTAL . . . .–REVELATION 22:1

The crystal mentioned in the Bible was probably rock crystal, an almost transparent, usually colorless form of quartz. Some scholars have suggested that the word translated as "crystal" instead means "ice," "gypsum," or "glass," but others disagree. Glass, when available in the region, was usually somewhat opaque.

The Bible often uses *crystal* to indicate clarity, brilliance, and high value. Ezekiel sees divine creatures surmounted by a dome "shining like crystal" (Ezek 1:22). Job describes wisdom as more precious than crystal (Job 28:18).

A mason measures a cubit from the elbow to the tip of the middle finger.

CUBIT

THERE WERE ALSO FOUR TABLES OF HEWN STONE FOR THE BURNT OFFERING, A CUBIT AND A HALF LONG, AND ONE CUBIT AND A HALF WIDE, AND ONE CUBIT HIGH . . . .–EZEKIEL 40:42

A cubit was a unit of linear measurement based on the distance from the elbow to the tip of the middle finger. The precise measurement varied, but the standard cubit was about 18 inches. The royal, or long, cubit, used for Solomon's temple, was about 21 inches. Cubits could be used to indicate a person or object's size, as well as depth and distance. An average-size man was four cubits tall; thus Goliath was indeed a giant, with a height of "six cubits and a span" (1 Sam 17:4)—almost 10 feet. A span was half a cubit, or the distance of an outstretched hand from thumb to little finger. See also chart for MEASURES.

CUCUMBER

LIKE A SCARECROW IN A CUCUMBER BED, WHICH GUARDS NOTHING, SO ARE THEIR GODS OF WOOD . . . . –LETTER OF JEREMIAH 6:70

While wandering in the wilderness, the Israelites complained bitterly about their harsh new life and yearned for the foods they had left behind (Num 11:5). One was the cucumber, widely grown in biblical lands and a mainstay of the Egyptian diet. This was probably the ancient snake cucumber *(Cucumis melo)* and not the present-day version *(Cucumis sativus),* which originated in India. In the Holy Land watchmen guarded fields of cucumbers and other crops; they lived in crude wooden shelters that were abandoned once the growing season was over. This practice gave Isaiah a striking image of Jerusalem destroyed and left like a derelict "shelter in a cucumber field" (Isa 1:8).

CUMMIN

. . . BUT DILL IS BEATEN OUT WITH A STICK, AND CUMMIN WITH A ROD.–ISAIAH 28:27

An herb native to western Asia, cummin, or cumin, was cultivated throughout ancient times. Isaiah described how its aromatic seeds were harvested: the farmer walked through the field beating the stalks of the plant with a rod, careful not to crush the seeds under the weight of a cart (Isa 28:27). The seeds were used to spice food. Oil from cummin was used for medicinal purposes. Jesus branded the scribes and Pharisees as hypocrites for ignoring matters of "justice and mercy and faith" while insisting that "mint, dill, and cummin" be assessed to pay for the support of the temple and its priests (Mt 23:23).

Cup

"For truly I tell you, whoever gives you a cup of water to drink because you bear the name of Christ will by no means lose the reward."
–Mark 9:41

Although cups were usually made from pottery, some were formed of precious metals, such as gold and silver. They could resemble either modern cups or shallow bowls. People drank from them, but they also had other purposes. Joseph used a silver cup for divination (Gen 44:4–5), and the tabernacle's branched lampstand had cups shaped like almond blossoms (Ex 25:33). By New Testament times, glass cups—usually goblet-shaped—had been introduced. The cup used for the Last Supper was probably a pottery bowl big enough to hold some wine for all present.

When used figuratively in the Bible, a cup typically symbolizes a share of whatever good or bad awaits. When Jesus prayed "let this cup pass from me" (Mt 26:39), he was asking his Father if his imminent death might be averted. The book of Psalms warns that for the wicked, "a scorching wind shall be the portion of their cup" (Ps 11:6). A cup can also symbolize blessings, and an overflowing cup represents abundance (Ps 23:5).

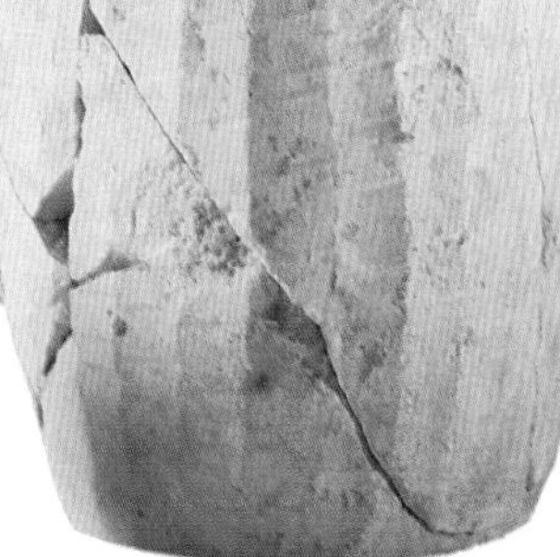

These limestone measuring cups have rough surfaces that were formed with a knife or adze. Cooks used the cups in the first century AD.

Cupbearer

Pharaoh was angry with his two officers, the chief cupbearer and the chief baker . . . .
–Genesis 40:2

A trusted member of the royal entourage, the cupbearer—or butler, in older Bible translations—poured the king's wine. He probably also functioned as an official taster, risking his own life to ensure that the king's drink was not poisoned. Cupbearers are depicted in Egyptian tomb paintings and in Assyrian and Canaanite art. Esteemed for their loyalty, they sometimes achieved exalted status; in close daily contact with the royal family, a cupbearer could become a valued confidant with the power to influence policy. For example, Nehemiah, as cupbearer at the Persian court, gained the ear of King Artaxerxes and won permission from him to rebuild Jerusalem.

Curds

For as pressing milk produces curds . . . so pressing anger produces strife.–Proverbs 30:33

Curds are coagulated sour or fermented MILK. In biblical times, they were made by adding some leftover curds to fresh milk in a goatskin and churning it until the mixture thickened. Curds and honey, considered signs of abundance, were often given to newly weaned babies. Adults enjoyed curds with honey and wine.

The soured milk, or strained yogurt, still consumed throughout the Near East corresponds to curds. Dried, it can be carried long distances, then mixed with meat or diluted into a beverage. Abraham probably served this drink, along with a freshly killed calf, to the angelic visitors who came to announce that his wife, Sarah, would bear a son (Gen 18:8).

A Bedouin woman churns goat milk in a sack, at top, to produce curds. She may then drain them of whey to create cheese, rolled into balls, above.

Curse

You are cursed with a curse, for you are robbing me—the whole nation of you!–Malachi 3:9

A curse is an utterance that calls down evil on a person, group, nation, place, or object. The act of cursing is also called execration. In the ancient Near East, curses invoked the power of a deity, and the words were believed to possess power if they accorded with God's will. Curses thus had power independent of the speaker's wishes, so a person had to be careful not to utter a curse thoughtlessly. Moreover, the Bible occasionally records that a curse was uttered but does not provide the words, lest they take effect on the scribe.

Curses were used in many contexts. They were uttered in vengeance against enemies who could not otherwise be attacked, and as punishments of criminals or subordinates who had angered the king. They were appended to treaties and contracts to guarantee compliance and were included on royal inscriptions to prevent defacement. After destroying Jericho, Joshua uttered a curse against anyone who might rebuild the city (Josh 6:26). When Hiel did so, he brought on his children's deaths (1 Kings 16:34). To be the object of habitual cursing—"the LORD make you an execration and an oath among your people" (Num 5:21)—was part of the punishment imposed on an adulterous wife. God cursed the serpent for causing the downfall of Adam and Eve and cursed the ground so that Adam would have to toil for his food (Gen 3:14, 17). See also BLESSING.

CURTAIN

HE SHALL TAKE A CENSER . . . AND HE SHALL BRING IT INSIDE THE CURTAIN . . . .–LEVITICUS 16:12

Tents, the movable dwellings used by the nomadic and seminomadic peoples of biblical times, were constructed out of cloths or skins that were often referred to as curtains. When the Israelites wandered in the wilderness, the ark of the covenant was housed in a portable tabernacle and was covered with "a curtain of blue, purple, and crimson yarns, and of fine twisted linen" (Ex 26:31) to "separate . . . the holy place from the most holy" (Ex 26: 33). At the moment Jesus died, the curtain that shielded the Holy of Holies from the rest of the temple was "torn in two, from top to bottom" (Mt 27:51), thus removing the barrier to God.

CYCLE OF NATURE

THE TONGUE . . . STAINS THE WHOLE BODY, SETS ON FIRE THE CYCLE OF NATURE, AND IS ITSELF SET ON FIRE BY HELL.–JAMES 3:6

The mysterious phrase "cycle of nature" appears only in the letter of James. The original Greek may also be translated as "wheel of birth." The author was probably referring to the continuous cycle of birth, deterioration, death, and renewal in nature. He may have borrowed the phrase from Hellenistic philosophers, who used it to mean the transmigration of souls—souls passing from one being to another at death. Though the meaning of the entire passage is unclear, it apparently involves the negative power of rash speech.

CYMBAL

PRAISE HIM WITH CLANGING CYMBALS; PRAISE HIM WITH LOUD CLASHING CYMBALS!–PSALM 150:5

In the Holy Land, the resounding cymbal was used to accompany hymns of praise, celebrations of victory, and festival dancing. Cymbals were among the instruments played in the temple. Musicians often joined them with such other percussion instruments as the tambourine (or timbrel), castanets (or sistrums), and bells, which were shaken rhythmically. In 1 Chronicles 13:8, the Israelites danced to "lyres and harps and tambourines and cymbals."

Cymbals were of two types. One consisted of two bronze plates, four to six inches in diameter, which were banged together. The other type was a metal cup that was held in place while its mate was struck against it.

CYPRESS

I AM LIKE AN EVERGREEN CYPRESS; YOUR FAITHFULNESS COMES FROM ME.–HOSEA 14:8

The wood of the cypress, a type of tall evergreen, is hard and fragrant, and it was highly prized in biblical times for building. Although according to older Bible translations God instructed Noah to make his ark of "gopher wood," modern translations generally assume that this was cypress (Gen 6:14), a favored shipbuilding material in those days. King Hiram of Tyre supplied cedar and cypress timber to Solomon (1 Kings 5:10) for the construction of the palace and the temple in Jerusalem in the 10th century BC. The temple's central room, the nave, was lined with cypress and covered with gold (2 Chr 3:5). In Hosea 14:8, the evergreen tree figuratively refers to God, who is everlasting.

This bronze pair of cymbals, played by the Israelites sometime during the Iron Age, was unearthed in Megiddo.

This clay tablet, inscribed in cuneiform and some Aramaic, is a document of a DEED. *Dating from the fifth century* BC, *it was found in the archives of a family involved in commerce and banking in the Babylonian city of Nippur.*

DAINTIES

THE RICH PERSON TOILS TO AMASS A FORTUNE, AND WHEN HE RESTS HE FILLS HIMSELF WITH HIS DAINTIES.
–ECCLESIASTICUS 31:3

Dainties were sweets and other delectable foods that were served in rich households. Proverbs cautions against coveting the foods of the wealthy and against eating the delicacies offered by deceitful rulers (Prov 23:3). However, dainties could be signs of blessed prosperity. Jacob predicts with satisfaction that the tribe of his son Asher will be rich, with Asher providing "royal delicacies" (Gen 49:20). Revelation lists dainties among the many things gone from the sinful, fallen city of Babylon: "The fruit for which your soul longed has gone from you, and all your dainties . . . never to be found again!" (Rev 18:14). However, some experts believe that in this case the original Greek word may refer not to food but instead more generally to luxuries.

DANCE

FOR EVERYTHING THERE IS A SEASON, AND A TIME FOR EVERY MATTER UNDER HEAVEN . . . A TIME TO MOURN, AND A TIME TO DANCE . . . .
–ECCLESIASTES 3:1, 4

Because 11 different words are used in the Old Testament for dance, experts infer that the steps and patterns of Hebrew dancing were elaborate. Numerous biblical references indicate that the practice was deeply rooted in Israel's religious and secular life, as it was in neighboring pagan countries. Women danced joyfully in celebration of martial victory, as Miriam did when Pharaoh's cavalry drowned in the Red Sea (Ex 15:20) and as the Israelite women did after David killed Goliath (see illustration). Less often, men performed dances that evoked religious ecstasy, as when David preceded the ark of the covenant into Jerusalem (2 Sam 6:14). Both men and women danced at harvest festivals, during which enamored youths sometimes selected wives at bride-choosing ceremonies in the vineyards. At wedding feasts and processions, dancing to honor the bride was a religious act. When the prodigal son returned in Jesus' parable, his father's household burst into a dance of celebration, much to the chagrin of his elder brother (Lk 15:25).

Accompanied by SONG and various musical instruments, dances in the Bible resembled popular folk or ethnic dancing that has survived in many regions of the Near East. They apparently involved twirling, leaping, jumping, and skipping, perhaps in rows and rings of performers. Men and women most likely danced separately, whether in groups or as individuals, and some children's games involved dancing. A very different matter was Salome's infamous dance for Herod's birthday (Mt 14:6), probably an exhibition that drew upon the Greek tradition of professional entertainment.

DANIEL, BOOK OF

THEN THE KING GAVE THE COMMAND, AND DANIEL WAS BROUGHT AND THROWN INTO THE DEN OF LIONS.–DANIEL 6:16

Written in both Hebrew and Aramaic, the book of Daniel is an apocalyptic text full of dreams and visions. It sheds important light on the world of angels and foreshadows the New Testament doctrine of resurrection.

Daniel, the hero of the book, was an Israelite nobleman taken captive by the Babylonians and trained for royal service. He was noted for his wisdom, his ability to interpret dreams, and his unswerving faith in God. Continuing to pray in defiance of a royal edict, he survived being thrown into a den of lions. Daniel predicted the eventual triumph of the kingdom of God over the power of opposing forces.

DARIC

ACCORDING TO THEIR RESOURCES THEY GAVE TO THE BUILDING FUND SIXTY-ONE THOUSAND DARICS OF GOLD . . . .
–EZRA 2:69

The daric, a gold coin, was probably introduced by and named for the Persian monarch Darius I, who ruled from 522 to 486 BC. On the face of the coin, the king is sometimes shown sprinting in martial fervor, carrying his bow and spear at the ready, or kneeling with a bow and arrow. The daric was worth four day's wages in the ancient Near East. Among the first coins used in the Holy Land, darics were contributed for the second stage of rebuilding the temple under Zerubbabel and Jeshua in 520 BC. The books of Ezra and Nehemiah both mention this event; according to the latter, the governor gave 1,000 darics.

DARKNESS

. . . THE LORD, MY GOD, LIGHTS UP MY DARKNESS.
–PSALM 18:28

Like other peoples of the ancient Near East, the Israelites felt that darkness represented death, devastation, and the underworld. It was part of the chaos out of which God made an orderly world, beginning with the creation of LIGHT. Darkness was often used in the Old Testament to suggest punishment or a curse, as in the plagues of Egypt. In the New Testament, darkness covered the land after Jesus was crucified (Mt 27:45). Biblical usage conveys an ethical dimension, as when sin is equated with walking in darkness. In contrast, God defeats ignorance by lighting the darkness. Both John's Gospel and the Dead Sea Scrolls link darkness psychologically and metaphysically with the forces of evil.

Women dance and play tamborines as they greet King Saul, David, and their warriors, who have triumphed over the Philistines. According to 1 Samuel 18:6, "the women came out of all the towns of Israel . . . with tamborines, with songs of joy, and with musical instruments." This type of display for victorious soldiers was customary.

Naomi takes the baby of her daughter-in-law Ruth, whose loyalty to the older woman was rewarded by God.

Daughter-in-law

. . . THE DAUGHTER RISES UP AGAINST HER MOTHER, THE DAUGHTER-IN-LAW AGAINST HER MOTHER-IN-LAW; YOUR ENEMIES ARE MEMBERS OF YOUR OWN HOUSEHOLD.–*MICAH 7:6*

Upon marrying, a woman typically left her family and became part of her husband's family. She assumed all the rights and responsibilities of a daughter and therefore was prohibited by Israelite law from later marrying her father-in-law. A daughter-in-law could be a valuable member of the household. Ruth's devotion was so renowned that she was described to Naomi as "your daughter-in-law who loves you, who is more to you than seven sons" (Ruth 4:15). Conversely, the prophet Micah uses a bad relationship between a woman and her daughter-in-law to demonstrate the breakdown of morality.

Dawn

AWAKE, MY SOUL! AWAKE, O HARP AND LYRE! I WILL AWAKE THE DAWN.
–PSALM 57:8

Sometimes translated as "dayspring," the dawn to the ancients was the first sign of morning light, while stars were still visible. In the Scriptures it is both the physical beginning of the day and a metaphor for spiritual renewal. In Luke's Gospel, Zechariah's prophecy about his son, John the Baptist, suggests that the coming of the Messiah will be a spiritual dawn (Lk 1:78). Matthew quotes Isaiah's vision of a redeemer's appearance when, in describing Jesus' ministry, he proclaims the "light has dawned" (Mt 4:16).

Day

AND THERE WAS EVENING AND THERE WAS MORNING, THE FIRST DAY.–GENESIS 1:5

The biblical day traditionally began at sundown. It was originally not divided into hours, but the night had three or four "watches." The days of creation described in Genesis were mirrored in the days of the week. Only the seventh day, when God rested from all the work that he had done, was named: it was called the sabbath (Ex 20:11). Weekdays were simply numbered, and the sabbath might also be referred to by its number. The day could also be identified as a particular day of the MONTH.

Certain days were designated for festivals, such as the Day of Atonement. The word *day* was also used to indicate a period of time, such as the "day of the plague" (Num 25:18) or the "day of salvation" (Isa 49:8; 2 Cor 6:2).

Day of Atonement

. . . THE DAY OF ATONEMENT . . . SHALL BE A HOLY CONVOCATION FOR YOU: YOU SHALL DENY YOURSELVES AND PRESENT THE LORD'S OFFERING . . . .–LEVITCUS 23:27

The Day of Atonement was the most sacred day of the ancient Israelite calendar, a time of repentance for sin. The law required fasting and prohibited doing any work. On this solemn day, the tenth day of the seventh month (September/October), the high priest entered the temple's usually unapproachable Holy of Holies and offered blood from sacrificial animals. A live GOAT, the so-called scapegoat, was sent into the wilderness, symbolically bearing the people's sins.

The New Testament associates these priestly traditions with Jesus' death, whereby "he entered once for all into the Holy Place, not with the blood of goats and calves, but with his own blood, thus obtaining eternal redemption" (Heb 9:12).

Day of Preparation

IT WAS THE DAY OF PREPARATION, AND THE SABBATH WAS BEGINNING.
–LUKE 23:54

On the day before the sabbath and other holy days, such as the Passover, the Israelites readied themselves for the observance. They started early because when the holy day began, at sunset, work was to stop. So in the preceding daylight hours, they gathered firewood, cooked, bathed, and changed into festive clothing.

Even the Romans recognized the importance of this day: Jews did not have to appear in court after 3 PM on the day of Preparation. In Jerusalem priests marked the start of preparations by blowing trumpets. It was on such an afternoon that Jesus died on the cross (Jn 19:31).

Day of the Lord

*See, the day of the LORD comes,
cruel, with wrath and fierce anger,
to make the earth a desolation . . . .
–Isaiah 13:9*

The "day of the Lord" meant different things in different eras. Depending on the setting, the phrase could mean deliverance or doomsday for Israel. Biblical writers also used the phrase or others like it—such as "that day"—to speak of the destruction of Israel's neighbors, the end of the world, and the second coming of Christ.

Amos was the first biblical prophet to use the phrase. Speaking to those in the northern kingdom of Israel, he asked, "Why do you want the day of the LORD? It is darkness, not light" (Am 5:18). God would again act in history, Amos said, but because the nation had become sinful, he would come as Israel's executioner, not as its deliverer. This prophecy reached fulfillment some 30 years later: Assyria conquered the northern kingdom in 722 BC and deported much of the population. Most of the exiles never returned, so they became known as the 10 lost tribes of Israel.

Later prophets used the concept of the day of the Lord to warn the southern kingdom of Judah that God would empower a foreign nation to punish them as well. Joel announced, "Blow the trumpet in Zion; sound the alarm on my holy mountain! Let all the inhabitants of the land tremble, for the day of the LORD is coming, it is near" (Joel 2:1). He described it as "a day of clouds and thick darkness! Like blackness spread upon the mountains a great and powerful army comes" (Joel 2:2).

The prophets also used the phrase to describe the doom that awaited a long list of neighboring states, including Babylon and Egypt. Isaiah's message for Babylon employed horrifying imagery: "Their infants will be dashed to pieces before their eyes" (Isa 13:16). Jeremiah offered this prophecy about Egypt's day of the Lord: "The sword shall devour and be sated, and drink its fill of their blood" (Jer 46:10). Indeed, Isaiah said the whole world would suffer:

On the day of the Lord, Jesus reigns serenely amid the turmoil. This 15th-century stained-glass window, part of Freiburg-im-Breisgau Cathedral in Germany, shows both demons and angels awaiting God's judgment of humans at "the end of the age" (Mt 24:3).

"Now the LORD is about to lay waste the earth and make it desolate, and he will twist its surface and scatter its inhabitants" (Isa 24:1). Some of the graphic word pictures that the prophets painted are reminiscent of the destructive flood. But the prophets assured their listeners that after God turned creation into chaos, he would restore both the earth and Israel, making a new creation.

Some Jews who lived in the centuries that elapsed between the accounts of the Old and New Testaments concluded that God was going to wipe the earth clean of sin and build a new and peaceful WORLD. They began writing about "the day of judgment," a phrase that appears in Jewish writings preserved in the Apocrypha. It also occurs in the New Testament: the authors of the letters of Peter and John use it, as does Jesus in Matthew's Gospel.

New Testament writers employed "the day of the Lord" or "the day of Christ" as a synonym for the second coming of Christ, which is simply called "the coming" in some Bible translations. This event would herald the end of human history, when Jesus would return to judge the world. Jesus himself seemed to make this connection. When questioned by his disciples about signs indicating his return, Jesus drew from the imagery of Isaiah, Ezekiel, and Joel in declaring that "the sun will be darkened, and the moon will not give its light; the stars will fall from heaven, and the powers of heaven will be shaken. Then the sign of the Son of Man will appear in heaven . . . and they will see 'the Son of Man coming on the clouds of heaven' with power and great glory" (Mt 24:29–30). Early Christians wanted to know when this would happen; Paul's reply to them was that "the day of the Lord will come like a thief in the night" (1 Thess 5:2). It may be that he was also referring to this time when he spoke about "the impending crisis" (1 Cor 7:26).

Deacon

Deacons likewise must be serious, not double-tongued, not indulging in much wine, not greedy for money . . . .
–1 Timothy 3:8

The Greek word for deacon is sometimes translated as "servant" or "minister." The term appears chiefly in Paul's first letter to Timothy. Deacons were church officers who apparently served as assistant ministers among the early Christians. Paul's letter implies that they needed to be temperate in speech and personal habits and able to manage money honestly. They may have visited the sick, aided the poor, and handled church finances. The office may also have been held by women; in some Bible translations Phoebe is identified as a deacon (Rom 16:1).

Deaf

Bring forth the people who are blind, yet have eyes, who are deaf, yet have ears!
–Isaiah 43:8

Mosaic law enjoined the Israelites not to insult the deaf (Lev 19:14). Physical deafness, like blindness, could be caused by God, who reminded Moses of this in Exodus 4:11. As a symbol, deafness could represent defiance toward the Lord and resistance to his message or refusal to listen to one's enemies because of reliance on God (Ps 38:13). As Isaiah prophesied that the coming of God's kingdom would restore hearing to the deaf (Isa 35:5), Jesus' healing of the deaf was seen by Luke and Matthew as proof that he was the Messiah. But the only Gospel writer who actually described Jesus' cures of deafness was Mark, who attributed one victim's affliction to an "unclean spirit" (Mk 9:25). See also DEMON.

Death

" . . . anyone who hears my word and believes him who sent me has eternal life, and . . . has passed from death to life."
–John 5:24

The ancient Semitic peoples believed that human beings, unlike gods, were perishable by nature, with death to be expected. An excerpt from the epic of Gilgamesh—a hero who sought immortality—reflects Babylonian and Assyrian beliefs on death: "When the gods created humanity, they established death for mankind; they kept life in their own hands." In Genesis, humans are created from dust and receive life only from the breath of God. In the end they must "return to the ground, for . . . you are dust, and to dust you shall return" (Gen 3:19). Death was grievous for the Israelites because they did not believe in a personal, immortal soul. This view was in sharp contrast to that of some Greek philosophers, who held that the body and soul were separate and that the latter survived after death. For the Israelites, death extinguished all strength and vitality, although a vague shadow or shade of the departed person went to Sheol, the realm of the dead, and slept with the ancestors. Yet the very inevitability of death was a source of some comfort. Death was part of the natural process, to be endured after having lived a full lifespan and produced children to carry on the family name. However, it was viewed as a terrible calamity to die young or without children. The concept of conquering death—"Many of those who sleep in the dust of the earth shall awake"(Dan 12:2)—came to fulfillment in the New Testament with Jesus' death and resurrection. Consequently Paul was able to proclaim, "'Where, O death, is your victory? Where, O death, is your sting?'" (1 Cor 15:55).

Death Sentence

On the evidence of two or three witnesses the death sentence shall be executed . . . .
–Deuteronomy 17:6

Under Israelite law, certain crimes were considered serious enough to warrant a death sentence, including intentional homicide and cursing or striking one's parents. Willful negligence that resulted in death, such as letting an ox run loose until it gored someone (Ex 21:29), was also a capital offense. The death penalty could be given for adultery, incest, or rape of a betrothed woman (Deut 22:25). Capital offenses against God included idolatry, approaching holy things in an unclean state, and blasphemy. Among the Israelites, EXECUTION was usually carried out by stoning.

After death came burial, but methods varied. At left are pottery sarcophagi from about the 14th century BC. Found near the city of Gaza, the coffins stand about six feet tall and show a definite Egyptian influence.

Debt

And out of pity for him, the lord of that slave released him and forgave him the debt.
–Matthew 18:27

Because debts in ancient Israel resulted from poverty, creditors were expected to be generous. Indeed, lending was considered a charitable gesture toward a neighbor experiencing temporary difficulty. There was also a religious dimension attached to the act: "Whoever is kind to the poor lends to the LORD" (Prov 19:17).

Charging interest to fellow Israelites was denounced. Since Israel was primarily agricultural, the borrower might pledge land, domestic animals, or a household member as guarantee of payment. Default could result in property loss, imprisonment, or enslavement of the debtor or a relative who had been the guarantee. However, creditors had to observe some legal restrictions when securing compensation. For example, they had to leave the debtor with sufficient means to ensure his daily survival.

Instead of making a pledge, the borrower might persuade a third party to provide surety, although it is not clear whether the guarantor assumed responsibility for the debt itself or for making the defaulting debtor available for prosecution. The law called for all outstanding debts of Israelites to be canceled every seventh year (Deut 15:1–3). See also LOAN.

Decree

In those days a decree went out from Emperor Augustus that all the world should be registered.–Luke 2:1

A decree, or edict, was a written public order given by a king or other empowered official. Caesar Augustus decreed that a census be taken, and in Babylon King Cyrus issued an edict that directed the rebuilding of the temple in Jerusalem (Ezra 5:13). When an order prohibited an action, it was called a ban or an interdict, as in Daniel 6:7. In the Old Testament, God, as king of the earth, issued decrees regulating both nature and human conduct. In reference to these, Psalm 19:7 states that "the decrees of the LORD are sure, making wise the simple."

DEDICATION

NOW AT THE DEDICATION OF THE WALL OF JERUSALEM THEY SOUGHT OUT THE LEVITES . . . TO CELEBRATE THE DEDICATION WITH REJOICING . . . .
–NEHEMIAH 12:27

When Israelites dedicated something to God, they were offering to let him use it for any purpose that he wanted. Often they were also seeking God's blessing upon the offering, such as when they dedicated their homes, fields, or the walls of Jerusalem. At other times they released to God's service the object of dedication, such as when they donated the spoils of war to the tabernacle worship center. Dedications apparently were accompanied by rituals and offerings. When Solomon dedicated the temple in a seven-day ceremony, he sacrificed 22,000 oxen and 120,000 sheep (2 Chr 7:5).

DEED

I SIGNED THE DEED, SEALED IT, GOT WITNESSES, AND WEIGHED THE MONEY ON SCALES.
–JEREMIAH 32:10

The book of Jeremiah gives a detailed description of Jeremiah's purchase of a field at Anathoth from his cousin Hanamel. Jeremiah and witnesses signed the deed of purchase "containing the terms and conditions" (Jer 32:11). Then he put the sealed deed and an unsealed copy—both papyrus scrolls—in an earthenware jar. Buying land at a time when Israel was threatened with exile demonstrated Jeremiah's faith that God would restore the nation.

In the Bible, a deed can also be an action, such as when the apostle Paul writes in his letter to the Colossians, "And whatever you do, in word or deed, do everything in the name of the Lord Jesus" (Col 3:17). See also DOCUMENT.

DEEP

. . . THE EARTH WAS A FORMLESS VOID AND DARKNESS COVERED THE FACE OF THE DEEP . . . .
–GENESIS 1:2

To the ancient Israelites, the deep was the primeval ocean. Before the creation, its waters spread over the whole earth. Then God made the dome of the sky to separate the waters above the earth—the source of precipitation—from the waters below, which gave rise to the seas, rivers, and lakes. Psalm 104:6–9 graphically describes the Creator's power over the waters: he rebukes them, puts them in their places, and sets their boundaries.

When referring to the waters after creation, the term *the deep* means the subterranean waters or the sea. The deep could be either destructive or beneficial to humankind. It was the source of the flood, which rose when "the fountains of the great deep burst forth, and the windows of the heavens were opened" (Gen 7:11). Those people who "went down to the sea in ships" saw the Lord's "wondrous works in the deep," including terrifying storms (Ps 107:23–25). The bottommost parts of the sea were known as the depths, but that term was also used in connection with SHEOL, believed to be the realm of the dead (Ps 86:13).

DEER

AS A DEER LONGS FOR FLOWING STREAMS, SO MY SOUL LONGS FOR YOU, O GOD.–PSALM 42:1

Several kinds of deer lived in biblical lands: red, fallow, and roe, or roebuck. In the Old Testament, deer were considered ritually clean animals that the people could eat (Deut 14:5). The list of daily foodstuffs required by King Solomon's court included deer and specifically mentioned roebucks (1 Kings 4:23). Proverbs 7:22 speaks figuratively of the hunted stag. A psalm thanking God for rescuing David from enemies celebrates the strength of the deer: "He made my feet like the feet of a deer, and set me secure on the heights" (Ps 18:33). Proverbs compares a wife with "a lovely deer, a graceful doe" (Prov 5:19).

The spotted fallow deer, a small species now often kept in parks, roamed the wilderness during biblical times. Its antlers grow quite large.

Joseph provided deliverance from famine for his people by giving his brothers grain to take back from Egypt. In the lower left of Ghiberti's "The Doors of Paradise," part of a baptistry, the silver cup that he placed in Benjamin's sack of grain is discovered.

DELIVERANCE

"NO ONE SHALL BE PUT TO DEATH THIS DAY, FOR TODAY THE LORD HAS BROUGHT DELIVERANCE TO ISRAEL." –1 SAMUEL 11:13

In the Bible, deliverance usually means rescue from evil or danger, although the word *deliver* is sometimes used to describe handing a person over to his enemies. Deliverance often refers to victory in battle, as when the judges Othniel and Ehud save the Israelites from their oppressors (Judg 3:9, 15). Reuben delivers Joseph when he convinces their brothers not to kill him (Gen 37:21). When Esther hesitates to intervene for her people, Mordecai tells her, "For if you keep silence . . . relief and deliverance will rise for the Jews from another quarter, but you and your father's family will perish" (Esth 4:14).

In the Old Testament, God is called the deliverer of his people. Though he often works through human agents, it is God himself who makes deliverance possible. In the New Testament, Jesus is the intermediary "who gave himself for our sins to set us free from the present evil age" (Gal 1:4). Even his name expresses his role as the one sent by God as a deliverer: *Jesus* is the Greek form of a Hebrew name that is translated as "savior."

DEMON

AND JESUS REBUKED THE DEMON, AND IT CAME OUT OF HIM, AND THE BOY WAS CURED INSTANTLY.–MATTHEW 17:18

Demons are mentioned quite often in the New Testament but seldom in the Old Testament. Nevertheless, belief in the existence and power of spirits was virtually universal in the ancient world. Isaiah, referring to God's day of vengeance, spoke of "goat-demons" and Lilith, a spirit that haunted deserted places (Isa 34:14). Demons had the power to bring catastrophe to humans: in the Aprocrypha, a demon killed every man who married Sarah until an angel intervened, "setting her free from the wicked demon" (Tob 3:17). Even common ills, such as toothaches, were attributed to evil spirits. In some instances, these mysterious beings were able to act only because God permitted it, such as when "God sent an evil spirit" to stir up dissension (Judg 9:23). Certain Israelite ritual practices, such as the noisy blowing of ram's horns, may have been derived from ancient methods to ward off demons

By the first century AD, the view of demons had changed. Instead of being regarded mostly as independent spirits, they were seen as Satan's agents. The New Testament uses numerous references to demons and exorcism to indicate that Satan is organizing his forces to oppose Jesus. In the Gospels, Jesus often acts as an EXORCIST and authorizes his apostles to cure demoniacs as well (Mt 10:8). Modern commentators have theorized that such episodes of possession by demons actually involved illnesses like epilepsy, but the authors of the Gospels would not have drawn such a distinction.

DENARIUS

"SHOW ME A DENARIUS. WHOSE HEAD AND WHOSE TITLE DOES IT BEAR?" –LUKE 20:24

A Roman silver coin called a penny in the King James Version of the Bible, the denarius was considered a standard day's pay for a Roman soldier or an ordinary worker in the Holy Land. In Matthew 20:2, *denarius* is translated as "the usual daily wage" from the Greek text. Since many coins of lesser value were in use, it is possible that laborers were sometimes paid by the hour or other part of the day. Mentioned more often in the New Testament than any other coin, the denarius carried the emperor's portrait. Its worth was halved when Nero devalued currency in the first century AD.

Desert

He turns a desert into pools of water, a parched land into springs of water.—Psalm 107:35

The deserts of biblical lands were not completely arid; they had some rainfall each winter. The rain could lead to sudden floods, but it occasionally sustained vegetation briefly. Among the deserts featured in the Bible are the plateau east of the Jordan River, eastern Judah near the Dead Sea, and the Sinai desert, or wilderness, where the Israelites wandered. Dangerous animals, including wolves, leopards, and snakes, roamed these areas. The Israelites regarded the desert with both dread and longing for the spiritual renewal attainable in its isolation. Isaiah implored the people to "make straight in the desert a highway for our God" (Isa 40:3). Jesus withdrew to deserted places to pray.

The desert, such as this area near the Dead Sea, was prominent in the lives of the Israelites. The dry lands became a powerful symbol that was often used by the prophets.

Destroyer

The destroyer shall come upon every town, and no town shall escape . . . .—Jeremiah 48:8

The Bible describes the destroyer as either an invading army, as in Jeremiah, or an avenging ANGEL. On the night of the Israelites' exodus from Egypt, God sent the destroyer to slay the firstborn child in every home not marked with lamb's blood (Ex 12:23). A divine messenger also slaughtered the Assyrian army that had laid siege to Jerusalem (2 Kings 19:35). In the New Testament, Satan was God's agent of destruction. When Paul advised Christians, "And do not complain as some of them did, and were destroyed by the destroyer" (1 Cor 10:10), he may also have meant Satan.

Deuteronomy, Book of

These are the words that Moses spoke to all Israel . . . .—Deuteronomy 1:1

Deuteronomy, the fifth book of the Old Testament, and the preceding four books set out Mosaic law. Collectively they are referred to as the Pentateuch. The word *Deuteronomy* comes from the Greek for "second law"—the first law being the commandments handed down at Mount Sinai.

Deuteronomy is structured as a series of addresses given by Moses to the second generation of the people of Israel on the eve of their entry into the long-awaited Promised Land. Moses gives them guidelines on how to live their lives in their new home. He calls upon the Israelites to renew their covenant with God, warning them that their future success depends on their remaining obedient to his divine will.

Deuteronomy recounts the teachings of Moses, who is shown in a medieval statuette by Nicolas of Verdun.

Devoted Thing

. . . every devoted thing is most holy to the LORD.—Leviticus 27:28

The law of the Israelites deemed something devoted to God as irrevocably his. Taboo for secular use, the object either was used for sacred purposes or was destroyed. This practice generally was associated with Israel's conquest of Canaan. Conquered cities were "devoted to destruction," meaning that the Israelites were to kill every being that breathed and set fire to everything that would burn, except for valuables that were to be saved for tabernacle use. When Achan took for himself gold and other spoils of Jericho, he brought God's vengeance down upon his family and all of Israel (Josh 7).

Dew

"May God give you of the dew of heaven, and of the fatness of the earth . . . ."
–Genesis 27:28

Moisture condensed from the air on cool nights, dew was vital to the survival of crops during the Holy Land's rainless summers. Modern field studies have confirmed its value to the region. The ancient Israelites considered dew a divine blessing, as important as rain. They observed it closely, noticing that it falls swiftly and stays all night but disappears in the morning. Dew figures in many biblical metaphors. For Gideon a fleece soaked with dew was a sign from God (Judg 6:37–38). Isaiah uses dew as a symbol of resurrection: "O dwellers in the dust, awake and sing for joy! For your dew is a radiant dew, and the earth will give birth to those long dead" (Isa 26:19).

Dial

"See, I will make the shadow cast by the declining sun on the dial of Ahaz turn back ten steps."–Isaiah 38:8

The dial mentioned in Isaiah 38:8 was not a sundial but rather a staircase on which the shadow of a nearby object moved upward as the sun passed overhead. God used it to give a sign to Isaiah that he would fulfill a twofold promise, whereby Hezekiah, king of Judah at the end of the eighth century BC, would recover from a serious illness, and Jerusalem would escape destruction by the army of Assyrian king Sennacherib. God told Isaiah that as a sign, the shadow's movement on the staircase would reverse, retreating 10 steps, or intervals, after first advancing that distance (2 Kings 20:9). After making this miracle occur, God fulfilled his promise: Hezekiah recovered, and the invading army perished.

Diamond

. . . with a diamond point it is engraved on the tablet of their hearts . . . .–Jeremiah 17:1

Modern diamonds were apparently not known in biblical lands before the first century AD, so scholars are unsure about what kind of stone metaphorically engraved the sin of Judah on the people's hearts in the book of Jeremiah. The prophet may have meant flint, adamant, or emery—a kind of corundum used in engraving and probably the hardest material that was then available.

Another stone called a diamond in some Bible translations appears in the description of the high priest's ceremonial breastplate (Ex 28:18) and among the costly jewels worn by the king of Tyre (Ezek 28:13). Modern translations generally call this JEWEL a moonstone, although jade, emerald, and other gems have also been suggested.

Dill

"Woe to you . . . hypocrites! For you tithe mint, dill, and cummin, and have neglected the weightier matters . . . ."–Matthew 23:23

The aromatic seeds and leaves of the annual dill plant *(Anethum graveolens)* were used to flavor foods and to freshen the breath. They were also used medicinally to relieve gas pains. Dill was subject to a tithe in the time of Christ. Jesus angrily indicted the scribes and Pharisees, who were more concerned about carefully tithing plants than tending to their relationships with other people and with God. Isaiah described harvesting dill seeds with a stick rather than threshing the plant (Isa 28:27); however, botanists now think that the prophet was actually referring to black cummin *(Nigella sativa)* rather than to dill.

Dill, a hardy member of the parsley family, grew wild in biblical lands but was also cultivated for its leaves and seeds.

Dinner

Better is a dinner of vegetables where love is than a fatted ox and hatred with it.
–Proverbs 15:17

An important daily MEAL for the Israelites, dinner was eaten in the evening, after work was over. Usually a common pot containing vegetable stew was placed on a mat or a table. The family gathered around it, scooping the stew from the pot with pieces of bread; cutlery was rarely available. Fruit followed, and wine was drunk from clay cups or bowls. The wealthy dined more elegantly: the Assyrian general Holofernes invited Judith to a table set with "silver dinnerware" (Jdt 12:1). In New Testament times, houses of aristocrats had silver and gold utensils (2 Tim 2:20). Dinner guests were common; Jesus was a guest of Levi (Mk 2:15) and others.

In a 19th-century painting by Edward Armitage, Jesus calls James and John, who are mending nets with their father, to be his disciples.

DISCIPLE

"WHOEVER DOES NOT CARRY THE CROSS AND FOLLOW ME CANNOT BE MY DISCIPLE."—LUKE 14:27

The word *disciple* is almost absent from the Old Testament. In the New Testament, it occurs often in the Gospels and in Acts of the Apostles. The word is used for many different groups in the Bible, from Jesus' inner circle of 12 followers to adherents of Moses, Isaiah, and John the Baptist, as well as Christians and the Pharisees. Disciples in the New Testament were often a large group of both men and women from a variety of backgrounds who followed Jesus and tried to learn from his teaching. They resembled those who today follow the Jewish tradition of going regularly to one rabbi to learn that person's interpretations of the law through discussion and study. Indeed, the original Greek word translated as "disciple" actually means "learner." The four Gospels portray Jesus' disciples in a variety of ways. Mark, depicting them as doubtful and afraid, uses their lack of comprehension to explain Jesus' message to his readers. In contrast, Matthew shows disciples who understand and live in accordance with Jesus' message and are thus authoritative teachers. See also APOSTLE.

DISCIPLINE

"HOW HAPPY IS THE ONE WHOM GOD REPROVES; THEREFORE DO NOT DESPISE THE DISCIPLINE OF THE ALMIGHTY."—JOB 5:17

An important task of Israelite parents was to discipline their children, combining teaching and guidance with rebuke and punishment. Although discouraged from being harsh, parents did not "spare the rod" (Prov 13:24); they believed such discipline would help children learn to live useful lives sanctioned by God. Prophets and rabbis also disciplined their followers, correcting them until they had learned their masters' teachings. God was considered a disciplinarian who loved his children but made his salvation available to them only through their obedience to his will.

DISEASE

HE SAID TO HER, "DAUGHTER, YOUR FAITH HAS MADE YOU WELL; GO IN PEACE, AND BE HEALED OF YOUR DISEASE."—MARK 5:34

The many diseases mentioned in the Scriptures—not always readily identifiable in today's medical terminology—troubled ancient peoples spiritually as well as physically. Was sickness a divine punishment for sin or an affliction caused by Satan or his demons? Would God allow the righteous to suffer? Because biblical writers were more interested in these

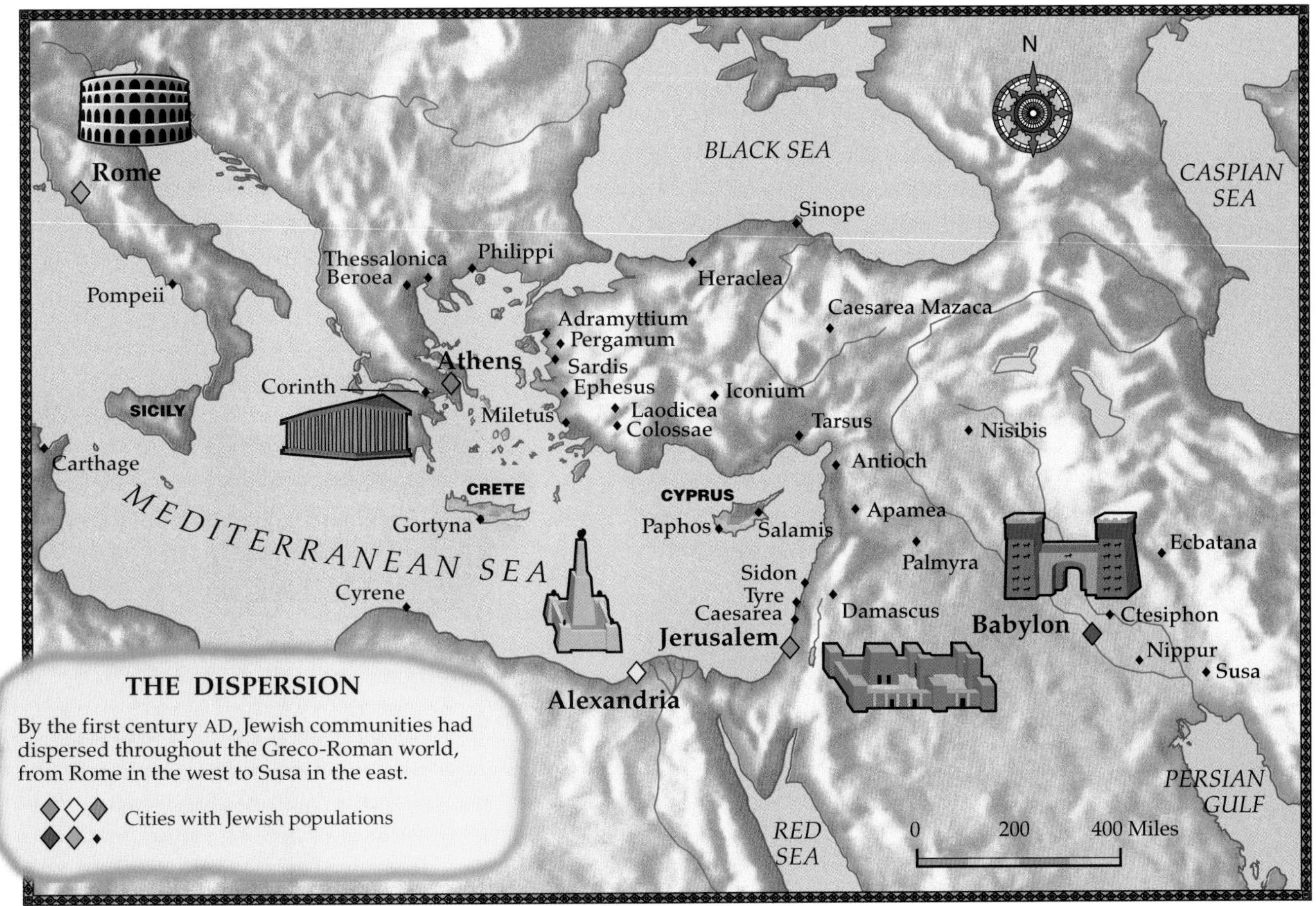

questions than in medical exactitude, ailments were not described in clinical detail. Likewise treatments, such as BALM from Gilead, were typically noted without much explanation.

At a time when bacteria, viruses, and most internal functions of the body were unknown, diseases were essentially distinguished by outward signs, by touch, and by what the sufferer could report. These limitations affected the potential for both accurate diagnosis and precise classification. For example, edema—the accumulation of bodily fluid once known as dropsy—was considered a distinct disease, but it is actually a symptom of disorders in various internal organs. The word *gangrene* can either have the modern meaning or refer to an ulcer. Even the term *leprosy,* mentioned so frequently in ancient writings, covers myriad skin maladies. Ailments known today and possibly referred to in the Bible include poliomyelitis, bubonic plague, chronic dysentery, and menorrhagia (perhaps the "hemorrhages" of Matthew 9:20). Evidence from archaeological digs suggests that tapeworms and whipworms caused intestinal infections. Descriptions of abnormal behavior may indicate mental illnesses, such as depression and manic-depressive disorder.

DISH

THE LAZY PERSON BURIES A HAND IN THE DISH, AND WILL NOT EVEN BRING IT BACK TO THE MOUTH.
–PROVERBS 19:24

A dish could be a plate, a platter, or a shallow or deep BOWL. Most dishes were used to hold or serve food and were made of pottery. Wooden dishes were highly valued, and those made of gold and other precious metals were used in the households of the rich and in the sanctuary. Medicines were measured and compounded in a deep bowl. This same type of dish played a role in Jesus' identification of his betrayer at the Last Supper (Jn 13:26).

DISPERSION

. . . TO THE EXILES OF THE DISPERSION . . . MAY GRACE AND PEACE BE YOURS IN ABUNDANCE.
–1 PETER 1:1–2

The first Dispersion, or Diaspora, took place in 721 BC, when the Assyrians conquered the northern kingdom of Israel and exiled many Israelites to Mesopotamia. In 597 BC the Babylonians conquered Judah; within 15 years, they had deported much of its population to Babylon. When the Persian king Cyrus allowed the Judeans to return home in 538 BC, many chose to remain in Babylon, forming the first permanent Dispersion community.

Wars fought during the Greco-Roman period in Palestine drove more of the people from their homeland. By the time of the New Testament, Jewish communities flourished throughout the Mediterranean area and Asia Minor (see map, p. 107). Nearly every city that Paul visited on his journeys contained a Jewish synagogue. In the first century AD the philosopher Philo noted that a million Jews lived in Egypt, and the Greek geographer Strabo wrote, "It is not easy to find any place in the habitable world which has not received this nation."

DISTRICT

. . . SET ASIDE FOR THE LORD A PORTION OF THE LAND AS A HOLY DISTRICT . . . .–EZEKIEL 45:1

The Bible uses the word *district* in several senses: an area with distinct boundaries, such as ancient tribal lands; an administrative division of a province or country, such as "the district of Galilee" (Mt 2:22); or a sacred precinct, as in Ezekiel's vision of a restored Jerusalem. Writing from exile in Babylon, the prophet gave measurements for the "holy district" and specified that it would contain the temple and houses for the priests (Ezek 45:1–6). See also ALLOTMENT.

DIVIDED KINGDOM

". . . IT SHALL BE A DIVIDED KINGDOM . . . ."–DANIEL 2:41

While interpreting a dream, Daniel alluded to competing factions of the Greek empire. However, the term *divided kingdom* usually refers to the Israelites' split into northern and southern realms, with separate kings and religious practices. After Solomon's death in 922 BC, his son Rehoboam, already recognized as king in the south, traveled to the north to be confirmed king there. He quickly angered northern leaders, and the north seceded, creating the northern kingdom of Israel and anointing its own king. The southern kingdom of Judah included Jerusalem and continued to be ruled by the Davidic dynasty. Both monarchies ended unhappily: the northern kingdom was overrun by the Assyrians in 721 BC, and the southern kingdom fell to the Babylonians in 597 BC.

DIVINATION

NO ONE SHALL BE FOUND AMONG YOU . . . WHO PRACTICES DIVINATION . . . .–DEUTERONOMY 18:10

Divination is the attempt to see the future, discern God's will, or sense the occurrence of distant events. One common method used by

Diviners in Babylon used this clay model of a liver, inscribed with omens and formulas, about the 17th century BC.

diviners was to examine the entrails of a slaughtered animal—particularly the liver of a sacrificial sheep—to look for distinctive marks or shapes. Other forms of divination included interpreting dreams, throwing sticks or lots, and astrology. Soothsayers claimed to find meaning in the onset of storms, the baying of dogs, and the slithering of snakes. Telling the

future by such natural signs is called augury.

Records of divination by Babylonians are abundant. Referring to its use by Nebuchadnezzar, Ezekiel 21:21 states that "the King of Babylon stands . . . at the fork in the two roads, to use divination." The prophet reports that the king inspected an animal's liver and tossed arrows with the names of different towns on them to determine which town he should attack.

Israelite law prohibited divination. Leviticus 19:26 says, "You shall not practice augury or witchcraft." The book of Deuteronomy calls "abhorrent to the LORD" such practices as consulting ghosts and seeking oracles from the dead (Deut 18:11–12). Cautioning Israel that although "these nations . . . do give heed to soothsayers and diviners, as for you, the LORD your God does not permit you to do so" (Deut 18:14), the book nevertheless assures the people that God will raise up a true prophet among them. See also MAGIC.

DIVORCE

. . . I HAD SENT HER AWAY WITH A DECREE OF DIVORCE . . . . –JEREMIAH 3:8

Israelite law allowed a man to divorce his wife if "she does not please him because he finds something objectionable about her" (Deut 24:1), whereas a mistreated wife could leave her husband but not divorce him. The Romans allowed both men and women to divorce their spouses.

By the time of the New Testament, rabbis disagreed about what constituted the "objectionable" behavior mentioned in Deuteronomy. Some thought that only adul-

This document, a fourth-century BC *papyrus scroll, is studded with clay sealings called bullae. It was found in a Judean desert cave.*

tery qualified, but others believed a man could divorce his wife for any reason. When the Pharisees tried to draw Jesus into the controversy, he replied in part that "'what God has joined together, let no one separate'" (Mt 19:6).

To divorce his wife, a man wrote out a bill of divorce—also called a certificate or decree of divorce or a certificate of dismissal in the Bible—and gave it to her. This legal document allowed her to marry again; however, she could never remarry her first husband. The divorced man may have been required to return the dowry and pay other sums to his former wife. Still, a divorced woman's life was not easy. She had to leave her children with her former husband, and she had few options if she did not remarry. Some women could return to their parents' homes, but for others prostitution was the only means of survival.

Doctrine

We must no longer be children, tossed to and fro and blown about by every wind of Doctrine . . . . –Ephesians 4:14

The term *doctrine* applies to teaching. According to the Gospels, Jesus' teachings were often unconventional, as he interpreted Mosaic law in far less rigid ways than did many of the Pharisees. Refuting criticism from the Pharisees, Jesus referred to Isaiah 29:13, charging them with "teaching human precepts as doctrines" (Mk 7:7).

The basic doctrine spread by the apostles was that Jesus was the Messiah, that he had risen from the dead, and that salvation was possible only through believing in his name. Teachers imparted these principles to new converts, and by the second century AD, the beliefs were widely enough accepted to be considered "sound doctrine" (Titus 2:1).

Document

. . . on that sealed document are inscribed the names of our officials, our Levites, and our priests.–Nehemiah 9:38

A document could be a letter, a decree (Ezra 5:17–6:1), a deed of purchase, a divorce certificate, or a family register. The earliest documents, written on clay, date from about 3500 BC in Mesopotamia. In the ancient Near East, some documents were recorded with a stylus on soft clay or wooden tablets with a wax surface. Others were written in ink on papyrus, leather, or a potsherd—a piece of broken pottery. A SEAL was used to witness a document.

Royal documents or laws were often carved into stone, such as the Code of Hammurabi and the ten commandments. In Egypt, historical inscriptions were chiseled into temple walls.

Dog

But whoever is joined with all the living has hope, for a living dog is better than a dead lion. –Ecclesiastes 9:4

People domesticated dogs and kept them as pets as far back as the Stone Age. The ancient Egyptians revered and even mummified them. Yet the Bible views the animals with contempt, usually describing them as scavengers that roam the streets in search of garbage and even dead bodies. Dogs lick Lazarus' sores (Lk 16:21), as well as human blood (1 Kings 22:38); they also eat the flesh of Jezebel (2 Kings 9:36).

The word *dog* is often used figuratively as a derogatory term for enemies and wicked people. When Isaiah chastises the religious leaders and prophets of Israel, accusing them of incompetence and greed, he calls them "dogs [who] have a mighty appetite; they never have enough" (Isa 56:11). In Revelation 22:15, the vision of the future kingdom of God specifically excludes "dogs," or evildoers—they will remain outside the gates of the city along with the "sorcerers and fornicators and murderers and idolaters."

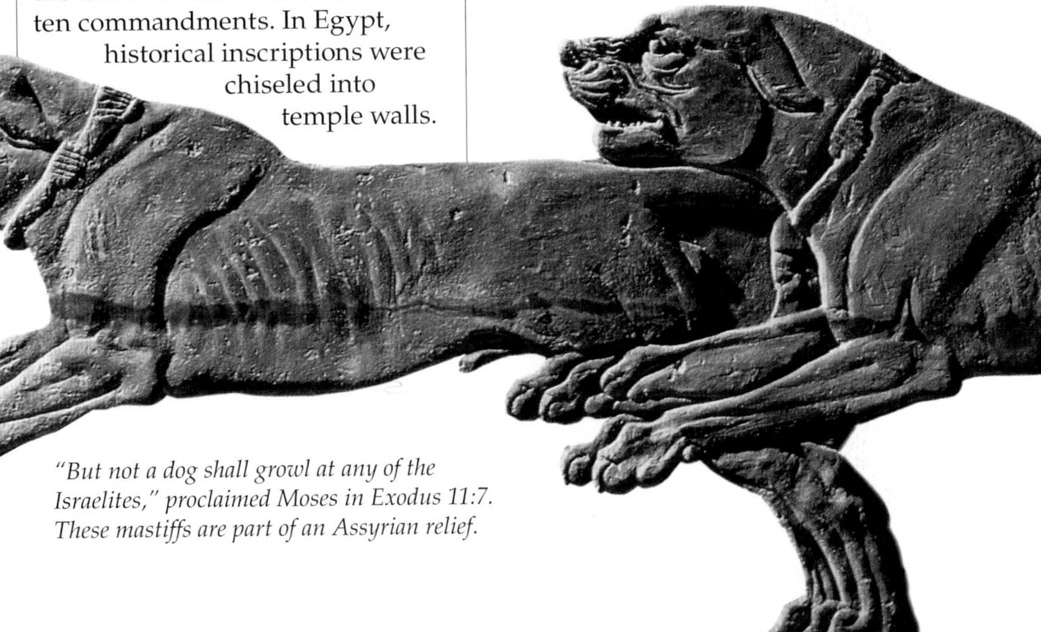

"But not a dog shall growl at any of the Israelites," proclaimed Moses in Exodus 11:7. These mastiffs are part of an Assyrian relief.

Dominion

. . . HIS DOMINION SHALL BE FROM SEA TO SEA, AND FROM THE RIVER TO THE ENDS OF THE EARTH.
–ZECHARIAH 9:10

In the beginning, God granted humankind dominion, or lordship, over his creation by decreeing that they be given "'dominion over the fish of the sea, and over the birds of the air'" (Gen 1:26). Some individuals also claimed God-given dominion, or power, over others, often causing feelings of jealousy and resentment. In the book of Genesis, Joseph's brothers angrily asked him, "'Are you indeed to have dominion over us?'" (Gen. 37:8). The Bible also mentions kings who assert political dominion over the land and people they rule (Jer 34:1). Psalm 22:28 states, however, that ultimate dominion is God's alone.

Donation

IF A MAN EATS OF THE SACRED DONATION UNINTENTIONALLY, HE SHALL ADD ONE-FIFTH OF ITS VALUE TO IT . . . .–LEVITICUS 22:14

When people gave an offering dedicated to the Lord—money, an animal sacrifice, or other gift—the Bible sometimes broadly describes it as a donation (Num 15:19–21).

At the behest of Johash, king of Judah, the priests took up a special collection to repair the temple (2 Kings 12:4–5). They placed a guarded chest at the temple entrance, and people dropped donations in a hole in its lid.

Sacred donations were the offerings that officiating priests were allowed to keep for themselves (Num 5:9–10). Often these donations were the consecrated parts of of an animal SACRIFICE. This meat could come from a person's tithe of livestock, as a tenth of every flock was given to God.

A familiar sight along the cobblestone streets of Jerusalem, the donkey—domesticated for thousands of years—is a hardy, stalwart animal used throughout the Near East to carry heavy loads.

Donkey

. . . "AM I NOT YOUR DONKEY, WHICH YOU HAVE RIDDEN ALL YOUR LIFE . . . ?"
–NUMBERS 22:30

The domesticated ass, which is translated as "donkey" in modern English-language Bibles, was the all-purpose beast of burden used by the seminomadic peoples of biblical times. A little over three feet tall, the sure-footed ass could be loaded down with a vast array of goods slung across its back (Gen 45:23). Men and women, both rich and poor, rode donkeys; the number one owned was a measure of wealth (Job 1:3). According to Mosaic law the donkey, which does not have a cloven foot or chew the cud, was considered unclean and therefore unfit to eat. Donkeys, like oxen, rested on the sabbath (Ex 23:12). Jesus, the humble messenger of peace, made his triumphant ride into Jerusalem "on a donkey's colt" (Jn 12:13–15).

Door

"... SEARCH, AND YOU WILL FIND; KNOCK, AND THE DOOR WILL BE OPENED FOR YOU."
–MATTHEW 7:7

During the Israelites' nomadic period, the doors of their tents were flaps of coarse cloth over the tent opening. Later, doors of houses in villages and cities were made of wood. They were very heavy, had bars for protection on the inside, and could be locked with bolts.

The Israelites carved their doorposts with lines of Scripture, heeding the instruction in Deuteronomy to "write [God's commandments] on the doorposts of your house" (Deut 6:9). On the first Passover, they sprinkled the blood of a lamb on their doorposts to ward off the DESTROYER, or angel of death (Ex 12:7).

The threshold, or doorstep, of the doorway was often made of stone and was higher than the floor to prevent flooding and keep out dirt. A house's threshold and cornerstone were considered sacred. Above the door was a stone or wooden lintel. Metal pegs set into the threshhold and the lintel allowed the door to swing inward.

The size of a doorway depended on the building. The doorway to a home was usually so low that an adult would have to stoop to walk through it. The entrances to palaces and temples were much larger and were made of wood or covered with copper. The elaborate doors of the temple were overlaid with gold (2 Kings 18:16). Fortified cities were entered through very wide doors or gates. The Bible often uses the word *door* symbolically, as in "sin is lurking at the door" (Gen 4:7).

Doorkeeper

I would rather be a doorkeeper in the house of my God than live in the tents of wickedness.
–Psalm 84:10

In the world of the Bible, the job of protecting the entrance to important places was held by people known variously as doorkeepers, gatekeepers, and keepers of the THRESHOLD. Eunuchs were employed as doorkeepers, or guards of the threshold, by the king of Persia (Esth 2:21). Special guards or gatekeepers were chosen from among the priestly Levites to watch over the ark of the covenant when it was brought to Jerusalem (1 Chr 15:23–24). The temple doorkeepers, referred to as "keepers of the threshold," had an important job that included collecting money from the people (2 Kings 22:4). Women could also serve as doorkeepers: after Jesus was arrested and led away, Peter was questioned by a woman who was guarding the gate to the high priest's courtyard (Jn 18:16–17).

Dove

. . . and the Holy Spirit descended upon him in bodily form like a dove.–Luke 3:22

In the Bible, many different kinds of pigeons were called doves. Seemingly gentle and innocent, doves came to represent purity. After the birth of a child in biblical times, an offering of a turtledove, or pigeon, was part of the purification ritual for the mother (Lev 12:6); doves were sold for that purpose in the outermost court of the temple. Mary made such an offering after the birth of Jesus (Lk 2:22–24). Following an ancient tradition among sailors, Noah sent out a dove to ascertain if the floodwaters had receded. After its second trip out the bird returned with an olive leaf in its beak, a sign of dry land (Gen 8:8–11). The apparent steadfastness and loyalty of a mated pair of doves was such that the word *dove* became a synonym for a loved one: "My dove, my perfect one, is the only one" (Song of S 6:9). Similarly, in Psalm 74 Israel is equated with a dove; seeking God's help in a time of national crisis, the psalmist begs, "Do not deliver the soul of your dove to the wild animals" (Ps 74:19).

As a sign that the flood had ended, a dove returns to Noah's ark with an olive branch in its beak in a 13th-century manuscript.

Dowry

. . . Pharaoh king of Egypt had gone up and captured Gezer . . . and had given it as dowry to his daughter . . . .
–1 Kings 9:16

A dowry was a gift of property that a bride brought to her marriage. It could be money, land, cattle, or servants and varied in size according to her father's social and economic standing. Pharaoh gave his daughter a city when she married King Solomon. If a girl was very poor or an orphan, her community provided her dowry. The bridegroom, in turn, paid a bride price to the bride's father to compensate for the loss of his daughter. This gift was kept for her in case her husband died or abandoned her. The payment of the bride price also made the union legal.

Dragon

The great dragon was thrown down, that ancient serpent, who is called the Devil and Satan . . . .
–Revelation 12:9

Fearsome dragons, or monsters, played a significant role in the ancient myths of the Near East. Symbols of chaos and evil, they were described as both serpents and sea monsters in the Bible and were variously called Rahab or LEVIATHAN. Several Old Testament passages, including Isaiah 27:1, depict God in a constant primordial struggle with this creature. Before God began the orderly act of creation, he imposed order upon the anarchy of the dragons. The psalmist sang to God: "You divided the sea by your might; you broke the heads of the dragons in the waters" (Ps 74:13). Israel's enemy Egypt was referred to as Rahab (Ps 87:4), and Pharaoh was described as a "dragon in the seas"

The seven-headed dragon of Revelation 12:3, depicted here with the body of a wild cat, emerges from the watery abyss in a detail from an Italian mural.

(Ezek 32:2). The book of Revelation describes a symbolic vision of the enemy—"a great red dragon, with seven heads and ten horns, and seven diadems on his heads" (Rev 12:3)—waging war with the angels in heaven in a battle between good and evil. The monster, which is identified as Satan or the devil, and his cohorts are expelled from heaven and cast down to earth. In the end they are "thrown into the lake of fire and sulfur, where . . . they will be tormented day and night forever" (Rev 20:10).

Drawers of Water

"Now therefore you are cursed, and some of you shall always be slaves, hewers of wood and drawers of water for the house of my God."–Joshua 9:23

Servants assigned to draw and carry water were considered at the very bottom of the social hierarchy. Joshua spared the Gibeonites in war but forced them into menial labor as hewers of wood and drawers of water. The covenant enacted in Moab encompassed Israel's entire community, even the lowliest members of society—"those who cut your wood and those who draw your water" (Deut 29:11). As part of their daily chores, women also drew water from wells (Gen 24:11). Meetings at a WELL led to three betrothals in the Old Testament: Isaac to Rebekah, Jacob to Rachel, and Moses to Zipporah.

Dream

Once Joseph had a dream, and when he told it to his brothers, they hated him even more.–Genesis 37:5

Throughout the ancient Near East, people believed that the gods communicated to humans through dreams, or "vision of the night" (Job 33:15). Some people sought divine insight by sleeping in holy places, such as temples. Some dreams presented clear and direct messages, while others were symbolic and required an expert to unravel their meaning. Egyptians and Assyrians wrote books on how to interpret dreams.

The Israelites believed that their own God communicated through dreams, to both the righteous and the unrighteous. The Bible offers many examples. The first instance is found in Genesis, when King Abimelech took Sarah from Abraham to add to his harem, not knowing that Sarah and Abraham were married. That night God spoke to the king in a dream, threatening to kill him if he approached Sarah. The next morning the king awoke, terrified. He

In a village outside of Jerusalem, a woman draws fresh water from an underground well. In the hot, dry desert, people's lives depend on the water obtained from such wells.

released Sarah and made his peace with Abraham by presenting him with gifts of slaves, livestock, and silver (Gen 20:1–18).

God used dreams throughout the Old Testament to communicate to people including Laban (Gen 31:24), Solomon (1 Kings 3:5), and King Nebuchadnezzar (Dan 2:3), as well as Jacob, Joseph, Pharaoh, Pharaoh's butler and baker, and a Midian soldier. In some instances, the message was painfully clear, as when Joseph recounted his dream to his older brothers: "There we were," he said, "binding sheaves in the field. Suddenly my sheaf rose and stood upright; then your sheaves gathered around it, and bowed down to my sheaf" (Gen 37:7).

Other more complex dreams might require the advice of interpreters or diviners. Pharaoh had two such dreams, which baffled his wise men. Pharaoh dreamed of seven gaunt cows eating seven fat cows, and then of seven withered ears of corn eating seven full ears. Joseph correctly interpreted the dreams as a warning from God that Egypt would experience seven years of bounty followed by seven years of famine (Gen 41).

Not all dreams mentioned in the Old Testament were from God. Moses warned against dreams that led people to worship false gods (Deut 13:1–5). Jeremiah harshly criticized false prophets who presented their dreams as the word of God (Jer 23:25–32).

Most revelatory dreams that appear in the New Testament are reported in the Gospel of Matthew. There are five dreams that specifically relate to the birth of Jesus. In one, God warned the wise men not to tell Herod where the baby Jesus could be found (Mt 2:12). The other dreams revealed God's instructions to Joseph. Also according to Matthew, Pilate's wife urged her husband not to become involved in the crucifixion of Jesus. "Have nothing to do with that innocent man," she pleaded, "for today I have suffered a great deal because of a dream about him" (Mt 27:19). See also DIVINATION.

Rebekah draws water from a well, at left, so that Abraham's servant and his camels can drink before they set out on their journey, at right, in this 12th-century mosaic.

DRINK

. . . FOR I GIVE WATER IN THE WILDERNESS, RIVERS IN THE DESERT, TO GIVE DRINK TO MY CHOSEN PEOPLE . . . .
–ISAIAH 43:20

The ancient Israelites regarded drinking water, which was essential to life, as a gift of God. Isaiah called the water that flowed from a rock struck by Moses in the desert a sign of divine favor (Isa 48:21). In the Apocrypha, water, milk, and "the blood of the grapes," or wine, are listed among "the basic necessities of human life" (Sir 39:26).

Israel's drinking water came chiefly from wells, springs, and cisterns built to retain rainwater during the long dry season. Some cities had pools for water storage, including Jerusalem, where an extraordinary tunnel brought water from the Gihon spring outside the walls (2 Kings 20:20).

Offering drink to visitors and strangers was a sign of HOSPITALITY and compassion. Rebekah's generous response to a request for water identified her as a suitable wife for Isaac (Gen 24:12–22). In the New Testament, giving drink to the needy meant serving Christ: "I was hungry and you gave me food, I was thirsty and you gave me something to drink" (Mt 25:35).

Milk was prized as a drink but, being difficult to preserve, was consumed sour or as cheese. The "strong drink" mentioned in the Bible as a source of strength or of danger (Isa 28:7) was either liquor or beer. The latter was made from barley and other grains.

DROSS

TAKE AWAY THE DROSS FROM THE SILVER, AND THE SMITH HAS MATERIAL FOR A VESSEL . . . .
–PROVERBS 25:4

Dross is the residue left when a metal, particularly silver, is refined by being heated in a furnace or crucible in a process called smelting. When the metal liquifies, the dross rises to the top and is skimmed off. As in the book of Proverbs, the Old Testament uses dross as a metaphor for moral impurity.

Metals combined with dross can represent the corruption of an entire nation. Ezekiel describes God's punishment of the Israelites as a form of smelting: "Because you have all become dross, I will gather you . . . into a smelter . . . so I will gather you in my anger and in my wrath, and I will put you in and melt you" (Ezek 22:19–20).

Drought

Drought and heat snatch away the snow waters; so does Sheol those who have sinned.–Job 24:19

The Israelites depended upon the dew and yearly rains for the success of their crops. A drought, which was a shortage of rain for a long period of time, could lead to agricultural failure, causing farmers and their families to fall into debt and servitude. An extended drought was greatly feared, as it inevitably produced FAMINE (1 Kings 18:1–2). Deuteronomy lists drought, along with consumption, "fiery heat," and other disasters, as a curse from God (Deut 28:22).

Among the natural causes of drought were the drying effect of the east wind—"and his fountain shall dry up, his spring shall be parched" (Hos13:15). Desert areas, with their minimal rainfall, were called lands of drought (Hos 13:5) or "waterless regions" (Lk 11:24).

When mentioned in the Bible, drought is often sent by God to punish the Israelites' sins, such as King Ahab's tolerance of a pagan god (1 Kings 17:1) and the Judean community's delay in rebuilding the temple after the Babylonian exile (Hag 1:11). After the sinner repents, the drought is ended. According to Job 24:19, "Drought and heat snatch away the snow waters; so does Sheol those who have sinned."

Unconscious from wine, Noah is mocked by his son Ham, at left, as his other sons hurry to cover their father's nakedness.

Drunkenness

. . . envy, drunkenness, carousing . . . those who do such things will not inherit the kingdom of God.–Galatians 5:21

The Bible consistently pictures drunkenness as shameful. Noah, the first planter of vines, drank too much wine and "lay uncovered in his tent" (Gen 9:21). Drunkards stagger, become violent, and lose their self-control, their perceptions, and their vigilance against enemies. Drunkenness was one of the sins of the incorrigible son whom Mosaic law condemned to death by stoning (Deut. 21:18–21).

Excessive drinking was not uncommon in the ancient Near East. Egyptian murals show reclining banqueters sipping wine through glass tubes until they collapsed. In the Bible, princes feasted "for strength, and not for drunkenness" (Eccl 10:17). Moderate drinking could symbolize joy and wisdom. In the book of Proverbs, Wisdom invites her guests: "'Come, eat of my bread and drink of the wine I have mixed. Lay aside immaturity, and live, and walk in the way of insight'" (Prov 9:5–6).

In New Testament times, Jesus' enemies spread false rumors that he was a drunkard (Mt 11: 19). The practice of prophesying and speaking in languages other than their own (Acts 2:4) sometimes made early Christians appear drunk (Acts 2:15), but their ideal was sober self-control. Temperance was always regarded as an important virtue.

Dung

Those slain by the LORD . . . shall not be lamented, or gathered, or buried; they shall become dung . . . . –Jeremiah 25:33

Usually animal excrement, dung was used for both fertilizer and fuel in ancient times. It was collected and deposited in a dunghill or dung pit, where it was mixed with straw and used as manure to fertilize plants. Dried animal dung was also used to heat ovens for cooking (Ezek 4:15).

During the years when the Israelites wandered in the wilderness, the dung and carcasses of animals sacrificied as sin offerings, whose blood was used to purge the shrine, had to be burned outside the camp according to law (Lev 16: 27). Similarly, humans had to excrete and bury fecal matter outside the boundaries of the camp (Deut 23:12–13). To the Israelites, leaving a corpse to rot "like dung on the field" (2 Kings 9:37) was a sign of dishonor. Such was the fate of Jezebel, whose corpse was ultimately consumed by dogs. The wicked were considered without merit or substance and would "perish forever like their own dung" (Job 20:7).

The "Dung Gate" (Neh 2:13) in Jerusalem's southwestern wall was one of 11 gates leading into and out of the city during the era of Nehemiah. The city's refuse was probably removed through that gate and disposed of elsewhere.

Drying in the sun, dung cakes made from manure and straw are used for cooking when other fuel is unavailable. The beehive-shaped houses of Haran appear in the distance.

Dust

. . . THE LORD GOD FORMED MAN FROM THE DUST OF THE GROUND, AND BREATHED INTO HIS NOSTRILS THE BREATH OF LIFE . . . . –GENESIS 2:7

Man's creation from dust emphasizes that humankind physically belongs to the EARTH, and the image of God molding man recalls the work of Near Eastern potters.

Dust—often carried to the Holy Land by hot, dry east winds—appears in many biblical metaphors. God tells Abraham, "I will make your offspring like the dust of the earth" (Gen 13:16), indicating enormous numbers. The prophet Isaiah says, "Even the nations are . . . accounted as dust on the scales" (Isa 40:15), meaning that they are as unimportant to God as dust particles are to someone weighing merchandise. Throwing dust expressed scorn (2 Sam 16:13); placing dust on the head was a sign of shame or mourning (Job 2:12). Shaking the dust off one's feet signified renouncing responsibility for a place and leaving it to its fate (Mt 10:14).

In death, man will return to dust. God reminds Adam when he expels him from the garden of Eden that "you shall . . . return to the ground, for out of it you were taken; you are dust, and to dust you shall return" (Gen 3:19). Ecclesiastes uses dust to picture death: "and the dust returns to the earth as it was, and the breath returns to God who gave it" (Eccl 12:7).

Dwarf

FOR NO ONE WHO HAS A BLEMISH SHALL DRAW NEAR, ONE WHO IS BLIND OR LAME . . .OR A HUNCHBACK, OR A DWARF . . . .–LEVITICUS 21:18, 20

In the ancient Near East, dwarfs—abnormally small or disproportioned people—were looked down upon. Their deformity seemed to contradict the belief that human beings were made in God's divine image. Deformed priests, although allowed to eat the holy food with other priests and Levites, were forbidden to make sacrificial offerings. The law required that just as the sacrifice must be unblemished, so too must be the officiant.

The Hebrew word translated as "dwarf" in Leviticus is translated elsewhere as "emaciated" or "thin," as in Genesis, when Pharaoh's dream foretells of the coming famine: "Then seven other cows, ugly and thin, came up out of the Nile after them" (Gen 41:3).

Dwelling

MY DWELLING PLACE SHALL BE WITH THEM; AND I WILL BE THEIR GOD . . . . –EZEKIEL 37:27

A dwelling was a place where someone lived, whether it was a HOUSE, a tent, or a territory. God's closeness to man is illustrated in the Bible through the naming of his many dwellings in their midst. God tells Moses to have the Israelites "make me a sanctuary, so that I may dwell among them" (Ex 25:8). God's sublime nature is revealed when he says, "I dwell in the high and holy place" (Isa 57:15). God is also a dwelling place (Ps 90:1), where people take refuge in his eternal protection. Psalm 43:3 exhorts the Lord, "O send out your light and your truth; let them lead me; let them bring me to your holy hill and to your dwelling."

dyeing

Royal purple dye was the most expensive and most coveted dye in the ancient world. Perhaps because the Phoenicians guarded the recipe and the dye-making process so fiercely, myths surrounding the discovery of purple dye have proliferated for centuries. In one tale, Hercules discovered the source of the color purple during a shoreside walk, when his dog crushed a snail in his jaws, staining his muzzle a brilliant purple. Cloth dyed purple from the glands of the murex snail was worth its weight in gold and was usually worn only by royalty. Each spring and fall, when the seas were calmest, men scoured the seafloor along the eastern shore of the Mediterranean for the snail. Writing in the first century BC, *Pliny recorded a recipe for making dye from the murex snail, which offers insight into ancient dyeing techniques.*

1. Working from small boats just offshore, fishermen lower netted baskets baited with cockles, a mollusk that murex snails were known to feed on, into the Mediterranean Sea. As the snails attempt to reach the tasty cockles inside the basket, the cockles snap shut on the snails' probing tongues, trapping them. The baskets are then hoisted aboard the boat with the snails clinging to them. This procedure is repeated again and again.

2. On shore, the men deposit the snails into rock pools, where they are kept alive until enough snails have been collected. The purple dye is produced from a liquid secreted in the snail's hypobranchial gland. Because each snail yields only a tiny droplet of this liquid, it takes thousands of snails to make just one gallon of the precious dye. These men use metal tools to break open the snail and extract its gland; smaller snails are crushed shell and all. The entire mixture is then steeped in salt.

3. *After soaking for three days, the mixture is thinned with water and then simmered in lead vats. When the dye has cooked for nine days, the resulting extract is approximately 1/16 of its original volume. The liquid is strained to remove impurities; only then is it considered suitable for dyeing. The man pictured here carefully skims mucous from the snails off the surface of the boiling dye. Because the lengthy dyeing process produced a foul odor, the industry was usually located outside of towns, away from where people lived.*

4. *After the dye is strained, the extract is diluted with water. A single piece of fleece is dipped in the dye as a test. The wool initially turns yellow, but as it oxidizes it develops a purplish hue. Satisfied with the color, dyers immerse the wool into the dye as shown above, where it is left to soak. Finally the artisans wring the wool, returning the precious excess dye to the vats. As the wool dries in the hot Mediterranean sun, it reaches a deep shade of purple.*

DYE

THEN JUDAS RETURNED TO PLUNDER THE CAMP, AND THEY SEIZED . . . CLOTH DYED BLUE AND SEA PURPLE . . . .
–1 MACCABEES 4:23

The Israelites commonly dyed fabric for garments and furnishings for the tabernacle (Ex 26:1). The small size of the basins and vats found by archaeologists in the Holy Land suggest that thread was dyed more often than cloth (see box). Thread was first steeped in dye, then dried; this process was repeated until the desired color was achieved.Wool was used more frequently than linen, which was difficult to dye; the wealthy favored dyed silk.

Although the process of dyeing is never specifically referred to in the Bible, colored yarns, dyed stuffs, and dyed garments are mentioned in Exodus 39:1, Judges 5:30, and Job 38:14. Solomon asked the king of Tyre to send him a man "skilled to work in . . . purple, crimson and blue fabrics" (2 Chr 2:7). Purple was the most popular color in biblical times—as well as the most expensive—but skilled artisans also dyed yarn in black, green, red, yellow, blue, and white.

Dyes were produced from a number of natural sources, including insects and plants, which were dried and crushed into powder, as well as minerals. The Israelites used ground pomegranate rind to make the color yellow, which the Phoenicians produced from safflower and turmeric. The color blue came from the indigo plant, and coveted purple dye was extracted from the murex mollusk found along the eastern coast of the Mediterranean. The color red was produced from vegetables, reddish-colored minerals, and insects. Black dye was obtained from the berry of the myrtle. See also box for COLOR.

EF

An agrarian table inscribed in ancient Hebrew script, this Gezer calendar from the 10th century BC *records the months of the* FARMING *year by the agricultural tasks.*

EAGLE

THEIR HORSEMEN COME FROM FAR AWAY; THEY FLY LIKE AN EAGLE SWIFT TO DEVOUR.–HABAKKUK 1:8

A number of species of eagles either nested in or passed through the Holy Land during biblical times. The same Hebrew word is also sometimes translated as "vulture" because the two birds were difficult to distinguish from each other at a distance. In the Holy Land, eagles built their nests "in the fastness of the rocky crag" (Job 39:28). The eagle had an enormous wingspan that sometimes stretched more than eight feet. It was noted for the power and speed of its flight, which was often used as a metaphor in the Bible (Lam 4:19). The eagle was also revered for the care it took of its offspring. God's loving protection of the Israelites was compared with the eagle "who hovers over its young" (Deut 32:11). As a bird of prey, however, the eagle was considered unclean and could not be eaten (Lev 11:13).

EAR

THE HEARING EAR AND THE SEEING EYE—THE LORD HAS MADE THEM BOTH.–PROVERBS 20:12

The human ear is used symbolically throughout the Bible. The listening ear suggests attentiveness, obedience, or the desire for understanding (Rev 2:7); closed or heavy ears represent an inability or unwillingness to hear (Jer 6:10). Unlike the statues of other deities (Ps 115:6), the Lord has ears to hear, and his revelations are said to open the ear (Isa 50:5). A psalmist yearning for God's help pleads: "Incline your ear to me" (Ps 102:2).

The ear's symbolic connection with obedience probably explains two ancient Israelite customs: piercing the ear of a slave at the master's door with an awl, which bound him in servitude for life (Ex 21:6), and smearing blood on the right ear of a priest at his consecration (Ex 29:20). Lepers were ritually cleansed by having blood and oil spread on their right ear (Lev 14:14–17). See also DEAF.

EARRING

THEN GIDEON SAID TO THEM, "LET ME MAKE A REQUEST OF YOU; EACH OF YOU GIVE ME AN EARRING HE HAS TAKEN AS BOOTY." –JUDGES 8:24

Like other Near Eastern peoples, the ancient Israelites—both male and female—wore jewelry, including earrings. Archaeological sites in the Holy Land have yielded earrings made of silver, gold, or other metals. Frequently worn in only one ear, many were crescent-shaped and fitted with pendants.

In the Old Testament, Ezekiel personified Jerusalem as God's favored bride, whose adornments included earrings (Ezek 16:12). But earrings could also represent excess or temptation: Jacob buried his household's gold earrings as part of a divinely ordered purification (Gen 35:4), and Aaron used the Israelites' gold earrings to create the calf whose worship was punished as idolatry (Ex 32:2–4).

These gold Canaanite earrings from the 15th century BC *were found at Tel el-Ajjul, near Gaza.*

EARTH

GOD CALLED THE DRY LAND EARTH, AND THE WATERS . . . SEAS. –GENESIS 1:10

The ancient Israelites may have imagined the earth as a flat strip of LAND resting upon pillars (1 Sam 2:8). As such the earth was "the foundations of the heavens" (2 Sam 22:8), bearing the weight of the firmament, which arched above it. In the Bible, the word for earth had several meanings. It was the entire physical world, created at the same time as the heavens but separate from them. It was also dry land as opposed to water. God ordered the fertile earth to "bring forth" plants, trees, and most other living things (Gen 1:11, 24). Although the Bible emphasizes God's personal relationship with the earth and its inhabitants, he is pictured as looking down upon the "circle of the earth"—apparently a reference to the horizon—from such a great height that people on its surface "are like grasshoppers" (Isa 40:22).

The earth was also the land where the Israelites and other peoples lived. Jerusalem was considered not only the political and religious capital of Israel but also the geographical "center of the earth" (Ezek 38:12). In the Bible, references to "the four corners of the earth" (Isa 11:12) may suggest that biblical peoples believed that the earth had concrete boundaries or outer limits.

EARTHQUAKE

AND THERE CAME . . . A VIOLENT EARTHQUAKE, SUCH AS HAD NOT OCCURRED SINCE PEOPLE WERE UPON THE EARTH . . . .–*REVELATION 16:18*

Biblical descriptions of earthquakes are often metaphors for God's judgment. Such imagery is not surprising, as the Holy Land is geologically unstable, experiencing many tremors and a few major earthquakes each century.

Some Old Testament narratives record actual quakes. An earthquake in northern Galilee mentioned in the books of Amos and Zechariah, for example, has been confirmed by excavations at the town of Hazor (Am 1:1; Zech 14:4–5). Earthquakes also mark several accounts of miraculous events in the Bible. "The earth shook, and the rocks were split" (Mt 27:51) when Jesus was crucified. An earthquake also preceded Jesus' resurrection (Mt 28:2).

This massive crevice in the steps leading to the ancient ritual baths at Qumran is a testament to the earthquake of 31 BC.

EAST

. . . AFTER JESUS WAS BORN IN BETHLEHEM . . . WISE MEN FROM THE EAST CAME TO JERUSALEM . . . . –*MATTHEW 2:1*

East was the primary direction for the ancient Israelites rather than north, which is used today as a point of orientation on maps and compasses. The Bible sometimes refers to the east simply as "the rising of the sun" (Isa 45:6). The term *front* stands for the east, too, since one is presumably facing eastward (Ex 27:13). Wisdom was associated with the east in biblical times, perhaps in recognition of the advanced civilization of Mesopotamia to the east of the Holy Land.

Other less defined areas are called the east country. The sons of Jacob's concubines are sent to the "east country" (Gen 25:6), which is probably the desert. God promises to save his people "from the east country and from the west country" (Zech 8:7), meaning the whole earth.

ECCLESIASTES, BOOK OF

FOR EVERYTHING THERE IS A SEASON, AND A TIME FOR EVERY MATTER UNDER HEAVEN . . . .–*ECCLESIASTES 3:1*

The book of Ecclesiastes is one of the wisdom books. Its original Hebrew title was "Preacher," although the book is less a religious text than a philosophical one. The author grapples with the question of the meaning of LIFE in the face of fickle chance and certain death and comes to the conclusion that there is a plan that only God understands. He commends the enjoyment of all things in moderation, because by celebrating the ordinary things in life day by day, people bring glory to God.

ECCLESIASTICUS, BOOK OF

HAPPY IS THE PERSON WHO MEDITATES ON WISDOM . . . . –*ECCLESIASTICUS 14:20*

Also known as the book of Sirach after its author, Jesus the son of Sirach, Ecclesiasticus presents proverbs and advice on many subjects. The author was a Hebrew scribe and teacher of law who gave religious instruction in early second-century BC Jerusalem. His advice touches upon ethics, the duties of the rich, social skills, and the pursuit of wisdom. But the source of all human ethics and wisdom, according to Sirach, is the Lord, and the bedrock of morality is the fear of the Lord. In the third century AD Christian writers gave the work the Latin name *Ecclesiasticus,* or the "church's book."

EDUCATION

. . . [BROTHERS] GROW STRONGER FROM . . . BOTH GENERAL EDUCATION AND OUR DISCIPLINE IN THE LAW OF GOD.
—4 MACCABEES 13:22

Through his spokesman Moses, God charged the Israelites to teach his commandments to their children: "Recite them to your children and talk about them when you are at home" (Deut 6:7). Many Israelites taught their children in the home. Fathers educated sons in all aspects of the Israelite faith and in the family trade, such as farming. Mothers educated daughters about household responsibilities, including laws dealing with food preparation. The very wealthy sometimes hired guardians or teachers to instruct their children (2 Kings 10:6).

Scholars are not certain when formal schools began to emerge in Israel. Schools may have been in existence as early as the time of David, about 1000 BC. Archaeologists have unearthed tablets inscribed with school exercises from that period. By the first century BC, Jews had set up elementary schools in synagogues and homes throughout Israel, which trained boys to read, write, and memorize Scripture; secular topics such as mathematics and astronomy generally weren't taught. Older students sometimes sought master teachers who would educate them in the intricacies of Bible interpretation and Jewish tradition. In Jerusalem, Paul found such a teacher in Gamaliel, a respected member of the Sanhedrin, or supreme court (Acts 22:3).

ELDER

ARE ANY AMONG YOU SICK? THEY SHOULD CALL FOR THE ELDERS OF THE CHURCH AND HAVE THEM PRAY OVER THEM . . . .—JAMES 5:14

In the ancient societies of Greece, Rome, Egypt, and Israel, men described as "elders" were figures of authority in communities, clans, and the central government. They were usually, but not necessarily, old: the Hebrew word for elder comes from the root meaning "chin" or "beard," suggesting an adult male.

Pursuing their religious education, these young boys sit on a hard dirt floor at the feet of their instructor in a Moroccan village school.

Elders were figures of authority in the tribes of Israel from the earliest historical times. According to the Bible, their status was already well established by the time the Israelites were enslaved in Egypt, where God commanded Moses to "assemble the elders of Israel" (Ex 3:16). During the Israelites' wanderings in the desert, the Lord commanded Moses to gather together 70 of the elders of Israel. He intended to impart to them a portion of the authority he had already bestowed on Moses in order for them to "bear the burden of the people along with you so that you will not bear it all by yourself" (Num. 11:17).

As later Jewish tradition evolved, the elders were called upon to make oral interpretations of the law of Moses, and their pronouncements carried great weight. Elders served as judges of personal disputes, leaders in time of war, and representatives of the people. Eventually, each synagogue had its own council of elders.

Following Jewish practice, the early Christian church was guided by groups of elders, known in the New Testament by the Greek word *presbyter*. When Paul established Christian churches, he appointed elders for each one (Acts 14:23). By the end of the first century AD, an elder was also called a BISHOP (Titus 1:5–9) or a DEACON.

ELECTION

. . . AS REGARDS ELECTION THEY ARE BELOVED, FOR THE SAKE OF THEIR ANCESTORS . . . .—ROMANS 11:28

When God chooses a person or group to receive his favor and fulfill his purpose, he elects them. The Israelites were elected God's chosen people not because of anything they had done but "because the LORD loved you and kept the oath that he swore to your ancestors" (Deut 7:8). He also chose individuals such as Abraham (Gen 12:7), Moses (Ps 106:23), and the kings (1 Sam 10:24), priests, and prophets for specific functions; those elected were obligated to live according to his will.

The early Christians viewed themselves as inheriting or sharing Israel's election. In the New Testament Jesus was considered the elect one (Lk 9:35), through whom God would bring salvation.

Organs were removed and stored in jars during embalming; jars such as these linked organs to animals, like the stomach to the jackal. Anubis, the funerary god, prepares a body for burial, below.

Elements

. . . YOU NEED SOMEONE TO TEACH YOU AGAIN THE BASIC ELEMENTS OF THE ORACLES OF GOD.–HEBREWS 5:12

In New Testament times, elements could be several different things. They could be rudimentary principles, as in the above passage from Hebrews. They could also be the four elements of the natural world: earth, air, water, and fire. The term *elemental spirits* is used in the Bible to include not only physical elements but the celestial spirits behind them, who the Greeks and Romans believed ruled the universe. When Paul wrote in his letter to the Galatians, "While we were minors, we were enslaved to the elemental spirits of the world" (Gal 4:3), he was referring to false gods. See also SPIRIT.

Eleazar sacrifices himself to slay the royal elephant (1 Macc 6:46) in this engraving.

Elephant

. . . WITH EACH ELEPHANT THEY STATIONED A THOUSAND MEN ARMED WITH COATS OF MAIL . . . . –1 MACCABEES 6:35

The ivory obtained from elephants has always been considered extremely precious. King Solomon's ships traveled vast distances and returned with a cargo of "gold, silver, ivory, apes, and peacocks" (1 Kings 10:22). Egyptian and Assyrian accounts of elephant hunts confirm that Indian elephants once existed in the Near East. However, the increasing demand for ivory caused their extinction in the area by the middle of the first millennium BC. Apparently elephants were also used in warfare during the Hellenistic age; 1 Maccabees recounts that the Syrian forces arrayed against the Jews in 163 BC included 32 elephants (1 Macc 6:30).

Embalm

JOSEPH COMMANDED THE PHYSICIANS IN HIS SERVICE TO EMBALM HIS FATHER. –GENESIS 50:2

The ancient Egyptians originated the art of preserving corpses—both human and animal—from decay by an elaborate process of embalming called mummification that took as many as 70 days to complete. The practice of embalming was rarely, if ever, used by the ancient Israelites, as evidenced by the condition of bodies unearthed from Holy Land tombs. In Genesis both Jacob and Joseph died and were embalmed in Egypt, indicating their prominence in that country and the desire to preserve their bodies for burial in Canaan. Spices were sometimes used for purifying, but not for preserving, dead bodies before burial (Jn 19:39–40).

Emblem

"IT SHALL SERVE AS A SIGN ON YOUR HAND AND AS AN EMBLEM ON YOUR FOREHEAD THAT BY STRENGTH OF HAND THE LORD BROUGHT US OUT OF EGYPT."–EXODUS 13:16

The word *emblem* refers to a small leather box containing passages of the Bible; the Israelites wore one on the forearm and another between the eyes at prayer time. Also called frontlets, the emblems held the specific passages from Exodus and Deuteronomy that stipulated they be worn in this manner. The passages were written on tiny scrolls of parchment.

Later, in the New Testament, emblems were called phylacteries. They were bound to the forehead and to the upper left arm with thongs, signifying that God's law should be constantly on the mind and near the heart.

Embroidery

THESE TRADED WITH YOU IN CHOICE GARMENTS, IN CLOTHES OF BLUE AND EMBROIDERED WORK . . . . –EZEKIEL 27:24

The art of decorative needlework, embroidery probably originated in Babylon; the Bible mentions Egypt and Edom as embroidery producers (Ezek 27:7, 16). Embroidered clothing, considered a luxury, was worn mostly by royalty and by the high priests (Ex 28:39).

The tabernacle curtains were ornamented with embroidery. The book of Exodus also describes the screen for the entrance to the court of the tabernacle as being "embroidered with needlework in blue, purple, and crimson yarns and fine twisted linen" (Ex 38:18). The work was apparently done by Oholiab, of the tribe of Dan, an "engraver, designer, and embroiderer" (Ex 38:23). Needles were made from bronze, bone, and ivory.

The emperor Augustus celebrates the military triumph of Tiberius, who will succeed him, in this onyx cameo.

Emperor

FEAR GOD. HONOR THE EMPEROR. –1 PETER 2:17

The Israelites did not use the term *emperor* to refer to any of their native rulers. The title, of Roman military origin, was bestowed as a temporary honor on successful field generals. Julius Caesar was the first to use it as a permanent title; after that, it was adopted by his successors.

In many areas of the ancient world, rulers were often thought to be divine in some way. Julius Caesar was worshiped as a god in parts of Asia, and after his death the Roman Senate voted to deify him. The cult of emperor worship later brought persecution to the early Christians, who were sometimes required to prove their loyalty by offering wine and incense before an image of the emperor.

Enemy

HE DELIVERED ME FROM MY STRONG ENEMY . . . .–PSALM 18:17

In biblical lands, enemies, or foes, often appeared as invading armies or as adversaries competing for territory, but another meaning of the term in the Scriptures connotes disobedience to the will of God or opposition to his people. Satan is the enemy because he has so assiduously worked against God throughout time. Indeed, the Hebrew word for Satan literally means "adversary." Because death is unknowable and implacable, it also is considered among the foremost of enemies (1 Cor 15:26).

Jesus' well-known commandment to love one's enemies is an amplification of such Old Testament teachings as Proverbs 24:17, which says, "Do not rejoice when your enemies fall." Jesus' resurrection defeats both of humankind's ancient enemies, Satan and death.

Engagement

"SO NOW LISTEN TO ME, BROTHER, AND TONIGHT WE SHALL SPEAK CONCERNING THE GIRL AND ARRANGE HER ENGAGEMENT TO YOU." –TOBIT 6:13

In biblical times, an engagement was as legally binding as a wedding. In a ceremony before witnesses, the bridegroom paid a bride price, or *mohar,* to the father of his fiancée; this transaction sealed the couple's union. The engagement typically lasted a year. During this time the pair was considered husband and wife, so they could be separated only by a formal divorce. When Joseph discovered Mary's expectant state during their engagement, he planned to divorce her quietly. But in a dream, an angel revealed to him that the conception of Mary's child was a miracle, brought about by the Holy Spirit (Mt 1:20). See also MARRIAGE.

Engraving

"HE IS TRAINED . . . TO DO ALL SORTS OF ENGRAVING AND EXECUTE ANY DESIGN . . . ."–2 CHRONICLES 2:14

The skill of engravers in the ancient world is apparent in the many materials that they carved. Glass, jewels, precious metals, clay writing tablets, stone, and wood were all engraved by the application of an iron stylus. When Jeremiah says of Judah's sin, "with a diamond point it is engraved on the tablet of their hearts" (Jer 17:1), the prophet may be referring to a hard stone, such as FLINT, as the carving instrument.

Wealthy people often used signet rings engraved with their name or personal symbol, and royal seals were sometimes engraved with winged discs or winged scarabs.

Ephesians, Letter of Paul to the

Therefore be imitators of God, as beloved children, and live in love, as Christ loved us . . . .
–Ephesians 5:1–2

One of the most important statements of the Christian faith, Paul's letter to the Ephesians may have been intended for general circulation among the early churches. Paul speaks of the great gift of redemption from death and sin and proclaims that Christ brought this gift to all peoples, thus expanding the old covenant and bringing Jews and Gentiles into spiritual union. He describes the duties of Christian family life and the proper relationship between weak and strong, rich and poor. He exhorts Christians to avoid selfishness, licentiousness, and anger in favor of love, humility, and holiness.

Ephod

I chose him out of all the tribes of Israel to be my priest . . . to wear an ephod before me . . . .
–1 Samuel 2:28

The ephod, an apronlike garment woven from yarns of various colors (Ex 28:6), was worn by the high priest during sacred rituals. It was placed over a blue tunic fringed with golden bells and embroidered pomegranates.

The ephod was fastened at the shoulders by two onyx clasps engraved with the names of the 12 tribes of Israel and was cinched at the waist with an intricately decorated band. Over that was a breastplate, bound "by its rings to the rings of the ephod with a blue cord" (Ex 39:21). The breastplate contained 12 jewels, which held the lots called Urim and Thummim. In the time of the judges, Gideon made an ephod that was used as an idol (Judg 8:27).

The apronlike ephod was an important part of the high priest's vestments, shown in a 19th-century engraving.

Esdras, 1&2

"The righteous, therefore, can endure difficult circumstances . . . ."
–2 Esdras 7:18

Although the apocryphal books 1 and 2 Esdras (the Greek form of Ezra) share a name, they have no connection. A historical book, Esdras 1 is a second-century BC compilation of materials largely drawn from the book of Ezra. A highlight is a debate among Persian guardsmen as to what is the most powerful force in the world. Their proposals are wine, the king, women, and truth, with truth finally winning out against the others. Three works are gathered in 2 Esdras—one Jewish and two Christian—written in the first century AD and later. These apocalyptic writings present visions that explore many issues, including life after death and the sufferings of the righteous.

Esther, Book of

In every province and in every city . . . there was gladness and joy among the Jews, a festival and a holiday.
–Esther 8:17

Set in Persia, the book of Esther tells of the marriage of Esther, a Jewish woman, to King Ahasuerus, who was probably Xerxes I. It describes how Esther and Mordecai, her cousin and adoptive father, thwart an attempt by one of the king's officials to massacre the Jews, their triumph sparking celebrations upon which the festival of Purim is based. This book is unusual in that it does not directly mention God. Subsequent authors inserted passages about the visions and prayers of Esther and Mordecai, asserting God's active role in the Jews' rescue. These additions to Esther are collected in the Apocrypha.

Eternal Life

For the wages of sin is death, but the free gift of God is eternal life in Christ Jesus our LORD.–Romans 6:23

The ancient Israelites did not have elaborate views of life after death. The Wisdom of Solomon says, "God created us for incorruption, and made us in the image of his own eternity" (Wis 2:23), but by sinning, humans brought about death. Some Israelites believed that after death the spirits of both the good and the evil descended to Sheol while their bodies decayed in the grave or tomb; others considered death the end of existence.

By the time of Jesus, many Jews believed in an afterlife, either as the immortality of the soul or in the form of the body coming back from the dead to new life. A biblical reference to the latter occurs in the book of Daniel: "Many of those who sleep in the dust of the earth shall awake, some to everlasting life, and some to shame and everlasting contempt" (Dan 12:2). Jesus' resurrection from the dead made eternal life an essential element of Christian doctrine.

Eunuch

Blessed also is the eunuch whose hands have done no lawless deed . . . . –Wisdom of Solomon 3:14

Males who had been castrated or who had been without the power to procreate from birth served as officials in royal households in the Near East. They were commonly in charge of the HAREM—the Greek word for eunuch means "keeper of the bed"—but they might have had different responsibilities. Acts of the Apostles tells of the conversion of an Ethiopian eunuch who had charge of the queen's treasury (Acts 8:27–39).

Philip baptizes the Ethiopian eunuch after telling him the "good news" about Jesus.

Despite their high status at court, eunuchs were regarded as socially and religiously inferior. However, God promises that even though they lack offspring, eunuchs devoted to him will receive "an everlasting name that shall not be cut off" (Isa 56:5).

Evangelist

The gifts he gave were that some would be apostles, some prophets, some evangelists, some pastors and teachers . . . . –Ephesians 4:11

An evangelist was a gifted preacher, skilled at telling the good news about Jesus to those who had not heard it. The word, which means "one who proclaims good news," is mentioned only three times in the Bible. Writing to the Ephesians, Paul says that evangelists are people called by God for a special task. The other references single out Philip and Timothy as evangelists (Acts 21:8; 2 Tim 4:5). Both men served as itinerant ministers. Philip took the gospel to the Samaritans and then to the Ethiopian eunuch. Timothy assisted Paul in starting churches in Asia Minor and Greece.

Execution

But if someone . . . kills another by treachery, you shall take the killer from my altar for execution. –Exodus 21:14

In the Holy Land, execution for a capital offense was ordinarily done by stoning. At least two witnesses to the crime were required, and they had to throw the first stones. Another form of execution was burning, used for incest or prostitution when committed by a priest's daughter. Criminals might also be killed by spear or bow and arrow. Those who insulted a king, as when John the Baptist chastised Herod, could be beheaded. In New Testament times, Romans carried out the punishment of CRUCIFIXION for treason and other crimes.

Exile

So Judah went into exile out of its land. –2 Kings 25:21

The threat of exile, or deportation, has a long history among the rulers of the ancient world. Conquerors commonly enforced their victories by banishing entire communities, or at least those elements likely to lead a rebellion. In 732 BC, the Assyrians deported part of the northern tribes of Israel. Eleven years later, Sargon II recorded sending 27,290 Israelites into exile when he captured Samaria, Israel's capital. Most of these people were unable to preserve their heritage among the Assyrians, and they are remembered as the 10 lost tribes.

The Babylonian captivity was the exile in the sixth century BC of many from the southern tribe of Judah (see map), including "deserters who had defected to the king of Babylon" (Jer 52:15). Through the prophet Jeremiah, God told them to rebuild their lives in Babylon, "for in its welfare you will find your welfare" (Jer 29:7). This group managed to maintain its identity, incorporating oral and written traditions into new writings.

EXODUS, BOOK OF

AT THE END OF FOUR HUNDRED THIRTY YEARS, ON THAT VERY DAY, ALL THE COMPANIES OF THE LORD WENT OUT FROM THE LAND OF EYGPT.
–EXODUS 12:41

The term *exodus* refers to the Israelites' flight out of Egypt and their journey to the Promised Land. As described in the book of Exodus, Moses relayed God's command to Pharaoh to let the Israelites go, but Pharaoh refused. In response, God sent 10 plagues against the Egyptians. The final and most horrible plague was the slaughter of the firstborn child of every Egyptian household. After this, Pharaoh at last relented and allowed the Israelites to leave. Once they had left, however, Pharaoh pursued them with his charioteers and army. God again intervened by parting the Red Sea for his people, then letting the waters rush back and swallow up Pharaoh and the Egyptians.

The Israelites—afflicted by hunger, thirst, and dissension—set out across the Sinai desert. When they finally reached the border of Canaan, they heard that the land was inhabited by giants, and they reviled God and Moses. As punishment, God forced them to wander in the WILDERNESS for 40 years. Only their children and a

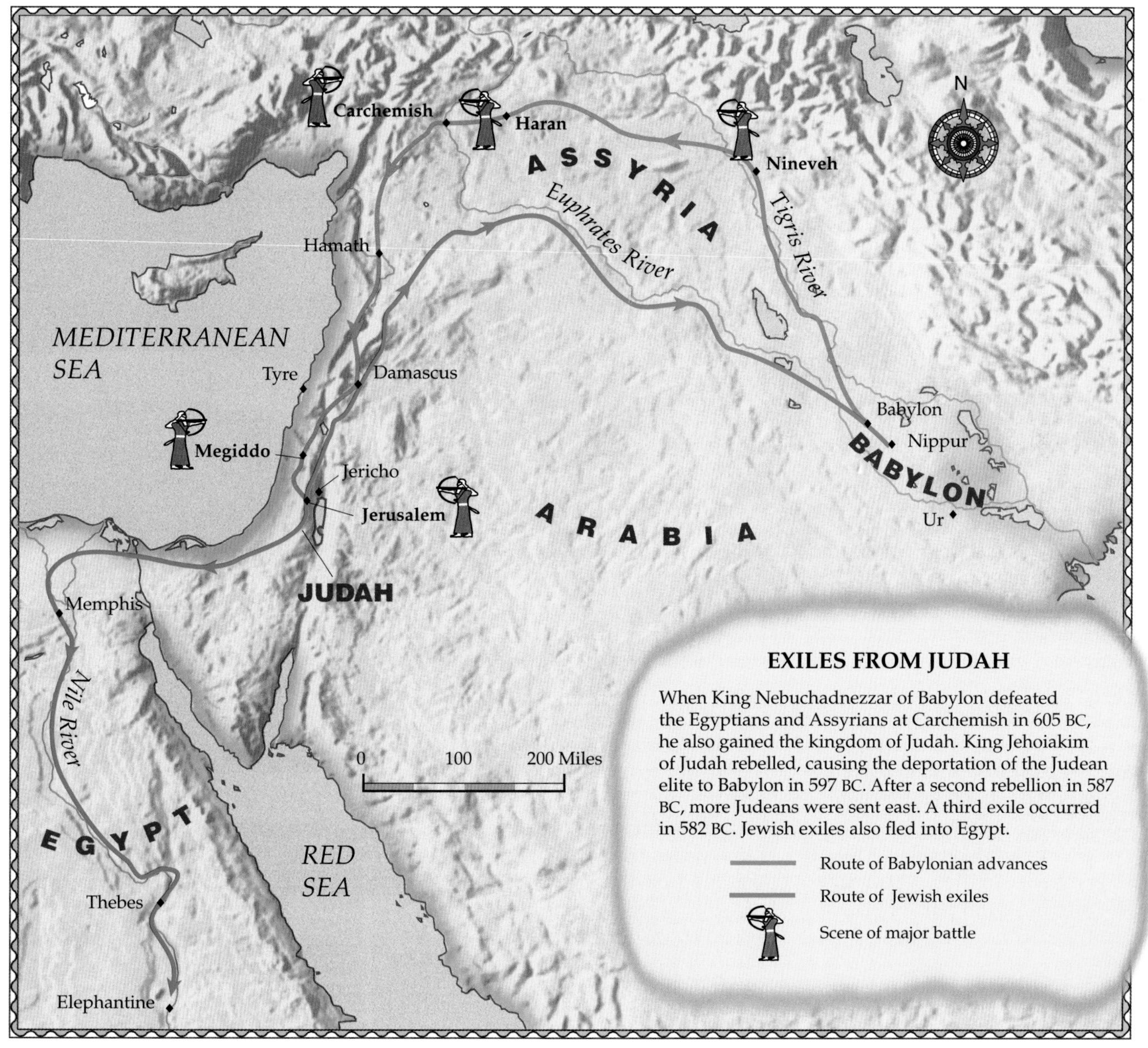

EXILES FROM JUDAH

When King Nebuchadnezzar of Babylon defeated the Egyptians and Assyrians at Carchemish in 605 BC, he also gained the kingdom of Judah. King Jehoiakim of Judah rebelled, causing the deportation of the Judean elite to Babylon in 597 BC. After a second rebellion in 587 BC, more Judeans were sent east. A third exile occurred in 582 BC. Jewish exiles also fled into Egypt.

few of the adults who had remained faithful to God ever saw the Promised Land.

Besides being a narrative of the deliverance of the Israelites from bondage in Egypt, the book of Exodus tells the story of Moses' life. It also contains some of the theological foundations of the Bible. The book declares God's presence among his people and his active care for them in time of need, exemplified by the miraculous fall of manna and quail during the wanderings in the wilderness. In Exodus God appears to Moses in the burning bush and reveals his name as "I AM WHO I AM" (Ex 3:14). God also proclaims the ten commandments, provides the rituals of worship, and decrees basic civil laws. He institutes his covenant with the nation of Israel, telling its members that "if you obey my voice and keep my covenant, you shall be my treasured possession out of all the peoples" (Ex 19:5).

EXORCIST

"NOW IF I CAST OUT THE DEMONS BY BEELZEBUL, BY WHOM DO YOUR EXORCISTS CAST THEM OUT?"
–LUKE 11:19

In the ancient world, illnesses and misfortunes were believed to be the work of demons, who could be exorcised, or expelled, by those who knew the proper rituals and occult incantations. Records survive of exorcisms in Babylon and Assyria. In one, the exorcist made a figurine of the demon and uttered special words while destroying the image. In another, the exorcist made a figurine of the possessed person and asked the demon to leave the body of the person and instead occupy the figure.

Casting out demons was a common practice in the first century AD and was a central part of Jesus' ministry. After Jesus' death, non-Christian exorcists tried to use his name to drive out an evil spirit, but "the evil spirit said to them in reply, 'Jesus I know . . . but who are you?'" (Acts 19:15).

EXPIATION

THEY PLEDGED THEMSELVES . . . TO OFFER RAMS IN EXPIATION OF THEIR ERROR.
–1 ESDRAS 9:20

God's covenant with Israel required the people to obey his laws or suffer punishment. If they didn't obey, however, they could find forgiveness by offering sacrifices that expiated their sins. Thus expiation is the cleansing or forgiving of sin through the blood of a sacrifice. The act of making an offering restored the person's covenant relationship with God, bringing about RECONCILIATION and God's pardon instead of his retribution.

Many of the New Testament writers taught that Jesus' sacrifice of his own life atoned for the sins of everyone, thereby rendering obsolete the old covenant and its sacrificial system.

EYE

"THE EYE IS THE LAMP OF THE BODY."–MATTHEW 6:22

Biblical references to the human eye are often figurative, as when those who lack understanding are described as being blind. The eye frequently stands for the whole person, thus revealing needs and emotions. The watchful eye of God is a symbol of divine protection. In Proverbs 7:2, the famous expression "apple of your eye" refers to the pupil. Apart from literary use, the actual eye was considered particularly important. Priests were disqualified for BLINDNESS (Lev 21:18), a slave blinded by his master was freed (Ex 21:26), and gouging out the enemies' right eyes disgraced their entire nation (1 Sam 11:2). The expression "an eye for an eye" (Mt 5:38) referred to retaliation for an injury (Lev 24:20).

EZEKIEL, BOOK OF

. . . THE WORD OF THE LORD CAME TO THE PRIEST EZEKIEL . . . AND THE HAND OF THE LORD WAS ON HIM THERE.–EZEKIEL 1:3

Combining harsh, doom-laden prophecies with a message of hope for Israel's ultimate redemption, Ezekiel is one of the most intriguing books of the Bible. A priest who prophesied to his fellow exiles in Babylon, Ezekiel presents a dark view of Israel's history, although he begins with a glorious vision of God appearing on a fiery chariot. The prophet portrays the Israelites as being rebellious toward God, which led to the punishment of exile. He then shifts tone, describing God's continuing love for his people and predicting the restoration of the temple. This book includes the famous passage that describes dry bones becoming alive again, prefiguring the idea of resurrection.

The book of Ezekiel contains the vision of God breathing life into skeletons, depicted in a detail of a sculptured menorah.

The book of Ezra describes the rebuilding of the temple in Jerusalem after the exiles returned from Babylon. This diorama reconstructs some of the activities involved, such as hauling the huge stones to the temple site, in the upper left, hoisting them into place, and cutting decorations into them, as shown in the middle foreground. Foremen with plans, in the upper right, oversee the work.

EZRA, BOOK OF

FOE WE ARE SLAVES; YET OUR GOD HAS NOT FORSAKEN US IN OUR SLAVERY, BUT HAS EXTENDED TO US HIS STEADFAST LOVE . . . .
–EZRA 9:9

The book of Ezra is a continuation of the historical narrative in 1 and 2 Chronicles. Together with the book of NEHEMIAH, it describes the return of the Jews from Babylon and the rebuilding of the temple. Some of the book is based on personal memoirs written by Ezra, a priest and scribe.

After the Persian king Artaxerxes placed him in charge of religious affairs in Judah, Ezra led one of the groups of exiles returning to Jerusalem, probably about 458 BC. Portions of the book of Ezra were written in Aramaic, which was the official language of the Persian Empire, rather than in Hebrew.

FACE

. . . DISHONOR HAS COVERED OUR FACE, FOR ALIENS HAVE COME INTO THE HOLY PLACES OF THE LORD'S HOUSE.–JEREMIAH 51:51

In the ancient Near East, a reference to the face might actually mean the whole person; thus, the Hebrew word for face is often translated as "person." Since an individual's countenance can reveal such feelings as joy and sadness, the face could also represent someone's emotional state.

Because the connection between the face and character was so close, actions involving the face were often significant. When a person lowered his face, he was signaling surrender. To spit in someone's face was to show disdain, while veiling the face showed reverence or modesty. To lift up another person's face could mean to grant a request. God's face, a significant theme in Old Testament writing, represented the divine presence, which mortals could not usually experience and survive without mediation. God could shine his face on an individual to confer blessing, set his face in judgment, or mercifully hide his face from human sin, although the hidden face of God might also mean disapproval.

In figurative language, the Bible speaks of the visible surfaces of the earth and the seas as faces.

FAITH

NOW FAITH IS THE ASSURANCE OF THINGS HOPED FOR, THE CONVICTION OF THINGS NOT SEEN.
—HEBREWS 11:1

In the Bible, faith means trusting in God by believing that he exists, that he embraces humanity with steadfast love, and that he is faithful to his word. Abraham is the enduring model of faith. In Genesis, God instructs him to "Go from your country . . . and your father's house to the land that I will show you" (Gen 12:1). Although Abraham did not know where he was going, still he went. Repeatedly Abraham obeyed God's word, and God caused him to prosper.

In the New Testament, Jesus taught that there was enough power in faith to cause physical HEALING (Mt 9:22) and even to move mountains (Mt 17:20). Jesus stressed faith especially to those in crisis. He told the crowds not to worry about food or clothing, because "your heavenly Father knows that you need all these things. . . . and all these things will be given to you" (Mt 6:32–33).

In the face of death, faith means believing that God sent his son so that everyone "may have eternal life" (Jn 3:16). Although people are saved by faith in Jesus, that faith must be expressed in actions, for "faith by itself, if it has no works, is dead" (Jas 2:17).

FAMILY

THIS IS THE STORY OF THE FAMILY OF JACOB.
—GENESIS 37:2

Unlike the modern notion of the family as a narrowly defined, limited social unit, the family in the Old Testament was a more fluid,

The evening meal was traditionally eaten in the company of one's family. Above, an Israelite father seated at right beside his grandson discusses the day's events with his sons. The mother pours wine for her eldest son, whose wife serves sweet figs.

open group (see illustration), closer to today's term *household*. In ancient times the oldest male who headed the family often had more than one wife, so families could be very large: Jacob, for example, had several wives and a family of 66 people (Gen 46:26). As large families were considered advantageous for economic reasons, most families of the time probably included wives, children, grandparents, grandchildren, slaves, and servants. Various laws against incest and adultery (Lev 18:6–20) helped to preserve the integrity and sanctity of the family.

The father wielded much of the authority in the family. He arranged his children's marriages (1 Sam 18:17–18) and could end his own for almost any reason. To obtain a DIVORCE, he wrote a "certificate of divorce," after which his wife had to leave his house (Deut 24:1). But divorce was sometimes criticized, as in Malachi 2:16.

A wife's primary functions were to bear children and provide food and clothing for the members of her family. According to the Bible, a competent wife should be treasured, as she was "far more precious than jewels" (Prov 31:10).

Children were considered proof of God's love. Sons—especially the eldest—were highly valued because they perpetuated the family line. Children were expected to honor and obey their parents—even into old age—and their failure to do so could, in some cases, be considered a capital offense: "Whoever curses father or mother shall be put to death" (Ex 21:17).

By New Testament times, most husbands were monogamous, and wives were to be loved and honored. "Husbands, love your wives," Paul advised the Ephesians, "just as Christ loved the church and gave himself up for her" (Eph 5:25). Jesus preached that marriage should be monogamous and permanent, but he spoke of the physical family as being less important than the community of believers in God, which Paul called "the family of faith" (Gal 6:10). While the father still headed the family, members of the early Christian church considered God to be the family's true leader. The emphasis on human ancestors was reduced, as Christians now traced their lineage to God. Jesus said, "And call no one your father on earth, for you have one Father—the one in heaven" (Mt 23:9).

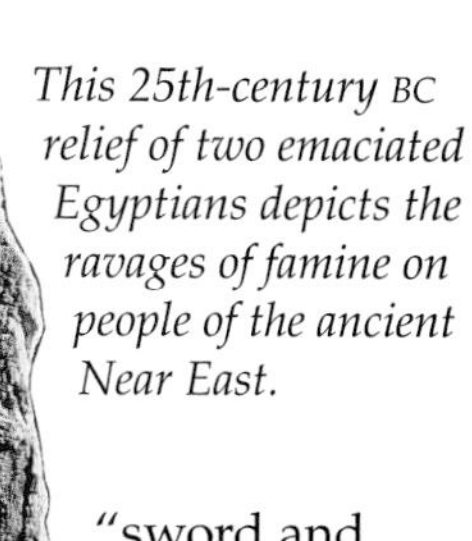

This 25th-century BC *relief of two emaciated Egyptians depicts the ravages of famine on people of the ancient Near East.*

FAMINE

AT DESTRUCTION AND FAMINE YOU SHALL LAUGH, AND SHALL NOT FEAR THE WILD ANIMALS OF THE EARTH.
–JOB 5:22

Famines, or extreme food shortages, are mentioned often in the Bible, reflecting the hard reality of life in the dry lands of the ancient Near East. The most common cause of famine was DROUGHT—a lack of moisture in the rainy season—but other natural forces, such as locusts, wind, hail, and "blight and mildew" (Am 4:9), could destroy crops and cause widespread hunger. Famine and warfare were also inevitable partners. Deuteronomy warns of a siege so terrible that starving parents would devour their children (Deut 28:47–53); in Jeremiah, false prophets face destruction by "sword and famine" (Jer 14:15). The best-known biblical famine takes place in Genesis 41: when Pharaoh has a dream about fat cows being consumed by thin cows, Joseph correctly divines that Egypt will see seven years of bounty and seven years of famine. The famines of the Old Testament were usually caused by God to punish humanity for its disobedience. If God so chose, he could send "not a famine of bread" but a want "of hearing the words of the LORD" (Am 8:11). In the New Testament, famine serves as a harbinger of the last judgment. The black horse of Revelation, whose rider holds a pair of scales, symbolizes famine. As it appears, a voice calls out that "a quart of wheat" will now cost a day's pay (Rev 6:6).

FARMING

DO NOT HATE HARD LABOR OR FARM WORK, WHICH WAS CREATED BY THE MOST HIGH.–ECCLESIASTICUS 7:15

Dating from at least 10,000 years ago, farming, along with breeding livestock, has been a foundation of the economy in the Holy Land. The laws of Israel closely regulated this essential activity (Lev 19:9).

Unlike the farmers of mighty Egypt and Mesopotamia, who had to irrigate their desert crops,

Israelite farmers could generally depend upon the winter rains (Deut 11:10–11), but drought occasionally brought disaster. Rough weather and various pests (1 Kings 8:37) were hazards too. The terrain was rocky and had to be cleared

In the Near East, men and women share the farm work. Above, a woman gathers wheat near Hebron during the harvest.

and hillsides terraced before planting, which began with the first rains. Sometimes using a team of draft animals pulling a single-handled wooden plow, the farmer broke the hard-baked soil, smashed the clods, and then smoothed the plowed ground with a hoe (Isa 28:24–25). The introduction of iron plows, in the late second millennium BC, raised crop yields. Seeds were sown by hand: they could be planted individually or scattered before or after plowing. At times, the fields were fertilized with dung. Growing conditions ranged widely throughout Israel, making possible a variety of crops. Grain, especially wheat for making bread, was a primary crop, as were olives and grapes. Other crops included beans, peas, onions, and melons. See also HARVEST.

FASTING

MY KNEES ARE WEAK THROUGH FASTING; MY BODY HAS BECOME GAUNT.
–PSALM 109:24

Biblical law required people to refrain from eating or drinking one day a year—from sunrise to sunset on the Day of Atonement (Lev 16:29–34). But people fasted several days or more, though sometimes taking liquids, when they mourned or when they sought God's help in a crisis. When Saul and his sons died fighting the Philistines, many Israelites fasted for a week (1 Sam 31:13). When the Jews feared a holocaust at the hands of the Persians, Queen Esther asked her people to fast for three days before she pleaded their case to the king (Esth 4:16).

By New Testament times, some Jews fasted every Tuesday and Thursday. Jesus accepted fasting as a spiritual discipline, but he criticized hypocrites who used fasting as a way to parade their PIETY (Mt 6:16). Jesus is reported to have fasted for 40 days before beginning his public ministry (Mt 4:2). Yet he did not require his disciples to fast, saying that their time together was short and an occasion for rejoicing (Mk 2:18–20). Later, members of the early Christian church fasted before making important decisions, such as ordaining ministers.

FATE

. . . THE SAME FATE COMES TO ALL, TO THE RIGHTEOUS AND THE WICKED, TO THE GOOD AND THE EVIL . . . .
–ECCLESIASTES 9:2

When biblical writers spoke of fate, they were usually referring to humanity's common destiny—death. Some of the prophets and sages of the Old Testament warned that the fate awaiting the wicked was an early or violent death. Indeed, argued one of Job's comforters, they "are destined for the sword" (Job 15:20, 22).

The Israelites believed that the timing and manner of death were in the hands of a sovereign and just God. Greek philosophers taught that humans were predestined by the gods to endure a course of events that no one could change. A similar view is found in the book of Ecclesiastes.

FATHER

. . . "ABBA, FATHER, FOR YOU ALL THINGS ARE POSSIBLE . . . ."
–MARK 14:36

In the Old Testament, the term *father* referred to the head of a family, a people, a town, a profession, or even to a grandfather. A high governmental official was also called a father, as was a prophet. When used in the plural, the term denotes past generations, as in "you, a brood of sinners, have risen in place of your fathers" (Num 32:14). According to the law, a father, as head of the household, had specific duties such as overseeing the religious education of his children.

In the New Testament, the term is most commonly used to refer to God. God is not only the father of Jesus Christ but also the father of believers and of all people. All, Jesus said, are "children of your Father in heaven" (Mt 5:45). Jesus

In this stained-glass window, God the Father supports the lifeless body of his son, Jesus, as the Holy Spirit hovers nearby.

frequently addressed God warmly as "Father" and used this intimate term when he taught his followers the well-known prayer, which in Luke's Gospel begins, "Father, hallowed be your name" (Lk 11:2). See also ABBA.

FATLING

. . . AND WHEN THOSE WHO BORE THE ARK OF THE LORD HAD GONE SIX PACES, HE SACRIFICED AN OX AND A FATLING.
–2 SAMUEL 6:13

Animals were often fattened as food for special occasions. In Luke a fatted calf—or fatling—was slaughtered in the parable of the prodigal son to celebrate his safe return (Lk 15: 23–24). As meat was rarely served in biblical times, fatted animals symbolized affluence or abundance.

Fatlings were also considered appropriate sacrificial offerings to God. Leviticus dictates specific rules for such sacrifices, saying, "All fat is the LORD'S," and details how the animal's fat must be removed and offered (Lev 3:14–17).

FELLOWSHIP

. . . AND TRULY OUR FELLOWSHIP IS WITH THE FATHER AND WITH HIS SON JESUS CHRIST.
–1 JOHN 1:3

From the exodus onward, the Israelites were bound together in fellowship with one another and with God, who also enjoyed fellowship with a few chosen individuals, but the concept is more clearly present in the New Testament.

Before Jesus, the Pharisees set an example by dining together weekly in order to discuss religious and legal issues. The similarly close relationship between Jesus and his disciples was a model for the early Christian concept of fellowship (Acts 2: 42–47). Early believers found themselves bound together by a common purpose and devotion, which included a shared belief in the message of the Gospels, as well as the ultimate acceptance of Jesus Christ as Lord (1 Cor 1:9). The outward expression of these tenets was essential.

Communion, or the Lord's supper, became the chief ritual expression of Christian fellowship (1 Cor 11:23–27). Paul exhorted believers, whether Jew or Gentile before conversion, to share both spiritual and material blessings. Separate from the Lord's supper, the love feast (Jude 1:12), or agape meal, was characterized by festive joy and welcomed the poor and hungry to participate in spiritual fellowship.

FESTAL GARMENTS

HE KILLED THIRTY MEN OF THE TOWN, TOOK THEIR SPOIL, AND GAVE THE FESTAL GARMENTS TO THOSE WHO HAD EXPLAINED THE RIDDLE.
–JUDGES 14:19

The term *festal garments* can refer to either a change of clothing or clothing that is clean, pure, or white. Such items were to be saved and worn only for special occasions. In biblical times, possessing more than one set of clothes was a sign of wealth. Thus, Samson at his wedding promises to reward his Philistine guests with "thirty festal garments" (Judg 14:12) if they can solve the riddle he poses. In Zechariah, an angel clothes Joshua in "festal apparel" (Zech 3:4), white robes that symbolize his consecration as the one who will remove the sins of his people and prepare for the coming Messiah.

FESTIVAL

THIS DAY SHALL BE A DAY OF REMEMBRANCE FOR YOU. YOU SHALL CELEBRATE IT AS A FESTIVAL TO THE LORD; THROUGHOUT YOUR GENERATIONS YOU SHALL OBSERVE IT . . . .
–EXODUS 12:14

The ancient biblical calendar was punctuated with various sacred feasts and festivals, which commemorated events in the relationship between God and the Israelites (see chart, pp. 132–133). Some festivals were closely aligned with the changing seasons, often paralleling an important annual event, such as the harvest (Ex 23:16). These were sacred occasions, which, according to God, "you shall celebrate at the time appointed for them" (Lev 23:4). The sabbath was observed weekly on God's appointed day of rest, which was the seventh day of the week (Ex 20:9–11).

Festivals were usually times of thanksgiving and joyous celebration often accompanied by singing and dancing, music, elaborate meals, and ritual sacrifices. PASSOVER, the remembrance of God's liberation of Israel from Egyptian captivity (Num 9:1–5), was a cause for great joy. Some festivals, such as the DAY OF ATONEMENT, were times of self-denial and sober reflection (Lev 23:27–28).

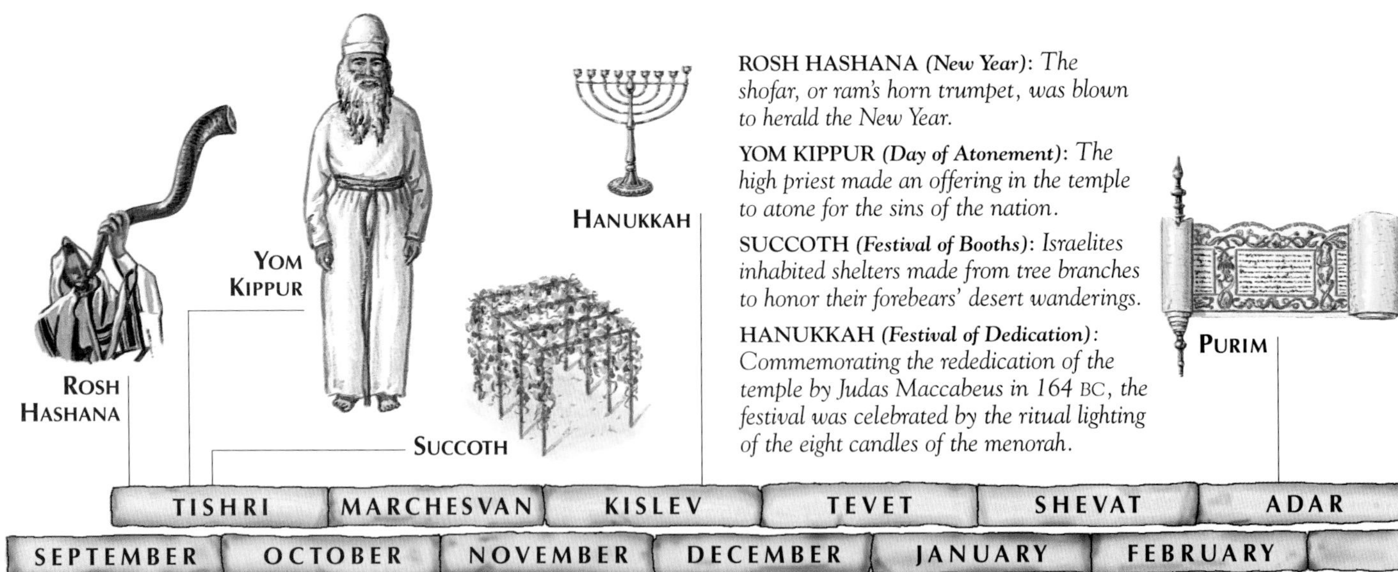

Festival of Booths

. . . On the fifteenth day of this seventh month, and lasting seven days, there shall be the festival of booths to the Lord.–Leviticus 23:34

The Festival of Booths, known also as the Festival of Ingathering (Ex 23:16) or Tabernacles, was a joyful festival that coincided with the annual fall harvest of crops. According to the law of Moses, on the 15th day of the seventh month, the Israelites were to live for seven days in temporary huts—booths—made of branches (Neh 8:13–18). These were to remind them of the dwellings they lived in while wandering in the desert, and of God's eternal protection. During the festival, booths were erected in the streets or on roofs, and offerings were made to God.

Festival of Dedication

At that time the festival of the Dedication took place in Jerusalem. It was winter . . . . –John 10:22

Jesus answered questions from an angry crowd as he attended the Festival of Dedication, a celebration not found in the Hebrew Bible. The festival commemorated the purification by Judas Maccabees in 164 BC of the second temple in Jerusalem, which had been defiled by the idolatrous Seleucids. The story is told in 1 Maccabees 4 and 2 Maccabees 10. Also called Hanukkah, which means "dedication" in Hebrew, or the feast of lights, the December festival lasted eight days, on each of which a candle was lit and sacrifices were offered to celebrate the victory over religious persecution.

Fetters

His feet were hurt with fetters . . . .–Psalm 105:18

In biblical times, the hands and feet of prisoners were often confined in fetters, or shackles—restraints that curtailed free movement. Fetters were made of wood, iron, or bronze, and wearing them was painful. When Samson was betrayed by Delilah and shorn of his strength-giving hair, the Philistines "bound him with bronze shackles" (Judg 16:21). A person whose fetters were joined by a CHAIN would be even further hobbled. Such was the condition of the man with an "unclean spirit," who was "bound with chains and shackles" to contain his demon and keep him from injuring himself (Mk 5:2–4; Lk 8:29).

Field

"The kingdom of heaven is like a mustard seed that someone took and sowed in his field . . . ." –Matthew 13:31

The word *field* usually refers to an open piece of land for growing crops or raising cattle, in contrast to a camp or a vineyard, which was generally enclosed. The BOUNDARY of a field was delineated by landmarks. Fields were also the site of battles (Judg 9:43) and burial grounds for the dead (2 Chr 26:23). The most famous field in the Bible is the Hakeldama, or Field of Blood, which is associated with Jesus' betrayer, Judas Iscariot (Mt 27:3–10; Acts 1:18–19). Phrases such as "animal of the field" (Gen 2:19) and "plant of the field" (Gen 2:5), usually refer to wild, undomesticated species.

Fig

. . . and they knew that they were naked; and they sewed fig leaves together and made loincloths for themselves.–Genesis 3:7

Cultivated throughout the Holy Land for their sweetness, figs were a basic part of the diet of biblical peoples. Figs were eaten fresh or dried and pressed into cakes

PURIM ***(Festival of Lots)***: *The book of Esther was read to commemorate the victory of the Jews and Queen Esther's bravery.*

PASSOVER: *The Festival of Unleavened Bread and Passover merged, and unleavened bread was eaten in memory of the exodus.*

SHAVUOT ***(Pentecost/ Feast of Weeks)***: *Originally a harvest festival, Shavuot has come to mark the day that Moses received God's laws on Mount Sinai.*

SHAVUOT

PASSOVER

FEASTS & FESTIVALS

Beginning with the celebration of the New Year in the month of Tishri, the ancient Israelite year was filled with feasts and festivals. Some important biblical holidays shown here, in chronological order from left to right, have been known by different names over the centuries but continue to commemorate the Israelites' faith in God's providence and devotion to God's laws.

NISAN | IYYAR | SIVAN | TAMMUZ | AV | ELUL

MARCH | APRIL | MAY | JUNE | JULY | AUGUST

(1 Sam 25:18). The large palmate leaves of the fig tree covered Adam and Eve's nakedness (Gen 2:7) and shaded Nathanael from the sun

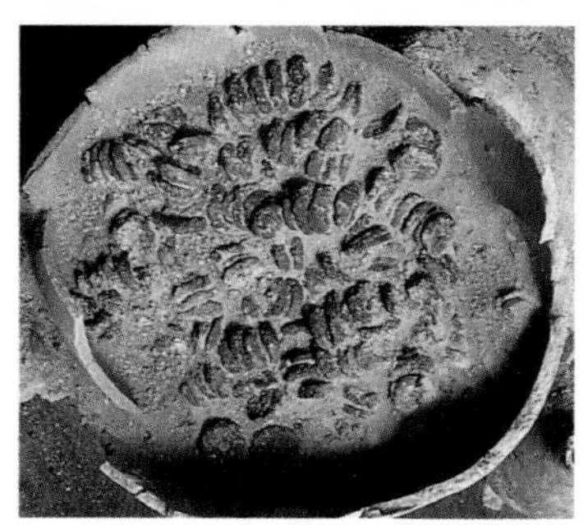

This clay jar of figs was preserved for 3,000 years before it was excavated intact from the ruins of Ekron in 1994.

(Jn 1:48, 50). Often planted with grape vines, the fig tree stood for peace and prosperity. The Lord sometimes threatened this happy combination when Israel was disobedient: "I will lay waste her vines and her fig trees" (Hos 2: 12).

FINGER OF GOD

WHEN GOD FINISHED SPEAKING WITH MOSES ON MOUNT SINAI, HE GAVE HIM THE TWO TABLETS OF THE COVENANT . . . WRITTEN WITH THE FINGER OF GOD.–EXODUS 31:18

Although the phrase "finger of God" appears only four times in the Bible, it is a colorfully potent symbol of God's incontrovertible power over all his creations. In Exodus it is used to demonstrate that God alone created the ten commandments. Pharaoh's magicians, when confronted with Aaron's plague of GNATS, finally conceded that they must be the work of God and not of man, and exclaimed to their leader, "This is the finger of God!" (Ex 8:19). Jesus said he cast out demons "by the finger of God" (Lk 11:20) to demonstrate God's power over evil spirits.

FIR TREE

". . . YOUR BUILDERS MADE PERFECT YOUR BEAUTY. THEY MADE ALL YOUR PLANKS OF FIR TREES FROM SENIR . . . ." –EZEKIEL 27:4–5

A tall evergreen of the pine family with cones and needle-like leaves, the fir tree was used for shipbuilding all over the eastern Mediterranean. In the above-cited lamentation, the prophet Ezekiel compares the Phoenician city of Tyre before its plunder by Nebuchadnezzar with a beautiful ship whose planks were made of fir trees. Stringed musical instruments, such as the harp, were also fashioned from the wood of the fir tree. The Hebrew word for fir is also translated as "cypress" and "juniper." See also CYPRESS.

FIRE

THEN THE ANGEL TOOK THE CENSER AND FILLED IT WITH FIRE FROM THE ALTAR AND THREW IT ON THE EARTH . . . . –REVELATION 8:5

The image of fire appears throughout the Bible as a symbol of God's power and wrath. When God first appears to Moses, it is in the form of a burning bush (Ex 3:2). Later he warns the Israelites that "the LORD your God is a devouring fire, a jealous God" (Deut 4:24). When Aaron is consecrated as a high priest, fire from the Lord consumes the sacrifice, a sign that God has approved the offering (Lev 9:24). God also uses fire to punish: Sodom and Gomorrah are destroyed by "sulfur and fire from the LORD" (Gen 19:24). Indeed, according to the book of Revelation, all evil will perish in a fire sent by God.

In addition to its normal uses for cooking and heating, fire was a main component of religious rituals. A holy fire was to be kept burning continuously on the altar (Lev 6:12–13) as a symbol of God's everlasting presence and love. Other fires, called "unholy fire" (Lev 10:1), were unacceptable for burnt offerings. According to Jewish tradition, no fire—even that used for cooking—could be kindled on the sabbath (Ex 35:3).

FIREBRAND

BUT ALL OF YOU ARE KINDLERS OF FIRE, LIGHTERS OF FIREBRANDS. –ISAIAH 50:11

Firebrands—pieces of wood set on fire—were hurled over city walls in times of siege. They may have been ignited like torches by setting fire to a cloth wrapped around one end and soaked in olive oil. In Amos 4:11—"you were like a brand snatched from the fire"—they symbolize those who have found salvation: Proverbs 26:18–19 likens a person who deceives a neighbor to a "maniac" throwing firebrands.

Commanded by God to "observe . . . the first fruits of wheat harvest" (Ex 34:22), Israelite farmers offered up the the best of their crops to the Lord.

FIREPAN

THEY TOOK AWAY . . . ALL THE BRONZE VESSELS USED IN THE TEMPLE SERVICE, AS WELL AS THE FIREPANS AND THE BASINS. –2 KINGS 25:14–15

Temple priests used metal firepans in sacrificial rituals, although it is uncertain how. The Bible mentions firepans only when listing the sacred utensils used in the tabernacle and later in the temple. Priests may have used these pans to carry away the ashes of sacrifices and to serve as censers holding live coals. The priests would sprinkle incense on the coals as a fragrant offering to God. The firepans were made of bronze when Israel worshiped at the portable tabernacle. But when Solomon built the temple, the firepans and other sacrificial utensils were of gold.

FIRST DAY OF THE WEEK

. . . ON THE FIRST DAY OF THE WEEK, WHEN THE SUN HAD RISEN, THEY WENT TO THE TOMB.–MARK 16:2

The Gospels note that Jesus was resurrected on the first day of the week; thus the phrase "the Lord's day" stands for Sunday. For Christians, Sunday was a day for rejoicing over the new life promised by Jesus' resurrection. It was named a day of rest after Christianity became the official religion of the Roman Empire. Many early Christians celebrated both the first day of the week and the last, which was the sabbath, or Saturday. In Revelation the author's vision of Christ comes on the first day of the week: "I was in the spirit on the Lord's day, and I heard behind me a loud voice like a trumpet" (Rev 1:10).

FIRST FRUITS

THE CHOICEST OF THE FIRST FRUITS OF YOUR GROUND YOU SHALL BRING INTO THE HOUSE OF THE LORD YOUR GOD. –EXODUS 23:19

As Israelite farmers harvested their first crops of the season, they brought to the temple the finest barley, wheat, grapes, olives, and other produce that their fields had to offer. The offering of these "first fruits" was a national celebration that occurred in late spring at the Festival of Weeks, or PENTECOST, and was repeated throughout the summer as later crops were harvested. With these offerings, the people showed gratitude for God's provision. The offerings also reminded Israel that they were only tenants on land that belonged to God (Lev 25:23).

FIRSTBORN

. . . THE FIRSTBORN OF HUMAN BEINGS YOU SHALL REDEEM . . . . –NUMBERS 18:15

After delivering the Israelites out of Egypt, God said to Moses, "Consecrate to me all the firstborn; whatever is first to open the womb among the Israelites, of human beings and animals, is mine" (Ex 13:2). In conveying the message to the Israelites, Moses made clear that it was firstborn males that had this special significance; they belonged to God and were to be offered up to him.

To fulfill the edict, firstborn male animals (also called firstlings) were sacrificed to God, and firstborn male children, at the age of one month, were presented to God in the temple. In the ceremony of redemption, a father then "bought back" his child by paying five shekels to a priest.

As the firstborn son, Jesus was taken to the temple by Mary and Joseph "to present him to the Lord" (Lk 2:22). Paul's letter to the Colossians refers to Jesus as the "firstborn of all creation" (Col 1:15), meaning that as God's son he oversees all created things. Both Colossians and Revelation call him the firstborn of the dead (Col 1:18; Rev 1:5), in reference to his resurrection. See also BIRTHRIGHT.

FISH

. . . HE SAID TO THEM, "HAVE YOU ANYTHING HERE TO EAT?" THEY GAVE HIM A PIECE OF BROILED FISH . . . .
–LUKE 24:41–42

The word *fish* appears many times in the Bible, but specific kinds are never mentioned. The only distinction noted is between fish that are clean and unclean. Fish with fins and scales were considered clean, and the unclean were all other aquatic creatures.

The Israelites' access to the Mediterranean Sea was limited by Philistine and Phoenician control of the coast, and the supply of freshwater fish from the Sea of Galilee—which was actually a lake—was readily exhausted by local markets. Nevertheless, fish was a popular food. Even during their sojourn in the desert, the Israelites longed for it: "We remember the fish we used to eat in Egypt for nothing" (Num 11:5).

Fish was prepared in a variety of ways: roasting, boiling, broiling, steaming, frying, pickling, salting, and drying. Indigenous species identified by modern zoologists include varieties of carp, catfish, and eel.

The story traditionally referred to as Jonah and the Whale describes not a whale but a great fish capable of swallowing a man whole: "Jonah was in the belly of the fish three days and three nights" (Jon 1:17). Jesus alludes to this tale in Matthew 12:40; here some Bible translations use the term *whale,* although others prefer *sea monster.* Since the whale is relatively rare in the Mediterranean Sea, where the story takes place, the word may have been used simply to emphasize the enormity of the creature that ingested Jonah.

In Christianity's early centuries, the fish became a symbol for Jesus. This was because the Greek word *ichthys,* meaning "fish,"could be used as an acronym for the Greek phrase meaning "Jesus Christ, Son of God, Savior." The fish symbol is still used to represent Christ.

This fishhook, found in Israel near the Mediterranean Sea, was used for fishing during the time of Roman rule.

FISHING

SIMON PETER SAID TO THEM, "I AM GOING FISHING."
–JOHN 21:3

Fishing was an important occupation during biblical times, and some enterprises thrived on the Sea of Galilee (see reconstruction, pp. 136–137). The Fish Gate in Jerusalem's city wall was so named because of its proximity to the fish markets.

Fishing was arduous labor. Fishermen hauled and mended heavy nets, rowed cumbersome wooden boats, and sorted and prepared their catch for transport to distant markets, often working through the night. They used the dragnet—a large, weighted net thrown from a boat and then dragged toward shore, sometimes with help from another crew. This method was employed at night, when the cooling water drew fish to the surface. Another net—the casting net—could be handled by a single man on shore or in shallow water. It was thrown in a wide arc over visible fish. Spears and harpoons were also used, as well as fishhooks attached to lines.

Simon Peter, Andrew, James, and John were among the apostles of Jesus who were fishermen; Philip, Thomas, and Nathanael probably were as well. Jesus used fishing as a metaphor in his preaching, such as when he compared the kingdom of heaven with a net that catches "fish of every kind" (Mt 13:47).

FLAX

SHE HAD, HOWEVER, BROUGHT THEM UP TO THE ROOF AND HIDDEN THEM WITH THE STALKS OF FLAX . . . .
–JOSHUA 2:6

A much-cultivated plant, flax was prized as the raw material for LINEN and for linseed oil, which was used in paint and medicines. Making linen from flax was a woman's task, alluded to in Proverbs 31:13. The process included soaking the flax in water to separate the fibers and then drying it. The drying took place on the roof of a house. In the book of Joshua, the prostitute Rahab uses the stalks of flax on her roof to hide Joshua's spies from men sent by the king of Jericho.

FISHING

"PUT OUT INTO THE DEEP WATER AND LET DOWN YOUR NETS FOR A CATCH."—LUKE 5:4

This town, like many others on the shores of the Sea of Galilee, built breakwaters to create a harbor; the waterfront has been finished with a stone quay and promenade. Fishermen who sailed out of the harbor at night have now returned with their catch at dawn, anchoring their boats and securing them to the mooring stones at the side of the quay. Here they unload the fish that is for immediate sale into small tanks filled with water that are built into the pavement. Most of the catch is intended for trade, however, and will be dried and salted. Nets are spread out on the promenade to dry.

FLESH

". . . THE SPIRIT INDEED IS WILLING,
BUT THE FLESH IS WEAK."
–MARK 14:38

The Bible draws a distinction between the flesh and the SPIRIT. When used in reference to the body as a whole, the term *flesh* often alludes to physical appetites that can distract human beings from performing God's will. This inherent weakness of the body makes it greatly susceptible to temptation.

According to God's original plan in the garden of Eden, flesh was simply a material substance free from any implication of evil. Only after Adam and Eve disobeyed God's command did flesh become connected with the taint of sin.

Jesus had a fleshly body but resisted its temptations, thus making salvation possible for humankind, who could choose to forego sins of the flesh and live in the spirit (Rom 8:9–11). According to Paul's writings, the flesh is not necessarily to be scorned; it is to be recognized as earthly yet able to be directed toward spiritual goals. He links flesh in a negative way to the law of Israel, contrasting it to faith in the spirit (Gal 3:2–5).

Occasionally *flesh* is used in scriptural writing to refer to male sexual organs or to sexual union.

A Bedouin woman tends a flock of sheep in the northern Negeb, a region extending southward from Judah, where herdsmen have grazed their flocks since biblical times.

FLIES

"'FOR IF YOU WILL NOT LET MY
PEOPLE GO, I WILL SEND SWARMS
OF FLIES ON YOU, YOUR OFFICIALS,
AND YOUR PEOPLE . . . .'"
–EXODUS 8:21

A scourge of flies was the fourth plague inflicted on Egypt before Pharaoh agreed to release Israel from bondage. When he did, Moses asked God to remove the swarms of flies, which then disappeared. But Pharaoh went back on his word, leading to worse plagues.

Ecclesiastes 10:1 mentions the insects: "Dead flies make the perfumer's ointment give off a foul odor; so a little folly outweighs wisdom and honor."

FLINT

LIKE THE HARDEST STONE,
HARDER THAN FLINT, I HAVE
MADE YOUR FOREHEAD . . . .
–EZEKIEL 3:9

The hard quartz known as flint is commonly found in the chalky ground of the Holy Land. Flint can be worked to produce a very sharp edge, and from prehistory into biblical times people shaped pieces of flint into tools and weapons. Moses' wife used "a flint" to circumcise their son (Ex 4:25). People also struck flint against iron to ignite a fire. The Bible stresses flint's extreme hardness. Setting one's face "like flint" was a sign of determination (Isa 50:7); causing water to flow from flinty rock, as God did to provide for the Israelites in the desert, was a miracle (Deut 8:15).

Flint provided excellent material for hand axes, left, as well as knives and other tools.

FLOCK

SHEPHERD YOUR PEOPLE
WITH YOUR STAFF, THE FLOCK
THAT BELONGS TO YOU . . . .
–MICAH 7:14

A flock is usually a group of SHEEP or goats. The word is often used in the book of Psalms and the New Testament to refer to the people of God. In Psalm 78:52, for example, the psalmist says that God led the Israelites "in the wilderness like a flock." In Matthew 26:31, when predicting that his disciples would

desert him, Jesus paraphrases the prophecy that the Lord would call for his shepherd to be killed and his flock scattered (Zech 13: 7). In John 10:14–16, Jesus identifies himself as the "good shepherd" and looks to the time when "there will be one flock, one shepherd."

FLOGGING

AFTER THEY HAD GIVEN THEM A SEVERE FLOGGING, THEY THREW THEM INTO PRISON . . . .
–ACTS OF THE APOSTLES 16:23

Flogging—beating someone with a whip or a rod—was an accepted means of punishment. Deuteronomy stipulates no more than 40 lashes for a guilty individual, lest the person be "degraded"(Deut 25:3). The number of strokes was later reduced to 39; Paul received this punishment several times. In the Gospel of Luke, Pilate recommends that Jesus be given a flogging as a warning to halt his preaching; however, Mark and Matthew indicate that the flogging that Jesus received was probably the severe chastisement given to a person who was condemned to be crucified.

The flogging of Jesus is depicted on the bronze doors of a basilica from the 11th or 12th century.

FLOOD

"FOR MY PART, I AM GOING TO BRING A FLOOD OF WATERS ON THE EARTH . . . ."
–GENESIS 6:17

The dramatic story of the flood as recorded in Genesis, in which God deluged the world with water to destroy human beings for their sinful ways, echoes earlier tales in the ancient Near East. From its many similarities to Mesopotamian flood stories—which also featured a virtuous hero, an ark, and animals, for example—there little doubt that the Old Testament version takes its inspiration from other earlier epics.

Was there ever such a devastating flood, one that may have inspired these stories? Overflowing waters were common in the low region between the Tigris and Euphrates rivers, but archaeologists and geologists have found no evidence that a massive deluge ever took place. Nor have archaeologists found an ark.

Although earlier flood stories were told to illustrate problems of overpopulation, the biblical flood story portrays God's displeasure with humankind's moral misdeeds. In Genesis, God says to Noah, "I have determined to make an end of all flesh, for the earth is filled with violence because of them" (Gen 6:13). See also ARK.

FLOOR

"HIS WINNOWING FORK IS IN HIS HAND, TO CLEAR HIS THRESHING FLOOR . . . ."–LUKE 3:17

Floors in ancient homes and other structures varied according to the economic status of the owner. The simplest floors consisted of tamped or rolled dirt; others were of pebble or stone. The wealthiest people could afford intricate mosaics. Solomon's temple had a cypress wood floor overlaid with gold (1 Kings 6:15, 30). A floor for THRESHING was usually a flat, hard surface used communally by farmers to process their harvests. Grain, such as wheat and barley, was piled atop the floor and then crushed to remove the seed coverings prior to winnowing.

FLOWERS

THE FLOWERS APPEAR ON THE EARTH; THE TIME OF SINGING HAS COME, AND THE VOICE OF THE TURTLEDOVE IS HEARD IN OUR LAND.
–SONG OF SOLOMON 2:12

The Holy Land was blessed with numerous wildflowers. The sudden coming of spring that carpeted the brown hills with colors inspired biblical poets; however, they were soon reminded within a few weeks—when the beauty of the flowers withered as the summer sun parched the soil—of the brevity of life. Still, there was a reality more enduring than the short-lived blooms: "The grass withers, the flower fades; but the word of our God will stand forever" (Isa 40:8).

In these three examples of ancient flutes, two are made of reed and a fragment of one is made of bone.

Flute

... YOU WILL MEET A BAND OF PROPHETS COMING DOWN FROM THE SHRINE WITH HARP, TAMBOURINE, FLUTE, AND LYRE PLAYING IN FRONT OF THEM ....
–1 SAMUEL 10:5

The flute, also translated as "pipe" (Job 21:12), is the primary wind instrument mentioned in the Bible. It was used during biblical times in religious ceremonies as well as on other occasions. Most ancient Near Eastern flutes consisted of two pipes of ivory, reed, or metal joined together, each with a reed mouthpiece. The reed was single, as in the modern clarinet, or double, as in the oboe. The pipes usually had three to five finger holes, which were covered and then released simultaneously to produce varying sounds. Since the two flute pipes were played together, one probably provided a kind of droning background. Flute players trilled brightly at joyous feasts and festivals but also wailed plaintively at funerals (Mt 9:23).

On the gateway of a German cathedral is a scene from the parable of the ten bridesmaids. The foolish maids, right, went to get oil for their lamps and were shut out of the wedding upon their return (Mt 25:1–13).

Food

"THEN PREPARE FOR ME SAVORY FOOD, SUCH AS I LIKE, AND BRING IT TO ME TO EAT ...."
–GENESIS 27:4

Bread, olive oil, and wine were standard fare for people living in the biblical era (Sir 39:26). Milk and cheese were provided by herds of sheep and goats. Because MEAT was expensive, the Israelites' diet was largely vegetarian. It included fruits—especially grapes and figs—and vegetables, such as beans, garlic, onions, and cucumbers. Lentil stew, for which the hungry Esau traded his birthright (Gen 25:29–34), was a common dish. On the special occasions when meat, such as a fatted ox, was served, it had to be butchered in accordance with strict dietary laws. Nuts and wild honey were considered delicacies.

Fool

THE HEART OF THE WISE INCLINES TO THE RIGHT, BUT THE HEART OF A FOOL TO THE LEFT.
–ECCLESIASTES 10:2

According to the Bible, anyone who denies the existence of God or who ignores God's laws is a fool. More than merely simple-minded, these unwise, ungodly people who live lives of folly stand in contrast to the faithful, who choose WISDOM in the knowledge of God: "The fear of the LORD is the beginning of knowledge; fools despise wisdom and instruction" (Prov 1:7).

Throughout the Bible the foolish person is depicted as one who is self-centered and thoughtless, living a reckless life in ignorance of God and his teachings. Says the book of Proverbs, "Doing wrong is like sport to a fool, but wise conduct is pleasure to a person of understanding" (Prov 10:23).

Those who see the errors of their way and deliberately continue to live foolish lives by sinning against God's laws are damned. Nevertheless, branding someone a fool was not to be done lightly. Anyone who does, said Jesus, "will be liable to the hell of fire" (Mt 5:22).

Foot

Do not swerve to the right or to the left; turn your foot away from evil.
–Proverbs 4:27

Because most ancient roads were not paved, feet became dirty quickly, and many of the customs recorded in the Bible developed as a result. A guest was welcomed by having his feet washed (Judg 19:21) or even anointed with oil. This service was performed by the lowest of the household slaves. Thus when Jesus washed the feet of his disciples (Jn 13:5–16), he was providing them with a vivid example of humble service to others.

Dusty SANDALS were removed and the feet were bathed before entering sacred precincts. Going barefoot could be a part of the mourning ritual. Moses was commanded to remove his sandals when standing on holy ground (Ex 3:5), and Isaiah similarly was ordered to take off his sandals as a symbol that Egypt would be conquered (Isa 20:2–4).

As removing even a particle of dust from a place was likely considered a kind of bond, a person could show contempt for a city or its people by shaking off its dust from his feet (Lk 9:5). The term *feet* could also represent the entire person, as in "'Their feet are swift to shed blood'" (Rom 3:15). Sitting at the feet of another person denoted great respect, and falling at a person's feet was an act of supplication.

Molded bronze strips adorned the ninth-century BC palace door of the Assyrian king Shalmaneser III, shown above with his entourage of attendants and footmen.

Footmen

So Jehoahaz was left with an army of not more than fifty horsemen, ten chariots and ten thousand footmen . . . .
–2 Kings 13:7

In some biblical passages, footmen were specifically infantry; in others, they were soldiers of all kinds. The word also may have referred to any male who was subject to military conscription. In the early days of the kingdom, a body of 50 footmen ran before the royal chariot to protect Absalom (2 Sam 15:1) and guarded royal or military precincts. They also served as court messengers, running throughout the kingdom with important messages committed to memory. Eventually the courier system employed by the Persian emperor Cyrus was adopted, and messages were written down (Esth 3:13).

Forced Labor

King Solomon conscripted forced labor out of all Israel . . . .
–1 Kings 5:13

When Israel conquered Canaan, some of the native inhabitants were conscripted into forced labor in menial work or building projects (Judg 1:28,30). King David instituted a government ministry of forced labor, and Solomon greatly expanded its reach, forcing people to labor in the building of the temple (2 Chr 2:2) and his royal palace. Farmers, palace workers, and craftsmen were enrolled in his projects. Under Solomon's son Rehoboam, plans to continue conscription among the northern tribes were apparently a major factor contributing to the revolt that split the nation into two kingdoms.

Throughout the ancient Near East, defeated peoples could be forced to supply labor to their conquerors, and noncitizens were liable to conscription. In Egypt, the Israelites had been conscripted into labor gangs. In Assyria, citizens owed public service to the empire, as soldiers or laborers, on state projects such as the construction of buildings and canals, but could evade the obligation by paying someone else to do the job.

FOREHEAD

BIND THEM AS A SIGN ON YOUR HAND, FIX THEM AS AN EMBLEM ON YOUR FOREHEAD . . . .
–DEUTERONOMY 6:8

In the Bible, the forehead was said to reveal a person's personality by conveying defiance or rebelliousness. A hard forehead indicated determination not to change or, as in Ezekiel 3:8–9, God-given courage. Examining the forehead was one of the ways a priest diagnosed leprosy (Lev 13:42–43). An EMBLEM worn on the forehead was a sign of loyalty to God (Deut 11:18). Throughout the ancient Near East, the forehead was often covered by a band or other headpiece, but the lower brow remained exposed.

FORERUNNER

WE HAVE THIS HOPE . . . A HOPE THAT ENTERS THE INNER SHRINE BEHIND THE CURTAIN, WHERE JESUS, A FORERUNNER ON OUR BEHALF, HAS ENTERED . . . .
–HEBREWS 6:19–20

In biblical times, a forerunner was a military scout or FOOTMAN. In the letter to the Hebrews, its author called Jesus the forerunner who went ahead of humankind to sit at the right hand of God. Military commanders often sent scouts ahead of the army to make way for its advance. Although not called a forerunner, by declaring that "one who is more powerful than I is coming after me" (Mt 3:11), John the Baptist performed the role in announcing the coming of Jesus.

FOREST

WAIL, OAKS OF BASHAN, FOR THE THICK FOREST HAS BEEN FELLED!
–ZECHARIAH 11:2

In biblical times the hillsides of the Holy Land were green with forests, which covered the central hill country and extended to Galilee and Bashan. To the north, Lebanon was renowned for its majestic cedars and cypress trees. King Solomon used so much cedar in the construction of his palace complex that a part of it was called the House of the Forest of the Lebanon (1 Kings 7:2–5). Timber was used domestically for fuel and construction, as well as exported. Forests were also valuable in time of war: the foothills west of Jerusalem had thick woods that frustrated invaders.

FORGIVENESS

". . . FOR THIS IS MY BLOOD OF THE COVENANT, WHICH IS POURED OUT FOR MANY FOR THE FORGIVENESS OF SINS."–MATTHEW 26:28

The Bible uses an array of vivid images to explain what it means to forgive someone and to be forgiven by God. Perhaps the clearest example is found in the prophet Micah's expression of gratitude to the Lord: "You will cast all our sins into the depths of the sea" (Mic 7:19). Isaiah takes the theme of divine forgiveness even further by speaking on behalf of God, saying, "I will not remember your sins" (Isa 43:25).

In the Bible, a person forgiven is a person whose sins are said to be "blotted out" (Isa 6:7) or "washed away" (Acts 22:16)

In forgiveness, a relationship shattered by an offense is restored to health. This restoration, in Old Testament times, took place only after the offending person confessed the sin and offered a sacrifice set by law. If the offender had damaged someone's property, the law required RESTITUTION. Compensation for one slaughtered sheep, for example, was four sheep.

New Testament writers proclaimed that after the sacrifice of Jesus, further sacrifices were no longer necessary. Instead, wrote John, "If we confess our sins, he who is faithful and just will forgive us our sins" (1 Jn 1:9). Jesus encouraged people to forgive one another. When Peter asked him if seven times was often enough, Jesus suggested "seventy-seven times" (Mt 18: 21–22)—meaning that there was no limit to forgiveness—yet he also claimed blasphemy against the Holy Spirit was an unforgivable sin (Mk 3:29–30). Some scholars assert that Jesus was referring to a spiritual callousness that refuses to acknowledge God, as he made the statement after scribes attributed his miracles to Satan.

Forgiveness is the message in this detail depicting the return of the prodigal son.

Fornication

The body is meant not for fornication but for the Lord and the Lord for the body.
–1 Corinthians 6:13

The word *fornication* appears only in the New Testament and Apocrypha, where it carries the broad meaning of "sexual immorality." Although Jesus taught the crowd in the temple that "the prostitutes are going into the kingdom of God ahead of you" (Mt 21:31), he nonetheless called fornication "an evil intention" (Mk 7:21). Paul repeatedly denounced sexual immorality, partly because of the loose lifestyles of the people he sought to convert. The Old Testament sets out specific rules for sexual behavior, forbidding ADULTERY as well as incest, homosexuality, and perverse sexual practices (Lev 18).

Only ruins remain today of the fortified city of Megiddo. Because of its strategic location, the city was destroyed and rebuilt dozens of times in the course of 3,000 years.

Fortification

He directed those who were doing the work to build the walls and encircle Mount Zion with squared stones, for better fortification . . . .–1 Maccabees 10:11

The oldest known fortifications in the Holy Land were at Jericho, dating from about 7000 BC. These fortresses predate all others by some 4,000 years. Fortified cities were common by 3000 BC, as their inhabitants increasingly found themselves under attack by the marauding armies of great empires. Walls, towers, and gates of mud brick were raised upon stone foundations to repel enemies.

David and Solomon created Israel's first nationwide system of forts, using field stone for foundations and walls. Such forts stood guard over vulnerable mountain passes, main highways, or border sites. During the frequent invasions of biblical times, people came from miles around to gain protection inside city walls. Fortified cities also served as important administrative or military centers for their surrounding regions. Specialized forts included chariot cities, where the chariot corps was stationed, and store cities that functioned as military supply centers. In Solomon's day, well-cut limestone blocks known as ashlars were often used in double-wall construction. Herod the Great enclosed Jerusalem and other cities with massive walls of stone that had corner towers and buttresses.

Foundation

When the builders laid the foundation of the temple of the LORD, the priests . . . were stationed to praise the LORD with trumpets . . . .
–Ezra 3:10

In the Bible, the word *foundation* is used both literally and figuratively. A foundation was the base upon which a building or even a city was constructed. The word was also used as a figure of speech. As the psalmist sang of God, "Righteousness and justice are the foundation of your throne" (Ps 89:14).

For laying the foundations of ancient structures, builders preferred bedrock. The best alternative was a platform of several layers of carefully cut, tight-fitting rocks. King Solomon ordered stonecutters to build the foundation of the temple with quarried, trimmed blocks (1 Kings 5:17). Most homes rested on one or more layers of rough rocks, covered with dirt. Laying the foundation of a building was often considered a time for rejoicing.

Biblical writers spoke of God laying the "foundation of the earth" (Job 38:4), referring to creation. In the New Testament, Jesus was described as the foundation of the church (1 Cor 3:11). Paul wrote that the rich, through generosity and good deeds, were building for themselves in the next age "a good foundation" (1 Tim 6:19).

FOUNTAIN

THE FEAR OF THE LORD IS A FOUNTAIN OF LIFE, SO THAT ONE MAY AVOID THE SNARES OF DEATH.
–PROVERBS 14:27

Created by the extensive limestone deposits of the Holy Land, fountains are springs of WATER flowing from the earth. The Promised Land, Moses assured his people, was "a good land, a land . . . with springs and underground waters" (Deut 8:7). Israel's wealth of fountains drew both nomads and permanent settlers, and as a result many place names contain the Hebrew root *en*, meaning spring. The Fountain Gate of Jerusalem was named for its proximity to the En-rogel springs.

Fountains can represent chaos in the Bible: the flood is partly caused by an upsurging of the "fountains of the great deep" (Gen 7:11) Yet a fountain can also stand for God's bounty. The description of God as a "fountain of living water" (Jer 2:13) is echoed by Jesus, who promises the Samaritan woman at the well "a spring of water gushing up to eternal life" (Jon 4: 13–14).

In the marshes along the banks of the Nile, a fowler uses heron decoys and a throwing-stick as a lure to snare his prey in this detail from a 15th-century BC Egyptian tomb painting.

FOWLER

FOR SCOUNDRELS ARE FOUND AMONG MY PEOPLE; THEY TAKE OVER THE GOODS OF OTHERS. LIKE FOWLERS THEY SET A TRAP; THEY CATCH HUMAN BEINGS.
–JEREMIAH 5:26–27

Fowlers, or bird catchers, were common in biblical times. They provided birds as food, caged pets, and sacrifices. Fowling was also considered a sport and a source of amusement.

Because fowlers often hunted birds by capturing them in traps, the word is sometimes used in the Bible as a warning of danger. A psalmist rejoices, "We have escaped like a bird from the snare of the fowlers" (Ps 124:7), and Proverbs 6:5 advises a youth to "save yourself . . . like a bird from the hand of the fowler." The passage cited from Jeremiah compares those who exploit others to gain wealth with fowlers who snare edible fowl beyond their needs.

FOX

HE SAID TO THEM, "GO AND TELL THAT FOX FOR ME, 'LISTEN, I AM CASTING OUT DEMONS AND PERFORMING CURES . . . .'"
–LUKE 13:32

The fox, a swift, doglike animal similar to the JACKAL, is often used as a symbol for cunning and resourcefulness. When Jesus was warned to leave Galilee because Herod Antipas wanted him killed, he compared Herod with a fox, which in this context meant sly and deceitful. The Hebrew word for fox may also imply insignificance. As Nehemiah rebuilt Jerusalem's walls, a critic taunted, "That stone wall they are building—any fox going up on it would break it down!" (Neh 4:3). Ezekiel likens false prophets to "jackals" that lurk among ruins (Ezek 13:4).

FRAME

YOU SHALL MAKE UPRIGHT FRAMES OF ACACIA WOOD FOR THE TABERNACLE.
–EXODUS 26:15

The Bible describes several kinds of frames, most of which are associated with the tabernacle. One was the framework for the tent tabernacle itself—45 feet long and 15 feet wide and high—across which the curtains were spread. Another was a brace that supported the legs for a tabernacle table that held the sacred bread. A third was a leather-covered frame for carrying tabernacle lamps and utensils. Another usage of *frame*—"you knit me together in my mother's womb. . . . My frame was not hidden from you" (Ps 139:13, 15)—refers to a human embryo.

FRANKINCENSE

. . . OPENING THEIR TREASURE CHESTS, THEY OFFERED HIM GIFTS OF GOLD, FRANKINCENSE, AND MYRRH.
–MATTHEW 2:11

Used to make perfumes and incense, frankincence was a costly gum resin imported from Arabia. It had important religious uses as an ingredient of holy anointing oil, as part of the burnt offering, and as part of the flour mixture for the grain offering (Lev 2:1). Frankincense, along with oil, was specifically banned as part of the sin offering, perhaps because of its festive associations (Lev 5:11). The gifts of the Magi who came to worship the Christ child included frankincense. The gift of frankincense has been interpreted as referring to Jesus' symbolic priesthood.

Frankincense, an aromatic resin, oozes from the cut bark of the boswellia tree and hardens into yellowish white beads, above.

FREEDOM

NOW THE LORD IS THE SPIRIT, AND WHERE THE SPIRIT OF THE LORD IS, THERE IS FREEDOM.
–2 CORINTHIANS 3:17

Freedom from oppression is among the major themes of the Bible, but the people of ancient times perceived freedom differently from the way it is understood today. For example, they did not believe that all individuals had an inalienable right to unfettered freedom of thought and action. Rather, freedom was mainly understood as liberty from slavery. The liberation of the descendants of Jacob from slavery in Egypt is the great theme sounded in the book of Exodus, and it echoes throughout the Bible. God's love and mercy liberated the Israelites, who by remaining faithful to his laws could retain their freedom in the face of onslaughts by foreign oppressors from Egypt, Assyria, and Babylon.

The New Testament presents a variation on this theme in its claim that Jesus Christ brought liberation from sin and death for those who abide by his teachings (Jn 8:34–36, 51). Paradoxically, human beings gain the blessings of freedom through bondage to God and his commandments. See also SLAVERY.

FRUIT

. . . SHE TOOK OF ITS FRUIT AND ATE; AND SHE ALSO GAVE SOME TO HER HUSBAND, WHO WAS WITH HER, AND HE ATE.–GENESIS 3:6

The Holy Land was rich in fruit, such as olives, figs, and grapes. According to Mosaic law, the fruit of a newly planted tree could not be eaten until after the fourth year, when it was dedicated to the Lord (Lev 19:23–25). Fruit was often used as a metaphor for the consequences of human actions: the fruit of obeying God was a reward, but sin yielded punishment. Isaiah foresaw Damascus lying in ruins, where just a few olives at the top of a fruit tree offer scant food for gleaning (Isa 17:6).

FUEL

THROUGH THE WRATH OF THE LORD . . . THE PEOPLE BECAME LIKE FUEL FOR THE FIRE . . . .–ISAIAH 9:19

The Israelites relied on many kinds of fuel to stoke the fires, braziers, and ovens they used for cooking and heating. Wood and charcoal were the most common sources. Charcoal, which burned hotter, was the fuel of choice for metalworking. Grass, vines, branch trimmings, thorn bushes, and shrubs were also used as fuel. The Israelites burned animal DUNG to heat their bread ovens, using human waste only in extreme circumstances. Whenever the Bible refers to coal, which was unknown in the Near East of biblical times, charcoal is the fuel that is meant.

FULLER

FOR HE IS LIKE A REFINER'S FIRE AND LIKE FULLERS' SOAP . . . .
–MALACHI 3:2

Fullers of biblical times had the task of shrinking, cleansing, and thickening new wool and cloth (see box, p. 146). To prepare wool or cloth for dying, the fuller washed it with lye and treaded on it. The cloth was then spread on a field to be bleached in the sun. Fullers' fields were located outside of towns because of the odor the process produced. Fullers also washed clothing and sometimes traded in textiles. Reference was made to the fuller's trade in the account of the transfiguration, when Jesus' clothes "became dazzling white, such as no one on earth could bleach them" (Mk 9:3).

Fulling

When cloth comes from the loom, it is stiff and unattractive. Fulling helps to fluff and shrink the fibers and create a supple, beautiful cloth. In the ancient Mediterranean world, as in these depictions of the Roman period, cloth of linen or cotton was beaten with wooden mallets to make it soft, but wool was usually trampled. Linen and cotton were bleached in the sun; wool was bleached by the fumes of sulfuric acid.

1. To finish woolen cloth, fullers first wash it by treading it in tubs filled with water and an alkali such as soda or fuller's earth. The agitation softens and felts the fibers. The cloth is rinsed to clean and shrink it further.

2. The damp cloth is brushed to create a nap. The paddle-shaped brush has bristles of sharp thorns.

3. The cloth is draped over a padded table, and a worker uses large shears to clip the nap to a uniform height. This gives the cloth a luxurious surface and helps to hide any flaws or irregularities in the weaving.

4. Bleaching woolen cloth, such as these togas, is done outdoors. Workers spread the cloth over wicker frames and expose it to fumes of burning sulfur coming from buckets under the frames.

5. The folded cloth is placed between boards and pressed. The pressure gives the cloth a smooth surface and enhances its luster, especially if it has been washed in fuller's earth.

6. As an added service, many fulleries dye their cloth. Here a customer selects a length of colorful, finished fabric.

FURNACE

SEE, I HAVE REFINED YOU, BUT NOT LIKE SILVER; I HAVE TESTED YOU IN THE FURNACE OF ADVERSITY.
–ISAIAH 48:10

Depending on the scriptural context, a furnace could be an oven for baking bread, a kiln for firing pottery, or a crucible for smelting metal. The furnace into which King Nebuchadnezzar's guards cast Shadrach, Meshach, and Abednego (Dan 3:19–20) was probably a large kiln normally used to make bricks or smelt ores. The Bible uses the idea of the red-hot furnace to describe the testing of a person's faith or to suggest divine punishment. In Matthew 13:42, Jesus depicts hell as "the furnace of fire."

FURNITURE

AND I WAS VERY ANGRY, AND I THREW ALL THE HOUSEHOLD FURNITURE OF TOBIAH OUT OF THE ROOM.–NEHEMIAH 13:8

Israelite homes had little furniture. A poor family might own straw mats or animal skins for sleeping and basic kitchen equipment, such as jars for food and water, a stone and clay oven, and a grinding mill for preparing grain. In lieu of chairs, a low ledge generally ran along one or more sides of a room. Richer people might have thick, woven mattresses supported by wood or bronze bedsteads, chairs, a low table or two, and storage chests. Although Amos mentions wooden pieces inlaid with ivory, most furniture was functional rather than aesthetic.

The tabernacle contained furniture. The court contained an altar and a LAVER; the outer room, or holy place, housed the table of the bread of the Presence, a lampstand, and the altar of incense; and the inner room, or most holy place, held the ark of the covenant.

This lead weight has an inscription in GREEK *that refers to the "Inspector of Markets." The weight dates from* AD *23 and was apparently from the city of Gaza, located on the southeastern coast of the Mediterranean Sea.*

Galatians, Letter of Paul to the

You foolish Galatians! Who has bewitched you?
–Galatians 3:1

Paul's letter to the Galatians was addressed to Gentile churches apparently on the brink of abandoning his teaching that salvation comes only through faith in Christ. Paul had started these churches in what is now central Turkey. Jewish Christians who arrived after him, however, began teaching that the Gentiles needed to enter the covenant that God made with Abraham by converting to Judaism and obeying Jewish laws, such as those involving circumcision. Paul wrote the Galatians that Abraham had been declared righteous and blessed by God before such laws had been given, and that through Jesus' crucifixion, God's promises had been fulfilled. The apostle explained, "There is no longer Jew or Greek . . . if you belong to Christ, then you are Abraham's offspring" (Gal 3:28–29).

Galbanum

Take . . . stacte, and onycha, and galbanum, sweet spices with pure frankincense . . . and make an incense . . . .–Exodus 30:34–35

Galbanum, a brownish yellow gum resin, was obtained from the sap of plants growing in Persia. The resin has a strong, pungent smell, which has been compared to that of balsam, and a bitter taste. During biblical times, galbanum had a medicinal use as an antispasmodic.

As given in Exodus, God's instructions to Moses for making sacred incense were very specific. They called for equal parts of galbanum and two other spices, stacte and onycha, as well as frankincense. These ingredients were to be blended and then seasoned with salt.

In the book of Ecclesiasticus, the personified figure of Wisdom refers to the spice—"and like choice myrrh I spread my fragrance, like galbanum, onycha, and stacte, and like the odor of incense in the tent" (Sir 24:15).

Galilean

When Pilate heard this, he asked whether the man was a Galilean.
–Luke 23:6

After being under foreign rule for about 750 years, Galilee had retained a Gentile population that exerted considerable cultural influence in the time of Jesus. Jewish inhabitants of the region, located in the northern part of the Holy Land, were misunderstood by mainstream Jews. Although sometimes considered unruly, Jewish Galilee was stable economically and politically. Accepting Greek culture in varying degrees, Galileans were dismissed as religiously lax or even sinful, but the area later became a major center of Jewish learning. Thought to be provincial farmers and fishermen, many Galileans actually lived in densely settled areas crossed by international commercial routes, and they engaged in trade and some manufacturing.

Gall

. . . they offered him wine to drink, mixed with gall; but when he tasted it, he would not drink it.
–Matthew 27:34

According to Matthew, when Jesus was about to be crucified he was offered wine laced with gall, a bitter-tasting herb thought to reduce pain. In Mark's Gospel, the drink contained myrrh (Mk 15:23), also believed to be a narcotic. Some presume that Jesus refused the drink because he wanted to remain conscious until his death.

In the Bible, *gall* can also refer to bile, the fluid secreted by the liver (Job 16:13). Peter uses the word figuratively when he tells a former magician, "I see that you are in the gall of bitterness and the chains of wickedness" (Acts 8:23).

Gallery

. . . the chambers rose gallery by gallery in three stories.
–Ezekiel 42:3

The temple that the prophet Ezekiel saw in a vision had an architectural feature that is translated as "gallery." But the meaning of the Hebrew word, used only in the book of Ezekiel, is uncertain. Some scholars have speculated that a gallery was a terrace or ledge. Thus, when Ezekiel spoke of the priests' rooms rising three stories, "gallery by gallery," he may have been describing balconies or the terraced levels of the building, with each floor smaller than the one beneath it. He states that the three "upper chambers" were narrower than chambers that had no galleries and that they "had no pillars like the pillars of the outer court" (Ezek 42:6).

According to other interpretations, the word may refer to a corridor outside the rooms or a hillside rock formation protruding into the building and incorporated into the design.

Games

When the quadrennial games were being held at Tyre and the king was present, the vile Jason sent envoys . . . .
–2 Maccabees 4:18

Games of different kinds, including athletic competitions and board games, enjoyed varying degrees of popularity. Although biblical passages indicate that the Israelites were familiar with footraces, wrestling matches, and archery contests, sporting events are virtually absent from the Old Testament. The Greeks and Romans, by contrast, were enthusiastic about sports, including boxing, javelin- and discus-throwing, and horse- and chariot racing. The quadrennial games mentioned in 2 Maccabees were athletic contests held every four years in Tyre, a port north of the Holy Land. They date at least from the time of Alexander the Great.

Archaeologists have found a number of board games, indicating their wide popularity in ancient Near Eastern cultures. A game board with 14 round playing pieces was found at Ur, dating from the 26th century BC. The board consists of squares inlaid with bold geometric patterns fashioned of shells. The oldest known board, a clay tablet marked with squares that was unearthed in Egypt, dates from 4000 BC and features cone-shaped pieces. One of the most popular board games was a version of checkers, which differed from the modern version in one respect: players did not choose their own moves, which were instead determined by tossing dice or other objects. Games of chance made use of dice, bones, or sticks. A popular game called hounds and jackals had pieces in the shape of those two creatures, which were moved around a board according to the toss of animal knucklebones. Archaeologists have unearthed examples of this game in Egypt and Mesopotamia.

In the two examples of ancient senet games from Arad, above, pieces were placed in holes. Game boards scratched into a segment from the courtyard of Herod's temple, right, were possibly made by Jesus' guards.

Garden

. . . therefore the LORD God sent him forth from the garden of Eden, to till the ground from which he was taken.
–Genesis 3:23

Created by God, the first garden, called Eden, was beautiful and abundant—a perfect paradise specially designed for human needs. Like the human owner of an earthly garden, the Lord strolled there in the cool air of evening. When Adam and Eve disobeyed his command, God not only cast them out of the garden but also cursed the ground, which would now bring forth "thorns and thistles" (Gen 3:18). Genesis 2:8 says that Eden was "in the east," perhaps putting it somewhere near the head of the Persian Gulf; however, Ezekiel places it on "the holy mountain of God" (Ezek 28:14), which may refer to Mount Zaphon. Down through the ages, the garden of Eden has remained a symbol of divine blessing. To some biblical prophets, this paradise was also an image of the restored Israel after the Babylonian exile.

Typically, the lush gardens of the ancient Near East were protected by hedges or walls of stone or mudbrick. Situated near the owner's dwelling, the enclosure often had a single gate that could be locked. In biblical lands, a nearby and reliable source of water was essential. In Egypt workers dug shallow ditches for IRRIGATION through the beds or used watering vessels.

Aside from producing vegetables, fruits, and spices, gardens were prized for their flowering beauty, midday coolness, and solitude. A person could retreat to the garden to pray and meditate or invite friends and relatives there for a joyous feast. The Israelites' neighbors sometimes offered sacrifices or held other religious ceremonies in their gardens. The tombs of ancestors were often built within garden compounds. According to the Gospel of John, Joseph of Arimathea and Nicodemus buried Jesus in a "new tomb" in a garden (Jn 19:38–42), recalling the tradition of laying the kings of Judah to rest in garden tombs.

The largest gardens were owned by royalty, who employed many gardeners to seed and water the grounds. The most celebrated was King Nebuchadnezzar's so-called Hanging Gardens of Babylon, apparently built within his palace walls on terraces and considered one of the seven wonders of the ancient world. Other monarchs in Mesopotamia and Egypt maintained gardens; the most notable near the Holy Land belonged to the Canaanite kings at Ugarit, where an opulent royal palace boasted a courtyard garden. In Jerusalem, the well-known "king's garden," which was near one of the city gates, provided a covert route of escape. The garden of Gethsemane was not only the site of Jesus' arrest but also a favorite meeting place for him and his disciples.

Egyptian women make garlands from roses in this detail from an early 20th-century painting.

GARLAND

THE CROWN OF THE WISE IS THEIR WISDOM, BUT FOLLY IS THE GARLAND OF FOOLS.
–PROVERBS 14:24

A garland is a wreath placed on the head. Winning athletes often received laurel wreaths to wear as crowns. In the Bible, a "fair garland" (Prov 1:9) can stand for both wisdom and the benefits conferred by wisdom; it also signifies joy and honor. The book of Isaiah compares God's granting of salvation to the nation of Israel with a wedding at which "a bridegroom decks himself with a garland" (Isa 61:10).

An incident that takes place in Acts of the Apostles reflects the fact that artists of the time often portrayed Greek gods wearing garlands: when Paul performs a miracle in Lystra, he and the apostle Barnabas are proclaimed to be gods, and a priest of Zeus brings oxen and garlands to please them (Acts 14:8–13).

GARLIC

"WE REMEMBER THE FISH WE USED TO EAT IN EGYPT FOR NOTHING, THE CUCUMBERS, THE MELONS, THE LEEKS, THE ONIONS, AND THE GARLIC . . . ."–NUMBERS 11:5

Wandering endlessly in the desert toward Canaan, the Israelites complained bitterly to Moses that there was no meat and nothing but MANNA to eat. They missed the food they had eaten during their captivity in Egypt. Garlic, related to the onion and a member of the lily family, was one of the foods the Israelites had enjoyed in Egypt, where the plant grew profusely.

The bulbous vegetable added its very strong aroma and flavor to other foods when used as a seasoning. Garlic was also believed to have medicinal value.

GARRISON

DAVID WAS THEN IN THE STRONGHOLD; AND THE GARRISON OF THE PHILISTINES WAS THEN AT BETHLEHEM.
–1 CHRONICLES 11:16

A garrison was a body of defense forces that often occupied enemy or subject territories. Garrisons were essential to political and military policy in ancient times. The Philistines set up several in Israel in the 11th century BC, presenting a tough challenge for King Saul. In fact, the first victory in the war against the Philistines was his son Jonathan's defeat of the garrison occupying Geba. According to 1 Samuel 13:3, the king, in celebration of Jonathan's victory, "blew the trumpet throughout all the land, saying, 'Let the Hebrews hear!'" Later King David established garrisons that consolidated his control of Syria and Edom.

GATE

YOU SHOULD NOT HAVE ENTERED THE GATE OF MY PEOPLE ON THE DAY OF THEIR CALAMITY . . . .
–OBADIAH 1:13

People entered walled cities, palaces, and the temple complex through what the Bible calls gates. The city gate became a combination community center, city hall, and market square. It was there that people met to talk with friends, city elders and kings held court, and merchants displayed their wares. The merchandise sold sometimes spawned the name of the gate, such as Jerusalem's Fish Gate, Sheep Gate, and Horse Gate.

Throughout the Bible, the word *gate* also symbolizes security and strength. Most city gateways featured massive double doors made of wood, some plated with bronze or iron to protect them from being set on fire by attacking soldiers. Others were crafted of solid stone slabs. The first-century Jewish historian Josephus wrote that the Beautiful Gate in Herod's temple was made of solid bronze. The other nine temple doors were plated with silver and gold.

When invading armies targeted a fortified city, they often focused their attack on the gate, because it was usually the weakest part of the wall. City builders knew this and designed the doors so that a gatekeeper, or DOORKEEPER, could quickly swing them closed and secure them with timber or metal bars. On the walls above each side of the gate were towers that held squads of defenders.

Larger cities often built small forts around the gate. Once invaders got past the outer gate, they found themselves surrounded by walls and blocked by an even more formidable inner gate. Beyond the main doors and beneath the towers lay a narrow corridor. In gateways from King Solomon's day, this entrance was usually about 10 yards long, with three rooms on each side for soldiers and supplies in times of war and for legal and commercial transactions in other times.

GAZELLE

. . . TURN, MY BELOVED, BE LIKE A GAZELLE OR A YOUNG STAG ON THE CLEFT MOUNTAINS.
–SONG OF SOLOMON 2:17

The gazelle, a small antelope, was so notable for its grace and comeliness that it was used as a symbol of love and beauty. Fawn-colored, light-footed, and with large, dark eyes, the gazelle was not only a delight to behold but also a source of meat, having been ruled a clean animal under Israelite dietary laws.

The hunted gazelle is used metaphorically in Proverbs 6:5 and Isaiah 13:14. However, the animal's speed made it hard to catch. For this reason, the fleet-footed youth Asahel was described "as swift of foot as a wild gazelle" (2 Sam 2:18).

A major gate in the wall of the Hittites' capital city, King's Gate had two sections. The armed deity sculpted into the gate in the left foreground offered additional protection.

Dry, scaly skin protects the hardy gecko from dehydration in the hot sun.

Gecko

. . . THE GECKO, THE LAND CROCODILE, THE LIZARD, THE SAND LIZARD, AND THE CHAMELEON. THESE ARE UNCLEAN . . . .
–LEVITICUS 11:30–31

The gecko, a member of the lizard family, was one of the animals specifically forbidden as food, according to Mosaic law. Known for the rapid chirping sounds it makes, which echo eerily across the desert floor, this reptile is found in great numbers in the Sinai and other desert areas. It has a dark, scaly skin covered with tough, wartlike bumps. The gecko is also known as a wall lizard because its suction-padded feet enable it to climb walls and scurry nimbly across ceilings. It is a night feeder, which searches the darkness for spiders and other INSECTS.

Genealogy

. . . THIS IS THE GENEALOGY OF THOSE WHO WENT UP WITH ME FROM BABYLONIA . . . .
–EZRA 8:1

Lists that chart the descent of a person or group, genealogies were common in biblical times. Perhaps the most famous examples of ancient genealogies are royal family trees. A kind of genealogy from 1800 BC, the Sumerian King List, names all the kings of Babylon back to the time of the flood. Others cover periods of up to 1,000 years and are not limited to royalty. Biblical genealogies take their form from these earlier examples. Among the more than 20 genealogies in the Old Testament, the most extensive—which covers the first nine chapters of 1 Chronicles—details the descendants of Adam up to the sixth century BC and includes hundreds of names.

Genealogies are usually traced through the male and are organized according to an ascending or descending scale. The genealogy of Jesus in Luke 3:23–38 is an ascending genealogy, which was commonly used to trace the ancestry of an individual back to an important historical figure. Conversely, descending genealogies begin with an ancestor and trace the generations forward in time. These generally include more information about the descendants, such as their age and accomplishments. Genesis 5:3, which begins, "When Adam had lived one hundred thirty years, he became the father of a son," 1 Chronicles 1–9, and Matthew 1:1–17 are examples of descending genealogies.

Because society was organized along familial and tribal lines in biblical times, genealogical records were important for establishing a person's lineage. Proving that one was related to a respected forefather was a way of ensuring social or religious prestige. For example, since only descendants of Aaron could become priests (Ex 28:1), temple officials examined a candidate's genealogy before approving him. Old Testament genealogies were also tangible reminders to the Israelites of their history as the chosen people.

Biblical genealogies are not exact or complete and should not be taken as historical fact. For example, the list of Aaron's descendants in 1 Chronicles 6:3–15 includes names that do not appear in Aaron's genealogy in Ezra (Ezra 7:1–5). Genealogies were included in the Old Testament primarily to establish a link with the past.

There are only two genealogies in the New Testament. The books of Matthew and Luke trace the ancestry of Jesus back to Abraham and Adam, respectively. Though there are many differences between the two genealogies, both were included in the Gospels to emphasize that Jesus was a son of David—the necessary lineage for the Messiah. See also ANCESTOR.

Jesus' descent from David is traced through Mary's lineage in Genealogy of the Virgin *by French painter Gerard David.*

GENERATION

. . . FROM GENERATION TO GENERATION WE WILL RECOUNT YOUR PRAISE.–PSALM 79:13

In the Old Testament, the word *generation* reflects a loosely defined time span rather than a specific number of years. For example, in Genesis a generation is said to be 100 years long, while in Numbers it is 60. Job, who lived 140 years, "saw his children, and his children's children, four generations" (Job 42:16), making each generation roughly 35 years long. A generation may denote a period from the birth—or death—of a father through the birth—or death—of his son. The term can refer generally to past ages (Isa 51:9) or to all of the people who were living at a certain time (Jer 2:31). In the New Testament, it may mean a specific group of people. For example, Jesus describes the scribes and Pharisees as "an evil and adulterous generation" (Mt 16:4).

GENESIS

IN THE BEGINNING WHEN GOD CREATED THE HEAVENS AND THE EARTH, THE EARTH WAS A FORMLESS VOID . . . . –GENESIS 1:1–2

The first book of the Bible, Genesis begins with the creation of the world and of the first human beings and ends with the death of Joseph and the settling of the Israelites in Egypt. The first chapters (Gen 1–11:9) recount the history of humanity through the stories of Adam and Eve, Noah, and the tower of Babel. They describe humankind's fall from God's favor, the near destruction of the world, and the scattering of people all over the earth. The final chapters (Gen 11:10–50:26) are the story of the patriarchs Abraham, Isaac, Jacob, and Joseph and their progeny. God summons Abraham to become father of the nation of Israel; through his descendants, "all the families of the earth shall be blessed" (Gen 12:3). Ancient tradition claims Moses as the author of Genesis, although modern scholars suggest it is made up of writings from various periods.

GENTILE

". . . IF YOU, THOUGH A JEW, LIVE LIKE A GENTILE AND NOT LIKE A JEW, HOW CAN YOU COMPEL THE GENTILES TO LIVE LIKE JEWS?" –GALATIANS 2:14

A Gentile is a non-Jew—one who is not a member of God's covenant nation of Israel. The term initially denoted a NATION, and Bible translators have also rendered it as "pagan" and "heathen," particularly when referring to religious practices of non-Jews. When God told Abraham, "I will make of you a great nation" (Gen 12:2), Abraham and his descendants were singled out for God's favor. Yet it was not until the Israelites were led to Sinai—where God revealed to Moses that they would be "a priestly kingdom and a holy nation" (Ex 19:6)—that they understood that they were uniquely separate from other peoples.

In the Promised Land the Israelites found and conquered seven nations, which they considered idolatrous and immoral. Deuteronomy counseled: "Do not intermarry with them . . . break down their altars, smash their pillars, hew down their sacred poles" (Deut 7:3, 5). After the period of exile, the Israelites' sense of themselves as an elect people grew even stronger, and the name of Gentile came to be applied to individuals as well as groups.

Despite prohibitions, Jews and Gentiles probably intermingled in many areas of daily life, including politics, trade, and even religion. In a postexilic prophecy, Israel was charged to be "a light to the nations" (Isa 42:6), bringing God's teaching and message to all. Although the leaders Ezra and Nehemiah commanded men to divorce their non-Jewish wives (Ezra 10:10–11; Neh 10:30), the edicts against intermarriage were not strictly followed: the Bible relates that Boaz wed the Moabite Ruth, and Esther's union with the Persian King Ahasuerus is nowhere condemned.

By the first century AD, distrust of Gentiles by some Jews was apparently so pronounced that the Roman historian Tacitus wrote, "[Jews] regard the rest of mankind with all the hatred of enemies." Herod the Great's temple in Jerusalem contained an outer "court of the Gentiles," beyond which no non-Jew was permitted to go. Nonetheless, some Gentiles were drawn to Jewish tenets and morality and became proselytes—converts to the Jewish faith. Others, who were sympathetic to Judaism

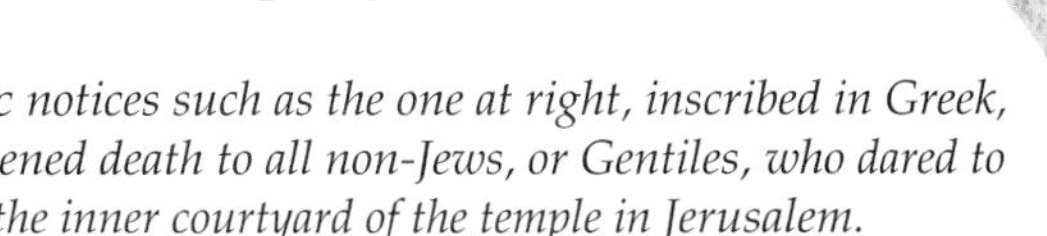

Public notices such as the one at right, inscribed in Greek, threatened death to all non-Jews, or Gentiles, who dared to enter the inner courtyard of the temple in Jerusalem.

but unwilling to be circumcised, earned themselves the name of God-fearers.

During his infancy, Jesus was proclaimed "a revelation to the Gentiles" (Lk 2:32), and as an adult, he is reported to have reached out to non-Jews in his ministry (Mt 8:5–13; Jn 4:4–29). Later, in the early days of the church, Paul undertook two missions among the Gentiles of Asia Minor. Paul believed that conversion to Judaism should not be required of people seeking to become Christians, and according to Acts of the Apostles, he won his case about AD 49. This victory helped to establish Christianity as a religion that was increasingly separate from Judaism.

Gesture

So Paul stood up and with a gesture began to speak.
–Acts of the Apostles 13:16

The people of the ancient Near East employed a rich variety of HAND, facial, and full-body gestures to enhance their spoken expression and to symbolize feelings, attitudes, and psychological states. The "lifting up" of the hands was often understood as a gesture of prayer (Neh 8:6). Standing while reading from Scripture was considered a gesture of respect; the act of spitting on someone was understood to be a profound insult (Deut 25:9; Mk 10:34). To seal an agreement, negotiators smacked their hands together, and mediators laid their hands on the heads of the opponents. A person in despair let his hands fall to his sides; a victor planted his foot upon the body of his vanquished foe. The verbal act of taking an oath might be accompanied by a physical gesture, such as placing the hand underneath the thigh of another (Gen 24:9).

Ghost

. . . your voice shall come from the ground like the voice of a ghost . . . .
–Isaiah 29:4

It was widely believed in biblical times that when a person died, the disembodied spirit went to Sheol, the place of the dead. Some people thought these ghosts could return to earth and take revenge for wrongs done to them in life. There is no evidence in the Bible, however, of avenging ghosts, although ghosts were apparently feared. When the disciples of Jesus saw him walking on water, as they sailed in the early hours of the morning, "they were terrified, saying, 'It is a ghost!' And they cried out in fear" (Mt 14:26). A thousand years earlier, a MEDIUM at Endor had conjured the spirit of Samuel at Saul's request; when Samuel's spirit appeared before her, the woman screamed (1 Sam 28:12).

Giant

These four were descended from the giants in Gath; they fell by the hands of David and his servants.
–2 Samuel 21:22

Like other ancient literature, the Bible contains many stories about giants, or beings of extraordinary stature. Genesis relates how, in the times before the flood, a race of huge people—"warriors of renown" (Gen 6:4)—lived on earth. These Nephilim were the descendants of sons of God who had married human women. When the Israelites struggled to conquer the tribes that occupied Canaan, they identified some of their enemies as Nephilim, such as the Anakim—a people so tall that the Israelites who spied on them felt "like grasshoppers" (Num 13:33).

Another race of giants the Israelites encountered were the Rephaim, whose name means "the hale ones" or "the healers." The last of the Rephaim was Og, king of Bashan, whom God delivered to the Israelites. After the slaughter, Og's gigantic iron bed was said to have been displayed in the city of Rabbah (Deut 3:1–11).

The best-known biblical giant is Goliath, the champion of the Philistines who was slain by the future king David (1 Sam 17:50–51). There is no archaeological evidence, however, that the Israelites' enemies were giants.

David stands triumphantly over the severed head of the the giant Goliath, as depicted on this leather shield.

GIFT

EVERY GENEROUS ACT OF GIVING, WITH EVERY PERFECT GIFT, IS FROM ABOVE, COMING DOWN FROM THE FATHER . . . .
–JAMES 1:17

In biblical times a gift might be freely given as part of a festive occasion or as a gesture of kindness; it might also be given under duress. Tribute that had to be paid to a conquering ruler was often referred to as a gift. A gift was also payment for services rendered. When Daniel correctly interpreted Nebuchadnezzar's dream, the grateful monarch rewarded Daniel with gifts (Dan 2:48). Allies were courted with presents, and astute diplomats knew their value: "A gift opens doors; it gives access to the great" (Pr 18:16). Even bribes were called gifts. As Isaiah lamented, "Everyone loves a bribe and runs after gifts" (Isa 1:23).

Gifts, in the form of sacrificial offerings, were also bestowed on God (Num 6:14). In turn, God showered humankind with endless gifts. Among these were life itself and all that supports it; the Old Testament covenants and the delivery of the Israelites to the Promised Land; and, in the New Testament, the ultimate gift of salvation through his own Son.

GLASS

"GOLD AND GLASS CANNOT EQUAL IT, NOR CAN IT BE EXCHANGED FOR JEWELS OF FINE GOLD."
–JOB 28:17

Until the time of the Romans, glass was a rare commodity in the Holy Land. The word appears in only two books of the Bible, and the above quotation from Job indicates that glass was considered as precious as gold and jewels. The art of glassmaking, first practiced in Egypt, dates from about 2600 BC. By 1500 BC, craftsmen in Egypt and Phoenicia created perfume bottles by wrapping tubes of glass around a sand and metal core. Because of impurities in its basic materials, the earliest glass was not transparent; the glass vessels imported into Syria and the Holy Land were opaque.

After glassblowing was invented, glass was a material that often compared in price with finely crafted pottery. Blown glass was used for table services, beakers, flasks, bowls, goblets, and bottles. Revelation refers to a "sea of glass mixed with fire" (Rev 15:2) in heaven. The description may mean that the surface of the sea was smooth and tranquil, or that it was highly polished, like one type of blown glass.

Three blown-glass Roman vessels from the first century BC, left, and the core-made glass container, below, once stored cosmetics and perfumes.

GLEANING

SO SHE STAYED CLOSE TO THE YOUNG WOMEN OF BOAZ, GLEANING UNTIL THE END OF THE BARLEY AND WHEAT HARVESTS . . . .
–RUTH 2:23

Still practiced today in some regions of the East, gleaning was an Israelite custom that allowed the POOR, widowed, alien, or others who had no property of their own to share in the harvest bounty. They gathered wheat or barley left behind by reapers, in spring or early summer, or olives and grapes left by pickers in the late summer and fall. Mosaic law required that growers purposely leave enough produce behind for the unfortunate to make a living: "You shall not reap to the very edges of your field, or gather the gleanings of your harvest; you shall leave them for the poor and for the alien" (Lev 23:22). In the Bible, the ancient practice of gleaning is illustrated by the story of Ruth, who was allowed by law to glean wheat in the fields owned by Boaz because she was both a foreigner and a widow related to him by marriage.

GLORY

O LORD, OUR SOVEREIGN, HOW MAJESTIC IS YOUR NAME IN ALL THE EARTH! YOU HAVE SET YOUR GLORY ABOVE THE HEAVENS.
–PSALM 8:1

In the Bible the word *glory,* when applied to humans, indicates honor, power, or wealth (Isa 61:6), but it is often used to characterize the power and influence of God.

God's glory—the manifestation of his nature and presence on earth—often demonstrates itself in storms or fires that announce his presence but also conceal him. In the book of Exodus, God led the Israelites as "a pillar of cloud by day . . . and in a pillar of fire by night" (Ex 13:21). The Lord spoke to Moses from a burning bush and appeared on Mount Sinai "like a

In a Byzantine mural, God's glory is made manifest in the risen Jesus, who releases Adam and Eve from Hell.

devouring fire" (Ex 24:17). At the dedication of the temple in Jerusalem, the glory of God appeared as a cloud that filled the new place of worship and marked it as his DWELLING place on earth (1 Kings 8:10).

Humans had no right to see God. Indeed, anyone who looked on him faced death. God warned Moses not to let the Israelites "break through to the LORD to look; otherwise many of them will perish" (Ex 19:21). When Moses asked for permission to see him, God replied, "'You cannot see my face; for no one shall see me and live'" (Ex 33:20). There are instances reported in the Bible, however, in which people apparently did see God and survive. The prophet Isaiah claimed, "I saw the Lord sitting on a throne, high and lofty; and the hem of his robe filled the temple" (Isa 6:1). In Ezekiel's vision of God, he described "something that seemed like a human form" sitting upon a sapphire throne (Ezek 1:26).

New Testament writers record the glory of God as expressing itself in the presence and deeds of Jesus. Shepherds were terrified when at his birth, "the glory of the Lord shone around them" (Lk 2:9). John noted of Jesus: "And the Word became flesh and lived among us, and we have seen his glory, the glory as of a father's only son" (Jn 1:14). Jesus' resurrection and ascension are also described as manifestations of the glory of God in the person of his Son. After his resurrection, Jesus appeared to his apostles and asked them, "Was it not necessary that the Messiah should suffer these things and then enter into his glory?" (Lk 24:26). In the New Testament Jesus is presented as both a reflection of God's glory and the personification of that glory itself, giving his followers a role model for redemption.

GLUTTON

DO NOT BE AMONG WINEBIBBERS, OR AMONG GLUTTONOUS EATERS OF MEAT; FOR THE DRUNKARD AND THE GLUTTON WILL COME TO POVERTY . . . .
–PROVERBS 23:20–21

In the Bible, the behavior of a glutton—one who eats to excess—was often linked with DRUNKENNESS. Both behaviors were condemned as rebellious, disobedient, and wasteful and could carry a stiff punishment. Parents of a drunken, defiant, and gluttonous son, "who does not heed them when they discipline him" (Deut 21:18), were to bring him before the elders of the town, who could order that the wastrel be stoned to death. Jesus' enemies observed that "the Son of Man came eating and drinking" and accused him of being "a glutton and a drunkard, a friend of tax collectors and sinners!" (Mt 11:19).

GNASHING OF TEETH

"THERE WILL BE WEEPING AND GNASHING OF TEETH WHEN YOU SEE . . . ALL THE PROPHETS IN THE KINGDOM OF GOD, AND YOU YOURSELVES THROWN OUT."
–LUKE 13:28

Gnashing refers to the grinding or snapping of one's teeth, and in the Old Testament it symbolizes the physical manifestation of anger, fear, or hatred. When Job complains that God "has gnashed his teeth at me" (Job 16:9), he means that God in his anger is treating him as an adversary and as unrighteous. In Lamentations 2:16, Jerusalem's enemies similarly show their contempt when "they hiss, they gnash their teeth." The phrase is also used by Matthew and Luke in the New Testament to describe the frustration and torment, rather than anger, of those punished in the afterlife. As they suffer horrendous agonies, these sinners gnash their teeth—perhaps also to show their stubborn determination not to repent of their wickedness.

GNATS

". . . 'STRETCH OUT YOUR STAFF AND STRIKE THE DUST OF THE EARTH, SO THAT IT MAY BECOME GNATS THROUGHOUT THE WHOLE LAND OF EGYPT.'"
–EXODUS 8:16

In the Gospel of Matthew, Jesus criticized the scribes and Pharisees for paying attention to such little details as tithing their herbs while ignoring important issues like justice, mercy, and faith. He compared the insignificant details with the gnat, a tiny insect, and the weightier things to the camel (Mt 23:23–24). Gnats were so ubiquitous that milk, water, and other liquids used for drinking had to be strained to remove them. In the book of Exodus, the third plague that God wrought on Egypt was a cloud of voracious gnats.

GOAD

HOW CAN ONE BECOME WISE WHO HANDLES THE PLOW, AND WHO GLORIES IN THE SHAFT OF A GOAD . . . ?
–ECCLESIASTICUS 38:25

Farmers controlled slow-moving oxen by prodding them with a long, pointed stick that annoyed the lethargic animals enough to make them move forward. Goads were eight- or nine-foot-long wooden poles sharpened at one end or tipped with an IRON point. At the other end there was often a flat piece of iron, which was used to scrape mud from the plowshare. Figuratively, the words of wise men acted as goads to prod others into action (Eccl 12:11).

In times of war a pointed ox goad was sometimes used to spear or batter enemy soldiers, which the judge Shamgar did very effectively: "After him came Shamgar son of Anath, who killed six hundred of the Philistines with an oxgoad" (Judg 3:31).

GOAT

AARON SHALL PRESENT THE GOAT ON WHICH THE LOT FELL FOR THE LORD, AND OFFER IT AS A SIN OFFERING . . . .
–LEVITICUS 16:9

In biblical times, the goat was a source of meat, milk, leather, and fabric, as well as being a sacrificial animal. Two male goats were chosen on the Day of Atonement. One was killed and offered to God for the sins of the people. The second—the scapegoat—was symbolically laden with Israel's sins and sent "into the wilderness to Azazel" to bear those sins away (Lev 16:10). According to Mosaic law, the young goat, or kid, was considered a suitable offering to God only if it remained with its mother for at least seven days after birth (Lev 22:27). Goats' hair was used in the curtains for the tent of the tabernacle (Ex 26:7). Most goats in the Holy Land had black hair, long ears, curved horns, and bearded chins. Tame goats and sheep pastured together, but the wild goat, or ibex, ran free. The strutting demeanor of the he-goat was compared with that of a rooster and a king (Prov 30:31). In Jesus' parable about judgment, the sheep inherited the kingdom and the goats went to hell: "He will separate people one from another as a shepherd separates the sheep from the goats" (Mt 25:32).

An artisan fashioned this goat from bronze in the second millennium BC, exaggerating the large, backward-curving horns for which both male and female mountain goats were known.

GODLINESS

. . . GODLINESS IS VALUABLE IN EVERY WAY, HOLDING PROMISE FOR BOTH THE PRESENT LIFE AND THE LIFE TO COME.
–1 TIMOTHY 4:8

The Greek word translated as "godliness" describes the character of a person who worships the gods and respects the leaders sanctioned by the gods, such as temple priests and the emperor. This association may be why the New Testament writers rarely used the word, preferring terms with a similar meaning, such as RIGHTEOUSNESS, faithfulness, and holiness.

Some writers did, however, occasionally use *godliness* to describe the Christian lifestyle (2 Pet 1:7). This was more than a private spiritual experience. Godliness expressed itself to others through an individual's attitude and behavior. It was often linked with other admirable characteristics, such as faith, righteousness, humility, love, and gentleness, as in 1 Timothy 6:11.

Though the word *godliness* does not appear in the Old Testament, the word *godly* is used, in much the same way, to describe people who are righteous in their relationship with God. In Psalm 12:1, the psalmist laments a world that has lost its faith and fallen into wickedness. He pleads: "Help, O LORD, for there is no longer anyone who is godly; the faithful have disappeared from humankind."

Gods

"Now I know that the LORD is greater than all gods . . . ."
–Exodus 18:11

The monotheism professed by the Israelites stood in sharp contrast to the dominant religious beliefs of the surrounding cultures, all of which worshiped a profusion of deities. Many gods were associated with specific places. Marduk, for example, was a god of Babylon, and Assyria was named for its protective deity, Ashur. In Egypt there were numerous local deities: Ptah was the patron of the city of Memphis; Thoth presided over Hermopolis; and the goddess Hathor was the protective deity of Dendera. Gods who were closely associated with a specific city or region were believed to have their primary power in that place.

Rulers proclaimed their connection to a national deity by incorporating a divine name into their own. Thus, the names of several Israelite kings, such as *Abijah, Hezekiah,* and *Josiah,* contain within them an element of God's name, *Yahweh*. Several Assyrian rulers had the name *Shalmaneser,* which means "the god Shulman is chief." Gods were associated with the sun, moon, and other celestial bodies, with natural phenomena, and with seasons. They were also patrons of crafts and various endeavors.

The number of deities was immense. Babylonian scribes compiled detailed records of the names of gods, their titles, and the temples where they were worshiped. By the seventh century BC, the number of gods known to the Babylonians was more than 2,500, although some of these were Sumerian gods that had been absorbed into the Babylonian pantheon, and not all of these deities were actively worshiped.

The Israelites were nominally monotheistic, but their popular folk beliefs were polytheistic. When they arrived in Canaan after their bondage in Egypt, the Israelites encountered the worship of the Canaanite gods, and this became a source of temptation for them. Moses condemned sacrifices the Israelites made "to deities they had never known, to new ones recently arrived" (Deut 32:17). The golden calves that some Israelites made and worshiped may have been associated with the cult of the powerful Canaanite god Baal. Among his other acts, Baal brought the spring rains and thus the fertility of the fields. Sometimes called Rider of the Clouds, Baal was associated with thunderstorms and used lightning as his weapon. The prophets railed against worship of Baal; in the famous contest on Mount Carmel, Elijah forced the people to choose between Baal and God (1 Kings 18). Another deity that enjoyed a certain following among the Israelites was the fertility goddess ASHERAH, who was symbolized by wooden cultic objects. King Solomon himself worshiped another fertility goddess called Astarte (1 Kings 11:5).

Also venerated in the temple, as indicated by Ezekiel 8:14, was Tammuz, the Near Eastern god who was associated with springtime fertility. When the spring vegetation faded, Tammuz' followers lamented, believing that he had gone to the underworld. The book of Isaiah condemned those who worshiped deities such as Fortune and Destiny by setting food before their idols or by pouring wine offerings (Isa 65:11); it also alluded to the ignominious fall of the Canaanite god Day Star, son of Dawn (Isa 14:12).

The Jews came into contact with the Olympian pantheon of the Greeks in the second century BC, when the Seleucid ruler Antiochus IV converted the temple into a shrine to Zeus, the chief Olympian god. By that time, however, monotheism was so firmly rooted in Jewish belief that the presence of the Greek shrine was not a temptation to them but rather was perceived as a deep affront; to tamper with the temple in this manner was to "pollute" it (2 Macc 6:2).

Canaanite gods included the fertility goddess Astarte, represented by the clay figure above, and Resheph, probably the deity depicted by the bronze statue at right.

Gold

How much better to get wisdom than gold!
–Proverbs 16:16

The precious metal that appears first, and most often, in the Bible is gold. As early as 3200 BC, gold objects were being produced in Syria. The mining of gold—as distinct from its discovery in the gravel of streambeds—did not become widespread until about 2500 BC. The finest gold came from Ophir, a place whose location is still unknown; Psalm 45:9 speaks of "the queen in gold of Ophir." Gold was also found in Egypt, Asia Minor, Arabia, and the Aegean islands. When the Israelites fled Egypt, they took quantities of gold with them (Ex 12:35).

A goldsmith was a skilled ARTISAN who fanned his small furnace with a blowpipe and practiced the techniques of lost-wax casting, in which the metal replaced wax in a clay mold, as well as filigree, cloisonné, and inlay.

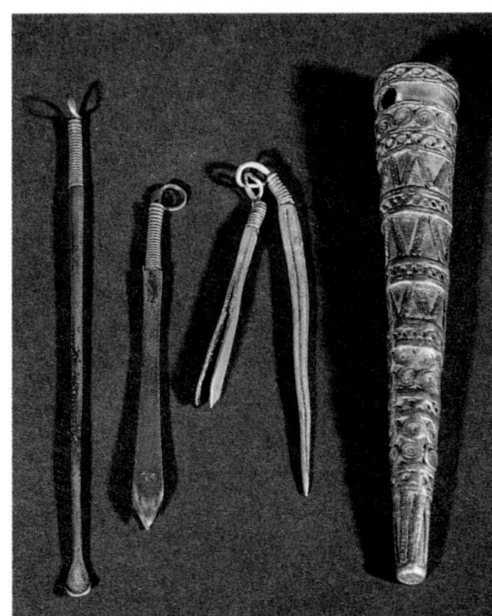

These gold ornamental pins and case from the third millennium BC were unearthed at Ur. Jewelry and other articles of gold are often mentioned in the Bible.

Gold's beauty and malleability made it a suitable material for jewelry, money, and religious objects. Moses' ark of the covenant was made of acacia wood, with an overlay of pure gold and assorted gold fittings (Ex 25:11–13). The golden calves fashioned and worshiped by Aaron and Jeroboam (Ex 32:2–4; 2 Kings 10:29) may have been gold-plated wood. In Psalm 45:13, the princess prepares for her wedding in "gold-woven robes"—clothing embroidered with gold thread.

GOSPEL

". . . THOSE WHO LOSE THEIR LIFE FOR MY SAKE, AND FOR THE SAKE OF THE GOSPEL, WILL SAVE IT."
–MARK 8:35

From the Old English word *godspell,* the word *gospel* means "good news." It translates a term that the Greeks used to describe news that a messenger brought of military victory or escape from danger. A Roman inscription dated 9 BC used the same word to describe the birthday of the emperor Augustus Caesar as "the beginning of good news for the world."

In the New Testament the "good news" was that Jesus was the Messiah, who brought salvation to humankind. Matthew wrote of the "good news of the kingdom," emphasizing that the gospel was about the kingdom of God—one of the main themes of Jesus' Sermon on the Mount (Mt 5–7). Mark spoke of the "good news of Jesus Christ" and the "good news of God," highlighting both the messenger and the source of the message. In letters to the early Christians, Paul similarly referred to the "gospel of God," "the gospel of his Son," and the "gospel of Christ"; however, he often mentioned "gospel" by itself, without adding any kind of description, suggesting that by the time he wrote the letters, Christians were already familiar with the term.

Some first-century Jewish Christians probably associated the word *gospel* with the prophetic promise of a coming MESSENGER "who announces peace, who brings good news, who announces salvation" (Isa 52:7). Within about a century after the death of Jesus, Christians started applying the term to the books in the New Testament that presented the good news about Jesus and his message in the writings of Matthew, Mark, Luke, and John, among others.

GOURD

. . . HE FOUND A WILD VINE AND GATHERED FROM IT A LAPFUL OF WILD GOURDS . . . .
–2 KINGS 4:39

A hard-rinded fruit related to the squash, the gourd grows on long vines in the Holy Land. The gourd is sometimes confused with the castor bean plant, whose seeds produce an oil used in biblical times for lamp fuel. Both plants were used as laxatives.

Gourds are not edible because they produce poisonous seeds, as Elisha's servant learned when he put them in a stew for guests; then, "while they were eating the stew, they cried out, 'O man of God, there is death in the pot!'" (2 Kings 4:40). The cedar-lined walls inside King Solomon's temple "had carvings of gourds and open flowers" (1 Kings 6:18).

GOVERNMENT

THE GOVERNMENT OF THE EARTH IS IN THE HAND OF THE LORD . . . .
–ECCLESIASTICUS 10:4

Ancient Near Eastern governments were typically empires or kingdoms, with well-developed bureaucracies to administer financial, military, and religious affairs in the homeland and in conquered provinces. However, the earliest mode of political organization may have been a loosely formalized democracy. Both nomads and settled farmers who clustered in towns governed themselves through assemblies of free men, led in some instances by elders. In time of war or other crisis, the assembly might invest special powers in one person, but these powers lapsed when the crisis passed. By the third millennium BC, permanent monarchies had emerged in Mesopotamia. In contrast, the Israelites resisted the institution of earthly kingship, because their covenant with God recognized the Lord as their king. God also provided the Israelites with a national identity that other peoples derived from a monarchy, decreeing that "you shall be for me a priestly kingdom and a holy nation" (Ex 19:6). Although singled out by God to lead the Israelites, Moses never held the title of ruler; rather, he presided over a federation of the 12 tribes of Israel and worked in consultation with the elders. The Israelites maintained their tribal federation despite being surrounded by monarchies in Moab, Edom, and Ammon, city-states in Canaan, and the warrior aristocracy of the Philistines.

Roman government was imposed upon the Israelites following the capture of the temple by the Roman army in 63 BC.

After Moses and his successor, Joshua, a series of judges—with civil, military, and judicial authority—led the federation, but not all the tribes accepted their authority at all times. Surrounded by powerful enemies, the Israelites at last desired to have a king and petitioned the judge Samuel to name one. Samuel opposed the idea, saying that a king would do nothing but oppress the people (1 Sam 8:1–17), but he finally relented and anointed Saul as the first king. Saul's troubled reign and tragic death in battle seemed to confirm Samuel's doubts about kingship, but Saul's successor, David, put the monarchy on a firm foundation.

Under the Israelite monarchy a new governmental bureaucracy appeared, which included courtiers, ambassadors, tax collectors, military officials, scribes, counselors, and a host of personal attendants for the king. However, the old village and tribal institutions continued to function as a parallel government, handling local issues.

In the 10th century BC, a political dispute resulted in the nation splitting into two kingdoms—Israel to the north and Judah to the south—with separate rulers. Assyrian conquest ended the northern kingdom in the eighth century BC, and Babylonian conquest extinguished the southern kingdom less than two centuries later. When the Jews returned from the Babylonian exile by permission of the Persian king Cyrus, they entered a long period of foreign domination by the Persians, the Greeks, and the Romans.

With some exceptions, foreign rulers granted a limited autonomy to the Jews in managing their internal affairs and religious matters. Elders continued to wield influence and authority over local matters, and Jewish councils handled some administrative and judicial functions. Great power was concentrated in the priestly community, because religious laws had to be observed as scrupulously as civil laws. For a time the high priest was also the governor; later, during the Roman period, the high priest's status was such that Jesus reportedly was tried both by the high priest's religious court and the Roman governor. By acceding to their judgments, Jesus demonstrated the duty of people to accept proper authority. But he also asserted that earthly government was separate from the divine kingdom when he said, "Give to the emperor the things that are the emperor's, and to God the things that are God's" (Mk 12:17).

Governor

And the LORD stirred up the spirit of Zerubbabel son of Shealtiel, governor of Judah . . . .–Haggai 1:14

A governor—sometimes called an ethnarch—administered a specific region or PROVINCE at the behest of a king or emperor. Pharaoh appointed Joseph governor after his prediction of famine came true (Gen 41:39–44); in this case the position probably meant chief overseer of Egypt and included responsibility for all of the country's food supplies. After the Babylonian exile, the Persian king appointed Nehemiah governor of Judah and gave him permission to rebuild Jerusalem's walls. In order to reach the city of Jerusalem safely, Nehemiah asked the king to write letters for him to give to the governors of the provinces along the way. Once in Judah, Nehemiah took pains to avoid oppressing the population, in contrast to his predecessors, who "laid heavy burdens on the people, and took food and wine from them" (Neh 5:15).

Pontius Pilate, the most prominent governor in the Bible, washed his hands of Jesus' death before an angry mob (Mt 27:24–26); another Roman governor sought a bribe to release the apostle Paul from prison (Acts 24:26). Nevertheless, the first letter of Peter exhorted Christians to obey governors for the Lord's sake (1 Pet 2:13–14).

GRAIN

"LET ME GO TO THE FIELD AND GLEAN AMONG THE EARS OF GRAIN . . . ."–RUTH 2:2

The most important edible grains in the Bible are the cereal crops wheat and barley, but millet and spelt (or emmer), grains of lesser quality, are occasionally mentioned. Flour ground from all of these grains was the principal ingredient in BREAD and other cooked products. Millet, the smallest of all cereal grains, was usually used in combination with other grains for bread; it also provided animal feed. Spelt, a kind of wheat also translated as "rye," was used to make bread in Egypt. Because spelt and wheat develop later than other crops, they survived the plague of hail (Ex 9:32).

Meal was ground grain, which was used both as an offering to God and as food; the prophet Elijah asked a poor widow to make a cake of meal for him (1 Kings 17:12–13). Jesus' disciples were criticized for violating the sabbath by plucking off heads of grain from the fields to eat (Mt 12:1–2).

GRAPES

THE GRAPES SHALL RIPEN, BUT WHO WILL TREAD THEM? –2 ESDRAS 16:26

Cultivated for at least 5,000 years in the Holy Land, grapevines during biblical times were prized for producing clusters of sweet black or green grapes. This fruit could be eaten fresh, providing essential iron and other minerals. Dried in the baking sun, the grapes became raisins, another important food. Raisins, rich with sugar, supplied quick energy to hungry guests and made a convenient gift. Grape leaves were also eaten, and stalks and vines were fed to domestic animals or used in tanning hides.

The principal use of grapes was in making wine, which was both an anesthetic and a beverage. A vinegary, or sour, wine was a common drink of poorer people and Roman soldiers. See also VINEGAR.

A farmer near Bethlehem winnows grain with a wooden fork, above. The pottery vessels at right stored grain about 3000 BC; the second jar from the left still holds grain from that time.

GRASS

THE GRASS WITHERS, THE FLOWER FADES, WHEN THE BREATH OF THE LORD BLOWS UPON IT . . . . –ISAIAH 40:7

The Bible often uses grass as a symbol. Because it is green only during the Holy Land's brief springtime, grass became a metaphor for human weakness, the shortness of life, and the inevitable destruction of enemies. Hills covered with green grass conveyed the serenity and peace of a benevolent God. Desolate or infertile ground without grass might signal God's anger; lush grass could symbolize abundance, such as when Job is told that "your descendants will be many, and your offspring like the grass of the earth" (Job 5:25).

Grass was eaten by animals such as the ox and the "wild ass" (Job 6:5).

GRASSHOPPER

MULTIPLY YOURSELVES LIKE THE LOCUST, MULTIPLY LIKE THE GRASSHOPPER!
–NAHUM 3:15

The book of NAHUM warned Nineveh—perhaps satirically—that in the face of destruction, it needed to increase its population like the grasshopper. Grasshoppers flourished in such large numbers that Isaiah likened them to the people of the earth as seen from God's perspective (Isa 40:22). The teeming insects could be very destructive to vegetation, but they did not arrive in a swarm like locusts. Although the grasshopper was able to fly long distances and jump vigorously when young, Ecclesiastes 12:5 speaks of the time when "the grasshopper drags itself along," making the insect a metaphor for human beings in their old age. Ritually clean (Lev 11:22), the thorax of the grasshopper was eaten dried or broiled.

GREEK

MANY OF THE JEWS READ THIS INSCRIPTION . . . AND IT WAS WRITTEN IN HEBREW, IN LATIN, AND IN GREEK.
–JOHN 19:20

The language and culture of the Greeks had a powerful impact on the ancient Mediterranean and Asian world. Greece at that time did not exist as a single political entity; Greek-speaking people inhabited the Greek mainland, but many important Greek city-states were spread along the Aegean coast of Turkey, north to the Black Sea, and as far west as southern Italy and Spain. In the fourth century BC, the conquests of Alexander the Great toppled the Persian Empire and spread Greek ideas and institutions from the Aegean Sea to India.

On this AD 23 lead weight, the Greek word for justice surrounds Justice herself, who holds scales and a cornucopia.

Although Rome subsequently conquered much of this territory and Latin became the language of government, Greek continued to be the international language of commerce, philosophy, literature, and religion. Evolved from older Greek dialects dating from 3000 BC, this international dialect of Greek was known as Koine, or "common," Greek. The New Testament authors wrote in Koine, which could be understood in large parts of Asia, Europe, and Africa, thus contributing to the rapid spread of Christianity. Pontius Pilate had an inscription placed on Jesus' cross that read "Jesus of Nazareth, the King of the Jews" in Greek, as well as in Hebrew and Latin.

GREETING

BUT SHE WAS MUCH PERPLEXED BY HIS WORDS AND PONDERED WHAT SORT OF GREETING THIS MIGHT BE.
–LUKE 1:29

In ancient times, the greeting that one person offered another upon meeting was a serious matter. Rank was a determining factor: in approaching a ruler, a person might kneel or lie prostrate, kiss the earth, clasp the sovereign's feet, and wish him eternal life. Visitors to Joseph, who held a high position in Egypt, "bowed to the ground before him" on greeting him (Gen 43:26). In the presence of elders, a person was expected to rise as a mark of respect; when Solomon's mother arrived, the king "rose to meet her, and bowed down to her" (1 Kings 2:19). On a busy street, men of superior age, position, or prestige had to be greeted; thus the scribes and Pharisees expected to be "greeted with respect in the marketplaces" (Mt 23:7). Mary did not understand the meaning of the angel Gabriel's first words to her, which indicated prestige: "Greetings, favored one! The Lord is with you" (Lk 1:28).

In Hebrew or Aramaic, the usual verbal salutation invoked a blessing of peace: "Peace be to you, and peace be to your house, and peace be to all that you have" (1 Sam 25:6). The Greek greeting was "hail" or, translated literally, "rejoice." Salutations similar to these were used in letters.

GRIDDLE

IT SHALL BE MADE WITH OIL ON A GRIDDLE . . . .
–LEVITICUS 6:21

Leviticus speaks of grain offerings to God being cooked on a griddle—a thick metal or clay plate. Often set on stones that formed a stand over a fire, the griddle was used for making bread as well. To prevent the flat, round cakes of bread from sticking, small depressions or holes were made in the griddle's surface. Unlike an oven or flat stones, which the Israelites also employed to make bread, a griddle was easily portable. The prophet Ezekiel was told to use "an iron plate," or griddle, to create a symbolic representation of the coming siege of Jerusalem (Ezek 4:3).

GRIEF

MY JOY IS GONE, GRIEF IS UPON ME, MY HEART IS SICK.
–JEREMIAH 8:18

The main cause of grief in biblical times was the death of a loved one, though such pain could be brought on by other calamities. The plight of the poor made Job grieve (Job 30:25), and "a foolish child" could aggrieve a mother (Prov 10:1). Even God experienced grief, brought on by humanity's wickedness: "And the LORD was sorry that he had made humankind on the earth, and it grieved him to his heart" (Gen 6:6). People expressed grief publicly with tears, shrieks, and lamentations; with the beating of the breast, the tearing of clothes, and the wearing of sackcloth and ashes. Grief was debilitating. "My eye has grown dim from grief," Job lamented, "and all my members are like a shadow" (Job 17:7). Therefore it eventually had to end: "For grief may result in death, and a sorrowful heart saps one's strength" (Sir 38:18). See also MOURNER.

GROVE

YET HE DEMOLISHED ALL THEIR SHRINES AND CUT DOWN THEIR SACRED GROVES . . . .–JUDITH 3:8

A grove was a stand of trees or a restful place like an oasis or an orchard. The Bible mentions both palm and olive groves. These apparently could be quite dense; 2 Esdras 16:28 speaks of people hiding in the "thick groves." A grove was often the location for a HIGH PLACE, an elevated area used for religious rituals. In these sacred groves, the Canaanite storm god Baal and the fertility goddess Asherah were worshiped. Living trees—as well as wooden poles—were cultic symbols for Asherah, and Moses warned the Israelites against establishing or maintaining such groves: "You shall not plant any tree as a sacred pole beside the altar that you make for the LORD your God" (Deut 16:21).

GUARANTEE

TO GUARANTEE LOANS FOR A STRANGER BRINGS TROUBLE, BUT THERE IS SAFETY IN REFUSING TO DO SO.
–PROVERBS 11:15

The Israelite system of borrowing required that guarantees or pledges to back up a loan be reasonable and interest-free. A guarantee was generally a personal item, a mortgage of property, or the word of a third party. Giving one's word could be strengthened by taking an oath, which was considered a very serious matter under the law (Num 30:2), as well as a sacred act witnessed by the Lord. Throughout the Old Testament, God affirmed his promises by oaths, which, according to Christian belief, Jesus fulfilled by bringing salvation to humankind.

A guarantee could also be the first payment of a purchase by installments. This down payment obligated the purchaser to pay the entire amount. It was this custom that Paul invoked when he pictured the gift of the Spirit as the guarantee, or first payment, on the reward of eternal glory (2 Cor 5:5).

GUARD

SO WE PRAYED TO OUR GOD, AND SET A GUARD AS A PROTECTION AGAINST THEM DAY AND NIGHT.
–NEHEMIAH 4:9

A guard was an individual or troop assigned to protect a place or person. Most guards were soldiers, and the Bible often mentions the CAPTAIN of the guard. The first guards to appear in the Scriptures are angels: God placed cherubim at the garden of Eden with a flaming sword "to guard the way to the tree of life" (Gen 3:24), and he sent an angel to protect the Israelites on their way to the Promised Land (Ex 23:20). A guard could be held personally responsible for his prisoner, even to the extent that "if he is missing, your life shall be given for his life, or else you shall pay a talent of silver" (1 Kings 20:39). Under house arrest in Rome, Paul lived with his sole guard and may have been chained to him (Acts 28:16, 20).

Grief was expressed in many ways in the Holy Land. These clay figurines of mourners are from the seventh century BC.

GUARDIAN

. . . they remain under guardians and trustees until the date set by the father.
–Galatians 4:2

In the ancient Near East, guardians, or trustees, were people responsible for the care and training of young charges and were often grouped together with elders in biblical passages (2 Kings 10:5).

A different kind of caretaker, "guardians of the thresholds," were those who guarded the entry to sacred places (1 Chr 9:19). *Guardian* was also used by the prophet Ezekiel in reference to the cherub who drove humankind out of the garden of Eden (Ezek 28:16); in Genesis 3:24, CHERUBIM were guardians of the tree of life.

In the New Testament, Peter speaks of Christ as a "guardian" of souls. Conversely, in his letter to the Galatians, Paul uses the term to mean the "elemental spirits of the world" (Gal 4:2–3), which were the cosmic powers of the universe that were worshiped by humans before God sent his Son.

GUEST

Be content with little or much, and you will hear no reproach for being a guest.
–Ecclesiasticus 29:23

Persons invited to attend a feast or spend the night in another's house were guests, who were entitled to special protection and care in biblical times (see illustration). In the ancient Greek culture described in Homer's epics, wayfaring strangers who were offered lodging enjoyed the status of friends of the host.

A similar cultural attitude is revealed in the book of Judges: when a guest was threatened by a group of ruffians, his host pleaded, "since this man is my guest, do not do this vile thing" (Judg 19:23). Guests were traditionally given the best room in the house, often specially prepared for

Extending hospitality toward a guest was a custom rooted in the nomadic way of life. Here a weary traveler is welcomed by the head of the household, who provides water to bathe his feet. Later he will join the family for the evening meal and be given a place to sleep for the night.

them by the host (2 Kings 4:10), although in the hot season an honored visitor might be offered a bed on the roof, which was often the coolest place to sleep (1 Sam 9:25).

GUILE

RID YOURSELVES, THEREFORE, OF ALL MALICE, AND ALL GUILE, INSINCERITY, ENVY, AND ALL SLANDER.—1 PETER 2:1

In the Bible, guile—deceit, trickery, or duplicity—is understood to be a reprehensible sin. Because such importance is placed on honesty and truthfulness, people who act dishonestly are considered to be among the godless—those who have turned away from God's word. Proverbs describes an enemy as "harboring deceit within" and cautions that "though hatred is covered with guile, the enemy's wickedness will be exposed" (Prov 26:24, 26).

In the New Testament, Paul encourages Christians "to be wise in what is good and guileless in what is evil" (Rom 16:19). In the passage cited above, 1 Peter also counsels people to rid themselves of evil intent and insincerity.

GUILT

FOR YOUR NAME'S SAKE, O LORD, PARDON MY GUILT, FOR IT IS GREAT.—PSALM 25:11

The concept of guilt was as complex an issue in biblical times as it is today. Guilt was sometimes a sense of remorse or shame—the equivalent of "feeling guilty"—but more often it was a state that a person entered into after committing a sin against a neighbor or against God. In the Old Testament, the same Hebrew word is sometimes translated as "guilt," "sin," or "punishment," stressing the close relationship among the three ideas.

Gymnasiums like the one above, in the ancient city of Sardis in Asia Minor, often had an open courtyard surrounded by rooms for learning, dining, exercising, and bathing.

Guilt was a collective as well as an individual matter, for one who sinned caused the whole community to fall into a state of guilt. During the siege of Jericho, God forbade the Israelites to seize booty for themselves. This command was broken by Achan, who stole God's "devoted things" for his own use, bringing guilt and God's anger upon all Israelites (Jos 7:1, 11–15).

To remove the burden of guilt, a wrongdoer offered RESTITUTION, either by paying a fine or performing a sacrifice. The purpose of a guilt offering—one of five forms of sacrifice described in Leviticus—was to make reparations for acts such as committing sacrilege or perjury. The person seeking to atone brought "a ram without blemish" to the priest and had to pay back any money that had been stolen, adding an extra "one fifth" for damages (Lev 5:15–16).

In the New Testament, Paul writes that everyone is "under the power of sin" (Rom 3:9), or guilty. 1 John describes Jesus as "the atoning sacrifice for our sins" (1 Jn 2:2)—one that has expiated the guilt of the world and repaired humankind's relationship with God. See also SIN.

GYMNASIUM

SO THEY BUILT A GYMNASIUM IN JERUSALEM, ACCORDING TO GENTILE CUSTOM . . . AND ABANDONED THE HOLY COVENANT.—1 MACCABEES 1:14–15

Based on the Greek word *gymnos*, meaning "naked," the gymnasium was an integral part of ancient Greek culture. Originally a place where young Greek men trained for the Olympic games and other sporting events, by the close of the fourth century BC the gymnasium had become a center where aristocratic male youths received both rigorous physical and intellectual training.

When Palestine was under the control of Syrian rulers in the second century BC, a concerted effort was made to Hellenize the Jews. As part of that campaign, a gymnasium was built in Jerusalem—an act that outraged pious Jews. Some found the gymnasium particularly objectionable because the young men exercised in the nude; some Jews became self-conscious and tried to hide their circumcisions. The gymnasium and its attendant practices were contributing factors that helped spark the Maccabean rebellion in 167 BC.

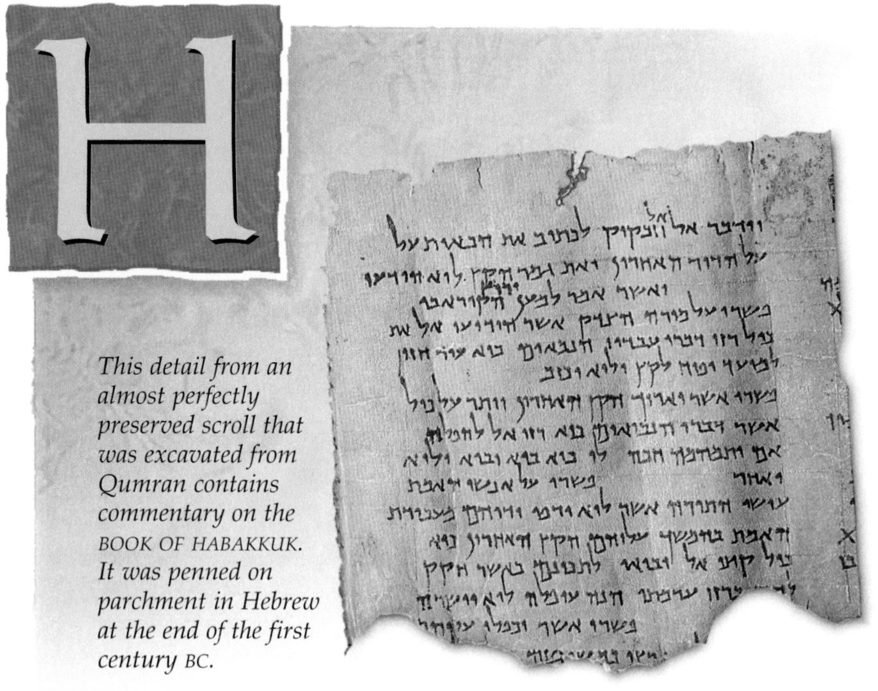

This detail from an almost perfectly preserved scroll that was excavated from Qumran contains commentary on the BOOK OF HABAKKUK. *It was penned on parchment in Hebrew at the end of the first century* BC.

Habakkuk, Book of

Though the fig tree does not blossom, and no fruit is on the vines . . . I will rejoice in the LORD; I will exult in the God of my salvation. –Habakkuk 3:17–18

The book of Habakkuk was written by and named after a PROPHET who lived in Judah apparently during the decade before the Babylonian invasion of 597 BC. His visions of the coming disaster left him perplexed and terrified, so he took his questions to the Lord. What puzzled Habakkuk the most was how God could permit the Babylonians to destroy the righteous along with the wicked. In response, God promised the prophet that he would punish the invaders in time. Meanwhile, God proclaimed, "the righteous live by their faith" (Hab 2:4). Habakkuk responded with a majestic poem of unconditional trust in God, promising that no matter what happened, "I will exult in the God of my salvation" (Hab 3:18).
An addition to the book of Daniel, the story of Bel and the Dragon mentions Habakkuk; some scholars have attributed the tale's authorship to the prophet.

In the biblical story of Bel and the Dragon, an angel carries the prophet Habakkuk—as shown in the upper right-hand corner of this 12th-century illumination—who bears food to Daniel in the lion's den.

Haggai, Book of

Is it a time for you yourselves to live in your paneled houses, while this house lies in ruins?–Haggai 1:4

After the Babylonian exile, the prophet Haggai called on the Jews to rebuild the temple in Jerusalem. The book of Haggai preserves his message, which moved the nation to finish the project they had started—and abandoned—about 20 years earlier.

The people had stopped work on the temple apparently so that they could plant crops. Yet they suffered a string of droughts that led to agricultural disaster, which the book of Haggai proclaims to be punishment from God for leaving the temple in ruins. The prophet rebukes the Israelites for leading lives of self-indulgence and not heeding the words of the Lord. He promises that when the temple is finished, the nation will prosper once again and God will reestablish the reign of David through Zerubbabel, governor of the Persian province of Judah.

The restoration of the temple, which began in 520 BC, was completed within five years, in 515 BC.

Hail

See, the Lord has one who is mighty and strong; like a storm of hail . . . . –Isaiah 28:2

The seventh of the 10 plagues that God visited on Egypt was "such heavy hail as had never fallen in all the land of Egypt since it became a nation" (Ex 9:24). The overwhelming storm destroyed the early crops and killed everyone who had not sought shelter. Modern research has confirmed that such a storm could indeed have occurred along the Nile, although according to Exodus it was a supernatural rather than a natural event. In the New Testament, hail is also a sign of God's punishment. The "hail and fire, mixed with blood" (Rev 8:7) that fall in Revelation recall the hailstorm of Exodus and signal the last judgment.

HAIR

[CHRIST'S] HEAD AND HIS HAIR WERE WHITE AS WHITE WOOL, WHITE AS SNOW . . . .
–REVELATION 1:14

In biblical times the Israelites—both male and female—wore their hair long. Barbers existed (Ezek 5:1), but they apparently trimmed hair rather than cut it short. Absalom had hair so long and luxuriant that each year he cut off "two hundred shekels" (2 Sam 14:26)—about six pounds. Samson wore his long hair, the source of his strength, in seven locks (Judg 16:13).

Hair was considered an important component of feminine beauty, and by the first century AD rabbis decreed that a woman must shield her hair from public view as a sign of modesty. Unkempt hair was generally considered a mark of mourning or shame; a woman accused of adultery would have her hair disheveled by a priest (Num 5:18).

The way hair was styled often had religious significance. Priests could trim but not shave their hair, nor could they cut the hair above their ears. The practice of wearing forelocks—ringlets near the ear—is still observed by some Orthodox Jews. The nazirites, who were especially devoted to God, were forbidden to cut any of their hair until they had fulfilled a vow, at which time the hair was shaved off. The book of Leviticus decreed that a person cured of skin disease must undergo a ritual purification, which included shaving the entire body (Lev 14:8).

By New Testament times, men tended to wear their hair much shorter than women, imitating Roman hair styles, which were cropped close to the head. Though many Jews also kept their hair fashionably short, they continued to allow their side locks to remain uncut. Paul warned that long hair on a man was "degrading to him" (1 Cor 11:14). Christ's hair was said to be "white as snow"—a mark of divine presence. See also BALDNESS.

The head of a young woman with braided hair was carved from marble in the second century AD.

HALL

[SOLOMON] MADE THE HALL OF THE THRONE WHERE HE WAS TO PRONOUNCE JUDGMENT, THE HALL OF JUSTICE . . . .
–1 KINGS 7:7

In biblical times a hall was not a narrow corridor connecting rooms but rather a large room itself. Often the largest room in a building, the hall was where kings rendered judgment on COURT cases and meetings and where banquets were held. The Babylonian king Belshazzar became terrified in the royal banquet hall when a human hand appeared out of nowhere and began writing on the wall (Dan 5:5–9). Paul preached in "the lecture hall of Tyrannus" (Acts 19:9) in Ephesus after he was no longer welcome to do so in the synagogue. It was in "the audience hall" (Acts 25:23) of a public building where Paul later defended himself before King Agrippa, who ruled part of Palestine.

HAMMER

IS NOT MY WORD LIKE FIRE, SAYS THE LORD, AND LIKE A HAMMER THAT BREAKS A ROCK IN PIECES?
–JEREMIAH 23:29

The first hammers were hand-held rocks that were used as pounding tools. About 3000 BC, a hole was bored in the rock so that a handle could be added. In biblical times, hammers often resembled broad mallets, and their handles were made of wood or bone. The bronze worker was "the one who smooths with the hammer" (Isa 41:7). Hammers were also used by stonemasons. For Jael, who killed Sisera by driving a PEG through his temple, a hammer served as a weapon (Judg 4:21). Gold objects of "hammered work" (Num 8:4) graced the ark of the covenant.

HAMSTRING

". . . YOU SHALL HAMSTRING THEIR HORSES, AND BURN THEIR CHARIOTS WITH FIRE."
–JOSHUA 11:6

As Joshua led the tribes of Israel in the military conquest of Canaan, the Lord commanded him to hamstring the enemy's horses. To cut the leg tendons, or hamstrings, of captured horses crippled their ability to draw the two-wheeled chariots used in warfare. Similarly, when King David conquered the kingdom of Zobah, he captured "one thousand seven hundred horsemen, and . . . hamstrung all the chariot horses" (2 Sam 8:4).

HAND

. . . WE HAVE SUCH A HIGH PRIEST, ONE WHO IS SEATED AT THE RIGHT HAND OF THE THRONE OF THE MAJESTY IN THE HEAVENS . . . .
–HEBREWS 8:1

Used nearly 2,000 times in the Bible, the word *hand* refers not only to the part of the body but also to the left or right side. It conveys power and may represent an individual's actions or thoughts.

The hand of God was an important symbol in the Old Testament, as well as in early Christianity. The divine hand created the world and controlled the course of history, such as in delivering Israel from Egypt (Ex 7:4–5). Wielding almighty authority, the hand of God led the righteous and punished the undeserving.

The hand's functions were often generalized to take on broader meanings. Because one takes possession of an object with the hand, the word was used to suggest ownership or dominion. For example, God is said to have delivered the Israelites from "the hand of Pharaoh" (Deut 7:8). To give one's hand to another was to make a pledge or promise obedience.

In biblical times, people spoke of the right or the left hand, often meaning the right or left side of the body. Jesus is at God's right hand because that is the side of power and authority and therefore a place of honor (Mk 16:19). By contrast, the left hand, which is typically the weaker physically, is often linked with negative attributes that range from foolishness to wickedness (Mt 25:41). Those who cannot distinguish the right hand from the left are thought to be like children, lacking knowledge or moral perception (Jon 4:11).

In the Old Testament, one's sins were transferred by the hands to the sacrificial animal (Lev 16:21). Before a blasphemer was stoned to death, all who heard him profane God put their hands on his head (Lev 24:14). In the New Testament, "the laying on of hands" transmitted power in acts of healing, blessing, ordination, and baptism.

Hands reach skyward in prayer toward the symbols of a Canaanite moon god on this 13th-century BC stele.

HANGING

THE GOD OF OUR ANCESTORS RAISED UP JESUS, WHOM YOU HAD KILLED BY HANGING HIM ON A TREE.
–ACTS OF THE APOSTLES 5:30

The Bible contains many references to hanging, yet criminals and betrayers of God's law were not executed by this means. The Israelites used STONING as capital punishment; once the victim had died he was suspended, or hanged, from a tree as an act of desecration and as a deterrent to potential wrongdoers. Deuteronomy states that such exposed corpses must be removed and buried before sundown to prevent the defiling of God's land (Deut 21:22–23).

The Egyptians apparently followed the same practice, for the imprisoned Joseph predicted that Pharaoh's baker would be hanged "on a pole" (Gen 40:19). In the book of Esther, the death of Haman—on the same gallows he had built for Mordecai—may not have been by hanging (Esth 7:10). "Gallows" is the translation of the Hebrew word meaning "pole" or "stake," suggesting that Haman died from impaling. The New Testament passage cited above refers to Jesus' crucifixion as his "hanging" and his cross as a "tree." Judas, who betrayed Jesus, committed suicide by hanging himself, according to Matthew 27:5.

HARD-HEARTED

HAPPY IS THE ONE WHO IS NEVER WITHOUT FEAR, BUT ONE WHO IS HARD-HEARTED WILL FALL INTO CALAMITY.
–PROVERBS 28:14

In the Bible, the term *hard-hearted* is used to describe a person who is stubborn, especially one whose hard heart prevents him from accepting God's will. A heart is hardened either by an individual's actions or, less often, by God's (Ex 8:15). The term also implies skepticism. When his disciples worried about not having enough bread to eat, Jesus reminded them of how he fed 4,000 people with only seven loaves of bread and asked, "Why are you talking about having no bread? Do you still not perceive or understand? Are your hearts hardened?" (Mk 8:17).

HAREM

". . . GATHER ALL THE BEAUTIFUL YOUNG VIRGINS TO THE HAREM . . . ."
–ESTHER 2:3

A harem—literally "the house of the women"—was the secure, private section of a house designated for women. Sequestering women was a custom practiced in ancient Semitic cultures. Esther was one of a number of young virgins who were gathered into a harem at the royal Persian court. Under the supervision of a EUNUCH, the virgins were cared for and given cosmetic treatments for a year; then, one by one, they spent the night with the king. From then on they were concubines and were secluded in a second harem (Esth 2:12–14). King Solomon had a harem of "seven hundred princesses and three hundred concubines" (1 Kings 11:3).

Condemned for keeping a large harem of foreign women in the book of 1 Kings, Solomon reclines happily among them in this 19th-century painting by James Tissot.

HARVEST

SO LET US NOT GROW WEARY IN DOING WHAT IS RIGHT, FOR WE WILL REAP AT HARVEST TIME . . . .
–GALATIANS 6:9

There were two main harvest seasons in biblical times, each lasting about seven weeks: the grain harvest in spring and early summer, and the fruit and vegetable harvest in late summer through early autumn. Crops planted in the hot desert or in coastal areas bore fruit earlier than crops planted in hilly or mountainous regions. Typically barley was gathered from April to May and wheat from May to June. These grains were either cut with sickles or pulled whole from the ground. The stalks were bound into sheaves and carried to the threshing floor by donkey or camel. Grapes, cucumbers, and melons were picked by hand in August and September, and olives were collected from mid-September to mid-November by knocking the trees with sticks.

Everyone in the family joined in the work of the harvest, which was an occasion for rejoicing. Many festivals corresponded to the yearly harvests, and the FIRST FRUITS were ritually offered to the Lord (Ex 23:16). Like nearly all aspects of farming, the harvest is mentioned figuratively in the Bible. In Galatians, reaping the harvest is used as a metaphor for the reward of eternal life.

Men harvest olives in this scene on a sixth-century BC Greek vase.

HASIDEANS

. . . A COMPANY OF HASIDEANS, MIGHTY WARRIORS OF ISRAEL . . . OFFERED THEMSELVES WILLINGLY FOR THE LAW.
–1 MACCABEES 2:42

Mentioned only in the Apocrypha, the Hasideans, or "pious ones," were a group of Jews who zealously observed Mosaic law. When Syrian invaders tried to force Israel to abandon Judaism and adopt Greek customs, the Hasideans joined other Jewish groups in the successful Maccabean guerrilla war to regain their independence. The Hasideans sought only religious FREEDOM, unlike other Maccabeans, who demanded political liberty as well. Most scholars believe that the Hasideans later split into two sects: the biblical Pharisees, who tried to win others to their views, and the Essenes, some of whom withdrew into isolated communities in order to wait for what they thought was the approaching end of the world.

HAWK

"Is it by your wisdom that the hawk soars, and spreads its wings toward the south?"
–Job 39:26

Common in the Holy Land, hawks probably included the sparrow hawk and several other species. Being carnivorous, these birds were considered "an abomination" unfit to eat (Lev 11:13, 16). Hawks, which nested in tall trees and on rocky cliffs, were associated with desolate terrain. In predicting the end of Israel's enemy Edom, Isaiah declared that "the hawk . . . shall possess" the ruins of that country (Isa 34:11). Yet the sight of hawks flying over the Jordan River valley on their southern migratory route was an inspiring one, and in the book of Job, God counts the soaring bird among his wondrous creations.

Because it is a bird of prey, the hawk was considered unclean according to Mosaic law.

HEAD

Blessings are on the head of the righteous . . . .
–Proverbs 10:6

The head was considered the source of life and energy rather than the seat of intelligence, which was believed to be the heart. Thus, covering the head with ashes or the hand was a display of grief. The importance of the head is reflected in the battlefield custom, practiced throughout the ancient Near East, of insulting a slain enemy by cutting off his head. David presented Goliath's head to Saul, whose own head would later be severed by the avenging Philistines. Other customs affirmed the importance of the head in a positive way, such as laying hands on the head to confer blessings or anointing the head with oil to signify happiness and prosperity. A person conventionally showed humility by bowing his head. Laying hands upon the head of a sacrificial offering transferred sins to the animal.

The Bible treats the head not only as the foremost part of the human BODY but also as a metaphor for a regional or family leader. Paul speaks of Jesus as the head of his church (Col 1:18). These symbolic references emphasize that the body cannot exist without the head.

HEALING

Do all possess gifts of healing? Do all speak in tongues? Do all interpret?
–1 Corinthians 12:30

Healing in the ancient Near East could involve folk medicine, treatment by physicians, prayers to a deity, or any combination thereof. The medical knowledge of the day was often considered inferior to the power of a holy man who was able to heal, such as Elijah, Jesus, and Paul. These healers, much like similarly gifted people mentioned in nonscriptural writings, might employ special gestures, material aids, and foreign words. Typically they practiced the "laying on of hands," for the hands were believed to have the power to confer wholeness. They could heal DISEASE, restoring the afflicted to health through God's intervention. So-called miracles involved an immediate, permanent cure.

Relatively few instances of healing occur in the Old Testament, except during the exodus and in the time of Elijah and Elisha. In the New Testament, however, there are many such occurrences. The Gospels tell of Jesus healing numerous people, sometimes in groups. He often used traditional healing methods, such as making clay from spittle to put on blind eyes. When curing a man of both deafness and a speech impediment, he commanded, "Ephphatha" (Mk 7:34), an Aramaic word meaning "be opened." Acts of the Apostles and the apostles' letters refer to healings by Jesus' followers (see illustration).

HEART

Pour out your heart like water before the presence of the Lord!–Lamentations 2:19

The heart, taken to mean the inner organs in a general sense rather than the specific muscle that causes blood circulation, was associated by the Israelites with such concepts as personality, mind, and character. Biblical references to thinking—such as remembering, concentrating, and pondering—were thought to be actions of the heart. Feelings, too, emanated from the heart, ranging from sorrow to ecstasy, from hate to love. Scriptural writers believed that because God could see clearly into the heart, he could discern the truth about hidden thoughts, intents, and emotions. Perhaps most important, however, is the spiritual function of the heart as God's dwelling. Calls made for repentance and conversion in the New Testament are a continuation of pleas in the Old Testament for the human heart to change. It is "the pure in heart" who "will see God" (Mt 5:8).

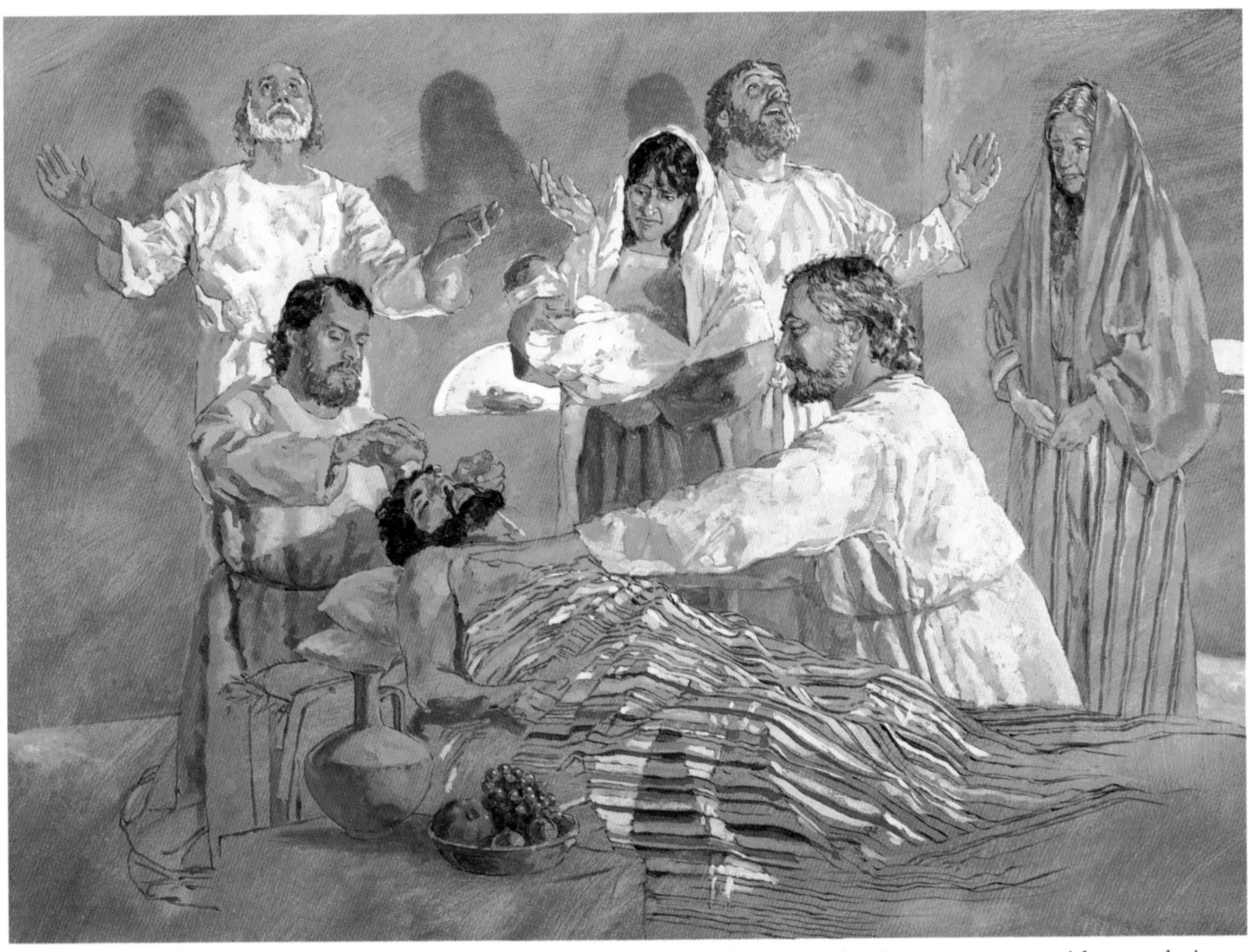

Church leaders often performed healing acts among the early Christians. Above, elders of the church attempt to cure a sick man, who is being watched over by his family. Two of the elders stand over his sickbed and pray for the restoration of his health. A third anoints his head with oil, and a fourth lays his hands upon the patient in order to transmit divine healing power to him.

HEARTH

THE BURNT OFFERING ITSELF SHALL REMAIN ON THE HEARTH UPON THE ALTAR ALL NIGHT. . . .
–LEVITICUS 6:9

Sacrifices, or offerings—including incense, grain, and portions of slaughtered animals—were burnt on the upper portion of an altar known as the altar hearth. The hearths described in Ezekiel were used to "boil the sacrifices of the people" (Ezek 46:23–24).

Hearths were also features of simple homes. Often merely a depression in the floor, a hearth held a fire that was used for both cooking and heating. Ancient houses had no chimneys, so the smoke from the hearth had to be dispersed through an open window or door, or the hearth could be in an open-air courtyard.

HEAVEN

. . . SEE IF I WILL NOT OPEN THE WINDOWS OF HEAVEN FOR YOU AND POUR DOWN FOR YOU AN OVERFLOWING BLESSING.
–MALACHI 3:10

Like all other ancient peoples, the Israelites formed their concept of the universe from unaided visual observation. To them, the entire universe consisted of heaven—a huge transparent dome where God and his hosts lived—and earth. Air, space, and sky were included in their idea of heaven, or the heavens (although the Hebrew term for heaven is plural, it referred to a single place). The sky was blue because great waters were held back by the firmament—a kind of partition that separated God's realm from the human world. Through its windows fell RAIN. Not only rainfall but also other weather phenomena, such as snow, hail, and wind, were stockpiled in God's heavenly "storehouses" (Job 38:22; Ps 135:7). Birds flew in the heavens, which were supported by "pillars" (Job 26:11) or "foundations"

(2 Sam 22:8) that may have been the earth itself. Biblical writers used such vivid images to describe the universe; it may be, however, that not everyone of the time took them literally.

Like the rest of creation, the heavens are subservient to God alone, not teeming with lesser gods as in other religions. When Jesus speaks of the "kingdom of heaven" in the Gospel of Matthew, this is equivalent to the "kingdom of God" that Mark and Luke use in parallel passages. In Acts of the Apostles, Jesus himself ascends into heaven (Acts 1:9–11). Some New Testament writings present a vision of a heavenly home that will also accommodate the faithful. "In my Father's house there are many dwelling places," Jesus tells his disciples in John 14:2. Paul writes to the Corinthians that "we have a building from God, a house not made with hands, eternal in the heavens" (2 Cor 5:1).

HEBREW

AND THEY ASSEMBLED THEM AT THE PLACE THAT IN HEBREW IS CALLED HARMAGEDON. –REVELATION 16:16

Hebrew is one of the Northwest Semitic group of languages, along with Ugaritic, Phoenician, Aramaic, and others. Its origins are obscure, but it probably developed from Canaanite toward the end of the second millennium BC. The word *Hebrew* is rarely used by biblical writers for the language, which is also called "the language of Judah" (Neh 13:24) and "the language of Canaan" (Isa 19:18). In the Bible, the term usually refers to a person such as Abraham or a descendant who is living outside traditional territory—for example, the Israelites who lived in Egypt before the exodus.

The Old Testament was written in Hebrew, except for Aramaic portions of the books of Daniel and Ezra. The Hebrew alphabet—consisting of 22 characters, with text written from right to left—was probably adapted from the Phoenician alphabet. It is difficult to reconstruct the ancient pronunciation of Hebrew because all the letters were originally consonants; not until the 10th century BC were some letters also used to mark vowel sounds at the end of words.

Hebrew inscriptions on pottery fragments list, at left, provisions for soldiers and, below, the price of gold from Ophir—30 shekels.

As a spoken language, Hebrew was largely supplanted by Aramaic, which was originally the language of ancient Syria but was widely used for international commerce in the Near East by the middle of the first millennium BC. When Nehemiah returned to Jerusalem from captivity in Babylon in the fifth century BC, he complained that some of the Jewish children "could not speak the language of Judah" (Neh 13:24). However, priests and other educated persons continued to use Hebrew. A number of Hebrew words, including *myrrh* and *jubilee,* have come into the English language.

HEBREWS, LETTER TO THE

LONG AGO GOD SPOKE TO OUR ANCESTORS IN MANY AND VARIOUS WAYS BY THE PROPHETS, BUT IN THESE LAST DAYS HE HAS SPOKEN TO US BY A SON . . . .–HEBREWS 1:1–2

An unknown author wrote the New Testament letter to the Hebrews, apparently to persuade Jewish Christians that God's new covenant, through Jesus, supersedes that of the old covenant. Drawing heavily from Old Testament books, especially Leviticus, the writer presents a detailed analysis intended to show that Jesus is superior to Moses, the prophets, and priests. He calls Jesus "the pioneer of . . . salvation" (Heb 2:10) and portrays his sacrifice—his death—as supplanting Old Testament sacrifices, which had to be repeated and only atoned for the sins of those involved in the rituals. The letter concludes by calling on all believers to emulate the characteristics of Jesus: faith, love, and perseverance.

HEDGE

THE BEST OF THEM IS LIKE A BRIER, THE MOST UPRIGHT OF THEM A THORN HEDGE.–MICAH 7:4

Prickly PLANTS grew wild in the arid countryside of the Holy Land, a constant threat to people and animals. But when cultivated as hedges, they protected vineyards by fencing out wild animals and human intruders. The prophet Isaiah spoke of this protection when comparing Israel with a vineyard: "I will remove its hedge, and it shall be devoured" (Isa 5:5). Similarly, Hosea recorded God's plan to keep Israel—here his "wife"—away from the temptation of idolatry: "I will hedge up her way with thorns . . . so that she cannot find her paths" (Hos 2:6).

This medieval illumination, a page from the prayer book of a European duchess, offers a fantastical view of hell.

HELL

"... FEAR HIM WHO, AFTER HE HAS KILLED, HAS AUTHORITY TO CAST INTO HELL."–LUKE 12:5

Jesus warned his disciples of a hell with "eternal fire prepared for the devil and his angels" (Mt 25:41). He also spoke of humans being thrown into hell and "salted with fire" (Mk 9:49), and he said that God could "destroy both soul and body in hell" (Mt 10:28). In one confrontation, Jesus asked Pharisees and Jewish scholars, "How can you escape being sentenced to hell?" (Mt 23:33).

The Old Testament does not speak of a place where the wicked are tormented after death. From Genesis through the books of the prophets, biblical writers used the Hebrew word *Sheol,* which has several different meanings: death, the grave, and the underworld abode of all the dead—wicked and righteous alike. Hades, which Jesus refers to in the parable of Lazarus and the rich man, also means a dwelling place for souls of the dead. The Old Testament does, however, contain a seed for the later Jewish and Christian understanding of hell. Daniel speaks of a resurrection of everlasting life for some and "everlasting contempt" for others (Dan 12:2).

As early as the third century BC, Jewish writers began referring to a place of punishment for sinners, using the same word that Jesus, according to some biblical translations, used: *Gehenna,* from a Hebrew phrase meaning "valley of Hinnom." This ravine, south of Jerusalem, is mentioned in the Old Testament as a place where children were passed through fire as an offering to the god Molech (2 Kings 23:10). Perhaps because of this, Gehenna became a metaphor for the place of eternal damnation.

Revelation says that at the end of human history, Death and Hades will be thrown into the "lake of fire"—also called the second death—along with everyone whose name is not written in the BOOK OF LIFE (Rev 20:14–15).

HELMET

SAUL CLOTHED DAVID WITH HIS ARMOR; HE PUT A BRONZE HELMET ON HIS HEAD ....–1 SAMUEL 17:38

Soldiers wore helmets as early as the third millennium BC. Helmets were made of various materials—usually metal or leather but sometimes cloth, felt, or wood—and in different styles. Assyrian armies used conical helmets with elongated neck pieces; Romans relied on snug-fitting models often decorated with plumes or hair. The variation in design helped soldiers to distinguish their enemies more readily during combat. The helmet could be a symbol of protection against evil spiritual forces: "Take the helmet of salvation, and the sword of the Spirit, which is the word of God" (Eph 6:17).

An iron helmet from about AD 100 has earflaps and a neck guard.

HEM

... I SAW THE LORD SITTING ON A THRONE, HIGH AND LOFTY; AND THE HEM OF HIS ROBE FILLED THE TEMPLE.–ISAIAH 6:1

The word *hem* in the Bible usually refers to the border or the skirts of a garment. Aaron's priestly ROBE had a hem decorated with gold bells and "pomegranates of blue, purple, and crimson yarns" (Ex 39:24). In some Bible translations, *hem* signifies "fringes" or "tassels," the gathered threads that Israelite men wore at the "corners" (possibly formed by vertical bands of cloth) of their outer robes to remind them of God's law (Num 15:37–41). Jesus' power to heal was so strong that a woman suffering from hemorrhages was cured by touching the "fringe" of his cloak (Mt 9:20).

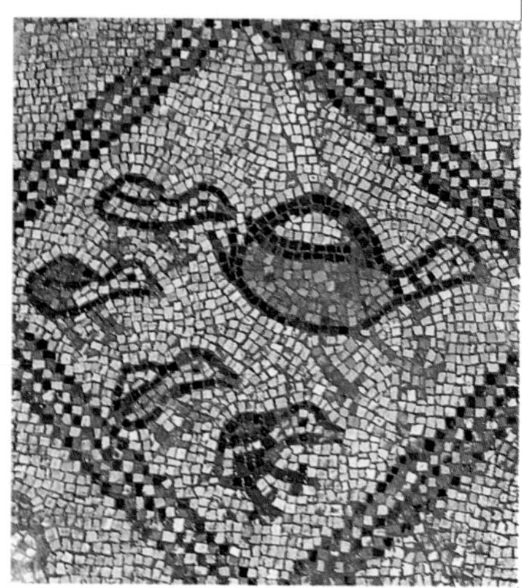

A hen and her chicks form part of the mosaic floor of a sixth-century AD *synagogue.*

Hen

"How often have I desired to gather your children together as a hen gathers her brood under her wings, and you were not willing!"–Luke 13:34

Chiding Jerusalem for its rejection of God's messengers, Jesus compared his love for its inhabitants with the motherly protection that the hen provides for her young. Originally from India, the domesticated chicken had been brought to the Holy Land as early as the middle of the second millennium BC.

In 2 Esdras 1:30, the writer of the apocryphal book may have been echoing the words of Jesus when he wrote of God saying to Israel, "I gathered you as a hen gathers her chicks under her wings."

Herald

In the first year of King Cyrus of Persia . . . he sent a herald throughout all his kingdom . . . .
–2 Chronicles 36:22

A herald was a government official who proclaimed the news. He was responsible for announcing royal proclamations to the public; he could also carry official pronouncements to other courts.

Noah's life was so exemplary that he is called a "herald of righteousness" (2 Pet 2:5). In his letters to Timothy, Paul refers to himself metaphorically as a herald, whose job it is to proclaim the message from God. In the second letter, he says, "For this gospel I was appointed a herald and an apostle and a teacher" (2 Tim 1:11).

Herb

For neither herb nor poultice cured them, but it was your word, O Lord, that heals all people.
–Wisdom of Solomon 16:12

The author of the Wisdom of Solomon, alluding to an incident described in Numbers 21, recalls that the Israelites, when bitten by snakes as a warning from God, were cured not by medicinal herbs but by the word of God.

Many herbs were used as medicines and as ingredients in cooking and in preparing cosmetics. Among those mentioned in the Bible are coriander, cummin, dill, mint, and rue. See also BITTER HERBS.

Herd

". . . he was loath to take one of his own flock or herd to prepare for the wayfarer . . . ."–2 Samuel 12:4

An animal from the herd was often used for a meal or a sacrifice to God. Almost any group of domesticated animals—sheep, goats, or swine—could be called a herd, though the word was most often used for cattle. Joseph saved the starving Egyptians by buying their cattle, but the following year they were again lamenting that "our money is all spent; and the herds of cattle are my lord's" (Gen 47:18). The person in charge of the herd was called a herdsman, which was Amos' occupation before he became a prophet (Am 7:14–15).

Hewn

. . . you have built houses of hewn stone, but you shall not live in them . . . .–Amos 5:11

To hew is to cut or shape by means of a heavy cutting instrument, such as an ax or a chisel. When God brought the Israelites into Canaan, he provided "hewn cisterns that you did not hew" (Deut 6:11), thereby sparing them the labor of cutting through rock. God forbade his people to build an altar of "hewn stones" (Ex 20:25), which would too closely resemble the Canaanite altars. "Hewers of wood" (Josh 9:21) may have cut wood or simply gathered firewood, a lowly task often reserved for slaves or foreigners. See also DRAWERS OF WATER.

High Place

He burned the high place, crushing it to dust . . . .
–2 Kings 23:15

Mountains, hilltops, and other natural elevations were used as places of worship by the Canaanites and, later, the Israelites. The term *high place* can refer to such a location or to an altar erected on a plain or in the midst of a town. Here religious practices were carried out: animal sacrifices were offered to various deities—including the God of Israel—

incense was burned, and statues and other cult items were set up.

Although Moses directed the Israelites to destroy the Canaanite high places (Deut 12:2–3), not all the people obeyed his order; some used the sites for their own worship. According to 1 Kings 3:2, "The people were sacrificing at the high places . . . because no house had yet been built for the name of the LORD."

With King Solomon's construction of the temple at Jerusalem, worship was centralized and the continued use of high places was condemned. High places once again became associated with rituals for false idols; however, Solomon himself built them so that his foreign wives would be able to worship their gods (1 Kings 11:7–8). Several centuries later—in the seventh century BC—King Josiah of Judah launched a great religious reform, during which he systematically destroyed the high places. He defiled them and "burned the bones" of the priests who had carried out rites there (2 Chr 34:3–7).

Archaeologists have excavated numerous high places, notably at Megiddo and Dan.

The rolling hill country of the Holy Land includes the region of Samaria, shown above.

High Priest

THOSE WHO HAD ARRESTED JESUS TOOK HIM TO CAIAPHAS THE HIGH PRIEST . . . .–MATTHEW 26:57

The high priest had the greatest authority of the temple priests and was the only one allowed to perform the holiest rite of the year. On the Day of Atonement he entered the most sacred room in the TEMPLE and sprinkled the blood of a goat on the ark of the covenant to atone for the sins of Israel.

The high priesthood was a lifetime position reserved for firstborn descendants of Zadok, a descendant of Aaron and a priest when Solomon built the first temple. Like other priests, the high priest had to be free of physical defects, but he was held to a higher degree of ritual purity. Unlike other priests, he could not touch corpses, including those of his parents, nor could he show customary signs of grief, such as tearing his clothes. His garments also set him apart. Over the priest's traditional white robe, the high priest added a blue robe fringed with golden bells. On his chest hung a breastpiece of 12 stones representing the tribes of Israel, and on his head rested a turban with a golden rosette inscribed "Holy to the LORD" (Ex 28:36).

When the Jews returned from the Babylonian exile without a king, the high priest assumed greater political prominence. After the Jewish revolt for freedom in the second century BC, the office of king was reestablished and combined with that of high priest. Thus a Hasmonean ruler became high priest, ending Israel's long tradition of the Zadokite priesthood. After Herod the Great crushed the Hasmonean dynasty, he took the liberty of appointing high priests whenever he wanted. The Romans did the same, with Caiaphas being one of their appointees, until they destroyed the temple in AD 70, thus ending the need for a high priest.

Hill

WHO SHALL ASCEND THE HILL OF THE LORD? AND WHO SHALL STAND IN HIS HOLY PLACE?–PSALM 24:3

The Bible uses *hill* and *hill country* to refer to elevated areas of the Holy Land, but it is not always clear whether a single hill or a range of hills is meant. The raised spine of land that runs between the Mediterranean coastal plain and the Jordan River valley is called hill country, as is the hilly area along the Jordan's east bank. In the Gospel of Luke, "the brow of the hill" describes a cliff (Lk 4:29); when Jesus offends the people in the Nazareth synagogue, a mob pursues him to a hill outside town and attempts to hurl him from it.

This detail from a 19th-century German painting depicts Jacob's fierce struggle on the bank of the Jabbok River with an angel, who strikes him on the hip.

Hip

The sun rose upon [Jacob] as he passed Penuel, limping because of his hip.
–Genesis 32:31

Jacob wrestled stubbornly all night with an angel beside the Jabbok River at Peniel, earning the new name *Israel*, or "the one who strives with God." His struggles ceased at daybreak, when his hip was dislocated. The resulting limp symbolized Jacob's submission to divine will. As a ritual commemoration of this unusual face-to-face meeting with the Lord, biblical dietary laws forbade eating the THIGH muscle at the hip socket of an animal (Gen 32:32). In ancient Hebrew, the expression "hip and thigh" signified utter destruction, such as when Samson slaughtered a band of Philistines (Judg 15:8).

Hiss

All your enemies open their mouths against you; they hiss, they gnash their teeth, they cry . . . .
–Lamentations 2:16

The sharp hissing sound created by forcing breath between the teeth and tongue was both a form of derision and an expression indicating amazement in biblical times. The word comes from the Hebrew root meaning "to whistle." Sometimes hand clapping, the GNASHING OF TEETH, or the shaking of the head or fist accompanied the hissing. Defeated enemy lands and cities were hissed at, as was the city of Jerusalem and its temple, which were laid to waste: "they hiss and wag their heads at daughter Jerusalem; 'Is this the city that was called the perfection of beauty, the joy of all the earth?'" (Lam 2:15).

Holiness

"Who is like you, O LORD, among the gods? Who is like you, majestic in holiness, awesome in splendor, doing wonders?"
–Exodus 15:11

The Bible refers to several kinds of holiness. One is the righteous and morally perfect nature of God; another is the sacredness of places, objects, and days such as the sabbath, which are dedicated to the Lord. Still another is the saintly character of people who devote themselves to obeying God.

The holiness of God stems from his moral perfection and uniqueness. "Holy, holy, holy is the LORD of hosts," said the seraphs who appeared in Isaiah's vision (Isa 6:3). Scholars are not certain where the term *holy* originated, but throughout the Scriptures the word usually designates something separate from the ordinary, both hallowed and revered.

Because God is holy and righteous, everything associated with him is required to be holy as well. In the Old Testament, objects of worship were rendered holy and sacred through rituals God prescribed. "Anoint the tabernacle and all that is in it," God told Moses. "Consecrate it and all its furniture, so that it shall become holy" (Ex 40:9). The people of Israel were holy because God set them apart from other nations, choosing them to become his treasured possession. They could keep their holy status only by complying with the laws God gave them through Moses. In part, this involved maintaining distance from other nations by not intermarrying (Deut 7:3–4) or joining in military alliances.

Sites visited by God also became holy because of his presence. When appearing to Moses in the burning bush, God said, "Remove the sandals from your feet, for the place on which you are standing is holy ground" (Ex 3:5). Similarly, the ark of the covenant, which held the ten commandments and symbolized the presence of God among the Israelites, was kept in the inner sanctum of the temple—the most holy place. The high priest entered this room only once a year, on the Day of Atonement, to offer sacrifices to the Lord to expiate the sins of the nation.

In the New Testament, holiness was no longer dependent upon sacrificial rituals. Christians believed that with the death of Jesus, the new covenant that Jeremiah prophesied had arrived. God had spoken through the prophet: "I will put my law within them, and I will write it on their hearts" (Jer 31:33). Christians further believed that through the guidance and power of the Holy Spirit dwelling within them, they could live a good and loving life, even in a world marred by evil. They did not feel the need to separate themselves from the ungodly. Rather, they were to be a shining light that would draw the world to Christianity. In so doing, they were presenting themselves "as a living sacrifice, holy and acceptable to God" (Rom 12:1).

Holy Convocation

Six days shall work be done; but the seventh day is a sabbath of complete rest, a holy convocation . . . .
–Leviticus 23:3

The Lord described in detail to Moses all the FESTIVAL days that he commanded the people of Israel to celebrate. In each case, the congregation was to be called together in "holy convocation" to begin worship, and all regular work was to be put aside. The signal to assemble was the sound of silver trumpets. The days designated by God as holy convocations were the weekly sabbath, the first and seventh day of Passover, the Festival of Weeks, the first day of the month of Tishri, the Day of Atonement, and the first and eighth days of the Festival of Booths.

Bees return to their hives to make sweet honey in this illumination.

Honey

Your lips distill nectar, my bride; honey and milk are under your tongue . . . .
–Song of Solomon 4:11

The seductive sweetness of honey made it a favorite food and a symbol of fruitfulness in Old Testament times. People collected wild honey and honeycombs from holes in the ground, crevices between rocks, and even from animal carcasses (Judg 14:9). Beekeeping was probably not practiced in Palestine before the fourth century BC, when hives were made of wicker and straw.

During the spring, bees in the Black Sea region of Asia Minor produced "mad honey," which had intoxicating and even poisonous effects. The spring blossoms of the rhododendron, azalea, and oleander plants, from which the bees collected nectar, were its apparent source. When the Bible described the Promised Land as "flowing with milk and honey" (Ex 3:8), the word translated as "honey" probably meant a syrup made from fruits, such as grapes or dates, rather than honey made by bees. Possibly because it tended to ferment, honey could not be used in burnt offerings to God (Lev 2:11).

Hook

With hooks they put him in a cage, and brought him to the king of Babylon . . . .
–Ezekiel 19:9

The people of biblical times used hooks for many purposes, from hanging curtains to subduing wild animals. In the book of Exodus, hooks of gold or silver fixed the hangings of the court of the tabernacle to pillars (Ex 26:32; 27:10). Because animals, both tame and savage, were led by hooks put in their noses, God asked Job whether the monster Behemoth might be captured "with hooks" (Job 40:24). Similarly, military victors led captives by means of small hooks or thongs inserted in their noses or jaws. Less gruesome uses for these implements were as fishhooks and as "pruning hooks" (Isa 18:5), which were small, sickle-shaped knives used to trim vines. In time of war, however, pruning hooks could be converted into spears (Joel 3:10).

The iron tip of an ancient piercing tool is flanked by two iron hooks, excavated from the city of Dor.

HORN

Arise and thresh, O daughter Zion, for I will make your horn iron and your hoofs bronze; you shall beat in pieces many peoples . . . .
–Micah 4:13

Horns, the pair of curved bony organs that grow out of the heads of animals such as the ram, goat, or ox, were used as containers for oil, as sturdy but flexible material for bows, and as musical instruments. A ram's horn, or shofar, figured in Joshua's successful attack on Jericho, an important battle in his conquest of Canaan. God ordered Joshua to have the priests blow trumpets of ram's horn as a signal to the people to shout (Josh 6:5). This instrument, also translated as "trumpet," was blown on the New Year festival (Lev 23:24), the Day of Atonement (Lev 25:9), and other major holy days (Ps 81:3).

Since animals fought with their horns, biblical writers used the horn as a symbol of strength: God promised to make Zion's horn iron so that she might have power over her enemies. Cutting off a horn signified that power was lost (Jer 48:25). Horns were often placed at the corners of an altar (Ex 27:1–2), and one could seek sanctuary by clutching them (1 Kings 1:50).

HORNETS

"I sent the hornet ahead of you, which drove out before you the two kings of the Amorites . . . . "
–Joshua 24:12

Sometimes called a wasp, the hornet was a large flying insect that was feared because of its painful sting. Common in the desert, the hornet could madden horses and cattle into a terrifying stampede. Hornets were sent by the Lord to harass Israel's enemies, such as in the book of Joshua, although the Bible sometimes uses the phrase "the pestilence" to refer to these persistent insects (Ex 23:28; Deut 7:20). One writer interprets God's sending wasps to plague the Canaanites as a kind of leniency: because they worked "little by little," the Canaanites might have time to repent (Wis 12:8–10).

HORSE

Harness the horses; mount the steeds! Take your stations with your helmets, whet your lances, put on your coats of mail!
–Jeremiah 46:4

Horses were first introduced in the Holy Land in the second millennium BC, although they were not commonly used by the Israelites until the time of Solomon. A symbol of strength and speed, the horse was used in war principally to pull chariots and later to carry fighting men. The Bible passage cited above, in which Jeremiah mockingly calls the Egyptians to arms, gives a vivid description of the way in which horses were used on the battlefield.

The book of Deuteronomy cautions the king not to acquire too many horses (Deut 17:16). Samuel warned those who were in favor of a monarchy that a king would build an army and take away their sons to drive his chariots (1 Sam 8:11). David kept horses for 100 chariots but chose to HAMSTRING captured horses (2 Sam 8:4); Solomon kept thousands of them (2 Chr 9:25). In Apocalyptic literature, horses bearing symbolic colors marked the end of time (Zech 6:1–8; Rev 6:1–8).

This eighth-century BC horse was finely crafted with saddle and reins.

HOSANNA

So they took branches of palm trees and went out to meet him, shouting, "Hosanna! Blessed is the one who comes in the name of the Lord . . . ."
–John 12:13

The word *hosanna* means "save us, please!" and comes from the Hebrew phrase *Hoshia-na* in Psalm 118:25. The Israelites recited this psalm and waved palm branches during the annual procession at the Festival of Booths. The people came to associate this psalm with the Messiah, who they hoped would restore Israel's golden age.

The cry of hosanna was raised in only one biblical scene, when the multitude greeted Jesus as he entered Jerusalem on the Sunday before his crucifixion. The crowd's use of another messsianic phrase—"Hosanna to the Son of David!"—implied that they believed Jesus was the Messiah (Mt 21:9).

HOSEA, BOOK OF

. . . the LORD said to Hosea, "Go, take for yourself a wife of whoredom . . . for the land commits great whoredom by forsaking the LORD."
–Hosea 1:2

The prophet Hosea, to whom this Old Testament book has been attributed, lived during the last years of the northern kingdom of Israel, before Assyria conquered the land in 722 BC. At the time, the Israelites had forsaken God. In their desire for bountiful crops and large families they worshiped Baal, the Canaanite god of fertility. Further, Israel's leaders so feared an invasion that they formed alliances with other nations instead of obeying the prophets, who urged them to trust God for protection. Hosea violently condemned the people for their unfaithfulness.

In the book of Hosea, the prophet's marriage to a prostitute, who left him for a lover, was a symbol of Israel's broken covenant with God. Hosea described God as the husband and Israel as the adulterous wife. Just as Hosea had a legal right to execute his wife for her adultery, so too—according to the covenant agreement—could God destroy Israel for her unfaithfulness. However, God instructed Hosea to love his wife as much as God loved his chosen people, promising that Hosea's love would redeem his wife, just as God's love would restore Israel.

Hospitality

Do not neglect to show hospitality to strangers, for by doing that some have entertained angels without knowing it.
–Hebrews 13:2

As there were few inns in ancient times, it was common courtesy to welcome travelers into private homes as honored guests. Providing a stranger with food and shelter in one's house was a highly commended practice throughout the ancient Mediterranean world. It was customary for the host to wash the feet of a guest and anoint his head with oil. The Israelites—once nomads and strangers themselves in Egypt—were commanded to open their homes and "love the alien as yourself" (Lev 19:34). In the book of Isaiah, hospitality—especially when extended to the poor—was portrayed as more virtuous than fasting.

Abraham humbly offers his hospitality to God's messengers, above, who reveal that Sarah will bear a son (Gen 18:1–9).

Even though travel was easier and safer by New Testament times, hospitality was still highly valued. Jesus and his disciples were dependent on the hospitality of faithful strangers as they spread the gospel (Mt 10:40–42). Early Christians also opened their homes for worship (1 Cor 16:19), and these house churches became the foundation for the young, fast-growing church. See also INN.

Host of Heaven

"To all of them you give life, and the host of heaven worships you."
–Nehemiah 9:6

The celestial bodies and angelic beings in the heavens were visualized by the Israelites as resembling earthly armies, organized under God in his role as "the LORD of hosts" (1 Sam 17:45). In Deuteronomy 33:2, "myriads of holy ones" were assembled at God's right. No clear distinction was drawn between the invisible supernatural entities and the visible stars, planets, sun, and moon.

The vast forces of nature were also included in these heavenly legions, which were created and sustained by God. The worship of these celestial entities, which was prevalent in other lands such as Assyria and Babylon, was forbidden in ancient Israel (Deut 17:3–5).

Hour

"Keep awake therefore, for you know neither the day nor the hour."–Matthew 25:13

Because the length of days varied according to the seasons and effective time-keeping devices did not exist, it was difficult to reckon hours precisely in ancient times, although sundials were sometimes used in the post-exilic period. By Roman times, an hour was $^{1}/_{12}$ of the daylight starting at sunrise and ending at sunset. Specific hours of the DAY, such as five o'clock and nine o'clock, are cited in the New Testament; three o'clock in the afternoon is called the "hour of prayer" (Acts 3:1).

Units of time like seconds and minutes were unknown, but the Roman concept of counting hours was familiar to Jews in New Testament times. The Roman civil day ran from midnight to midnight, but the Bible does not indicate whether Paul and other missionaries followed this system. Usually, the term *hour* referred to a generalized time of day or an appointed meeting. A repeated theme in the Gospel of John is the "hour" of Jesus' glory—the period beginning with his entry into Jerusalem and climaxing in his resurrection. The period between the assumption and the second coming is "the last hour" (1 John 2:18).

Mosaic pavements were common features in the houses of the wealthy in Jerusalem. Designs built on geometric or rosette patterns in red, white, yellow, and black decorated the floors of bathrooms and other rooms where water was used, as well as in hallways. Other rooms, such as the main reception area, were frequently floored with elaborate mosaics.

Limestone pedestal tables were also common fixtures in the houses of the Jewish quarter. These tables would have been laden with serving wares, as shown above, made from bronze, glass, or a glossy red type of pottery known as terra sigilata*. Large stone jars beneath the table held water or wine. Objects made from stone were more durable but also more expensive than those made from clay.*

Antiques, glassware, and painted pottery were displayed in niches set into walls in the main receiving rooms, where guests could admire their beauty. A cupboard might also safeguard vessels containing special perfumes or oils.

A HOUSE OF RICHES

". . . THE FLOODS CAME, AND THE WINDS BLEW AND BEAT ON THAT HOUSE, BUT IT DID NOT FALL, BECAUSE IT HAD BEEN FOUNDED ON ROCK." —MATTHEW 7:25

The prosperity of the Herodian dynasty, which lasted from 37 BC to AD 70, was reflected in the opulent houses of Jerusalem's Jewish quarter. These spacious homes were built of dressed stone and elegantly decorated with beautiful objects crafted locally or imported from abroad. Many of the quarter's well-to-do Jewish residents lived in houses similar to the one in the illustration at left, which is based on findings from extensive excavations in Jerusalem. As in other houses in the Near East, the rooms were built around a central courtyard, which is paved with flagstone in this example. As was typical, the house consisted of three stories. Public rooms such as the reception hall, which was decorated with an elaborate mosaic, were on the ground floor, and family rooms were situated on the first and second floors. Narrow stairways led to the lower level, or basement, which housed the kitchen, storage rooms, reservoirs, bathrooms, and a pool for ritual cleansing. The walls of the more luxurious rooms were brightly frescoed with geometric or floral patterns and borders, as seen in the room in the top right-hand corner. The ceilings were finished in stucco with decorative raised patterns.

HOUSE

UNLESS THE LORD BUILDS THE HOUSE, THOSE WHO BUILD IT LABOR IN VAIN.–PSALM 127:1

Differences in house construction existed during the Old Testament period, but a standard style did evolve, as excavations have shown. Although a very poor family might have only one or two rooms, the typical Israelite house contained four, which formed a rectangle. The back room ran the width of the house, and three long parallel rooms led to it. Houses were made of sun-dried mud bricks or stone. Most included a courtyard, where families cooked in clay ovens; it was located on the east side of the house so that the prevailing westerly winds could blow away the oven smoke. The courtyard was also sometimes used as a place for animals. Since the house provided little space for furniture, which the poor could not afford anyway, inhabitants slept on mats rolled out on the floors, which might be made from beaten earth or mud and lime plaster.

Modest houses, often referred to as "nests," had few, if any, windows and were dark and hot in summer. Flat roofs, constructed of wooden beams covered with brushwood and clay, provided an escape from the dark interiors and were usually reached by an outside stairway or ladder. People went to their roofs to sleep when it was too warm indoors, as well as to pray and to dry everything from fruits and vegetables to flax and laundry. A parapet surrounded the roof's edge, as Mosaic law dictated, so that no one would fall off (Deut 22:8).

Well-to-do families had larger houses—often two or more stories high—built of cut stone around a central courtyard (see reconstruction, pp. 180–181). These houses frequently had a second courtyard with adjoining rooms. Floors in the more expensive houses might be covered with mosaics, and walls were plastered, often with frescoes. Only the wealthiest could afford rooms paneled with wood, such as cedar. Windows were closed in with lattices and covered with shutters or curtains; glass was rare until the Roman period. Fixed wooden doors opened inward and could be bolted for security. Moveable beds were rare, even in the houses of the rich; a platform covered with cushions doubled as a bed and couch. Chests held clothes and bedding.

The Bible sometimes uses the word *house* in the sense of a family or an ancestral line, such as the house of Joseph or David. See also BUILDING.

In this relief, God creates Eve from the rib of Adam, the first human being.

HUMAN BEING

FOR WHAT HUMAN BEING KNOWS WHAT IS TRULY HUMAN EXCEPT THE HUMAN SPIRIT THAT IS WITHIN? –1 CORINTHIANS 2:11

Although the ancient Israelites believed that a human being consisted of both body and soul, or spirit, they saw not two separate elements but one entity. In their view, the existence of the spirit did not mean personal immortality. Later, under the influence of Greek philosophy, some Jewish thinkers postulated the idea of a soul that might survive death.

One of the fundamental themes of the Bible is the special relationship of the human race with God. This relationship is a defining characteristic of humankind, setting it apart from the animal kingdom and nature. Genesis depicts human beings as superior to nature; indeed, God calls upon them to subdue the earth and fill it with their offspring (Gen 1:28). Genesis does not explain the mystery of how humans are made in the IMAGE OF GOD, although humankind's ability to reason might be one trait it shares with its creator. Also, Adam and Eve may have possessed a higher form of humanity, closer to God's image, before they disobeyed God.

HUMILITY

AND ALL OF YOU MUST CLOTHE YOURSELVES WITH HUMILITY IN YOUR DEALINGS WITH ONE ANOTHER . . . . –1 PETER 5:5

The message that humility is one of the most important qualities for the virtuous runs throughout the Scriptures. Biblical writers emphasize that to be humble, one must recognize God's power and one's own powerlessness and sinfulness. "Remember the long way that the LORD your God has led you these forty years in the wilderness, in order to humble you," Moses told his people. "He humbled you by letting you hunger" (Deut 8:2–3).

In the New Testament, Jesus provided an example of true humility. "Learn from me," he said, "for I am gentle and humble in heart" (Mt 11:29). Preaching the need for humility, he warned his listeners that "all who exalt themselves will be humbled, and all

A hunting scene carved into a slab of black stone was found in the palace of Sargon II, who ruled Assyria in the eighth century BC. At left, a beardless man aims an arrow, probably at a bird. The middle figure carries a bow and arrows, and the hunter at right takes away his game.

who humble themselves will be exalted" (Mt 23:12).

The Bible also places high value on meekness, a quality that combines humility with gentleness. The meeker a person is, the closer to God he is—and the greater his reward. Indeed, as Jesus promised in his Sermon on the Mount: "Blessed are the meek, for they will inherit the earth" (Mt 5:5).

HUNTER

. . . ESAU WAS A SKILLFUL HUNTER, A MAN OF THE FIELD, WHILE JACOB WAS A QUIET MAN, LIVING IN TENTS.–GENESIS 25:27

The Bible seldom mentions hunting and hunters, perhaps because the ancient Israelites were mainly herders or farmers. The Israelites' dietary laws, however, covered wild game as well as domestic animals (Deut 14:4–7)—proof that some hunting occurred. The Israelites killed game encountered by chance and slew lions or bears that threatened their flocks, but most did not choose hunting as a pastime. The first hunter mentioned in the Bible is Nimrod, the "mighty hunter before the Lord" (Gen 10:9). Another notable hunter is Esau, the "man of the field," who is tricked by his brother Jacob out of his birthright. The book of Genesis notes that their father, Isaac, "loved Esau, because he was fond of game" (Gen 25:28).

Among the Egyptians, Phoenicians, and Assyrians, hunting was a popular occupation. Hunters often used dogs and cats to pursue game and birds, and some also struck out after larger beasts, such as lions and hippopotamuses. Josephus, a Jewish historian of the first century AD, noted that Herod the Great, king of Judea, was fond of hunting on horseback.

The hunter's kit included bows and arrows, slingstones, nets, snares for trapping birds, and pits for bears and other large prey.

HUSBAND

"THE LORD GRANT THAT YOU MAY FIND SECURITY, EACH OF YOU IN THE HOUSE OF YOUR HUSBAND."–RUTH 1:9

The role of husband was basically the same in both Old and New Testament times. A husband had authority over his WIFE and was responsible for providing her with material necessities as well as fulfilling her emotional and sexual needs. Israelite law dictated these duties, referred to in Exodus 21:10. The law allowed men to be polygamous, but by New Testament times, monogamy was the norm.

In the Old Testament, God is often described as the husband of Israel, who is sometimes seen as "a faithless wife" (Jer 3:20). Perhaps drawing on this metaphor, the author of the book of Revelation describes the "new Jerusalem" as "coming down out of heaven from God, prepared as a bride adorned for her husband" (Rev 21:2).

Hyena

Is the hyena greedy for my heritage at my command?
–Jeremiah 12:9

Hyenas are indigenous to the Holy Land. Large, striped carnivores with powerful heads and shoulders, they roam at night in search of carrion. Like the jackal, the hyena is a rapacious scavenger. The book of Isaiah pairs these animals as symbols of desolation, prophesying that Babylon will be a place where "hyenas . . . cry in its towers, and jackals in the pleasant palaces" (Isa 13:22). Similarly, Jeremiah predicts, "wild animals shall live with hyenas in Babylon" (Jer 50:39). In Jeremiah 12:9, God laments Judah's destruction and likens its enemies to the hyena.

Hymn

When they had sung the hymn, they went out to the Mount of Olives.
–Mark 14:26

A hymn is a song written to honor God. The first one mentioned in the Bible is the song of Moses, which he and the Israelites sang after they crossed the Red Sea. The lyrics, which are preserved in the book of Exodus, begin: "I will sing to the LORD, for he has triumphed gloriously" (Ex 15:1). The melody remains a mystery, as is true of all the songs in the Bible.

The book of Psalms is a collection of hymns that the Israelites recited or sang during public worship. The theme of a PSALM might be jubilant praise, anguished regret, or a cry for help. Priests sang these hymns in the temple courtyard each day during the sacrifices. Pilgrims traveling to Jerusalem to attend religious festivals sang psalms about the Holy City. Jesus and his disciples sang a hymn during the Last Supper, a Passover meal (Mk 14:26).

Christians continued the tradition of singing psalms in their worship services, adding songs about Jesus and doctrinal beliefs. Many scholars believe that New Testament writers occasionally quoted these hymns. Philippians 2:6–11, for example, is widely accepted as part of such a song. Perhaps the most famous hymn in the New Testament is the Magnificat, Mary's song of praise that begins: "My soul magnifies the Lord" (Lk 1:46).

Tambourine players accompany a singer performing a hymn, as depicted by figurines from the ninth or eighth century BC.

Hypocrite

"You hypocrite, first take the log out of your own eye, and then you will see clearly to take the speck out of your neighbor's eye."
–Matthew 7:5

Some biblical translations use the term *hypocrite* in Old Testament passages to refer to someone who is opposed to God, or "godless." In the New Testament, however, the word describes someone who pretends to be a better person than he really is. Jesus berates hypocrites, who pray and fast ostentatiously, seeking praise (Mt 6:5, 16). He accuses the scribes and the Pharisees of hypocrisy, saying that "they do not practice what they teach" (Mt 23:3), and compares them with "whitewashed tombs, which on the outside look beautiful, but inside they are full of the bones of the dead and of all kinds of filth" (Mt 23:27).

The hyssop shrub, left, produces flower-filled branches, right, that were used as natural brushes.

Hyssop

So they put a sponge full of the wine on a branch of hyssop and held it to his mouth.
–John 19:29

A small, bushy shrub, the hyssop has a cluster of tiny flowers at the end of each stem. In Exodus 12 the Israelites use the plant to mark the doorways of their houses with BLOOD from the Passover lamb. The Gospel of John specifies that a hyssop branch (rather than the "stick" of Matthew and Mark) is used to place wine on Jesus' lips. Here John calls to mind the scene from Exodus; he may be indicating that Jesus, the "Lamb of God" (Jn 1:29), is the new Passover sacrifice. Hyssop was also used to sprinkle liquids in purification rituals, such as those for lepers (Lev 14:2–7).

I J K

A Latin INSCRIPTION appears on a stone from a Roman aqueduct. It speaks of the emperor Hadrian, who ruled from AD 117 to 138.

Idleness

Put him to work, in order that he may not be idle, for idleness teaches much evil.
–Ecclesiasticus 33:28–29

The Bible condemns people who are willfully idle, refusing to work to support themselves. Eccesiasticus, or Sirach, compares an idler with "a filthy stone," so despised that "every one hisses at his disgrace," and to "the filth of dunghills" (Sir 22:1–2). Tobit proclaims that idleness leads to poverty and is "the mother of famine" (Tob 4:13). According to Proverbs, "The appetite of the lazy craves, and gets nothing, while the appetite of the diligent is richly supplied" (Prov 13:4).

In the New Testament, Paul chides church members who are not doing their part: "For we hear that some of you are living in idleness, mere busybodies, not doing any work" (2 Thess 3:11). Disdain for laziness, however, does not extend to those who are unable to find employment (Mt 20:1–16).

Idol

What use is an idol once its maker has shaped it— a cast image, a teacher of lies?
–Habakkuk 2:18

Idols are images intended to represent gods or goddesses. In ancient biblical lands, idolatry—the worship of idols—was almost universal. The sole exception was the nation of Israel, which God sternly forbade to make images of anything, even himself (Ex 20:4).

Although biblical writings suggest that the Israelites' neighbors believed that an idol was the actual deity, in fact they believed that the idol was a sort of house in which the god resided. Through the idol, the god could communicate with worshipers, hear their prayers, smell the sweet savor of incense, and taste and eat the mystical essence of the foods that were offered. The idol—and the god it contained—were believed to go to sleep each night and awaken with the sun each morning. Once awake, the idol could "speak," responding to its devotees' pleas through omens, prophecies, or the casting of lots, which could be manipulated or interpreted by priests to give the desired answer.

Rulers consulted the idol in matters of statecraft and war; ordinary people consulted it for personal problems. Whoever controlled an idol also controlled the god that dwelt within it; therefore, capturing an enemy's idols was a major goal of warfare.

Idols were made of many materials—carved in stone or wood, molded in clay, or cast in metal. The King James Version of the Bible refers to graven and molten images. Idols could take the form of humans, mammals, birds, fish, or human-animal hybrids. There were even idols that were nonrepresentational, such as simple stone or wood pillars, in which the gods were thought to be present. In the Old Testament, wooden pillars—*asherim* in Hebrew—were sacred to the great mother goddess Asherah. The stone pillars were sacred to the god Baal, whose name means "the master" and who controlled the vital rain, according to Canaanite belief.

Cities and states had important idols to whom everyone made sacrifices. Ordinary households had their own private idols—figures called teraphim—to which household members offered humble sacrifices. When moving, people took these idols with them. Before the Babylonian exile, many Israelites also kept teraphim. Rachel went so far as to steal the household GODS of her father, Laban, when she departed with her husband, Jacob (Gen 31:19). Michal, David's first wife, easily found an idol to put in her husband's place in bed to deceive the assassins that were sent by her father, King Saul (1 Sam 19:13–16).

The Israelites sometimes lapsed into idolatry as a nation, the most flagrant example being the golden calf that they made in the desert. Scholars are not certain whether the Israelites were worshiping God in the shape of a calf or whether the calf represented God's throne.

King Ahab, influenced by his foreign wife, Jezebel, built an altar and temple to Baal and set up the sacred pole of Asherah (1 Kings 16:31–33). The wicked King Manasseh even had an image of Asherah set up in the temple in Jerusalem (2 Kings 21:7). On at least one occasion God himself told his people to make an image: when he sent poisonous snakes to afflict the Israelites in the wilderness, he instructed Moses to make a bronze effigy of a SERPENT and mount it on a pole as a talisman against the venom (Num 21:8–9).

Israel's priests and prophets denounced idols in scathing terms. "Destroy all their figured stones, destroy all their cast images," God commanded Moses in Numbers 33:52. Epithets used in the Bible for idols include "scarecrows in a cucumber field" (Jer 10:5) and "detestable things" (Ezek 5:11). The book of Isaiah makes its point by describing the actions of an idol maker: "He plants a cedar and the rain nourishes it. Then it can be used as fuel. Part of it he takes and warms himself; he kindles a fire and bakes bread. Then he makes a god and worships it, makes a carved image and bows down before it" (Isa 44:14–15).

Image of God

So God created humankind in his image, in the image of God he created them . . . . –Genesis 1:27

As the Hebrew word for image signifies a physical likeness, some biblical scholars interpret God's creating human beings "in his image" to mean that people resemble him physically. Others take this to mean that God's image is reflected in the person's whole nature, both body and soul. Whatever the meaning of the term, some scholars speculate that God created humans in his own likeness so that there would be creatures with whom he could have a relationship.

In the New Testament, Paul alludes to the concept of man being made in the likeness of his creator. When writing about head coverings during prayer, he says, "For a man ought not to have his head veiled, since he is the image and reflection of God" (1 Cor 11:7). In Colossians 1:15, however, it is clear that Jesus has preeminently assumed this role, being described as "the image of the invisible God, the firstborn of all creation."

Elijah, shown in an 18th-century Russian icon, escaped death and achieved immortality by the power of God.

Immortality

It is he alone who has immortality and dwells in unapproachable light, whom no one has ever seen or can see . . . . –1 Timothy 6:16

To the Israelites, only their "living God" (Deut 5:26) was inherently immortal—imperishable, eternal, and beyond the power of death. This was in contrast to foreign gods and to human beings. God had proclaimed that Adam and his descendants would be mortal creatures: in Genesis 3:19, God told Adam, who has disobeyed him, that "you are dust, and to dust you shall return." The Israelites believed that death was final but that it might be postponed by good deeds.

In Christian belief, God provided a way for humankind to escape punishment for sin and defeat death by sending Jesus to earth, where he took the place of all human beings and died for their sins. Jesus offered the promise of immortality to believers, declaring that "anyone who hears my word and believes him who sent me has eternal life" (Jn 5:24). According to 2 Timothy 1:10, Jesus "abolished death and brought life and immortality to light."

Import

Solomon's import of horses was from Egypt and Kue . . . . –1 Kings 10:28

The Holy Land, located at the crossroads connecting Asia to both Europe and Africa, was a prime passageway for international trade. The Israelites exported grain, oil, and wine overland via a CARAVAN or by sea; in turn, their imports included spices, incense, precious stones, and wood. King Solomon imported vast quantities of gold (2

Chr 8:18) and such exotica as "ivory, apes, and peacocks" (2 Chr 9:21). According to 2 Chronicles 9:25–28, Solomon acquired 12,000 horses, some imported from Egypt, despite the prohibition that the king "must not acquire many horses for himself, or return the people to Egypt in order to acquire more horses, since the LORD has said to you, 'You must never return that way again'" (Deut 17:16).

INCENSE

THEY OFFER TO THE LORD EVERY MORNING AND EVERY EVENING BURNT OFFERINGS AND FRAGRANT INCENSE . . . .–2 CHRONICLES 13:11

An expensive mixture of fragrant spices and plant resins, incense was burned as an offering during worship. This practice was not unique to the Israelites; indeed, incense was used by people throughout the ancient Near East, and archaeologists have unearthed incense altars from many cultures in the region. A frequent complaint of the prophets was that Israel had adopted the Canaanite ritual of burning incense to Baal, god of rain and fertility.

According to Exodus 30:34–36, God gave Moses detailed instructions about making incense. A skilled perfumer was to grind into powder what appear to be ingredients collected from mountain, desert, and sea. The formula called for blending stacte (possibly the hardened sap of myrrh trees from southern Arabia), onycha (perhaps a spice from the shells of mollusks found in the Red Sea), GALBANUM (resin from the roots of a mountain plant), and frankincense (another Arabian tree sap).

Priests alone were allowed to burn this incense, a ritual they performed every morning and evening by sprinkling the powder onto coals burning on top of a gold-plated altar inside the sanctuary. When arrogant King Uzziah burned an offering himself, he was stricken with leprosy for the rest of his life (2 Chr 26:19–21). As part of the annual offering on the Day of Atonement, the high priest went into the temple's inner sanctum and poured two handfuls of incense onto coals that he carried in a portable censer. The smoke protected him from catching a fatal glimpse of God (Lev 16:13).

In the New Testament, both the smoke of incense and the prayers of saints "rose before God from the hand of the angel" (Rev 8:4).

Incense burners could be quite elaborate. Images of musicians and a sphinx decorate this bronze model from about 1100 BC.

INHERITANCE

"'. . . ALL ISRAELITES SHALL RETAIN THE INHERITANCE OF THEIR ANCESTRAL TRIBES.'"–NUMBERS 36:7

The inheritance of property for the Israelites was governed by numerous laws and customs. When a man died, his eldest son was entitled to a double portion of the family heritage, with the remainder divided equally among the other sons. According to the laws God handed down to Moses, "If a man dies, and has no son, then you shall pass his inheritance on to his daughter. If he has no daughter, then you shall give his inheritance to his brothers. If he has no brothers, then you shall give his inheritance to his father's brothers. And

On a medieval altar plaque, the dying Jacob apportions an inheritance to each of his sons.

if his father has no brothers, then you shall give his inheritance to the nearest kinsman of his clan" (Num 27:8–11).

If a man had a son by a concubine, he had to arrange for an adoption to leave the child an inheritance. If a daughter inherited land, she was required to marry a member of her father's clan (Num 36:6–9)—preferably someone in the family of one of her father's brothers—to keep it within the tribe. The same concern generated the practice of levirate marriage, in which a widowed, childless woman would marry her brother-in-law, and their first son would be considered the dead husband's heir. As a fail-safe mechanism, every 50th year—called the jubilee year—each tribe would repossess any property it had lost during that period.

In the New Testament, the inheritance that Jesus gives is salvation. Hebrews 9:15 states that "those who are called may receive the promised eternal inheritance."

INK

I have much to write to you, but I would rather not write with pen and ink; instead, I hope to see you soon . . . . –3 John 13–14

The Greek word for ink comes from the root meaning "black." In biblical times, lampblack, or soot, was mixed with gum arabic to create black ink for writing on papyrus. The carbon mixture was dried into cakes; when a scribe was ready to write, he rubbed a moistened PEN on it. Because carbon ink did not adhere well to parchment, a different ink was made by crushing nut galls and mixing them with iron sulfate and water. In one of Ezekiel's visions, a man "clothed in linen" possessed a "writing case" typical of those worn by scribes to carry pens and inks (Ezek 9:2). Colored inks were sometimes used—particularly red ink, which was made from red ocher or iron oxide. The Dead Sea Scrolls are evidence that biblical scribes could produce an ink of remarkable permanence and legibility.

The bronze inkwell, top, equipped with folding handles, was excavated from Qumran, where the Dead Sea Scrolls were found. Above, a fifth-century BC Egyptian writing palette contains two hollows—the empty one may have held water to be mixed with the black ink stored in the lower compartment.

INN

And she gave birth to her firstborn son . . . and laid him in a manger, because there was no place for them in the inn. –Luke 2:7

Buildings specially constructed as inns, in the modern sense, probably did not exist in Old Testament days, although lodging places are mentioned occasionally. By the New Testament period, the imperial needs of the Persians, Greeks, and Romans had led to the establishment of public inns in the Holy Land. Whether a walled space built around a well or a series of modest rooms lining a courtyard, inns generally offered little comfort to the weary guest aside from providing water and a space upon which to lay down one's own bedding, although some did offer food. Travelers rested alongside their domestic and pack animals. Comfort was less an issue than safety, however, since robbery and even murder were not uncommon. See also reconstruction for JOURNEY.

An innkeeper could be a man or woman and, as in the story of the Good Samaritan in Luke 10:34–35, might even be paid to act as caretaker in a kind of hospice for the wounded. In the New Testament a guest room in a private house (Mk 14:14; Lk 22:11) might also have been considered a type of inn; either form of accommodation apparently eluded Mary and Joseph in their search for lodging in Bethlehem.

INQUIRY

Concerning this salvation, the prophets who prophesied of the grace that was to be yours made careful search and inquiry . . . . –1 Peter 1:10

In the Bible, people often sought information from God regarding the outcome of an illness or a dispute, for example, or whether to fight a particular battle and who would win. Answers were sought in several ways. People might consult a priest, who could answer yes-or-no questions by manipulating sacred objects called Urim and Thummim, although exactly how these items were used remains a mystery. In later times, people also sought answers from the prophets. Early Christians searched for direction from God through prayer and fasting or by casting lots, which was the method employed by the apostles to choose Judas' replacement (Acts 1:26).

INSCRIPTION

Pilate also had an inscription written and put on the cross. It read, "Jesus of Nazareth, the King of the Jews." –John 19:19

Inscriptions are words or letters cut into or written on a durable surface. Ancient inscriptions were often incised on temple walls, tombs, and other public structures; Hammurabi's famous code of laws was carved on a stela. One of the oldest Hebrew inscriptions is the Gezer calendar, an agricultural record from the 10th century BC. Pontius Pilate had an inscription put on Jesus' cross "written in Hebrew, in Latin, and in Greek" (Jn 19:20). At crucifixions, Roman officials often displayed inscriptions announcing the crime that had been committed.

This remnant of an ancient synagogue in Jerusalem from the time of Herod bears an inscription in Greek that commemorates the generosity of its builder, Theodotos.

Insects

All winged insects that walk upon all fours are detestable to you.
–Leviticus 11:20

In ancient times, as today, some insects were useful, such as honeybees and silkworms, and even the lowly maggot helped eliminate decaying matter. But other insects were pests. Locusts and cicadas, which were common in the Near East, could destroy vast regions of crops and spread famine throughout the land; fleas carried bubonic plague and other deadly diseases to people and animals. Ants, flies, and gnats are other insects mentioned in the Bible. The Old Testament forbade the Israelites to eat any insects except "those that have jointed legs above their feet" (Lev 11:21)—that is, locusts, crickets, and grasshoppers. To ensure that they did not accidentally swallow an unclean insect, the Pharisees were said to strain their drinking water through a cloth (Mt 23:24).

By far the most destructive of biblical insects, locusts were known for their voracious appetite. Above, a horde of locusts feeds on savory leaves.

Insult

I gave my back to those who struck me . . . I did not hide my face from insult and spitting.
–Isaiah 50:6

One person insulting another, whether by word or deed, is condemned in the Bible, as is insulting God, even indirectly by exploiting the needy. Representatives of God were sometimes subject to scorn and insults; such was the case of Isaiah in the passage cited above, and of Jeremiah, who lamented, "I have become a laughingstock all day long; everyone mocks me" (Jer 20:7). In the face of such derision, the book of Proverbs counsels patience: "Fools show their anger at once, but the prudent ignore an insult" (Prov 12:16).

In Matthew 5:21, Jesus warned that anyone who treated another with insolence could be brought before the Sanhedrin, which was a local council of leaders and elders that functioned as the Jewish high court. But during his trial and crucifixion, Jesus bore in silence the many insults hurled at him, setting an example for his followers. See also LAUGHTER.

Intercession

Consequently [Jesus] is able for all time to save those who approach God through him, since he always lives to make intercession for them.
–Hebrews 7:25

In the Bible, intercession is a request that someone makes of God on behalf of another, such as when Abraham asks God to spare any righteous people living in Sodom (Gen 18:23–33). Later, when God threatens to destroy the Israelites for worshiping a golden calf, Moses implores God to turn from wrath. As a result, "the LORD changed his mind" (Ex 32:14). The New Testament encourages Christians to intercede for one another in PRAYER, activating in turn the intercession of Christ and the Holy Spirit. Christ's ultimate act of intercession on behalf of humankind came when he sacrificed himself to "bear the sins of many" (Heb 9:28).

INVADERS

THEY WILL SET APART MEN TO PASS THROUGH THE LAND REGULARLY AND BURY ANY INVADERS WHO REMAIN ON THE FACE OF THE LAND, SO AS TO CLEANSE IT . . . .
–EZEKIEL 39:14

In biblical times, invaders attacked fortified or walled cities with bows and arrows, as well as spears, javelins, and battering rams (see illustration). They also used assault ramps. By filling a moat with earth or rubble, they could build ramps to the top of the city wall. Troops protected by shields moved up the ramps while archers and slingers fired over the wall. The Assyrians and Babylonians were among the Holy Land's major invaders, and from about 732 BC to 587 BC Israel and Judah faced assaults from these Mesopotamian superpowers. Later the Romans invaded the Holy Land and took control of Judah in 63 BC, followed by the capture of Jerusalem in 70 AD. See also ARMY.

IRON

AND THERE SHALL BE A FOURTH KINGDOM, STRONG AS IRON; JUST AS IRON CRUSHES AND SMASHES EVERYTHING, IT SHALL CRUSH AND SHATTER ALL THESE.
–DANIEL 2:40

In the mid-second millennium BC, the Hittites developed a superior technology for smelting iron ore into the hardest metal known in ancient times. After the collapse of their empire about 1200 BC, this technology gradually spread throughout the eastern Mediterranean, during the period that archaeologists call the Iron Age. Farmers preferred iron PLOW tips, because they were more durable than bronze. Similarly, iron weapons—including swords, daggers, and spearheads—gave armies a strategic military advantage. The spearhead of the giant Goliath reportedly weighed "six hundred shekels of iron" (1 Sam 17:7), or more than 15 pounds.

IRRIGATION

FOR THE LAND THAT YOU ARE ABOUT TO ENTER IS NOT LIKE THE LAND OF EGYPT . . . WHERE YOU SOW YOUR SEED AND IRRIGATE BY FOOT LIKE A VEGETABLE GARDEN.
–DEUTERONOMY 11:10

Although irrigation practices in the ancient Near East varied according to the local climate and terrain, without some form of irrigation the

Led by King Sennacherib, the Assyrian army attacked the city of Lachish in 701 BC, as depicted here. Alhough Lachish was heavily fortified, its double walls and archers were defenseless against the invaders, who used battering rams and ladders to conquer the city.

great cities in that part of the world could not have flourished as they did. In rain-starved Egypt, for example, the life-giving Nile rose every year, flooding the wide flat croplands and then ebbing to leave behind a layer of fertile mud. This predictable overflow, which occurred from July to September, provided the basis for a system of canals and catch basins that could store water for agricultural use throughout the dry season. The water was often lifted from a storage basin or canal to the fields above by means of a movable pole balanced with a bucket and weight hanging at opposite ends.

In contrast, the Holy Land was generally mountainous and streams were few and relatively small, but heavy dew in the summer months and periods of heavy rain, particularly from October through April, meant that irrigation was not essential. Nevertheless, from as early as the third

millennium BC, efficient irrigation systems were in place, which principally relied on springs to distribute water to fields and orchards during the two growing seasons—early spring and summer—when rainfall was low.

Irrigation was much more complex in the Mesopotamian lands near the Tigris and Euphrates, whose floods could be capricious and destructive. A highly sophisticated system of reservoirs, dikes, and canals as wide as 25 yards was maintained both to control floodwaters and to keep out the eight- to nine-foot tides from the Persian Gulf, which in spring could ruin the soil by allowing salt water to flood the fields. See also FARMING.

Isaiah appears on a stained-glass window from Exeter Cathedral in Devon.

Isaiah, Book of

Then I heard the voice of the Lord saying, "Whom shall I send, and who will go for us?" And I said, "Here am I; send me!"–Isaiah 6:8

The book of Isaiah is a collection of words and predictions attributed to the prophet for whom the book is named. The book addresses three distinct eras: Isaiah's lifetime, more than 150 years before Babylon conquered Judah in 587 BC; the exile in Babylon; and the Holy Land after the exile. Because of varied settings and writing styles, many scholars believe the book is the work of several writers.

When Isaiah began his ministry about 742 BC in Jerusalem, the divided kingdoms of Israel and Judah were both prospering. But the people's faith was waning. Worship had eroded to insincere rituals, and injustice was commonplace. God told Isaiah to warn the Israelites that both kingdoms would be destroyed unless they repented. When Isaiah inquired how long he should warn them, God's reply was ominous: "Until cities lie waste without inhabitant" (Isa 6:11). Twenty years later, Assyria conquered the northern kingdom of Israel, exiled the survivors, and annexed the land. Judah survived but only as a nation in servitude. Isaiah continued to warn its people, while also trying to reassure them that God would eventually restore both kingdoms.

Island

Your fame reached to far-off islands, and you were loved for your peaceful reign. –Ecclesiasticus 47:16

In Bible translations, the Hebrew for "regions with borders on the sea" is rendered as "islands," as well as "coast" or "coastlands." The biblical islands, or isles, were those found along the coast of the Mediterranean Sea and its branches. Although the Israelites were not a seafaring people, they were aware of many distant coastland areas, such as those mentioned in Jeremiah 31:10 and Ezekiel 27:3.

A psalm asking for God's blessing on the king expressed the hope that his DOMINION would be so vast and far-flung that the "isles" would "render him tribute" (Ps 72:10). God the creator was described as being so powerful that "he stilled the deep and planted islands in it" (Sir 43:23), and his dominance over his creation was such that he could pick up "the isles like fine dust" (Isa 40:15). In the New Testament, numerous islands, including Crete, Malta, and Rhodes, are mentioned by name. Paul stopped at many of the Mediterranean islands on his extensive missionary travels, and while in exile on the island of Patmos (Rev 1:9), John received visions that are recorded in Revelation.

This eighth-century BC ivory carving depicts a man bearing gifts that he will offer as tribute.

IVORY

. . . THEY BROUGHT YOU IN PAYMENT IVORY TUSKS AND EBONY. –EZEKIEL 27:15

Since prehistoric times ELEPHANT herds roamed throughout northern Syria, but the great herds were extinct by 800 BC. Elephant tusks were the source of most ivory in Syria and the Holy Land, although some came from India. According to 1 Kings 10:22, Solomon's ships of Tarshish returned to the Holy Land laden with ivory every three years. Ivory was a luxury item that was used to decorate thrones, to panel walls in palaces, and to create intricately inlaid furniture. Excavations at Ugarit and Megiddo have yielded ladies' combs, decorative boxes, and figurines carved from ivory.

Elephant tusks and objects made from ivory were valued spoils of war. When the Assyrian king Sennacherib listed the tribute that had been given to him by Hezekiah, the king of Judah, it included chairs and beds inlaid with ivory. The prophet Amos showed his scorn for the decadent upper classes of Samaria and Jerusalem by calling them "those who lie on beds of ivory" and warned that "they shall now be the first to go into exile" (Amos 6:4, 7).

JACKAL

. . . YOU HAVE BROKEN US IN THE HAUNT OF JACKALS, AND COVERED US WITH DEEP DARKNESS. –PSALM 44:19

The jackal resembles its relatives, the wolf and the fox, in appearance. Smaller than the wolf, it hunts in packs, which gives it a fearsome reputation. In the Bible, the "haunt of jackals" is either the desert, where jackals live, or a place of devastation, where they scavenge. Similarly, when a city or state is called the "lair of jackals," it means that it is destroyed or deserted (Jer 9:11). Referring to their plaintive howl, the prophet Micah said, "For this I will lament and wail . . . I will make lamentation like the jackals" (Mic 1:8).

A member of the dog family, the jackal, seen here in its winter coat, is a wily scavenger.

JAMES, LETTER OF

. . . I BY MY WORKS WILL SHOW YOU MY FAITH.–JAMES 2:18

Though short, the letter of James brims with practical advice on how to live as a Christian. Like the book of Proverbs, it addresses a variety of practical issues, which has led some scholars to call it Christian wisdom literature. The book encourages believers to speak kindly of one another, to resist the temptation to favor the rich over the poor, and to view difficult circumstances as opportunities to grow stronger in their faith.

Perhaps the most notable of James' teachings is that genuine Christian faith expresses itself in good deeds: "So faith by itself, if it has no works, is dead" (Jas 2:17). The author of this letter identifies himself only as James. But an early Christian tradition claims that he was the brother of Jesus and the leader of the Jerusalem church who was martyred a few years before the Romans destroyed Jerusalem in 70 AD. The letter of James is addressed to "the twelve tribes in the Dispersion" (Jas 1:1), apparently in response to problems common among Jewish Christians throughout the Roman Empire.

JEREMIAH, BOOK OF

THE DAYS ARE SURELY COMING, SAYS THE LORD, WHEN I WILL MAKE A NEW COVENANT WITH THE HOUSE OF ISRAEL AND THE HOUSE OF JUDAH.–JEREMIAH 31:31

The prophet Jeremiah warned Judah that there were only two ways in which they could avoid complete destruction for their sins: by returning to the faith of their ancestors or by accepting the demands placed on them by the Babylonians. The people did neither. Instead, they branded Jeremiah a traitor and accused him of demoralizing a nation yearning for independence.

The book of Jeremiah is primarily a collection of the prophet's oracles and pronouncements against Judah. It also contains oracles against Judah's enemies and stories about Jeremiah's ministry, which spanned 40 years. Jeremiah lived to see his main prophecies fulfilled with the defeat of Judah, the destruction of Jerusalem, and the stripping of Solomon's temple in 586 BC. The northern kingdom of Israel had been conquered by Assyria 150 years earlier; likewise, according to the prophet, Judah and Jerusalem had fallen because the people had broken their covenant with God (Jer 11:10–11). God promises through Jeremiah, however, that he will renew his covenant with Israel, "and I will will be their God, and they shall be my people" (Jer 31:33).

JEREMIAH, LETTER OF

. . . GODS OF SILVER AND GOLD . . . CANNOT SAVE THEMSELVES FROM RUST AND CORROSION.–LETTER OF JEREMIAH 11–12

The apocryphal letter of Jeremiah is addressed to the Judeans facing imminent exile in Babylon and warns them not to fear or worship the idols they will encounter. "Their tongues are smoothed by the carpenter," says the writer, "and they themselves are . . . false and cannot speak" (Let Jer 8). The authorship of the letter is attributed to the prophet Jeremiah, possibly in keeping with the custom of crediting a work to the person who inspired it. The letter, written perhaps 300 years after the book of Jeremiah, seems to expand on the prophet's assurance: "The gods who did not make the heavens and the earth shall perish" (Jer 10:11).

JEW

"YET ALL THIS DOES ME NO GOOD SO LONG AS I SEE THE JEW MORDECAI SITTING AT THE KING'S GATE." –ESTHER 5:13

A Jew is a person descended from the biblical Israelites or one who practices Judaism. The word is derived from the southern kingdom of Judah. Originally it described Judean citizens, but after the Babylonian exile in 587 BC the term applied to all, including those of the Diaspora, who traced their descent from or identified with this ethnic or religious group, regardless of race or nationality. In the Bible *Jew* often appears in contrast to *Gentile,* or non-Jew. Jesus and most of his followers were Jews. Christianity was at first considered a sect of Judaism. See also DISPERSION.

Esther, seen here kneeling before King Ahasuerus, saved the Jews from extermination.

JEWEL

. . . THE LIPS INFORMED BY KNOWLEDGE ARE A PRECIOUS JEWEL. –PROVERBS 20:15

Jewels were not a natural resource of the Holy Land, and their rarity made them all the more valuable. Cut and polished gems were important plunder in war and were used as currency in the ancient Near East before coins came into use about the sixth century BC.

Gems were used primarily by priests and royalty since they were too costly for the ordinary citizen. The wealthy often wore jewelry made of gold or silver studded with precious stones. The ephod, or sacred garment, of the high priest had an onyx stone set in gold filigree on each shoulder (Ex 28:9–12). Aaron's breastplate contained 12 precious stones, one for each of the tribes of Israel, including carnelian, turquoise, amethyst, and BERYL (Ex 28:17–20). Gems also decorated crowns and royal garments.

In the New Testament, the new Jerusalem is depicted as God's bride, with "a radiance like a very rare jewel" (Rev 21:11). The foundations of the city wall are adorned with sapphires, emeralds, topaz, and other gems, and each gate is a single pearl (Rev 21:19–21).

JEWELRY

SHE PUT . . . ON HER ANKLETS, BRACELETS, RINGS, EARRINGS, AND ALL HER OTHER JEWELRY. –JUDITH 10:4

In biblical times men and women of all classes wore jewelry. Archaeologists' finds have included necklaces made of various metals or drilled beads, bracelets of gold and silver, EARRINGS, carved brooches, and ivory and bone pins. Both sexes wore earrings, necklaces, bracelets, and rings. Israelite women wore nose rings and sometimes ankle bracelets. Signet rings were used to seal documents and as a sign of authority.

For most people, jewelry would likely have been made of bronze or iron, but the rich could afford gold or silver. High priests and royalty adorned their garments with semiprecious and precious stones,

Among the jewelry excavated at Beth Shean was a necklace whose 37 carnelian pendants appear above.

sometimes set in gold filigree. Ezekiel describes the garment of the king of Tyre as ornamented with "carnelian, chrysolite, and moonstone, beryl, onyx, and jasper, sapphire, turquoise, and emerald" (Ezek 28:13).

One kind of gold necklace probably symbolized power. When Joseph became the chief minister of Egypt, Pharaoh "put a gold chain around his neck" (Gen 41:42), and King Belshazzar announced that the person who could interpret the mysterious writing on the wall should "have a chain of gold around his neck, and rank third in the kingdom" (Dan 5:7).

The kings of Midian wore crescents, which may have been a royal emblem, and pendants (Judg 8:26). Amulets were widely worn. These good luck charms often represented animals or people or even gods, in violation of the commandment: "You shall not make for yourself an idol" (Ex 20:4). Amulets were sometimes placed on animals to ward off evil spirits on journeys.

Job, Book of

"I will say to God, Do not condemn me; let me know why you contend against me."
–Job 10:2

The book of Job is the story of a righteous man who suffers a string of catastrophes because of a challenge to God from Satan. Again and again Job's faith is tested: raiders steal part of his vast herds, and a mysterious fire from heaven burns the rest. A windstorm collapses his house, killing his 10 children inside. Then Job is covered from head to foot with sores.

Three friends come to comfort and advise Job during his misery. In a series of poetic dialogues, they argue that tragedy of this magnitude reveals that God is punishing Job for some sin, and they urge him to confess. Job vows that he has not sinned and is dismayed that God could be so unjust.

Finally God speaks to Job from a whirlwind, cataloguing the wonders of creation, and Job apparently concedes that he was wrong to challenge God. The story concludes with Job being blessed by God with 10 more children and even greater wealth than before. Many scholars think that the authors of the book used Job as a vehicle to discuss the suffering of the innocent following the destruction of Jerusalem by the Babylonians in 587 BC (see Ezekiel 14:14).

Joel, Book of

I will repay you for the years that the swarming locust has eaten . . . .
–Joel 2:25

The book of Joel is a compelling prophecy about a series of catastrophic events. The book can be broken into two distinct parts. In the first (Joel 1:1–2:27), a swarm of locusts devours the land like a marauding army, stripping bark from trees and laying waste to the vines. The prophet Joel may have witnessed one of the locust infestations that periodically blighted the Holy Land and then used the imagery to warn the Israelites of what awaited them: "For the day of the LORD is near, and as destruction from the Almighty it comes" (Joel 1:15). Joel calls on the people, the priests, and the elders to ask for the Lord's mercy. But the army of locust continues to wreak havoc: it enters a "garden of Eden" but leaves it a "desolate wilderness" (Joel 2:3). Finally God promises to drive away the locusts and restore fertility to the land.

In the second part (Joel 2:28–3:21), the apocalyptic theme, focusing on the "day of the LORD," is continued. According to the prophet, God will bring judgment on the evil nations who have driven his people into exile, and he will restore Israel, "for the LORD dwells in Zion" (Joel 3:21).

John, Gospel According to

In the beginning was the Word, and the Word was with God, and the Word was God.
–John 1:1

The Gospel According to John, which relates the life of Jesus, is dramatically different from the Gospels of Matthew, Mark, and Luke. Many of the familiar parables and miracles, the story of the birth of Jesus, and even the Sermon on the Mount and the Lord's Prayer are absent from John. Rather, the author of this Gospel based his narrative on seven miraculous signs that revealed Jesus as "the Messiah, the Son of God" (Jn 20:31). These miracles—such as raising Lazarus from the dead and turning water into wine—appear nowhere else in the Bible. The stories are punctuated with Jesus' self-revelations. After feeding the 5,000, Jesus said, "I am the bread of life.

This title page of the Gospel According to John is from the seventh-century AD Lindisfarne Gospels.

Whoever comes to me will never be hungry" (Jn 6:35). At the raising of Lazarus, Jesus said, "I am the resurrection and the life. Those who believe in me, even though they die, will live" (Jn 11:25).

Since about the second century AD, the church has attributed this anonymous Gospel to John, one of Jesus' dearest apostles. Traditionally he is also thought to be the author of Revelation and the three letters of John. But because John was described as an unlearned man (Acts 4:13), some scholars today conjecture that John's followers may have drawn from his sermons and written the Gospel for him. The primary purpose of John is to proclaim Jesus as the savior (Jn 20:31). Therefore it is significant that the Gospel, which was finished by about 100 AD, was conceived and written at a time when synagogue leaders and the Jewish-Christian community were in a fierce battle over who Jesus was.

JOHN, 1–3

WHO IS THE LIAR BUT THE ONE WHO DENIES THAT JESUS IS THE CHRIST?–1 JOHN 2:22

The three letters of John form a unit and share common language, writing style, and topics. First John, which echoes the style and content of the Gospel of John, was written to a church in which questions of faith were threatening to divide it. Some members of the church whom 1 John identifies as "antichrists" (1 Jn 2:18) denied that Jesus was the son of God and that he had "come in the flesh" (1 Jn 4:2). The letter calls the church back to fundamental Christian beliefs, pleading for love and unity.

Second John is addressed to "the elect lady and her children"—presumably a church and its members. It urges believers to love one another and to shun false teachers.

Third John is written to a man known as Gaius, commending him for showing hospitality to strangers and warning him about a lying and mean-spirited churchman named Diotrephes.

Some Christians have thought that the disciple John wrote the three short letters of John; however, as in the case of the Gospel of John, scholars have suggested that followers of John may have written the letters, perhaps about 100 AD.

JONAH, BOOK OF

. . . JONAH WAS IN THE BELLY OF THE FISH THREE DAYS AND THREE NIGHTS.–JONAH 1:17

The book of Jonah is a prophetic work whose principal character is an eighth-century BC prophet mentioned in 2 Kings 14:25. When God instructed Jonah to go east to warn the Assyrian capital of Nineveh that it would be overthrown, he instead boarded a ship headed west. A violent storm erupted and Jonah was thrown overboard for inciting God's wrath. God directed a great FISH to swallow Jonah. But when Jonah prayed to God, the fish spewed him ashore. The prophet took God's message to Nineveh, whose people repented and were spared. The book of Jonah is generally interpreted as a story depicting God's universal love and mercy.

JOSHUA, BOOK OF

". . . MOSES IS DEAD. NOW PROCEED TO CROSS THE JORDAN, YOU AND ALL THIS PEOPLE, INTO THE LAND THAT I AM GIVING TO THEM . . . ." –JOSHUA 1:2

The book of Joshua tells the story of the Israelite conquest of Canaan and the fulfillment of God's promise to Abraham (Gen 12:1–4). Its hero, Joshua, is the warrior who succeeded Moses and led the nation into battle for that land, beginning with Jericho. The first half of Joshua (Josh 1–12) describes the many battles of the campaign, but the message is that Canaan was won by faith in God rather than by military prowess. Before the Israelites crossed into Canaan, God told Joshua, "Every place that the sole of your foot will tread upon I have given to you" (Josh 1:3).

The remaining chapters of the book tell how Joshua divided the land among the 12 tribes (Josh 13–21) and called the nation together to renew its pledge of loyalty to God (Josh 22–24). Although the book's author is unnamed, Jewish tradition ascribes most of it to Joshua; the closing section is attributed to Aaron's son, the priest Eleazar.

Jonah emerges from the mouth of the sea monster in this detail from a 13th-century Italian mosaic.

JOURNEY

HE ORDERED THEM TO TAKE NOTHING FOR THEIR JOURNEY EXCEPT A STAFF; NO BREAD, NO BAG, NO MONEY IN THEIR BELTS . . . .
–MARK 6:8

In biblical times, people journeyed by themselves or in groups (see reconstruction, pp. 198–199) to trade goods, seek employment or medical treatment, attend games and religious festivals, visit relatives, and, occasionally, to migrate due to war or famine. Because of the great variety of terrain and traveling conditions in the Near East, a "day's journey" was an imprecise phrase often used to indicate a short distance that could be covered easily in a day. A "sabbath day's journey" (Acts 1:12), by contrast, was 2,000 cubits—about 3/5 of a mile—which was the limit that a person was allowed to walk on the sabbath. See also TRAVEL.

JUBILEE, YEAR OF

IN THE YEAR OF JUBILEE THE FIELD SHALL RETURN TO THE ONE FROM WHOM IT WAS BOUGHT . . . .
–LEVITICUS 27:24

To ensure that the people did not oppress, enslave, or exploit one another or accumulate unreasonable wealth, God told Moses that every 50th year would be a year of jubilee. At this time all land would be given back to its original owner without payment, all indentured servants were to be released from their obligation, and all cultivated land was to lie fallow. Although it is unlikely that these dicta were ever carried out, the jubilee served to remind Israel that everything ultimately belonged to the Lord: "The land shall not be sold in perpetuity, for the land is mine" (Lev 25:23).

JUDE, LETTER OF

FOR CERTAIN INTRUDERS HAVE STOLEN IN AMONG YOU, PEOPLE WHO . . . PERVERT THE GRACE OF OUR GOD INTO LICENTIOUSNESS . . . .
–JUDE 4

The letter of Jude is a 25-verse work written to warn one or more churches about immoral newcomers. It draws from the Old Testament, the Apocrypha, other Jewish traditions, and apostolic teaching to condemn the intruders. It reminds believers that false teachers will come, and that God has a long history of punishing such ungodliness. The author identifies himself as Jude—short for Judas—brother of James. But according to tradition, Jude was also the brother of Jesus. Both James and Judas are named among Jesus' brothers in Mark 6:3.

JUDGE

YOU SHALL APPOINT JUDGES AND OFFICIALS THROUGHOUT YOUR TRIBES . . . AND THEY SHALL RENDER JUST DECISIONS FOR THE PEOPLE.
–DEUTERONOMY 16:18.

The word *judge* was used in various ways in different biblical periods. At first Moses decided all disputes between the Israelites and gave them God's instructions. Then, exhausted by the demands of the people, who "stood around him from morning until evening" (Ex 18:13), he took the advice of his father-in-law, Jethro, and appointed judges to decide the minor cases, reserving only the most difficult controversies for himself.

After settlements were established, city elders sat in judgment at the city gate, where they heard indictments, settled lawsuits, and imposed penalties for crimes. Particularly difficult cases were decided in conjunction with priests or the supreme judge. Deuteronomy described the conduct required of judges: "You must not distort justice; you must not show partiality; and you must not accept bribes, for a bribe blinds the eyes of the wise and subverts the cause of those who are in the right" (Deut 16:19). But there are numerous examples in the Old Testament of judges committing these and other injustices, and the prophet Zephaniah called the judges of Jerusalem "evening wolves that leave nothing until the morning" (Zeph 3:3).

The book of Judges chronicles the period between Joshua and Samuel, when Canaan was periodically invaded by foreign armies. It is said that God appointed judges who were leaders during peace and military commanders in times of war, although some seem to have had judicial functions as well. There were 12 of these judges, including one woman, Deborah. See also JUDGES, BOOK OF.

During the monarchy the king was the highest judge. He appointed local judges who not only settled disputes but also acted as governors of a sort, keeping the peace, collecting taxes, and supplying information. In the ninth century BC, Jehoshaphat appointed judges to all the major cities of Judah. After the return from exile, Artaxerxes charged the priest Ezra to "appoint magistrates and judges who may judge all the people in the province Beyond the River who know the laws of your God; and you shall teach those who do not know them" (Ezra 7:25).

Abraham called God "the Judge of all the earth" (Gen 18:25). Jesus forbade his followers to judge another's sins when they had sinned themselves: "Can a blind person guide a blind person? Will not both fall into a pit?" (Lk 6:39).

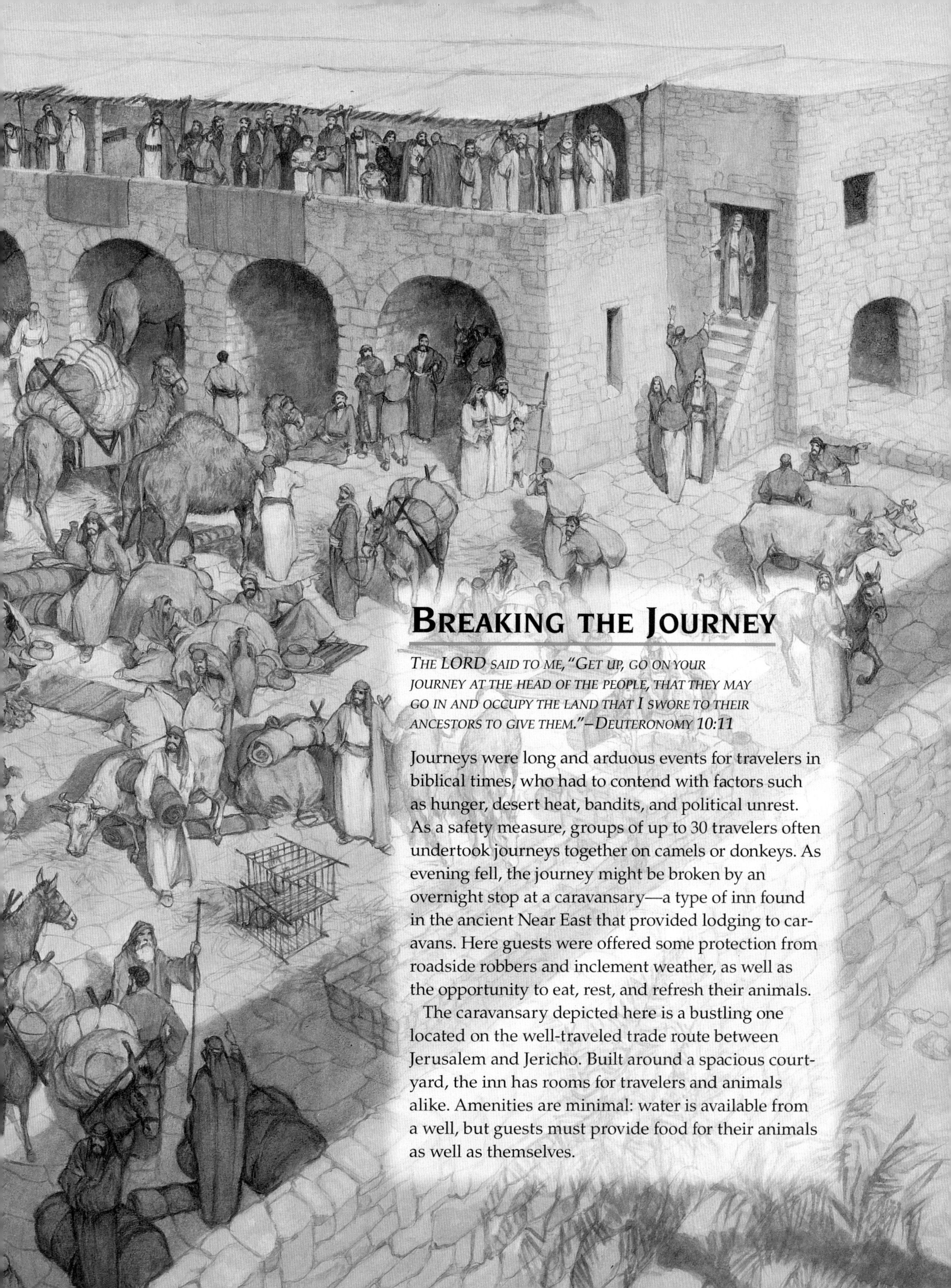

BREAKING THE JOURNEY

THE LORD SAID TO ME, "GET UP, GO ON YOUR JOURNEY AT THE HEAD OF THE PEOPLE, THAT THEY MAY GO IN AND OCCUPY THE LAND THAT I SWORE TO THEIR ANCESTORS TO GIVE THEM."—DEUTERONOMY 10:11

Journeys were long and arduous events for travelers in biblical times, who had to contend with factors such as hunger, desert heat, bandits, and political unrest. As a safety measure, groups of up to 30 travelers often undertook journeys together on camels or donkeys. As evening fell, the journey might be broken by an overnight stop at a caravansary—a type of inn found in the ancient Near East that provided lodging to caravans. Here guests were offered some protection from roadside robbers and inclement weather, as well as the opportunity to eat, rest, and refresh their animals.

The caravansary depicted here is a bustling one located on the well-traveled trade route between Jerusalem and Jericho. Built around a spacious courtyard, the inn has rooms for travelers and animals alike. Amenities are minimal: water is available from a well, but guests must provide food for their animals as well as themselves.

In the book of Judges, the prophetess Deborah, depicted in a Gustave Doré engraving, gives military and legal advice.

Judges, Book of

Then the LORD raised up judges, who delivered them out of the power of those who plundered them.–Judges 2:16

A collection of stories, the book of Judges primarily tells about 12 Israelite leaders, or judges. These inspired heroes led various tribes in battles with enemies during the period of about two centuries between Joshua's death and the selection of the first Israelite king.

Israel was a loose confederation of tribes, each of which was supposed to conquer and subdue the territory in Canaan assigned to it. Instead, the Israelites learned to live with the Canaanites. (Archaeological evidence suggests that many Canaanites lived in fertile valleys, while the Israelites settled mostly in the rocky highlands.) As a result, a pattern developed: the Israelites worshiped Canaanite deities, and God sent enemy invaders as punishment. When the Israelites repented and pleaded for help, God raised a deliverer to drive away the oppressor. These deliverers—the judges—often continued to serve as tribal leaders and arbitrators even after the oppressors were vanquished. The 12 judges were Othniel, Ehud, Shamgar, Deborah, Gideon, Tola, Jair, Jephthah, Ibzan, Elon, Abdon, and—the most famous of all—Samson.

Stories that close the book show Israel engulfed in spiritual and political anarchy. A Levite serves as hired priest in the home of a man who has idols (Judg 17–18). The tribe of Benjamin is nearly wiped out by the other Israelite tribes in retaliation for the gang rape and murder of a Levite's concubine (Judg 19–20). The book's last sentence seems to imply that Israel desperately needs the unifying influence of a king.

Although the author of Judges is unnamed, the book has been attributed to Samuel, the prophet who anointed Saul and David as the first and second kings of Israel.

Judgment Seat

For we will all stand before the judgment seat of God.–Romans 14:10

In the Roman Empire, a judgment seat was a raised bench or platform on which the MAGISTRATE or other official sat with his counselors to deliberate cases. It was commonly set up in a public place, such as when Pontius Pilate "brought Jesus outside and sat on the judge's bench at a place called The Stone Pavement" (Jn 19:13). In the Gospel of Matthew, the judgment seat was the place where Pilate's wife sent word to him: "Have nothing to do with that innocent man" (Mt 27:19). In his letters, Paul used the term to allude to God's final judgment of all human beings.

Judith, Book of

No one ever again spread terror among the Israelites during the lifetime of Judith . . . . –Judith 16:25

The apocryphal book of Judith tells the story of a beautiful widow who saves her Judean town from a besieging Assyrian army. She does it by seducing the commander, Holofernes, and decapitating him as he lies drunk in bed; at daybreak, the Jews attack, and the Assyrians flee in confusion. Errors in the story, such as identifying Nebuchadnezzar as king of Assyria instead of Babylon, may have been intentionally introduced to show that the work is fiction. The author is unknown, but details of the story suggest it was written in the second century BC to provide a model for Jewish resistance to oppression.

Judith holds the head of Holofernes, as shown in a Renaissance painting.

KEEPER

THE LORD IS YOUR KEEPER; THE LORD IS YOUR SHADE AT YOUR RIGHT HAND.
–PSALM 121:5

In English translations of the Bible, the word *keeper* stands for a number of different Hebrew words. It sometimes denotes a person working at an occupation or task, such as a shepherd (1 Sam 17:20) or a watchman who guards an orchard or vineyard (Song of S 1:6). Certain officials were also called keepers. The keepers of the threshold (2 Kings 22:4) supervised the temple treasury, collected money from the people, paid workmen, and purchased supplies. Doorkeepers and gatekeepers guarded important entrances, such as a city GATE. Palace officials might include the keeper of the king's forest (Neh 2:8) and the keeper of the wardrobe (2 Kings 22:14).

The underlying concept of being a keeper is that of responsibility, particularly for the welfare of others. When God queries Cain about Abel's whereabouts, Cain sarcastically replies, "I do not know; am I my brother's keeper?" (Gen 4:9). In Isaiah 27:3, God is pictured as the keeper of the people of Israel, guarding them "night and day."

KEY

I WILL PLACE ON HIS SHOULDER THE KEY OF THE HOUSE OF DAVID . . . .–ISAIAH 22:22

Although keys and locks were common in biblical times, the word *key* is used almost exclusively in a figurative sense in the Bible. The sole exception is in the book of Judges, where the servants of King Eglon of Moab use a key to open the locked chamber in which their master lies slain (Judg 3:25).

Because keys controlled access to important buildings, they were a symbol of power and authority. Keys to palaces and large houses were given only to trusted servants. In the Gospel of Matthew, Jesus tells his apostle Peter, "I will give you the keys of the kingdom of heaven" (Mt 16:19).

Actual keys and locks were probably made of wood. A sturdy bolt, which secured the door, passed through a block—the lock—which had holes bored in its upper half. When the bolt was shoved into position, pins in the holes of the block dropped down into matching holes in the bolt, keeping it in place. The key had pins that matched those in the lock. The key was slid into a hollow in the bolt until its pins met those of the lock. It was then raised to push the locking pins clear, at which point the bolt could be slid back.

Excavated keys from the Roman period include one worn as a ring and one that opened a house door.

KIDNEYS

YOU SHALL TAKE . . . THE TWO KIDNEYS WITH THE FAT THAT IS ON THEM, AND TURN THEM INTO SMOKE ON THE ALTAR.
–EXODUS 29:13

Along with other body parts high in fat, the kidneys of sacrificial animals were essential for burnt offerings in rites of purification, restitution, and the consecration of priests. The law forbade eating these choice organs, which, along with the blood, were believed to contain the very life of the animal.

Human kidneys could symbolize inner qualities such as conscience and intelligence. Emotions were thought to spring from the kidneys, since that area of the body is physically sensitive. Kidneys were linked with the bowels and the HEART, which represented all the inner organs, as the center of individual will and personality.

KIN

YOU SHALL NOT HATE IN YOUR HEART ANYONE OF YOUR KIN . . . .
–LEVITICUS 19:17

To the Israelites, *kin,* or kindred, meant blood relatives; the Hebrew word translated as "kin" literally means "brother." The nuclear family was the basic unit of kinship, with the father as the head. Next came the extended family, which was several nuclear families that were all descended from the same patriarch. A number of extended families were aligned in a clan, often living in close proximity, and 50 or more clans formed a tribe.

Members of an extended family had certain obligations to one another. If a wrong was done to a member of the family, the closest male relative, or next of kin, was expected to avenge it. If a childless man died, the custom of levirate marriage required that his brother marry the widow to produce an heir for the deceased, "so that his name may not be blotted out of Israel" (Deut 25:6). When poverty forced a member of an extended family to sell property, it was the responsibility of the closest relative to buy it back (Lev 25:25). The same principle applied if a kinsman or kinswoman was sold into slavery (Lev 25:47–49).

KING

GOD IS KING OVER THE NATIONS; GOD SITS ON HIS HOLY THRONE.–PSALM 47:8

Hereditary kings ruled over most territorial entities in the ancient Near East. In Egypt the king, or pharaoh, was recognized as a god; in Mesopotamia the institution of kingship was believed to be not only divinely ordained but also as old as creation itself.

The Israelites came late to the idea of a monarchy. God was considered the one true king of Israel, and his covenant with his people was a kind of treaty between the ruler and his subjects. When threatened by powerful enemies, however, Israel felt the need to strengthen itself politically and militarily. The nation's elders went to Samuel, a prophet and leader, asking him to "appoint for us . . . a king to govern us, like other nations" (1 Sam 8:5). At God's command, he chose Saul and anointed him as the first king.

Despite the new monarchy, Israel remained at heart a theocracy, with the king being the prime instrument of God. In addition to the important religious role he fulfilled, the king was the supreme military leader and judge. Yet Israelite kings possessed less than absolute dominion over their subjects; even David, later regarded as the greatest of the kings, made a covenant with the tribal leaders that may have set limits on his power (2 Sam 5:3). The king was also subject to the existing code of civil and religious laws. For example, he could not appropriate land at will (1 Kings 21). Furthermore, the king was required, at least in theory, to possess an edition of the laws of Deuteronomy, copied for him in the presence of the levitical priests. The king was expected to keep these laws always at hand and to read them each day, "so that he may learn to fear the LORD his God, diligently observing all the words of this law and these statutes, neither exalting himself above other members of the community nor turning aside from the commandment" (Deut 17:19–20).

A 12th-century illumination features events in the lives of Israel's first two kings, Saul and David. At top, King Saul leads the army of Israel as David fights and then beheads Goliath. At bottom, left, David plays the harp for Saul and, at right, is anointed king.

Despite the restrictions placed on the monarchs, they frequently lapsed into excess and lawlessness. Manasseh, a king of Judah during the era of the DIVIDED KINGDOM, practiced idolatry and became a symbol of evil. Even David, the model of kingship, deeply "displeased the LORD" (2 Sam 11:27) when he arranged for the death of Bathsheba's husband. In so doing, he brought down the curse of "the sword shall never depart from your house, for you have despised me" (2 Sam 12:10) upon himself and his family.

Solomon succeeded David, his father, as king. After his death, the kingdom divided, with separate rulers in the north and south. Centuries after Assyria and Babylon, respectively, defeated those two kingdoms, the Maccabees led a Jewish revolt against Greek rule. This family then became Judea's kings and high priests; theirs was called the Hasmonean dynasty. The Romans conquered this kingdom in 63 BC, and about 25 years later Herod the Great became king of Judea.

Jesus was born during Herod's reign. When the wise men came looking for a child "who has been born king of the Jews" (Mt 2:2), Herod, fearing for his throne, tried to have the child killed. In Christian belief, the Old Testament promise that a new king—the Messiah—would appear in the future was brought to fulfillment with Jesus' birth. Throughout the New Testament runs the theme that Jesus, a descendant of the royal Davidic line, is a ruler or king.

Kingdom of God

. . . "The time is fulfilled, and the kingdom of God has come near; repent, and believe in the good news."–Mark 1:15

At the heart of Jesus' message was the good news that all people could enter the kingdom of God, or the kingdom of heaven, if they turned away from sin. He warned, however, that whereas little children and those who emulated them would possess the kingdom, the rich would have a difficult time entering it (Mk 10:14–15, 23). Jesus used the PARABLE of the mustard seed (Mk 4:30–32), among others, to try to describe this kingdom. He sometimes indicated that the kingdom of God had already arrived through him, but he also spoke of it as a promise for the future.

Kings, 1&2

. . . they have done what is evil in my sight and have provoked me to anger . . . .
–2 Kings 21:15

The Old Testament's two books of Kings recount the history of the Israelite monarchy from its apex to its demise. They begin with Solomon's reign, a period of prosperity highlighted by the construction of the Jerusalem temple. Yet Solomon's extravagances and frailties, including the worship of other gods, sowed the seeds of disaster (1 Kings 11:1–13). Solomon's son succeeded him, but the kingdom then split into the northern state of Israel and the southern state of Judah. According to the authors of Kings, Israel succumbed to pagan influences and was vanquished by the Assyrians (2 Kings 17) in 721 BC. Judah, also undermined by unfaithfulness, was occupied by Babylon in 597 BC. A decade later Jerusalem and its temple were destroyed as the Babylonians carried out a second wave of deportation of the people (2 Kings 25:1–11).

The books of Kings are part of a history that extends from the Israelites entering the Promised Land up to the Babylonian exile. They are written from a theological perspective, in which rulers and events are judged by the Deuteronomic code: unfaithfulness to God is the ultimate sin and accounts for the tragic history of the monarchy.

Kiss

Greet one another with a holy kiss.
–1 Corinthians 16:20

In Near Eastern culture the kiss was a gesture of love, friendship, homage, or worship. Kissing on the lips expressed the erotic attraction between lovers, as described in an opening verse of Song of Solomon: "Let him kiss me with the kisses of his mouth!" (Song of S 1:2). But kissing did not always have sexual significance. Samuel kissed Saul when he anointed him the first king of Israel (1 Sam 10:1). Relatives and friends kissed each other affectionately on greeting (Gen 29:13) or parting. A kiss could mean forgiveness and reconciliation, such as when the prodigal son returned home and his father "ran and put his arms around him and kissed him" (Lk 15:20). To signify obeisance or respect, a person might kiss the hands or feet of a leader or teacher. The kiss could also work as a tool of deception: Joab was able to stab his rival Amasa because he put him off guard with a kiss (2 Sam 20:9–10), and Judas bestowed a kiss upon Jesus at the moment of his betrayal (Mk 14:45). The early Christians greeted each other with a "holy kiss" that signified the love filling the entire community.

Kitchen

. . . "These are the kitchens where those who serve at the temple shall boil the sacrifices of the people."
–Ezekiel 46:24

This verse from Ezekiel contains the only biblical reference to the kitchen. Except for the residences of royalty and the rich, houses did not have a separate room for COOKING. Most people cooked outside in the courtyard using a clay oven or, in bad weather, inside the house using a charcoal brazier. Ezekiel's vision of the ideal temple included two cooking areas: one in the outer court, to serve the common people, and one in the priestly quarters, reserved for the priests (Ezek 46:20).

A kiss is the sign by which Judas identifies Jesus to his enemies in a German oak carving from the early 16th century.

KITE

THEY SHALL NOT BE EATEN; THEY ARE AN ABOMINATION: THE EAGLE, THE VULTURE, THE OSPREY, THE BUZZARD, THE KITE OF ANY KIND . . . . –LEVITICUS 11:13–14.

Several species of kites, members of the hawk family, were found in the Holy Land in ancient times. Two still seen in this area are the common kite and the black kite. The common kite migrates to the Mediterranean coast in winter, and the black kite settles in summer near villages, where it lives on refuse. Kites also eat field mice, rats, and moles. The Old Testament lists them among 20 unclean "birds" (including the bat, actually a mammal), perhaps because they are carnivores and scavengers and may therefore come into contact with dead bodies.

KNEADING BOWL

BLESSED SHALL BE YOUR BASKET AND YOUR KNEADING BOWL. –DEUTERONOMY 28:5

The kneading bowl (called a trough in some Bible translations) was a common cooking utensil—a large, shallow container used to mix flour, water, and oil into bread dough. Made of wood, pottery, or bronze, kneading bowls were handily portable. When the Israelites left their bondage in Egypt, they carried "their kneading bowls wrapped up in their cloaks on their shoulders" (Ex 12:34). Later, as they were about to enter the Promised Land, Moses referred to this mundane but highly important object—along with another household container, the BASKET—when conveying the blessings or curses that would come from God for keeping or breaking his commandments (Deut 28:5, 17).

A baker, portrayed by a third-century BC clay figurine, makes dough in a kneading bowl; the other bowl may be for additional flour.

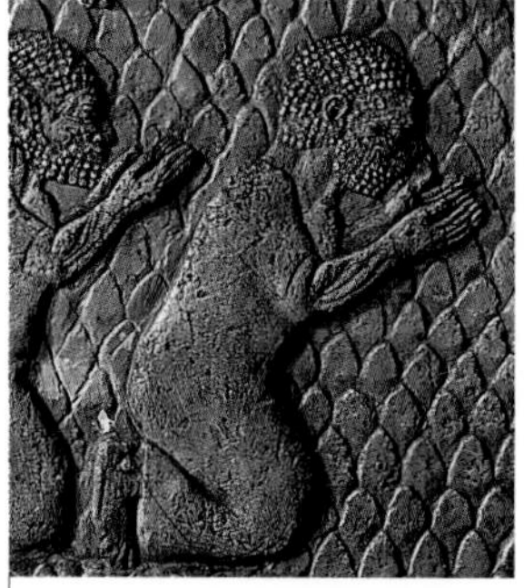

Judean captives of the Assyrian king show submission by kneeling in a palace relief from about 700 BC.

KNEELING

A LEPER CAME TO HIM BEGGING HIM, AND KNEELING HE SAID TO HIM, "IF YOU CHOOSE, YOU CAN MAKE ME CLEAN." –MARK 1:40

A position assumed when praying, kneeling demonstrated respect and reverence. Therefore, at the dedication of the temple, Solomon "knelt on his knees . . . and spread out his hands toward heaven" before speaking to God (2 Chr 6:13). When asking Jesus to heal them, people often knelt in front of him, as did the mother of the sons of Zebedee when requesting a favor for her children (Mt 20:20). "At the name of Jesus every knee should bend" (Phil 2:10) wrote Paul to the Philippians, indicating the homage that should be accorded to Jesus' divine status.

KNEES

HIS LIMBS GAVE WAY, AND HIS KNEES KNOCKED TOGETHER. –DANIEL 5:6

In the Bible, the knees—by their trembling, knocking together, or growing frail—could signify fear or weakness. In Isaiah 35:5, God is beseeched to "make firm the feeble knees." The word *knees* sometimes means the lap, as when Job, lamenting that he was ever born, asks, "Why were there knees to receive me?" (Job 3:12). In Genesis, Rachel tells her husband to go in to her maid, "that she may bear upon my knees and that I too may have children through her" (Gen 30:3); here the mention of the knees probably concerns an ADOPTION ritual. Many references to the knees involve bowing or kneeling in prayer or deference to an earthly superior. Jesus tells of a slave falling on his knees to plead with his master for forbearance (Mt 18:26).

KNIFE

. . . WHEN ISAAC SAW HIS FATHER'S HAND WIELDING A KNIFE AND DESCENDING UPON HIM, HE DID NOT COWER. –4 MACCABEES 16:20

People made knives from flint, copper, bronze, and later, iron. Most knives uncovered in the area of the Holy Land are about 6 to 10 inches long.

The figure of the jackal, a funerary god, indicates that this bronze Egyptian knife belonged to an embalmer.

Some knives during biblical times were longer, resembling short swords. Others were the length of a pen knife and were used for small jobs, including shaving and sharpening reed pens. Most knives were not weapons but rather tools for various chores, such as cutting food, pruning trees, and killing and skinning animals. Animals were often slaughtered by knife as offerings to God; Genesis 22 tells the story of Abraham's willingness to sacrifice his son Isaac in a similar manner.

The potsherds at right, inscribed with Hebrew names, are believed to be the LOTS *used at Masada in* AD *73 by Jewish rebel leaders to determine who would kill the others when the Romans overcame them.*

Laborer

"Do not human beings have a hard service on earth, and are not their days like the days of a laborer?" –Job 7:1

Laborers ranked low on the social scale in the biblical world; one of the Hebrew words translated as "laborer" also means "servant" and "slave." Work seems to have been regarded as God's punishment for Adam and Eve's disobedience (Gen 3:17–19). Yet biblical writers depict Adam before the fall as the caretaker of the garden of Eden (Gen 2:15) and God himself as an artisan who created the world (Ps 102:25).

Mosaic law included rules to protect laborers. An employer was obligated to pay his workers promptly rather than to withhold wages until the next morning (Lev 19:13). Laborers, including resident aliens and even slaves, had the sabbath off (Ex 20:10).

Jesus filled his parables with allusions to humble workers such as vineyard laborers, shepherds, and slaves. He told his disciples who were about to go out on a mission to take provisions from those who offered them, "for the laborer deserves to be paid" (Lk 10:7).

Ladder

And he dreamed that there was a ladder set up on the earth, the top of it reaching to heaven . . . . –Genesis 28:12

To go up and down heights, people built stairways from stone and made ladders from wood, metal, or rope. They used ladders to climb onto rooftops or into storerooms lacking doors and, during warfare, to scale walls, as shown on Egyptian friezes dating as far back as the third millennium BC. In 1 Maccabees 5:30, the army attacking a Jewish stronghold carried "ladders and engines of war." The "ladder" in Jacob's dream was probably a staircase like that of a ziggurat, or step PYRAMID. On it "angels of God were ascending and descending" (Gen 28:12).

Lamb of God

. . . "Here is the Lamb of God who takes away the sin of the world!" –John 1:29

In the Gospel of John, when John the Baptist saw Jesus approaching, he declared him to be "the Lamb of God." Biblical scholars have proposed various interpretations of this phrase, which is not used in the other Gospels. It may mean that, charged with fulfilling the divine plan for the redemption of humankind, Jesus acted as a symbolic sacrificial lamb for the atonement of all sins, much like the actual sheep sacrificed in the temple to redeem the individual sinner. Similarly, John's image may have recalled the Israelite ritual on the annual Day of Atonement, when a goat, or scapegoat, bore the transgressions of the people out into the wilderness. Using either interpretation, John is prefiguring the redemptive death and resurrection of Jesus. Another theory holds that John was referring to the lambs slaughtered for the feast at Passover (Ex 12:3), which Jesus celebrated the night before he died, or to the horned ram that led a flock, a traditional symbol for the king of Israel. The book of Revelation repeatedly identifies Christ in his glory as "the Lamb" but never as "the Lamb of God."

A medieval stained-glass window presents the lamb as a symbol of Jesus.

An 18th-century British stained-glass window shows Peter healing a lame man.

LAMENESS

BUT IF IT HAS ANY DEFECT—ANY SERIOUS DEFECT, SUCH AS LAMENESS OR BLINDNESS—YOU SHALL NOT SACRIFICE IT TO THE LORD YOUR GOD . . . .
–DEUTERONOMY 15:21

Lameness was a ritual blemish under Mosaic law. Since according to Scripture, humans were created by God in his image (Gen 1:27), the physical deformity was considered inappropriate in worship. Therefore no lame animal could be offered as a sacrifice to God, nor could a crippled priest offer sacrifices (Lev 21:17–18). However, the lame among Aaron's descendants, who comprised the hereditary caste of priests, were allowed to eat the priestly share of sacrificial offerings (Lev 21:22).

In the New Testament, Jesus and his disciples frequently healed the lame, and the physical cure simultaneously reinstated the afflicted to the community of worship. When Peter and John healed a crippled beggar beside the Beautiful Gate, for example, the man immediately entered the temple to offer praise to God (Acts 3:1–8).

LAMENTATIONS, BOOK OF

HOW LONELY SITS THE CITY THAT ONCE WAS FULL OF PEOPLE!
–LAMENTATIONS 1:1

The book of Lamentations is a set of sorrowful dirges mourning the destruction of Jerusalem by the Babylonians. Though traditionally attributed to Jeremiah, authorship is not certain. Lamentation over a destroyed city was an old Near Eastern literary form, with precedents in the literature of Sumer. The emotional force of such dirges came from the realization that the guardian deity was responsible for the catastrophe, a belief that pervades Lamentations. Despite the destruction, however, the author pleads with God not to abandon his people but rather to grant their restoration (Lam 5:21–22).

LAMP

"NO ONE AFTER LIGHTING A LAMP PUTS IT IN A CELLAR, BUT ON THE LAMPSTAND SO THAT THOSE WHO ENTER MAY SEE THE LIGHT."
–LUKE 11:33

Lamps were the principal source of indoor illumination in biblical times. The earliest lamps were stone bowls filled with melted animal fat, in which floated a wick of twisted plant fibers. These were replaced by pottery bowls, the lamps mentioned in the Bible. In the Near East, the principal fuel for these lamps was olive oil. Oil gave off less smoke than fat, smelled better (fat quickly went rancid), and perhaps burned slightly brighter. Over the course of centuries, the form of the lamp changed from an open bowl to a more efficient, semi-closed shape, with a spout to hold the wick. Some lamps had multiple wicks around their circumference for greater lighting power. Lanterns were used for outdoor illumination. The typical lantern was a container of pottery or METAL with one open side; it held a lamp, which it shielded from wind and rain.

Household lamps burned day and night, not only because most houses were dark inside but also as an aid in lighting fires. The lamp was usually placed on a lampstand or shelf for better light. Domestic lampstands were commonly made of wood or ceramic, but those for the tabernacle and the temple were gold. The tabernacle lamps were shaped like the calyxes and petals of flowers, perhaps for esthetic or symbolic reasons.

Lamps had great symbolic importance: they stood for life, good fortune, God's favor, and learning and wisdom. In the New Testament they sometimes represented Jesus and his teachings, as in Revelation 21:23.

A lamp from the Second Temple period has a large hole for oil and a small one for the wick.

LAND

. . . THEN I WILL DWELL WITH YOU . . . IN THE LAND THAT I GAVE OF OLD TO YOUR ANCESTORS FOREVER AND EVER.–JEREMIAH 7:7

The close relationship of humans to the land began at creation, when God fashioned Adam from "the dust of the ground" (Gen 2:7). The fate of Adam and all his descendants was bound to the land: God ordained that they should till the ground until they returned to it at death (Gen 3:17–19, 23).

As an agricultural people, the Israelites had an intimate relationship with the land (see map). Land brought forth food and life; to possess barren soil therefore was a terrible misfortune. The OWNERSHIP and proper use of land were governed by law and morality. It was a sin for owners to cheat the people who worked the land for them or to obtain land by causing the death of its owner. Job says God should cause his land to bring forth thorns rather than wheat "if I have eaten its yield without payment" (Job 31:39).

Not only the fate of individuals but also that of nations was tied to land. For a nation to have an identity, it had to be rooted in a homeland, which God provided to Israel as part of his covenant with Abraham. He commanded Abraham to go to the place where the Canaanites dwelled, "to the land that I will show you" (Gen 12:1). There he proclaimed, "To your offspring I will give this land" (Gen 12:7).

This area was the Promised Land, which the Israelites claimed after God redeemed them from slavery in Egypt. Because the people rebelled during their journey in the wilderness, God caused an entire generation to die before reaching the Promised Land. However, he turned over the region to their children and grandchildren after prescribing regulations about their inheritance (Num 27:5–11; 36:5–9). See also ALLOTMENT.

The rich land was "flowing with milk and honey" (Ex 3:8) and filled with "vineyards, olive orchards, and fruit trees in abundance," signifying God's "great goodness" (Neh 9:25). The fertility of the land was tied to following God's commandments. For those who obeyed, "blessed shall be . . . the fruit of your ground" (Deut 28:4), but a curse would fall on the ground of those who disobeyed (Deut 28:18). Possession of land was a gift that God could withdraw; those who violated his laws were warned by the prophet Amos that "your land shall be parceled out" (Am 7:17).

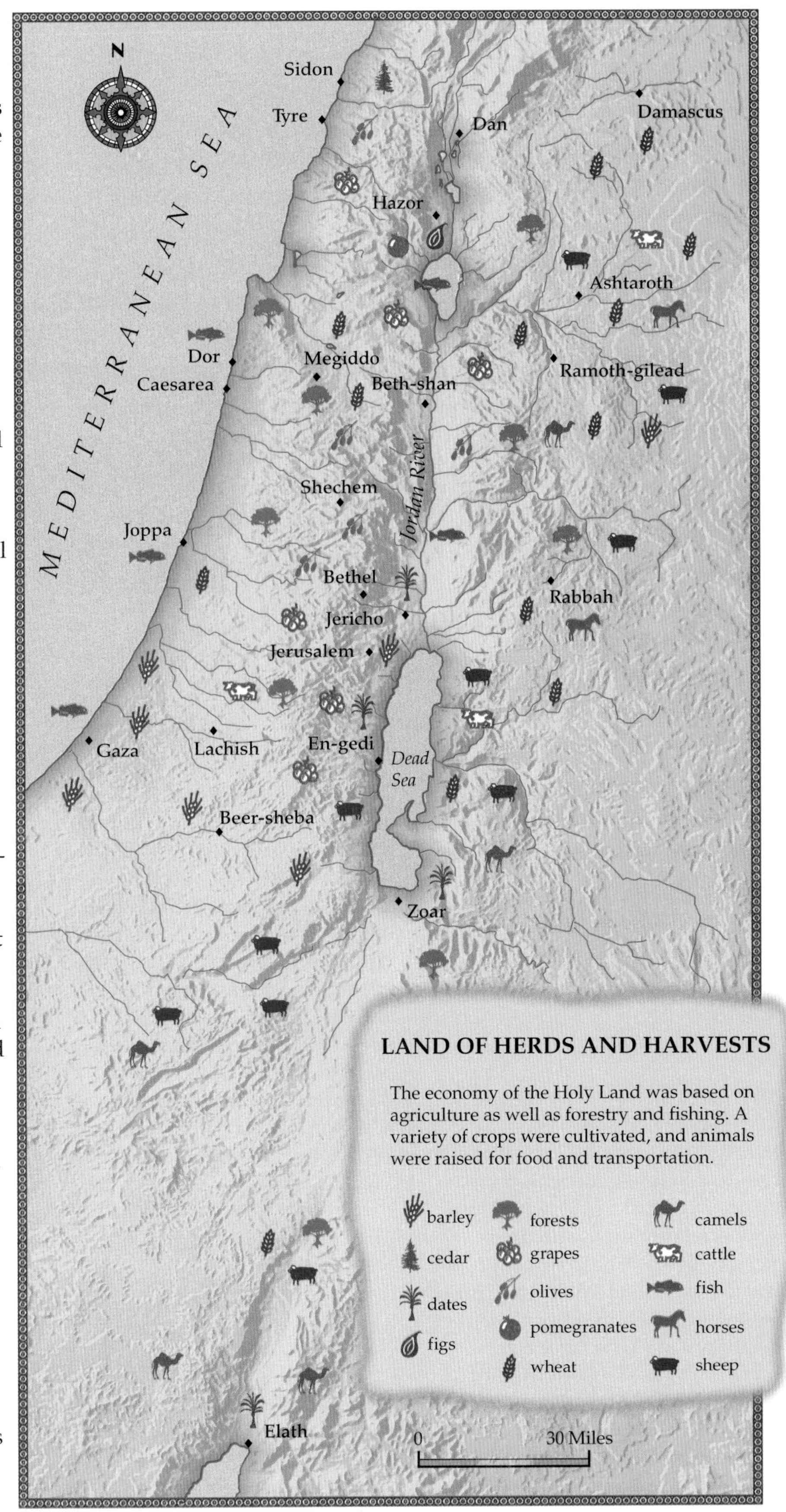

LAND OF HERDS AND HARVESTS

The economy of the Holy Land was based on agriculture as well as forestry and fishing. A variety of crops were cultivated, and animals were raised for food and transportation.

LANGUAGE

Now the whole earth had one language and the same words.–Genesis 11:1

According to Genesis, the diversity of languages that sprang up in the ancient world was divine punishment for human arrogance in building the tower of Babel (Gen 11:1–9). Foreign languages could also be symbolic of oppressors: the Assyrians, for example, were called "insolent people . . . stammering in a language that you cannot understand" (Isa 33:19). HEBREW was the main language of the Israelites of the Old Testament, but during postexilic times the Jews adopted Aramaic, the international language of the Persian Empire, for daily use, while retaining Hebrew for their religious writings. Subsequent political changes eventually made Greek the international language of commerce and culture and Latin the language of the Roman government. However, Aramaic continued in general use, and Jesus probably spoke an Aramaic dialect.

LATTICE

For at the window of my house I looked out through my lattice . . . .
–Proverbs 7:6

The word *lattice* occurs only in the Old Testament, where it refers to a balustrade at a WINDOW or to a window as a whole, rather than to the criss-crossed strips of wood that appeared during the Roman period. Balustrades, probably made of stone or wood, were built into window frames to provide security against burglars and a measure of protection from the heat and rain. They also allowed a person to look out a window without being seen clearly from the outside. In Song of Solomon 2:9, the maiden watching her beloved from her house observes that "he stands behind our wall, gazing in at the windows, looking through the lattice." A woman staring out a window is a familiar theme in art from Old Testament times (see illustration). For young women to do this, however, was considered unseemly, because prostitutes sat at their windows. The author of the book of Ecclesiasticus advised any readers with a "a headstrong daughter" to "see that there is no lattice in her room, no spot that overlooks the approaches to the house" (Sir 42:11).

In the Old Testament, lattice *might refer to an entire window or simply to the balustrade connected to one. Here a woman of the ancient Near East peers out of a recessed window in which the lattice consists of a balustrade of limestone columns.*

LAUGHTER

Feasts are made for laughter . . . .
–Ecclesiastes 10:19

Laughter was variously an expression of joy, contempt, or disbelief. Abraham was incredulous when God told him that his wife, Sarah, who was 90 years old, would give birth to a son; his response was laughter. Because of this, God instructed that the child be named Isaac, which in Hebrew means "he laughs" (Gen 17:19). Laughter could also be a sign of derision. After having been humiliated by enemies, Israel became a "laughingstock among the peoples" (Ps 44:14). Job, in his trials, called himself a "laughingstock to my friends" (Job 12:4).

While the Bible recognizes that there is a place for laughter (Eccl 3:4), it also speaks of fools whose "laughter is wantonly sinful" (Sir 27:13). The letter of James says that submitting to God means, among other things, to "let your laughter be turned into mourning and your joy into dejection" (Jas 4:9). Though this and other passages contrast laughter with sadness, the book of Proverbs indicates that these emotions are not always far apart: "Even in laughter the heart is sad, and the end of joy is grief" (Prov 14:13).

Laver

Then King Ahaz . . . removed the laver from them . . . .
–2 Kings 16:17

Before offering sacrifices at the tabernacle altar, Aaron and other priests purified themselves by washing their hands and feet in the water of a bronze basin known as a laver. If they failed to do this, they would die (Ex 30:21). The tabernacle had only one such basin, which the Bible describes as resting on a bronze stand (Ex 30:18) and being crafted from the mirrors of women "who served at the entrance to the tent of meeting" (Ex 38:8).

In Solomon's temple this laver was replaced by the MOLTEN SEA, which held approximately 11,000 gallons of water, and 10 smaller, mobile basins, each containing about 220 gallons (1 Kings 7:23–39). It was the molten sea that King Ahaz dismantled to help pay his tribute to the king of Assyria.

Law

And what other great nation has statutes and ordinances as just as this entire law that I am setting before you today?
–Deuteronomy 4:8

The first five books of the Bible are sometimes called the book of the law or the law of Moses. They contain the rules that God gave to Moses. These ordinances, which God laid down so that his people could live in a covenant relationship with him, became the Israelites' legal code. The code addressed all aspects of community life: in addition to civil and criminal laws, its rules encompassed religious requirements, moral standards, dietary traditions, and social customs. Around the written law grew a body of oral law, called "the tradition of the elders" by the scribes and Pharisees (Mt 15:2), which determined the manner in which the laws would be applied.

The laws were of two types. Categorical laws, such as the ten commandments, were general pronouncements on how people should live. Casuistic, or case, laws determined specific crimes and often set penalties and compensation, such as "When someone steals an ox or a sheep, and slaughters it or sells it, the thief shall pay five oxen for an ox, and four sheep for a sheep" (Ex 22:1).

In the New Testament, the law often became a source of discussion between Jesus and his critics. When asked to name the greatest commandment, Jesus named the first and second commandments—to love God wholeheartedly and to love one's neighbor as oneself—adding that "on these two commandments hang all the law" (Mt 22:40). Jesus argued against focusing on the law's minute details rather than its essence. When the Pharisees disparaged his disciples for picking grain on the sabbath, Jesus reminded them that David had once broken the law by eating holy bread. He said, "The sabbath was made for humankind, and not humankind for the sabbath" (Mk 2:27). See also DEUTERONOMY.

A parchment scroll from the 15th century contains the first five books of the Bible, also called the law of Moses. This scroll was used for services in a German synagogue.

Law of Moses

"Therefore be very steadfast to observe and do all that is written in the book of the law of Moses . . . ."
–Joshua 23:6

The law of Moses refers to the first five books of the Old Testament. Also called the Pentateuch (meaning "five scrolls") or the Torah ("the law"), they consist of the books of Genesis, Exodus, Leviticus, Numbers, and Deuteronomy. Although Moses has traditionally been considered the author of the Pentateuch, today many scholars believe that this section of the Bible was written by a number of authors at different times.

These books cover the period from the creation until Moses' death. They include God's instructions to the Israelites so that they might live according to his will. In the books are the ten commandments as well as a wide variety of laws dealing with specific situations. The laws are presented in various overlapping codes. Leviticus, for example, contains a group of laws sometimes called the holiness code because of God's command within it: "You shall be holy, for I the LORD your God am holy" (Lev 19:2). It speaks to priests as well as to ordinary people.

LAWGIVER

HUMAN SUCCESS IS IN THE HAND OF THE LORD, AND IT IS HE WHO CONFERS HONOR UPON THE LAWGIVER.
–ECCLESIASTICUS 10:5

A lawgiver is one who gives a code of laws to a people. In biblical times, this person might be a king,

Often called a lawgiver, Moses holds stone tablets in a French illumination.

military commander, priest, or other leader. The word is frequently associated with Moses, but the Bible does not identify him in this way. When Jesus asked, "Did not Moses give you the law?" (Jn 7:19), he was referring to Moses handing down God's commandments to the Israelites rather than to Moses creating the law himself. Jesus is sometimes thought of as the originator of a new law; he, however, told his followers, "Do not think that I have come to abolish the law or the prophets; I have come not to abolish but to fulfill" (Mt 5:17).

The letter of James warns people not to judge one another because only in God the father is there "one lawgiver and judge who is able to save and to destroy" (Jas 4:12).

LAYING ON OF HANDS

DO NOT NEGLECT THE GIFT THAT IS IN YOU, WHICH WAS GIVEN TO YOU THROUGH PROPHECY WITH THE LAYING ON OF HANDS BY THE COUNCIL OF ELDERS.
–1 TIMOTHY 4:14

The laying on of hands, which occurs in both the Old and New Testaments, was a symbolic act. It often involved an offering made to God, in which the priest laid his hands on the head of an animal, such as a bull or ram, before it was killed as a sacrifice. On the Day of Atonement, the high priest placed his hands on a goat to transfer the sins of the people to the animal, which was then sent into the wilderness to carry them away (Lev 16:21). When someone ceremonially laid one or both of his hands on another person, he might be giving his blessing or transferring a divine commission (Gen 48:14; Num 27:23). Jesus often used the gesture when healing the sick, perhaps to convey the idea of a blessing. The New Testament also links the laying on of hands with baptism and the gift of the Holy Spirit (Acts 19:5–6).

Throughout the missionary period, church elders or congregations commissioned evangelists, bestowed the gift of prophecy, or consecrated those given special tasks by the laying on of hands. Elsewhere in the Bible, laying hands on a person could refer to a capture (2 Chr 23:15; Mk 14:46).

LEAD

YOU BLEW WITH YOUR WIND, THE SEA COVERED THEM; THEY SANK LIKE LEAD IN THE MIGHTY WATERS.
–EXODUS 15:10

A soft, dense, gray metal, lead was plentiful in the ancient world. In Ecclesiasticus 47:18, Solomon was said to have "amassed silver like lead." Evidence of the use of lead dates back to 3000 BC. Lead objects were among the booty the Israelites captured in battle with the Midianites (Num 31:22). Mined in areas around the Mediterranean Sea, the metal was a trade item; Ezekiel 27:12 speaks of Tarshish exchanging silver, iron, tin, and lead for the wares offered by Tyre. Lead was too pliable to be used alone for tools or jewelry, but its heaviness made it suitable for plumblines, sinkers on fishing lines, and weights, such as the basket cover in Zechariah 5:7–8. Another important use of lead was in the refinement of SILVER (Jer 6:29). Exodus 15:10 underscores lead's heaviness by comparing the metal with Pharaoh's army sinking into the Red Sea.

LEADER

MOSES SPOKE TO THE ISRAELITES; AND ALL THEIR LEADERS GAVE HIM STAFFS, ONE FOR EACH LEADER, ACCORDING TO THEIR ANCESTRAL HOUSES . . . .–NUMBERS 17:6

A leader was one vested with religious or secular authority. Israelite tribal chiefs were leaders, as were judges and kings. Individuals held leadership positions among Levites and priests (Neh 11:16; 12:7), and Nehemiah speaks of a "leader of the singers" in the days of King David (Neh 12:46). Leaders were to be respected: "You shall not revile God, or curse a leader of your people" (Ex 22:28).

In the Roman era, ultimate authority rested with the EMPEROR and his representatives, who could "punish those who do wrong" (1 Pet 2:14). Although the Bible urged obedience to earthly leaders, it also demanded that they be humble. Jesus advised his disciples that "whoever wishes to be great among you must be your servant" (Mt 20:26).

Leather Working

Leather was widely used in the ancient world for clothing, weaponry, and a variety of other items. It provided material for sandals, belts, shields, sword sheaths, helmets, scrolls, furniture, chariot wheel covers, harnesses, buckets, and containers to hold wine or make butter. Tanneries were located outside of town, where they were usually positioned so that the prevailing westerly winds could carry the stench away.

1. After hides are delivered to the tannery, the tanners wash them in wooden tubs to remove the dirt and blood. The hides are then beaten, trod upon, and soaked again in order to loosen the hair.

2. When the hides have been cleaned and the hair loosened, the tanners scrape and stretch them to remove the hair and excess flesh; this also softens them for the tanning process. They might shave some of the hides to produce a thinner leather, which would be more suitable for bags.

3. The hides are put in tanning pits and soaked in vegetable tannins made of pine, sumac, oak galls, acorns, roots, berries, or pomegranate rinds, which impart to the leather a hue of tan, yellow, crimson, dark brown, or black. After a few weeks, the men remove the hides from the pits and carry them up to the roof to dry.

LEATHER

OVER THE GOLDEN ALTAR THEY SHALL SPREAD A BLUE CLOTH, AND COVER IT WITH A COVERING OF FINE LEATHER . . . .–NUMBERS 4:11

Humans have prepared the hides of animals such as sheep and goats since earliest times (see box, p. 211). In the ancient Near East, clothing made of leather was worn by prophets and other ascetics, and nearly everyone wore leather sandals. Soldiers went into battle with helmets and shields made of leather that was well oiled to repel arrows and prevent cracking. Skins were sewn together and fashioned into containers for water and wine, and fine leather was used to make beds and other furnishings for the homes of the wealthy. Documents were often written on leather, as were many of the Dead Sea Scrolls.

LEAVEN

YOU SHALL BRING FROM YOUR SETTLEMENTS TWO LOAVES OF BREAD AS AN ELEVATION OFFERING . . . THEY SHALL BE OF CHOICE FLOUR, BAKED WITH LEAVEN, AS FIRST FRUITS TO THE LORD. –LEVITICUS 23:17

God instructed Moses that the people should thank him for their wheat harvest by celebrating on the 50th day after the Passover sabbath. This day was called the Festival of Weeks—or Pentecost—commemorating the seven weeks between the barley and the wheat harvests. The first fruits of wheat were presented to the Lord as two loaves of bread baked from the new wheat flour and leavened with a piece of dough reserved from a previous baking. Since the fermentation in leavened bread was considered a form of corruption, the loaves could not be burnt on the altar but were waved horizontally back and forth over it. Eating UNLEAVENED BREAD during Passover symbolized the Israelites' hasty escape from Egypt. The absence of the corruption of leaven stood for the moral purity of the redeemed people, who were admonished that, during the festival, "no leavened bread shall be seen in your possession" (Ex 13:7).

LEGION

THEN JESUS ASKED HIM, "WHAT IS YOUR NAME?" HE REPLIED, "MY NAME IS LEGION; FOR WE ARE MANY."–MARK 5:9

By the time of Jesus, reorganization of the Roman army under the Emperor Augustus had produced legions of some 4,500 to 6,000 of the finest troops, made up of Roman citizens. A legion was built upon centuries of 100 men each, which were grouped into cohorts of 600 men each, or a total of 10 cohorts. A few of the empire's 28 legions were stationed in Syria, but they were rarely seen in the Holy Land until 66 AD, when the Jews rebelled against their oppressors. In Matthew *legion* symbolizes the great power and numbers of God's angels (Mt 26:53). In the passage cited above and also in Luke 8:30, when a possessed man told Jesus his name was Legion, he meant that a huge number of demons was teeming within him.

LEOPARD

A LEOPARD IS WATCHING AGAINST THEIR CITIES; EVERYONE WHO GOES OUT OF THEM SHALL BE TORN IN PIECES . . . .–JEREMIAH 5:6

Although leopards are now a vanishing species in the Middle East, in biblical times these large cats were plentiful in Lebanon and the Holy Land. Leopards inhabited mountainous terrain and forests, and their stealth and great speed posed a threat to shepherds and

A detail from the mosaic floor of a fifth-century BC synagogue in the northern Negeb depicts a leopard.

the herds they tended. Indeed, when Isaiah uses the example of a leopard lying peacefully with a kid, it illustrates the harmony of the rule of an ideal king (Isa 11:6). Habakkuk's description of horses "swifter than leopards" (Hab 1:8) may refer to cheetahs, which were once trained for hunting.

LEPROSY

[JESUS] STRETCHED OUT HIS HAND AND TOUCHED HIM, SAYING, "I DO CHOOSE. BE MADE CLEAN!" IMMEDIATELY HIS LEPROSY WAS CLEANSED. –MATTHEW 8:3

Biblical references to leprosy include a wide variety of skin ailments from eczema and psoriasis to modern leprosy, or Hansen's disease, with its running sores, white patches, and the loss of toes and fingers. Suspected lepers were quarantined for seven days, then examined by a priest. If the condition persisted, they were confined for another seven days (Lev 13:4–5). Those still afflicted were cast out from the community, but those who spontaneously healed were ritually restored by ceremonies during an eight-day period (Lev 14:1–32). Finally the healed person was daubed with oil and the blood of a sacrificial lamb on the right ear lobe, thumb, and big toe.

Healthy people avoided any contact with the leper so that they themselves would not become ritually unclean. Leviticus also addresses the spread of the disease to cloth and warns "if the disease shows greenish or reddish in the garment" (Lev 13:49), it is leprous. The second temple had a chamber set aside for healed lepers to undergo purification rites. Houses could also be deemed leprous, probably because of dry rot, lichens, or mold, which polluted anyone who entered. Jesus did not regard lepers as unclean and healed them without hesitation, commanding his disciples to follow his example.

Letter

When they gathered the congregation together, they delivered the letter. –Acts of the Apostles 15:30

In biblical times, letters were written both by professional scribes and by common people. They were inscribed on a variety of surfaces: clay tablets, pottery fragments, prepared animal skins, and papyrus sheets. Papyrus was used by the Egyptians and also in the Holy Land before the Persian period; the sheets were folded or rolled up and often sealed to keep the contents private. In 2 Samuel 11:14–15 Uriah unwittingly carried a message to Joab that plotted his own death.

The king's seal on a letter lent it royal force, "for an edict written in the name of the king and sealed with the king's ring cannot be revoked" (Esth 8:8). By the sixth century BC, the Persians had created an official postal system. The Greeks and Romans had a similar service for state mail. The rich had slaves or couriers to deliver personal mail; common people relied on travelers or traders.

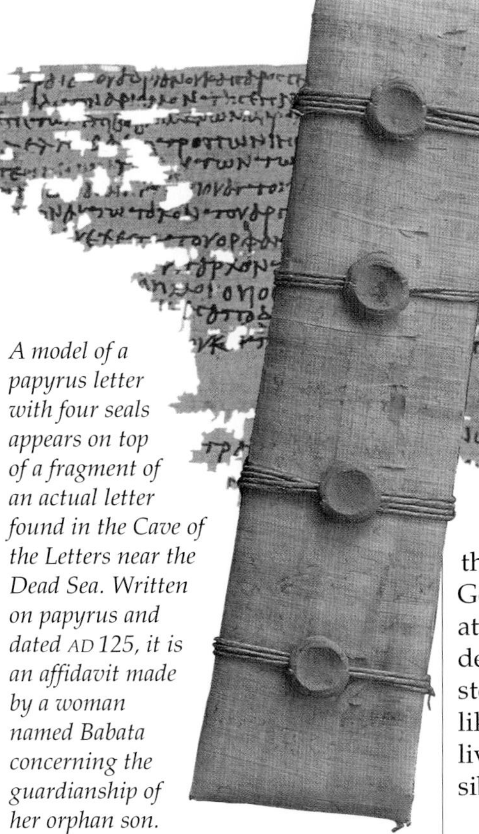

A model of a papyrus letter with four seals appears on top of a fragment of an actual letter found in the Cave of the Letters near the Dead Sea. Written on papyrus and dated AD 125, it is an affidavit made by a woman named Babata concerning the guardianship of her orphan son.

Greek teachers such as Plato used letters as a form of communication and to broadcast their beliefs to a large audience. Such instructional letters, or epistles, make up much of the New Testament. To maintain his far-flung ministry, the apostle Paul wrote many didactic letters intended to be read to entire congregations in his absence.

Leviathan

On that day the LORD . . . will punish Leviathan the fleeing serpent, Leviathan the twisting serpent, and he will kill the dragon that is in the sea.–Isaiah 27:1

In ancient mythology, Leviathan was a primeval sea monster that battled with the gods. Ugaritic literature describes Baal defeating the seven-headed sea creature Lothan, another name for Leviathan. This legend reappears in the Old Testament, where Leviathan, or DRAGON, symbolizes the watery forces of chaos that God had to defeat in order for creation to take place. An elaborate description of this primeval monster is given in Job 41. Ezekiel likens Pharaoh to a dragon that lives in the Nile (Ezek 29:3–5), possibly referring to the crocodile.

Leviticus, Book of

Speak to the people of Israel and say . . . keep my statutes and my ordinances . . . . –Leviticus 18:2, 5

Leviticus is the third of the five books of the Pentateuch and was called the Priests' Manual in postbiblical Jewish literature. Leviticus gives detailed instructions to priests, who were from the tribe of Levi, and to all of Israel regarding how to worship God. It describes various sacrifices acceptable to God, as well as what to sacrifice and for what purpose. Leviticus also establishes laws about ritual cleanliness, ordination of priests, religious holidays, and ethical behavior, including what Jesus called the second great commandment—"love your neighbor as yourself" (Lev 19:18; Mt 22:39). Many scholars suggest that editors compiled Leviticus from several ancient sources, although it was traditionally attributed to Moses.

LIFE

. . . THE LORD GOD FORMED MAN FROM THE DUST OF THE GROUND, AND BREATHED INTO HIS NOSTRILS THE BREATH OF LIFE; AND THE MAN BECAME A LIVING BEING.
–GENESIS 2:7

The vital force that causes people to move, act, and feel was seen as God's gift of life. Animals were also seen as having life, and even water bubbling out of a spring was said to be living in a figurative sense because it moved. The almighty God alone could create and sustain life, but God also brought death. Deuteronomy taught that Israel had to decide between life and death by choosing good or evil (Deut 30:15, 19–20). By loving God and obeying him, Israel chose life.

According to Genesis 2, God formed the first HUMAN life from the dust of the earth. But only God's breath made him a living being; without God's breath, or spirit, no life was possible. Blood was also strongly associated with life: Mosaic law prohibited blood from being eaten because it was seen even as life itself (Gen 9:4). Accordingly, rules for animal slaughter prescribed that the blood be removed before the flesh could be eaten.

Life was preferable to death under any circumstances, for in life there was hope. In his search for the meaning of life, Ecclesiastes concluded that "a living dog is better than a dead lion" (Eccl 9:4).

God parts dullish clouds to allow brilliant light to shine forth in this rendition of the creation of light by Raphael. The painting is part of a series in the Vatican known as Raphael's Bible.

LIGHT

THE PEOPLE WHO WALKED IN DARKNESS HAVE SEEN A GREAT LIGHT; THOSE WHO LIVED IN A LAND OF DEEP DARKNESS— ON THEM LIGHT HAS SHINED.
–ISAIAH 9:2

Light is the symbol of God's presence in the Jewish Festival of Dedication, which celebrates the return of the defiled temple in Jerusalem to the worship of God. Figuratively, light stands for joy, spirit, and good, and darkness represents death, gloom, and evil.

Because God is totally rightous, pure, and holy, he is defined as light, and there can be no darkness in him. Evildoers do their deeds in DARKNESS and hate the light because it reveals their sins. The book of Psalms describes God's word as a lamp lighting one's path through life (Ps 119:105).

For Christians, Jesus brought the light of God into a world darkened by sin and doubt. In the Gospel of John, Jesus made reference to his own God-given divinity when he said, "I am the light of the world. Whoever follows me will never walk in darkness but will have the light of life" (Jn 8:12).

LIGHTNING

"FOR AS THE LIGHTNING COMES FROM THE EAST AND FLASHES AS FAR AS THE WEST, SO WILL BE THE COMING OF THE SON OF MAN."
–MATTHEW 24:27

In the Holy Land, lightning and thunderstorms are frequent occurrences during the cool season. Ancient mythology used lightning to signal the wrath of the gods, and in the Old Testament it heralded God's arrival on Mount Sinai (Ex 19:16). Lightning was also a sign of God's power. Besieged by enemies, a psalmist implored God to "make the lightning flash and scatter them" (Ps 144:6). It could symbolize momentous events, such as when Jesus said, "I watched Satan fall from heaven like a flash of lightning" (Lk 10:18).

LILY

I AM A ROSE OF SHARON, A LILY OF THE VALLEYS. AS A LILY AMONG BRAMBLES, SO IS MY LOVE AMONG MAIDENS.
–SONG OF SOLOMON 2:1–2

The ancient Near East boasted a variety of lilies, plants from the Liliaceae family, which are characterized by bulbs. However, the biblical lily, a symbol of beauty, could also refer to other showy flowers. The "lilies of the field" in Matthew 6:28 may refer to the vivid scarlet blooms of the crown anemone, a wildflower that grows profusely on the hillsides of the Holy Land. Solomon's temple had pillars topped with a decorative lily motif. This "lily-work" (1 Kings 7:19) was probably based on Egyptian designs, which frequently used the lotus, or water lily, in art and architectural detail.

Though most commonly red, the blooms of the crown anemone can also be yellow, blue, or purple.

LINE

The carpenter stretches a line, marks it out with a stylus, fashions it with planes, and marks it with a compass . . . .
–Isaiah 44:13

A line was a cord or tool used to ascertain distance, depth, or length. A line was used to survey a city (Jer 31:39), to parcel out land (Am 7:17), and, along with a plummet, to ensure precision in building. Metaphorically, a line served as a measure of judgment: "I will make justice the line, and righteousness the plummet" (Isa 28:17). In battle, soldiers were drawn up into lines (Judg 20:20).

A different Hebrew word also translated as "line" represents the descent from a common ancestor. Promising to uphold the house of David in perpetuity, God declares in Psalm 89:29: "I will establish his line forever."

LINEN

"There was a rich man who was dressed in purple and fine linen and who feasted sumptuously every day."
–Luke 16:19

Linen, a fabric used in biblical times for clothing, fine furnishings, and ships' sails, comes from the flax plant. Flax was widely grown in Egypt, where the silty soil was especially suitable for its cultivation. Biblical references to "fine linen" usually meant the highly desirable Egyptian linen, which resembled silk. A symbol of purity, fine linen was used to make priests' garments (Lev 16:32) and the tabernacle curtains (Ex 26:1). Egyptian mummies were wrapped in hundreds of yards of linen, and Jewish burial customs also involved wrapping a body in linen cloth (Jn 19:40).

LION

They are like a lion eager to tear, like a young lion lurking in ambush.
–Psalm 17:12

Asiatic lions disappeared from the Holy Land about the 14th century AD, though they remained in Mesopotamia and Syria until the 19th century. Lion hunting was a popular royal sport in ancient times, and one pharaoh is said to have kept lions as pets. But to shepherds, lions were a dangerous foe. David told Saul that he had protected his father's sheep from lions and bears (1 Sam 17:34–35). Daniel was thrown into a lions' den but emerged unharmed (Dan 6:23). Israel is portrayed as a fierce nation when Balaam compares its people with a lion (Num 23:24).

LIPS

"Your own mouth condemns you, and not I; your own lips testify against you."
–Job 15:6

Often used in the Old Testament to reveal someone's feelings or character, the lips could express righteousness or joy, deceit or fear. They were usually considered to be directly controlled by the heart or mind, although in figurative language they occasionally seemed to act on their own. Covering the upper lip generally indicated a sense of grief (Ezek 24:17, 22). Like the mouth or the tongue, the lips were sometimes used to symbolize language or speech. In some English-language versions of the Bible, the phrase translated as "uncircumcised lips" was used by Moses to plead that he was inarticulate (Ex 6:12).

LIVER

Moses took . . . the appendage of the liver, and the two kidneys with their fat, and turned them into smoke on the altar.
–Leviticus 8:16

According to Mosaic law, the "appendage of the liver" (Ex 29:13)—probably its fatty part or the pancreas—was prescribed as one of the select parts of sacrificial animals to be offered to God in burnt offerings, always in conjunction with the KIDNEYS. Ancient cultures believed that future events could be divined by scrutinizing the liver's internal markings, a practice mentioned only once in the Bible, when Nebuchadnezzar examined a sheep's liver to determine his next military move (Ezek 21:21). In the Apoc-

A child's linen tunic, found in a Bar-Kokhba cave, has tied sacklike pockets to hold items such as herbs and seeds.

"And God said, 'Let the waters bring forth swarms of living creatures . . . .'" (Gen 1:20). Not as fanciful as the metamorphic creatures seen by Ezekiel, the living creatures in this Pompeiian mosaic include a hippopotamus, a snake, a bird, a dragonfly, and ducks.

rypha, a fish's liver is burned with its heart as medicine (Tob 6:7). The word *liver* does not appear the New Testament.

Living Creatures

. . . and in the middle of the fire . . . was something like four living creatures.
–Ezekiel 1:4–5

Ezekiel saw a vision of God's GLORY in the flashing lightning of a desert storm. The wind came swirling down from the north, and in its turmoil the prophet saw what seemed to be living creatures in human form—each with four faces and four wings. Revelation 4:6–9 speaks of "living creatures" that are described as six-winged beings who offer perpetual praise and glory to God. In the books of Genesis and Leviticus, the term is used to refer in general to God's creatures on earth.

Loan

On loans to a foreigner you may charge interest, but on loans to another Israelite you may not charge interest . . . .
–Deuteronomy 23:20

Ever mindful of their past bondage in Egypt, the Israelites of the Old Testament felt that the unfortunate should be helped, not exploited. Loans of money or goods were considered a sharing of the Lord's bounty, and lending was deemed a righteous act. Therefore, interest was illegal on loans to other Israelites, and the pledge given to secure a loan was never to be burdensome or humiliating (Deut 24:6). Every seventh year, the sabbath year, debts between Israelites were supposed to be forgiven. In reality, as with any law, there were violations of these generous guidelines. The book of Ezekiel rails against anyone who "takes advance or accrued interest"; if he should, "he shall surely die" (Ezek 18:13).

These loans were made in a primarily agricultural society by merchants, landowners, and other private individuals. But in Babylon and other Near Eastern cultures, systems had been devised to regulate commercial loans in the modern sense. The standard yearly interest rates for loans of silver and grain were from 20 percent to 30 percent. By the time of Jesus, the Jews had adopted the practice of buying goods on credit and gave loans of money for interest. See also DEBT.

Locust

The locusts came upon all the land of Egypt and settled on the whole country . . . .
–Exodus 10:14

A small insect resembling a cricket or grasshopper, the locust migrates in swarms, which often appear in the sky as immense black clouds. Since ancient times, the locust has

been a menace in the Near East, where great numbers of the insect periodically descend upon the land to devour all the vegetation in their path.

In the Bible, locusts are often a sign of divine wrath. They were the eighth PLAGUE God sent to punish Pharaoh for refusing to free the enslaved Israelites (Ex 10). In Joel the locust is a harbinger of the day of the Lord (Joel 1:4). The Bible also uses plagues of locusts to symbolize large, mighty armies. Jeremiah predicts the invasion of Egypt by the Babylonians, who are described as being "more numerous than locusts" (Jer 46:23).

Considered "clean" insects by the ancient Israelites, locusts were thought to be suitable for food. The Gospels of Matthew and Mark report that John the Baptist "ate locusts and wild honey" (Mt 3:4; Mr 1:6) in the wilderness of Judea. Locusts are still consumed by some tribes in the Near East when other food is in scarce supply.

LOINS

BUT YOU, GIRD UP YOUR LOINS; STAND UP AND TELL THEM EVERYTHING THAT I COMMAND YOU. –JEREMIAH 1:17

Comprised of the body's midsection, including the hips and lower back, the loins are mentioned in both literal and figurative senses throughout the Bible. A type of girdle known as a loincloth was a basic male garment in ancient times, worn alone or with other items of clothing as an undergarment. It might be made of cloth or LEATHER; the prophets Elijah and John the Baptist emphasized their lack of pretense by wearing rough leather loincloths. This garment was probably loosened but not taken off at night. To gird up one's loins—that is, to raise up trailing lower garments and wrap them around the hips or waist—was to prepare for making a journey.

In figurative language, the phrase indicated a sense of preparedness, although modern translations do not always retain the imagery. The loins could also be the source of one's progeny (Heb 7:10). In the Old Testament, one's physical strength was thought to be located there; in Nahum 2:1 the prophet exhorts Judah: "Gird your loins; collect all your strength." By the same token, loosed or shaking loins might indicate helplessness.

LOOM

. . . LIKE A WEAVER I HAVE ROLLED UP MY LIFE; HE CUTS ME OFF FROM THE LOOM . . . . –ISAIAH 38:12

Since ancient times, a loom has been used to weave interlacing threads into cloth. Cloth could be woven in long strips for curtains, or a garment could be made in one piece like Jesus' seamless tunic (Jn 19:23). In the Holy Land and Greece, a loom consisted of two vertical beams with a crossbeam at the top, from which the thread hung. The Egyptians used the more portable horizontal loom, which Bedouin tribes still use today. It was probably this type of loom that Delilah used to weave the sleeping Samson's hair (Judg 16:14). See also WEAVING.

LORD

THE KING OF ISRAEL ANSWERED, "AS YOU SAY, MY LORD, O KING, I AM YOURS, AND ALL THAT I HAVE."–1 KINGS 20:4

The word *lord* was a term of respect for someone who exercised power over another. Moses was called "my lord" (Num 32:25); a master was the lord of his slaves; and tribal heads or rulers of nations also were referred to as lords. Belshazzar gave a splendid feast "for a thousand of his lords" (Dan 5:1) or courtiers. The ancient Near Eastern gods were believed to control the fate of humankind; thus they were lords.

Two different Hebrew words are translated as "lord": *adon* and *baal.* Their meanings overlap and could signify either that the authority figure had a personal relationship with his subjects or exercised total control over others, such as women or slaves.

In accordance with Jewish tradition, throughout the Old Testament, LORD is substituted for the divine name of Yahweh. In the New Testament, this term of respect refers to God as well as to Jesus. Used as a verb in Nehemiah 5:15—"even their servants lorded it over the people"—the phrase could indicate an abuse of power.

This wooden Egyptian figurine is clad in a loincloth, a basic garment in ancient times.

LORD'S SUPPER

WHEN YOU COME TOGETHER, IT IS NOT REALLY TO EAT THE LORD'S SUPPER. . . . EACH OF YOU GOES AHEAD WITH YOUR OWN SUPPER . . . .
–1 CORINTHIANS 11:20–21

The Lord's supper is a ritual inaugurated by Jesus when he ate his last meal, known as the Last Supper, with his disciples. Jesus called the bread and wine his body and blood, offered as a sacrifice to establish God's new covenant with humanity. He then asked the disciples to consume the bread and wine "in remembrance of me" (Lk 22:19). When the early Christians met for communal meals, they included a ritual observance of this act. Paul chided some church members for partaking of the Lord's supper "in an unworthy manner" (1 Cor 11:27).

LOTS

SO THEY CAST LOTS, AND THE LOT FELL ON JONAH.–JONAH 1:7

In both Old and New Testament times, people often made difficult decisions by casting lots on the ground or drawing them from a container. They believed that the outcome was a reflection of divine will. The lots may have been potsherds, stones, sticks, dice, or other materials.

In order to divide the Promised Land among the tribes, God instructed Moses that "the land shall be apportioned by lot; according to the names of their ancestral tribes they shall inherit" (Num 26:55). The organization of the temple priests was also determined by lots (1 Chr 24:5). According to 1 Samuel 10:21, lots were used in selecting Saul as the first king of Israel. All four Gospels say that the Roman soldiers who crucified Jesus divided his clothing among themselves by casting lots, an act seen as a fulfillment of Psalm 22:18.

The Hebrew word for lot can also mean "destiny." Isaiah warns foreign nations of "the lot of those who plunder us" (Isa 17:14).

LUKE, GOSPEL OF

". . . I AM BRINGING YOU GOOD NEWS OF GREAT JOY . . . ."–LUKE 2:10

The Gospel of Luke, the longest book in the New Testament, is the first part of a two-volume work that includes the Acts of the Apostles. Authorship of the book is traditionally attributed to Luke, "the beloved physician" (Col 4:14) and a companion of Paul. Writing with the detail of a historian, Luke gives "an orderly account" of the events concerning Jesus (Lk 1:3). His audience seems to have been Gentile Christians, and his Gospel stressed that Jesus' message was directed to all, including Gentiles, sinners, the poor, and women.

A French painting depicts two elders, driven by lust, accosting Susanna as she bathes.

LUST

". . . BEAUTY HAS BEGUILED YOU AND LUST HAS PERVERTED YOUR HEART."–SUSANNA 56

The English word *lust* originally meant any strong desire, whether good or evil. Early translations of the Bible reflect this, using the word to mean a positive desire or longing, such as when Paul says to the Philippians, "My desire is to depart and be with Christ" (Phil 1:23).

Modern translations define *lust* more narrowly as sexual craving or an intense longing for power or possessions. In the apocryphal book of SUSANNA, lust causes two elders to perform evil actions. In the Gospel of Matthew, Jesus warns that anyone who lusts for a woman has already committed adultery in his heart (Mt 5:28). The letters of Peter speak of lust, or licentiousness, which is placed first in a list of Gentile vices (1 Pet 4:3).

Lewdness is a synonym for lust in the Bible, and the two words are sometimes used concerning idolatry. In fertility cults in Egypt, Mesopotamia, Asia Minor, and other lands outside Israel, sexual intercourse may have been part of ceremonial worship. God says of the idolatrous inhabitants of Jerusalem, "They were well-fed lusty stallions, each neighing for his neighbor's wife" (Jer 5:8).

LYRE

. . . MAKE MELODY TO OUR GOD ON THE LYRE.–PSALM 147:7

The lyre was a stringed instrument in the alto range, which was used to accompany religious or secular songs. About 20 to 23 inches high and with two curved arms—one longer than the other—it became the main instrument in the temple orchestra after the Babylonian exile. Sheep's small intestines were probably used for its strings, which were equal in length but varied in number. David's skill on the lyre was legendary.

The harp, a related instrument, was played less frequently in Israelite music. Precious metals and rare woods might be used in both instruments, which were popular with members of the upper classes.

The book of Daniel contains a mysterious message: MENE, MENE, TEKEL, and PARSIN. Mene *is Aramaic for the Babylonian mina, the small stone weight shown at right. The inscription says that this weight is a replica of another made by Nebuchadnezzar II.*

MACCABEES, 1–4

ANYONE FOUND POSSESSING THE BOOK OF THE COVENANT, OR ANYONE WHO ADHERED TO THE LAW, WAS CONDEMNED TO DEATH BY DEGREE OF THE KING.
–1 MACCABEES 1:57

The four books of Maccabees, part of the Apocrypha, are ancient Jewish writings. Although the books are separate and distinct, they all deal with the problem of the persecution of Jews during the Hellenistic period.

The first two books of Maccabees are historical works that recount the horrors imposed on faithful Jews in the second century BC, when the Holy Land was under the domination of Syria's Greek rulers. The ruthless Antiochus IV tried "to compel the Jews to forsake the laws of their ancestors and no longer to live by the laws of God; also to pollute the temple in Jerusalem" (2 Macc 6:1–2). In response, a pious priest named Mattathias, along with his five sons, led a REBELLION that eventually succeeded in cleansing the desecrated temple and driving the Syrians out of the country. The first book of Maccabees is generally considered more historically accurate than the second, but it has a clear political bias. It attempts to legitimize the ruling family that emerged from the rebellion, which became the Hasmonean dynasty. The second book is more concerned with theological matters.

The third book of Maccabees bears no relation to the first two; instead it deals with the Egyptian king Ptolemy IV's attempt to exterminate the Jews in his country in the third century BC. The Jews were rounded up and were about to be trampled by hundreds of elephants when two angels from God intervened and rescued them (3 Macc 5:1–2; 6:16–21). The frightened king repented and became the Jews' protector.

The fourth book is a philosophical treatise on the power of reason to rule passion, drawing on the story of the martyrs in 2 Maccabees to illustrate the point.

MADNESS

THE WORDS OF THEIR MOUTHS BEGIN IN FOOLISHNESS, AND THEIR TALK ENDS IN WICKED MADNESS . . . .
–ECCLESIASTES 10:13

In ancient times, such mental illnesses as depression and schizophrenia were not defined or understood. To the Israelites, outside forces caused abnormal behavior, such as when the "evil spirit from the LORD" provoked King Saul's homicidal rage against David (1 Sam 19:9–10). Ironically, Saul's servants had brought in David to play the lyre to soothe Saul when he was first tormented by this spirit (1 Sam 16:14–23). In this case and others, according to the Old Testament, God allowed a destructive power to take possession of an individual. While making his escape from Saul, David himself found it expedient to pretend to be a madman: "He scratched marks on the doors of the gate, and let his spittle run down his beard" (1 Sam 21:13).

The artist William Blake interpreted the madness of Babylonian king Nebuchadnezzar (Dan 4:33) in this watercolor.

The New Testament attributed both madness and epilepsy to demonic possession. Physical signs that commonly revealed "madness" included erratic movements, foaming at the mouth, and rolling of the eyes.

For most victims of madness, the only treatment was isolation, perhaps accompanied at times by abuse. The afflicted might also be stoned to death, apparently to cleanse the community of the effects of the illness.

MAGIC

Now a certain man named Simon had previously practiced magic in the city and amazed the people of Samaria . . . .
–Acts of the Apostles 8:9

People in the ancient world, both Gentile and Jewish, believed firmly in the power of magic. Magic, which could be a component of religion, began as an attempt to control the forces of nature that favored or threatened human existence: rain and sun; the fertility of crops and flocks; tempests, hail,

From the eighth or seventh century BC, figurines of sages dressed in fish skins were used as objects of magic.

and floods; plagues of locusts or disease. Both magic and religion attempted to influence the gods who were believed to control these forces. Religion did so by trying to please the gods with sacrifice and prayer; magic employed rituals and formulas to compel the gods (or their subordinate spirits) to grant the desired result.

Magic could be used to attract good luck, cure disease, ensure fertility, and pronounce or counteract a curse. For example, King Balak of Moab hired the prophet-magician Balaam to curse the Israelites (Num 22:5–6). However, in both the Old and New Testaments, magic was used primarily for divination, or foretelling events.

The Bible distinguishes between "magic art" (Wis 17:7) and a MIRACLE. Miracles occurred by God's will, but magic was opposed to it. In Exodus, God proved to be a superior force to Pharaoh's magicians (Ex 7:8–9:11). In Acts of the Apostles, the magician Simon was so impressed by the "great miracles" of Peter and John that he offered them money for their powers (Acts 8:13–19). Because it was assumed that magicians worked with the aid of evil spirits, priests and prophets condemned them. Nevertheless, they flourished because of popular demand for their services.

MAGISTRATE

"Thus, when you go with your accuser before a magistrate, on the way make an effort to settle the case . . . ."
–Luke 12:58

A magistrate was a local government official who had both administrative and judicial authority. When organizing the restoration of the postexilic Jewish community in Jerusalem, the Persian king Artaxerxes commissioned Ezra to "appoint magistrates and judges who may judge all the people" (Ezra 7:25). A magistrate might have handled matters particular to the state, while a JUDGE would cover traditional cases of law. In the cities of the Roman Empire, the chief officials were commonly called magistrates; they commanded lesser authorities called police. When Paul and Silas were falsely accused of causing a disturbance in the city of Philippi, they were brought before magistrates, who ordered them to be stripped, beaten, and jailed (Acts 16:20–23).

MALACHI, BOOK OF

. . . Judah has profaned the sanctuary of the LORD . . . and has married the daughter of a foreign god.
–Malachi 2:11

Malachi, which means "my messenger" or "my angel" in Hebrew, is the name of the last prophetic book in the Old Testament. Nothing is known about the individual named Malachi; some believed that the book was composed by an angel. Directed to the postexilic Jews of the fifth century BC, the book warned that God was unhappy with ritual laxity, including the offense of "offering polluted food on my altar" (Mal 1:7), and with the prevalence of divorce and mixed marriages. However, the book also revealed that God would send a messenger to purify the nation before the last judgment.

MALLOW

They are exalted a little while, and then are gone; they wither and fade like the mallow . . . .
–Job 24:24

Any plant belonging to the genus *Malva,* the mallow is common around Jerusalem. In late spring the pink blossoms of the *Malva sylvestris* are conspicuous, but the flowers quickly die. Thus the book of Job compares the wicked with the mallow, which might enjoy a moment of glory but would soon fade. In another passage, Job uses *mallow* to refer to an altogether different plant—probably the *Atriplex halimus,* a shrub that grew in salt marshes near the Dead Sea or the Mediterranean Sea. Here Job describes the poor, who are reduced to eating the salty and unpleasant-tasting plant "through want and hard hunger" (Job 30:3).

Manasseh, Prayer of

O Lord, according to your great goodness you have promised repentance and forgiveness to those who have sinned against you . . . .
–Prayer of Manasseh 7

The Prayer of Manasseh was probably written by a pious Jew in the second or first century BC. This short apocryphal book was supposedly the remorseful appeal to God by Manasseh, the seventh-century BC king of Judah. According to 2 Kings, Manasseh's rule was marked by idolatry and unfaithfulness, and his sins—"more in number than the sand of the sea" (Pr Man 9)—brought on the wrath of God, leading to the nation's downfall (2 Kings 21:11–15). The book of 2 Chronicles says that when the contrite Manasseh, a captive in Babylon, offered his prayer, "God received his entreaty, heard his plea, and restored him again to Jerusalem and to his kingdom" (2 Chr 33:13).

Mandrake

In the days of wheat harvest Reuben went and found mandrakes in the field, and brought them to his mother Leah.–Genesis 30:14

An illustration shows clearly the forked root of the mandrake.

A perennial HERB found throughout the eastern Mediterranean region, the mandrake has been reputed to have medicinal and magical powers since antiquity. In the spring the plant produces a yellow-red fruit, which was used as a narcotic or purgative. The mandrake, also called the love apple, has a long, divided root that looks vaguely like a human body; perhaps for this reason it was believed to be an aphrodisiac and to induce fertility. In Genesis, Rachel bargains with Leah for mandrakes to help her to conceive; later she does become pregnant, although the Bible does not specifically attribute this outcome to the mandrakes (Gen 30:14–24).

In the Prayer of Manasseh, King Manasseh of Judah repents of his many transgressions. The writer of 2 Kings 21 believed that Manasseh's evil actions ultimately caused the southern kingdom to fall and its citizens to be deported. In the 19th-century British painting By the Waters of Babylon, *the Judeans lament their long exile and pray for deliverance.*

MANGER

"THIS WILL BE A SIGN FOR YOU: YOU WILL FIND A CHILD WRAPPED IN BANDS OF CLOTH AND LYING IN A MANGER."–LUKE 2:12

Also referred to as a crib (Isa 1:3), a manger was a feeding trough used by livestock. In the Holy Land people often brought their animals inside in the winter, and the livestock stayed in an area of the house below the family's sleeping quarters. This area usually contained a stone or masonry manger. Animals and their troughs might also be kept in the courtyard, under the house, or in a nearby field, and mangers were frequently hewn out of CAVE walls. According to the Gospel of Luke, Mary laid Jesus in some kind of manger after his birth, "because there was no place for them in the inn" (Lk 2:7).

His mantle slung over his shoulder, Eliza curses King Ahab and Jezebel, whose mantles are brightly colored. Jezebel plotted the death of Naboth to gain his vineyard for Ahab (1 Kings 21).

MANNA

"YOU GAVE YOUR GOOD SPIRIT TO INSTRUCT THEM, AND DID NOT WITHHOLD YOUR MANNA FROM THEIR MOUTHS . . . ."
–NEHEMIAH 9:20

When the Israelites complained bitterly of their hunger to Moses while wandering in the desert, God said, "I am going to rain bread from heaven for you" (Ex 16:4). The Israelites called this food manna. Similar to the coriander seed, it rained down on the desert at night in the form of a fine, white, grainy flake. At dawn the people would go out to gather up normally one omer (about two quarts) each, but two omers were collected the day before the sabbath. They prepared the manna by grinding and boiling it. Made into thin cakes, it had a honeylike taste.

Aside from manna, God provided only occasional QUAIL for the Israelites to eat during their 40-year sojourn in the wilderness. The showers of manna ended when the people reached Canaan. In the Gospel of John, Jesus referred to his body and blood as a kind of spiritual manna: "This is the bread that came down from heaven . . . the one who eats this bread will live forever" (Jn 6:58).

MANTLE

THEN ELIJAH TOOK HIS MANTLE AND ROLLED IT UP, AND STRUCK THE WATER; THE WATER WAS PARTED . . . .
–2 KINGS 2:8

A mantle, or cloak, was an outer garment, perhaps worn over the robe, that provided protection from rain and cold. Like the robe, it could be used as a cover for sleeping outdoors. The tearing of the hem of the mantle, which was often made of wool, was a sign of grief. A mantle of rich fabric, color, or decoration demonstrated wealth. It might be fastened with a buckle, such as the golden one mentioned in 1 Maccabees 10:89.

The prophet Elijah used his mantle to miraculously part the Jordan River. He also designated Elisha as his successor by throwing his mantle over the future prophet as he plowed a field (1 Kings 19:19).

MARBLE

"SO I HAVE PROVIDED FOR THE HOUSE OF MY GOD . . . ALL SORTS OF PRECIOUS STONES, AND MARBLE IN ABUNDANCE."
–1 CHRONICLES 29:2

A metamorphic form of limestone, marble has been prized since ancient times for the ease with which it can be carved and for the beautiful luster it takes on when polished. King David provided his son Solomon with marble, along with gold and precious stones, for the decoration of the first temple. A symbol of luxury, marble is otherwise mentioned only in the description of the palace of King Ahasuerus in the book of Esther (Esth 1:6) and in the book of Revelation, where it appears in a list of commodities associated with the sinful city of Babylon (Rev 18:12). See also STONE.

Mark

And the LORD put a mark on Cain, so that no one who came upon him would kill him.
–Genesis 4:15

The word *mark* has a variety of meanings in the Bible. A drawn line indicated, or marked, a boundary (Num 34:7–8) or a carpenter's measurements (Isa 44:13). Roads were designated by being marked (Ezek 21:19), and the dead were put in marked graves (2 Esd 2:23). A mark could be a target, as in "he bent his bow and set me as a mark for his arrow" (Lam 3:12).

A distinguishing physical sign that set a person apart was also a mark. Circumcision served to single out Jews as God's people (Gen 17:7–14), and the mark God put on Cain after the murder of Abel warned others not to hurt him (Gen 4:15). In the book of Ezekiel, God orders the scribe to mark the foreheads of the righteous in Jerusalem, presumably to spare them from destruction (Ezek 9:4). People branded or tattooed their slaves; in Revelation 13:16, those "marked on the right hand or the forehead" by the second beast were in effect slaves to the false prophet.

The word *mark* could also be used as an exhortation to pay close attention. When instructing Ezekiel, God commanded: "Mortal, mark well" (Ezek 44:5).

A French illumination from the early 11th century pictures the author of the Gospel of Mark.

Mark, Gospel of

Then he began to teach them that the Son of Man must undergo great suffering . . . .
–Mark 8:31

Most scholars believe that the Gospel of Mark is the earliest of the four Gospels and that it served as a source for the Gospels of Matthew and Luke. Early Christian tradition attributes the work to the apostle Peter's assistant, a man named John Mark, who wrote down Peter's preachings. He may have been directing his Gospel toward Gentile Christians in danger of persecution. A dominant theme in the book is the suffering of Jesus; the writer spends approximately a third of the text on the last week of Jesus' life. He also shapes the narrative in such a way that despite Jesus' miracles and preaching, his divine identity is not truly understood by those around him until after his death.

A modern Italian sculpture captures the alienation of Cain, who received a mark from God to protect him in his wanderings.

Marketplace

. . . ruin is in its midst; oppression and fraud do not depart from its marketplace.
–Psalm 55:11

During biblical times in the Holy Land, city plans, consisting generally of narrow streets clogged with buildings, did not always include large public spaces within the city or TOWN. Thus merchants ran shops in their own homes or in the bazaar, which was a cluster of booths set up near the gates to the city. This marketplace was either just within the city gates, in an open square just outside the gates, or in both places. The square was also used for public gatherings: when Assyria threatened Jerusalem, King Hezekiah of Judah rallied his troops "in the square at the gate of the city" (2 Chr 32:6), and the victorious Philistines displayed the bodies of Saul and his son Jonathan in the square at Beth-shan (2 Sam 21:12).

By the Roman period, many of the ancient cities had been rebuilt in the Greek style and included a large *agora,* meaning "place of assembly." This new type of marketplace was the commercial and social center of town (see reconstruction, pp. 224–225). Here, surrounded by the markets, people idled (Mt 20:3), children played (Mt 11:16), the sick were brought to Jesus for healing (Mk 6:56), and arrogant scribes walked about waiting to be paid respect (Mk 12:38).

Marketplace of Luxury Goods

"When he went out about nine o'clock, he saw others standing idle in the marketplace . . . ."–Matthew 20:3

Marketplaces in the Galilean city of Sepphoris, located just four miles northwest of Nazareth, were commercial areas filled with a wide variety of both local and imported goods. The Romans were rebuilding this provincial capital during the first century AD, and many products from throughout the Mediterranean region were available in the time of Jesus. The illustration shows a marketplace in Sepphoris that specializes in expensive items. As a Roman soldier stands guard, merchants sell from stalls under a portico and from tables and mats out in the open. They offer wares that include hair combs, glass, and fabrics. Shoppers use baskets to carry such items as oil lamps and small pots. At right, a servant helps a Roman matron with mats and other purchases, some of which were bought at different marketplaces, while the woman looks at bronze mirrors and at bottles for perfumes and precious oils.

Marriage

Let marriage be held in honor by all, and let the marriage bed be kept undefiled . . . .
–Hebrews 13:4

Marriage was one of the cornerstones of ancient Israelite society. It provided social stability, strengthened family solidarity, and produced children. Held up as the ideal state for both men and women, it was often used as a metaphor for the relationship between God and Israel.

Marriage was also an economic arrangement, as families strove to improve their status by alliances with those possessing wealth and position. It was accepted that marriages were arranged by parents, after prolonged discussion of ancestry, property, and the size of the dowry and bride price. Nevertheless, a young man or woman usually had some choice in the matter, even if only to decline a particular partner. To keep wealth within the extended family, parents tried to marry their children to relatives.

Although intermarriage with non-Israelites did occur, during some periods it was discouraged for fear that the Israelite partner would turn away from God to foreign deities (Deut 7:3–4; Josh 23:12–13; Ezra 9:14).

To signify that the families of both the BRIDE and bridegroom had an interest in seeing the marriage preserved, each put up a financial stake. The bridegroom's family made a present, called the bride price, to the woman's parents to compensate them for the loss of their daughter's services, or the bridegroom might substitute a term of labor for cash or goods, as Jacob did with Laban (Gen 29:15–30). The bride's family made a larger gift—the dowry—to the woman to bring to her marriage. In the case of divorce, the wife may have been allowed to take back the dowry, which could have included money, jewelry, clothing, household goods, slaves, and land. The families often used written contracts to spell out the terms of the marriage.

The wedding was a time of feasting and rejoicing. Splendidly dressed, the bridegroom paraded to the bride's house with his companions, one of whom served as his best man. The bride, also beautifully clothed and bejeweled and wearing a veil over her face, awaited him with her bridesmaids. The couple and their attendants then formed a procession, with much singing and dancing, through the streets; if darkness fell, the bridesmaids and others lit oil lamps and torches that they carried (Mt 25:1–13). They all made their way to the home of the bridegroom or that of his parents; there the wedding feast took place (see illustration). The festivities, with plentiful food and wine, lasted a week or more, depending on the wealth of the family. On the wedding night, the parents and friends of the young couple blessed them and wished them well.

The law spelled out rights and duties within marriage. The husband had to provide his wife with food, clothing, and shelter. Her "marital rights" (Ex 21:10) included sexual relations. Polygamy was permitted and was found especially

The wedding feast was an extravagant, joyous affair during biblical times. Here a bride and bridegroom, wearing garlands of flowers, sit surrounded by friends and family. They all enjoy fine food and drink as, at right, more jugs of wine are prepared. Hands joined, the bridesmaids in the background dance to musical accompaniment.

among royalty and the prosperous. The patriarchs Abraham and Jacob both had more than one wife, as well as concubines. In later times monogamy became the ideal.

Adultery was considered a grave sin for women. A wife who committed this act could be condemned to death at the hands of the community (Lev 20:10), but an erring husband received no penalty. A man could divorce his wife if he found "something objectionable about her" (Deut 24:1).

Although the Israelites exalted marriage, some early Christians considered it secondary to the pursuit of God, perhaps because they believed the end of the world was at hand. Paul advised, "To the unmarried and the widows I say that it is well for them to remain unmarried as I am" (1 Cor 7:8). However, the author of the first letter to Timothy criticizes overly ascetic groups who "forbid marriage" (1 Tim 4:3).

In the marshlands where the Tigris and Euphrates rivers meet, people today live much as the original Mesopotamians did.

MARSH

"UNDER THE LOTUS PLANTS IT LIES, IN THE COVERT OF THE REEDS AND IN THE MARSH."
–JOB 40:21

Wetlands are rare in the Holy Land, existing only at some river mouths and some locations along the Jordan River and the Dead Sea. During the Maccabean revolt, the pious Jonathan and his forces were attacked after taking refuge in the "marshes of the Jordan" (1 Macc 9:42), but they managed to escape the enemy. The prophet Ezekiel had a vision in which the Dead Sea turned into fresh water, except for "its swamps and marshes" (Ezek 47:11); saline marshes were essential for providing salt. According to the book of Job, as cited above, the mighty BEHEMOTH roamed the marshes lining the Jordan River.

MASON

KING HIRAM OF TYRE SENT MESSENGERS TO DAVID . . . AND MASONS AND CARPENTERS TO BUILD A HOUSE FOR HIM.
–1 CHRONICLES 14:1

Skilled masons were apparently not used in Israel until the time of King David, who had to hire masons from Tyre to build his palace. The Tyrians may have also trained Israelites in the art of shaping and fitting stones for construction, as the Bible makes no further mention of foreign masons.

As skilled craftsmen, masons probably belonged to a guild. The mason's primary tools were the hammer, punch, and chisel. To make smooth cuts, the mason used special saws. After cutting and shaping the stones, he rubbed the rough areas with sandstone. To lay out straight lines, he used a taut string loaded with chalk or paint. He checked vertical alignment with a plumb line and horizontal alignment with a cord stretched between cornerstones.

Masonry was costly because of the amount of skilled work involved. Therefore, shaped stone was seldom used except for great public places, such as palaces and temples. See also QUARRY.

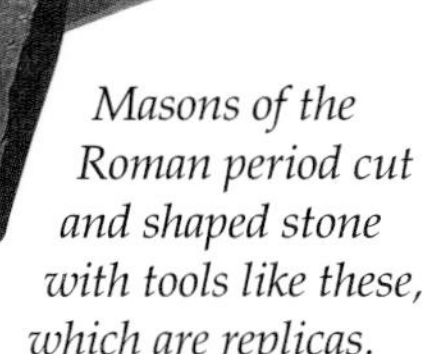

Masons of the Roman period cut and shaped stone with tools like these, which are replicas.

MASTER

. . . ANYONE WHO TAKES CARE OF A MASTER WILL BE HONORED.
–PROVERBS 27:18

Owners of property, heads of households, and persons in authority were referred to as masters or mistresses. Those words were also used metaphorically to describe powerful nations. Isaiah 47:5 says Chaldea "shall no more be called the mistress of kingdoms." The apostles called Jesus Master as a title of respect. When Simon Peter first spoke to him, he used this form of address, even though he did not know who Jesus was (Lk 5:5). The term was also used by the early Christians; the letter of Jude speaks of "our only Master and Lord, Jesus Christ" (Jude 1:4).

MATTHEW, GOSPEL OF

AND JESUS CAME AND SAID TO THEM, "ALL AUTHORITY IN HEAVEN AND ON EARTH HAS BEEN GIVEN TO ME."
–MATTHEW 28:18

Though attributed to the apostle Matthew, the Gospel of Matthew was probably written by an anonymous Greek-speaking scribe, who was perhaps a Jewish Christian, at the end of the first century AD in Antioch. In recounting the life and death of Jesus, the text emphasizes that he was the Son of God, which means that his activities and teachings were the works of the Lord. This Gospel emphasizes that a person finds favor with God by becoming a disciple of Jesus, and that Jesus' message, intended for all humanity, must be spread by missionary work: "Go therefore and make disciples of all nations" (Mt 28:19).

MEADOW

ONCE I SAW EPHRAIM AS A YOUNG PALM PLANTED IN A LOVELY MEADOW . . . .
–HOSEA 9:13

A grassy open field, a meadow was useful as pasture land for grazing sheep (Zeph 2:6). Broad, luxuriant meadows that supplied excellent fodder for fattening animals were considered part of God's bounty and a sign of his blessing. In Psalm 65:13, the psalmist proclaims that "the meadows clothe themselves with flocks, the valleys deck themselves with grain, they shout and sing together for joy." Conversely, turning away from God would result in the end of abundance. The prophet Hosea, condemning the unfaithfulness of Israel, contrasts the image of a meadow in the passage above to the dire punishment to come.

For centuries the lush meadows of the Holy Land have provided nourishment for livestock. Springtime draws a flock of sheep, above, to graze in the Judean hills.

MEAL

SO WHENEVER HE PASSED THAT WAY, HE WOULD STOP THERE FOR A MEAL.
–2 KINGS 4:8

In biblical times, most people ate two main meals a day—breakfast and dinner, or supper—and sometimes a light refreshment in between. Breakfast might be a piece of flat bread and olives or cheese. At midday, farm workers might rest in the shade and have bread soaked in sour wine with some parched grain and perhaps a piece of fruit, which was the repast that Ruth enjoyed with the reapers in the field (Ruth 2:14). Dinner was the evening meal, which was prepared during the day by the women at home, often with the help of their children. This more leisurely meal usually consisted of a vegetable stew, bread, fruit, and wine. The Israelites saved meat for special occasions, and they followed laws that regulated which foods they could eat.

Meals, such as those of FELLOWSHIP, often had symbolic significance, in both Old and New Testament times. They could celebrate God-given abundance, cement friendships, or seal agreements. The Pharisees criticized Jesus for eating with tax collectors and sinners (Mt 9:11). Meals were an important part of Passover and some other religious feasts.

MEASURES

YOU SHALL NOT HAVE IN YOUR HOUSE TWO KINDS OF MEASURES, LARGE AND SMALL.
–DEUTERONOMY 25:14

Quantitative measures were used in the ancient marketplace, but the system varied in different places and times, and standards were hardly rigid. "Handfuls of barley" (Ezek 13:19), for example, was imprecise, and distances were sometimes calculated by the length of a bowshot (Gen 21:16) or the distance traveled in a day (Num 11:31).

When the Bible speaks generally of "measures" of flour, barley, or other items, it may mean *seahs* or other common units (see chart). Cheating by measuring falsely was deemed "an abomination to the LORD" (Prov 20:10). Deuteronomy warned against not having "a full and honest measure" (Deut 25:15).

Ancient Measures

The chart below lists the units of measure common in Old and New Testament times and their approximate modern equivalences. Throughout Mesopotamia, Egypt, and the Holy Land, the cubit was the basic unit for measuring short distances. It continued to be used in the Greco-Roman world, along with linear measurements of Greek and Roman origins. The Israelites based their units of capacity on the measurements used by the Egyptians, Assyrians, and Babylonians. They later also adopted Greek and Roman measures for liquids and dry volumes, such as grains.

Old Testament

Linear Measure

UNIT	APPROXIMATE EQUIVALENCE: METRIC SYSTEM	APPROXIMATE EQUIVALENCE: US SYSTEM
finger	1.85 CM	¾ IN
palm	7.4 CM	3 IN
span	26.2 CM	8¾ IN
cubit	44.4 CM	1 FT 6 IN
royal cubit	52.5 CM	1 FT 9 IN

Dry Measure

UNIT	APPROXIMATE EQUIVALENCE: METRIC SYSTEM	APPROXIMATE EQUIVALENCE: US SYSTEM
kab	1.2 L	2⅓ DRY PTS
omer	2.2 L	2 DRY QTS
seah	7.33 L	⅕ BUSHEL
ephah	22 L	⅗ BUSHEL
homer/cor	220 L	6¼ BUSHEL

Liquid Measure

UNIT	APPROXIMATE EQUIVALENCE: METRIC SYSTEM	APPROXIMATE EQUIVALENCE: US SYSTEM
log	0.3 L	⅓ QT
hin	3.66 L	4 QTS
bath	22 L	5½ GAL
homer/kor	220 L	58 GAL

New Testament

Linear Measure

UNIT	APPROXIMATE EQUIVALENCE: METRIC SYSTEM	APPROXIMATE EQUIVALENCE: US SYSTEM
cubit	44.4 CM	1 FT 6 IN
long cubit	52.5 CM	1 FT 9 IN
fathom	1.78 M	5 FT 10 IN
stade	178 M	600 FT
mile (Roman)	1482 M	0.92 MI

Dry Measure

UNIT	APPROXIMATE EQUIVALENCE: METRIC SYSTEM	APPROXIMATE EQUIVALENCE: US SYSTEM
litra (Greek) libra (Latin)	0.45 KG	1 LB
modion (Greek) modius (Latin)	6.8 KG	15 LB

Liquid Measure

UNIT	APPROXIMATE EQUIVALENCE: METRIC SYSTEM	APPROXIMATE EQUIVALENCE: US SYSTEM
xestes (Greek) sextarius (Latin)	0.54 L	1 PT
choinix (Greek)	1.08 L	1 QT
metretes (Greek)	39 L	10⅓ GAL

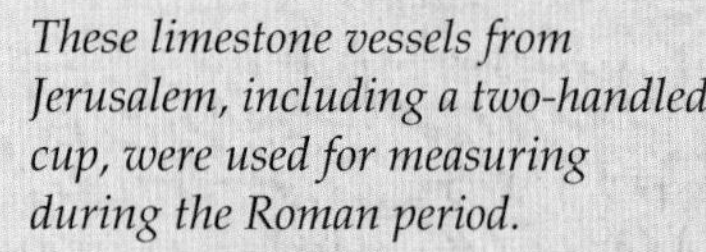

These limestone vessels from Jerusalem, including a two-handled cup, were used for measuring during the Roman period.

MEAT

. . . HE DISTRIBUTED TO EVERY PERSON . . . A LOAF OF BREAD, A PORTION OF MEAT, AND A CAKE OF RAISINS.
–1 CHRONICLES 16:3

Biblical dietary laws concerning meat were very strict. Oxen, cattle, sheep, and goats were "clean"—that is, suitable for sacrificial use and human consumption. However, young goats could not be eaten if boiled in their mother's milk. Pigs, camels, rabbits, and rock badgers were unclean, as were birds that ate prey.

The Israelites seldom ate meat. When they did cook a calf, lamb, or kid, it was usually for guests (2 Sam 12:4) or to celebrate a religious feast or a special occasion, such as the return of the prodigal son in Jesus' parable (Lk 15:23).

A stone frieze from the second century BC portrays a Roman butcher cutting meat in his shop.

MEDIATOR

FOR THERE IS ONE GOD; THERE IS ALSO ONE MEDIATOR BETWEEN GOD AND HUMANKIND, CHRIST JESUS, HIMSELF HUMAN . . . .
–1 TIMOTHY 2:5

In his letter to the Galatians, Paul described Moses as the mediator, or go-between, through whom God communicated the law to Israel (Gal 3:19). In similar fashion, the first letter to Timothy and the letter to the Hebrews called Jesus the mediator between God and humanity, who was the only one able to bridge the gulf because he was both divine and human. These texts portrayed Jesus as the mediator of a new covenant that went far beyond the original covenant mediated by Moses.

Mosaic law rewarded obedience to God, but it punished disobedience, sometimes by death. The new covenant instead promised unconditional mercy and forgiveness of sins to those who had faith. The sacrifices prescribed by the law were no longer necessary, because Jesus Christ had given himself as a sacrificial ransom for the sins of all: "For this reason he is the mediator of a new covenant, so that those who are called may receive the promised eternal inheritance, because a death has occurred that redeems them from the transgressions under the first covenant" (Heb 9:15).

MEDIUM

THEN SAUL SAID TO HIS SERVANTS, "SEEK OUT FOR ME A WOMAN WHO IS A MEDIUM, SO THAT I MAY GO TO HER AND INQUIRE OF HER."
–1 SAMUEL 28:7

A medium foretold events by calling up the ghosts of the dead rather than by interpreting a DREAM or an omen. This ability gave mediums a dangerous connection to the worship of underworld deities and spirits. Biblical law dealt harshly with these diviners. Leviticus 20:27 decreed: "A man or a woman who is a medium or a wizard shall be put to death." (A wizard also practiced necromancy as well as other forms of magic.) King Saul consulted a medium—a woman who was sometimes called the witch of Endor—before his fatal battle with the Philistines.

The medium of Endor, at left, brings forth Samuel's spirit for King Saul in an 18th-century painting by Benjamin West.

MEMORIAL

"SO THESE STONES SHALL BE TO THE ISRAELITES A MEMORIAL FOREVER."–JOSHUA 4:7

Memorials, which could be simple objects or complex rituals, served as reminders that God would take care of his people in the future as he had done in the past. When God stopped the flow of the Jordan River so that the Israelites could cross into the Promised Land, he told them to memorialize the event by setting up a monument of 12 stones taken from the riverbed. The feast of Passover was instituted to remind later generations that God had delivered their ancestors from Egyptian slavery. In the New Testament, Jesus requested that his disciples reenact the Last Supper as a memorial "in remembrance of me" (Lk 22:19).

MENE, MENE, TEKEL, AND PARSIN

"AND THIS IS THE WRITING THAT WAS INSCRIBED: MENE, MENE, TEKEL, AND PARSIN."
–DANIEL 5:25

The book of Daniel recounts a feast during which the Babylonian king and others drank from vessels that had been taken from the Jerusalem temple. Disembodied fingers suddenly appeared and wrote, "MENE, MENE, TEKEL, and PARSIN" on the wall (Dan 5:25). Only Daniel was able to interpret this message for the king: "MENE, God has numbered the days of your kingdom and brought it to an end; TEKEL, you have been weighed on the scales and found wanting; PERES, your kingdom is divided and given to the Medes and Persians" (Dan 5:26–28).

Mene, tekel, and *parsin* are Aramaic for units of weight: a mina (about 50 shekels), a shekel, and two half-minas, respectively. The words are also similar to those meaning "number," "weigh," and "divide." *Peres* meant one half-mina, but it, too, sounded like an Aramaic word for Persia. Daniel's interpretation used wordplay to convey God's judgment on the Babylonian kingdom and to predict its demise.

MERCY

DO NOT, O LORD, WITHHOLD YOUR MERCY FROM ME; LET YOUR STEADFAST LOVE AND YOUR FAITHFULNESS KEEP ME SAFE FOREVER.
–PSALM 40:11

In the Bible both God and people show mercy by helping those in need. Several Hebrew words are translated as "mercy"; one is related to the word for womb, indicating that the strong love a mother feels for her children is at the heart of mercy. The metaphor of a parent's love is used to describe the ongoing mercy and compassion that God feels for his chosen people, despite their weaknesses. In Jeremiah 31:20, the Lord says, "Is Ephraim my dear son? Is he the child I delight in? As often as I speak against him . . . I will surely have mercy on him." God remained ever faithful to his people as they wandered in the desert, inspiring the prophet Nehemiah to write: "You in your great mercies did not forsake them in the wilderness" (Neh 9:19). God expected his people to emulate his example by showing "kindness and mercy to one another" (Zech 7:9). According to the New Testament, God's mercy included sending Jesus to save humanity: "But God, who is rich in mercy . . . made us alive together with Christ" (Eph 2:4–5).

MERCY SEAT

YOU SHALL PUT THE MERCY SEAT ON THE ARK OF THE COVENANT IN THE MOST HOLY PLACE.
–EXODUS 26:34

The centerpiece of Israelite worship was the ARK OF THE COVENANT, a wooden chest containing the ten commandents that God had given to Moses. The cover of the ark was called the mercy seat, which formed a throne for the invisible God (Lev 16:2; Num 7:89). The mercy seat, made of pure gold, was decorated on the ends with two hammered-gold cherubim facing each other and "overshadowing the mercy seat with their wings" (Ex 37:9). On the Day of Atonement, the high priest sprinkled blood from sacrificial animals onto the mercy seat (Lev 16:14–15).

MESSENGER

SEE, I AM SENDING MY MESSENGER TO PREPARE THE WAY BEFORE ME . . . .
–MALACHI 3:1

Messengers went forth with written or oral communications from one person to another. The word *angel* is derived from the Greek *angelos,* meaning "messenger"; in the Bible angels frequently come to earth with messages from God. Prophets and priests were also God's spokespersons; thus, "the lips of a priest should guard knowledge, and people should seek instruction from his mouth, for he is the messenger of the LORD of hosts" (Mal 2:7). Imbued with the Holy Spirit, early Christian leaders carried the message of Jesus as they ventured into the world on their mission to spread the teachings of the gospel. (Acts 1:8). See also AMBASSADOR.

The good Samaritan, depicted in a Swiss painting, shows mercy toward a man who has been stripped and beaten. Jesus used the story to illustrate the concept of loving one's neighbor.

Messiah

Then the high priest said to him, "I put you under oath before the living God, tell us if you are the Messiah, the Son of God."
–Matthew 26:63

After God chose David as the anointed one—or Messiah—to rule as Israel's KING, he made a covenant with him that ensured his descendants would govern Israel forever. David chose his son Solomon to succeed him (1 Kings 1:30). But the Davidic succession ended with the Babylonian conquest in 587 BC. Centuries passed as many Jews longed for a Messiah descended from King David who would restore their independence.

According to Luke, when Jesus was born, a man named Simeon recognized the baby as the Messiah (Luke 2:25–32). But it was not until Jesus began his ministry that people suggested that he might be descended from David. His preaching and miraculous deeds attracted attention, but Jesus did not call himself Messiah until his trial. According to Mark, when the high priest asked, "Are you the Messiah?" Jesus answered, "I am" (Mark 14: 61–62). His response is more equivocal in Matthew and Luke (Mt 26:64; Lk 22:67–68).

Metal

. . . his mother took two hundred pieces of silver, and gave it to the silversmith, who made it into an idol of cast metal . . . .–Judges 17:4

Seven metals are mentioned by name in the Bible: gold, silver, copper, iron, lead, bronze, and tin. By a process known as refining, or smelting, these metals were prepared and then formed into various objects (see box). Prized for their beauty and rarity, gold and

2. and 3. A smith's assistant heats the iron to red-hot, as shown at right. Below, smiths hammer the iron on the anvil. The forging process—alternately heating and hammering the metal—removes impurities and air bubbles but leaves the iron soft. While heating, the iron combines with the carbon in the burning charcoal. The addition of small amounts of carbon strengthens the iron and produces steel. The smiths gradually work the iron into a durable blade.

Metal-working

In the ancient Near East, the most common type of furnace used in metalworking was the bowl furnace, a clay-lined or stone-lined hole set into the ground. Charcoal was the preferred fuel because it produced a hotter flame than wood. A bellows or draught system was used to keep the fire hot. This type of furnace was sufficient for melting copper and bronze for casting, but it could not reach the extreme temperatures needed to melt iron (1530°C). Through trial and error, metalworkers learned to smelt iron ore and to heat, hammer, quench, and cool the iron to produce a hard, strong, and resilient material known as steel.

1. Laborers deliver dull and broken tools and weapons such as sword and knife blades, axheads, chisels, and scythes to the metalworking area, at left, for sharpening and repair. On an anvil—the iron block upon which metals are shaped—the smith pictured here in the background straightens a blade that he has softened over the furnace.

4. The smith quenches the blade by plunging it into cold water, as pictured at right. Quenching produces an extremely hard but brittle metal. Next, the smith will temper the blade by reheating it and allowing it to cool slowly. Tempering gives steel flexibility but sacrifices some of its hardness.

silver were used for decoration, jewelry, and money. The Bible often refers to cast metal images and idols, as in Judges 17:3–4.

Copper was mined and smelted in several areas in the Near East. When mixed with tin—which was imported from as far away as Spain—it became bronze, an alloy that is much stronger and more durable than pure copper. Copper and bronze were the chief metals from which the Israelites' tools, weapons, and utensils were produced until iron was introduced about 1200 BC.

Known today as a copper and zinc alloy, the word *brass* may refer to any copper alloy when used in the Old Testament (Isa 48:4). Lead was often fashioned into weights and used for plumb lines and sinkers for fishing nets.

MICAH, BOOK OF

ALAS FOR THOSE WHO DEVISE WICKEDNESS AND EVIL DEEDS ON THEIR BEDS! WHEN THE MORNING DAWNS, THEY PERFORM IT . . . .
–MICAH 2:1

The book of Micah is a collection of the oracles and prophecies of Micah, one of the 12 Minor Prophets. A contemporary of the prophet Isaiah, Micah lived in the eighth century BC. He traveled from the small town of his birth to Jerusalem, where he delivered a series of speeches condemning immorality, official CORRUPTION, the abuse of the poor, and hypocritical piety. The book of Micah foretells God's punishment for this wickedness: the destruction of Jerusalem, which would become "a heap of ruins" (Mic 3:12). But it also stresses God's unending love for his people and promises ultimate salvation, predicting the coming of a new king, or Messiah, from the city of Bethlehem (Mic 5:2).

MIDWIFE

WHEN SHE WAS IN HER HARD LABOR, THE MIDWIFE SAID TO HER, "DO NOT BE AFRAID; FOR NOW YOU WILL HAVE ANOTHER SON."
–GENESIS 35:17

Drawing on traditional knowledge and personal experience, midwives assisted women in childbirth. The Hebrew word literally means "one who helps to bear." Midwives comforted and advised the mother, received the baby at BIRTH, cut its umbilical cord, washed and rubbed it with salt (which was believed to act as a disinfectant), and wrapped it in swaddling clothes. Midwives were trained by apprenticeship to experienced practitioners. In Exodus 1:15–20 Pharaoh ordered the midwives to kill all male Hebrew infants, but they refused.

Midwives attend the birth of John the Baptist in this bronze relief.

MILDEW

I STRUCK YOU WITH BLIGHT AND MILDEW; I LAID WASTE YOUR GARDENS AND YOUR VINEYARDS . . . .
–AMOS 4:9

Mildew, from the Hebrew word for paleness, is a common fungus that often causes a whitish growth on plants. In the Old Testament mildew was a punishment that the Lord dispensed for unfaithfulness (Deut 28:22). Though mildew attacks crops in wet conditions, in the Bible it was always coupled with "blight," or blasting winds, which withered and ruined crops. Solomon prayed that if mildew or other plagues were loosed upon the land, God would hear the prayers of those who repented and forgive them (1 Kings 8:37–39). Mildew also may have referred to a condition that rendered clothing or a house unclean, or "leprous" (Lev 13:47–59; 14:34–53).

MILK

"INDEED, I KNOW THEIR SUFFERINGS, AND I HAVE COME DOWN TO DELIVER THEM . . . TO A GOOD AND BROAD LAND, A LAND FLOWING WITH MILK AND HONEY . . . ."
–EXODUS 3:8

Milk and milk products were among the dietary staples of peoples of the Bible. Milk was obtained from sheep, goats, cows, and sometimes from camels. Since milk was quick to turn sour, it was frequently made into butter and cheese. The prohibition against boiling a kid in his mother's milk (Ex 34:26) led to the Jewish dietary law forbidding the consumption of dairy products at the same meal in which meat is eaten. In the passage above, when God told Moses that he would free the people from Egyptian captivity and lead them to the Promised Land, he called it "a land flowing with milk and honey" to describe how prosperous it would be.

In the New Testament, the word *milk* is used figuratively to symbolize early learning. When Paul taught in Corinth, he preached only the elementary principles of Christianity to the congregation, explaining, "I fed you with milk, not solid food, for you were not ready for solid food" (1 Cor 3:2).

MILL

NO ONE SHALL TAKE A MILL OR AN UPPER MILLSTONE IN PLEDGE, FOR THAT WOULD BE TAKING A LIFE IN PLEDGE. –DEUTERONOMY 24:6

Grinding GRAIN into flour in a mill was a burdensome task performed by women or slaves. So essential was the mill to daily life that the passage above declares it could not be taken as collateral, since to do so would deprive a family of its means of sustenance. The simplest household mill was a saddle-shaped stone on which grain was placed and ground into coarse flour by a smaller stone. The handmill—about $1^1/_2$ feet in diameter—was a pair of round stones; the top one was fitted with a handle so that one woman could rotate it while another poured grain into a hole in the center of the millstone. Large mill houses were often run by the state. The drudgery of grinding grain was part of Samson's punishment when he was captured by the Philistines (Judg 16:21).

MILLO

SOLOMON BUILT THE MILLO, AND CLOSED UP THE GAP IN THE WALL OF THE CITY OF HIS FATHER DAVID. –1 KINGS 11:27

The Hebrew word translated as "millo," meaning "the fill," describes an artificial, earthen terrace supported by retaining walls, which was used as a platform on which to erect one or more buildings. The word appears only in the Old Testament, often as a proper name referring specifically to the Millo in the city of David. Even before King David conquered Jerusalem, the local Canaanites had enlarged the growing city by building millo terraces on the eastern slope of the hill of Ophel.

This topographical map from the 12th century BC—one of the world's oldest surviving maps—plots the locations of the ancient gold mines of Wadi Hammamat in Egypt.

MINES

NOW JUDAS HEARD OF THE FAME OF THE ROMANS . . . AND WHAT THEY HAD DONE IN THE LAND OF SPAIN TO GET CONTROL OF THE SILVER AND GOLD MINES THERE . . . . –1 MACCABEES 8:1–3

Mineral deposits were scarce in ancient Israel, and most METAL had to be imported. Under King David and King Solomon the Israelites produced copper at mines in the rich beds in the Arabah Valley, south of the Dead Sea. There were also iron ore mines in the region of Gilead and elsewhere, but their production never filled the demand for these metals. Mining was a difficult and dangerous occupation, and as a result it was done mostly by slaves, convicts, and prisoners of war. The Roman emperor Tiberius, who ruled from 14 to 37 AD, sent 4,000 Jewish captives to the silver and iron mines in Sicily.

Miners worked in narrow shafts and tunnels, using picks and hammers of bronze to hack out passageways and extract the ore, which was carried out in skin bags. Their only light came from flickering, feeble oil lamps. The workers were endangered by rockfalls and plagued by bad air. Despite these conditions, the book of Job marvels at the technology of mining and provides a colorful description of the mining process (Job 28:1–11).

MINISTER

. . . TYCHICUS WILL TELL YOU ALL THE NEWS ABOUT ME; HE IS A BELOVED BROTHER, A FAITHFUL MINISTER, AND A FELLOW SERVANT IN THE LORD.–COLOSSIANS 4:7

The Bible speaks of many types of ministers, secular and religious. Broadly, a minister is anyone who serves. This individual could be a household servant, the king's cupbearer, or an angel. In the Old Testament, a minister was usually a person who served God in some assigned role, most commonly as a PRIEST, such as the sons of Aaron (Num 3:3), chosen to serve God by working in the temple. A priest's ministry included offering sacrifices, burning incense, maintaining the temple and its furnishings, and settling disputes among the people.

In the New Testament, ministers included Christians who took care of the physical or spiritual needs of others. Church leaders, such as the the apostle Paul, were called ministers of Christ (Rom 15:16). The act of ministry required humble and unselfish service. With this understanding, New Testament writers encouraged all Christians to serve the hungry, the naked, the sick, and the imprisoned. As the ultimate model of ministry, the Gospels pointed to Jesus, who "came not to be served but to serve" (Mt 20:28).

MINT

"FOR YOU TITHE THE MINT AND RUE AND HERBS OF ALL KINDS, AND NEGLECT JUSTICE AND THE LOVE OF GOD . . . ."
–LUKE 11:42

Mint is an aromatic herb. In biblical times its leaves were used to season food, relieve indigestion, and freshen the air in synagogues. The Pharisees, who were meticulous about observing every detail of the law, tithed even the smallest contents of their herb gardens, which were the least costly of their possessions. Jesus rebuked them, not for tithing their mint, rue, and other herbs, but rather for putting such obligations on the same level with weightier concerns such as their relationship with God and their neighbors.

In this detail of a fresco by Raphael, as the Israelites reach shore, Moses performs a miracle. By raising his staff, he reverses the waters of the Red Sea and drowns Pharaoh's army.

MIRACLES

THEY FORGOT WHAT HE HAD DONE, AND THE MIRACLES THAT HE HAD SHOWN THEM. IN THE SIGHT OF THEIR ANCESTORS HE WORKED MARVELS . . . .
–PSALM 78:11–12

Miracles—deeds beyond the normal range of human power to enact—are chronicled throughout the Bible, from God's creation of the world to the coming of Jesus and his resurrection. Both the Old and New Testaments use various words to convey the concept of miracles, such as *signs*, *works*, or *acts*.

Some miracles, such as the appearance of God to Moses as a burning bush (Ex 3), confirmed Israel as his chosen people. Other kinds of miracles included those of divine rescue, such as when the Lord saved Daniel from death in the lions' den (Dan 6:22). The plagues that God sent to Egypt were miraculous demonstrations of his power both to redeem and to punish. At other times God bestowed on individuals, such as Moses, Joshua, Elijah, and Elisha, miraculous powers with which to act on his behalf.

In the New Testament, Jesus is the principal worker of miracles, athough miraculous deeds are also credited to his disciples. Jesus performed many miracles of HEALING and exorcism, demonstrating the presence of God within himself. But he asked that these acts not be spoken of and refused demands that he work miracles simply to prove his divine power, insisting that faith in God was all that mattered. When Jesus appeared in Nazareth, the lack of faith of the people made it impossible for him to perform anything but a few minor healings (Mark 6:5).

MIRROR

FOR NOW WE SEE IN A MIRROR, DIMLY, BUT THEN WE WILL SEE FACE TO FACE.
–1 CORINTHIANS 13:12

Mirrors were made of polished metal, usually bronze or copper; the wealthy might have mirrors of gold and silver. They were used by Israelite women at least as far back as the exodus, when the women were said to have donated them to make the bronze basin and stand of the tabernacle (Ex 38:8). Glass mirrors were not made until the first century AD. Whether metal or glass, these early mirrors presented a dim, often fuzzy reflection, as indicated by the passage cited from 1 Corinthians. Figuratively, the mirror image may refer to a partial and imperfect understanding of God.

MOLECH

ANY OF THE PEOPLE OF ISRAEL . . . WHO GIVE ANY OF THEIR OFFSPRING TO MOLECH SHALL BE PUT TO DEATH . . . .
–LEVITICUS 20:2

A variation on the Hebrew word for king, *Molech* was a name given to a Canaanite god to whom children were sacrificed. The nature of the sacrifice, which involved the passing of a child through fire, is much debated. One interpretation is that the children were actually burned; another is that the children were neither burned nor even sacrificed but only dedicated to a foreign god in a fire ceremony. Two Israelite kings, Ahaz and Manasseh, are said to have participated in this unlawful practice (2 Kings 16:3; 21:6).

MOLTEN SEA

THEN HE MADE THE MOLTEN SEA; IT WAS ROUND, TEN CUBITS FROM RIM TO RIM, AND FIVE CUBITS HIGH.–2 CHRONICLES 4:2

According to 2 Chronicles, temple priests purified themselves with water drawn from a bronze bowl 15 feet wide, 7 feet high, and 3 inches thick. This basin, which was known as the molten sea, held about 11,000 gallons of water and sat in the courtyard of Solomon's temple, resting on the backs of a dozen bronze oxen. The 12 oxen, perhaps representing the tribes of Israel, were clustered in groups of three, with each group facing either north, south, east, or west. The Babylonians broke up the molten sea and took the bronze when they defeated Jerusalem in 587 BC (2 Kings 25:13, 16). See also LAVER.

This miniature replica of the bronze basin called the molten sea was made in the 19th century.

MONEY

FOR THE LOVE OF MONEY IS A ROOT OF ALL KINDS OF EVIL . . . .
–1 TIMOTHY 6:10

In Old Testament times, goods, livestock, or quantities of precious metal were considered forms of money, but barter transactions were also quite common. A man's wealth was calculated in terms of his possessions, such as cattle. Metals used as money were silver and gold, in the form of ingots, rings, foil, pins, or earrings; value was determined according to their weight in the presence of a witness.

In the Bible, money is often mentioned in regard to temple taxes, land prices, and temptations to corruption. Monies paid to the temple were essential in maintaining or repairing the property (2 Kings 12:4–5) and providing for the priests and other personnel. Taxation by civil authorities was begun about 1000 BC to support the monarchical government and to raise tributes exacted by foreign powers.

These coins with the head of Alexander the Great were minted in the fourth century BC.

Coinage legitimized by governments was in standard use in the Holy Land since the Persian period (see chart, p. 238). Three types of currency were accepted: money issued locally, imperial Roman coinage, and money struck in the Greek style by cities such as Tyre and Antioch. The value of these coins can only be estimated and certainly fluctuated over time. As payment for betraying Jesus, Judas Iscariot was said to have received 30 pieces of silver (Mt 26:15).

Money in the Holy Land

Most coins used in the Holy Land were produced by a process called striking, in which molten gold, silver, or bronze was poured into a mold with several shallow, connected depressions for blanks of coins. When cool, strips of the blanks were removed. The reheated strips were placed between two dies, each engraved with a design or inscription. A strong hammer blow against the top die left an impression on each side of the coin. The coins were then cut apart with pliers or a chisel and might also be stamped with the date and the symbol of the minting authority. To deter counterfeiters, the Romans added serrated edges to silver coins to show that there was no copper core.

PERSIAN

538 BC–332 BC

Gold and silver coins issued by the Persians, such as this gold daric, were the first official coins used in Judah. The Persian rulers also permitted the high priests to produce small silver coins, known as Yehud coins.

HELLENISTIC

332 BC–142 BC

The silver tetradrachma showing Zeus seated, left, was minted by Alexander the Great. His successor, Ptolemy I, broke with the practice of not showing a living ruler and issued coins bearing his own likeness, as on the gold tetradrachma, right.

HASMONEAN

135 BC–37 BC

During the Hasmonean dynasty, Jewish national coins were struck in Jerusalem after 135 BC. These were in small denominations, often in bronze, with an inscription in Aramaic, Greek, or old Hebrew, as on the coin above.

HERODIAN

37 BC–AD 95

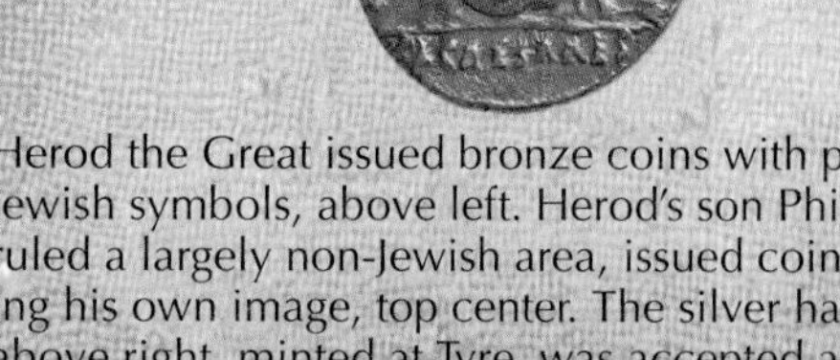

Herod the Great issued bronze coins with pagan or Jewish symbols, above left. Herod's son Philip, who ruled a largely non-Jewish area, issued coins showing his own image, top center. The silver half-shekel, above right, minted at Tyre, was accepted as payment of the temple tax. The silver denarius, bottom, circulated throughout the Roman Empire.

FIRST JEWISH REVOLT

AD 66–70

During the first war with Rome, the Jews produced silver shekels inscribed "Jerusalem the Holy," above right, and coins inscribed "For the redemption of Zion," above left. The emperors Vespasian, Titus, and Domitian each issued Judea Capta coins, bottom, commemorating the defeat of the rebellion in AD 70.

Jesus drives the money changers from the temple in a 14th-century fresco by Giotto.

MONEY CHANGER

HE ALSO POURED OUT THE COINS OF THE MONEY CHANGERS AND OVERTURNED THEIR TABLES.
–JOHN 2:15

By the time of Jesus, so many different cultures had been brought together under Roman rule that virtually every village in the Holy Land had its own money changer. This person made exchanges between locally accepted currencies and the great variety of other monies passing through. Since foreign traders and Jewish pilgrims to the temple carried money in large denominations for convenience, money changers also provided change. Both types of transaction were subject to a small surcharge, perhaps 4 percent to 8 percent. In violation of Mosaic law, money changers sometimes also acted as bankers, holding a client's funds on deposit and returning a fixed rate of interest. The annual interest varied greatly, ranging from 20 percent to 300 percent.

The specialized class of money changers at the temple was necessary because only coins from Tyre were accepted for buying offerings and paying the annual temple tax. The Passover festival was under way when Jesus routed the money changers from the temple; this would have been an especially busy season for exchanges, which were sometimes fraudulent. Archaeologists recently uncovered possible remains of the kiosks set up by money changers in an outer court of the temple, which was probably the Court of the Gentiles.

MONTH

THIS MONTH SHALL MARK FOR YOU THE BEGINNING OF MONTHS; IT SHALL BE THE FIRST MONTH OF THE YEAR FOR YOU.
–EXODUS 12:2

A biblical month began with the appearance of the new moon's slender crescent at sunset. The month was tied to the phases of the moon, and the lunar calendar was based on months averaging 29½ days, for a total of 354 days in the YEAR. The Israelites eventually learned from the Babylonians to reconcile this system with the lengthier agricultural, or solar, year of 365¼ days by adding a 13th month to the calendar every two or three years. The Israelites also adopted Babylonian names for the months. For example, the first Babylonian month, Nisanu, became Nisan in Hebrew. This was the month referred to in Exodus 12 as the time of the Passover festival. Before the Babylonian exile, it was called Abib.

MOON

"IT SHALL BE ESTABLISHED FOREVER LIKE THE MOON, AN ENDURING WITNESS IN THE SKIES."–PSALM 89:37

According to the book of Genesis, God created the moon, "the lesser light to rule the night," on the fourth day (Gen 1:16). To the Israelites, the moon in its phases marked the months and so was the basis of their calendar. The full moon signaled the start of two of their most important festivals: the Festival of Booths in autumn and Passover in spring. A minor holiday was observed at the beginning of each month, when the new moon appeared; special offerings were brought to the temple, and trumpets were sounded in celebration (Num 10:10). The returning moon symbolized both rebirth in nature and the promise of redemption for Israel. Mosaic law specified that the day when the new moon appeared in the seventh month was to be observed as "a day of complete rest, a holy convocation" (Lev 23:24).

The moon god called Sin appears, along with his crescent symbols, on an Assyrian limestone stele from the eighth century BC.

Some peoples, including the Canaanites, worshiped the moon as a male god. Under the name *Sin,* he was the patron deity of Ur, the homeland of Abraham's father, Terah. However, Moses warned the Israelites not to "bow down and serve" the moon, the SUN, or any other celestial body (Deut 4:19).

The moon normally represented permanence (Ps 72:5; 89:37). The Israelites and other ancient peoples perceived its disappearance during an eclipse as an ominous sign.

MORSEL

"... LET ME SET A MORSEL OF BREAD BEFORE YOU."
–1 SAMUEL 28:22

A morsel in the Bible is usually a small piece of bread broken from a loaf. Though it might be eaten by itself, a bread fragment could also be used for dipping into wine (Ruth 2:14) or for scooping up food. When several people ate from the same bowl, the breaking of the bread into morsels signified close friendship. Proverbs 18:8 uses the word metaphorically to warn that gossip and slander can be as irresistible as delicious tidbits of food: "The words of a whisperer are like delicious morsels; they go down into the inner parts of the body."

MORTAR

THE PEOPLE WENT AROUND AND GATHERED IT, GROUND IT IN MILLS OR BEAT IT IN MORTARS ....
–NUMBERS 11:8

People of biblical times crushed grains or herbs by placing them in the hollow of a stone vessel called a mortar and grinding them with a pestle. While in the wilderness, the Israelites used mortars to prepare manna for food. A neighborhood in Jerusalem was called the Mortar (Zeph 1:11) because it lay in a bowl-shaped depression.

From about 12,500 to 8500 BC, the mortar developed from the crude example at right, with pestle, to the more finished example at left.

Mortar was also a material used by a MASON for binding stones or bricks. It could be sticky bitumen (Gen 11:3) or a mixture of water and mud, clay, lime, or sand.

MOSAIC

THERE WERE COUCHES OF GOLD AND SILVER ON A MOSAIC PAVEMENT OF PORPHYRY, MARBLE, MOTHER-OF-PEARL, AND COLORED STONES.–ESTHER 1:6

Mosaics were well known in the ancient Near East; their use dates from at least 2900 BC in Sumer. Small pieces of stone, ceramic, or other hard materials typically formed the inlaid decorations; the use of mother-of-pearl, such as in the palace floor of King Ahasuerus of Persia (Esth 1:6), was unusual. There is little evidence of mosaics in the Holy Land during Old Testament times, but there are splendid examples from the Roman period.

MOTH

"... STORE UP FOR YOURSELVES TREASURES IN HEAVEN, WHERE NEITHER MOTH NOR RUST CONSUMES ...."
–MATTHEW 6:20

Along with the butterfly, the moth belongs to the order *Lepidoptera* and is any of a large number of winged insects. The Holy Land has many species of moths, but the Bible refers only to the kind that eats through clothing. The insect is associated with the weakness of humanity (Job 13:28), the destructiveness of sin (Ps 39:11), and the impermanent nature of the material world. Jesus spoke of spiritual goods that were invulnerable to the moth, and the letter of James warned the wealthy, "Your riches have rotted, and your clothes are moth-eaten" (Jas 5:2).

MOTHER

HONOR YOUR FATHER AND YOUR MOTHER, AS THE LORD YOUR GOD COMMANDED YOU, SO THAT YOUR DAYS MAY BE LONG ....
–DEUTERONOMY 5:16

One of God's ten commandments was to honor both parents. In Israelite society, the mother was further revered as the bearer of children. Childbirth was considered a woman's most important duty because she was assuring the continuation of the family line.

A stained-glass Yorkshire chapel panel shows the mother of Jesus carrying the infant as the family flees to Egypt.

Although the father ruled the household during biblical times, the mother was second in command. She was responsible for the care and training of the children when they were small. The father took over the training of sons as they grew older, but the mother remained in charge of the daughters until they married and left the home to have their own children.

Some biblical passages use the term *mother* figuratively. The prophet Deborah is called "a mother in Israel" (Judg 5:7) for her role in defeating a Canaanite army. In the New Testament, the apostle Paul speaks of Jerusalem as the heavenly mother of Christians (Gal 4:26). See also BARRENNESS.

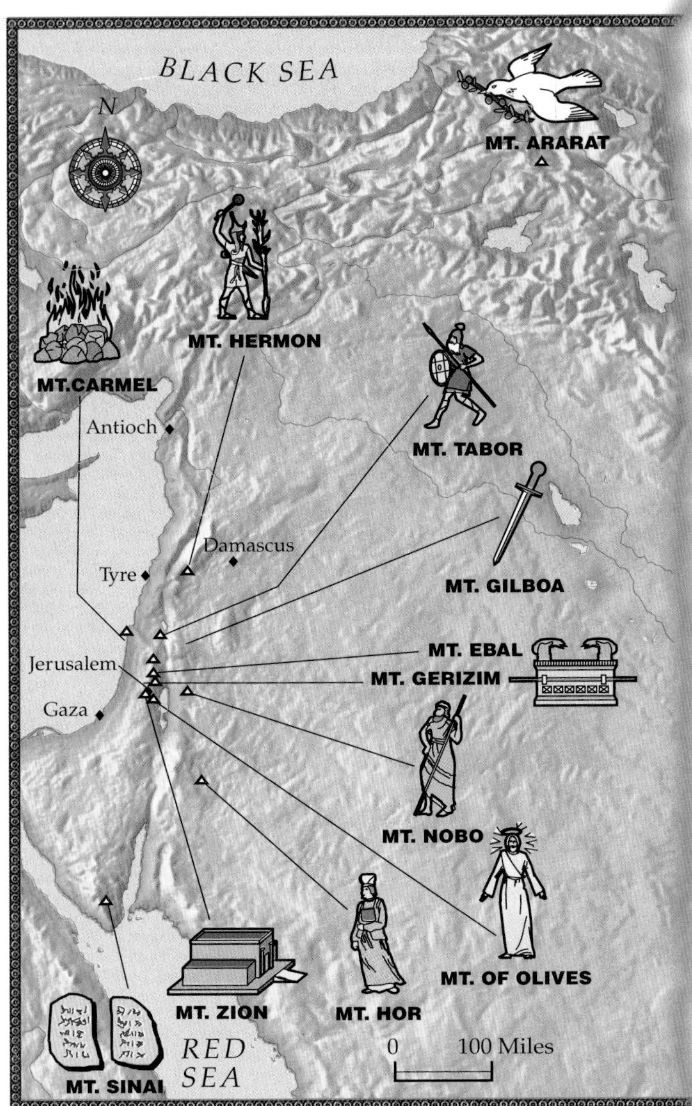

MOUNTAINS OF THE BIBLE

In the Old and New Testaments, mountains are often the site of important religious and historical events. The mountains shown on the map at left were especially significant in biblical times.

Mt. Ararat: The receding flood left Noah's ark on a mountain in Ararat, sometimes identified as the volcano Mt. Ararat (Gen 8:4).

Mt. Carmel: On Mt. Carmel, the prophet Elijah challenged Jezebel's prophets of Baal to summon their god to burn their sacrifice. When they failed, Elijah successfully summoned God to do the same (1 Kings 18:19–40).

Mt. Ebal and Mt. Gerizim: When the Israelites returned to the Promised Land, they reconfirmed their covenant with God at Mt. Ebal and Mt. Gerizim (Deut 11:29; Josh 8:30–35).

Mt. Gilboa: The Israelites, led by Saul, were defeated by the Philistines at Mt. Gilboa. Rather than risk capture, Saul chose death by his own sword (1 Sam 31:1–7).

Mt. Hermon: Many ancient peoples revered high, snowcapped Mt. Hermon as the dwelling place of gods (Deut 3:8–9).

Mt. Hor: According to tradition, Mt. Hor is the burial place of Moses' brother Aaron. At the summit, Moses transferred Aaron's priestly vestments to Eleazar, Aaron's son (Num 20:22–29; 33:38–39).

Mt. Nebo: God commanded Moses to ascend Mt. Nebo to look across the valley of Jericho and into Canaan but forbade him to enter the land with the Israelites (Deut 34:1–4).

Mt. of Olives: Many of the events in the last week of Jesus' life occurred on the Mt. of Olives, located just east of Jerusalem on the road to Bethany. According to Acts of the Apostles, 40 days after his resurrection Jesus ascended to heaven from this holy hill (Acts 1:3–12).

Mt. Sinai: God revealed his presence on Mt. Sinai with a thick, smoky cloud, trumpet blasts, and lightning, and gave the law to Moses (Ex 19–24). Tradition equates Mt. Sinai with Jebel Musa.

Mt. Tabor: Mt. Tabor was the scene of battles in the Old Testament. In a battle led by Deborah and Barak, Israelite foot soldiers drove Canaanite charioteers from the mountain (Judg 4:14–15). A fourth-century tradition assigns Mt. Tabor as the site of the transfiguration of Jesus (Mk 9:2).

Mt. Zion: Zion, a fortified hill in pre-Israelite Jerusalem, was captured by David and renamed the City of David (2 Sam 5:7).

MOUNTAIN

. . . THE LORD SUMMONED MOSES TO THE TOP OF THE MOUNTAIN, AND MOSES WENT UP.–EXODUS 19:20

Mountains form an important part of the landscape in the Holy Land. Parallel chains of rugged mountains and hills flank the Dead Sea and the VALLEY of the Jordan River. Though the mountains are not nearly as high in elevation as some ranges, they appear otherwise, precipitously falling into deep valley rifts and dramatically abutting the Dead Sea, which lies about 1,300 feet below sea level. Within these ranges are summits that are called mounts. A mount can also be an isolated peak, such as the traditional site of the biblical Mount Sinai, which rises about 7,500 feet.

Canaanite mythology deemed Mount Zaphon the sacred mountain of the storm god Baal, and the Caananites used mountaintops as sites for worship. Similarly, mountains and summits were associated with God in the Old and New Testaments (see map). Moses first encountered God at Mount Horeb, referred to as the "mountain of God" (Ex 3:1). In the Bible this site is alternatively called Mount Sinai. It was considered so sacred that God commanded Moses to "set limits around the mountain and keep it holy" (Ex 19:23). Here God gave Moses the ten commandments. In a later time, Jerusalem was sometimes referred to as Mount Zion, the place where God dwelled (Ps 48:1–2).

In the New Testament, Jesus was tempted on a "very high mountain" (Mt 4:8). Mountains were the scenes for Jesus' Sermon on the Mount (Mt 5:1), his transfiguration (Mk 9:2), his agony the night before his death (Mk 14:26–36), and his ascension (Acts 1:9–12).

MOURNER

. . ."PRETEND TO BE A MOURNER; PUT ON MOURNING GARMENTS, DO NOT ANOINT YOURSELF WITH OIL . . . ." –2 SAMUEL 14:2

In the event of a death, the family and friends of the deceased began elaborate mourning rituals; upon the death of a king, an entire nation took part. These mourners gave vent to their sadness with loud wailing and lamentation, as well as beating of breasts and tearing of clothes, during the funeral procession. However, they might also hire professional mourners, who were often women, to add to the public display of grief. These mourners, accompanied by flute players, sang or wailed traditional laments or poems written especially for the dead. People paid them for their services because of their expertise.

The prophet Jeremiah describes God's impending destruction of Judah as a death that will require such professional mourners: "Call for the mourning women to come; send for the skilled women to come; let them quickly raise a dirge over us, so that our eyes may run down with tears, and our eyelids flow with water" (Jer 9:17–18). See also BURIAL.

MOUTH

TRUE INSTRUCTION WAS IN HIS MOUTH, AND NO WRONG WAS FOUND ON HIS LIPS. –MALACHI 2:6

The Scriptures usually mention the mouth in regard to speech. In this sense it was very important because it had the power to produce good or evil: "You will find no wickedness in me; my mouth does not transgress," asserts Psalm 17:3. Jesus told his followers, "What comes out of the mouth proceeds from the heart" (Mt 15:18). Because of this connection between the mouth and the inner self, a person might acknowledge shame by covering the mouth with the hand (Mic 7:16). The Bible also uses the word *mouth* to refer to an opening, such as that of a cave or well. It sometimes pictures the underworld, or Sheol, as a voracious beast with a gaping mouth (Isa 5:14).

MULE

". . . HAVE MY SON SOLOMON RIDE ON MY OWN MULE, AND BRING HIM DOWN TO GIHON."–1 KINGS 1:33

The mule, the offspring of a female horse and a male DONKEY, was valued for its strength and stamina but not for its temperament or level of intelligence; Psalm 32:9 says it is "without understanding." As Mosaic law prohibited the interbreeding of species (Lev 19:19), the Israelites may have had to import the hybrid animals into the Holy Land. Mules were used as pack animals and were ridden by ordinary people as well as royalty. Solomon rode on King David's mule en route to being anointed king.

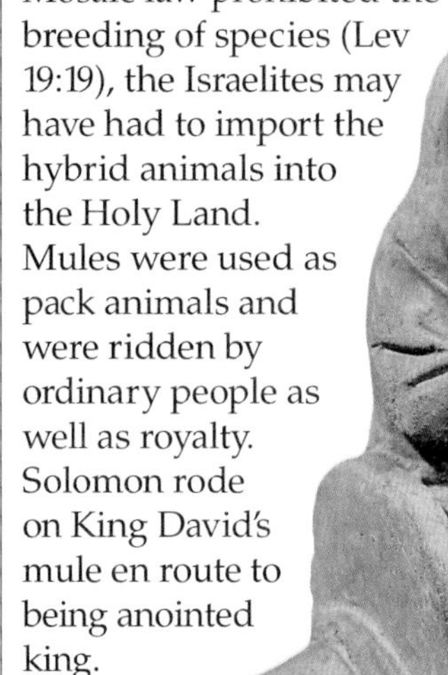

This first-century BC terra-cotta figurine from the Greek isle of Lemnos shows a woman on a mule.

MURDER

YOU WANT SOMETHING AND DO NOT HAVE IT; SO YOU COMMIT MURDER.–JAMES 4:2

The ten commandments, the heart of God's covenant with Israel, prohibited murder (Ex 20:13). The penalty for a person who intentionally killed another, except during war or in self-defense, was EXECUTION, conducted by one of the victim's relatives, who was called the "avenger of blood" (Num 35:19).

Someone who claimed to have killed accidentally could flee to one of six cities of refuge scattered throughout the Holy Land. There the accused was entitled to a trial before city elders. If the elders found the person guilty of premeditated murder—a verdict that required the testimony of at least two witnesses—they turned the slayer over to the avenger. But if they determined that the killing was indeed unintentional, they granted the slayer refuge as long as the person stayed in the city. Only if the high priest died could the individual safely leave the city; apparently the priest's death atoned for the killing or substituted for the death of the slayer.

In Ezra's day, after the Jews returned from exile in Babylon, state officials took charge of murder trials and executions. In New Testament times, Roman law prohibited the Jews from conducting executions. The Romans crucified or beheaded those who committed murder.

Music

. . . I will solve my riddle to the music of the harp. –Psalm 49:4

The melodies of ancient Israelite music are lost because they were probably passed down only orally. However, the Scriptures frequently convey scenes of victory, worship, mourning, or joy that are alive with the sounds of singing and musical instruments.

The Bible ascribes the invention of music to Jubal (Gen 4:21) and mentions music as part of Israel's religious practice, yet not until 1 Chronicles is there a full account of the use of music in worship. That book describes music as a highly regulated part of the services, with Chenaniah, "leader of the Levites in music" (1 Chr 15:22), and others appointed as directors of it. By the time the Jews returned from exile in Babylon, music, performed by members of professional guilds, had become essential to worship and funerals. Borrowing from royal models, the temple orchestra included a large choir, a great number of one or two types of stringed instruments, and one or more cymbals as percussion. Many of the psalms suggest that a HYMN might be sung or perhaps chanted in parts, with two choirs responding in turn to each other or to the congregation.

A female musician is depicted playing the harp. This scene is part of a wall painting in the tomb of Rekhmere, a vizier for two Egyptian pharaohs of the 18th Dynasty.

Musical Instruments

And the priests stood arrayed in their vestments, with musical instruments and trumpets . . . . –1 Esdras 5:59

Many musical instruments are mentioned in the Scriptures. Although the ram's horn, or shofar, could sound only two or three different notes, it was a very important instrument that was used to signal danger, announce or highlight ritual functions, and mark the deaths of important people. The piercing, high notes of pairs of long metal trumpets, which were considered sacred items of the temple, rang out before ceremonies such as sacrifices. Other instruments, too, were assigned specific functions in Israelite religious or secular life or were associated with particular types of music. For example, tambourines were typically used for joyful music, and the high priest's robe was hemmed with jingling, clapperless bells. Other instruments named in the Old Testament include the lyre, harp, pipes, flute, and cymbals. Since the New Testament lacks detailed references to traditional Jewish festivals and temple services, fewer instruments are mentioned specifically. In the first letter to the Corinthians, Paul refers to the "noisy gong" (1 Cor 13:1), which was probably used in pagan worship, and the bugle, which was sounded to announce battle (1 Cor 14:8).

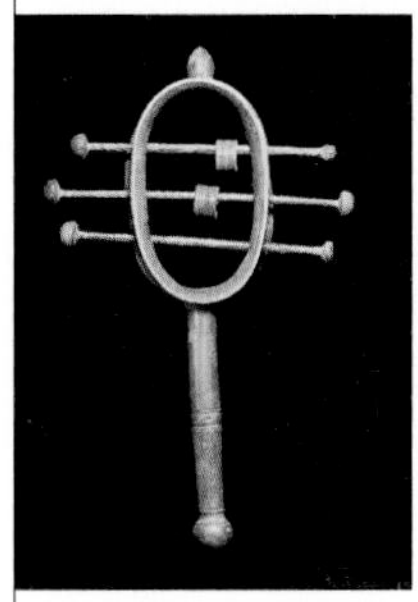

The rattle-like sistrum was a metal musical instrument of Egyptian origin used during biblical times.

Musician

"To the sound of musicians at the watering places, there they repeat the triumphs of the LORD . . . ." –Judges 5:11

Jubal, the first musician mentioned in the Bible, was the forerunner of many different kinds of professional performers: wandering minstrels who sang war ballads, court musicians who enlivened the feasts of the wealthy, and members of Levite guilds, founded by David to play in temple rituals. The guilds increased greatly in influence in the second-temple period, performing both instrumental and vocal music and ensuring that all instruments were ritually pure. Women also created and performed music in Old Testament times, from Miriam and Deborah to groups of women praising David's battlefield triumphs. David himself was well known as a musician and was summoned when King Saul needed someone "skillful in playing the lyre" (1 Sam 16:16).

Mustard Seed

"It is like a mustard seed that someone took and sowed in the garden; it grew and became a tree . . . ."
–Luke 13:19

Mustard seeds were cultivated for their oil during biblical times and were ground into powder for both culinary and medicinal purposes. The tiny mustard seed, once mistakenly believed to be the smallest seed of all, quickly grows into a large annual plant, sometimes as high as six feet. To illustrate how rapidly God's kingdom would grow, Jesus told the parable of the mustard seed blossoming into a tree large enough for nesting birds. He also used the seed to describe the power of even a small amount of faith, which, he said, enabled a person to move a mountain (Mt 17:20).

The mustard seed of the Bible may refer to the species called black mustard, or Brassica nigra.

Mute

But I am like the deaf, I do not hear; like the mute, who cannot speak.
–Psalm 38:13

In the Bible the inability to speak is often seen as the result of divine intervention or demonic possession. In the Old Testament, God rendered Ezekiel partially mute for more than seven years, allowing the prophet to speak only of Israel's coming destruction (Ezek 3:26–27). In the New Testament, the angel Gabriel took away Zechariah's power of speech when he expressed doubt that he and his wife, both "on in years," would produce a child (Lk 1:18–20). Jesus cured many mutes, sometimes by exorcising demons; after these miracles, witnesses were amazed to hear the mute speak (Mt 9:33).

Myrrh

Take the finest spices: of liquid myrrh five hundred shekels, and of sweet-smelling cinnamon half as much . . . .
–Exodus 30:23

Myrrh is a fragrant gum resin derived from a shrub or tree, especially the *Commiphora abyssinica,* which is native to southern Arabia and eastern Africa. Egyptian royal tombs dating from the 15th century BC contain art depicting myrrh trees. The resin, a highly valued commodity in ancient times, was used to purify corpses (Jn 19:39) and as an ingredient in "sacred anointing oil" (Ex 30:23–25), beauty treatments (Esth 2:12), and scents for clothing (Ps 45:8). Myrrh was among the offerings presented to the infant Jesus as a GIFT (Mt 2:11). During his crucifixion, Jesus was offered wine mixed with myrrh as a sedative (Mk 15:23).

Mystery

Then the mystery was revealed to Daniel in a vision of the night, and Daniel blessed the God of heaven.
–Daniel 2:19

God's plans were an enigma to the people of the Bible, though they were sometimes divulged in dreams and visions. In the Old Testament the word *mystery* occurs only in the book of Daniel, where it refers to the "deep and hidden things" of God (Dan 2:22). God enables Daniel to interpret a dream of Nebuchadnezzar, thus informing the king of Babylon of future events. "The great God has informed the king what shall be hereafter," Daniel tells Nebuchadnezzar, who then calls Daniel's God "a revealer of mysteries" (Dan 2:45, 47).

In the New Testament, Jesus makes known, to some extent, God's design. Asked by his disciples why he preaches in parables, Jesus says, "To you it has been given to know the secrets of the kingdom of heaven, but to them it has not been given" (Mt 13:11). The letters to the early Christians use the word *mystery* at times to refer to Jesus himself, the mystery "revealed in flesh" (1 Tim 3:16).

Myths

Have nothing to do with profane myths and old wives' tales.
–1 Timothy 4:7

As used in the New Testament, the term *myths* (from the Greek word for story) means incorrect or deceptive beliefs or narratives. The first letter to Timothy warns about the danger of "myths and endless genealogies that promote speculations rather than the divine training that is known by faith" (1 Tim 1:4), and the letter to Titus speaks of "Jewish myths" (Titus 1:14). These may be allusions to sections of the Pentateuch or to Gnostic ideas, which involved an esoteric knowledge leading to salvation and which attracted some Jews and early Christians.

Christian belief was considered to be different, because it was based on direct knowledge of Jesus: "For we did not follow cleverly devised myths when we made known to you the power and coming of our Lord Jesus Christ, but we had been eyewitnesses of his majesty" (2 Pet 1:16).

This fragment is from a Dead Sea Scroll that contains a commentary on the book of NAHUM. The commentary was written in Hebrew about 50 BC by the religious community identified as the Essenes. It tries to find meaning in the biblical book that relates specifically to the community.

Nahum, Book of

Your people are scattered on the mountains with no one to gather them.–Nahum 3:18

The book of Nahum is a prophecy of the destruction of Nineveh, the capital of Assyria. The only information that the book gives about the writer is that he was "Nahum of Elkosh" (Nah 1:1), a city that may have been in southwestern Judah.

The prophet probably delivered his message sometime between the 663 BC Assyrian capture of Egypt's capital at Thebes, mentioned in Nahum 3:8, and the 612 BC fall of Nineveh to the Babylonians and Medes. During much of this period, Assyria dominated the kingdom of Judah; the formidable nation had already, in 721 BC, decimated the northern kingdom of Israel. Nahum condemned the terrorism and "endless cruelty" (Nah 3:19) of Assyria's conquests. Using vivid images of devastation, he assured his people that God would punish Assyria with total ruin.

Nails

David also provided great stores of iron for nails for the doors of the gates . . . . –1 Chronicles 22:3

Being made of metal, nails were costly in biblical times. The first nails were bronze, an alloy that becomes brittle if hammered excessively. When iron became available, it was used for large, heavy-duty nails; however, smaller nails were still made of bronze. Builders might use wooden pegs instead of nails and would drive them into holes bored into the wooden pieces to be joined.

In New Testament times, the Romans, when executing a criminal by CRUCIFIXION, sometimes fastened the person's hands and feet to the cross with nails. According to John 20:25, this was done to Jesus.

The Bible uses the word *nails* to signify fingernails in only a few instances. Deuteronomy 21:12 states that if an Israelite wants to marry a woman taken captive in war, she must shave her head and pare her nails, a rite that conferred a new identity upon her. Daniel 4:33 describes Nebuchadnezzar, when stricken with madness, as growing nails like birds' claws.

Nakedness

I spread the edge of my cloak over you, and covered your nakedness . . . . –Ezekiel 16:8

In the Old Testament, the term *nakedness*, often a euphemism for genital organs, is associated with shame. After their disobedience, Adam and Eve realized they were naked and immediately clad themselves in loincloths (Gen 3:7). When Ham discovered Noah drunken and naked, he failed to cover his father's body, whereas his brothers respectfully laid a garment upon the old man as they avoided looking at him (Gen 9:22–23). In the holiness code set out in Leviticus to distinguish the Israelites from other nations, the phrase "uncover the nakedness" usually refers to having sexual intercourse; the code specifies types of sexual relations proscribed by law (Lev 18:6–23). See also LAW OF MOSES.

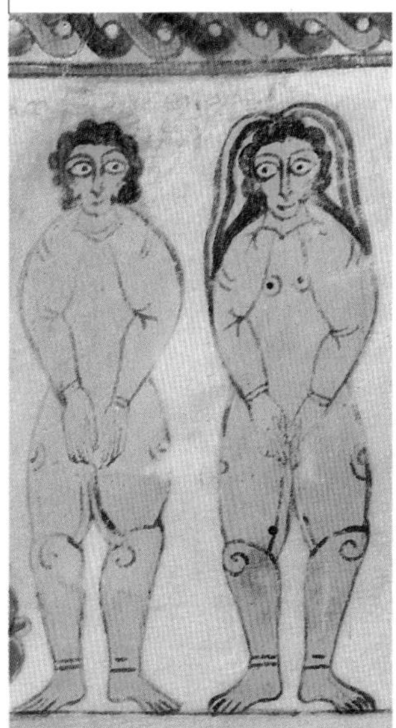

Adam and Eve became aware of their nakedness after they ate the forbidden fruit. This illustration of the first man and woman appears on a Spanish genealogical table from about AD 950.

A Renaissance painting depicting the birth of John the Baptist shows Zechariah, rendered mute by the angel Gabriel, writing on a tablet. At the baby's circumcision, relatives were ready to name the child after his father, but Zechariah wrote, "His name is John" (Lk 1:63).

NAME

THEY SHALL SEEK REFUGE IN THE NAME OF THE LORD . . . .
–ZEPHANIAH 3:12

Throughout the ancient Near East, names were of great significance. Names for people, places, or things were supposed to capture the essence of their nature. Adam named his wife *Eve*; in Hebrew *Eve* is related to the word for life, reflecting Eve's role as "the mother of all living" (Gen 3:20). Babies were generally named at birth by their mother or father. Infants' names might convey the particulars of their birth, personality, or even their destiny. This is especially evident in the naming of the children of Jacob by Leah and Rachel (Gen 29:32–35; 30:6–24; 35:18) and of the sons of Joseph (Gen 41:51–52), as well as in the naming of John the Baptist by his father (Lk 1:63) and of Jesus by Joseph (Mt 1:21, 25). Not all biblical names are so significant: *Deborah,* for example, simply means "bee."

Names sometimes changed. In one instance in the Old Testament, a mysterious man who wrestled with Jacob renamed him *Israel* (Gen 32:28), that is, "one who strives with God." Kings might be given different names when they assumed the throne (2 Kings 23:34; 24:17). In the New Testament, Jesus changed Simon's name to *Peter* (Jn 1:42), meaning "rock."

God revealed his own name as *Yahweh,* interpreted as meaning "I AM WHO I AM" (Ex 3:13–14). By doing so, he indicated an intimate relationship with his people. The name of God was holy and not to be misused (Ex 20:7). It was also powerful. God declared that the prophets "shall speak in my name" (Deut 18:19), and enemies feared Israel because it was "called by the name of the LORD" (Deut 28:10). In the New Testament, Jesus told his Father, "I have made your name known" (Jn 17:6).

NARD

WHILE THE KING WAS ON HIS COUCH, MY NARD GAVE FORTH ITS FRAGRANCE.
–SONG OF SOLOMON 1:12

Nard, or spikenard, was a costly OINTMENT made from the roots and stems of an aromatic herb, *Nardostachys jatamansi,* native to the Himalayas in India. In the Gospels, Jesus was anointed with nard on two occasions, at the homes of Simon the leper and of Lazarus. Onlookers criticized the women who anointed Jesus, asking why the ointment was not instead sold for 300 denarii—roughly the yearly income of a laborer—and the money given to the poor. According to John 12:8, Jesus responded, "You always have the poor with you, but you do not always have me."

NATION

"I WILL MAKE OF YOU A GREAT NATION, AND I WILL BLESS YOU, AND MAKE YOUR NAME GREAT, SO THAT YOU WILL BE A BLESSING." –GENESIS 12:1

Genesis contains what is called the Table of Nations. Chapter 10 of that book uses genealogies stemming from the three sons of Noah to chart the history of ancient nations and their relationship to one another. The line of Shem is particularly important because it eventually includes Abraham. In addition, the term *Semitic* is derived from Shem's name.

Abraham becomes the progenitor of a new nation, that of Israel. When God calls Abraham to leave his land and start anew in Canaan

An Armenian illumination uses the tents of the 12 tribes to symbolize the nation of Israel.

(Gen 17:8), he tells him that his descendants will be a blessing to all other nations: "Abraham shall become a great and mighty nation, and all the nations of the earth shall be blessed in him" (Gen 18:18). Israel, God's chosen people, is to be a "light to the nations" (Isa 42:6). The New Testament echoes these words, substituting the term *Gentiles* (Lk 2:32; Acts 13:47). It stresses that salvation is open to human beings "from every tribe and language and people and nation" (Rev 5:9) and that God has power over all nations.

NATURE

EVEN THOUGH OUR OUTER NATURE IS WASTING AWAY, OUR INNER NATURE IS BEING RENEWED DAY BY DAY.–2 CORINTHIANS 4:16

The word *nature* does not appear in the Old Testament. In the New Testament, it usually refers to human or divine nature. In 2 Corinthians 4:8–18, Paul contrasts the innermost self—the spiritual being—with an exterior self that is "afflicted in every way"; his words may reflect the philosophical discussions of that time. The second letter of Peter asserts that Christians can transcend their humanity through Jesus: "You may escape from the corruption that is in the world . . . and may become participants of the divine nature" (2 Pet 1:4). In the Gospel of John, Jesus uses the word concerning the devil: "When he lies, he speaks according to his own nature" (Jn 8:44).

NAVE

THE NAVE HE LINED WITH CYPRESS, COVERED IT WITH FINE GOLD, AND MADE PALMS AND CHAINS ON IT. –2 CHRONICLES 3:5

The Hebrew word that generally means "palace" or "temple" is sometimes translated as "nave." This was the largest room in Solomon's TEMPLE: about 35 feet wide and 70 feet long. It connected a vestibule, which was the entrance area, with the inner sanctuary, or Holy of Holies—a 35-foot cube that held the ark of the covenant. The nave contained a small cedar and gold altar for incense, 10 golden lampstands, and a table for the bread of the Presence. Only priests could enter this room, and some of the rituals they performed took place there.

In a Doré engraving, Samson tells Delilah of his nazirite vow not to cut his hair.

NAZIRITE

". . . I WILL OFFER HIM AS A NAZIRITE FOR ALL TIME." –1 SAMUEL 1:22

Nazirites were men and women devoted to special service to God, either through their own VOW or that of their parents. There were three special rules observed by nazirites: to abstain from wine or any fruit of the vine; not to allow one's hair to be cut; and not to go near a dead body, even that of a family member (Num 6:2–7). Nazirites who accidentally came into contact with a corpse had to perform an elaborate purification ritual to become reconsecrated.

Most nazirites served for a limited period, but others occupied this holy state for their entire lives. The most famous was Samson, who was declared a nazirite by an angel before his birth. Samson broke every one of his vows. He took part in a drinking feast, touched the body of a dead lion, and revealed the secret of his strength to Delilah by declaring, "If my head were shaved, then my strength would leave me" (Judg 16:17)—thus causing his hair to be cut off.

NECK

ON THAT DAY,
SAYS THE LORD OF HOSTS,
I WILL BREAK THE YOKE
FROM OFF HIS NECK . . . .
–JEREMIAH 30:8

Figuratively, the neck is often associated in the Scriptures with submission or its direct opposite, disobedience. A person might either bow the neck in surrender, for example, or defiantly stand "stiff-necked" (Ex 32:9) in secular or spiritual matters. Similarly, enforced servitude can be seen as a chain or yoke upon the neck, and freedom is won by casting off the yoke. The neck played a role in Near Eastern customs. On the battlefield, the victor set his foot upon his defeated enemy's neck to affirm his supremacy. When a weeping Esau embraced his estranged brother, Jacob, and "fell on his neck" (Gen 33:4), he was using a customary gesture of deep tenderness.

Nehemiah directs the rebuilding of Jerusalem after the exile, from Beno Elkan's sculptured menorah in the parliament garden in Jerusalem.

NEEDLE

"IT IS EASIER FOR A CAMEL TO GO THROUGH THE EYE OF A NEEDLE THAN FOR SOMEONE WHO IS RICH TO ENTER THE KINGDOM OF GOD."–MARK 10:25

Needles were essential for sewing clothes and other items made of cloth or leather. They were also used for elaborate EMBROIDERY, such as for priests' vestments (Ex 39:29). In the earliest days, needles were made of bone or ivory. Later bronze came into use as well.

Jesus' example of a camel going through the eye of a needle was meant to capture the attention of his listeners. Some interpreters have suggested that he was referring to a narrow gate in Jerusalem called the Needle's Eye; however, the existence of such a gate is not known.

NEHEMIAH, BOOK OF

"COME, LET US REBUILD THE WALL OF JERUSALEM . . . ."
–NEHEMIAH 2:17

Along with the book of Ezra, the book of Nehemiah narrates the reconstruction of the Jews' homeland after their exile. This book may have been written by the author of 1 and 2 CHRONICLES, but the main source is an account by Nehemiah himself. Nehemiah, a Jew, held a high position of wine server in the court of King Artaxerxes of Persia. At Nehemiah's request, the king allowed him to rebuild the walls of Jerusalem, appointing him governor of the province of Judah. Nehemiah went to Jerusalem in 445 BC, about a century after many of the Jews had returned from Babylonian captivity. The book tells of the Jews restoring the walls in 52 days and of Nehemiah instituting religious reforms in the community.

NEIGHBOR

DO NOT PLAN HARM AGAINST YOUR NEIGHBOR WHO LIVES TRUSTINGLY BESIDE YOU.
–PROVERBS 3:29

In the Old Testament, the word *neighbor* can refer not only to a person living nearby but also to any fellow Israelite. The ten commandments specifically proscribe crimes against neighbors: "You shall not bear false witness against your neighbor. You shall not covet your neighbor's house; you shall not covet your neighbor's wife . . . or anything that belongs to your neighbor" (Ex 20:16–17). Leviticus further decrees that "you shall love your neighbor as yourself" (Lev 19:18). Treachery toward one's people—"They all speak friendly words to their neighbors, but inwardly are planning to lay an ambush" (Jer 9:8)—was sinful and would bring down God's punishment.

In the New Testament, a lawyer asked Jesus, "Who is my neighbor?" (Lk 10:29). Jesus answered with the parable of the good Samaritan. A man was set upon by robbers, beaten, and left half-dead; a priest and a Levite passed by the victim without helping, but a Samaritan—a member of a group that was widely despised by Jews—stopped and saved the man. When

A Bedouin man uses a net to fish the Red Sea off the Sinai peninsula. In biblical times, fishermen cast similar nets from shore and waited for their catches.

questioned by Jesus, the lawyer acknowledged that of the three passersby, the alien Samaritan was the true neighbor, for he showed MERCY. Then Jesus commanded, "Go and do likewise" (Lk 10:37).

NET

BUT THE OTHER DISCIPLES CAME IN THE BOAT, DRAGGING THE NET FULL OF FISH . . . .–JOHN 21:8

Nets of strong cord were the chief implements used for FISHING during biblical times. They were of different types. Habakkuk 1:15 refers to the seine, a weighted net thrown from shore. The Gospels also mention such casting nets, which were cone shaped (Mt 4:18; Mk 1:16). Other nets were thrown from a boat and, when fish had been caught, hauled into the boat or into shore by wading fishermen. The dragnet, or trawl, was pulled behind a boat. Nets were also used to hunt game animals and birds, particularly the huge flocks of quail that passed through the Near East when migrating.

NETTLE

. . . MOAB SHALL BECOME LIKE SODOM . . . A LAND POSSESSED BY NETTLES AND SALT PITS, AND A WASTE FOREVER. –ZEPHANIAH 2:9

Nettles are prickly plants belonging to the family *Urtica*. Some types have stinging hairs that can produce a skin rash when touched. Because they often spring up in neglected or destroyed areas, they are used in the Bible as signs of dereliction or devastation. The book of Isaiah pictures Edom in ruins: "Thorns shall grow over its strongholds, nettles and thistles in its fortresses" (Isa 34:13). Nettles can also represent a harsh judgment. Because the Israelites are unfaithful, "nettles shall possess their precious things of silver" (Hos 9:6). A shiftless worker brings desolation down upon himself: "I passed by the field of one who was lazy . . . the ground was covered with nettles" (Prov 24:30–31).

The Roman nettle, or Urtica pilulifera, *is one of several species of nettle that grow in the Holy Land.*

NEW COVENANT

AND HE DID THE SAME WITH THE CUP AFTER SUPPER, SAYING, "THIS CUP THAT IS POURED OUT FOR YOU IS THE NEW COVENANT IN MY BLOOD."–LUKE 22:20

When Jesus spoke of the new covenant at the Last Supper, he was reminding his followers that his life and imminent death were a fulfillment of God's promise in the book of Jeremiah: "I will make a new covenant with the house of Israel" (Jer 31:31). This agreement between God and his people differed from their previous COVENANT. Rather than putting his laws on tablets of stone, as he did through Moses with the ten commandments, God said he would "put my law within them, and . . . write it on their hearts" (Jer 31:33). In the Old Testament, the Israelites sacrificed oxen to God to produce "the blood of the covenant" (Ex 24:8). In the New Testament, Jesus offered his own blood as that of the new covenant, and the early Christians commemorated this act in their ritual called the Lord's supper. According to the letter to the Hebrews, Jesus, the "mediator," rendered the original pact obsolete through his sacrifice, "so that those who are called may receive the promised eternal inheritance, because a death has occurred that redeems them from the transgressions under the first covenant" (Heb 9:15).

Night

And God said, "Let there be lights in the dome of the sky to separate the day from the night . . . ."–Genesis 1:14

The Israelites considered the night to be divided into three "watches" from sunset to sunrise, though by New Testament times the Roman system of four watches was used. Night constituted the first half of each DAY, which extended from sunset to sunset. In the Bible, *night* is most often used to indicate time. Used figuratively, however, *night* is variously associated with death, sorrow, and the absence of God. By contrast, the new Jerusalem pictured in Revelation knows no night, since God, who is light, is eternally present everywhere (Rev 1:23–25). Night also affords an opportunity for dreams or visions inspired by the Lord (Dan 2:19; Mt 2:13–14) or for acts of divine deliverance.

As in biblical times, modern nomads must endure a life of constant wandering in search of water and grazing lands. Pictured above is a Bedouin camp in the mountains of Judea.

Nomad

By the waysides you have sat waiting for lovers, like a nomad in the wilderness. –Jeremiah 3:2

Wandering herders, or nomads, who lived in tents and moved according to the pasturing needs of their horses, asses, camels, sheep, or goats, were commonplace throughout the Near East in biblical times. The farmer Cain was doomed to become a "wanderer on the earth" (Gen 4:12) for murdering his brother, Abel. Cain's descendants led to Jabal, the forefather "of those who live in tents and have livestock" (Gen 4:20).

The ancestors of Israel—Abraham, Isaac, and Jacob—lived a seminomadic herding life, their wandering periodically interrupted by stays in agricultural villages and cities. After killing a cruel overseer, Moses fled Egypt and lived among the Midianites, who were nomadic descendants of Abraham. The Israelites wandered in the wilderness for 40 years until they entered the Promised Land, when their nomadic life ended with settlement in Canaan. The prophets would later hark back to that wilderness period, when the Israelites were utterly dependent on God, as a time of innocence. Isaiah uses a nomadic image to portray the prosperity of postexilic Jerusalem: "Enlarge the site of your tent, and let the curtains of your habitations be stretched out" (Isa 54:2). See also TENT.

North

Up, up! Flee from the land of the north, says the LORD . . . . –Zechariah 2:6

The Hebrew word for north means "left," because when the Israelites thought in terms of direction, they always imagined themselves facing east. Thus west, where the sun set, lay behind them, with south on the right and north on the left. The psalmist who sang, "The north and south—you created them" (Ps 89:12), was using those two directions to indicate the extreme limits of the world, all of which God created. Invaders of Israel, such as Assyria and Babylon, often came from the north; Jeremiah's references to the "evil from the north" (Jer 4:6) signified Babylon.

Nose

They shall cut off your nose and your ears, and your survivors shall fall by the sword.–Ezekiel 23:25

The word *nose* is mentioned only in the Old Testament, which relates its role in certain ancient Near Eastern customs. An adulteress in Assyria could have her nose cut off as punishment. Sometimes war captives were similarly mutilated or led into captivity by hooks pierced through their nostrils. Both women and men adorned themselves with nose jewelry, and the Ishmaelites were famous for their gold nose rings. The connection between the nose and the lungs—a word not in the Bible—was apparently not understood. Biblical people thought of the nose rather than the lungs as the organ of breathing. Symbolically, human nostrils are linked with the breath of life, and the Lord's nostrils sense the misdeeds of the wicked.

Number

The total number of people born to Jacob was seventy.
–Exodus 1:5

Methods for recording numbers existed as early as the seventh millennium BC. By 3000 BC, the Egyptians and Sumerians had developed more complex systems: the Egyptians used a decimal system based on 10, and the Sumerians used both a decimal and a duodecimal system based on 6 and 12. Remnants of the Sumerian method have survived until today. Time is divided into 12 hours comprised of 60 minutes; a year is broken into 12 months; and a foot is made up of 12 inches.

Beyond their numerical value, numbers also had symbolic meaning in antiquity. The number three had sacred connotations, as many ancient religions had triads of gods. Prayers were said three times a day (Ps 55:17), and the temple was divided into three sections (1 Kings 6:6).

The number four represented all of creation to Semitic peoples, as there were four cardinal directions. The river in the garden of Eden flowed into four branches, which watered the entire known world (Gen 2:10–14); the Israelites dispersed in exile would be reunited "from the four corners of the earth" (Isa 11:12).

Seven—the sum of four and three—indicated wholeness and perfection. Thus creation took place over six days, with the seventh day a day of rest (Gen 2:2). God's promises were described as the highest-quality silver that had been "purified seven times" (Ps 12:6). Multiples of seven were even more significant. When asked how often one person should forgive another, Jesus replied: "Not seven times, but . . . seventy-seven times" (Mt 18:22). Large numbers were sometimes used in the Bible to indicate comprehensiveness and were not always meant to be taken at face value.

Hebrew numbers are legible on potsherds dating from the seventh century BC, at left. Egyptian hieratic script also appears on these ancient fragments.

Numbers, Book of

Take a census of the whole congregation of Israelites . . . .
–Numbers 1:2

The fourth book in the Pentateuch, Numbers records a variety of historical, legal, and poetic traditions. In Hebrew the book of Numbers is called In the Wilderness, which is appropriate both because the phrase appears in the first verse and because the book opens with Israel in the Sinai wilderness. Numbers spans 40 years and ends with Israel on the east bank of the Jordan, poised to enter Canaan. The name of the book comes from two censuses that were taken—first of the generation that didn't trust God to lead them to Canaan (Num 1) and was therefore denied entry, and second of the generation that Joshua led into the land (Num 26).

The book of Numbers relates that Israelite spies returned from Canaan bearing grapes, as seen in this wood engraving.

Nurse

Then Naomi took the child and laid him in her bosom, and became his nurse.
–Ruth 4:16

In a typical Israelite household, mothers nursed and cared for their own children. But members of the upper class and royalty sometimes hired wet nurses and governesses for their children. Moses' mother was hired as his wet nurse (Ex 2:7–9) after Pharaoh's daughter discovered him on the river and decided to raise him as her son.

A nurse could be a relative, such as Naomi, who nursed her own grandson, or a hired servant, who often became an honored member of the family. CHILDREN were traditionally breast-fed until the age of two or three, and weaning was sometimes a cause for celebration. Genesis 21:8 relates that "Abraham made a great feast on the day that Isaac was weaned."

Because a nurse symbolized nurturing and responsibility, Moses compared himself with one when he accused God of abandoning the Israelites and leaving them in his care: "Did I give birth to them, that you should say to me, 'Carry them in your bosom, as a nurse carries a sucking child,' to the land that you promised on oath to their ancestors?" (Num 11:12).

OAK

. . . [JOSHUA] TOOK A LARGE STONE, AND SET IT UP THERE UNDER THE OAK IN THE SANCTUARY OF THE LORD. –JOSHUA 24:26

An acorn-bearing hardwood, the oak tree includes more than 300 species. The most common oaks in the Holy Land are a hillside evergreen about the size of a shrub and a larger and deciduous species that dominated the once-lush forest east of the Sea of Galilee. Oak timber was sturdy and valued in construction; as such the tree was often a symbol of strength. The oak was also considered sacred: Abraham set up an altar to the Lord in a place called the oaks of Mamre (Gen 13:18), and Saul and his sons were buried beneath an oak (1 Chr 10:12).

OATH

BE ASHAMED OF BREAKING AN OATH OR AGREEMENT . . . . –ECCLESIASTICUS 41:19

An oath is a solemn promise to carry out certain obligations or a statement assuring the absolute truth of one's remarks. Veracity was of paramount importance in biblical society. Though oaths generally were spoken, they were sometimes sealed by a gesture such as raising the hands to the heavens to underscore the importance of the promise.

Oath-taking itself was a kind of religious ritual, often enacted with holy objects in a sacred place and in the presence of a priest. God was usually invoked to guarantee an oath: "Whoever takes an oath in the land shall swear by the God of faithfulness" (Isa 65:16). Taking God's name in a false oath was a serious offense and amounted to "profaning the name of your God" (Lev 19:12).

Those "who stand by their oath even to their hurt" (Ps 15:4) were praised in the Old Testament, but those who "despised the oath and broke the covenant" (Ezek 17:18) were severely punished. In contrast, it was believed that God would never break the covenant that he made with David and his successors: "The LORD swore to David a sure oath from which he will not turn back" (Ps 132:11).

In the New Testament, Jesus railed against the scribes and Pharisees, who regarded some oaths as more binding than others (Mt 23:16–22). He set up a new standard based on simple, honest speech rather than on oaths (Mt 5:34, 37). See also VOW.

OBADIAH, BOOK OF

. . . EDOM . . . . I WILL SURELY MAKE YOU LEAST AMONG THE NATIONS . . . . –OBADIAH 1–2

Obadiah is the shortest book in the Old Testament. Other than his name, Obadiah, which means "servant of the Lord," nothing is known about the prophet who wrote it. But the message preserved in its 21 verses suggests that he lived in the years just after 587 BC, when Babylon vanquished Judah by capturing Jerusalem and exiling the survivors. The prophet condemned neighboring Edom for looting Jerusalem and gloating over its demise. Edom and all other nations that hurt Judah would face the WRATH of God, Obadiah promised: "As you have done, it shall be done to you" (Ob 15). Afterward, Obadiah said, the exiles would return home and dominate the entire region.

This ancient deity was worshiped by the Edomites, against whom Obadiah railed bitterly.

OBEDIENCE

NOW THAT YOU HAVE PURIFIED YOUR SOULS BY YOUR OBEDIENCE TO THE TRUTH . . . LOVE ONE ANOTHER . . . . –1 PETER 1:22

In the Old Testament the word *obedience* is translated from the Hebrew word meaning "to hear," and it implies listening to and submitting to the word of God. God's ancient covenant with the Israelites was founded on obedience. He assured his chosen people that "if you obey my voice and keep my covenant, you shall be my treasured possession out of all the peoples" (Ex 19:5). When the Israelites failed to hear God's words, they were exiled.

Jesus taught his followers to give obedience to God. Though he often struggled with spiritual temptations, Jesus was faithful in his own submission to God's will. Death on the cross was his ultimate act of obedience, whereby "he learned obedience through what he suffered; and having been made perfect, he became the source of eternal salvation for all who obey him" (Heb 5:8–9).

OBEISANCE

JOAB PROSTRATED HIMSELF WITH HIS FACE TO THE GROUND AND DID OBEISANCE, AND BLESSED THE KING . . . .
–2 SAMUEL 14:22

The act of kneeling and bowing one's face to the ground, obeisance signified respect and submission to a superior. The same Hebrew word is translated as "obeisance" when the homage is directed toward another person and as "worship" when it is directed toward God. Prostrating oneself before the king acknowledged one's inferior status. It was also performed in the hope of receiving the monarch's approval, as when Joab paid obeisance to David in the passage above and declared, "Today your servant knows that I have found favor in your sight" (2 Sam 14:22). Obeisance could acknowledge worthy deeds, such as when Judith beheaded Holofernes. Achior "threw himself at Judith's feet, and did obeisance to her" (Jdt 14:7).

When Moses came down from Mount Sinai and discovered the people worshiping a golden calf, he ordered the sons of Levi to slaughter them for their offense (Ex 32:27).

ODOR

. . . THE WHOLE CONGREGATION SHALL OFFER ONE YOUNG BULL FOR A BURNT OFFERING, A PLEASING ODOR TO THE LORD . . . .
–NUMBERS 15:24

In the Bible, the word *odor* usually appears in the often-used phrase "a pleasing odor to the LORD," referring to a burnt sacrifice that is acceptable to God. These sacrifices included animals, crops, or grain mixed with oil and aromatic gums such as FRANKINCENSE. But to be pleasing and acceptable to God, the sacrifice had to be offered in a spirit of obedience and worship. God declared that if Israel persisted in its disobedience, sacrifices would mean nothing. In such a case, God warned, "I will not smell your pleasing odors" (Lev 26:31).

New Testament writers used the concept as a metaphor. When Philippian Christians sent a gift to Paul while he was in prison, he thanked them for their "fragrant offering, a sacrifice acceptable and pleasing to God" (Phil 4:18). In a letter to Christians at Ephesus, Paul encouraged them to forgive and love one another "as Christ loved us and gave himself up for us, a fragrant offering and sacrifice to God" (Eph 5:2).

Incense was offered as a "pleasing odor to the Lord" in bronze stands, such as these from the 13th century BC.

OFFENSE

THOSE WITH GOOD SENSE ARE SLOW TO ANGER, AND IT IS THEIR GLORY TO OVERLOOK AN OFFENSE.
–PROVERBS 19:11

In the Bible, *offense* generally means a legal crime, a sin, or an action that provokes disgust. When Laban angrily reproached Jacob for fleeing his house with Leah and Rachel, Jacob answered Laban's accusations by asking, "What is my offense?" (Gen 31:36). When Jesus tried to preach to the people of his hometown in their synagogue, Matthew reported that they "took offense" (Mt 13:57) at his presumption. When Paul claimed that the "cross"—Jesus' sacrifice and death—constituted an "offense" (Gal 5:11), he was using the term in the sense of "scandal." This word aptly described the way many Jews and Gentiles characterized the Christian doctrine that God could allow his only Son to suffer and die.

Office

. . . whoever aspires to the office of bishop desires a noble task. –1 Timothy 3:1

In the Old Testament, several Hebrew words are translated as "office." The term is used to signify various positions held by people such as judges (Deut 17:9) or gatekeepers (1 Chr 9:22).

The New Testament mentions offices such as those of apostle, bishop, evangelist, prophet, priest, elder, and deacon. Some were established positions; others were less defined. The first letter to Timothy sets forth the various qualifications for the offices of bishop and deacon (1 Tim 3:2–13). In the early Christian church, offices were not just posts to be filled but also the means by which the faithful exercised the specific gifts they had received from God.

At right is a limestone carving of a royal scribe and officer of the Egyptian treasury during the 19th Dynasty.

Officer

The king shall appoint officers in all the provinces of his kingdom . . . . –Additions to Esther 2:3

In the Bible many Hebrew words have been translated as "officer." Generally the word refers to people who serve in the government, the temple, and the military. These officials performed many different functions, reflecting the complexity of ancient Near Eastern societies. The term denoted people of both modest and high status, ranging from field overseers in Egypt to powerful deputies, who ruled in the king's place as regents. Some important officers at royal courts were eunuchs, who were employed to guard the king's harem (Esth 2:14).

When Solomon created 12 districts in his kingdom, he placed an officer in charge of each, with responsibility for administrative functions and tax collection. In Persia a handful of men enjoyed immense power; only seven high officials had direct access to the king (Esth 1:14). Isaiah referred to "dignitaries" (Isa 9:15) who, along with ELDERS, wielded undue influence in public affairs. Jeremiah entrusted a prophecy to an official called the quartermaster, who accompanied the king of Judah on a journey to Babylon (Jer 51:59).

According to 1 Chronicles 26:30, 1,700 officers, referred to as "men of ability," were in charge of secular and religious affairs in the area of Israel west of the Jordan River. To administer the affairs of fewer than three tribes there were 2,700 officers (1 Chr 26:32).

Although certain officials acted in the name of the king and were subject to royal authority, there were occasions when corrupt officials were able to frustrate the will of the king. Ezra, for example, states that non-Jews bribed Persian provincial officials to prevent the rebuilding of the temple in Jerusalem, a project that had been personally authorized by the Persian ruler, Cyrus (Ezra 4:4–5).

Oil

"The olive tree answered them, 'Shall I stop producing my rich oil by which gods and mortals are honored . . . ?'" –Judges 9:9

From the olive, grown on trees that are often gnarled and hundreds of years old, comes an all-purpose oil. It takes an OLIVE TREE 15 to 20 years to begin producing a mature crop, but once it does, the tree can generate 10 to 20 gallons of oil each harvest. Throughout biblical times, people used olive oil as food, rubbed their bodies with it, burned it to produce light, and used it in religious rituals. Almost every time the Bible mentions oil, it is referring to olive oil.

Along with grain, dairy products, and wine, olive oil was one of the dietary staples in ancient Near Eastern homes (Sir 39:26). Olive oil was spread on bread, used in cooking, and mixed with flour to make bread (Ex 29:23). A widow on the brink of starvation told the prophet Elijah that she had only "a handful of meal in a jar, and a little oil in a jug" (1 Kings 17:12).

Olive oil was used as a religious offering (Lev 2:4), as a remedy for stomach distress, and as a balm to heal wounds. It was also used as

Oil poured into the hole at the top of this Roman pottery lamp from the first century AD *reached its 21 chambers by means of a thin chamber bordering the underside of the lamp.*

fuel for lamps in homes and in the temple. The sanctuary lamp in the tent of the meeting was lit with the "pure oil of beaten olives" (Lev 24:2). Soldiers often worked oil into leather shields to keep the hide from turning brittle. Oil was traded internationally throughout the Near East. Solomon used olive oil as a kind of currency: he sent 20,000 baths, or 120,000 gallons, of oil to king Hiram of Tyre as partial payment for cedar and cypress trees imported from Lebanon to build the temple (2 Chr 2:10).

ANOINTING a person with oil could have powerful religious significance. Some people chosen by God for special services were anointed. For example, Samuel took a horn filled with oil and anointed the boy David "in the presence of his brothers; and the spirit of the LORD came mightily upon David from that day forward" (1 Sam 16:13). Kings were anointed with olive oil (1 Sam 10:1), as were honored guests (Ps 23:5). The term *Messiah*—meaning "anointed one"—later came to refer to a descendant of David who would lead the people of Israel into an age of peace.

OINTMENT

"YOU DID NOT ANOINT MY HEAD WITH OIL, BUT SHE HAS ANOINTED MY FEET WITH OINTMENT."–LUKE 7:46

In the hot, dry climate of the Holy Land, men and women alike rubbed olive oil on their skin as a moisturizer. Perfume makers used oil as a base for fragrant ointments, boiling the oil and then adding a sometimes secret blend of root and bark powders, tree resins, and spices. Myrrh, frankincense, cinnamon, and aloe were among the many additives that could turn fine-grade olive oil into a jar of ointment worth a laborer's yearly salary. Costly ointments were often sealed in small ALABASTER jars (Mt 26:7). To preserve the delicate scent, the owner would not break the seal until he was was ready to use the ointment—perhaps to welcome an honored guest or treat the corpse of a loved one. It was such an ointment that a woman "who was a sinner" (Lk 7:37) used to anoint Jesus.

OLIVE TREE

HIS SHOOTS SHALL SPREAD OUT; HIS BEAUTY SHALL BE LIKE THE OLIVE TREE . . . .
–HOSEA 14:6

Since antiquity the olive tree—a small evergreen cultivated for the oil-bearing olives it produces—has been a ubiquitous presence in the Holy Land, thriving even on rocky hillsides. Though its most productive years are at age 40 to 50, an olive tree will produce olives for hundreds of years.

Olives and the OIL extracted from them (see box, pp. 256–257) were important cash crops in biblical times. Hundreds of thousands of gallons of oil flowed from the presses of Ekron, a seventh-century BC industrial city 22 miles west of Jerusalem. Excavators have found more than 100 olive-press installations: rectangular stone vats, circular pressing jars, boulders with holes drilled through them to act as weights, and the ashes of beams to which the boulders were secured.

Olive wood was used for fine cabinetwork; the two cherubim guarding the temple's inner sanctuary were made of olive wood (1 Kings 6:23). The olive tree symbolized fertility and peace. The dove released by Noah returned with an olive branch, the first sign of life after the flood (Gen 8:11).

ONE GOD

. . . FOR US THERE IS ONE GOD, THE FATHER, FROM WHOM ARE ALL THINGS . . . .–1 CORINTHIANS 8:6

Most of the nations around Israel worshiped a number of gods, but the Israelites had only one deity. In the early days, their special convenant with God did not stop them from believing that other deities existed or even from using parts of other religions' mythologies. But Israel's prophets increasingly insisted on the existence of only one God. The book of Isaiah proclaims on God's behalf: "I am the LORD, and there is no other; besides me there is no god" (Isa 45:5). By the time the Jews returned from the Babylonian exile, monotheism was the established practice.

A 14th-century icon portrays the dignity of Jesus, who was called the only Son of God.

ONLY SON

". . . NOW I KNOW THAT YOU FEAR GOD, SINCE YOU HAVE NOT WITHHELD YOUR SON, YOUR ONLY SON, FROM ME."–GENESIS 22:12

Abraham's willingness to obey God's command to sacrifice his "only son," Isaac, was indeed a show of faith, since it was considered crucial to have a son to carry on the family line. (Ishmael was discounted because he was Abraham's son by a concubine.) The New Testament describes Jesus as the only Son of God, making his death a unique sacrifice: "For God so loved the world that he gave his only Son, so that everyone who believes in him . . . may have eternal life" (Jn 3:16).

ONYX

"IT CANNOT BE VALUED IN THE GOLD OF OPHIR, IN PRECIOUS ONYX OR SAPPHIRE."–JOB 28:16

Onyx is a variety of quartz with microscopic crystals. Banded in white and black, brown, or red, and with a lustrous finish when polished, onyx has been prized since ancient times. Genesis 2:12 lists it among the precious resources of Eden. The high priest wore onyx on the shoulders of his ephod and on his BREASTPIECE. King David contributed "great quantities of onyx" (1 Chr 29:2) to the temple. The mineral, scarce and costly, was imported from as far away as India.

ORACLE

". . . THIS ORACLE CONCERNS THE PRINCE IN JERUSALEM AND ALL THE HOUSE OF ISRAEL IN IT." –EZEKIEL 12:10

In the Bible, oracles are messages from God. Although they sometimes occurred in response to a person's inquiry, God did not always choose to communicate directly: "As I live, says the Lord GOD, I will not be consulted by you" (Ezek 20:3). More frequently God communicated through a PROPHET. This human intermediary could receive an oracle in various ways, such as through visions, voices, or dreams. The person then relayed the message to its intended recipient, whether an individual or group. In

Olive Pressing

In biblical times, harvesting olives began in September, with green table olives, and continued through November, when the fully mature black olives were picked. To minimize crop damage from transport, olive presses—usually large stone basins—were often kept near the orchards. Two or more pressings produced oil of differing quality. The first pressing produced the finest grade, used in lamps and cosmetics and for ritual anointing. The second resulted in a lower-grade oil, used for cooking.

Found in Capernaum, this basalt olive press from the first century AD is also the type shown in the middle illustration at right. In earlier times, workers stomped on the olives or rolled stones over them by hand.

1. Farmers shake ripe olives from the tree by pulling on the branches or tapping them with a stick. As the men collect the fallen olives, they pick them up carefully to avoid bruising the fruit and releasing the oil. More than half the pulp of an olive is oil, which is extracted in at least two pressings.

2. After the olives are poured into the basin, the first pressing takes place. With this type of press, a man or donkey pushes the beam that rotates the millstone, which crushes the olives. Wedges and washers keep the stone from also crushing the olive pits, which can contaminate the oil with sediment. Workers scoop the crushed olives into loosely woven baskets and let the oil drain into storage vats.

3. The second pressing is for lower-grade oil. A stack of baskets filled with the crushed pulp is placed under a beam, which is anchored into the wall. A worker adjusts stone weights on the beam to flatten the baskets, forcing the last of the oil into a stone vat below. Heavier weights may then be added to produce an oil of even lower quality.

one case, God communicated through a foreign prophet. When Balaam was summoned by King Balak of Moab to curse the Israelite invaders, he instead uttered God's blessing on them (Num 23:7–12). Oracles could be long pronouncements, such as those recounted against foreign nations in the books of Isaiah and Jeremiah. In Isaiah the oracles and their subjects are formally announced, as in "The oracle concerning Babylon" (Isa 13:1). The author of the book of Malachi begins by calling his work "an oracle" (Mal 1:1).

ORCHARD

I WENT DOWN TO THE NUT ORCHARD, TO LOOK AT THE BLOSSOMS OF THE VALLEY, TO SEE WHETHER THE VINES HAD BUDDED . . . .
–SONG OF SOLOMON 6:11

In the Holy Land, orchards consisted of such nut or fruit trees as ALMOND, pomegranate, and olive. Productive orchards were a sign of God's bounty toward his chosen people in Canaan, where they found "all sorts of goods, hewn cisterns, vineyards, olive orchards, and fruit trees in abundance" (Neh 9:25). When the Israelites began clamoring for an earthly king, Samuel relayed God's warning of the losses they would suffer under a monarch. Among them were their orchards: "He will take the best of your fields and vineyards and olive orchards and give them to his courtiers" (1 Sam 8:14).

Almond trees, prized for their delicious nuts and delicate blossoms, grow in orchards in Galilee.

ORDAIN

YOU . . . SHALL ANOINT THEM AND ORDAIN THEM AND CONSECRATE THEM, SO THAT THEY MAY SERVE ME AS PRIESTS.
–EXODUS 28:41

The word *ordain* can refer to appointing someone to the priesthood. The Hebrew word for ordination means to "fill the hands," perhaps because an Israelite priest's hands were filled with offerings for the altar. Aaron and his sons—Nadab, Abihu, Eleazar, and Ithamar—were ordained as priests during an elaborate seven-day ceremony, in which they were bathed, clothed in special garments, and anointed with oil. The Levites were also named as priests. When Moses descended the mountain to find the Israelites worshiping a golden calf, he asked, "Who is on the Lord's side?" (Ex 32:26). Only those from the tribe of Levi responded. Because of their loyalty, Moses announced, "Today you have ordained yourselves for the service of the LORD" (Ex 32:29).

The 12 apostles were not formally ordained, but Jesus "gave them power and authority over all demons and to cure diseases" (Lk 9:1). The early Christians assigned special roles in the church by the LAYING ON OF HANDS; the author of the first letter to Timothy may have been alluding to this practice when he wrote: "Do not ordain anyone hastily" (1 Tim 5:22).

Ordain can also mean "establish" or "determine." Biblical writers made it clear that God had the authority to ordain all things. He was said, for example, to have "ordained" how King Ahaziah would meet his death (2 Chr 22:7). When the Israelites were held in captivity by the Babylonians, the author of Lamentations counseled the exiles to accept their punishment, reasoning: "Who can command and have it done, if the Lord has not ordained it?" (Lam 3:37).

ORDINANCE

THESE THINGS SHALL BE A STATUTE AND ORDINANCE FOR YOU THROUGHOUT YOUR GENERATIONS WHEREVER YOU LIVE.
–NUMBERS 35:29

In the Bible, an ordinance is a LAW, or decree, from God or from a human authority, such as a king. The word usually refers to a part of the body of law that the Israelites lived by, called the Mosaic code, on which hinged the nation's covenant with God. When speaking of the Passover, for example, Moses said: "You shall observe this rite as a perpetual ordinance for you and your children" (Ex 12:24). However, *ordinance* might also be used more generally to mean the entire code: "They were a nation that practiced righteousness and did not forsake the ordinance of their God" (Isa 58:2).

Kings sometimes added to Israel's basic laws. After relating a story in which David decided how the spoils of war should be divided, the author of 1 Samuel declared: "From that day forward he made it a statute and an ordinance for Israel; it continues to the present day" (1 Sam 30:25). Here *ordinance* is paired with *statute,* but the words are often synonymous.

Orphan

. . . do not oppress the widow, the orphan, the alien, or the poor . . . .
–Zechariah 7:10

A person who was fatherless was considered to be an orphan in biblical times. Although Mosaic law dealt with the rights of orphans, these children often had little recourse without a male parent to provide for them. Orphans were at risk of losing their property and livestock and were sometimes driven out of their homes and forced to beg for food. The psalmist even speaks of orphans being murdered (Ps 94:6). God charged Israel's rulers with protecting orphans and others who were needy, but some of the rulers, according to Isaiah, passed oppressive laws that victimized orphans instead (Isa 10:2).

Ostrich

. . . my people has become cruel, like the ostriches in the wilderness.
–Lamentations 4:3

Now extinct in the Near East, the ostrich once roamed the plains and deserts of Mesopotamia and Arabia, its mournful cry perfectly suited to its desolate home. An ostrich can grow to 8½ feet and run 40 miles an hour, but with its rudimentary wings, it cannot fly. The hunting of ostriches was a common scene in Assyrian art. The birds were eaten in ancient times, though not by the Israelites, who considered them unclean (Lev 11:16). The Old Testament describes the ostrich as stupid and as neglectful of its offspring: "For it leaves its eggs to the earth . . . forgetting that a foot may crush them . . . . It deals cruelly with its young, as if they were not its own" (Job 39:14–16).

Ovens were used not only for cooking food but also for firing pottery. A small potter's oven from the Roman period, above, was excavated at Tel Qasile in the Holy Land.

Oven

For they are kindled like an oven, their heart burns within them . . . .
–Hosea 7:6

Ovens used for baking bread varied somewhat. A common type was a simple cylinder of burnt clay, two or three feet in diameter, with a hole in the tapered top. The oven was fired with grass, animal dung, shrubs, wood, or charcoal. Potsherds were sometimes plastered onto the clay to help retain the heat. Depending on the kind of oven, the loaves of bread were placed in a compartment above the fire or directly against the inner walls of the oven. When a pot was put on top of it, an oven served as a stove for boiling or frying. The oven was usually in the courtyard of the house. See also box for BAKING.

Overseer

I will appoint Peace as your overseer and Righteousness as your taskmaster.
–Isaiah 60:17

An overseer supervised a particular enterprise. The type of operation involved could vary greatly. Potiphar, an Egyptian official, chose Joseph to manage his entire household, and "he made him overseer of his house and put him in charge of all that he had" (Gen 39:4). Pharaoh appointed overseers to supervise agricultural output (Gen 41:34). In building the temple, Solomon relied on forced labor controlled by overseers who would "make the people work" (2 Chr 2:18). Paul told the early church leaders that they were the ones in charge: "Keep watch over yourselves and over all the flock, of which the Holy Spirit has made you overseers" (Acts 20:28). Here the term may mean the equivalent of BISHOP.

Its large size ideal for a bottle, this ostrich egg has a bronze neck and handle.

Owl

I am like an owl of the wilderness, like a little owl of the waste places.
—Psalm 102:6

Several species of owls exist in the Holy Land. Those mentioned in the Bible include the screech owl and the little owl, but matching the original Hebrew words with particular species is problematic. Owls were considered unclean because they are predatory (Lev 11:17–18). Primarily nocturnal hunters, the birds use their sharp talons and beaks to catch small animals and insects. By day most owls sleep in out-of-the-way places, such as a tree hollow, an empty cave or building, or an abandoned nest.

The owl's predilection for secluded spots made it a symbol of abandonment, used to predict the destruction of foreign nations. The book of Isaiah says that Edom will one day be called No Kingdom There (Isa 34:12). Describing such a forsaken place, the prophet evokes the image of owls living among the ruins: "There shall the owl nest and lay and hatch and brood in its shadow" (Isa 34:15).

Ownership

. . . no one claimed private ownership of any possessions, but everything they owned was held in common.
—Acts of the Apostles 4:32

The concept of legally possessing property, especially land, was important in both Old and New Testament times. An early biblical example of land purchase occurs in Genesis 23, when Abraham buys a cave and the surrounding field from Ephron the Hittite for a burial place; although Ephron makes at least a perfunctory offer to give him the land, Abraham insists on paying 400 shekels to ensure that Ephron will fully relinquish ownership.

Israelite law concerning land ownership was based on the idea that all land belonged to God. The law's main purpose was to protect the allotments of the tribes that had settled Canaan. Ancestral land was not supposed to be sold outside of a family or clan; if this happened, however, the shift of ownership was to last only until the next year of JUBILEE, which occurred every 50 years, when each person was to return to his ancestral property (Lev 25:13). In Roman times such strictures no longer applied, although land was subject to taxation.

Besides land, significant property included houses, cattle, and slaves. Biblical law addressed the treatment of slaves, ownership disputes, and other related issues. Acts of the Apostles recounts how some Christians sold their property and helped to support other believers.

Ox

Where there are no oxen, there is no grain; abundant crops come by the strength of the ox.—Proverbs 14:4

Oxen are mature bovine animals or, more specifically, castrated bulls used for work. In the Bible, the word translated as "ox" can generally mean any type of large cattle, regardless of age or gender.

Oxen were essential as draft animals in the Holy Land. They drew plows, often in pairs, though the Israelites were forbidden to "plow with an ox and a donkey yoked together" (Deut 22:10). Oxen dragged heavy threshing sleds at harvest time and pulled wagons containing sacrificial offerings. The animals were highly valued: they were rested on the sabbath, were spared from being muzzled while "treading out the grain" (Deut 25:4), and were sacrificed to God as "offerings of well-being" (Ex 24:5). Oxen figured among the consequences for breaking the covenant: "Your ox shall be butchered before your eyes" (Deut 28:31). They could also be dangerous, as witnessed by the detailed laws that dealt with an ox goring a person (Ex 21:28–36).

Domesticated cattle were descended from wild species, whose strength and vitality were celebrated. The powerful God who rescued the Israelites from Egypt was compared with "the horns of a wild ox" (Num 23:22). The molten sea, the enormous basin in the temple courtyard, sat atop 12 oxen (2 Chron 4:2–4). In the book of Revelation, God's throne was said to be surrounded by four creatures, one of which was like the mighty ox (Rev 4:7).

Oxen were used in many countries of the Near East. This ox is from a limestone stele found in Tel el-Amarna, the capital city built by Pharaoh Akhenaten in the 14th century BC.

P Q

The Hebrew words on this fragment of a PHYLACTERY *parchment, discovered at Qumran, were copied from Scripture in the first century* AD. *Such parchments were folded to fit inside the tiny compartments of phylactery boxes.*

PALACE

SOLOMON DECIDED TO BUILD . . . A ROYAL PALACE FOR HIMSELF.
–2 CHRONICLES 2:1

Although the Israelites must have been familiar with palaces from their sojourn in Egypt, it was not until David became king that they began to build them. Until that time, their society was roughly egalitarian, with no striking contrasts between the houses of rich and poor. King Saul's dwelling at Gibeah, built about the end of the 11th century BC, was no more than a fortress of rough stone, made for defense rather than splendor. But King David's dwelling boasted costly beams of cedar imported from Lebanon, and Solomon spent 13 years building a much more elaborate palace—a complex that included the Hall of the Throne, the Hall of Justice, and separate residences for him and one of his wives, who was a pharaoh's daughter. Centuries later, King Herod built himself several magnificent palaces; the one in Jerusalem had beautiful gardens and a banquet hall that could accommodate hundreds of guests.

More than a luxurious dwelling for royalty, a palace was designed to impress the king's subjects and foreign potentates (see reconstruction, pp. 262–263). It was also a governmental and diplomatic center where the king met with his advisers, entertained supporters and visiting dignitaries in the great banquet hall, and dispensed justice. In the sixth century BC, the prophet Jeremiah was held in the Jerusalem palace's jail, called the court of the guard, where prisoners awaiting trial were kept (Jer 32:2).

PALM TREE

YOU ARE STATELY AS A PALM TREE, AND YOUR BREASTS ARE LIKE ITS CLUSTERS.
–SONG OF SOLOMON 7:7

The date palm, a hardy tree with a deep root system well suited to an arid environment, was cultivated in Mesopotamia at least 6,000 years ago. As palms live and produce fruit for a great many years, the tree became a symbol of prosperity: "The righteous flourish like the palm tree" (Ps 92:12). Its gracefulness also made it a symbol of beauty, such as in Song of Solomon. The elegant palm was a common decorative motif in the the ancient Near East's art and architecture, including Solomon's temple (1 Kings 6:29).

Typically, palm trees grew in oases. During their sojourn in the wilderness, the Israelites found a place to camp that had 70 of the trees (Ex 15:27). The date palm provided not only shade but also food for desert travelers; the dates could be eaten fresh or dried or made into cakes, and they were easy to transport. The rest of the tree was used in various ways: the sap for a fermented drink, the trunk for timber, the large leaves for roofing houses and constructing shelters for the FESTIVAL OF BOOTHS, and the smaller leaves for weaving into baskets or mats. In an expression of joy, crowds in Jerusalem held palm branches as they greeted Jesus (Jn 12:13).

These fruit-laden palm trees grow in an orchard in Israel. Among the earliest cultivated trees, the date palm takes 10 to 15 years to mature and lives up to 200 years.

The Palace in Samaria

*Now the rest of the acts of Ahab . . . and the ivory house that he built . . .
are they not written in the Book of the Annals of the Kings of Israel?—1 Kings 22:39*

For more than a century, Samaria, capital of the northern kingdom of Israel, was renowned for the opulence of its royal buildings. Omri, who became king in 876 BC, founded the city on a hill near Shechem. His successor, Ahab, completed most of the building. Old Testament texts mention Samaria's houses of ivory, and archaeological findings indicate that the palace furniture was decorated with carved ivories. The walls, paneled in cedar, may also have had ivory overlays. Phoenician and Syrian builders and artisans created many of the major building projects in the eastern Mediterranean region, including Samaria. Their techniques and designs show influences from Egypt and the Aegean area, especially in the use of such motifs as winged figures, twined lotus and papyrus blossoms, and stylized palms. In the palace room depicted here, the seated king receives a party of diplomats. The visitors honor the king by bowing and raising their arms. They also present tribute, which the scribe records: rare ebony wood, golden vessels, and gemstones.

PAPYRUS

"CAN PAPYRUS GROW WHERE THERE IS NO MARSH? CAN REEDS FLOURISH WHERE THERE IS NO WATER?"
–JOB 8:11

Papyrus refers not only to the aquatic plant that grows in marshy areas in the Near East, particularly along the Nile, but to the sheets of paper made from the plant and the manuscripts written on it. The Roman scholar Pliny the Elder declared: "Civilization—or at the very least human history—depends on the use of papyrus." Papyrus was used to make ropes, sandals, clothes, rugs, and medicine. Sails were made out of papyrus, as were seaworthy baskets and skiffs. The infant Moses was hidden in a papyrus basket on the banks of the Nile (Ex 2:3), and according to the book of Isaiah, ambassadors sailed the Nile "in vessels of papyrus"(Isa 18:2).

Paper made by pressing together strips of papyrus pith was invented in Egypt; throughout antiquity the Egyptians monopolized its commercial production. Books were written on papyrus rolls made from sheets of papyrus fastened end to end into a long strip, or scroll. A 30-foot-long roll was needed for a document such as the Gospel of Luke. See also BOOK.

PARABLE

JESUS TOLD THE CROWDS ALL THESE THINGS IN PARABLES; WITHOUT A PARABLE HE TOLD THEM NOTHING.–MATTHEW 13:34

Metaphorical stories that illustrate a point or teach a lesson, parables were central to Jesus' teaching. More than clever stories, they were proclamations of the gospel and vehicles to help his listeners understand the kingdom of God. However, the meaning of Jesus' parables was not always obvious. Indeed, he may occasionally have used parables to conceal his message from his opponents so that its true meaning was disclosed only to his disciples: "To you it has been given to know the secrets of the kingdom of God; but to others I speak in parables, so that 'looking they may not perceive, and listening they may not understand'" (Lk 8:10).

As seen in a stained-glass window, fishermen sort their catch in the parable of the dragnet (Mt 13:47–50).

Each of the more than 40 parables recorded in the New Testament has more than one level of meaning. First there is the story: drawn from everyday life, it is often entertaining and designed to engage the listener. Then there is the lesson. Sometimes it is evident from the story itself; at other times it is meant to compel the listener to think more deeply. Jesus often achieved this by concluding his lessons with a question. After telling Simon the parable of a creditor and his debtors, for example, Jesus asked, "Now which of them will love him more?" (Lk 7:42).

Some of Jesus' parables are related to passages in the Old Testament, Scriptures that Jesus drew from in his teaching. For example, the parable of the wicked tenants (Mt 21:33–44; Mk 12:1–11; Lk 20:9–18) is based on the song of the vineyard from Isaiah 5:1–7. The story is highly allegorical: the landowner is God; the vineyard is Israel; the tenants are the Israelites; the slaves are the prophets; and the son is Jesus. Jesus knew the power of parables to open the minds of his listeners, and centuries later his teachings are still being spread by way of these stories.

PARADISE

". . . THE FURNACE OF HELL SHALL BE DISCLOSED, AND OPPOSITE IT THE PARADISE OF DELIGHT."
–2 ESDRAS 7:36

The word *paradise* means a wooded park like the garden of Eden. It is a name for the place where the righteous go when they die. A garden was a compelling image, but there was some disagreement over whether paradise was a final resting spot or simply a way station before RESURRECTION. Its location was thought to be either concealed on earth or, according to Paul, in "the third heaven" (2 Cor 12:2). In Revelation, Christ vows to give "permission to eat from the tree of life that is in the paradise of God" (Rev 2:7) to those who are faithful.

The apocryphal book 2 Esdras describes the events leading up to the last judgment and contrasts paradise with hell.

Paralytic

When Jesus saw their faith, he said to the paralytic, "Take heart, son; your sins are forgiven."—Matthew 9:2

On several occasions the Gospels describe Jesus healing individuals who were paralyzed. The precise medical conditions, which may have been paraplegia, stroke, or palsy, are not readily identifiable in modern terms. In some cases, evidently, the victims had suffered from these afflictions for years. In the most notable incidents (Mt 9:2–8; Mk 2:3–12; Lk 5:18–26), Jesus' ability to free a person from paralysis is considered a tangible demonstration of his authority to forgive sins.

Parched Grain

You shall eat no bread or parched grain . . . until you have brought the offering of your God . . . .
—Leviticus 23:14

In biblical times, parched grain, which had been roasted over a fire for long-term storage, was often eaten by soldiers, refugees, and farm workers. In the book of Ruth, when Boaz invited Ruth to share a midday meal with the reapers, "he heaped up for her some parched grain" (Ruth 2:14). Among the peace offerings that Abigail loaded onto donkeys to bear to David were "five measures of parched grain" (1 Sam 25:18). In the passage cited from Leviticus, the Israelites were warned that parched grain could not be eaten until the second day of Passover, after a grain offering had been presented to the Lord.

Partridge

". . . the king of Israel has come out to seek a single flea, like one who hunts a partridge in the mountains."
—1 Samuel 26:20

A medium-size game bird, the partridge—particularly the species that inhabited the rocky regions of the Holy Land—was widely hunted in biblical times. When chased, the partridge traveled swiftly upon sturdy legs, preferring to run rather than fly, and cackled like a clucking hen. In Hebrew the word *partridge* means "the caller." Hunters had to be relentless in their quest for a partridge; thus Saul's unyielding pursuit of David in 1 Samuel was likened to a partridge hunt. Jeremiah compared those "who amass wealth unjustly" with "the partridge hatching what it did not lay" (Jer 17:11), accusing the partridge of usurping other birds' eggs.

Passion

Do not fall into the grip of passion, or you may be torn apart as by a bull.
—Ecclesiasticus 6:2

In the Bible, *passion*, or intense emotion, often refers to sexual longing. Holofernes' "passion" (Jdt 12:16) for Judith leads to his downfall; while he is sleeping, Judith cuts off his head (Jdt 13:2–8). Homosexual relations are described as "degrading passions" (Rom 1:26), and the New Testament warns against becoming "slaves to various passions and pleasures" (Titus 3:3). Christians must deny earthly temptations, for "those who belong to Christ Jesus have crucified the flesh with its passions and desires" (Gal 5:24). The King James Bible refers to the events surrounding the death of Christ as Christ's Passion. Newer translations use the phrase "his suffering" (Acts 1:3).

Passover

"'. . . It is the passover sacrifice to the LORD, for he passed over the houses of the Israelites in Egypt, when he struck down the Egyptians . . . .'"
—Exodus 12:27

Passover is one of the most important festivals of the year. Originally this ancient spring FESTIVAL was celebrated as two distinct festivals: Passover, which was the ritual sacrifice of an animal to ward off evil from the home, and the Festival of Unleavened Bread, which celebrated the barley harvest—the first harvest of the year. In the

Common in the Near East, the gray rock partridge would conceal itself among the rocks. These carved partridges decorated an eighth-century AD Muslim palace.

Bible these two festivals are brought together and celebrated concurrently to commemorate the Israelites' dramatic release from Egyptian slavery, which is related in the book of Exodus.

The Hebrew word for Passover, *pesach*, is derived from the verb

This 19th-century wood engraving by Gustave Doré reveals the dark side of Passover, in which the firstborn of the Egyptians were slain by the Lord.

that means "to pass over" or "to spare." In order to force the Egyptians to release the Israelites, God promised that he would pass through Egypt, killing firstborn humans and livestock. The Israelites were instructed to sacrifice a lamb or kid and mark the lintels and doorposts of their houses with the blood (Ex 12:6–7) so that God could identify and spare them. Then they were to roast the sacrificial animal whole and eat it with unleavened bread and bitter herbs. All future generations of Israelites were to celebrate the Passover meal. Moses told the elders, "You shall observe this rite as a perpetual ordinance" (Ex 12:24).

Passover, celebrated on the 14th day of the month of Nisan (March–April), became Israel's freedom festival, drawing thousands of pilgrims to the temple. All priests were pressed into service to help sacrifice each family's Passover lamb. The animal was killed and its blood was caught in a bowl. The priest then splashed this symbol of life on the altar. Levites skinned the lamb, wrapped the carcass in the skin, and returned it ready to roast for the family meal after Passover began at sundown.

Passover was an immensely popular festival in New Testament times, when Jews felt enslaved by their Roman occupiers. On what was later called Palm Sunday, when Jesus rode into Jerusalem, he was likely greeted by pilgrims who had arrived early to purify themselves for the Passover SACRIFICE (Jn 11:55). According to the synoptic Gospels, Jesus celebrated Passover with his disciples Thursday evening, at what became known as the Last Supper. On Friday during Passover, Jesus was crucified by the Roman governor Pilate in Jerusalem.

Christians memorialized the Last Supper and Jesus' death through the rite of communion, by eating bread and drinking wine that represented his body and blood (Mt 26:26–28; Mk 14:22–24; Lk 22:19–20). The resurrection that followed on the Sunday after the crucifixion inspired an annual Easter observance that eventually displaced Passover in what became a predominantly Gentile church.

PATH

KEEP STRAIGHT THE PATH
OF YOUR FEET, AND ALL YOUR
WAYS WILL BE SURE.
–PROVERBS 4:26

A path was a way for walking or riding. In the Bible, two different paths often symbolized different choices in life. The evil—those who disobeyed God—are depicted as walking a dark and crooked path that leads to death. In contrast, the path of the righteous is straight and "like the light of dawn, which shines brighter and brighter until full day" (Prov 4:18). The reward for choosing this path is eternal life with God, of which the psalmist sang, "In your presence there is fullness of joy; in your right hand are pleasures forevermore" (Ps 16:11).

Two travelers on a donkey cross over a winding path on a Judean hillside.

PATIENCE

. . . MAY YOU BE PREPARED TO ENDURE EVERYTHING WITH PATIENCE . . . .–COLOSSIANS 1:11

In the Bible, patience is not simply passive accommodation but also restraint in the face of opposition. Trusting in God's mercy, believers were to "wait patiently for him" (Ps 37:7) to act. God himself repeatedly demonstrated patience with his rebellious people, delaying his wrath to give them the opportunity to repent. God's patience is thus an aspect of his mercy; he is described as "slow to anger" (Ex 34:6), a characteristic echoed in a prayer of Ezra when the prophet declared, "Many years you were patient with them" (Neh 9:30).

According to the apocryphal book Prayer of Manasseh, even though King Manasseh was so evil that his conduct eventually led to the destruction of Judah, when he prayed for FORGIVENESS, God restored his kingdom. The king praised God as one of "great compassion, long-suffering, and very merciful" (Pr Man 7). In the New Testament, Christians were told to meet their tribulations with patience, following the examples set by the prophets, Job, and especially Jesus. They were also urged to "be patient . . . until the coming of the Lord" (Jas 5:7).

PATRIARCHS

. . . THOSE WHO DIE FOR THE SAKE OF GOD LIVE TO GOD, AS DO ABRAHAM AND ISAAC AND JACOB AND ALL THE PATRIARCHS.
–4 MACCABEES 16:25

Patriarch is a combination of the Greek words meaning "father" and "rule." It refers to the male head of a family or CLAN. In the Bible *patriarchs* refer specifically to the founding fathers of the nation of Israel—Abraham, Isaac, and Jacob. It was Jacob's 12 sons who headed the 12 tribes of Israel. The stories of the patriarchs and the matriarchs (Sarah, Rebekah, Leah, Rachel, Bilhah, and Zilpah) are found in Genesis, where they are portrayed as seminomadic herders. Scholars disagree as to when the ancestors of Israel lived or if they were historical figures, though their way of life generally reflects Near Eastern life in the second millennium BC.

The patriarchs were considered to be the first of the nation's ancestors to receive the divine promise. God established a covenant with Abraham and promised him many descendants: "Look toward heaven and count the stars. . . . So shall your descendants be" (Gen 15:5). Abraham's offspring would inherit land and a special blessing from God: "I will make of you a great nation, and I will bless you, and make your name great" (Gen 12:2). The ultimate test of Abraham's faithfulness came when God commanded him to sacrifice his son Isaac. Abraham proceeded, but Isaac was spared at the last moment by an angel (Gen 22: 11–12). God continued his promises through Isaac and his son Jacob, to whom he said: "Be fruitful and multiply; a nation and a company of nations shall come from you. . . . The land that I gave to Abraham and Isaac I will give to you, and I will give the land to your offspring after you" (Gen 35:11–12).

PAVILION

IT WILL SERVE AS A PAVILION, A SHADE BY DAY FROM THE HEAT, AND A REFUGE AND A SHELTER FROM THE STORM AND RAIN.
–ISAIAH 4:6

"Pavilion" is one of the translations of the Hebrew word *sukkah*. This word can mean anything from a humble shelter of branches to a marketplace BOOTH to a large and costly tent fit for a king on a military campaign (2 Macc 13:15). In Job 36:29 *pavilion* is used to describe God's heavenly home among the clouds, from which he thunders; the same Hebrew word is used in Psalm 18:11, where it is translated as "canopy."

PEACE

"AGREE WITH GOD, AND BE AT PEACE; IN THIS WAY GOOD WILL COME TO YOU."–JOB 22:21

In biblical times, peace—that which is opposite from WAR—was a familiar concept, though peace was far less common than war. Usually understood as the absence of strife, *peace* has a much

The phrase "Peace on Israel" is inscribed beneath a menorah in the mosaic floor of a fifth-century AD synagogue.

broader and richer meaning in the Bible. The Hebrew word *shalom* connotes completeness, wholeness, and well-being, religiously attained through a connection with God. True peace is inseparable from righteousness; both are divine attributes. Psalm 85:10 declares that "righteousness and peace will kiss each other," and Isaiah boldly states: "The effect of righteousness will be peace" (Isa 32:17). Similarly, there was a link between peace and justice: "The way of peace they do not know, and there is no justice in their paths" (Isa 59:8). Peace is a gift to the faithful from God, who promised to make "a covenant of peace" (Ezek 34:25). Peace also signifies prosperity or security from danger. Psalm 4:8 declares, "I will both lie down and sleep in peace; for you alone, O LORD, make me lie down in safety" (Ps 4:8).

The New Testament exhorts all believers to work together for peace among nations and also advances the concept of an inner, personal peace. The apostle Paul wrote that "the peace of God, which surpasses all understanding, will guard your hearts and your minds in Christ Jesus" (Phil 4:7). "Peace!" was also a common salutation in both the Old and New Testaments, expressing the speaker's wish that a richness of blessings would descend on the one thus greeted. According to the Gospel of John, Jesus declared, "Peace I leave with you; my peace I give to you" (Jn 14:27).

PEG

SO HE WENT INTO HER TENT; AND THERE WAS SISERA LYING DEAD, WITH THE TENT PEG IN HIS TEMPLE. –*JUDGES 4:22*

Wooden pegs were an indispensable article of daily life in biblical times. They fastened TENT ropes in place, were driven into house walls, and served to hang up clothes and other belongings. They also held together the wooden framing of the tabernacle (Ex 26:17), and they could even be used as weapons, as when Jael used a tent peg to kill the enemy general Sisera (Judg 4:21). The Hebrew word for peg is also translated as "pin,"a heavy wooden pin used by weavers to secure threads to a loom. Delilah used such a pin in one of her attempts to deprive Samson of his strength (Judg 16:13–14).

Flames from the Holy Spirit, depicted as a dove, descend upon the disciples as they gather for Pentecost.

PEN

I HAVE MUCH TO WRITE TO YOU, BUT I WOULD RATHER NOT WRITE WITH PEN AND INK . . . . –*3 JOHN 13*

In biblical times, WRITING was recorded on rock, clay tablets, pottery, leather, metals, and papyrus. The "iron pen" mentioned in Jeremiah (Jer 17:1) was probably a hard-pointed instrument that was used for inscribing metals or other hard surfaces. Fine-pointed pens were used to write on parchment, made from animal skins. In ancient Egypt, pens, ranging from 15 to 40 centimeters long, were cut from rushes and used to write with ink on potsherds or papyrus. In New Testament times, reeds were cut and dried, sharpened to a point, split like a quill pen, and manipulated like a brush. These pens were used to write on papyrus with ink, the "pen and ink" to which the author of 3 John refers.

PENTECOST

AT OUR FESTIVAL OF PENTECOST, WHICH IS THE SACRED FESTIVAL OF WEEKS, A GOOD DINNER WAS PREPARED FOR ME . . . . –*TOBIT 2:1*

The ancient Jewish festival of Pentecost derives its name from the Greek for 50, because it was celebrated 50 days after the religious offering of the barley harvest on the second day of Passover. Since it took place seven weeks, or a week of weeks (plus one day), after the barley offering, it came to be known as the Festival of Weeks.

Pentecost (or Festival of Weeks in the Old Testament) was a day of rejoicing that originally celebrated the WHEAT harvest. It was one of three annual festivals in ancient Israel when every able-bodied male was required to appear at the central sanctuary. There two loaves of bread made from the harvested grain were among the offerings presented to the Lord (Lev 3:17–19).

For the first Christians, Pentecost took on a new significance. According to Acts of the Apostles, when the disciples gathered for Pentecost 50 days after Jesus' death, "suddenly from heaven there came a sound like the rush of a violent wind" (Acts 2:2), and they began to speak in other tongues. Christians believe that this event signified the descent of the Holy Spirit upon the believers.

People of the Land

But neither he nor his servants nor the people of the land listened to the words of the LORD . . . .
–Jeremiah 37:2

In the Bible, the Hebrew term *'am ha'arez* means literally "people of the land" and refers to enfranchised male citizens of a certain area. Though who these people actually were has been much debated, the most likely interpretation is that the term originally designated a specific class of people who were distinguished by their economic, social, military, and political power and were often critical to the functioning of the state. These individuals were held in contrast to the the POOR, or peasants, but by the time of the exile, the phrase "people of the land" was sometimes used to refer to the poor or lower segments of the population (2 Kings 24:14).

Although "people of the land" most commonly refers to the Israelites, the phrase is also used to refer to Canaanites (Num 14:9), Egyptians (Gen 42:6), and Hittites (Gen 23:12). In this sense it means "the population of the land." Used in the plural, the phrase "peoples of the land" describes non-Israelites who had not been exiled but rather remained in the Holy Land (Ezra 10:11).

Perdition

. . . and, lo, almost all go to perdition, and a multitude of them will come to doom.
–2 Esdras 10:10

The word *perdition*, meaning destruction, refers to a state of utter ruin, death, or damnation. In the apocryphal book 2 Esdras, when an angel describes the final day of judgment to Ezra, the prophet responds: "For an evil heart . . . has alienated us from God, and has brought us into corruption and the ways of death, and has shown us the paths of perdition" (2 Esd 7:48). After escaping his enemies, David links perdition with the watery abyss of Sheol, or the underworld, and thus with death: "For the waves of death encompassed me, the torrents of perdition assailed me" (2 Sam 22:5). In Revelation 9:11 God's archenemy is called Apollyon, meaning "destroyer"—a form of *perdition.*

Perfume

Mary took a pound of costly perfume made of pure nard, anointed Jesus' feet, and wiped them with her hair.
–John 12:3

Perfumes—aromatic scents derived from flowers, spices, resins, roots, and bark—were highly prized in the ancient Near East, where they were used for cosmetic, religious, and even hygienic purposes. In the hot climate, perfumes served to mask body odors, and scented ointments, which protected the skin against the region's strong sun, were considered basic toilet items even for workmen and slaves. The task of creating perfumes and salves generally fell to women; Samuel warns the Israelites that a king would "take your daughters to be perfumers and cooks and bakers" (1 Sam 8:13). However, the sacred incense, or perfume, used in worship and in sacrifices could only be prepared by priests, who used special formulas (Ex 30:34–38).

Aromatic oils and spices were used in burying the dead. In 2 Chronicles, the bier of King Asa of Judah was "filled with various kinds of spices prepared by the perfumer's art" (2 Chr 16:14). Mourners, however, would refrain from using perfumes. The NARD with which Mary lavishly anointed Jesus' feet (Jn 12:3) was produced from the root of a flowering herb.

Perjury

For their worshipers either rave in exultation, or prophesy lies, or live unrighteously, or readily commit perjury . . . .
–Wisdom of Solomon 14:28

The word *perjury* appears twice in the apocryphal book Wisdom of Solomon. Elsewhere in the Bible, the term for the act of perjury—purposely to lie under OATH—is to *bear false witness*. The ten commandments prohibited the Israelites from swearing oaths in God's name that they did not intend to fulfill and from bearing false witness against their neighbors (Ex 20:7, 16). Being a witness included bringing charges as well as giving testimony against a wrongdoer, and the book of Deuteronomy stipulated that a malicious false witness, or perjurer, receive the same punishment that he hoped would befall the person he had wrongly accused (Deut 19:16–21).

When tilted, this ivory perfume flask from the 12th century BC would dispense drops of oil into the hollowed stopper on top.

PERSECUTION

"BUT THEY HAVE NO ROOT,
AND ENDURE ONLY FOR A WHILE;
THEN, WHEN TROUBLE OR PERSECUTION
ARISES ON ACCOUNT OF THE WORD,
IMMEDIATELY THEY FALL AWAY."
–MARK 4:17

The Bible contains many instances of persecution, which is abuse aimed against individuals or groups of people based on their beliefs. The book of Daniel describes the persecution of Shadrach, Meshach, and Abednego, who were thrown into a furnace for refusing to worship an idol (Dan 3:17–21). The books 1 and 2 Maccabees recount the revolt sparked by the attempt of the king of Syria, Antiochus IV, to suppress the Jewish faith through persecution.

In the New Testament, some of Jesus' contemporaries, such as the members of the Nazareth synagogue (Lk 4:29), harassed and threatened him. The persecution that Jesus endured culminated in his execution by the Romans. He predicted that his followers would also suffer for their faith in him: "If they persecuted me, they will persecute you" (Jn 15:20). These words were fulfilled in the deaths of the early CHRISTIAN martyrs. Stephen, the first martyr, linked his suffering with those of the ancient prophets: "Which of the prophets did your ancestors not persecute?" (Acts 7:52). His murder at the hands of Jewish authorities launched a general persecution in which Saul participated, "entering house after house; dragging off both men and women" (Acts 8:3).

Saul later converted and was called Paul; with Barnabas, "they strengthened the souls of the disciples and encouraged them to continue in the faith, saying, 'It is through many persecutions that we must enter the kingdom of God'" (Acts 14:22). According to tradition, Paul was put to death in Rome during the reign of Nero. Although Nero executed many Christians, records do not support the idea that there was a widespread persecution of the Christians by the Roman Empire at that time. Apparently, individual governors had the discretion to bring charges against sects thought to be dangerous to the state.

The Seleucid king Antiochus IV, shown on a silver coin, subjected Jews to persecution in the second century BC.

PERSEVERANCE

. . . LET US RUN WITH PERSEVERANCE
THE RACE THAT IS SET BEFORE US . . . .
–HEBREWS 12:1

Perseverance was a quality that believers needed to maintain their faith in the face of temptation, opposition, or persecution. The writer of the letter to the Hebrews likened the path to salvation to a race; he urged Christians to follow the example of Jesus, who, by his own perseverance, had won the prize and "taken his seat at the right hand of the throne of God" (Heb 12:2). In this letter and others in the New Testament, church leaders exhorted members to hold fast to their beliefs and to rely particularly on supplication. Paul told the Romans, "Rejoice in hope, be patient in suffering, persevere in prayer" (Rom 12:12).

PESTILENCE

BEFORE HIM WENT
PESTILENCE, AND PLAGUE
FOLLOWED CLOSE BEHIND.
–HABAKKUK 3:5

In the Scriptures, a pestilence is any kind of disastrous epidemic or PLAGUE. Sent by God, a "bitter pestilence" (Deut 32:24) could have a devastating effect on livestock (Ex 9:3) or on people: "So the LORD sent a pestilence on Israel; and seventy thousand persons fell" (1 Chr 21:14). Although God sometimes used pestilence to punish his people for failing to believe in him or for breaking their covenant with him, he also used it to help them. To facilitate the Israelites' entrance into the Promised Land, for example, God promised them, "I will send the pestilence in front of you, which shall drive out the Hivites, the Canaanites, and the Hittites from before you" (Ex 23:28).

PETER, 1&2

BUT, IN ACCORDANCE
WITH HIS PROMISE, WE WAIT FOR
NEW HEAVENS AND A NEW EARTH,
WHERE RIGHTEOUSNESS IS AT HOME.
–2 PETER 3:13

According to tradition, the two letters of Peter were written by the apostle Peter; however, some scholars believe they were written by other Christian leaders, perhaps after Peter's death. The first letter went out to the churches Peter had visited in what is today northern and western Turkey. Roman authorities in this and other regions had once been tolerant of Christianity because they considered it a Jewish sect, but they later treated it with a suspicion that could erupt into persecution. The author advised believers to conduct themselves honorably and to "accept the authority of every human institution" (1 Pet 2:13).

If persecution did occur, believers were to suffer for Jesus' sake, as he had suffered on their behalf.

One of Peter's followers may have written the second letter, using the apostle's name—a common practice among disciples—and theology to combat false teachers who emerged in the early church. Some of them advocated freedom from Christianity's moral strictures. The author calls them "slaves of corruption" (2 Pet 2:19).

PHARAOH

I AM AGAINST YOU,
PHARAOH KING OF EGYPT,
THE GREAT DRAGON SPRAWLING
IN THE MIDST OF ITS CHANNELS . . . .
–EZEKIEL 29:3

The term *pharaoh*, meaning "great house" in ancient Egyptian, was originally used to refer only to the royal palace. Starting in 1504 BC, with the reign of Thutmose III, it became identified with the ruler himself, as it is in every reference in the Bible. This usage was a courtly stratagem to avoiding saying any of the king's five "great names," which were considered too powerful to be spoken directly. Believed to be a god on earth, the Egyptian ruler was considered the incarnation of Horus, a falcon-headed deity, as well as the son of Re, the mighty god of the sun; after death, he would become Osiris, the god of the dead in the underworld.

An absolute monarch, the pharaoh was commander of the nation's armies, high priest of the state religion, and ultimate legal authority. His chief adviser in managing the huge, complex bureaucracy of the empire was a vizier, perhaps the position Joseph held. Old Testament writers mention 10 pharaohs, including four by name. The identities of others can be surmised, but scholars disagree on that of the pharaoh in Exodus. Many believe it was Ramses II, who ruled Egypt for much of the 13th century BC.

PHARISEE

". . . I HAVE BELONGED TO THE
STRICTEST SECT OF OUR RELIGION
AND LIVED AS A PHARISEE."
–ACTS OF THE APOSTLES 26:5

The Pharisees were a Jewish religious party that had wide influence in the Holy Land from about the second century BC to the first century AD. They were scholars who studied the Torah and developed the oral tradition that determined how the written law should be carried out. During the reign of Salome Alexandra (76–67 BC) in the Hasmonean period, the Pharisees dominated the government, but later the synagogues became their sphere of influence. By New Testament times, Pharisees numbered about 6,000.

Although the Pharisees were progressive enough to adapt the law to changing circumstances, they rigidly observed the rules concerning the sabbath, ritual purity, and tithing food. According to the Gospels, they argued with Jesus on such matters, at times provoking his wrath; he called them hypocrites and a "brood of vipers" (Mt 3:7). Nevertheless, Jesus dined with Pharisees (Lk 7:36; 11:37), and at least one of them, Nicodemus, became his follower.

The early Christian community included Pharisees (Acts 15:5). The apostle Paul was a member of the party (Acts 26:5; Phil 3:5). See also SADDUCEE.

In his celebrated altarpiece Maesta, *painted between 1308 and 1311, the artist Duccio included scenes from Jesus' life. Here, before Pilate, the Pharisees accuse Jesus of blasphemy.*

PHILEMON, LETTER OF PAUL TO

I AM APPEALING TO YOU FOR MY CHILD, ONESIMUS . . . .
–PHILEMON 10

After Paul converted a runaway slave named Onesimus, he sent him back to his owner, Philemon, as Roman law required. Onesimus carried with him a letter, which Paul wrote on his behalf from prison. Paul asked Philemon, a Christian who hosted church meetings in his home, to welcome Onesimus back "no longer as a slave but more than a slave, a beloved brother" (Philem 16). Paul stopped short of asking Philemon to free Onesimus, but he may have implied this request by calling for brotherly love, adding: "I wanted to keep him with me . . . but I preferred to do nothing without your consent, in order that your good deed might be voluntary" (Philem 13–14).

Remains of Philippi, an ancient Macedonian city, still stand. The letter of Paul to the Philippians was written to the Christians living in the city, then under Roman rule.

PHILIPPIANS, LETTER OF PAUL TO THE

I THANK MY GOD EVERY TIME I REMEMBER YOU . . . .
–PHILIPPIANS 1:3

While Paul was in prison, perhaps in Ephesus or Rome, Christians at the church he founded in Philippi, about 300 miles north of Athens, sent him a courier bearing gifts. Paul responded with written thanks that became the letter to the Philippians or perhaps part of it; some scholars contend that abrupt changes in tone and content, such as between the first two verses of chapter three, suggest an amalgam of two or three messages. Beyond expressing thanks, Paul warns the Philippians against those who insist that righteousness depends on observing Jewish laws. He also tells believers to honor Jesus by standing united and firm in their faith.

PHYLACTERY

"THEY DO ALL THEIR DEEDS TO BE SEEN BY OTHERS; FOR THEY MAKE THEIR PHYLACTERIES BROAD AND THEIR FRINGES LONG."
–MATTHEW 23:5

In the time of Jesus, Jewish men wore phylacteries—small, black leather boxes strapped to their forehead and left arm—while praying. Inside each box were Bible passages transcribed on tiny parchments. The passages included the ten commandments and a statement of loyalty to God (Deut 6:4–9). The custom of wearing phylacteries, which continues today, may have started as early as 250 BC, growing out of the command to take the words of God and "bind them as a sign on your hand, fix them as an EMBLEM on your forehead" (Deut 6:8).

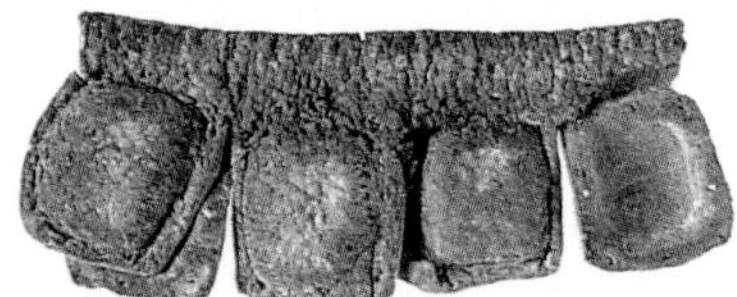

These four compartments, which hold tiny scrolls, fit into a phylactery box worn on the forehead.

PHYSICIAN

JESUS ANSWERED, "THOSE WHO ARE WELL HAVE NO NEED OF A PHYSICIAN, BUT THOSE WHO ARE SICK . . . ."–LUKE 5:31

The Old Testament scarcely mentions physicians, and those of Genesis 50:2 are apparently also embalmers. Little is known about the theories or practices of physicians in biblical lands, except that they set broken bones, applied curative or palliative salves and poultices, and used bandages. Medicines usually came from plants, animal products, or other natural substances such as salt and bitumen.

Among the instruments that a physician would have used in the Roman period were, from top to bottom, tweezers for removing objects, a spatula for applying salves, and a probe for exploring wounds, all found in Judea.

The Bible cites treatments of wine, oil, and even "a lump of figs" (Isa 38:21) for a boil.

Although the Israelites included in their laws important preventive measures, such as prohibiting foods that might carry DISEASE, ancient peoples knew little about bacteria and viruses or the inner workings of the human body. A correct diagnosis of most illnesses was therefore difficult, as was the application of a remedy. Medical practitioners nonetheless developed their craft throughout the Near East. Babylon's Code of Hammurabi included rules for doctors. In Egypt physicians specialized in treating particular parts of the body. The Greeks, most notably Hippocrates, stressed the need for training. By New Testament times, Greek physicians in Rome had made great strides in treatment and public hygiene; nevertheless, most doctors in the Holy Land probably still had insufficient means to deal with serious disease.

Traditionally, the person Paul calls "Luke, the beloved physician" (Col 4:14) has been identified as the author of the Gospel of Luke.

PIETY

"LET US NOT BE COWARDLY IN THE DEMONSTRATION OF OUR PIETY." –4 MACCABEES 13:10

The word *piety,* or religious devotion, is sometimes equated in the Bible with fear of God, which leads to a life of holiness. The book of Proverbs says, "The fear of the LORD is the beginning of knowledge" (Prov 1:7). Piety is the observance of all duties toward God; impiety involves the defiance of his commandments. The book of 4 Maccabees tells of seven brothers who were tortured and killed for refusing to eat "unclean" food; the author praises their "immortal spirit of devotion" (4 Macc 14:6), and he exhorts his readers to embrace their own faith with equal passion. In the New Testament, the writer of the second letter to Timothy tells the early Christians to be on guard against false teachers, whose words can erode such faith: "Avoid profane chatter, for it will lead people into more and more impiety" (2 Tim 2:16).

Pure motives are essential to true piety. Jesus warns against ostentation: "Beware of practicing your piety before others in order to be seen by them; for then you have no reward from your Father in heaven" (Mt 6:1).

PILGRIMAGE

". . . I WILL REJOICE OVER THE CREATION OF THE RIGHTEOUS, OVER THEIR PILGRIMAGE ALSO . . . ." –2 ESDRAS 8:39

The Israelites, among other ancient peoples, took pious journeys to holy sites, which were usually places where God or the prophets had appeared. After David installed the ark in Jerusalem, Israelite men were expected to go there for three annual festivals. When the nation split into two kingdoms, shrines were set up at Dan and Bethel in the north, but the southern kings Hezekiah and Josiah declared Jerusalem the only legitimate site of pilgrimage. When the pilgrims, who often included women and children, crowded the roads toward Jerusalem, they sometimes sang psalms in unison.

In the book of 2 Esdras, the writer uses *pilgrimage* to refer to the believer's ultimate return to God.

PILLAR

THE KING STOOD BY THE PILLAR AND MADE A COVENANT BEFORE THE LORD . . . .–2 KINGS 23:3

Pillars were used at least as early as 2600 BC to support the roofs of temples and palaces in Egypt and Mesopotamia, more than 1,600 years before King Solomon commissioned bronze pillars for his magnificent temple (1 Kings 7:15). Pillars were usually made of stone or wood; Solomon's palace had pillars of cedar (1 Kings 7:2). Some scholars believe that the Philistine temple pillars that Samson pushed down were made of wood, on footings of stone. Pilasters, an architectural feature similar to pillars, were often set into walls for ornamentation; the temple of Ezekiel's vision was furnished with pilasters carved with images of palm trees (Ezek 40:16).

Located near the Dead Sea, in the area of Sodom, the rock formation in the foreground resembles a pillar and so is called Lot's Wife.

Aleppo pine trees, such as these rising from Spanish cliffs, are native to the Mediterranean region, including the Holy Land.

Pillars of another type, consisting of one or more rough boulders, were used in Old Testament times to mark a boundary or serve as a MEMORIAL. Pillars also had religious significance: the Israelites erected them to signify God's dwelling place (Gen 28:22), and the Canaanites put up pillars on hilltops to represent their gods Baal and Asherah.

PILLAR OF CLOUD

"... YOU LED THEM BY DAY WITH A PILLAR OF CLOUD, AND BY NIGHT WITH A PILLAR OF FIRE ...."
–NEHEMIAH 9:12

God announced his presence and protected the Israelites during their escape from Egypt and throughout their desert wanderings by manifesting himself as a pillar of cloud or fire. In daylight he appeared as a pillar of cloud to guide his people and at night as a pillar of fire to provide them with light (Ex 13:21). The pillar of cloud revealed God's presence at the tent of meeting, when "the pillar of cloud would descend and stand at the entrance of the tent, and the LORD would speak with Moses" (Ex 33:9).

PINE

... THE BEAMS OF OUR HOUSE ARE CEDAR, OUR RAFTERS ARE PINE.
–SONG OF SOLOMON 1:17

Pine trees, particularly Aleppo pines growing on the hillsides of the Holy Land, were used in construction. Pine wood, being soft and straight-grained, was easy to work with. It was envisioned as part of the ideal home, such as in Song of Solomon, and as part of the postexilic temple: "The glory of Lebanon shall come to you, the cypress, the plane and the pine, to beautify the place of my sanctuary" (Isa 60:13). The trees were also used for shipbuilding—"they made your deck of pines from the coasts of Cyprus" (Ezek 27:6).

In the book of Isaiah, God says that when the Israelites return from their exile in Babylon, he will transform the arid wilderness by placing in the desert the pine and other trees (Isa 41:19).

PINNACLE

THEN THE DEVIL TOOK HIM TO THE HOLY CITY AND PLACED HIM ON THE PINNACLE OF THE TEMPLE ....
–MATTHEW 4:5

One of the temptations to which the devil subjected Jesus, according to the Gospels of Matthew and Luke, was to transport him to the Jerusalem temple's pinnacle and dare him to throw himself off and let God save him. Scholars do not know just where this highest point of the temple was located, since Roman occupying forces destroyed the temple in AD 70 and no plans survived; however, many believe that the pinnacle was the southeast corner of the great wall surrounding the temple. This corner overlooked the Kidron Valley and had a fearful drop combined with a magnificent view.

PIT

I CALLED ON YOUR NAME, O LORD, FROM THE DEPTHS OF THE PIT . . . .
–LAMENTATIONS 3:55

A pit is a natural or artificial hole in the ground. In the Bible, the word often refers to a well or a cistern, although pits were also used to house prisoners, trap animals, and bury the dead. Digging a pit was so common an occupation that the book of Exodus specifies the punishment for anyone whose uncovered pit causes the death of another person's animal (Ex 21:33–34).

Frequently *pit* carries a negative connotation. In Genesis, Joseph's jealous brothers cast him into a pit (Gen 37:24), and Proverbs characterizes a prostitute as "a deep pit" (Prov 23:27). Sheol, the underworld to which the souls of the dead are consigned, is often called the Pit, as in Isaiah 14:15.

In the book of Revelation, "the key to the shaft of the bottomless pit" (Rev 9:1) may belong to the fallen angel Apollyon; from this smoky pit issues first a plague of demonic locusts and then a warlike beast (Rev 9:1–12; 11:7). Eventually Satan is bound and thrown into the pit for 1,000 years "so that he would deceive the nations no more, until the thousand years were ended" (Rev 20:3).

PITCHER

THEN I SET BEFORE THE RECHABITES PITCHERS FULL OF WINE, AND CUPS . . . .
–JEREMIAH 35:5

Pitchers were usually made of pottery, but they might also be GLASS or stone. Most had a handle and a molded spout for pouring. Pitchers were used to carry water from a well or fountain and to hold wine and other liquids. When King David was at war with the Philistines and inexplicably craved water from the enemy's springs, two of his young soldiers, "respecting the king's desire, armed themselves fully, and taking a pitcher climbed over the enemy's ramparts" (4 Macc 3:12). Ecclesiastes 12:6 lists among its images of death "the pitcher . . . broken at the fountain."

This 12th-century BC pitcher is an ancient example of the Philistines' decorated pottery.

PLAGUE

". . . SEE, THE LORD WILL BRING A GREAT PLAGUE ON YOUR PEOPLE . . . ."
–2 CHRONICLES 21:14

The word *plague* in the Scriptures can refer to different kinds of calamity, such as the 10 plagues that God sent to Egypt because of its enslavement of the Israelites (Ex 7–11). These plagues included infestation by locusts and other creatures, disease suffered by livestock and people, punishing weather, and finally the killing of the Egyptian firstborn males. Viewed by the Israelites as God's way of revealing his power and purposes to Pharaoh, the miraculous plagues were distinct from natural disasters. However, some of them were rooted in natural phenomena. For example, huge numbers of migrating locusts often destroyed crops in that part of the world, and the plague of frogs was akin to the swarms of frogs that appeared when the annual flooding of the Nile River subsided.

Elsewhere in the Old Testament, plagues were portrayed as God's punishment for Israel (Ps 106:29) or for foreign nations (Zech 14:12). Joel described a plague of locusts that destroyed in successive waves (Joel 1:4). According to 2 Samuel 24:15, God sent a pestilence, or plague, that killed 70,000 Israelites after David took a census. The Philistines were afflicted by tumors after capturing the ark of the covenant. Advised by their priests to return the ark with a guilt offering to the Lord, the Philistines asked, "'What is the guilt offering that we shall return to him?' [The priests] answered, 'Five gold tumors and five gold mice, according to the number of the lords of the Philistines; for the same plague was upon all of you and upon your lords'" (1 Sam 6:4).

Some naturally occurring infectious diseases also were known as plagues; these may have been be the illnesses cured by Jesus in Luke 7:21. See also SCOURGE.

When Moses lifted his staff, God sent a plague of hail on Egypt (Ex 9:23), as shown in this 14th-century illumination.

PLAIN

"EVERY VALLEY SHALL BE LIFTED UP, AND EVERY MOUNTAIN AND HILL BE MADE LOW; THE UNEVEN GROUND SHALL BECOME LEVEL, AND THE ROUGH PLACES A PLAIN."
–ISAIAH 40:4

Level expanses of land, plains were a common feature in the varied landscape of the Holy Land and played a role in biblical events. With the exception of the marshy, coastal Plain of Sharon, Israel's plains were more fertile and easily traversed than its uplands and attracted both settlers and invaders. The Plain of Megiddo (or Valley of Jezreel), the gateway from the Mediterranean coast to the Jordan Valley, was the site of the Canaanites' failed attempt to conquer Israel (Judge 5:19). The "cities of the Plain" (Gen 13:12) that were settled by Lot—including Sodom and Gomorrah—were probably located on the southeastern shore of the Dead Sea.

PLANTS

YOU CAUSE THE GRASS TO GROW FOR THE CATTLE, AND PLANTS FOR PEOPLE TO USE, TO BRING FORTH FOOD FROM THE EARTH . . . .
–PSALM 104:14

All forms of plant life—including trees, bushes, herbs, vines, vegetables, fruits, and flowers—were thought to have been created by God for humankind's use and enjoyment. Immediately after making man, "the LORD God planted a garden in Eden . . . and there he put the man whom he had formed" (Gen 2:8).

A common metaphor in the Bible is of Israel as a plant; Jeremiah speaks of the Lord who "planted" Israel and called it "a green olive tree" (Jer 11:16–17). Flourishing plants were a sign of divine blessing (Ps 1:3); barren fields were a sign of God's wrath: "I struck you with blight and mildew; I laid waste your gardens and your vineyards" (Am 4:9). Abandoning God would bring utter devastation down upon the Israelites—"though you plant pleasant plants . . . yet the harvest will flee away in a day of grief and incurable pain" (Isa 17:10–11).

Many plants require seasonal care (Eccl 3:2). In Paul's first letter to the Corinthians, the spread of the Christian church is compared with the maturation of plants: both require careful tending by workers on earth, but both are ultimately divine gifts, for "only God . . . gives the growth" (1 Cor 3:7).

PLASTER

. . . A HUMAN HAND APPEARED AND BEGAN WRITING ON THE PLASTER OF THE WALL . . . .
–DANIEL 5:5

Plaster was used to smooth the rough stone interior walls of houses and to seal out the cold winds of winter. The poor made clay the base of their plaster, while the prosperous used a mixture of lime, sand, and hair or plant fibers. Even kings, who could afford smooth-cut stone for their palaces, liked plaster because it provided a flat surface on which to paint decorative murals. The purification of a house infected with "a leprous disease" (Lev 14:34)—probably mold or fungus—included scraping the plaster from the walls.

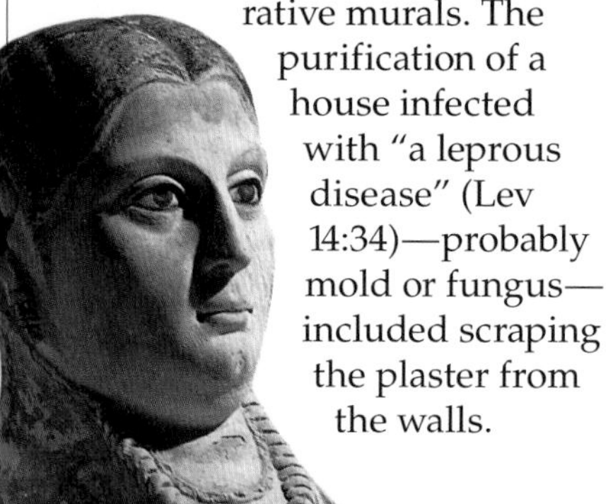

This painted plaster funerary mask from the first century BC, finely crafted with the features and hands of an Egyptian woman, likely served as the lid to a sarcophagus.

PLEDGE

WHEN YOU MAKE YOUR NEIGHBOR A LOAN OF ANY KIND, YOU SHALL NOT GO INTO THE HOUSE TO TAKE THE PLEDGE.
–DEUTERONOMY 24:10

The giving of a pledge as a guarantee for a LOAN was strictly regulated in Old Testament times. However, the frequent indictments in the books of Job, Ezekiel, and Amos of those who violated the laws of taking pledges suggest that abuses were not uncommon. Clothing, livestock, land, or human beings—including children (Job 24:9)—were considered suitable pledges, but a widow's clothing could not be taken as a pledge (Deut 24:17). The pledge on a defaulted loan was to be sold, but any monies that were made above the amount of the debt were to be returned to the debtor. A special kind of pledge was called the earnest—the first installment of an agreed series of payments—which was similar to a down payment.

PLOW

IT WAS INDEED WRITTEN FOR OUR SAKE, FOR WHOEVER PLOWS SHOULD PLOW IN HOPE . . . OF A SHARE IN THE CROP.
–1 CORINTHIANS 9:10

The plows that are used today by peasants in the Near East to prepare the ground for sowing seed are remarkably similar to those used in biblical times (see illustration). The plow's handle, crossbar, and other supports were wooden, sometimes fashioned from nothing more than a forked tree branch. The plow was attached to the center of a YOKE, which was fixed to the animal's shoulders. Usually oxen were used to pull plows and were prodded by a wooden stick or goad.

In biblical times, plowing began after the late October rains had softened the hard, rocky soil. With the ground wet, the farmer could begin to till the soil for his wheat or barley crop. Plowing was arduous work: only one furrow was plowed at a time, and it took both concentration and skill to keep the narrow trenches parallel. Above, a farmer carefully plows straight furrows in his field with a team of oxen, while his young son follows behind sowing seeds. After the seeds are sown, they are covered with soil.

The plowshare, the blade that is attached to the wooden beam of the plow and penetrates the ground, was made of harder material, such as bronze or iron. (Bronze eventually was replaced by iron after the Israelites settled in Canaan.) The Israelites who lived during the first millennium BC depended on the neighboring Philistines, who had superior iron technology, for sharpening their tools (1 Sam 13:19–21). In times of peace, swords were often converted into plowshares to conserve scrap metal. Thus, plowshares became a metaphorical image for peace: "They shall beat their swords into plowshares" (Isa 2:4).

PLUMB LINE

. . . THE LORD WAS STANDING BESIDE A WALL BUILT WITH A PLUMB LINE, WITH A PLUMB LINE IN HIS HAND.–AMOS 7:7

A simple but effective tool, a plumb line is a thin, strong cord with a weight, or plummet, at one end. It was used to check the vertical trueness of walls and columns. The weight was typically made of LEAD—hence the names *plumb* and *plummet*, from the Latin *plumbum*, meaning "lead." In the passage above from the book of Amos, God is depicted with a plumb line in his hand checking Israel, symbolized by a wall, like a careful builder. Though Israel was once solid, the sins of the people had made it crooked, and the Lord proclaimed that it would therefore be toppled and destroyed.

PLUNDER

THEY WILL PLUNDER YOUR RICHES AND LOOT YOUR MERCHANDISE . . . . –EZEKIEL 26:12

Plunder taken by victors in battle included booty—the loot seized by individual soldiers—and spoils, which were the prizes captured for the nation as a whole. Any valuable possessions were considered

Assyrian soldiers carry away items seized as plunder from a captured Elamite city in this seventh-century BC stone relief from the king's palace at Nineveh.

plunder, including livestock, clothing, jewelry, women, and children. According to the concept of holy war explained in Deuteronomy 20, God allowed the plundering of cities outside the Holy Land (Deut 20:12–15), but enemy cities within the Holy Land were to be totally destroyed to avoid the influence of their "abhorent things" (Deut 20:18). In either case, God prohibited the cutting down of food-producing trees (Deut 20:19–20).

Pods

He would gladly have filled himself with the pods that the pigs were eating; and no one gave him anything.–Luke 15:16

The carob—or locust—tree, which grows throughout Syria, Palestine, and Egypt, produces pods, or husks, which hold within them a dark, sweet syrup. These flat, horn-shaped pods can grow to as long as one foot and were frequently ground and fed to livestock. The poor also ate the sweet, ripe pods. In the wilderness, John the Baptist survived on a diet of "locusts and wild honey" (Mt 3:4). The locust he ate was perhaps the carob pod rather than the insect; thus the pods are also referred to as Saint John's bread.

Poison

"For the arrows of the Almighty are in me; my spirit drinks their poison; the terrors of God are arrayed against me."–Job 6:4

The Hebrew word for poison, *hema*, means "heat" and probably refers to the fiery sensation one feels after consuming poison or being stung. In biblical times, poison could be found in plants, snakes, water, or food throughout the Near East. Poison was a metaphor for evil in the Bible, and the wicked were said to "suck the poison of asps" (Job 20:16). Lies were also considered venomous, and the TONGUE was likened to a small fire with the power to destroy an entire forest: "But no one can tame the tongue—a restless evil, full of deadly poison" (Jas 3:8).

Pollution

"'The land that you are entering to take possession of is a land polluted with the pollution of the aliens . . .'"
–1 Esdras 8:83

In the Bible, the word *pollution* means ritual impurity or moral uncleanness, both of which were considered offenses against God. In the passage above, the "pollution of the aliens" refers to forbidden sacrifices made to idols by the inhabitants of the land of Canaan before the Israelites conquered it. Another OFFENSE tied to pollution was murder, "for blood pollutes the land" (Num 35:33). When priests in Jerusalem sacrificed blind, sick, or blemished animals, God accused them of "offering polluted food on my altar" (Mal 1:7) and refused the offering.

Pomegranate

Your cheeks are like halves of a pomegranate behind your veil.
–Song of Solomon 4:3

The pomegranate, a small, semi-tropical tree or bush that produces an edible red fruit, was indigenous to Persia but was grown throughout the Near East. The tree was cultivated in Egypt and already flourished in Canaan by the time the Israelites arrived (Deut 8:8). Its

Dating from the 11th century BC, this pomegranate-shaped clay vessel was discovered in Israel.

fruit was consumed to quench thirst, and the rind was used to make medicine and a red dye. A symbol of eternal life, as well as of fertility because of its many seeds, the round fruit was a decorative motif in Solomon's temple (1 Kings 7:18–20) and was embroidered on priestly robes (Ex 28:33).

During the rainy season, pools of water collect in gullies or ravines, such as Wadi Kelt in the Judean Desert, above, where reeds grow along the limestone embankment.

POOL

. . . THE BURNING SAND SHALL BECOME A POOL, AND THE THIRSTY GROUND SPRINGS OF WATER . . . .
–ISAIAH 35:7

After the winter rainy season ended in May, people of the Near East drew much of their water supply from pools. These pools could be either natural ponds that were found along the Nile but were rare in the Holy Land or man-made pools and cisterns cut into limestone. The pool of Gibeon was part of the elaborate water system for the city of Gibeon, north of Jerusalem. After applying mud to a blind man's eyes, Jesus told him to wash in the pool of Siloam (Jn 9:7), a reservoir in Jerusalem built by King Hezekiah, to cure his blindness. Jesus also healed a lame man at the pool of Beth-zatha (Jn 5:2–9).

POOR

YOU ALWAYS HAVE THE POOR WITH YOU . . . .–JOHN 12:8

In the Bible, the word *poor* refers both to those who are unable to obtain the basic necessities of life and to God's righteous people, who are also called the humble and meek. Though some passages fix the blame for poverty on the laziness of the poor themselves, the Old Testament recognizes that poverty also results from social inequity, injustice, and oppression by the wealthy and powerful.

Some of the poor in biblical times were unable to care for themselves because they were widowed, orphaned, old, or disabled; others worked but did not receive the full fruits of their labor. Isaiah castigated those who grew rich by exploiting the poor (Isa 3:14). God is described in Psalm 68:5–6 as the "Father of orphans and protector of widows" and the one who "gives the desolate a home."

The Bible is filled with injunctions to look after the poor, who were protected by the law. When fields and vineyards were harvested, for example, the owners were not to strip them bare but were to leave gleanings for the needy. So that debt would not be a lifelong BURDEN, all debts were to be forgiven every seven years—a practice called the "Lord's remission" (Deut 15:1–2).

In fulfillment of the ministry to which he was appointed by God—"he has anointed me to bring good news to the poor" (Lk 4:18)—Jesus urged charity toward the poor. In the Gospel of Luke, Jesus proclaimed, "Blessed are you who are poor, for yours is the kingdom of God" (Lk 6:20).

PORCH

WHEN HE WENT OUT TO THE PORCH, ANOTHER SERVANT-GIRL SAW HIM, AND SHE SAID TO THE BYSTANDERS, "THIS MAN WAS WITH JESUS OF NAZARETH."
–MATTHEW 26:71

During the Greco-Roman period, houses were often built with a covered entrance, or porch. It was in such a porch, as cited in the passage above, that Peter was accused of, and denied, knowing Jesus. In public buildings, a porch was usually a passageway with columns. In the House of the Forest of the

Lebanon—a palace built by King Solomon—there was "a porch in front with pillars" (1 Kings 7:6), which was a vestibule within the main building leading off to the sanctuary.

PORTION

THIS IS YOUR LOT, THE PORTION I HAVE MEASURED OUT TO YOU, SAYS THE LORD . . . .
–JEREMIAH 13:25

A portion is an allotment or share of food, possessions, or land. The Promised Land was divided among all the Israelite tribes except for the tribe of Levi, which had been chosen as priests and were to be given a "priestly portion" (Num 18:8) of temple offerings for their support instead of land. *Portion* also refers to the bond of love between God and Israel; thus "the Lord's own portion was his people" (Deut 32:9). Affirming that God's love is reciprocated in the hearts of his people, the book of Psalms proclaims that "the LORD is my chosen portion" (Ps 16:5).

POST

THE PRINCE SHALL ENTER BY THE VESTIBULE OF THE GATE FROM OUTSIDE, AND SHALL TAKE HIS STAND BY THE POST OF THE GATE.
–EZEKIEL 46:2

During biblical times, vertical, wooden posts were used in buildings as frames from which gates and doors swung (Judg 16:3). Similarly, the word *doorpost* refers to the frame of the doorway to a house (Ex 12:23). Most often, however, the word *post* is used in the Bible to denote the station or duty to which a person, such as a guard or an OFFICER, has been assigned. Those who are stationed at these posts are frequently referred to as gatekeepers or sentinels.

Stone posts frame the main gate of the third-century AD Bar Am synagogue in Galilee.

POT

. . . AND EVERY COOKING POT IN JERUSALEM AND JUDAH SHALL BE SACRED TO THE LORD . . . .
–ZECHARIAH 14:21

In biblical times, pots and other receptacles were made of baked clay. The earliest pots were formed by hand and left to dry in the sun. Because they were porous, however, these pots could hold only dry materials. By about 3000 BC, a rudimentary potter's wheel had been invented. The potter shaped the pot on the wheel, then let it dry to the hardness of leather, after which handles, spouts, and decorations were added. Earthenware was originally cooked in the ground and covered with burning fuel; later it was fired in a kiln. Most pottery was made to be used as common household items, such as cooking pots, kettles, water jars, jugs, lamps, bowls, and cups, the remains of which have been discovered in abundance throughout the Near East.

In the Book of Lamentations, Jerusalem's besieged inhabitants are alternately likened to precious jewels and to "earthen pots . . . of a potter's hands" that are thrown away when broken (Lam 4:1–2).

POTSHERD

WHOEVER TEACHES A FOOL IS LIKE ONE WHO GLUES POTSHERDS TOGETHER . . . .–ECCLESIASTICUS 22:9

Broken pieces of pottery, or potsherds, were typically thrown away; mounds of these discards have been found wherever ancient lands were inhabited. Potsherds were also used as paper for everyday notes, such as receipts of sale and letters; such potsherds are called ostraca. Large pieces of pottery were used to carry hot coals and to scoop water from a well. When Job was covered with sores, he "took a potsherd with which to scrape himself" (Job 2:8). God described the underbelly of the sea monster Leviathan as "like sharp potsherds" (Job 41:30). Potsherd Gate in Jeremiah 19:2 may have been the gate through which Jerusalem's garbage, including potsherds, was removed.

Pictured here are an assortment of household ceramic pots from the first millennium BC, which were excavated from the ruins of the City of David, part of the ancient city of Jerusalem.

Potter

Has the potter no right over the clay, to make out of the same lump one object for special use and another for ordinary use?–Romans 9:21

The potter was one of the busiest artisans in the ancient Near East: clay vessels and dishes of all kinds, sizes, and shapes flowed from his wheel (see box, p. 282). Since pottery broke easily, there was always a demand for his wares. The potter's craft involved the preparation of the clay—breaking it up, mixing it with water, and wedging it to remove air pockets—and shaping it with skillful hands on the wheel. The potter also had to judge when the vessels were dry enough for baking, because clay that was too damp would explode in the kiln.

The potter's chief aid was the wheel. Potters used a tournette, a stone turntable that they turned with one hand, leaving only one hand free to shape the clay. A later improvement was the "fast wheel," made from wood or stone, which the potters kicked with their feet. The Bible often likens God's creative power to the potter's skill at coaxing formless clay into a variety of shapes, as in Isaiah 64:8—"we are the clay, and you are the potter; we are all the work of your hand."

Imbued with the power of God, Jesus raises Lazarus from the dead as Mary and others look on (Jn 11:28–44), in this detail from a 14th-century fresco by Giotto.

Power of God

Jesus said to them, "Is not this the reason you are wrong, that you know neither the scriptures nor the power of God?"–Mark 12:24

Biblical writers believed that God alone had absolute power. Jeremiah declared, "There is none like you, O Lord; you are great, and your name is great in might" (Jer 10:6). God revealed his power in miraculous ways: by creating the world and everything in it; by bringing the enslaved Israelites out of Egypt and "giving them the heritage of the nations" (Ps 111:6)—the promised land of Canaan; and by performing various acts of SALVATION (Ps 106:8–12).

In the New Testament, Jesus manifests the power of God in his healings and especially in his death and resurrection. According to Paul, "He was crucified in weakness, but lives by the power of God" (2 Cor 13:4).

Praise

Praise the LORD, all you nations!–Psalm 117:1

Psalm 100:1 says, "Make a joyful noise to the Lord, all the earth," and the people of Israel willingly complied throughout biblical history. When God made the Red Sea swallow up Pharaoh and his army, the jubilant Israelites sang: "I will praise him, my father's God, and I will exalt him" (Ex 15:2). In Jerusalem, the temple rang with the voices of Levite choirs singing God's praises. Some of these poetic hymns are found in the book of Psalms, whose Hebrew title is translated as "Songs of Praise." The faithful also praised the Lord by offering sacrifices, through meditation and PRAYER, and by dancing, as when "David danced before the Lord with all his might" (2 Sam 6:14).

New psalms and hymns were created for worship in the early church, which were often modeled on earlier biblical prayers. Paul told the Colossians to "sing psalms, hymns, and spiritual songs to God" (Col 3:16). Refering to Isaiah 29:13, Jesus criticized insincere praise, such as that of the scribes and Pharisees: "This people honors me with their lips, but their hearts are far from me" (Mt 15:8).

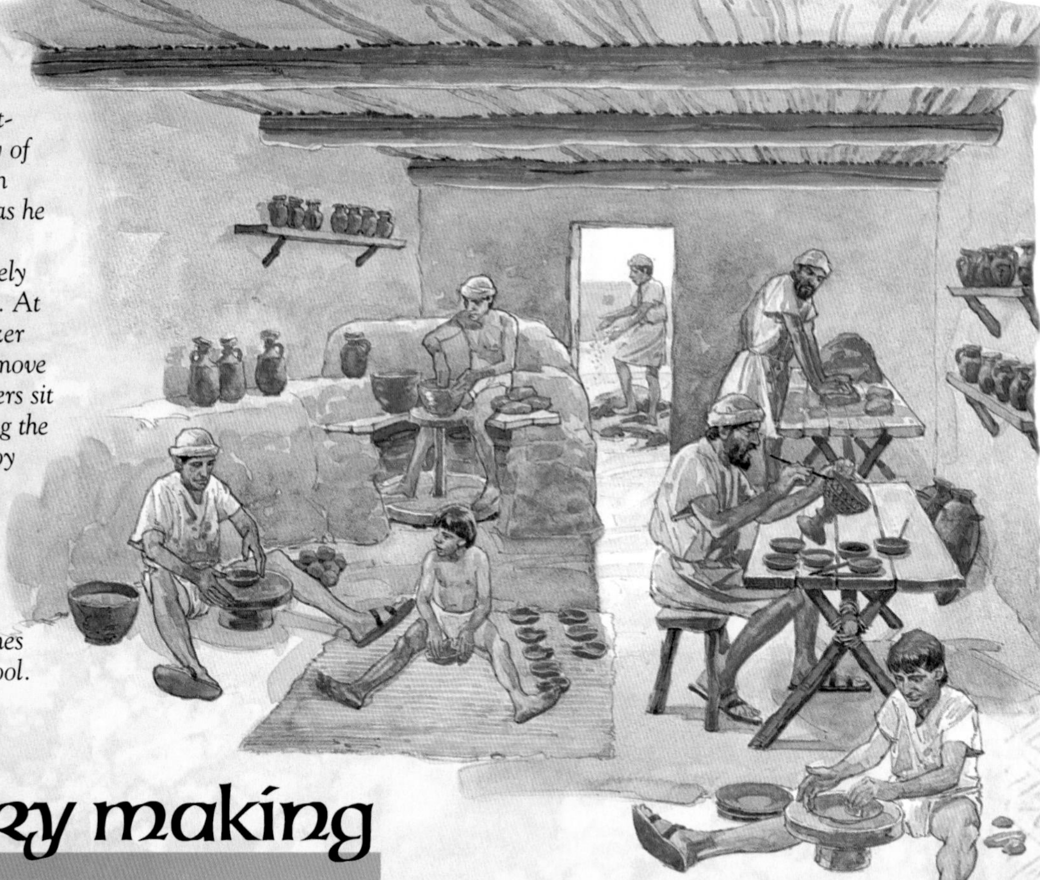

1. In a workshop, potters perform a variety of tasks. Outside, a man tramples on the clay as he adds an aggregate to make the clay less likely to break during firing. At a table inside, a worker wedges the clay to remove air bubbles. Two potters sit at their wheels shaping the clay into vessels; a boy helps by pinching the spouts of lamps. Near them, one worker paints designs on a goblet, while another burnishes a plate with a bone tool.

pottery making

Using clay collected from nearby riverbanks or streambeds, the village potter produced indispensable vessels for everyday life—water jugs, cooking pots, cups, bowls, plates, pitchers, jars, and lamps. In the Iron Age pottery workshop pictured above, two types of wheels are used to shape the clay: the potter sitting on the floor has a wheel that must be turned by hand; the potter seated by the door uses a later invention, a wheel that is turned with the feet, thus freeing the hands.

2. In the yard, a man stokes the fire, carefully keeping the kiln at the right temperature for firing pots. The finished pieces are placed in rows, ready to sell.

PRAYER

"... THUS SAYS THE LORD, THE GOD OF YOUR ANCESTOR DAVID: I HAVE HEARD YOUR PRAYER, I HAVE SEEN YOUR TEARS; INDEED I WILL HEAL YOU ...."
–2 KINGS 20:5

The Bible first mentions the concept of prayer when speaking of Adam and his children: "At that time people began to invoke the name of the LORD" (Gen 4:26). From then on, people addressed God directly through prayer. They praised him, made complaints and confessions, petitioned him on behalf of themselves and others, requested guidance and divine assistance, and offered thanks.

In singing of the goodness of God, a psalmist exhorted the people: "Enter his gates with thanksgiving, and his courts with praise" (Ps 100:4). The Israelites gathered for group prayer at the temple on special holy days, such as the sabbath and festivals. For those who had become impure, such as women who had given birth and anyone who had touched a corpse, PURIFICATION rituals were required before entering the temple precincts. Priests walked barefoot on the holy ground of the temple and wore a special head covering. Both men and women covered their heads when attending services, but among the early Christians, Paul instructed the men to remove their head coverings when praying (1 Cor 11:4).

Posture could indicate the intent of the prayer. Worshipers often prayed with their eyes looking up and their hands lifted toward heaven. Bowing the head was a sign of submission, and lying face down on the ground indicated extreme penitence.

Before and after the exile to Babylon, the religious center for the Israelites was the temple in Jerusalem. But in postexilic times many Jews lived too far from the temple to worship there regularly or at all, so they built synagogues. After Jesus' death, his disciples spread Christianity in part by traveling from one synagogue to another. As the new religion grew, Christians formed churches, initially in people's homes and much later in church buildings.

From a church in Verona, a panel painted by Andrea Mantegna shows Jesus at prayer in the garden of Gethsemane.

Jesus instructed his disciples, "Pray then in this way" (Mt 6:9), and he taught them the Lord's Prayer as a model of what a prayer should be. He began by glorifying God and ended with a plea for the necessities of daily life, for forgiveness, and for rescue from evil. In Gethsemane Jesus spoke to God three times, asking to be spared the suffering he foresaw. Concluding with a statement of submission—"yet not what I want but what you want" (Mt 26:39)—he ultimately bowed to his Father's will.

PREACHING

LET THE ELDERS WHO RULE WELL BE CONSIDERED WORTHY OF DOUBLE HONOR, ESPECIALLY THOSE WHO LABOR IN PREACHING AND TEACHING ....
–1 TIMOTHY 5:17

Considered important work in biblical times, preaching required people of integrity. In the Old Testament, the prophets were preachers, delivering messages from God. Jonah, for example, walked across Nineveh proclaiming: "Forty days more, and Nineveh shall be overthrown!" (Jon 3:4). The city's inhabitants took this prophecy so seriously that they repented of their sins, causing God to change his mind, much to Jonah's dismay.

In the New Testament, preaching usually meant proclaiming the good news, or GOSPEL. According to Luke 4:18–21, Jesus announced that his presence fulfilled a prophecy written in the book of Isaiah: "The LORD ... has sent me to bring good news to the oppressed, to bind up the brokenhearted, to proclaim liberty to the captives, and release to the prisoners" (Isa 61:1). Jesus chose the 12 apostles both "to be with him, and to be sent out to proclaim the message" (Mk 3:14). After Jesus' death, the core of the message preached by his disciples was that Jesus had died for the sins of humanity, had been resurrected, and would come again. Peter told an assembly of Gentiles in Caesarea that Jesus "commanded us to preach to the people and to testify that he is the one ordained by God as judge of the living and the dead" (Acts 10:42). In his letter to Titus, Paul wrote that a bishop of the early church must "have a firm grasp of the word that is trustworthy in accordance with the teaching, so that he may be able both to preach with sound doctrine and to refute those who contradict it" (Titus 1:9).

A 16th-century painting of the transfiguration shows Jesus flanked by Moses and Elijah. In the Gospels, Jesus explained that he was predestined to fulfill "everything written about me" (Lk 24:44) in Mosaic law and by the prophets.

PREDESTINATION

AND THOSE WHOM HE PREDESTINED HE ALSO CALLED . . . .
–ROMANS 8:30

To many Israelites, predestination meant that human beings had a destiny that followed a plan. Other nations believed that gods battled one another and the outcome determined the future of mortals. The Bible maintains that God has a plan for his people, collectively and individually. Genesis presents this view in the story of Joseph. When his brothers fear that Joseph might take revenge for their murder plot, he tells them that his fate was never in their hands: "Even though you intended to do harm to me, God intended it for good" (Gen 50:20).

God is seen as the designer of all things. According to Paul: "From one ancestor he made all nations to inhabit the whole earth, and he allotted the times of their existence and the boundaries of the places where they would live" (Acts 17:26). In the Old Testament, God exercises his will by creating a world that he controls and by selecting Israel as his chosen people. In the New Testament, Jesus' death becomes the means of human REDEMPTION "according to the definite plan and foreknowledge of God" (Acts 2:23). Indeed, those who persecuted Jesus did what God's "hand and . . . plan had predestined to take place" (Acts 4:28). Addressing any member of the Roman church who might question the justice of predestination, Paul wrote, "But who indeed are you, a human being, to argue with God?" (Rom 9:20).

PRIEST

"'I WILL RAISE UP FOR MYSELF A FAITHFUL PRIEST, WHO SHALL DO ACCORDING TO WHAT IS IN MY HEART AND IN MY MIND.'"
–1 SAMUEL 2:35

Priests in Israel supervised public worship and conducted sacrificial rituals. Before the nation came into being, no formal priesthood existed; family leaders such as Abraham, Isaac, and Jacob acted as priests by offering sacrifices. During the exodus, however, God assigned the male descendants of Jacob's son Levi to serve as priests and workers in the tabernacle and later the temple. Aaron and his descendants were consecrated as priests and supported by the other Levites. Those with physical defects, such as blindness, lameness, or skin disorders, were excluded from the priesthood. Also unacceptable were those who married widows, women who were divorced, or former prostitutes. In general, Levites who were not of Aaron's line served in nonpriestly roles, such as temple gatekeepers and musicians.

Levi's descendants received no allotment of land in Israel but rather lived in 48 cities scattered around the nation. For their services at God's sanctuary, they were supported by donations and portions of the offerings to God, including money, crops, and livestock.

Priests served primarily as mediators between God and humanity. In representing God, they taught the people how to worship and obey the law, and they pronounced God's blessing. In representing humanity, they alone poured on the altar the lifeblood of sacrifices that atoned for sin.

Several sections of the New Testament portray Jesus as the sacrifice that ended the need for the sacrificial system and the priesthood, which ceased when the temple was destroyed in AD 70. See also HIGH PRIEST.

PRINCE

THE GLORY OF A KING IS A MULTITUDE OF PEOPLE; WITHOUT PEOPLE A PRINCE IS RUINED. –PROVERBS 14:28

In the Bible, the term *prince* can have any of various meanings. It may indicate noble blood or royal authority, but it may also be used for a tribal chief, a political leader, or even someone who possesses extraordinary skill in warfare. A king, his heir, and important subordinate rulers could all be called princes, as could powerful figures in the supernatural world. One of the titles of the Messiah, the future king of Israel, was "Prince of Peace" (Isa 9:6). Ezekiel's idea of a Messiah similarly centered upon a prince reminiscent of David. "The Prince of princes" in Daniel 8:25 refers to God.

This yellow limestone bust of an Egyptian prince probably portrays Amenhotep III or his son Akhenaten from the 18th Dynasty.

PRISON

BRING ME OUT OF PRISON, SO THAT I MAY GIVE THANKS TO YOUR NAME.–PSALM 142:7

The first prisoner mentioned in the Old Testament is Joseph, who was incarcerated "where the king's prisoners were confined" in Egypt (Gen 39:20). During biblical times, people were rarely put in prison as a legal punishment; rather, like Joseph, they were confined while awaiting trial. Joseph's imprisonment differed from that of Pharaoh's cupbearer and baker, who as a result of displeasing their master were put "in custody" (Gen 40:3), a form of house arrest. For the prophet Jeremiah—accused of deserting to the Chaldeans, who were besieging Jerusalem—a deep cistern twice served as a dungeon (Jer 37:16; 38:6).

The New Testament speaks of John the Baptist's imprisonment under Herod because he spoke out against the king's marriage. It also tells of the apostle Paul's many arrests and confinements for preaching the gospel. After Paul was jailed along with Silas, another church leader, in the city of Philippi, the prison was shaken by a violent earthquake that opened all the doors and broke the prisoners' chains. The miracle persuaded the prison's jailer to convert to Christianity (Acts 16:23–34).

Throughout the biblical era, many prisons were dark, overcrowded, and beset with rats. People were sometimes permitted to remain under house arrest because of their high rank or other factors. For example, in Rome, "Paul was allowed to live by himself, with the soldier who was guarding him" (Acts 28:16), probably because the governor of Judea had spoken in his favor. Otherwise, prisoners were hobbled by chains or confined in painful stocks, as was the case with Paul and Silas in the jail at Philippi.

Among the ruins of Philippi is the prison that may have held Paul and Silas, who were kept in the "innermost cell" (Acts 16:24).

PROFANE

YOU SHALL NOT PROFANE MY HOLY NAME, THAT I MAY BE SANCTIFIED AMONG THE PEOPLE OF ISRAEL . . . . –LEVITICUS 22:32

In Old Testament times, a person who used a holy object in an ordinary way profaned it; similarly, an object that had not been made holy by God was described as profane. A holy item or place, such as the tabernacle, was one that had been set aside for God's exclusive use or for his worship. The Scriptures contain many rules about how priests should treat such objects and sites. A person who did not obey these laws was judged to have profaned God's name, as was anyone who swore a false oath (Lev 19:12). See also HOLINESS.

PROMISE

*. . . I am with you,
says the LORD of hosts,
according to the promise that
I made you . . . . –Haggai 2:4–5*

God made a number of promises in the Old Testament. He promised Abraham abundant offspring and a land for Israel, and he assured David that his descendants would rule perpetually. He told the Israelites that he would be their God and they would be his people.

In the New Testament, God's promises are fulfilled in Jesus. Lest the faithful grow impatient waiting for Christ's second coming, the second letter of Peter says, "The Lord is not slow about his promise . . . but is patient with you, not wanting any to perish, but all to come to repentance" (2 Pet 3:9).

PROPHET

*"I will raise up for them a
prophet . . . who shall speak to them
everything that I command."
–Deuteronomy 18:18*

In biblical times, prophets were people who received messages from God—often through a VISION, a dream, or spoken words—and then delivered those messages by speech, writing, or symbolic actions. Isaiah went naked for three years to warn Judah not to ally itself with Egypt and Ethiopia, as these two nations would soon become enslaved and be dragged away "naked and barefoot" (Isa 20:4).

Unlike kings and priests, prophets did not inherit their calling. God chose them individually, sometimes meeting with resistance. Moses, for example, argued that he had a speech impediment (Ex 4:11), and Jeremiah said that he was too young (Jer 1:6).

The recurring message of the prophets was that the Israelites had broken their covenant with God and that unless they repented of their idolatry, immorality, and oppression of the poor, the Lord would punish them.

Prophets spanned the biblical era, from the patriarch Abraham to John, the author of Revelation. They included women, such as Miriam and Deborah. For a time they banded together to form a guild called the company of prophets (2 Kings 4:38). False prophets abounded, and since anyone could claim that his message was from God, it was hard for people to distinguish between the authentic and the fraudulent. After Babylon conquered Jerusalem in 587 BC, prophets gradually lost their influence, perhaps because priests started delivering the message of God as revealed in the Scriptures.

The New Testament lists prophecy among the spiritual gifts. It names Jesus as a prophet, as well as Agabus, who predicted Paul's arrest in Jerusalem (Acts 21:10–11). Christian prophets also eventually lost their influence, when believers instead began turning for guidance to religious leaders.

PROSTITUTE

*"Only Rahab the prostitute
and all who are with her in
her house shall live because she
hid the messengers we sent."
–Joshua 6:17*

Prostitution was an accepted institution in biblical lands, although it was considered degrading. The Israelites were forbidden to make prostitutes of their daughters (Lev 19:29), and young men were warned to stay away from such women. A priest could not marry a prostitute, and the daughter of a priest who became a prostitute could be burned to death in punishment (Lev 21:7, 9). The Israelites were also forbidden to bring the wages of prostitutes "into the house of the LORD your God in payment for any vow" (Deut 23:18). Some translations speak of "temple prostitutes," who were thought to have engaged in idolatrous fertility rites, but most scholars now question their existence. Biblical writers used the term *whore of Israel* in reference to the nation's occasional worship of foreign gods.

When the prophet Isaiah lamented having "unclean lips," a seraph touched them with a burning coal to make them pure (Isa 6:5–7), as seen in this baroque painting.

The prostitute Rahab was held in esteem because she saved Joshua's spies in Jericho by hiding them when they were in danger (Josh 2:1–6). The Gospel of Matthew lists Rahab as an ancestor of King David and Jesus (Mt 1:5).

PROVERB

"AS THE ANCIENT PROVERB SAYS, 'OUT OF THE WICKED COMES FORTH WICKEDNESS'. . . ."
–1 SAMUEL 24:13

Proverbs, or popular sayings drawn from the conventional wisdom of the time, occur in the Scriptures. The prophet Ezekiel quotes several, including "Like mother, like daughter" (Ezek 16:44). The book of PROVERBS is a gathering of maxims attributed to wise Israelites, such as Solomon. These proverbs are insightful, sometimes witty commentaries on human and religious behavior and experience. They are often composed of couplets—an easily remembered form—with the second line restating in some fashion the idea of the first. They offer spiritual guidance, advice, and warnings, such as: "Pride goes before destruction, and a haughty spirit before a fall" (Prov 16:18).

Proverbs played a major teaching role in both the Old and New Testaments. The book of Proverbs begins with an explanation of how proverbs can edify the reader. Jesus recognized the power of proverbs, using them when preaching: "Doubtless you will quote to me this proverb, 'Doctor, cure yourself!'" (Lk 4:23).

In the Bible, bad behavior is often a lesson for others and so may become the subject of a proverb. In 1 Kings 9:7, God warns Solomon that if Israel turns away from him, the nation "will become a proverb and a taunt among all peoples."

This florid initial P begins the book of Proverbs in a medieval German Bible. It shows King Solomon, to whom much of the book was attributed.

PROVERBS, BOOK OF

HEAR, MY CHILD, YOUR FATHER'S INSTRUCTION, AND DO NOT REJECT YOUR MOTHER'S TEACHING . . . .–PROVERBS 1:8

The book of Proverbs is a collection of insights designed to help young people live good lives. According to the first verse, many of the adages are Solomon's; however, as it was a practice of the time to honor a great person by making such an attribution, scholars are not certain that Solomon was the real author. The book also mentions as contributors Agur, King Lemuel, and others called only "the wise" (Prov 24:23).

Throughout the many chapters, long and eloquent poems blend with pithy statements, addressing a wide array of practical and spiritual issues. Practical matters include instruction about disciplining children and the need to preserve landmarks. Spiritual matters include advice on the importance of obeying God and a litany of the perils of keeping bad company.

These teachings are built on the understanding that, in general, God rewards wisdom and righteousness and punishes foolishness and evil. Yet the authors also believed that God, being a sovereign power, could respond to individuals in unpredictable ways. To people who felt overly secure in their knowledge, the writers warned, "No wisdom, no understanding, no counsel, can avail against the LORD" (Prov 21:30).

PROVIDENCE

. . . THROUGH THE BLOOD OF THOSE DEVOUT ONES . . . DIVINE PROVIDENCE PRESERVED ISRAEL THAT PREVIOUSLY HAD BEEN MISTREATED.
–4 MACCABEES 17:22

The belief in God's providence—or guidance of events to a benevolent outcome—was a source of comfort to the faithful in biblical times. During the exile, the Israelites were sustained by the thought that God was with them, giving "power to the faint" (Isa 40:29). In the Sermon on the Mount, Jesus told his followers not to worry about how they would live, because God would take care of them just as he did the birds. He asked, "Are you not of more value than they?" (Mt 6:26). The passage above from 4 Maccabees refers to "those devout ones" martyred for Israel as agents of God's providence. See also PREDESTINATION.

PROVINCE

. . . HE SENT LETTERS TO ALL THE ROYAL PROVINCES, TO EVERY PROVINCE IN ITS OWN SCRIPT AND TO EVERY PEOPLE IN ITS OWN LANGUAGE . . . .–ESTHER 1:22

In the Old Testament, the word *province* denoted the division of Israel under governors and later into Babylonian and Persian administrative districts ruled by satraps. The Romans used a similar, though more refined system of jurisdiction over their empire, dividing it into administrative areas, or provinces, which became networks of cities. Imperial provinces—areas won by recent conquest where military control was needed—were governed by the emperor directly. Senatorial provinces, or peaceful areas that had long been part of the empire, were run by proconsuls.

This ancient Roman aqueduct, some six miles long, supplied water from springs on Mount Carmel to the city of Caesarea, capital of the Roman province of Judea.

PRUNING HOOKS

FOR BEFORE THE HARVEST, WHEN THE BLOSSOM IS OVER AND THE FLOWER BECOMES A RIPENING GRAPE, HE WILL CUT OFF THE SHOOTS WITH PRUNING HOOKS . . . . –ISAIAH 18:5

The pruning hook, which resembles a sickle but has a shorter and broader blade, is used for trimming and harvesting grape vines. The first pruning hooks had bronze blades and wooden handles; later they were made of iron. Because of its sharp metal blade, the pruning hook, like the plowshare, could be readily fashioned into a weapon in times of war and back into a hook in times of peace (Mic 4:3). Grapevines required great care; pruning vines channeled the plant's energy into producing luscious fruit. Jesus spoke of God doing the same to his followers: "Every branch that bears fruit he prunes to make it bear more fruit" (Jn 15:2).

PSALM

FOR GOD IS THE KING OF ALL THE EARTH; SING PRAISES WITH A PSALM. –PSALM 47:7

From the Greek word *psalmos*, meaning "song," a psalm is a poetic song of PRAISE, prayer, lament, or reflection. Often exquisitely composed, the psalms are among the most beautiful writing in the Scriptures. Psalms vary in terms of purpose and content. They include hymns, or songs of praise, which call people together to praise the Lord (Ps 8, 62); psalms of thanksgiving, which praise specific acts on God's part (Ps 21, 30, 75); and psalms of lament, in which an individual or nation petitions God for deliverance from suffering (Ps 6, 79).

PSALM 151

IT WAS HE WHO SENT HIS MESSENGER AND TOOK ME FROM MY FATHER'S SHEEP, AND ANOINTED ME WITH HIS ANOINTING OIL. –PSALM 151:4

Psalm 151, a book of the Apocrypha, begins with God's selection of the young shepherd David as RULER of the covenant people and ends with David's victory over Goliath. These events are described in 1 Samuel 16–17, but Psalm 151 retells them in what is alleged to be David's voice. The book is titled Psalm 151 partly because it follows Psalm 150 in some Greek Psalter manuscripts. Originally known in its Greek form, a Hebrew version of the psalm, dating from the first century AD, was discovered in 1956 among the Dead Sea Scrolls.

King David appears on the opening page of the book of Psalms from the 15th-century Rothschild Miscellany.

Psalms, Book of

Make a joyful noise to the LORD, all the earth. Worship the LORD with gladness; come into his presence with singing.–Psalm 100:1–2

In Hebrew, the book of Psalms is known as the book of Praises. It is the hymn book of ancient Israel—a collection of lyrics and prayers expressing the people's greatest joys, deepest hurts, and most daunting questions. David's name appears in the introduction to many of the psalms, reflecting the traditional view that he is their author, but many modern scholars think otherwise. The writings likely cover a span of some 600 years, from the time of David, until about 400 BC, a century after the Israelites returned from exile.

How people used the psalms in biblical times is uncertain, though headings at the beginning of some psalms indicate they may have been set to MUSIC, accompanied by assigned instruments—stringed instruments for Psalm 4, flutes for Psalm 5. Pilgrims traveling to Jerusalem may have sung psalms extolling the Holy City, such as Psalm 122. Crowds gathered at the temple may have joined Levitical choirs in singing other psalms, and priests may have recited some in the sanctuary. See also SELAH.

Punishment

. . . "My punishment is greater than I can bear!" –Genesis 4:13

In biblical times, any transgression—whether against a religious law or a civil statute—was considered a crime against God. The Old Testament prophets frequently used the word *punishment* to refer to divine punishment. The Lord inflicted punishment on nations, the faithless, and kings alike, with acts ranging from plagues (Ex 32:35) and exile (2 Kings 17:7–8) to "eternal punishment" (Mt 25:46).

Unlike some other ancient Near Eastern cultures, Israel did not impose the death penalty for crimes involving property. Capital punishment, which was commonly carried out by STONING, was reserved for offenses such as intentional homicide, idolatry, certain acts of sexual immorality, and blasphemy. A person who injured another was required under the law of retaliation ("eye for an eye") to pay compensation in kind (Ex 21:23–24; Deut 19:21).

During Roman rule, Jewish courts were apparently prohibited from levying capital punishment, although some scholars believe they did so. Crucifixion, which Jesus suffered, was a Roman form of punishment; Roman officials also authorized scourging, beheading, and lifetime sentences to labor in the mines.

Purge

. . . stone him to death. . . . Purge the evil from your midst . . . . –Deuteronomy 21:21

When people in ancient Israel broke a fundamental law, such as one prohibiting idolatry or murder, they were treated as moral impurities or infections that could contaminate the spiritual health and holiness of the community. As such, they were purged, or removed—sometimes by execution. The purpose of purging was to cleanse or purify. Thus, when King Josiah wanted to "purge Judah and Jerusalem," he cleared the land of places dedicated to the worship of idols (2 Chr 34:3–8). In Psalm 51:7, a sinner begs of God, "Purge me with hyssop, and I shall be clean."

Purification

Moses took the blood and with his finger put some on each of the horns of the altar, purifying the altar . . . . –Leviticus 8:15

Purification was the ceremonial cleansing of people and objects to make them fit for worship or service in the temple. Ritual purity was not only important for everyday life but especially for participation in holy rites. People became unclean if they touched a corpse or a person with a skin disease, or when they ate prohibited food, such as shellfish. Women were unclean during menstruation and after childbirth. A woman underwent "blood purification" for 33 days if she had a son or 66 days if she had a daughter (Lev 12:4–5).

In the Bible, a person who came in contact with a corpse was considered unclean. Using a branch from a hyssop shrub, a priest ritually purifies two people with the ashes of a red heifer and water, as prescribed in Numbers 19.

Biblical law prescribes various cleansing rituals, which often included a waiting period, a ritual bath, and sometimes a sacrificial offering. Holy objects, such as the temple altar, were sometimes purified with blood. Priests purified themselves by taking ritual baths before offering sacrifices (Num 19:7). On occasion, Jesus instructed people to fulfill the requirements of ritual purification but said that people are defiled only by what comes out of their hearts: "For out of the heart come evil intentions, murder, adultery, fornication, theft, false witness, slander. These are what defile a person" (Mt 5:19–20).

PURIM

. . . THESE DAYS OF PURIM SHOULD NEVER FALL INTO DISUSE AMONG THE JEWS . . . .–ESTHER 9:28

Purim, or the Festival of Lots, is celebrated on the 14th or 15th of Adar (February) to commemorate the deliverance of Persian Jews from massacre by the royal official Haman. The story is told in the book of ESTHER, named for Queen Esther, who declared the date of the intended massacre a holiday called Purim—from the Akkadian *pur*, meaning "lots"—because Haman and his co-conspirators had cast lots to select the date for the slaughter. On Purim charity is distributed, a festive meal is shared, and children shake rattles to drown out the name of Haman.

PURPLE

"ALAS, ALAS, THE GREAT CITY, CLOTHED IN FINE LINEN, IN PURPLE AND SCARLET, ADORNED WITH GOLD, WITH JEWELS, AND WITH PEARLS!" –REVELATION 18:16

In biblical times, the best purple, scarlet, and violet dyes were produced on the Syrian and Phoenician coasts, where artisans extracted them from the glands of mollusks. Because of their scarcity, such dyes were very valuable. In Exodus, purple fabrics were favored for priestly vestments and for the tabernacle; in Revelation, purple adorned the rich—but debauched—city of Rome. A less expensive purple dye, made from madder root, was manufactured in Thyatira in Asia Minor. Lydia, Paul's first convert to Christianity in Europe, was a native of Thyatira and a seller of purple cloth (Acts 16:14). See also DYE.

PURSE

"CARRY NO PURSE, NO BAG, NO SANDALS; AND GREET NO ONE ON THE ROAD."–LUKE 10:4

In the Bible, a purse is a small leather pouch in which money is carried. When Jesus sent out a group of 70 followers with instructions to "carry no purse," he was urging them to have FAITH that God would provide for them, often through the generosity of others. But on the eve of his crucifixion, Jesus said, "The one who has a purse must take it" (Lk 22:36), suggesting that his followers should be prepared for resistance to God's message. In John, the "common purse" held by Judas refers to communal monies used by Jesus and his disciples (Jn 12:6; 13:29).

PYRAMID

HE ALSO ERECTED SEVEN PYRAMIDS, OPPOSITE ONE ANOTHER, FOR HIS FATHER AND MOTHER AND FOUR BROTHERS. –1 MACCABEES 13:28

Pyramids were built in Egypt as monumental tombs for the wealthy and powerful. Though the Israelites would likely have seen pyramids when they were in captivity in Egypt, they are only mentioned in the apocryphal book 1 Maccabees. In an apparently odd gesture for a man intent on political and cultural independence for Jews, the Maccabean leader Simon built a monument to his family—a group of seven pyramids around which he erected a ring of mighty columns—in the second century BC. See also TOMB.

QUAIL

THEY ASKED, AND HE BROUGHT QUAILS, AND GAVE THEM FOOD FROM HEAVEN IN ABUNDANCE. –PSALM 105:40

Small, migrating gamebirds, quail flew in large numbers over the Holy Land and the Red Sea in biblical times en route to Europe after wintering in Africa. Fatigue would force these short-winged birds to the ground, making them easy targets. Considered a delicacy in

Egypt, quail were often pickled and potted. In the wilderness, when the Israelites complained bitterly of hunger, God promised to provide food for them. "Then a wind went out from the LORD, and it brought quails from the sea and let them fall beside the camp" (Num 11:31). The Israelites collected more than 50 bushels of quail per person. Biblical law classified quails as among the "clean" birds—those suitable as food.

Quarry

The house was built with stone finished at the quarry . . . .
–1 Kings 6:7

A quarry is an excavation where STONE is extracted from the earth to be used in building. In ancient times, the arduous and hazardous occupation of quarrying was carried out by criminals and captives. The methods used for taking stones from the rock mass varied. Typically, guidelines were laid to ensure that the stones would be of the approximate dimensions desired. Workmen drilled holes along the lines, using bronze or iron tools. Then wooden pegs were hammered into the holes, and water was added to soak the pegs. The force of the expanding wood split the stone free. This method worked well with easily split stone such as limestone and sandstone; for more durable rocks such as granite, workmen pounded deep grooves with balls and hammers.

Stone that has been exposed to the air is typically harder than freshly quarried stone, so masons strove to remove and shape the stone quickly. Hewn stones were dressed to final shape at the quarry or at the building site with hammer, chisel, and pick. Stone was also sawed with copper blades. Sawed stone was prized for its smooth finish. See also MINES.

Queen

Meanwhile King Solomon granted the queen of Sheba every desire that she expressed . . . .
–2 Chronicles 9:12

The queen was often the most powerful of the many wives and concubines of the KING. She alone had the right to produce an heir to the throne. Though queens occasionally ruled as sovereigns in other nations of the Near East, the only queen to rule in Judah before the exile was Athaliah, daughter of Ahab, who usurped the throne after her son, King Ahaziah, was killed (2 Kings 11:1–3). Frequently a woman became a queen in marriage to seal a political alliance with an important foreign ruler. If her son or grandson attained the crown, the queen might play the more important role of queen mother, as Bathsheba did before and during the reign of her son, Solomon (1 Kings 2:19–20).

One of the seven wonders of the world, the Egyptian pyramids of Giza, in the desert west of the Nile, were built about 2600 BC. The three large pyramids honor the pharaohs Mycerinus, Chephren, and Cheops.

R

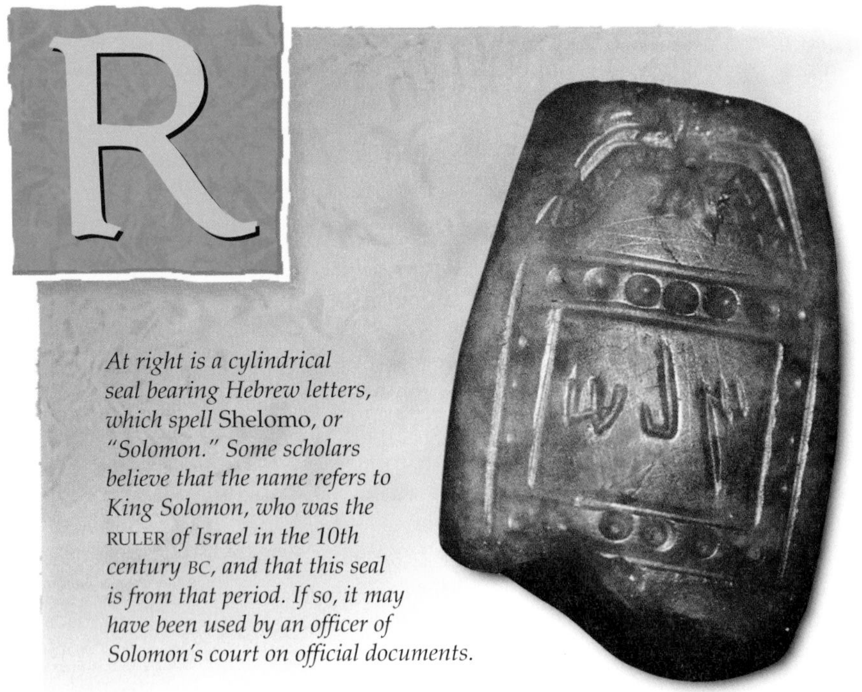
At right is a cylindrical seal bearing Hebrew letters, which spell Shelomo, *or "Solomon." Some scholars believe that the name refers to King Solomon, who was the* RULER *of Israel in the 10th century* BC, *and that this seal is from that period. If so, it may have been used by an officer of Solomon's court on official documents.*

RABBI

[THE SCRIBES AND THE PHARISEES] LOVE TO HAVE THE PLACE OF HONOR AT BANQUETS AND THE BEST SEATS IN THE SYNAGOGUES . . . AND HAVE PEOPLE CALL THEM RABBI.–MATTHEW 23:6–7

In New Testament times, Jews addressed their spiritual leaders with the respectful title of *Rabbi*. The word, derived from the Hebrew *rab*, meaning "Great One," came to mean "teacher" or "master," often referring to Pharisees and other experts in interpreting the laws recorded in the first five books of the Bible.

When people began using the term *rabbi* early in the first century AD, they were not speaking of an ordained person who had completed a prescribed course of study. In most cases, they were speaking of religious scholars who had served an apprenticeship with an older teacher and who were respected for the knowledge they had attained. Disciples and others frequently addressed Jesus as Rabbi, a title he did not reject. Even John the Baptist was called Rabbi by his disciples on at least one occasion (Jn 3:26). But Jesus sternly criticized scribes and Pharisees for wearing the title like a crown and believing that they deserved special treatment. Jesus told his disciples never to accept this honored title for themselves, warning that "all who exalt themselves will be humbled" (Mt 23:12).

RABSARIS

THE KING OF ASSYRIA SENT THE TARTAN, THE RABSARIS, AND THE RABSHAKEH WITH A GREAT ARMY FROM LACHISH . . . . –2 KINGS 18:17

The rabsaris was a chief attendant to a king of Assyria or Babylon. He served in high administrative positions and was often given important military and diplomatic assignments. In the passage cited above, the Assyrian siege of Jerusalem was led by the rabsaris and two other ministers, who attempted to convince King Hezekiah to surrender. Under Nebuchadnezzar, Sarsechim the Rabsaris took part in the destruction of Jerusalem (Jer 39:3). The word *rabsaris* means "chief eunuch" in Akkadian and Hebrew. Although scholars disagree about how literally the title is to be taken, eunuchs may have been favored by royal courts because their lack of heirs or other ties to regular society were presumed to ensure their single-minded loyalty to the king.

RAIN

THE FARMER WAITS FOR THE PRECIOUS CROP FROM THE EARTH, BEING PATIENT WITH IT UNTIL IT RECEIVES THE EARLY AND THE LATE RAINS. –JAMES 5:7

The Holy Land is a land of rainy winters and dry summers. The Bible's many references to rain show how important rain was to a society that was largely agricultural. Farmers counted on rainfall and dew to water their crops rather than on extensive irrigation systems, such as those used in Egypt and Mesopotamia. When the "early rain" (Deut 11:14) began in October, the farmer would plow his fields. The heaviest rains—about 70 percent of the yearly total—occurred between November and February. The rains of March and April, called the "later rain" (Deut 11:14), marked the end of winter; once they ceased, the farmer sowed his summer crops.

DROUGHT, which the Bible usually portrays as a punishment from God (Deut 11:17), was a constant threat. By contrast, abundant rainfall was considered a sign of God's favor. When the prophet Elijah forecast a drought, he did so to demonstrate that it was his God, rather than the Canaanite god Baal, who controlled the rain in Israel (1 Kings 17:1; 18:1).

Rainbow

And the one seated there looks like jasper and carnelian, and around the throne is a rainbow that looks like an emerald.
–Revelation 4:3

In the book of Genesis, God promises Noah that he will never again unleash a destructive flood. God's pledge is a "bow in the clouds . . . a sign of the covenant between me and the earth" (Gen 9:13). The Hebrew word for rainbow, the multicolored arc that is produced when sunlight is refracted

In this stained-glass window, Noah rejoices as the sun appears and a rainbow arcs across the sky.

through raindrops, is the same as that for a warrior's bow; thus, God's act of setting his spent bow in the clouds is the equivalent of laying his weapon aside. Elsewhere in the Bible the rainbow symbolizes divine glory, as in the passage above from Revelation.

Ransom

Shall I ransom them from the power of Sheol?
–Hosea 13:14

A ransom was the price paid to atone for wrongdoing or negligence. For example, should a man's ox gore someone and the owner be found guilty of negligence, "the ox shall be stoned, and its owner also shall be put to death"(Ex 21:29). But because the killing was not willful MURDER, the man could escape execution by paying a ransom in compensation for the victim's life (Ex 21:30). However, a ransom could not release a person found guilty of premeditated murder from the death penalty (Num 35:31). A ransom could be paid to free a slave. In Isaiah, the Israelites released from captivity were called "the ransomed of the LORD" (Isa 35:10). In the New Testament Jesus sacrificed, or ransomed, himself for humankind (Mt 20:28).

Raven

"Who provides for the raven its prey, when its young ones cry to God, and wander about for lack of food?"
–Job 38:41

A member of the crow family, the raven is a scavenger that generally inhabits wilderness areas. It can fly long stretches without resting, and it roosts on rocky perches. It was probably for these reasons that in Genesis Noah released a raven from the ark to seek out mountaintops newly emerged from the floodwaters. The Israelites considered ravens unclean and ominous: they lived in ruins (Isa 34:11) and would peck out human eyes (Prov 30:17). They were also a symbol of judgment in the Bible (Zeph 2:14). Yet God provided for all his creatures, even ravens; in turn, ravens were useful to God when they fed the prophet Elijah, who was in hiding (1 Kings 17:6).

A member of the crow family, the gray raven is native to Israel and a cousin of the black raven alluded to in Song of Solomon 5:11.

Razor

Your tongue is like a sharp razor, you worker of treachery.
–Psalm 52:2

In biblical times razors, or cutting instruments, were usually made from flint, obsidian, or iron. They could be very simple or elaborately decorated. God commanded Moses to tell the nazirites that "all the days of their nazirite vow no razor shall come upon the head" (Num 6:5). The Levites were commanded to "shave their whole body with a razor" (Num 8:7). In the passage above from Psalms, the tongue is compared with a "sharp razor" to warn of the destructive power of those who speak lies. Isaiah warns Israel that God's punishment will be delivered by "the king of Assyria,"described as a "razor hired beyond the River" (Isa 7:20).

Reapers

And it shall be as when reapers gather standing grain and their arms harvest the ears . . . .
–Isaiah 17:5

A dietary staple, grain was one of the primary crops of biblical times. Those who harvested it were called reapers. The barley crop was reaped from April to early May, and wheat from May to early June. Often entire families joined in the harvesting. Reapers moved through the fields gathering together the grain with one hand and cutting the ears off with a sickle held in the other. After being bundled into small sheaves, the ears of grain were carried off for THRESHING. Reaping was also used metaphorically in the Bible, as in "you reap whatever you sow" (Gal 6:7).

Rebellion

. . ."*Today, if you hear his voice, do not harden your hearts as in the rebellion.*"
–*Hebrews 3:15*

In the Bible, *rebellion* usually refers to disobedience to God's commands. During their wanderings in the wilderness, the Israelites rebelled and were chastised: "You have been rebellious against the LORD as long as he has known you" (Deut 9:24). The prophets saw this pattern continuing and urged the Israelites not be to "a rebellious people, faithless children, children who will not hear the instruction of the LORD" (Isa 30:9). Such behavior was also called apostasy, or a "falling away" from God. The letter to the Hebrews, quoting Psalm 95, recalls Israel's history of rebellion and warns Jewish Christians not to turn away from God as their ancestors did.

Rebellion also means disobedience to one's parents or revolt against the state (see illustration). In the Roman Empire, civil revolt was punishable by death. Jesus was charged with claiming to be "the King of the Jews" (Mt 27:37), which was considered an act of rebellion against Rome. He was crucified in place of Barabbas, who was "in prison with the rebels who had committed murder during the insurrection" (Mk 15:7).

Reconciliation

All this is from God, who reconciled us to himself through Christ, and has given us the ministry of reconciliation . . . .
–*2 Corinthians 5:18*

In the Old Testament, Moses continually warned the Israelites to obey the law and thus keep their special covenant with God. In the New Testament, Paul preached that Jesus had offered himself to end humanity's alienation from God. Both of these leaders aimed at the reconciliation of human beings with God, thus ending the separation that began with the disobedience of Adam and Eve in the garden of Eden.

The Day of Atonement reconciled the Israelites with God through sacrifices and fasting, which were meant to make amends for unintentional sins. However, these actions did not erase deliberate sins; each sinner had to confess his own transgressions and, through prayer, fasting, and sacrifices, attain personal reconciliation with God. Paul and other New Testament writers believed that the offering of sacrifices was no longer necessary because God had sent his ONLY SON, Jesus, through whom "God was pleased to reconcile to himself all things" (Col 1:20).

Red

"*Why are your robes red, and your garments like theirs who tread the wine press?*"
–*Isaiah 63:2*

The people of Bible times knew red as a common dye produced from vegetables, insects, or minerals and used for clothing. The COLOR had several symbolic associations. It was sometimes linked with bloodshed; in the book of Isaiah, God's robes were reddened when he trampled his enemies and "poured out their lifeblood" (Isa 63:6). Elsewhere in Isaiah, red is the color of sin (Isa 1:18). In Revelation, the "bright red" (Rev 6:4) horse and its rider stand for war, and the "red dragon" (Rev 12:3) is Satan.

During his reign (4 BC–AD 6), King Archelaus sent Roman troops to control the crowds in Jerusalem for the Passover festival. His action caused a rebellion that ended with about 3,000 deaths. At right, amid the chaos at the temple, the pilgrims throw stones at the soldiers.

Redemption

. . . AFTER THEY HAVE SOLD THEMSELVES THEY SHALL HAVE THE RIGHT OF REDEMPTION; ONE OF THEIR BROTHERS MAY REDEEM THEM . . . .
—LEVITICUS 25:48

The Old Testament frequently describes secular redemption, a legal or commercial process. In its common form, it involved the payment of a price to deliver someone from a difficult situation or to reclaim property. The act of redemption was carried out by another individual or entity because the person in difficulty was unable to do so. Often it was a family member who stepped forward to pay the price. Thus captives were redeemed by the payment of ransom, an object or person seized for debt was redeemed by a proper payment, and slaves were redeemed from bondage by payment of their worth. In some ancient Mediterranean societies, a slave who wished to purchase freedom could do so through a transaction involving a deity; the slave made payment to a god's temple and was freed, though the person was formally the slave of the god who "redeemed" him and became his protector.

The New Testament teaches that redemption came from Jesus' crucifixion, as seen in this illumination.

Since the essential purpose of redemption was often to deliver a person, the action became an appropriate metaphor for God's saving actions among humans. The Old Testament portrays God as the redeemer or savior who rescues the Israelites from bondage in Egypt and from exile in Babylon. The New Testament portrays Jesus as the redeemer of humanity. Here the element of a price being paid takes on great significance. Sinless himself, Jesus pays the ultimate price—his own life—to redeem human beings from their slavery to sin and death.

Reed

. . . "WHAT DID YOU GO OUT INTO THE WILDERNESS TO LOOK AT? A REED SHAKEN BY THE WIND?"
—MATTHEW 11:7

Reeds are true grasses with hollow stalks that can grow as tall as 15 feet. They are found near sources of water in the Near East, along with shorter, grasslike rushes. The King James Version of the Bible refers to both reeds and rushes as "flags." The prophet Isaiah created the image of a penitent whose bowed head looks "like a bulrush" (Isa 58:5) bent by the wind. He was probably referring to the PAPYRUS, the top of which bends, rather than breaks, in the wind. If too much weight is brought to bear on a reed, however, the stalk will break off jaggedly. Thus Isaiah warns against relying on Egypt, "that broken reed of a staff, which will pierce the hand of anyone who leans on it" (Isa 36:6). Israelites used reed stalks as measuring sticks, a standard length being six long cubits (Ezek 40:5). Reeds also served as pens, flutes, and fishing spears. As early as the fourth millennium BC, Egyptians crafted rafts out of reeds. Job refers to time rushing by "like skiffs of reed" (Job 9:26).

Reeds grow thickly along the banks of the Jordan River in the Holy Land. These abundant grasses were used for many purposes during biblical times.

Refiner

. . . HE WILL SIT AS A REFINER AND PURIFIER OF SILVER . . . .
—MALACHI 3:3

A refiner was a highly skilled craftsman who separated metals from accompanying impurities. SILVER was found, mixed with lead, primarily in the ore galena. The refiner extracted this prized metal by melting the lead and silver mixture in a clay crucible and blowing hot air on it with a bellows. The porous crucible absorbed the lead as it oxidized so that only the pure silver remained. When mixed with a different alloy from lead, silver was refined by melting it together with lead, again with an air blast. The lead absorbed the impurities as it oxidized. In one of his prophecies, Jeremiah referred to this process (Jer 6:27–30). Copper was refined by simply blowing air through the molten metal.

Remnant

". . . for from Jerusalem a remnant shall go out, and from Mount Zion a band of survivors. The zeal of the LORD of hosts will do this."
–2 Kings 19:31

God was stern in his punishment of the sinful and disobedient, but there was usually a faithful group, called a remnant, which he spared from destruction. Noah and his family, along with the animals in the ark, were the remnant that God permitted to survive the devastating flood. When Sodom was about to be destroyed, Abraham asked that the righteous be saved, and Lot and his two daughters became the remnant. This pattern is often repeated in the Bible. The very existence of such survivors indicated that God would not allow the annihilation of his people; nevertheless, he warned that if even the remnant disobeyed him, it could indeed be destroyed: "I will cast off the remnant of my heritage . . . because they have done what is evil" (2 Kings 21:14–15).

Isaiah predicted that only a minority of Israelites would be saved, despite the growth of the nation: "For though your people Israel were like the sand of the sea, only a remnant of them will return" (Isa 10:22). During the time of the divided kingdom, Hezekiah of Judah saw his land invaded by the Assyrians, who killed many Judeans. Hezekiah prayed to God and learned that the Assyrians would be unable to capture Jerusalem and that their king would not enter the city. Also, God would provide the survivors with the food they needed to recover over a three-year period so that "from Jerusalem a remnant shall go out" (2 Kings 19:31).

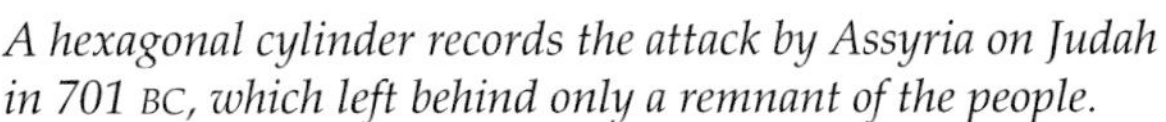

A hexagonal cylinder records the attack by Assyria on Judah in 701 BC, which left behind only a remnant of the people.

Repentance

"If another disciple sins, you must rebuke the offender, and if there is repentance, you must forgive."–Luke 17:3

In the Old Testament, repentance was a confession of wrongdoing, often signaled by public weeping, the tearing of clothes, and the wearing of sackcloth and ashes, as when Job cried: "I despise myself, and repent in dust and ashes" (Job 42:6). Though such gestures were effective symbols of guilt, in themselves they were not enough; sinners had to show that they had turned away from sin and toward purity and righteousness. To make ATONEMENT for wronging someone else, for example, an offering at the temple was required. The Day of Atonement called for a ceremonial sacrifice to atone for the entire nation's transgressions during the year. However, even these public offerings did not guarantee God's forgiveness. To receive that, the sinners' repentance had to be in their hearts and made evident by their actions toward others.

The concept of repentance is very important in the New Testament. John the Baptist made it a crucial part of his message, proclaiming, "Repent, for the kingdom of heaven has come near" (Mt 3:2) and baptizing believers "with water for repentance" (Mt 3:11). Jesus echoed the proclamation of his cousin (Mt 4:17) and stressed that he had come to save sinners. The overriding importance of repentance is clear in Jesus' parable of the Lost Sheep, when "there will be more joy in heaven over one sinner who repents than over ninety-nine righteous persons who need no repentance" (Lk 15:7). After his resurrection, Jesus appeared to his apostles and told them that they were to preach the message of repentance and forgiveness in his name (Lk 24:47).

Reptile

For every species of beast and bird, of reptile and sea creature, can be tamed and has been tamed by the human species . . . . –James 3:7

Reptiles are animals that usually crawl on short legs or slither on their bellies, including lizards, crocodiles, alligators, snakes, and turtles. According to biblical law, "Whatever moves on its belly, and whatever moves on all fours . . . all the creatures that swarm upon the earth, you shall not eat; for they are detestable" (Lev 11:42). Among the unclean reptiles specifically proscribed was "the land crocodile" (Lev 11:29–30), which may refer to the large desert monitor.

In the Holy Land the most common type of reptiles are lizards, with more than 40 species inhabiting the area. River crocodiles were found throughout the Nile in ancient times. See also SERPENT.

Reservoir

In his days a water cistern was dug, a reservoir like the sea in circumference. –Ecclesiasticus 50:3

In many lands where seasonal rains were the major source of water, reservoirs were used to catch and hold the rainwater. A reservoir could be natural, constructed with masonry, or cut from bedrock; a man-made type was called a CISTERN. Without reservoirs, the first Israelite villages in the dry hill country might not have survived. Some settlements had access to springs, but they still needed to collect water in case of drought or siege. Many houses had their own cisterns. The number of reservoirs increased during the second and first millennia BC, as people learned to plaster the inside of the storage units to keep the water from leaking out.

Solomon's Pools, reservoirs south of Bethlehem, have supplied water for centuries.

Restitution

Anyone who kills an animal shall make restitution for it, life for life. –Leviticus 24:18

Many of the ancient Israelites' laws were based on the notion of restitution. A person who stole or damaged property had to restore or replace the item and give something more as well. These conditions also applied to anything obtained fraudulently. Leviticus 6:5 stipulates that "you shall repay the principal amount and shall add one-fifth to it." If someone stole an ox or a sheep and then sold or slaughtered it, he had to pay the owner "five oxen for an ox, and four sheep for a sheep" (Ex 22:1); if the thief still possessed the living animal, he repaid double its worth. Besides giving recompense to the person wronged, the sinner had to make restitution to God for committing a transgression by making a "guilt offering" (Lev 6:6).

The New Testament does not refer to restitution, but in the Gospel of Luke, Zacchaeus the tax collector promises to atone for any unfair dealings by giving half of his goods to the poor and recompensing those whom he defrauded four times the amount taken from them (Lk 19:8).

Resurrection

By his great mercy he has given us a new birth into a living hope through the resurrection of Jesus Christ from the dead . . . . –1 Peter 1:3

The Old Testament has little to say about the afterlife except for occasional mentions of Sheol, the place where the vague shadow of a person went after death. An indirect reference to resurrection, the rising of the dead to life, occurs in Daniel: "Many of those who sleep in the dust of the earth shall awake, some to everlasting life, and some to shame and everlasting contempt" (Dan 12:2). The book of 2 Maccabees contains the first clear mention in the Bible of resurrection; the passage implies that it is only for those who have obeyed God (2 Macc 7:14).

In New Testament times, Jews were divided on the issue of resurrection. The Pharisees believed in it, but the Sadducees did not, perhaps because it was not in the Pentateuch. When the Sadducees questioned Jesus about it, he astounded them by using the Scriptures to support the concept of resurrection (Mt 22:23–33). According to the Gospels, Jesus told his disciples that he himself would "rise again" three days after being killed (Lk 18:33). After the miracle occurred, he appeared to believers several times before his ASCENSION. In his letters, Paul emphasized that Jesus' resurrection was essential to Christianity. Without it, he wrote, the belief that death could be defeated by a rebirth in Jesus was false; the resurrection provided knowledge that everyone would be raised from the dead and "made alive in Christ" (1 Cor 15:22).

RETRIBUTION

LISTEN, AN UPROAR FROM THE CITY! A VOICE FROM THE TEMPLE! THE VOICE OF THE LORD, DEALING RETRIBUTION TO HIS ENEMIES!–ISAIAH 66:6

Retribution is the practice of dealing out appropriate punishment for wrongful actions. Although the word appears infrequently in the Bible, the concept was an important one. The Israelite law that stipulated "eye for eye, tooth for tooth" (Deut 19:21) was based on retribution. Most often, however, requital was the province of God. In the book of Judges, after the Canaanite Adoni-bezek is maimed by the Israelites, he concedes that "as I have done, so God has paid me back" (Judg 1:7). The Bible also links retribution more directly to God, such as when he reveals, through Jeremiah, that he must "bring retribution" to Judah for its wickedness (Jer 5:29). In the New Testament, the concept of divine retribution usually refers to the DAY OF THE LORD, when everyone will be judged by God, and "he will repay according to each one's deeds" (Rom 2:6). In the Gospel of Matthew, Jesus specifies some of these deeds, such as giving food to the hungry or withholding it from them; he also speaks of people receiving either eternal punishment or eternal life (Mt 25:46).

REVELATION

"FOR YOU, O LORD OF HOSTS, THE GOD OF ISRAEL, HAVE MADE THIS REVELATION TO YOUR SERVANT . . . ." –2 SAMUEL 7:27

Revelation, God's communication with human beings, occurs in several ways in the Bible. One conduit is nature; Amos calls God "the one who forms the mountains, creates the wind, reveals his thoughts to mortals, makes the morning darkness, and treads on the heights of the earth" (Am 4:13). God also reveals himself through historical events, such as in the exodus (Ex 6:6–8) and in the use of other nations to punish Israel for violations of its covenant with God. Sometimes God communicates with people directly—even "face to face" (Ex 33:11)—and sometimes indirectly through messengers such as angels and "his servants the prophets" (Am 3:7).

In the Old Testament, human beings also sought God's revelation by consulting the Urim and Thummim, casting lots, and other forms of divination. For New Testament writers, Jesus was the definitive revelation of God, "destined before the foundation of the world, but . . . revealed at the end of the ages for your sake" (1 Pet 1:20).

REVELATION TO JOHN

THEN I SAW A NEW HEAVEN AND A NEW EARTH . . . . –REVELATION 21:1

The Revelation to John, also called the Apocalypse, is the last book of the New Testament. It announces the final victory of God over the forces of evil at the end of human history; this victory will usher in judgment day, followed by a new and eternal age of peace for God's people, when "Death will be no more" (Rev 21:4). Most scholars today doubt that the author, "John," was Jesus' apostle. Rather, he was probably a Jewish Christian writing during a time of persecution by Roman rulers to encourage his fellow Christians to remain true to their faith. He expressed this mes-

Part of a medieval Spanish commentary on the book of Revelation, this beautiful illustration centers on Christ as "the Lamb" (Rev 5:8).

sage by describing elaborate visions filled with symbolic characters and events, many with parallels in Old Testament writings.

Reward

"Do not be afraid, Abram, I am your shield; your reward shall be very great."
–Genesis 15:1

In the Bible, a reward is usually divine payment for good behavior. In Genesis, the king of Sodom offers Abram, the first Israelite patriarch, the spoils of battle, but Abram refuses, saying he has sworn to the Lord to take nothing. God then assures Abram that as a reward for his righteous action, he will receive a son. Boaz pronounces a BLESSING upon Ruth for her faithfulness: "May the LORD reward you for your deeds" (Ruth 2:12). In the Gospels, Jesus speaks to his believers of the reward that awaits them in the afterlife: "Rejoice and be glad, for your reward is great in heaven" (Mt 5:12).

Riddle

Samson said to them, "Let me now put a riddle to you."–Judges 14:12

A common form of entertainment in the ancient world, riddles were verbal puzzles that tested an audience's wits. They were popular diversions at banquets and feasts. The most famous riddle in the Bible was posed by Samson at his own wedding feast: "Out of the eater came something to eat. Out of the strong came something sweet" (Judg 14:14). Unable to solve the puzzle, the Philistine guests coerced Samson's wife into finding out the answer and later taunted Samson with it: "What is sweeter than honey? What is stronger than a lion?" (Judg 14:18).

The Bible notes that the ability to solve riddles was a mark of wisdom (Dan 5:11–12; Prov 1:6). To prove Solomon's wisdom, the Queen of Sheba tested him with "hard questions" (1 Kings 10:1).

The 12th-century Winchester Bible contains this illustration of Solomon and the Queen of Sheba, shown posing riddles to the king.

Some riddles that required interpretation were labeled "dark sayings," implying that their meaning was hidden behind symbols. When God spoke to Moses, he did so "clearly, not in riddles" (Num 12:8) to prevent any misunderstanding.

Righteousness

"I hold fast my righteousness, and will not let it go; my heart does not reproach me for any of my days."–Job 27:6

In the Bible, *righteousness* usually means being obedient to God's commands and is closely associated with integrity (Ps 7:8) and blamelessness (Prov 11:5). Several individuals are described as especially exemplifying the quality of righteousness, including Abraham (Gen 15:6), Noah, Daniel, and Job (Ezek 14:14), Jacob and Joseph (Wis 10:10, 13), John the Baptist (Mk 6:20), and Jesus (1 Pet 3:18).

As a legal concept, *righteousness* originally referred to an individual who was innocent of a crime. In the book of Amos, the Lord condemns those who "sell the righteous for silver, and the needy for a pair of sandals" (Am 2:7)—that is, those who accept a bribe to testify falsely against someone. The prophet Isaiah links righteousness with justice, pronouncing God's condemnation of Israel because "he expected justice, but saw bloodshed; righteousness, but heard a cry!" (Isa 5:7). As the "Judge of all the earth" (Gen 18:26), God shows righteousness by rewarding the good and punishing the wicked and by performing saving acts on behalf of Israel, his covenant partner.

In the New Testament, the concept of righteousness was central to Paul's argument as to whether or not Gentile Christians were bound by the law of Moses. Paul maintained that observance of the law was not necessary for righteousness, or justification, in God's eyes. Rather, he insisted that righteousness came only from faith "in him who raised Jesus our Lord from the dead" (Rom 4:24).

Ring

"You may write as you please with regard to the Jews, in the name of the king, and seal it with the king's ring . . . ."
–Esther 8:8

The rings mentioned in the Bible were worn both on the fingers and in the nose. Precious metals used as currency were often made into rings and other JEWELRY, which could be transported easily. Thus, the gold nose-

Gold rings worn by pharaohs include one decorated with ducks and another used to seal documents.

ring that Abraham's servant gave Rebekah was valued at "a half-shekel" (Gen 24:22). Signet rings, set with skillfully engraved semiprecious stones, were used by kings to stamp their royal seal on documents. In the book of Esther, King Ahasuerus gave his signet ring first to Haman and then to Mordecai (Esth 3:10; 8:2), enabling each man to issue binding decrees under the king's authority.

River

You visit the earth and water it, you greatly enrich it; the river of God is full of water . . . . –Psalm 65:9

In the Bible, the word *river* can refer to a long watercourse, to a riverbed or channel, or to an irrigation canal. The earliest civilizations in the Near East grew up along waterways—the Nile, Tigris, and Euphrates—that could support transportation and commerce. Other rivers in the biblical world were too small, or not sufficiently navigable, to serve these purposes. The Nile played a significant part in the early life of Moses and in the plagues that God visited upon Egypt (Ex 2:3–5; 7:15–24; 8:3). The serpentine Jordan River, which was generally unnavigable, was a barrier the Israelites had to cross to enter the Promised Land; it then served as a natural boundary between the tribes, and later the nations, on either side of it. Control of the fords, or crossings, of the Jordan was highly desirable. During his contest with the rebellious Absalom, David crossed the Jordan at "the fords of the wilderness" (2 Sam 15:28; 17:16).

The flowing waters of rivers and streams could also symbolize God's salvation (Rev 22:1); a cataract, or waterfall, suggested his power (Ps 42:7). See also BAPTISM.

This road in the Holy Land connects the Mount of Olives to the temple in Jerusalem. In the era of the Roman Empire, the system of roads in the region improved immensely.

Road

"If you let me pass through your land, I will travel only along the road . . . ." –Deuteronomy 2:27

In Old Testament times, the rise of nations and growth of trade necessitated routes for TRAVEL. The roads of the geographically challenging Near East were at first simply pathways created by clearing away such obstructions as boulders and trees. In the Judean and Negeb deserts, these routes had to circumvent the sites of wells and pasturage for cattle. In the central part of the Holy Land, the very steep hills, the dunes of the coastal plain, and the valleys susceptible to spring floods also had to be avoided.

The important north–south routes in the Holy Land were the coastal portion of the Great Trunk Road; a central road through Jerusalem and Beer-sheba; and King's Highway, on the east side of the Jordan (see map, p. 302). These routes fostered government and business travel, pilgrimages, and military actions. Fortresses were situated along some roads to keep them secure from invaders. By the time of Jesus, the Romans had begun to improve existing routes as well as to build new roads. Throughout the empire, they created a network of paved thoroughfares, some as wide as 26 feet, which joined other roads to provide both local and international links for the Jewish people.

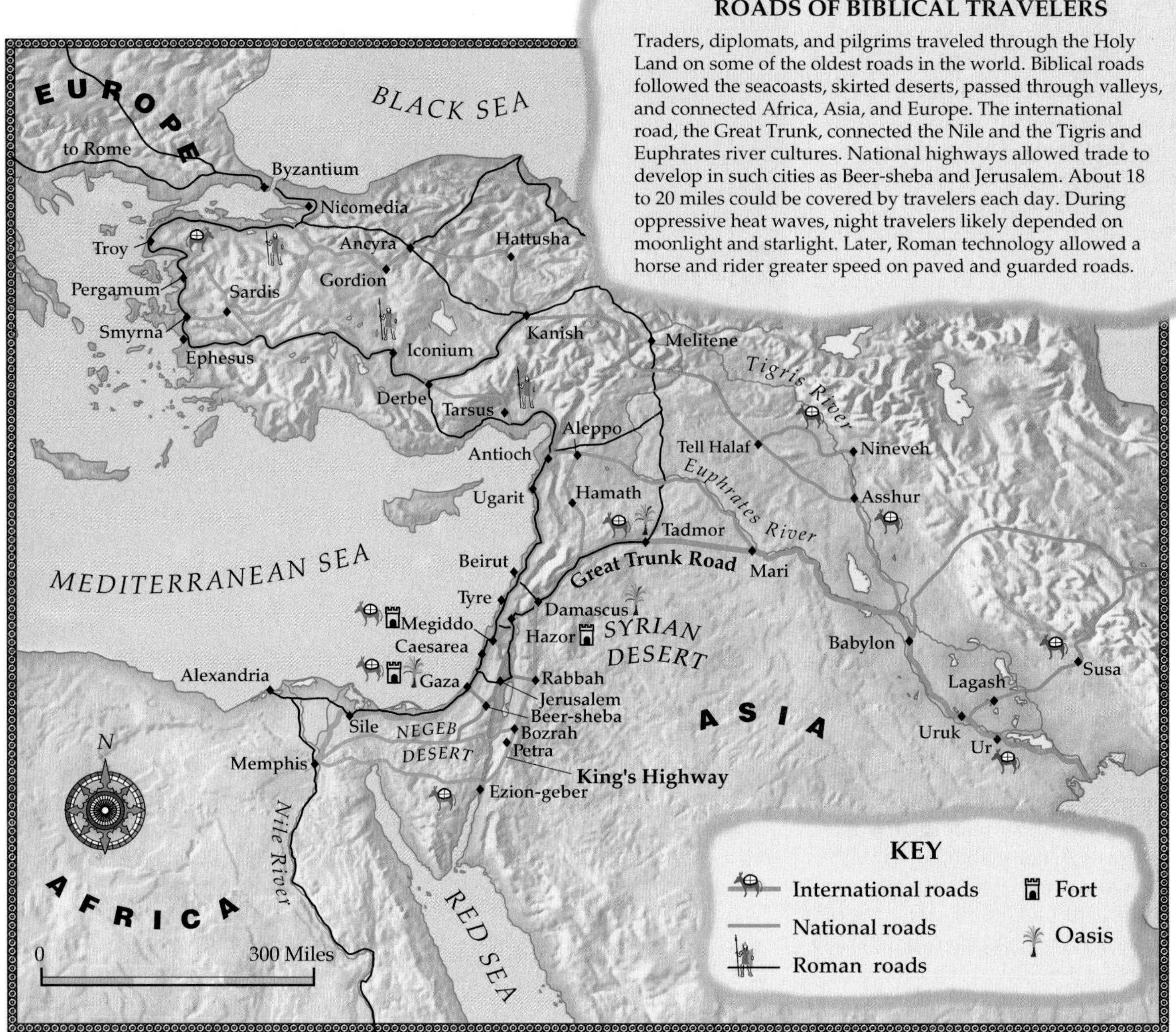

Robbery

For I the LORD love justice,
I hate robbery and wrongdoing . . . .
–Isaiah 61:8

The biblical prohibition against robbery, taking another's property without permission, is encompassed by the commandment "You shall not steal" (Ex 20:15). Some scholars believe this injunction originally applied to kidnapping, an offense punishable by death. Biblical law does not make the modern distinction between robbery, or stealing by force, and theft, which implies taking by stealth. A person who stole an animal was required to make restitution for it. In Leviticus, a robber is directed to make a guilt offering to God in addition to repayment (Lev 6:1–7). Scriptural references to robbery show that the act was considered a violation of another person's rights. According to Isaiah, those who make unjust laws "rob the poor," that is, the widows and orphans (Isa 10:2). In Malachi 3:8, God derides the Israelites for "robbing" him by failing to make full tithes and offerings. Because the people have held God in contempt, they are "cursed with a curse" (Mal 3:9).

Highway robbers, or bandits, are mentioned as early as the era of the judges (1200 BC). The motivation for these organized bands of thieves was often political; the book of Judges recounts that the lords of Shechem despoiled travelers to harm their enemy Abimelech (Judg 9:25). During Roman times, an extremist Jewish group known as the ASSASSINS, or *Sicarii*, robbed and murdered to finance their antigovernment activities. The Roman authorities, who could order crucifixion for slaves who had committed robbery, sometimes punished these troublemakers as thieves. Such was the situation of the "bandit" Barabbas, a Jewish rebel whom the mob voted to spare from crucifixion instead of Jesus (Jn 18:40).

ROBE

SO JESUS CAME OUT, WEARING THE CROWN OF THORNS AND THE PURPLE ROBE. –JOHN 19:5

The Bible's references to articles of CLOTHING are difficult to translate precisely. Generally, a robe was a flowing outer garment worn by both men and women over a short-sleeved or sleeveless tunic. Fine linen robes, dyed scarlet or purple, were the prerogatives of priests and royalty; thus Jesus' guards mocked him by giving him a purple robe. In the book of 2 Samuel, Tamar's "long robe with sleeves" signified that she was the virgin daughter of King David (2 Sam 13:18). Jacob gave his favorite son, Joseph, a similar robe (Gen 37:3), which the King James Version of the Bible calls "a coat of many colors."

ROCK

"THERE IS NO HOLY ONE LIKE THE LORD, NO ONE BESIDES YOU; THERE IS NO ROCK LIKE OUR GOD."–1 SAMUEL 2:2

The word *rock* appears throughout the Bible, often as a symbol of God's protective power. For an UNBELIEVER, however, God is "a rock one stumbles over" (Isa 8:14), whose wrath will make one's teeth "grind on gravel" (Lam 3:16). In the Gospel of Matthew, Jesus tells the parable of the wise man "who built his house on rock"(Mt 7:24). When Simon became a disciple, Jesus named him Peter (Jn 1:42), meaning "rock." He later said of the apostle, "On this rock I will build my church" (Mt 16:18).

ROD

EVEN THOUGH I WALK THROUGH THE DARKEST VALLEY, I FEAR NO EVIL; FOR YOU ARE WITH ME; YOUR ROD AND YOUR STAFF—THEY COMFORT ME. –PSALM 23:4

Also called a staff, the multipurpose wooden rod mentioned often in the Bible could be straight or crooked at one end. It might act as a defensive weapon, a walking stick, or a shepherd's crook, used to count, guide, and protect the flock. Many scriptural references suggest a punitive or disciplinary use, but the law explicitly forbade killing a servant with a rod. In Egypt the rods of Moses and Aaron were used to produce wonders to prove God's power to Pharaoh. Later, AARON'S ROD flowered and bore almonds to affirm the legitimacy of his family's leadership. As a symbol of authority, the rod prefigured the ceremonial royal scepter.

Like shepherds in biblical times, a present-day Yemenite shepherd near Jerusalem carries a rod to help guide his flock.

ROMANS, LETTER TO THE

THEREFORE, SINCE WE ARE JUSTIFIED BY FAITH, WE HAVE PEACE WITH GOD THROUGH OUR LORD JESUS CHRIST . . . .–ROMANS 5:1

Paul wrote the letter to the Romans, his longest epistle, as a way to introduce himself and his beliefs to previously established churches in Rome. The apostle said he hoped to visit the churches on his way to Spain, and he hinted that he would like their financial support in his endeavor to take the gospel to the western edge of the empire. Much of the letter is an explanation of God's plan of salvation. This salvation, Paul wrote, does not come from keeping Jewish laws, nor is it limited to Jews. Rather, it is available "through faith in Jesus Christ for all who believe" (Rom 3:22).

ROOF

THROUGH SLOTH THE ROOF SINKS IN, AND THROUGH INDOLENCE THE HOUSE LEAKS. –ECCLESIASTES 10:18

The roof was an integral living and working space in the cramped houses of the Holy Land. It was where people slept in hot weather, children played, and women did domestic tasks, such as putting out laundry to dry. People could socialize across the rooftops or look down from them to see what

A cutaway model of an ancient house shows the layers of the roof. This reconstruction is based on findings from excavations of the town of Arad in the northern Negeb Desert, which date from the first half of the third millennium BC.

was happening in the streets. Families sometimes gathered on the roof on hot evenings, and people went there to pray, as did the apostle Peter while staying at the HOUSE of a tanner (Acts 10:9). An outdoor ladder or stairway usually led to the roof.

Roofs were flat and made of a mat of branches laid over wooden beams; on top of this mat went a layer of clay packed down by heavy stone rollers to make a smooth, hard surface. Along the edge, a parapet was built to prevent falls, as required by biblical law (Deut 22:8). Roofs probably needed frequent repair during the wet season, but most of the time they kept out both the rain and sun.

The roof comes into play in several incidents in the Bible. Rahab hid the Israelite spies in Jericho under stalks of flax drying on her roof (Josh 2:6). David first saw Bathsheba from his palace rooftop (2 Sam 11:2). The friends of a paralyzed man removed the roof of a house and lowered him down to be healed by Jesus (Mk 2:4).

Root

"... SINCE THEY HAD NO ROOT,
THEY WITHERED AWAY."
–MATTHEW 13:6

Roots anchor plants to the ground and draw in the nutrients and water necessary for their survival. Biblical writers often used the root as a symbol. The book of Proverbs evokes the image of firmly established roots, which provide security and prosperity; "the root of the righteous" is not only immovable but also fruit-bearing (Prov 12:3, 12). Sin and faithlessness, however, bring about rootlessness and exile: "The LORD . . . will root up Israel out of this good land that he gave to their ancestors, and scatter them" (1 Kings 14:15). The New Testament urges Christians to be grounded in Jesus, "rooted and built up in him and established in the faith" (Col 2:7). Paul warns that "the love of money is a root of all kinds of evil" (1 Tim 6:10).

Rope

THEN SHE LET THEM DOWN BY
A ROPE THROUGH THE WINDOW . . . .
–JOSHUA 2:15

Ropes were indispensable in biblical times. They were used for such tasks as tying bundles, lashing loads onto pack animals, leading animals, hauling carts, restraining captives, and even dragging stones weighing many tons from quarries. Poor people also wore ropes as belts, and Joshua's spies climbed down a rope to leave Rahab's house unseen. Placing a rope circlet on the head was a sign of submission. Usually made of plant fibers or hair, ropes ranged in size from thin cords to cables as thick as a man's wrist. Rope makers used a wide variety of materials, including reeds, date-palm fibers, papyrus, flax, grass, and leather.

Discovered in a Judean Desert cave, this knotted rope was used in 7000 BC.

Many scholars believe that the "rose" mentioned in Ecclesiasticus 39:13 is actually the oleander, shown above.

ROSE

LISTEN TO ME, MY FAITHFUL CHILDREN, AND BLOSSOM LIKE A ROSE GROWING BY A STREAM OF WATER. –ECCLESIASTICUS 39:13

In the Scriptures, the word *rose* might refer to any of a number of colorful flowers. The maiden in Song of Solomon says, "I am a rose of Sharon" (Song of S 2:1). Researchers have long disagreed over that flower's precise identification; it has been variously called a CROCUS, lily, narcissus, anemone, rockrose, or tulip. In 2 Esdras 2:19, the roses growing on "seven mighty mountains" are probably Phoenician roses, which are wild roses that thrive at high elevations. Roses and similar flowers can be awe-inspiring objects of beauty; thus Simon son of Onias, praised for his "glorious" appearance, is compared with "roses in the days of first fruits" (Sir 50:5, 8).

RUBY

"THE STREETS OF JERUSALEM WILL BE PAVED WITH RUBY AND WITH STONES OF OPHIR." –TOBIT 13:16

The ruby, a deep red stone that is a variety of corundum, appears not to have been used in the Near East before the third century BC. Biblical references to the ruby may actually mean the carnelian, or sardius, red coral, or even the pearl, according to the particular translation. When the "ruby" is mentioned, it is as a highly valued jewel. Ezekiel 27:16 includes rubies among the items that Edom traded with Tyre, and Isaiah 54:12 describes the restored Jerusalem as having pinnacles made of rubies.

RULER

WHEN A LAND REBELS IT HAS MANY RULERS; BUT WITH AN INTELLIGENT RULER THERE IS LASTING ORDER. –PROVERBS 28:2

The Bible uses the general term *ruler* for a person in a position of power over others. A ruler might be a tribal leader, a city magistrate, or an overseer of some kind; King Nebuchadnezzar made Daniel "ruler over the whole province of Babylon" (Dan 2:48). The book of Nehemiah mentions rulers of districts and even rulers of "half the district" (Neh 3:9). The term also describes people of supreme authority, such as kings and emperors. Samuel proclaimed to Saul, "The LORD has anointed you ruler over his people Israel" (1 Sam 10:1). God and other deities named in the Bible are also spoken of as rulers.

Possibly crafted in Solomon's time, this seal depicts a ruler with a scepter.

RUST

YOUR GOLD AND SILVER HAVE RUSTED, AND THEIR RUST WILL BE EVIDENCE AGAINST YOU . . . .–JAMES 5:3

In many Bible translations, *rust* simply means corrosion of some type, and it is used as a symbol of corruption, impurity, and decay. The prophet Ezekiel denounced Jerusalem and its inhabitants as rust on a copper cooking pot (Ezek 24:6, 11). According to the Gospel of Matthew, Jesus used the image of rust to describe the vulnerablity of treasures on earth, as opposed to those in heaven (Mt 6:19–20). The letter of James lists one of the future miseries of the rich as being the rusting of their gold and silver.

RUTH, BOOK OF

"WHERE YOU GO, I WILL GO . . . YOUR PEOPLE SHALL BE MY PEOPLE, AND YOUR GOD MY GOD." –RUTH 1:16

The book of Ruth tells the story of a widow from Moab, a country east of the Dead Sea, who refuses to abandon her mother-in-law, Naomi. After Naomi's husband and sons die, Naomi decides to return to Judah, her native land. Ruth insists on going with her, even though Naomi tries to dissuade her. In Bethlehem, Ruth meets and marries Boaz, Naomi's kinsman. Ruth eventually becomes the great-grandmother of David and an ancestor of Jesus. The story, written anonymously, may have been preserved to establish the family tree of David or as a reminder that God's mercy extends to everyone, including non-Israelites. Ruth also serves as a model of loyalty. Scholars are uncertain as to whether the book was written before or after the exile. See also DAUGHTER-IN-LAW.

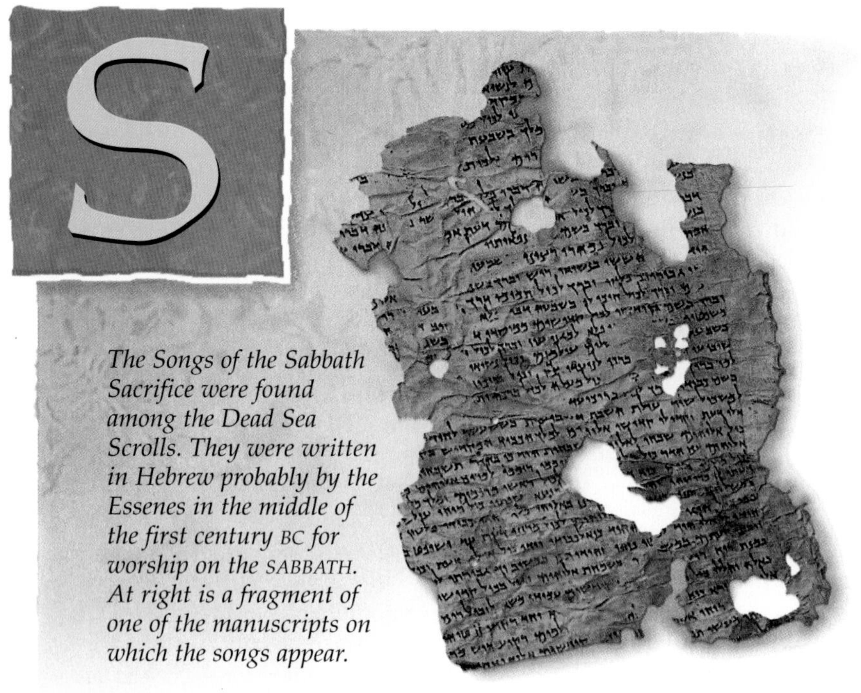

The Songs of the Sabbath Sacrifice were found among the Dead Sea Scrolls. They were written in Hebrew probably by the Essenes in the middle of the first century BC for worship on the SABBATH. At right is a fragment of one of the manuscripts on which the songs appear.

SABBATH

BUT THE SEVENTH DAY IS A SABBATH TO THE LORD YOUR GOD; YOU SHALL NOT DO ANY WORK . . . .
–DEUTERONOMY 5:14

The word *sabbath* is derived from a Hebrew word meaning "rest." The seventh day of the week was the sabbath, or day of rest—a memorial to the day that God rested after the labors of creation and a sign of Israel's covenant with God (Ex 31:13–17). The observation of the sabbath was the fourth of the ten commandments that Moses brought down from Mount Sinai; thus it was a cornerstone of God's law. Although the commandment prohibited work, biblical law specifically banned only plowing, harvesting, collecting food, and building a fire. On the day before the sabbath, the people gathered enough food for two days, and on the sabbath itself they generally did not leave their homes. When the Israelites were in the wilderness of the Sinai desert, a man was caught gathering sticks on the sabbath. God told Moses to have him killed, and the people stoned the man to death (Num 15:32–36).

For the observant, the sabbath was a day of joy and meditation as well as a time of rest for all family members, servants, and even animals (Deut 5:14). For those who needed to leave home on the seventh day, the law was later interpreted to permit a "sabbath day's journey" (Acts 1:12), defined as 2,000 cubits (about 1,000 yards) from the center of one's town.

SABBATH YEAR

. . . THEN THE LAND SHALL REST, AND ENJOY ITS SABBATH YEARS.
–LEVITICUS 26:34

Every seventh year was "a sabbath of complete rest" (Lev 25:4), when farmers were not to cultivate their fields but instead were to live off the previous year's harvest. According to Leviticus 25:6–7, whatever grew naturally could be eaten by humans, livestock, and wild animals; Exodus 23:11 limits the privilege to the poor and wild animals. Debts also were to be forgiven and slaves released. Like the year of JUBILEE, the sabbath, or sabbatical, year reminded the people that the land belonged to God. The sabbath year may have been created to prevent economic exploitation, but its full observance was probably infrequent.

SACKCLOTH

PUT ON SACKCLOTH AND LAMENT, YOU PRIESTS; WAIL, YOU MINISTERS OF THE ALTAR.–JOEL 1:13

To mourn a death or catastrophe or to display penitence, the people of the ancient Near East donned sackcloth, a coarse, dark material woven of camel or goat's hair. Some interpreters believe that *sackcloth* refers to a garment, while others think the term denotes simply the burlap-like material that was used to make grain bags. Jacob, believing that Joseph had been killed, "put sackcloth on his loins, and mourned for his son many days" (Gen 37:34). In the book of Jonah, the king of Nineveh orders that animals as well as people "be covered with sackcloth" (Jon 3:8) to entreat God's mercy.

SACRIFICE

". . . I HAVE COME TO SACRIFICE TO THE LORD; SANCTIFY YOURSELVES AND COME WITH ME TO THE SACRIFICE."
–1 SAMUEL 16:5

People in ancient Israel offered sacrifices of animals and crops to obtain God's forgiveness, to express their devotion to him, and to return to a state of purity, or cleanliness. The sacrificial offering, usually of a slaughtered animal, was the central act of worship.

The first seven chapters of Leviticus describe many kinds of sacrifices. The most common was the burnt offering, which atoned for sin and demonstrated loyalty to God. Each morning and evening, temple priests sacrificed a lamb as a burnt offering on behalf of the nation. Priests also officiated at private burnt offerings. Wealthier Israelites brought unblemished bulls, goats, or lambs, and the poor brought pigeons, doves, or grain mixed with oil.

If the offering was an animal, the worshiper brought it live to the altar and laid hands on its head, perhaps to symbolize that what was about to happen would express the individual's penitence or devotion. Either the priest or the offerer quickly killed the animal by cutting its throat so that the BLOOD flowed from it. (To slaughter birds, priests twisted their necks.) The priest caught some of the blood in a bowl and splashed it on the altar. In Leviticus 17:11, God explains the significance of this rite: "The life of the flesh is in the blood; and I have given it to you for making atonement for your lives on the altar." The animal (unless it was a bird) was skinned and quartered; the priest kept the hide as a contribution. The priest then put all the pieces into the fire on the altar, and the smoke produced a "pleasing odor to the LORD" (Lev 1:9).

A worshiper might also bring an offering of well-being, sometimes called a freewill offering. This was voluntary, rather than obligatory, and was performed in fulfillment of a vow, in simple devotion to God, or in gratitude for blessings, such as recovery from an illness. God's portion of the sacrifice, burned on the altar, was the liver, kidneys, and the fat covering the entrails. The priest kept the breast and right thigh. If the priest raised his portion in the air, he was dedicating it to God in what the Bible calls an elevation offering. The remainder of the meat went to the worshiper.

Another sacrifice was the sin or guilt offering, which atoned for unintentional sin or cleansed impurity, such as from touching a corpse. Atonement for the sin of a high priest required the sacrifice of a bull. Kings and other leaders had to sacrifice a male goat; people of the middle class could sacrifice a female goat or a lamb; and the poor could offer a pigeon, dove, or grain (see illustration). The offerer could not eat the meat of the sacrifice, which was given to the priest as a contribution. With God's portion, the priest burned the fat and dashed the blood on the altar.

Grain offerings frequently accompanied animal sacrifices, as did drink offerings of wine. The priest burned a handful of the grain; the remainder became his food. For a drink offering, he poured some of the wine at the base of the altar.

In New Testament times, Jews continued the long tradition of temple sacrifices, as did Jewish Christians. Peter and John went to the temple at 3 PM (Acts 3:1), when priests burned the evening sacrifice. Paul purified himself, preparing to offer a sacrifice (Acts 21:26). Yet even while observing the traditions of sacrifice, some Jewish Christians believed that Jesus "offered for all time a single sacrifice for sins" (Heb 10:12).

Sacrifices came to a halt when Rome destroyed the temple in AD 70. Jews began substituting prayer for sacrifice, a practice alluded to by the prophet Hosea: "Take away all guilt . . . and we will offer the fruit of our lips" (Hos 14:2). Similarly, Paul told Christians to live righteously, presenting themselves to God "as a living sacrifice, holy and acceptable to God" (Rom 12:1).

To restore a woman's purity after childbirth, biblical law required a burnt offering and a sin offering (Lev 12:1–8). Surrounded by family, the woman below has brought two doves, one for each sacrifice. Standing at the north side of the altar, the priest performs the burnt offering first. He begins by wringing the neck of the bird to kill it.

SADDUCEE

SOME SADDUCEES, WHO SAY THERE IS NO RESURRECTION, CAME TO HIM AND ASKED HIM A QUESTION . . . . –MARK 12:18

The Sadducees were a faction of Judaism in the Near East from the second century BC to the first century AD. They competed with another faction, the Pharisees, for influence in the courts and for control of the temple. The Sadducees believed in a literal interpretation of the laws of Moses. They rejected the ideas of resurrection, rewards and punishments after death, and angels and spirits. They also disagreed with the Pharisees on the issue of purity. Unlike the Pharisees, the Sadducees believed that only priests performing temple rituals should be held to the highest standards of ritual purity.

Though opponents, the Pharisees and the Sadducees are depicted as joined in their efforts to discredit Jesus. The Pharisees resisted Jesus because he would not accept the teachings of the oral law as binding. The Sadducees, whose members included priests and Levites, rich landowners, and merchants, opposed Jesus because supporting him might threaten their wealth and position. See also PHARISEE.

SAINT

GREET EVERY SAINT IN CHRIST JESUS. THE FRIENDS WHO ARE WITH ME GREET YOU.–PHILIPPIANS 4:21

In the Bible, saints are those who are set apart from others, marked as God's chosen people. In the Old Testament such people are called holy people or a holy nation. The people of Israel came to be called holy because God made them so: "You shall be holy to me; for I the LORD am holy, and I have separated you from the other peoples to be mine" (Lev 20:26).

St. John of Patmos, author of the book of Revelation, dictates to a scribe in this panel from a Byzantine diptych.

The word *saint* appears almost exclusively in the New Testament and refers to Christians, who are considered holy because of their special relationship with God. The primary difference between the Old Testament idea of saints and that of the New Testament is the role played by Jesus. Saints are people, Jews and Gentiles alike, who follow Jesus Christ. Paul addressed his letter "To the church of God that is in Corinth, to those who are sanctified in Christ Jesus, called to be saints" (1 Cor 1:2). Although the moral nature of the term *saint* is less clear, saints are reminded to save themselves from impurity (Eph 5:3) and pattern their lives after the HOLINESS of God.

SALT

"YOU ARE THE SALT OF THE EARTH; BUT IF SALT HAS LOST ITS TASTE, HOW CAN ITS SALTINESS BE RESTORED?" –MATTHEW 5:13

Salt was a necessary seasoning for food and a preservative—without it, food spoiled easily in the hot desert climate. Rock salt was obtained from mines deep in the earth's surface. The Dead Sea produced an inferior salt, but its accessibility made it a major source of salt in the Holy Land. Salt was added to sacrificial offerings (Ezek 43:24), and infants were rubbed with it after birth (Ezek 16:4).

Jesus called his disciples the salt of the earth, likening their role to the preservative qualities of salt, which kept food free of contamination. Yet he cautioned them not to become worthless like salt that has lost its flavor (Mt 5:13).

It was a common practice to sow the earth of a conquered city with salt; hence soil that was too saline symbolized desolation in the Bible. The barren land around the Dead Sea, the location of Sodom and Gomorrah, was described as having "all its soil burned out by sulfur and salt . . . unable to support any vegetation" (Deut 29:23).

Its salinity nearly 10 times that of regular seawater, the Dead Sea cannot sustain plant or animal life. These salt clusters have formed at its southern end.

SALVATION

"THERE IS SALVATION IN NO ONE ELSE, FOR THERE IS NO OTHER NAME UNDER HEAVEN GIVEN AMONG MORTALS BY WHICH WE MUST BE SAVED."
–ACTS OF THE APOSTLES 4:12

In the Bible, *salvation* is used to mean deliverance from danger and has both religious and secular connotations. In the Old Testament, God is considered the primary agent of salvation. The psalmist sings of the Lord, "He alone is my rock and my salvation" (Ps 62:2). Israel repeatedly turns to God for protection from military defeat and bondage by other nations. Perhaps the greatest act of salvation was when "the LORD saved Israel that day from the Egyptians" (Ex 14:30).

In the New Testament, the idea of salvation takes a different form. The word refers primarily to the ultimate or eternal salvation of those who believe in Christ—the anointed one—as the savior. For believers, salvation was seen as the saving or rescuing of someone from a life of sin, which Jesus accomplished by sacrificing himself on the cross to atone for human sins. Acceptance of salvation through Christ involved a spiritual event described as a "new birth" (1 Pet 1:3).

SAMUEL, 1 & 2

THEN ALL THE ELDERS OF ISRAEL . . . CAME TO SAMUEL AT RAMAH, AND SAID TO HIM, "YOU ARE OLD . . . APPOINT FOR US, THEN, A KING . . . ."
–1 SAMUEL 8:4–6

The two books of Samuel, written by unnamed historians, tell of how Israel emerged from a loosely knit band of tribes to become a unified nation under the leadership of its first king, Saul, who was followed by David. The story begins with the birth of Samuel, who served Israel as a prophet, priest, and judge. When he became old, tribal elders asked him to appoint a king. He reluctantly took the request to God, who told him that "they have not rejected you, but they have rejected me" (1 Sam 8:7). God chose Saul as Israel's first king, but once crowned, Saul chose to disobey God. For this, God punished Saul by having David succeed him (1 Sam 15:28).

The story of David begins in 1 Samuel 16 and continues throughout 2 Samuel, detailing the rise of David from court musician to king. The nation rallies around David, who in his youth had been secretly anointed by Samuel as the next king. The four decades of his reign established a dynasty in Israel that endured for about 400 years.

SANCTIFICATION

BUT NOW THAT YOU HAVE BEEN FREED FROM SIN . . . THE ADVANTAGE YOU GET IS SANCTIFICATION. THE END IS ETERNAL LIFE.
–ROMANS 6:22

Sanctification means to make something holy by devoting it to God through the removal of sin or ritual impurity. In the Old Testament, Israel was sanctified by obeying God's commandments and observing Jewish rituals. These rituals, which marked Israel as uniquely devoted to God, included sacrificial offerings, ritual bathing, and sprinkling with water.

In times of crisis, leaders also called on the people to cleanse themselves of ritual impurity and sin. Before the Israelites crossed into the Promised Land, for example, Joshua said, "Sanctify yourselves; for tomorrow the LORD will do wonders among you" (Josh 3:5). The people probably observed battle purification rituals, which included abstaining from sexual activity. Objects and sites of worship, such as altars, could also be sanctified through cleansing rituals.

New Testament writers deemphasized the ritual aspect of sanctification but maintained its connection to faith, justice, and love of God. They also linked sanctification to Christ's death, the Holy Spirit, and other experiences of Christian life. Urging believers to express sanctification by living righteously, the apostle Paul wrote: "God did not call us to impurity but in holiness" (1 Thess 4:7).

Sanctuary

Judah became God's sanctuary, Israel his dominion. –Psalm 114:2

In the Bible, *sanctuary* is another word for TEMPLE or tabernacle. It is a place set aside for the worship of God. In priestly tradition, God's sanctuary was the place where sacrifices were offered and rituals were carried out, but in a broad sense it was the entire Promised Land that was God's home (Ex 15:17). Occasionally, *sanctuary* is used to refer to places where other gods were worshiped. God warns the people through the prophet Ezekiel that "because you have defiled my sanctuary . . . I will cut you down" (Ezek 5:11). Solomon built the "inner sanctuary" (1 Kings 6:16) of his temple to house the ark of the covenant.

Sand

They all come for violence, with faces pressing forward; they gather captives like sand. –Habakkuk 1:9

The abundance of sand along the Mediterranean coast, as well as in the Holy Land's desert regions, probably inspired biblical writers to use grains of sand as a symbol for limitless numbers. Thus, God tells Abraham that he will have offspring "as the sand that is on the seashore" (Gen 22:17). References to sand also suggest weight—Job's calamity was "heavier than the sand of the sea" (Job 6:3)—and the possibility of buried treasure (Deut 33:19). In one of his parables, Jesus likens those who ignore his message to "a foolish man who built his house on sand" (Mt 7:26).

A young woman's sandals from the second century AD were found perfectly preserved in a cave in the Judean Desert.

Sandals

How graceful are your feet in sandals, O queenly maiden! –Song of Solomon 7:1

The inexpensive sandal—a leather or wooden sole attached to the foot by means of thongs—was the most common footwear of biblical times. Shoes, which resembled soft slippers, were also worn, and Roman soldiers marched in laced or strapped boots. Before entering a house or a sacred place, and as a gesture of mourning, people removed their sandals or shoes. In early biblical times, giving one's shoe to another signified the sealing of a bargain. When Ruth's next-of-kin handed his sandal to Boaz, he was consenting to Boaz's plan to marry Ruth and to acquire the land belonging to Naomi (Ruth 4:7–8).

Satan

After he received the piece of bread, Satan entered into him. –John 13:27

Satan comes from the Hebrew word meaning "adversary." In the Old Testament, Satan is represented as one who accuses people of wrongdoings rather than as the embodiment of evil, and the word is variously rendered as "slanderer," "accuser," or "adversary." The prophet Zechariah describes a vision of the trial of Joshua, the high priest, in which Satan is "standing at his right hand to accuse him" (Zech 3:1).

The word *Satan* appears primarily in the book of Job, however, and it is from Job that an understanding of Satan as a celestial being is derived. In Job 1–2, Satan is depicted in debate with God over Job's faithfulness. Satan questions Job's motives for worshiping God and asks, "Does Job fear God for nothing?" (Job 1:9). God allows Satan, acting as his agent, to put Job's piety to the test.

In the New Testament, Satan is no longer an agent of God but rather a leader of the forces of evil, which stand in opposition to the kingdom of God. Satan is called variously the tempter, the devil, the deceiver, and the evil one, and he repeatedly tries to tempt Jesus. When Jesus is fasting in the wilderness, Satan challenges his identity as SON OF GOD and urges him to prove himself by turning stones into bread, but Jesus refuses (Mt 4:1–4). In the final battle between God and Satan, "the devil who had deceived them was thrown into the lake of fire and sulfur . . . and . . . tormented day and night forever and ever" (Rev 20:10).

A wall painting from the tomb of Nebamun in Thebes, dating from 1380 BC, shows a jewelry shop worker weighing finished ingots. The scales that he uses employ a plumb line suspended by a hook and a counterbalance, on the right, carved in the form of an animal.

SAWS

HE BROUGHT OUT THE PEOPLE WHO WERE IN IT, AND SET THEM TO WORK WITH SAWS AND IRON PICKS AND AXES.—1 CHRONICLES 20:3

The earliest saws, dating from prehistoric times, were flint blades with notched edges. Later, these were replaced by bronze saws, with handles, which were easier to control. By about 1200 BC, hardy iron saws came into use in the Near East. In the passage above from 1 Chronicles, saws apparently were used in the demolition of a conquered city. But saws were used more commonly in construction and carpentry to cut wood and freshly quarried stone. According to 1 Kings, the stone that was used in the construction of Solomon's temple was "cut according to measure, sawed with saws, back and front" (1 Kings 7:9).

SCALES

HONEST BALANCES AND SCALES ARE THE LORD'S; ALL THE WEIGHTS IN THE BAG ARE HIS WORK. —PROVERBS 16:11

Scales, instruments to determine weight, were used in antiquity for commercial dealings. The earliest scales were handheld. Two pans were suspended from a crossbeam; one pan held the object being appraised, the other a known weight that usually consisted of various-size stones. The balance between the pans indicated the weight. Tampering with scales was a serious crime. The prophet Micah protested, "Can I tolerate wicked scales and a bag of dishonest weights?" (Mic 6:11). The Bible also uses the word *scales* to denote the scales that cover fish. When Saul's temporary blindness was healed, "something like scales fell from his eyes" (Acts 9:18). Leviticus 11:9 declares that the only aquatic creatures the Israelites could consume were those with fins and scales. See also BALANCES.

SCEPTER

. . ."HOW THE MIGHTY SCEPTER IS BROKEN, THE GLORIOUS STAFF!" —JEREMIAH 48:17

The scepter probably originated in ancient times as a club used by rulers to smite foes. In the Bible, the scepter is most often a symbol of authority and oppression (Zech 10:11). In royal courts of the ancient Near East it was used as a ceremonial baton, often laden with gold and gems. In Egypt and Persia, a scepter was typically a long, slender staff with a decorative head. An ancient wall relief shows the Persian king Xerxes I bestowing

Four ibexes surround a goat with curved horns on this copper scepter from the fourth millennium BC.

royal favor on a subject with a golden scepter. In Assyria, rulers wielded a short-handled scepter shaped like a battle mace. The nation of Israel was described symbolically as God's scepter (Ps 60:7), representing his sovereignty on earth.

Scourge

Famine and plague, tribulation and anguish are sent as scourges for the correction of humankind.
–2 Esdras 16:19

In the Old Testament, *scourge* frequently refers to punishments visited on the Israelites, who have rejected God (Josh 23:13). Similarly, God's blessings protect those who have made God a refuge: "No evil shall befall you, no scourge come near your tent" (Ps 91:10).

A scourge is also an instrument used to administer a severe beating. A more deadly version of the whip, a scourge consisted of leather thongs attached to a handle; pieces of metal or bone might be added to the thongs to inflict more intense pain. The apocryphal book 4 Maccabees tells the story of the martyrdom of Eleazar, who is tortured violently by the army of Antiochus: "His flesh was being torn by scourges, his blood flowing, and his sides were being cut to pieces" (4 Macc 6:6).

In New Testament times, a person who was sentenced to be crucified would be scourged (or flogged) first, as was Jesus' fate, according to Matthew and Mark: "And after flogging Jesus, [Pilate] handed him over to be crucified" (Mt 27:26; Mk 15:15). By weakening the person and hastening death, the beating possibly shortened the agony. See also FLOGGING.

Scribe

He was a scribe skilled in the law of Moses that the LORD the God of Israel had given . . . .–Ezra 7:6

Scribes could read and write with proficiency. They wrote letters, drafted contracts, and kept accounts. Professional scribes were often hired by local villagers. They worked from dictation, as Baruch did in copying the prophecies of Jeremiah onto a scroll (Jer 36:4).

With the establishment of the Israelite monarchy, scribes rose to prominence in the central bureaucracy: they were responsible for records, TAXES, and foreign correspondence. Their role evolved further and began to overlap with that of priests and Levites during the dark days of exile and thereafter, when it became their task to preserve, copy, and teach the sacred texts. The faithful gathered around scribes such as Ezra to learn the Torah and other Hebrew texts (Neh 8:1–3). After the return to Jerusalem, scribes became the official interpreters of Jewish law. They were an intellectual elite who gained political power and served as judges in the Sanhedrin.

In the New Testament *scribe* is often synonymous with *lawyer*, and scribes are frequently portrayed discussing with Jesus points of law such as forgiveness (Lk 5:21) and purity regulations (Mk 7:2–5), as well as interpretation of Scripture (Mk 12:28). Most of the scribes

At right, a brush holder, a water pot, and a palette form a hieroglyph meaning "scribe." Below, a scribe sits before the Egyptian god of writing, Thoth.

were aligned with the Pharisees, a Jewish political-religious party. Jesus condemned both groups as hypocrites, for "they do not practice what they teach" (Mt 23:3).

Scripture

All scripture is inspired by God and is useful for teaching, for reproof, for correction, and for training in righteousness . . . .
–2 Timothy 3:16

The word *Scripture* is derived from the Latin for WRITING. The term refers generally to writings that a religious group considers authoritative or inspired. Christians and Jews use *Scripture* to refer exclusively to the writings that were approved by their religious leaders as authentic, or canonical. In the New Testament, almost all of the more than 50 references to Scripture denote the sacred writings of the Old Testament, which are considered the written record of God's message to his people. *Scripture* may refer to these writings as a whole or to a specific passage that is quoted. Apparently, by the time 2 Peter was written, Paul's letters were being treated as part of the Scripture in Christian worship (2 Peter 3:16).

Scroll

. . . "He dictated all these words to me, and I wrote them with ink on the scroll."
–Jeremiah 36:18

Before the invention of books, both Old Testament and New Testament writings were copied on scrolls, which were sheets of PAPYRUS or leather glued end to end and rolled up on rods. Papyrus scrolls, which had been manufactured in Egypt since 3000 BC, were made from thin strips cut from the papyrus reed, which grew readily along the Nile. Two layers of these strips, one in horizontal rows and one in vertical rows, were laid atop one another and bonded together to form thick, rough sheets of paper.

Leather scrolls were sewn together from prepared skins of calves, sheep, or goats. Most of the Dead Sea Scrolls discovered at Qumran were made from such skins. Scrolls are still used in Jewish worship: on the night before Purim, a scroll containing the story of Esther is read aloud in the synagogue. Some scrolls contained one book of the Bible, others more. In Jewish tradition the writings of the 12 Minor Prophets are referred to as "the Twelve" because they were written on one scroll.

The Mediterranean Sea laps the coast of Israel, seen here from the city of Achzib.

Sea

You will cast all our sins into the depths of the sea.
–Micah 7:19

The Israelites and their neighbors considered the Mediterranean Sea to be the most important body of water. In the Bible it is often referred to as the "Great Sea" (Josh 1:4). Despite its long coastline, Israel was not a seafaring country. Through most of Israel's history, the Mediterranean was controlled by the Philistines, Canaanites, and Phoenicians.

God and Jesus both demonstrated their power over the sea. In the book of Exodus, God saved the Israelites by parting the waters of the Red Sea (Ex 14:21). In the Gospel of Matthew, Jesus walked on the Sea of Galilee and calmed a strong wind (Mt 14:25–33).

Seal

So she wrote letters in Ahab's name and sealed them with his seal . . . .
–1 Kings 21:8

A seal is an object with a design engraved in reverse, which produces a mirror image when pressed into wax, clay, or other soft material. *Seal* may also refer to the impression itself. A seal was a guarantee of a document's authenticity: when Queen Jezebel sealed official letters with her husband's seal, it was to convince the recipients that King Ahab himself had ordered the death of Naboth. Seals also ensured that documents and containers were not opened by unauthorized persons.

Seals were distinctive and individual. The earliest seals bore simple geometric shapes. Later seals were engraved with mythic scenes, religious images, or inscriptions, which often included the owner's name. Some seals were of the stamp type—designed to be worn as a necklace, bracelet, or ring. Others were cylindrical and were rolled over the wax or clay to produce an impression. The best seals were made from semiprecious stones, but seals were also made from pottery, stone, and wood. See also SIGNET.

SEASON

For everything there is a season, and a time for every matter under heaven . . . .–Ecclesiastes 3:1

In the Holy Land, there are two distinct seasons: summer, a dry period lasting from mid-April to mid-October, with complete drought from mid-June to mid-September; and winter, characterized by heavy rainfall, which begins in October or November. Typically, December, January, and February are the months with the most rain. For farmers in biblical times, the moisture provided by the dews of May and early June were also essential.

The Israelites referred to various periods of the year in terms of farming activities, agricultural festivals, or prevailing weather, such as "the heat of summer" (Ps 32:4). Seasonal terms were more frequently used for times of the year than the names of months; thus, November and December were known as "seed time," April and June as "harvest." The Gezer calendar, a 10th century BC agricultural table, describes the months by their harvests.

The term *season* is also used to describe the proper time for events to occur or come to fulfillment. According to Psalm 104:27: "These all look to you to give them their food in due season."

Though the scorching sun of the summer season has left the ground of the wadi at the foot of the Qumran cliffs dried and cracked, wildflowers spring up after a seasonal winter rain shower.

SEAT

He took his seat on the throne of the kings.–2 Kings 11:19

In the Bible, a seat usually represents an exalted position and honor, such as the THRONE of a king or the seats of judges, teachers, and elders. A seated position also indicates importance: a king often sat while his subjects stood around him. In Solomon's court, Solomon's mother occupied the seat to the right of his throne (1 Kings 2:19), making her influence apparent to all. Special seats were set aside for respected figures in synagogues and at banquets. When Jesus told his disciples, "The scribes and the Pharisees sit on Moses' seat" (Mt 23:2), he meant that they were authorities on the law of Moses.

SEED

". . . the good seed are the children of the kingdom; the weeds are the children of the evil one . . . ." –Matthew 13:38

According to Genesis, after God separated the heavens from the earth, he then said, "'Let the earth put forth vegetation: plants yielding seed, and fruit trees . . . that bear fruit with the seed in it'" (Gen 1:11). Without seed, land would "become desolate" (Gen 47:19). Biblical law proscribed mixing different species, and it was forbidden to sow one's field "with two kinds of seed" (Lev 19:19). As a penalty for disobedience, God warned the Israelites: "You shall sow your seed in vain, for your enemies shall eat it" (Lev 26:16). Jesus used imagery of a seed sown in a field in several of his parables.

Selah

I cry aloud to the LORD, and he answers me from his holy hill. Selah –Psalm 3:4

The word *selah* appears 74 times in the Bible: 71 times in the book of Psalms and 3 times in Habakkuk. *Selah* probably was meant to indicate a pause in the singing. Because it often appears at the end of a psalm or a section of a psalm, it may be a musical or liturgical direction that was probably added to the original text. *Selah* may mean "lift up" and may have been a signal to the singers or orchestra to sing or play louder, or an instruction to the congregation to lift up their hands in prayer. Conversely, some scholars suggest that the word may have been a signal for the entire congregation to fall prostrate on the ground.

Seraph

Seraphs . . . said: "Holy, holy, holy is the LORD of hosts; the whole earth is full of his glory." –Isaiah 6:2–3

The word *seraph* is derived from the Hebrew root meaning "burn." Seraphs are supernatural creatures, possibly fiery beings who are serpentine in form but have human faces and feet. They were depicted in Isaiah's vision—their only appearance in the Bible—as guardians or attendants of God, and "each had six wings: with two they covered their faces, and with two they covered their feet, and with two they flew" (Isa 6:2).

Seraphs, shown here in red, attend the coronation of the Virgin Mary in this 15th-century illumination from a Book of Hours.

Seraphs, or seraphim, surround and worship God on his throne. One seraph is said to have cleansed Isaiah from sin by touching his lips with a hot coal from the altar (Isa 6:7). Postbiblical tradition of the early Christian church sometimes includes seraphim and CHERUBIM among the choirs of angels.

Serpent

At the last it bites like a serpent, and stings like an adder. –Proverbs 23:32

Serpents—a general term for snakes—variously inspired dread, loathing, and awe in ancient times. Although some snakes, including the viper, were poisonous, many were not. Nevertheless, the fear inspired by their venom caused serpents to be regarded as powerful figures. Snakes were religious symbols of fertility and protection: the sacred serpent on a pharoah's headdress guided him to victory. The Greek god Asclepius associated serpents with healing. Serpents could also symbolize evil: in Mesopotamian and Canaanite mythology, a primeval sea serpent represents the waters of chaos. In the Bible, this creature is called LEVIATHAN or dragon (Isa 27:1).

In the book of Genesis, the serpent was said to be "more crafty than any other wild animal that the Lord God had made" (Gen 3:1), and it successfully tempted Eve in the Garden of Eden, causing God to utter the curse: "Upon your belly you shall go, and dust you shall eat all the days of your life" (Gen 3:14).

Serpents could also be deadly menaces. To punish the Israelites in the wilderness, God sent "poisonous serpents" (Num 21:6), or literally "fiery" serpents, perhaps because of the burning sensation of their bites. Many people were killed, and the survivors begged for help. God instructed Moses to put a bronze serpent atop a pole, declaring that "everyone who is bitten shall look at it and live" (Num 21:8). The bronze serpent eventually became an object of worship, as in other ancient Near Eastern religions. According to 2 Kings, King Hezekiah destroyed the bronze serpent known as Nehushtan (2 Kings 18:4).

In the New Testament, Jesus addresses scribes and Pharisees as "you snakes, you brood of vipers!" (Mt 23:33). In the book of Revelation, Satan, "the deceiver of the whole world," is referred to as "that ancient serpent" (Rev 12:9).

The serpent is often depicted in ancient art. This 14th- to 13th-century BC serpent was unearthed at the copper mines of Timna, near the Gulf of Aqaba.

Seven stars (Rev 1:20) are central among the apocalyptic symbols from the book of Revelation, as illustrated by this 12th-century manuscript.

Servant

... "You are my servant, I have chosen you and not cast you off" ....–Isaiah 41:9

A servant was one who worked as a household domestic, messenger, guard, or attendant. One of the most common Hebrew words for servant is also translated "slave." Servants were both male and female: the Bible mentions a "servant-boy" (1 Sam 9:22) and "servant-girls" (Prov 27:27), although the latter were probably women. On the night Jesus was arrested, Peter denied knowing Jesus to several servant-girls (Mt 26:69–72). Maids could bear children on behalf of their mistresses. When Jacob's wife Leah could no longer conceive a child, her maid Zilpah bore two more sons for Jacob, and both babies were considered legally to belong to Leah.

In 2 Kings 8:13, Hazael, the future king of Aram, calls himself "a servant" before the prophet Elisha. Moses and David are referred to as servants of God, because God worked through them to achieve his aims: "'Through my servant David I will save my people Israel'" (2 Sam 3:18). Similarly, the nation of Israel was chosen to be God's servant (Isa 41:8). In the New Testament, followers of Jesus are "servants of Christ" (1 Cor 4:1).

Seven

The seven priests carrying the seven trumpets of rams' horns before the ark of the Lord passed on ....–Joshua 6:13

The number seven has religious significance, and it appears in the Bible hundreds of times. Some scholars believe that the importance of the number seven reflected the division of the lunar month into four seven-day weeks. God created the world in six days and rested on the seventh. Noah took seven pairs of every clean animal with him on the ark. Passover, the Festival of Weeks, and the Festival of Booths were seven-day festivals, and every seventh year was a SABBATH YEAR (Lev 25:4).

In Mark 8:6–8, Jesus fed the multitudes with "seven loaves" and a few small fish and had "seven baskets full" of leftover food. When Peter asked Jesus if he should forgive a sin as many as seven times, Jesus replied, "Not seven times, but I tell you, seventy-seven times" (Mt 18:22). The number seven also appears often in the apocalyptic literature. In the book of Revelation, there are seven churches (Rev 1:4), seven stars and seven lampstands (Rev 1:20), seven angels and seven trumpets (Rev 8:2), and seven seals (Rev 5:1).

Shadow

... for our days on earth are but a shadow.–Job 8:9

The term *shadow* is used as an image throughout the Bible that ranges from the gloomy to the comforting. Commenting on the brief, variable, and insubstantial nature of human life, Job observes: "A mortal ... comes up like a flower and withers, flees like a shadow and does not last" (Job 14:1–2). However, just as trees provide welcome shade from the intense midday heat of the Holy Land, so a good ruler is said to provide a shadow of protection (Lam 4:20). Moreover, spiritual refuge can be found "in the shadow of the Almighty" (Ps 91:1). Recent English versions of the Bible render the famed phrase "the valley of the shadow of death" as "the darkest valley" (Ps 23:4).

Sheep

Then he led out his people like sheep, and guided them in the wilderness like a flock.
–Psalm 78:52

Sheep were considered a source of wealth in ancient times. The Bible describes one man as being "very rich; he had three thousand sheep" (1 Sam 25:2). Sheep were prized for their MEAT, fat, milk, wool, and skins. The domesticated sheep were generally broad-tailed breeds; the tail, like the camel's hump, stored quantities of reserved fat and could weigh up to 30 pounds. Sheep were important in Israelite sacrifice, and the "fat tail" (Ex 29:22) was sometimes part of the offering.

Sheep were a common sight in the Holy Land as they grazed or were led to new pastures by a shepherd. Isaiah 53:6 compares humankind with sheep that are easily sidetracked and lost: "All we like sheep have gone astray." The shelters where sheep were kept—sometimes natural caves—were referred to as sheepfolds (1 Sam 24:3). Abel was described as a "keeper of sheep" (Gen 4:2), and Jacob is said to have manipulated the breeding process so that the ewes, or females, would produce lambs of a particular pattern (Gen 30:37–39). The sheep's fleece, or coat of wool, was cut off by a sheepshearer during a festive shearing season. Wool was highly valued: the king of Moab had to pay the king of Israel tribute that included "the wool of one hundred thousand rams" (2 Kings 3:4). The inner covering of the tabernacle was made of the tanned skins of rams, or male sheep (Ex 26:14). When "the priest Zadok took the horn of oil . . . and anointed Solomon" (1 Kings 1:39), the horn that contained the oil was that of a ram. A ram horn's mighty blast even brought down the walls of Jericho (Josh 6:2–20).

Shekel

. . . the man took a gold nose-ring weighing a half shekel . . . .
–Genesis 24:22

The word *shekel* is derived from the Hebrew root meaning "weight." The shekel was the basic measure of WEIGHT and was used in metal objects ranging from nose rings to silver basins and coins.

Late in the fifth century BC, coinage of silver shekels with reliable stamped values became the standard exchange for goods and services. Perhaps the most famous shekel was the Phoenician COIN produced in Tyre from 126 BC to about 56 AD. It was made of such high-quality silver that it became the preferred currency for use in paying the temple tax. The phrase "shekel of the sanctuary" (Num 7:13) occurs frequently in the Bible and may refer to the prevalent standard of currency in ancient Israel.

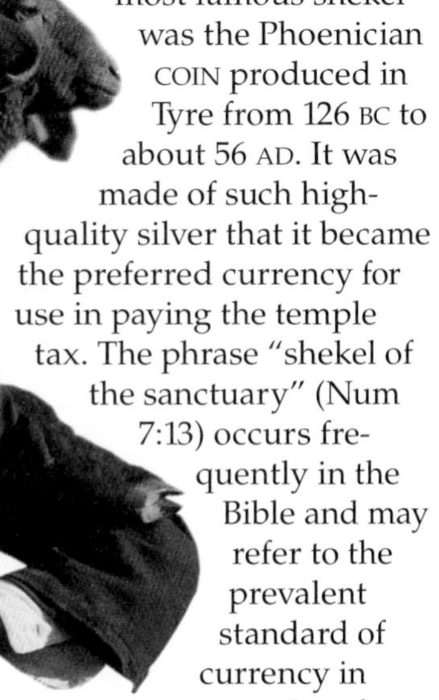

Though blind and enfeebled by age, this Bedouin shepherd supports one of his sheep on his shoulders, just as a father might a child.

Sheol

Though they dig into Sheol, from there shall my hand take them; though they climb up to heaven, from there I will bring them down.–Amos 9:2

The Israelites believed that the dead—wicked and righteous alike—dwelled in a place called Sheol, located in an underworld within the earth, also referred to as "the Pit" (Isa 14:15). According to Job, Sheol was a "land of gloom and deep darkness" (Job 10:21). It was described as insatiable: "Sheol has enlarged its appetite and opened its mouth beyond measure" (Isa 5:14). The evil Korah and his followers were swallowed up by it while still alive: "If . . . they go down alive into Sheol, then you shall know that these men have despised the LORD" (Num 16:30). In the New Testament, Sheol is known as Hades or HELL and is depicted as a place of torture and confinement for the wicked (Lk 16:23; 2 Pet 2:4).

Shepherd

. . . they were harassed and helpless, like sheep without a shepherd.–Matthew 9:36

Since sheep and goats can forage in nearly barren wastelands, they were the most ubiquitous domestic animals in the arid Holy Land. Shepherds were responsible for the care and safety of their own sheep and goats as well as those of their master. Moses, Abraham, Jacob, David, and the prophet Amos all worked as shepherds for at least part of their lives.

The shepherd's job required that he continually move his flock to new pastures, especially in the summer months, making sure the animals had water to drink at least once a day and rounding up strays. The shepherd also guarded his charges from attacks by lions,

Villages often hired a shepherd to watch the sheep of each household. If a sheep or goat was lost or stolen, the shepherd was required to repay its owner. In this illustration, a flock is attacked by a pack of wolves. A shepherd takes up his slingshot and hurls a rock at one of the wolves to drive the animals away. With practice, a leather slingshot could be deadly; it could also be used to redirect stray sheep. To guide their charges over hilly or rocky terrain, the shepherds have rods, or staffs.

bears, and other predators, often at the risk of his own life (see illustration). The search for new pasture often took the flock and shepherd far into the wilderness.

In ancient times, as today, shepherding was often an occupation of nomads, and shepherds were sometimes looked down upon by settled populations (Gen 46:32–34). Because both groups competed for the same land and water, there was often hostility between them, as the story of Cain and Abel (Gen 4:1–16) suggests.

References to God as a shepherd and Israel as his flock abound in the Old Testament (Gen 48:15; 49:24; Ezek 34:15). In the Gospel of John, Jesus describes his relationship to his followers: "I am the good shepherd. The good shepherd lays down his life for the sheep" (Jn 10:11). The image of the good shepherd leading his flock was so strongly embedded in the early Christian church that leaders of Christian congregations came to be known as pastors, from the Latin word meaning "shepherd."

Shibboleth

. . . they said to him, "Then say Shibboleth," and he said, "Sibboleth," for he could not pronounce it right.—Judges 12:6

The modern meaning of *shibboleth*, as a slogan of a sect or party, is derived from a story in the book of Judges. After the Gileadites defeated the Ephraimites, they took control of the Jordan River, preventing their foes from returning home. When the Ephraimites attempted to sneak across the river

by concealing their identity, the Gileadites made each suspect pronounce the password *shibboleth*. Because the Ephraimites spoke a different dialect of Hebrew, they could not pronounce the "sh" sound and instead said "sibboleth." Anyone who mispronounced the word was uncovered as an Ephraimite and slain.

Shield

Happy are you, O Israel! Who is like you, a people saved by the LORD, the shield of your help . . . . –Deuteronomy 33:29

The typical shield of biblical times was made of leather stretched over a wooden frame with inside handles. Leather shields had to be oiled frequently to prevent drying and cracking. Shields varied in size and shape: in David's time, spearmen preferred body shields, while archers often favored the smaller round shield that could be used with bow and arrow. Metal was generally used only as structural support, but decorative gold shields adorned the royal palace in Jerusalem (1 Kings 10:16–17). In times of warfare, shieldbearers often carried rectangular shields large enough to cover another soldier's entire body, and mounted shieldbearers were also assigned to CAVALRY archers.

Ship

Or look at ships: though they are so large that it takes strong winds to drive them, yet they are guided . . . wherever the will of the pilot directs.–James 3:4

Ships have plied the waters of the ancient Near East loaded with goods for TRADE since before 4000 BC. The earliest vessels were simple canoes made from sturdy reeds that were used to travel the many rivers and canals. By the third millennium BC, the Egyptians were making ships from wood. The absence of good timber in Eygpt caused cedar to be imported from Lebanon, and seagoing ships were invented. The Israelites had little direct experience with shipping. King Solomon, who ruled in the 10th century BC, nevertheless is said to have employed "ships of Tarshish" (1 Kings 10:22), which were probably Phoenician ships, for Mediterranean and Red Sea trading.

Cargo vessels were propelled by as many as 100 oarsmen in single-banked or double-banked galleys. A flutist or time beater set the cadence of the rowing strokes. Eventually, expanded trade necessitated the development of trading ships with a single square sail and a rounded hull. Storms and blanketing fogs of winter made sailing safest from late May to mid-September. Trading ships were under the command of a sailing master, or captain, hired by the ship's owner. Greek warships, built after 400 BC, might carry 200 men as crew.

Voyage by ship was apparently limited to freight ships, and because there was little cabin space, passengers probably slept on the open deck. In Acts of the Apostles, the apostle Paul went aboard trading ships in his travels throughout the Mediterranean. The further growth of shipping necessitated the construction of protected commercial harbors complete with artificial sea walls, piers, storehouses, and defenseworks such as those that Herod the Great built in Caesarea. See also illustration for VOYAGE.

Shrine

We have this hope, a sure and steadfast anchor of the soul, a hope that enters the inner shrine behind the curtain . . . .–Hebrews 6:19

In the Bible, the word *shrine* refers to a building devoted to the WORSHIP of a specific deity or to a box or container in which sacred objects are kept. Some shrines were also located in larger temples, often housed in a wall niche. *Shrine* can also refer to objects or places associated with the worship of other gods. King Josiah "removed all the shrines of the high places that were in the towns of Samaria" (2 Kings 23:19). Paul chastised the silversmith Demetrius for the sin of selling "silver shrines" (Acts 19:24), miniature versions of the temple of Artemis.

This seventh-century BC cult stand, unearthed at Ein Hatzeva in the Negeb Desert, was used in worship at an Edomite shrine.

Siege

Blessed be the LORD, for he has wondrously shown his steadfast love to me when I was beset as a city under siege.
–Psalm 31:21

In biblical times, a siege was a major military tactic that involved encircling a fortified city and then either attacking it or waiting for it to surrender. This method was highly effective because it cut the people off from food and water supplies and kept away any of their allies. Many cities prepared for such an event by storing food and by building cisterns for the collection of rainwater. However, sieges could last for long periods of time: according to 2 Kings 17:5, Assyria besieged Samaria for three years. Such lengthy isolation often led to starvation among the citizenry.

The book of 2 Chronicles describes Assyria's siege of Jerusalem. Once his army was encamped outside the city, King Sennacherib sent messengers to the Judean people to frighten them by telling them that their ruler, Hezekiah, was "handing [them] over to die by famine and by thirst" (2 Chr 32:11). Although God saved the city of Jerusalem from Assyria, Sennacherib destroyed most of the other cities of Judah. The king inscribed on a clay prism his winning strategy: "I besieged and conquered by stamping down earth-ramps and then by bringing up battering rams, by the assault of foot soldiers, by breaches, tunneling, and sapper operations."

Even the fortress of Masada, built atop a desert cliff, could not withstand a siege by Roman troops. Facing conquest, Jewish rebels in the fortress committed mass suicide in AD 73. Shown above are the remains of Masada and the Roman siege ramp, at right.

Sappers were mining engineers who dug tunnels. In AD 70, during the Roman siege of Jerusalem, Jewish Zealot sappers dug tunnels under the enemies' ramps, shored the tunnels up with wooden beams, and then set the beams on fire. Without the support timber, the tunnels caved in, undermining the ramps. In the end, however, the Romans captured the city, as foreseen by Jesus in the Gospel of Luke: "Indeed, the days will come upon you, when your enemies will set up ramparts around you and surround you, and hem you in on every side" (Lk 19:43).

Besides siege ramps, INVADERS used siege walls, apparently walls built to surround cities, and what the Bible calls siegeworks. These were towers or platforms from which soldiers could shoot arrows and cast spears and other weapons over the city's wall. According to Mosaic law, the Israelites could cut down "only the trees that you know do not produce food" to build siegeworks (Deut 20:20). Soldiers on the siegeworks were vulnerable to the city's defenders, who, from their position on top of their walls or towers, could assault the attackers with all sorts of weapons, including arrows, rocks, and even boiling water or hot oil.

SIEVE

FOR LO, I WILL COMMAND, AND SHAKE THE HOUSE OF ISRAEL . . . AS ONE SHAKES WITH A SIEVE, BUT NO PEBBLE SHALL FALL TO THE GROUND.–AMOS 9:9

A sieve is an agricultural tool used to separate grain from chaff. Biblical sieves were made of mesh woven from hair, grass, reeds, string, or fine leather. The mesh was attached to a flat, round wooden frame or was placed in a bowl. Although WINNOWING removed much of the chaff, the grain was sometimes sifted for further purification before being stored as food for humans. The impure grain was thrown into the sieve. The mesh retained stones, chaff, and other unwanted material but let the grain fall through. The chaff was burned, and the grain was stored in wide-mouthed earthenware jars in underground silos in the back room of the house or in storehouses. Large national silos may have existed to store grain from farmers as payment of taxes.

In the book of Amos, the sieve is used as a metaphor for God's discipline: the prophet warns that God will place Israel in a sieve from which no one will fall through, for none of the people are good grain. The book of Isaiah says that God will bring judgment on the nations, sifting them "with the sieve of destruction" (Isa 30:28).

SIGN

. . . "THIS IS THE SIGN OF THE COVENANT THAT I HAVE ESTABLISHED BETWEEN ME AND ALL FLESH THAT IS ON THE EARTH." –GENESIS 9:17

In the Bible a sign is often an object or event that reveals God's purpose. In the book of Genesis, God places a RAINBOW in the sky as a visible sign to Noah that the Lord will never again destroy the world by flood (Gen 9:12–17).

God called upon his people to perform certain practices as signs of their covenant with him, including circumcision (Gen 17:11) and the observance of the sabbath (Ex 31:13–17). He asked the Israelites to put blood on their doorways in Egypt as a sign for him to pass over their houses during the slaughter of the firstborn (Ex 12:13). God's actions on behalf of Israel against the Egyptians were among the many signs that he provided of his continuing care for his chosen people (Josh 24:17). The Israelites nevertheless displayed occasional weakness in their faith, prompting God to demand of Moses, "And how long will they refuse to believe in me, in spite of all the signs that I have done among them?" (Num 14:11).

Isaiah and other prophets used signs as vivid ways to communicate God's word. Isaiah "walked naked and barefoot" (Isa 20:3) as a portent of Egypt's future status. This was a warning to Judah to trust in God, rather than in other countries, for protection.

According to the Gospel of John, Jesus performed a number of signs that revealed his identity as God's son and as the Messiah. However, in one instance he chided, "Unless you see signs and wonders you will not believe" (Jn 4:48). Jesus also warned his disciples of false messiahs and prophets who would "produce great signs and omens, to lead astray, if possible, even the elect" (Mt 24:24).

In an ivory carving of the nativity, sculpted about AD 810, an angel tells the shepherds, "This will be a sign for you: you will find a child wrapped in bands of cloth and lying in a manger" (Lk 2:12).

SIGNAL

ALL YOU INHABITANTS OF THE WORLD, YOU WHO LIVE ON THE EARTH, WHEN A SIGNAL IS RAISED ON THE MOUNTAINS, LOOK! –ISAIAH 18:3

The signals commonly used in Old Testament days to warn of impending danger, announce great triumphs, or summon the community to gather were both auditory and visual, including whistles, shouts, trumpet blasts, hand-waving, fire, smoke, and signal posts or flagstaffs. Israelites on the march or their troops in battle were signaled to rally by the waving of a BANNER or flag. The prophet Jeremiah warned of an invasion by saying, "Blow the trumpet in Tekoa, and raise a signal on Beth-haccherem; for evil looms out of the north" (Jer 6:1). The book of Zechariah speaks of God signaling for his dispersed people as he prepares to bring them back home (Zech 10:8).

SIGNET

A STONE WAS BROUGHT AND LAID ON THE MOUTH OF THE DEN, AND THE KING SEALED IT WITH HIS OWN SIGNET AND WITH THE SIGNET OF HIS LORDS . . . .
–DANIEL 6:17

A signet is a small SEAL that was used for marking official documents. Often set into rings, signets were made from gemstones, both for beauty and for durability. They bore the owner's name or an identifying design, which the signet maker carved with tools of copper or iron, perhaps sometimes using a simple bow drill with a metal bit and abrasive powder. Like other gem cutters, the signet maker needed a good eye and a steady hand; he also had to have the ability to trace the design in reverse so that the signet's impression would read properly.

SILENCE

BUT THE LORD IS IN HIS HOLY TEMPLE; LET ALL THE EARTH KEEP SILENCE BEFORE HIM!
–HABAKKUK 2:20

Silence, or quietness, has various connotations in the Bible. It can be a sign of reverence, resignation, or peace. The prophets sometimes called for silence. For example, in an indictment of Israel, Amos says, "The prudent will keep silent in such a time; for it is an evil time" (Am 5:13). According to the Gospels, Jesus often warned witnesses of his healings not to talk about what they had seen, and he himself stood silent in the face of some of the accusations against him (Mk 14:61; 15:5). The letters to the Thessalonians urged the early Christians to live and work quietly (1 Thess 4:11; 2 Thess 3:12).

Silver was often used to make religious objects, such as this sixth-century BC incense altar from Persia.

SILVER

. . . ABRAHAM WEIGHED OUT FOR EPHRON THE SILVER THAT HE HAD NAMED IN THE HEARING OF THE HITTITES . . . .
–GENESIS 23:16

When Abraham bought a grave site for Sarah for 400 shekels of silver—"according to the weights current among the merchants" (Gen 23:16)—he was demonstrating one of silver's most important uses. Silver, rather than gold, was the chief medium of exchange in the Old and New Testament periods. The precious metal was originally exchanged in the form of ingots, jewelry, and other articles, but eventually the silver COIN became very common.

Silver was chiefly extracted from galena, a lead ore, in which it was present in small quantities. Because the Holy Land was poor in galena, silver had to be imported, either in refined or unrefined form. The main sources of the ore were in present-day Armenia, Crete, and Greece.

Silver was one of the first metals to be used by human beings. Since ancient times, it has been prized for its beautiful luster and for its malleability: silver can be bent, drawn into wire, and hammered into extremely thin sheets. Silversmiths took advantage of these qualities to make exquisite jewelry, drinking cups, and other articles, including ceremonial vessels and fittings for the tabernacle and Solomon's temple.

SIN

. . . "LET ANYONE AMONG YOU WHO IS WITHOUT SIN BE THE FIRST TO THROW A STONE AT HER."
–JOHN 8:7

Sin is disobedience to or rebellion against God. Although Genesis 3 does not contain the word *sin*, that biblical chapter does tell of Adam and Eve's violation of the one injunction that God had given them. Their sin leads to expulsion from the garden of Eden and such consequences as painful childbirth, hard labor, and death. In Genesis 4, God warns their son Cain to be wary of the power of sin: "If you do not do well, sin is lurking at the door; its desire is for you, but you must master it" (Gen 4:7).

Along with some neighboring peoples, the Israelites believed in the innate sinfulness of human beings. The book of Proverbs poses the question: "Who can say, 'I have made my heart clean; I am pure from my sin'?" (Prov 20:9). In the New Testament, Jesus stops the stoning of an adulteress when he calls upon the sinless in the crowd to cast the first stone (Jn 8:7–9).

Mosaic law set forth the standard for acting righteously in order to preserve the covenant with God. Recognizing that people would nevertheless commit both uninten-

Eve and Adam committed the first sin when they ate the fruit of "the tree that is in the middle of the garden" (Gen 3:3). A miniature from a medieval book of prayers depicts them beside the tree, entwined around which is the snake that tempted Eve.

tional and intentional sins, it also established an elaborate system of offerings and sacrifices by which sinners could make atonement to God. If a transgression hurt another person, the sinner also had to make RESTITUTION to the victim.

In the Gospels, Jesus calls upon victims to forgive those who wronged them in order to receive forgiveness from God for their own "trespasses" (Mt 6:14; Mk 11:25). The letter to the Hebrews describes Jesus as the only human being without sin; as such, he is the savior who can "remove sin by the sacrifice of himself" (Heb 9:26).

Sister

"WHOEVER DOES THE WILL OF GOD IS MY BROTHER AND SISTER AND MOTHER."
–MARK 3:35

Biblical writers used the word *sister* to mean someone's female sibling whether the two people had both parents in common or only one. According to his words in Genesis 20:12, Abraham married his half-sister, Sarah; however, that practice was later prohibited by the command, "You shall not uncover the nakedness of your sister" (Lev 18:9). *Sister* could also be used figuratively for any female relative or member of the same tribe. The singer in Song of Solomon speaks of his beloved when he says, "You have ravished my heart, my sister, my bride" (Song of S 4:9). In the New Testament, the term is used to express women's spiritual kinship within the Christian community.

Skin

YOU CLOTHED ME WITH SKIN AND FLESH, AND KNIT ME TOGETHER WITH BONES AND SINEWS.
–JOB 10:11

Scriptural references to human skin are usually linked to disease, most frequently to problems generally called LEPROSY. Skin maladies could cause ritual uncleanliness. Some of the Bible's most memorable expressions use *skin* figuratively, such as in Job 19:20: "I have escaped by the skin of my teeth."

Beginning with the hides that God gave Adam and Eve to cover their nakedness (Gen 3:21), animal skins—derived mainly from household flocks of sheep, goats, donkeys, and cattle—were essential to domestic life. Skin containers, usually made from goat hides, were used to hold water, milk, and wine. During the Israelites' sojourn in the desert, the tabernacle was covered by animal skins.

Jews who hid in the Cave of Letters during a revolt against Rome left behind this water skin of goat hide. Dating from about AD 135, it has been partially restored.

SKIRTS

ALSO ON YOUR SKIRTS IS FOUND THE LIFEBLOOD OF THE INNOCENT POOR . . . .
—JEREMIAH 2:34

In the Bible, *skirts* refers to the hem of a garment or to a loose item of clothing worn by women. The term is almost always used symbolically, such as when God sarcastically asks Job whether he (rather than God himself) has caused the dawn to "know its place, so that it might take hold of the skirts of the earth, and the wicked be shaken out of it?" (Job 38:12–13). Because they cover nakedness, skirts are associated with sin and harlotry. In Lamentations, the "uncleanness" of Jerusalem lies "in her skirts" (Lam 1:9). In Jeremiah, God threatens to "lift up" the skirts of Jerusalem, exposing the city's corruption (Jer 13:26).

SLANDER

PUT AWAY FROM YOU ALL BITTERNESS AND WRATH AND ANGER AND WRANGLING AND SLANDER . . . .
—EPHESIANS 4:31

The Bible explicitly condemns uttering slander (Lev 19:16), or false words intended to harm another. Mosaic law prohibited slander with the commandment against bearing "false witness against your neighbor" (Ex 20:16; Deut 5:20). Proverbs 30:10 warns specifically against slandering a servant to a master. In the New Testament, several of the letters to the early Christians list slander along with other transgressions. For example, the first letter of Peter advises, "Rid yourselves . . . of all malice, and all guile, insincerity, envy, and all slander" (1 Pet 2:1). Some interpreters suggest that the greatest slanderer in the Bible is Satan, whom Jesus called "the father of lies" (Jn 8:44).

SLAVERY

". . . I LED YOU UP FROM EGYPT, AND BROUGHT YOU OUT OF THE HOUSE OF SLAVERY . . . ."
—JUDGES 6:8

Slavery was commonplace in ancient times. A person could be forced into bondage if captured during war or if kidnapped. Slavery could also be imposed for failure to honor debts. Free people might voluntarily sell their children or themselves into slavery to avoid destitution. Slaves labored in fields, in mines, and on construction projects; some worked in the temple or in the government bureaucracy. A slave might also toil as a domestic SERVANT. Hagar, who became Abraham's concubine, was the "slave-girl" (Gen 16:1) of his wife, Sarah.

Slaves were recognized as being the master's chattel: "You may keep them as a possession for your children after you, for them to inherit as property" (Lev 25:46). Yet biblical law attempted to curb cruelty: "When a slaveowner strikes a male or female slave with a rod and the slave dies immediately, the owner shall be punished" (Ex 21:20). Slaves were not permitted to work on the sabbath (Deut 5:14). A fellow Israelite could be enslaved for only six years; in the seventh year the slave had to be released and the owner was to "provide liberally" for the newly freed person (Deut 15:13–14). Such generosity reflected God's own care: "Remember that you were a slave in the land of Egypt, and the LORD your God redeemed you" (Deut 15:15).

Slavery continued into later periods, and the New Testament never calls for its abolition. Paul urged slaves to "obey your earthly masters" (Eph 6:5) and the master to stop threatening his slaves, for "both of you have the same Master in heaven" (Eph 6:9). Elsewhere Paul used the concept of slavery metaphorically, proclaiming: "Christ has set us free" (Gal 5:1).

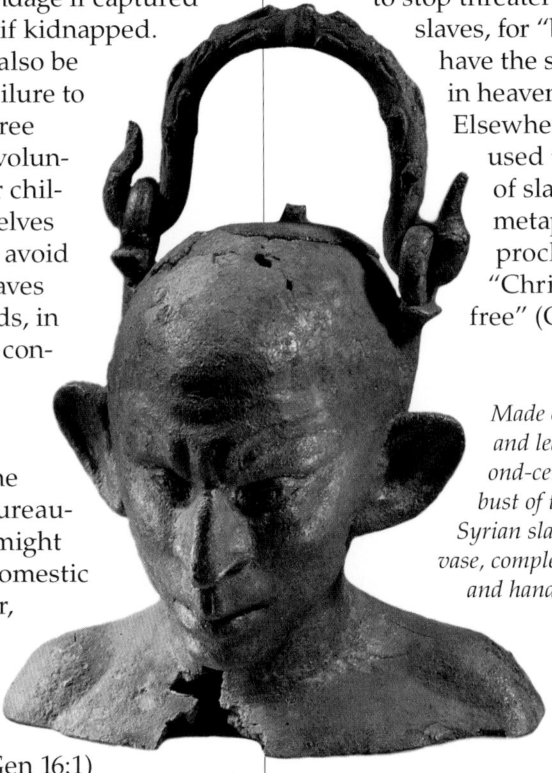

Made of bronze and lead, this second-century Roman bust of the head of a Syrian slave served as a vase, complete with cover and handle.

SLEEP

SO THE LORD GOD CAUSED A DEEP SLEEP TO FALL UPON THE MAN . . . .—GENESIS 2:21

In Genesis, God put Adam into a "deep sleep" before removing his rib to create Eve. This incident illustrates one of the numerous meanings of *sleep* that occur in the Bible. Adam's sleep was a supernaturally induced state, similar to the sleep that fell over Abraham (Gen 15:12) and Saul's soldiers (1 Sam 26:12). Visions were sometimes granted to those in such a deep sleep. *Sleep* is also a biblical synonym for physical or mental laziness and often for death. Lazarus was described as having "fallen

As Jesus prays, the apostles sleep in The Agony in the Garden *by Mantegna.*

asleep" (Jn 11:11). Jesus chided his disciples for sleeping while he prayed before his arrest in the garden of Gethsemane (Mt 26:40).

Sling

It is like binding a stone in a sling to give honor to a fool.—Proverbs 26:8

A long-range slingshot, or sling, was made from a pair of braided leather straps or thongs, which were joined at one end by a pad of leather or cloth large enough to hold a brook rock, a worked stone, or a fired piece of clay. Originally a shepherd's weapon for repelling predators, the sling became important on the battlefield, even into Roman times. The best slingers could use either hand to twirl the sling briskly, then release one strap to hurl the stone with enough force and accuracy to disable, stun, disarm, or kill the target. The tribe of Benjamin's left-handed slingers were especially noted for their deadly accuracy (Judg 20:16). By the Greco-Roman era, lead pellets had replaced stones.

Smith

So too is the smith, sitting by the anvil, intent on his iron-work . . . . —Ecclesiasticus 38:28

According to tradition, Cain is the ancestor of all smiths: his name is Hebrew for metalworker, and his descendant Tubal-cain is the first smith mentioned in the Bible (Gen 4:22). The smith was one of the essential craftsmen of ancient Israel. Among the wares he produced were metal tools, weapons, and cooking utensils, as well as ornaments of gold and silver for men and women.

Coppersmiths probably began to practice their craft about 4500 BC, making axes, knives, saws, and other articles. The blacksmith, or ironsmith, emerged about 1200 BC, when people learned to produce IRON from ore. The blacksmith heated the unformed blobs of metal produced by the iron smelter in a forge, aided by blasts of air from a goatskin bellows. When the metal became red-hot and soft enough to work, the smith placed it on an anvil and shaped it with blows from his hammer, or he twisted it with tongs. This arduous process is described in Ecclesiasticus 38:28. In the period of the judges and King Saul, the Philistines had a monopoly on metalworking, forcing the Israelites to take their tools to their enemies for repair (1 Sam 13:19–20).

Snare

For he will deliver you from the snare of the fowler and from the deadly pestilence . . . . —Psalm 91:3

According to the psalmist, anyone who trusts in God has nothing to fear from the hazards of life, as symbolized by the cunning snares and traps used by catchers of birds. The snare of a fowler often consisted of a NET arranged so that when a bird or other small animal took the bait, the net would fall and capture it. Another kind of snare was a rope noose, which caught the prey by its feet on the ground or fell from above and caught the bird or mammal around the neck. Larger animals were trapped when they fell into a concealed hole in the ground.

The Bible often refers to a snare or trap figuratively to mean the acts of the wicked or death. In the book of 2 Samuel, David says in reference to his enemies that "the snares of death confronted me" (2 Sam 22:6). The wiles of Satan are also called a snare (1 Tim 3:7).

An Egyptian tomb painting from about 1400 BC shows men catching geese in a papyrus thicket with a net snare. The man behind the thicket signals them to close the snare.

Though its climate is temperate, Israel occasionally has snow. Mount Hermon, seen above, has an elevation of more than 9,200 feet and is snowcapped year-round.

Snow

"For to the snow he says, 'Fall on the earth'. . . ."
–Job 37:6

The Bible mentions specific incidents of snowfall only rarely (2 Sam 23:20; 1 Macc 13:22), reflecting its infrequency in the Holy Land. However, snow was common enough in northern MOUNTAIN regions that when the Lord asked Jeremiah, "Does the snow of Lebanon leave the crags of Sirion?" (Jer 18:14), the question was clearly rhetorical: Sirion, or Mount Hermon, is perpetually snowcapped. The author of Job portrays snow, "the hoarfrost of heaven" (Job 38:29), as a natural force that God controls. Snow is also a metaphor for whiteness and for divine glory, as when the angel who appears at Jesus' empty tomb wears clothing "as white as snow" (Mt 28:3). Miriam, who was infected with a leprous disease, was also described as being "white as snow" (Num 12:10).

Snuffers

He made its seven lamps and its snuffers and its trays of pure gold.–Exodus 37:23

Priests apparently used metal tools called snuffers, which may have resembled scissors, tweezers, or tongs. The Bible does not say what snuffers looked like or how they were used. But the root meanings of the two Hebrew words identifying them are "trim" and "grasp," suggesting that priests used the snuffers either to trim the burnt wicks of the sacred menorah—a seven-branched lampstand that lit the sanctuary of the tabernacle and later the temple—or to pull out the stub of a spent wick and insert a fresh one. Special gold trays were used to carry away the remnants.

The shape of these 14th-century BC Egyptian snuffers suggests that they may have been used for trimming, grasping, or inserting objects.

Soldier

The LORD goes forth like a soldier, like a warrior he stirs up his fury . . . .
–Isaiah 42:13

Traditionally, all Israelite men, with the exception of the Levites, were expected to fight to protect the people, although some were exempt because of the stringent demands of ancient combat. Saul created the nation's first standing ARMY of trained and paid soldiers, which eventually included infantry, cavalry, and charioteers. When victorious, they typically received a share of the spoils. Soldiers in the New Testament were likely to be part of the occupying Roman army. Military imagery is used by Paul in the second letter to Timothy: "Share in suffering like a good soldier of Christ Jesus," the apostle urges his readers, because "the soldier's aim is to please the enlisting officer" (2 Tim 2:3–4).

Son

. . . "Now you have conceived and shall bear a son; you shall call him Ishmael . . . ."
–Genesis 16:11

The word *son* was used for both male offspring and adopted male children. It could also refer to a male descendent several generations removed. Sons ensured the continuation of the family line and received certain privileges within the family. For example, each son inherited an equal portion of his father's possessions except for the firstborn, who was due a double share (Deut 21:17) and became head of the family upon the death of the father.

Son was a polite way to address someone of inferior status, even when there was no family relationship. Students were often called "my son." In 1 Samuel 3:6, the elderly priest Eli used the phrase to address the child Samuel. The term *son of* indicated an association with a particular group or family. The Israelites—both men and women—were called the "sons of Israel" (Gen 42:5), that is, the descendants of Jacob. When Amos said, "I am no prophet, nor a prophet's son" (Am 7:14), he was denying membership in a professional prophets' guild.

Son of God

The tempter came and said to him, "If you are the Son of God, command these stones to become loaves of bread."–Matthew 4:3

In the New Testament, Jesus is identified as the "Son of God," though it is not clear whether he ever used the phrase himself. Jesus' unique relationship with God is stated in the Gospel of John: "Jesus is the Messiah, the Son of God" (Jn 20:31). This parent-child relationship is further revealed by Jesus' use of the word *Father,* or *Abba,* when addressing God, as in Mark 14:36. Though Jesus at times may have acted on his own authority, as with most sons, he ultimately owed obedience to God, his father. See also MESSIAH.

Son of Man

"Let these words sink into your ears: The Son of Man is going to be betrayed into human hands." –Luke 9:44

In the Gospels, Jesus repeatedly calls himself the Son of Man, and scholars believe this enigmatic term carries at least two possible meanings. In Matthew 8:20 and Luke 9:58, when Jesus refers to himself as "the Son of Man," he is perhaps identifying himself humbly as a human being. In other contexts, *Son of Man* might have been a messianic title that Jesus assumed to indicate his mission on earth: that of the "one like a human being" prophesied in Daniel 7:13, who would return at the end of the present age to rule the world throughout eternity.

Song

Sing to God, sing praises to his name; lift up a song to him who rides upon the clouds . . . . –Psalm 68:4

Song was an integral part of the lives of biblical peoples, and the pages of the Bible are filled with references to music. Work itself generated songs or chants: well diggers sang or chanted the "song of the well" as they dug (Num 21:17–18), and grape pressers shouted as they treaded the grapes (Jer 25:30).

Celebrations of all kinds, including religious festivals and weddings, were appropriate occasions for songs to be sung. Emotions often burst forth in song: after David's victory over Goliath, "the women came out of all the towns of Israel, singing and dancing . . . with songs of joy, and with musical instruments" (1 Sam 18:6). Mourning for the dead included song. Family and friends publicly wailed and chanted, and professional mourners sang dirges and laments. After Saul's death, David "intoned" (2 Sam 1:17) a moving lament called "The Song of the Bow" (2 Sam 1:18). The most famous

Zekhensef'ankh, the singer of Amon, plays the harp and sings a song to the Egyptian deity Horus in this painted wooden stele from the first millennium BC.

singer and musician in the Old Testament was David. Because of his reputation, many of the psalms, or poetic verses meant to be sung, were attributed to him. Professional musicians and singers performed in the royal court, and songs were raised in the Jerusalem temple: "When the burnt offering began, the song to the LORD began also" (2 Chr 29:27). See also PSALM.

SONG OF SOLOMON

HOW BEAUTIFUL YOU ARE, MY LOVE . . . .–SONG OF SOLOMON 4:1

The Song of Solomon is a collection of poems consisting mainly of private and erotic conversations between a young man and woman. The couple doesn't speak of God or

"I am a rose of Sharon, a lily of the valleys" (Song of S 2:1) is a verse from the Song of Solomon illustrated in this 20th-century illumination.

religion but rather delights in describing the beauties of nature, including each other's body. The first verse (Song of S 1:1), perhaps a late addition, names Solomon as the book's author. But a MUSICIAN may have written it to entertain at banquets or weddings. Known also as the Song of Songs, the lyrics are similar to ancient Egyptian love songs. Jews and Christians accepted the book into the canon in part because they saw in its passion an allegory of God's love for Israel and Christ's love for the church.

SONS OF GOD

WHEN PEOPLE BEGAN TO MULTIPLY ON THE FACE OF THE GROUND, AND DAUGHTERS WERE BORN TO THEM, THE SONS OF GOD SAW THAT THEY WERE FAIR . . . . –GENESIS 6:1–2

The phrase "sons of God" appears only two times in the Bible. In both cases—Genesis 6:2 and 6:4—it is used mythologically to refer to divine beings, perhaps including Satan, who were subordinate only to God. Metaphorically, *sons of God* also can designate individuals or groups who have a special relationship with God, either as his sons or more generally as his "children." In Deuteronomy 14:1, Moses tells the Israelites: "You are the children of the LORD your God." The same metaphor is used in the New Testament, when, for example, the apostle Paul tells the Galatians, "Because you are children, God has sent the Spirit of his Son into our hearts, crying 'Abba! Father!'" (Gal 4:6). See also ABBA.

SOUL

. . . LOVE THE LORD YOUR GOD WITH ALL YOUR HEART AND WITH ALL YOUR SOUL, IN ORDER THAT YOU MAY LIVE. –DEUTERONOMY 30:6

In biblical usage *soul* does not designate a part of a human being; rather, it refers to the whole person or self. Thus, the word *soul* may take the place of a pronoun, such as *I* or *you*. In the Bible, the exhortation of "save my soul"can also be translated as "save me."

In ancient Israel, the dualistic notion of a person composed of a mortal BODY and an immortal soul did not exist. This concept is derived from the Greeks, who used the word *psyche* for soul, and is found only in very late biblical passages and in the books of the Apocrypha. According to the Wisdom of Solomon, "a perishable body weighs down the soul" (Wis 9:15). A soul, however, is immortal because "the souls of the righteous are in the hand of God, and no torment will ever touch them" (Wis 3:1). The same understanding of the soul as distinct from the physical body is found in the New Testament. In 1 Peter 2:11, Christians are urged to "abstain from the desires of the flesh that wage war against the soul."

SOUTH

"IS IT BY YOUR WISDOM THAT THE HAWK SOARS, AND SPREADS ITS WINGS TOWARD THE SOUTH?" –JOB 39:26

In the Bible, *south* refers either to a direction or a geographic region. The ancient Israelites oriented themselves by facing east, toward the sunrise; the south therefore lay to their right. In Genesis, as Rachel was dying in childbirth, she named her new son *Ben-oni,* meaning "son of my sorrow." After her death, Jacob renamed his son *Benjamin* (Gen 35:18). This more auspicious name meant "son of the south" or "son of my right hand"—the right side being considered lucky. *South* is also a designation for the Negeb, the semi-arid region in the southern part of the Holy Land. The Queen of Sheba, who appears in 1 Kings 10:1–10, elsewhere in the Bible is referred to as "the queen of the South" (Mt 12:42; Lk 11:31).

The most frequently used word in the Bible for south is negeb, *which refers to the dry region that comprises the southern part of the Holy Land. A view of the Negeb Desert is seen, above, where the Red Canyon snakes its way through the Eliat Mountains.*

SOVEREIGNTY

FOR HIS SOVEREIGNTY IS AN EVERLASTING SOVEREIGNTY AND HIS KINGDOM ENDURES FROM GENERATION TO GENERATION.
–DANIEL 4:34

The Bible teaches that all things were created by and are dependent upon God, and that God has a purpose for his creation. This biblical concept of sovereignty upholds the absolute authority of God. God is "the blessed and only Sovereign, the King of kings and Lord of lords" (1 Tim 6:15). Similarly, God is described as "Judge of all" (Gen 18:25) and "the Almighty" (Gen 49:25). In one of only two instances in the Bible when the term is applied to anyone other than God, Solomon is called "sovereign over all the kingdoms" (1 Kings 4:21).

SOWER

". . . A SOWER WENT OUT TO SOW. AND AS HE SOWED, SOME SEEDS FELL ON THE PATH, AND THE BIRDS CAME AND ATE THEM UP."
–MATTHEW 13:3–4

In biblical times, seeds were sowed by hand. The sower walked across the field, flinging out handfuls of SEED from a container held in one hand until the field was covered. Wheat and barley were sowed in the late fall, when the first rains had softened the dry, hard soil enough for the primitive, lightweight plows to penetrate. Sometimes the sowing was done before the rain so that the soil could be turned and the seed buried at once; otherwise, the field was harrowed to break up clods of soil and bury the seeds. Sometimes livestock were driven across the newly sown field, their sharp hooves substituting for the prongs of the harrow.

Sowing is also used metaphorically in the Bible, as in Job 4:8 and Proverbs 11:18. Jesus often used the imagery of sowing seeds in his teachings, such as in the parable of the sower (Mt 13:3–9; Mk 4:3–9; Lk 8:4–8).

True to its name, the house sparrow of Israel often nests in or near buildings.

Sparrow

"ARE NOT FIVE SPARROWS SOLD FOR TWO PENNIES? YET NOT ONE OF THEM IS FORGOTTEN IN GOD'S SIGHT."–LUKE 12:6

Jesus spoke of a small bird called a sparrow, or sometimes a swallow, as a synonym for something insignificant and of little value. In the passage above, Jesus used sparrows to illustrate that God, in his omniscience, overlooked nothing, no matter how trifling. Sparrows were sold in markets as inexpensive food for the poor. According to Mosaic law, they were considered clean for eating or sacrifice. Longing for the sanctuary of the temple, a psalmist envied the freedom of the sparrow and the swallow to nest there (Ps 84:2–3).

Spear

SO ABNER STRUCK HIM IN THE STOMACH WITH THE BUTT OF HIS SPEAR, SO THAT THE SPEAR CAME OUT AT HIS BACK. –2 SAMUEL 2:23

The spear, with its triangular, pointed metal head fitted to a wooden or reed shaft, was typically thrust in close fighting. The javelin, a similar weapon though smaller and lighter, was hurled at the enemy at medium range. By about 1200 BC, both weapons usually had long, broad heads with a hole for the shaft and, along with the sword, were considered essential in battle. Spear-carriers led assaults on foot behind a wall of rectangular shields, in chariots, or on horseback. Spears were used by the soldiers of many Israelite tribes, including Judah and Naphtali (1 Chr 12:24, 34).

The spear was used even into Roman times. In the New Testament, it was the weapon employed by a Roman soldier to pierce the body of Jesus to ensure that he was dead (Jn 19:34). See also SHIELD.

Spice

. . . HOW MUCH BETTER IS YOUR LOVE THAN WINE, AND THE FRAGRANCE OF YOUR OILS THAN ANY SPICE!–SONG OF SOLOMON 4:10

Rare, expensive, and aromatic, spices were highly valued commodities in the ancient Near East. In addition to being a major component of sacred oil, incense, and perfume, spices were often used in cooking food and in preparing the dead for burial. They were also an important ingredient in some drugs and hygienic products. Many spices, including cinnamon, cummin, and saffron, did not grow in the Holy Land but rather had to be imported from India, Arabia, Egypt, Mesopotamia, Persia, and other eastern countries.

Gum, a pungent resin also called balm, was often mixed with spices. It was used for embalming in Eygpt and for medicinal purposes in other biblical lands. The balm of Gilead was a much-prized medicine made from the resin of a balsam tree found in a mountainous area east of the Jordan. It was brought by caravan "from Gilead, with their camels carrying gum, balm, and resin, on their way to carry it down to Egypt" (Gen 37:25).

These copper spearheads are from the early Canaanite period (3200–2200 BC).

Merchants amassed fortunes buying and selling spices not native to ancient Israel, including some of the spices shown above.

Spies

"BUT WE SAID TO HIM, WE ARE HONEST MEN, WE ARE NOT SPIES.'"–GENESIS 42:31

Spies surreptitiously obtained information about enemies. The Hebrew word for spy means "to travel by foot," suggesting the secrecy surrounding the spy's mission. Spies played an important role in Israel's history: Moses sent a dozen spies into Canaan to "see what the land is like, and whether the people who live in it are strong or weak" (Num 13:18). Before attacking Jericho, Joshua sent two spies into the land on a reconnaissance mission. Their presence was detected, but their lives were saved by a prostitute named Rahab, who hid them from the king (Josh 2:1–4). In the New Testament, Jewish leaders commissioned spies who unsuccessfully tried to lure Jesus into making antigovernment pronouncements (Lk 20:20).

SPINDLE

SHE PUTS HER HANDS TO THE DISTAFF, AND HER HANDS HOLD THE SPINDLE.
–PROVERBS 31:19

Spinning flax or wool into continuous thread or yarn for cloth was achieved by using two tools: the distaff and the spindle (see box). Raw fibers were wrapped loosely around a stick called a distaff, and strands of fiber were drawn out and attached to a spindle—a roughly foot-long rod with a hook to catch the fiber and a weighted disc, called a whorl, made of stone, pottery, or bone. The whorl gave momentum to the spindle as it was twirled to twist the strands into yarn. The yarn's quality—its thickness and evenness—was determined by the spinner's skill in manipulating the spindle.

Spinning was typically done by women, including those of the upper class. It often took months of spinning to generate enough thread to be woven into cloth. The book of Proverbs praises the wife who "seeks wool and flax and works with willing hands" (Prov 31:13), spinning to make cloth for her family and the marketplace (Prov 31:21, 24). To furnish the tabernacle during the exodus, "all the skillful women spun with their hands, and brought what they had spun in blue and purple and crimson yarns and fine linen" (Ex 35:25). See also WEAVER.

Spinning & Weaving

In biblical times, spinners and weavers typically worked with wool taken from the family's flocks. Many homes had a place set aside indoors for a loom. Besides producing yarn, spinners also combined strands of yarn to create strong, multi-ply cords.

1. A spinner draws fibers from the distaff tucked between her side and elbow while the hanging spindle turns. By spinning in a clockwise direction, she produces yarn with a Z-twist. The weight of the yarn wound on the spindle increases the spindle's momentum.

2. A loom holds lengthwise thread, called the warp, taut while a weaver uses a heddle rod to lift every other thread. She draws the crosswise threads—the weft or woof—which are attached to a shuttle, between the warp threads. As she works, the completed cloth is rolled onto the warp beam at the top of the loom.

Spirit

My spirit abides among you; do not fear. –*Haggai 2:5*

Biblical writers used the term *spirit* to mean the inner vitality of both human and divine beings and as a synonym for a supernatural being. The human spirit was described as superior to the vulnerable body, as in "the spirit indeed is willing, but the flesh is weak" (Mk 14:38).

In the Scriptures, a spirit, though invisible, has a dynamic force that may be experienced or even physically felt; indeed, the Hebrew and Greek words for spirit may also be translated as "wind" or "breath." Genesis 1:2 describes the beginning of creation as "a wind from God," or "the spirit of God," sweeping over the waters of the earth.

In the Old Testament, the spirit of God sometimes came upon people and could result in "a prophetic frenzy" (1 Sam 10:10). In the New Testament, the Holy Spirit, sometimes called the Spirit of God or simply the Spirit, manifested God's presence and inspired the faithful. When Jesus was baptized, "he saw the Spirit of God descending like a dove and alighting on him" (Mt 3:16). On Pentecost the disciples were "filled with the Holy Spirit" (Acts 2:4). The Gospels describe Jesus exorcising demons, which are sometimes called evil or unclean spirits. These spirits could cripple or blind a person, but they were powerless when confronted with the Spirit of God.

The "spirits in prison" (1 Pet 3:19), to whom Jesus is said to have preached after his crucifixion, may mean those who disobeyed God's laws in Old Testament times. See also MADNESS.

Spiritual Gifts

. . . since you are eager for spiritual gifts, strive to excel in them for building up the church. –*1 Corinthians 14:12*

The "spiritual gifts" that Paul referred to in his first letter to the Corinthians were the special skills and abilities with which God endowed the early Christians. These gifts were similar to those God had bestowed on elected people in Old Testament times, such as Samson's physical strength and Saul's prophetic activity. In his letter, Paul assured believers in Jesus that "in every way you have been enriched in him, in speech and knowledge of every kind . . . not lacking in any spiritual gift" (1 Cor 1:5, 7). These gifts, which included the ability to prophesy, to instruct, to heal, to interpret tongues, and to perform miracles, were all received through the Holy Spirit and were all meant to serve "the common good" (1 Cor 12:7). The first letter of Peter echoed this sentiment, urging the faithful to "serve one another with whatever gift each of you has received" (1 Pet 4:10).

Though every spiritual gift was considered valuable, Paul emphasizes that one—love—stood above the rest: "If I have all faith, so as to remove mountains, but do not have love, I am nothing" (1 Cor 13:2).

The Holy Spirit descends in the form of a dove on Mary and the apostles, as portrayed by Bernardino Pinturicchio in a late 15th-century fresco in the Vatican Palace.

Spit

"They abhor me . . . they do not hesitate to spit at the sight of me." –*Job 30:10*

Spitting at or into the face of another was a gesture of contempt. Religious leaders judging Jesus "spat in his face" (Mt 26:67), and soldiers taunted and spat on him before the crucifixion (Mt 27:30). Jesus reacted like the persecuted servant of God in the book of Isaiah: "I did not hide my face from insult and spitting" (Isa 50:6). Spittle could be a sign of degradation. Ecclesiasticus 26:22 says that "a prostitute is regarded as spittle," and David, feigning madness to escape danger, "let his spittle run down his beard" (1 Sam 21:13). Yet saliva was sometimes a part of healing practices: Jesus used it to cure the blind (Jn 9:6) and the deaf (Mk 7:33).

Stairs at the entrance to King Hezekiah's tunnel in Jerusalem lead to a spring.

Stairs

. . . one went up by winding stairs to the middle story, and from the middle story to the third.–1 Kings 6:8

In the Holy Land, stairs or ladders commonly went up the outside of houses to the second story or the roof, where people could retreat in the summer to catch a cool breeze. In public buildings—such as Solomon's temple, described in the passage above—stairs were constructed both inside and out. Steps were used in the steep streets of some cities to connect one level to another; Nehemiah 12:37 mentions "the stairs of the city of David." In Megiddo and other cities, extensive stairways were built to allow access to storage pits and water systems.

Star

. . . there, ahead of them, went the star that they had seen at its rising, until it stopped over the place where the child was.–Matthew 2:9

Gazing at the clear night skies of the Near East, the Israelites must have marveled at the sheer number of stars. However, unlike the Babylonians and Egyptians, they seem to have devoted little study to these luminaries, perhaps fearing that it could lead to the idolatry of star worship. The Israelites nevertheless knew that the travels of the stars and planets across the sky followed regular patterns, and they had sufficient knowledge of astronomy to regulate the calendar and determine the dates for holy days and festivals.

The most famous star in the Bible is the star of Bethlehem, which led the wise men to the child Jesus (Mt 2:1–10). Astronomers have theorized that this celestial body was a supernova or an unusual, brilliant conjunction of Jupiter and Saturn in the constellation Pisces. In its account of the star, Matthew's Gospel may have been alluding to the Old Testament prophecy that "a star shall come out of Jacob, and a scepter shall rise out of Israel" (Num 24:17).

Steward

. . . the steward had brought the men into Joseph's house, and given them water . . . .–Genesis 43:24

A steward managed the running of a large residence. Indeed, in Hebrew, the word *steward* means "one over the household." Joseph, while holding a high government position in Egypt, had a steward who greeted visitors when they arrived and took care of their needs and those of their livestock (Gen 43:19, 24).

A steward's duties could include supervising meals and banquets (Add Esth 1:8), managing financial and business affairs, and watching over the children and servants. Royal administrators who managed Israel's resources were called "stewards of King David's property" (1 Chr 27:31).

In the New Testament, Paul asked the church in Corinth to "think of us in this way, as . . . stewards of God's mysteries" (1 Cor 4:1). He added that a steward was required to be trustworthy. A bishop oversaw church affairs; thus he was "God's steward," who "must be blameless . . . hospitable, a lover of goodness, prudent, upright, devout, and self-controlled" (Titus 1:7–8). Christians were said to be "like good stewards of the manifold grace of God" (1 Pet 4:10), meaning that each person was endowed with a gift from God that was to be shared.

Stocks

Then Asa was angry with the seer, and put him in the stocks, in prison . . . . –2 Chronicles 16:10

Stocks were an instrument of punishment used in later Old Testament and Roman times. They generally consisted of two pieces of wood, with holes that restrained the feet and sometimes the neck and hands as well. For prophesying the destruction of Jerusalem, Jeremiah was said to have been put in the stocks (Jer 20:2), although some interpreters suggest he was simply confined in a small cell. Stocks such as those mentioned in Job 13:27 may have allowed for some mobility, in contrast to the Roman stocks that forced apart the legs of the imprisoned Paul and Silas (Acts 16:24).

A black granite statue attests to the piety of the Egyptian steward Dhewty, from the 18th Dynasty, who kneels before a base that probably held the image of a god.

Stone

He built the inner court with three courses of dressed stone to one course of cedar beams.—1 Kings 6:36

Stone, abundant in the Holy Land and along the Nile River, had a wide variety of uses. One of the most important was in the building of city walls, as well as houses, palaces, temples, and other public structures. King Solomon employed 80,000 stonecutters to build his temple (1 Kings 5:15). The different types of stone extracted from quarries for construction included limestone, sandstone, and granite (see illustration). The CORNERSTONE of a building was chosen carefully.

Stones were made into memorials and served as landmarks. They were also used as weights on scales and fashioned into axes, hammers, and mortars. The ten commandments and other important documents were carved on stone, and large stones often covered wells and entrances to tombs, such as the one in which Jesus was buried (Jn 20:1).

Stones could be deadly weapons when thrown by hand or launched by catapult. In the famous confrontation between David and Goliath, David put a smooth stone in his sling and fired it at the Philistine; then "the stone sank into his forehead, and he fell face down on the ground" (1 Sam 17:49).

Stones used for building projects were cut out of a quarry's rock face by chiseling a series of holes in the rock, driving a wooden stake into each hole, and then pouring water on the stakes. When the soaked stakes expanded, they broke the stone off from the rock face. In the illustration above, a man drives stakes into the rock, outlining blocks of stone. A second worker pours water from a goatskin bag onto the embedded stakes. Behind them, a third worker dresses a cut stone block with a hammer and chisel. In the background, a group of laborers struggles to move a large, dressed stone block for conveyance to a building site. The men use wooden levers, ropes, and logs to move the stone up a ramp and out of the quarry.

Stoning

David was in great danger; for the people spoke of stoning him . . . .—1 Samuel 30:6

Stoning was the most common form of capital punishment prescribed by Israelite law. It was imposed mainly for offenses against God, including blasphemy (Lev 24:16), worshiping false gods (Deut 17:2–7), toiling on the sabbath (Num 15:32–36), and sacrificing children to the god Molech (Lev 20:2). Rebelling against parental authority and committing adultery were also grounds for stoning (Deut 21:18–21; 22:21–24). Executions usually took place outside the city, after at least two witnesses presented evidence. The accusers were required to throw the first stones at the convicted person, with the community following suit if the victim remained alive. In the New Testament, Jesus prevented the stoning of an adulteress (Jn 8:3–11). His follower Stephen was stoned, thus becoming the first Christian martyr (Acts 7:59).

Storage

He built fortresses and storage cities in Judah.—2 Chronicles 17:12

Because drought, locusts, or blight could destroy the year's crops, people of the ancient Near East stored away the surplus of a good harvest against future lean times. They knew that famine might occur at any time, as shown by the story of Pharaoh's dream about the seven fat and seven lean ears of grain (Gen 41). Storage was also needed for the normal consumption of produce and for produce kept for sale. Barns, caves, and dugout chambers were all used for bulk storage. The standard containers were pottery jars, sometimes big enough for a person to hide in, in which olive oil, wine, grain, and documents such as the Dead Sea Scrolls were kept.

Rulers built storehouses and entire storage cities to keep their subjects from starving during times of famine; some have been excavated by archaeologists. Solomon and Jehoshaphat built numerous storage cities in their kingdoms. Royal storage cities were used for military equipment as well as food. Biblical writers speak of God's storehouses for rain, hail, snow, wind, and even the ocean. In the book of Deuteronomy, Moses assures the Israelites that if they obey God, he "will open for you his rich storehouse, the heavens, to give the rain of your land in its season and to bless all your undertakings" (Deut 28:12).

From about the 18th century BC, these terra-cotta models of silos for grain storage were found in an Egyptian tomb.

Stumbling Block

"Occasions for stumbling are bound to come, but woe to the one by whom the stumbling block comes!" –Matthew 18:7

A stumbling block, an obstacle someone can fall over, is used both literally and figuratively in the Bible. Leviticus 19:14 prohibits putting a physical hindrance in the path of a blind person. Sin is a metaphorical stumbling block. The silver and golden idols made by the Israelites are the "stumbling block of their iniquity" (Ezek 7:19). In Matthew 13:41, the Greek words translated as "causes of sin" mean "stumbling blocks." Isaiah assures the Israelites that God is the "the Rock of your refuge" (Isa 17:10) yet cautions that this rock can prove a stumbling block as well. If God's word is not heeded, "he will become a rock one stumbles over—a trap and a snare" (Isa 8:14).

Suffering

Rejoice in hope, be patient in suffering, persevere in prayer.–Romans 12:12

The Bible is filled with instances of people trying to come to terms with the idea that a powerful, good, and just God could allow suffering to come into their lives. The book of Genesis relates that the first human beings received a world free from worry and pain but that they introduced suffering into that world by disobeying God. Suffering thus became part of the human condition. Still, the question of why humans must suffer has no simple answer.

The book of JOB, in particular, explores the mystery of innocent people experiencing misery and evil. Job, a "blameless and upright" man (Job 1:1), refutes

New Testament writers warned followers of Jesus to be prepared to endure periods of suffering that could be extreme, as shown in Persecution of the First Christians, *a 19th-century painting by Giuseppe Mancinelli.*

the idea that his misfortunes are punishment for his sins and says that God "destroys both the blameless and the wicked" (Job 9:22). In the end, God rewards Job profusely. The message of the book may be that faith must transcend punishments and rewards.

For a Christian, suffering is inevitable. Jesus advises those who wish to follow him to "take up their cross" (Mk 8:34) to prepare for the difficulties that lie ahead. Some New Testament writers stress the value of suffering. Paul writes that "suffering produces endurance, and endurance produces character, and character produces hope" (Rom 5:4). He also reminds Christians that their anguish makes them joint heirs with Jesus: "We suffer with him so that we may also be glorified with him" (Rom 8:17). The letter of James goes so far as to say, "Whenever you face trials of any kind, consider it nothing but joy" (Jas 1:2). See also PERSECUTION.

SULFUR

THEN THE LORD RAINED
ON SODOM AND GOMORRAH SULFUR
AND FIRE . . . OUT OF HEAVEN . . . .
–GENESIS 19:24

Sulfur deposits are found in the valley of the Dead Sea and other areas of seismic and volcanic activity in the Near East. This highly flammable mineral can spontaneously combust during an earthquake, producing a scorching flame and an overpowering stench. The ancient Israelites thus associated it with God's fiery punishment of the wicked, such as the inhabitants of Sodom and Gomorrah. The Bible also uses the image of sulfur to indicate a barren land, as when Moses warns Israelites contemplating rebellion that their children will inherit a land with "all its soil burned out by sulfur and salt" (Deut 29:23). Some Bible translations use the word *brimstone* instead of *sulfur*.

SUN

LIGHT IS SWEET,
AND IT IS PLEASANT FOR THE
EYES TO SEE THE SUN.
–ECCLESIASTES 11:7

To the people of the Holy Land, the sun was a mixed blessing. It was the source of light and vital warmth, but its heat could also be deadly.

In this carving, the pharaoh Akhenaten appears with his family beneath a disk that represents the Egyptian sun god.

Farm workers tried to do their heaviest work in the cool of the morning to avoid heat exhaustion. In the book of Jonah, God provides a miraculous bush to protect Jonah from the sun near Nineveh (Jon 4:6).

The sun marked the seasons of the year and the time of day, which was judged roughly by the sun's warmth. For example, "the heat of the day" (Gen 18:1) corresponded to noon. The biblical day lasted from sunset to sunset.

The sun was worshiped as a god by many of Israel's neighbors. The Israelites themselves sometimes practiced sun worship (2 Kings 23:5), although it was forbidden to do so (Deut 4:19). As a god, the sun was considered the embodiment of justice. Scriptural writers sometimes spoke metaphorically of God as the sun, such as in Psalm 84:11. The book of Revelation describes "one like the Son of Man" (Rev 1:13), whose "face was like the sun shining with full force" (Rev 1:16).

SURETY

". . . WHO IS THERE THAT WILL GIVE SURETY FOR ME?"
–JOB 17:3

Giving surety meant pledging one's property or one's own person as assurance that someone else would repay a debt. It was ritually sealed with a type of handshake. Warning against this practice, Proverbs 17:18 says, "It is senseless to give a PLEDGE, to become surety for a neighbor." The precise obligations of the person giving surety are unclear. If the debtor defaulted, the person might have been forced to surrender personal property to the creditor, but he could in turn recoup his losses from the debtor. The individual providing surety might also have been obligated to reimburse the creditor for any expenses connected with collecting the debt.

SUSANNA

. . . THE TWO ELDERS CAME, FULL OF THEIR WICKED PLOT TO HAVE SUSANNA PUT TO DEATH.
–SUSANNA 28

One of the additions to the book of DANIEL, Susanna is a story in the Apocrypha about a beautiful married woman. Two lecherous elders told the woman, Susanna, that unless she committed adultery with them, they would say she had done so with a young man. When she refused, the elders carried out their threat and Susanna was sentenced to death. In response to Susanna's prayer for help, God inspired the young Daniel to expose the lie. Daniel asked each elder to name the kind of tree under which the crime took place. The answers differed, and the men were executed. After this, "Daniel had a great reputation among the people" (Sus 64).

SWINE

". . . DO NOT THROW YOUR PEARLS BEFORE SWINE, OR THEY WILL TRAMPLE THEM UNDER FOOT . . . ."
–MATTHEW 7:6

Swine were considered unclean, and pork was forbidden as food (Deut 14:8). It was a measure of his extreme degradation that the prodigal son had to accept work as a swineherd (Lk 15:15). In the passage above, Jesus used the pig as a symbol of base and evil people when warning his disciples to be discriminating about those with whom they shared the gospel "pearls." To cure two men possessed by demons, Jesus made the evil spirits enter a herd of swine, which then rushed into the sea and drowned (Mt 8:28–32).

SWORD

IT IS SHARPENED, THE SWORD IS POLISHED, TO BE PLACED IN THE SLAYER'S HAND.
–EZEKIEL 21:11

Mentioned more than 400 times in the Scriptures—more frequently than any other weapon—the bronze or iron sword, with its metal, wooden, or bone handle, was the primary offensive weapon of the ancient Near East. Some 5,000 years ago, combatants used a short, straight sword about 10 inches long for stabbing and a sharp-edged, sickle-shaped sword for cutting and striking at each other. By the second millennium BC, the sickle-shaped type was made with a handle twice as long as the blade; straight swords improved more slowly. About 1200 BC, because of better technology, longer and tougher metal blades, often made of iron rather than the less durable bronze, became common on the battlefield; swords included both the broadsword and a narrower saber. Israelite soldiers carried straight, double-edged iron swords, perhaps 30 inches long, with handles that conformed to the hand.

The image of the sword in the Bible represents many different concepts, including God's protection or punishment, the authority of the state, and harmful false witness. The "sword flaming and turning to guard the way to the tree of life" (Gen 3:24) is a symbol of humanity's separation from paradise. See also ARMS.

An elaborately decorated handle is part of a sword from a palace in Ugarit. The weapon dates from the early 13th century BC.

Sycamore Tree

So he ran ahead and climbed a sycamore tree to see him . . . .–Luke 19:4

In Luke's Gospel, Zacchaeus, a wealthy tax collector in Jericho, was so eager to see Jesus that he climbed a sycamore tree at the side of the road. The soft but durable wood of the sycamore tree was used for furniture and construction. Sycamores were frequently planted as shade trees. They bear a fruit similar to the FIG but smaller and inferior in taste, which was often eaten by the poor. Though Amos was chosen by God to prophesy to the Israelites, he denied it was his calling. He merely claimed to be a herdsman and a dresser of sycamore trees (Am 7:14), whose job it was to puncture the fruit to make it ripen.

Symbol

Behind the door and the doorpost you have set up your symbol . . . .–Isaiah 57:8

Although the word *symbol* is used infrequently, the Bible is rich with examples of symbols, which are objects used to stand for something else. Typically, there is a clear connection between the symbol and the idea it is intended to represent. For example, in the Bible warfare is frequently used as a symbol of the struggle between good and evil (Wis 5:17–20). Symbols also act as visible signs of the invisible, such as fire, which commonly represents God's presence (Ex 3:2).

Jews and Christians draw symbols from their cultural and historical backgrounds. For Jews, circumcision is a symbol of the admission of a child into a community of believers, as the rite of baptism is for Christians. The menorah, a seven-branched lampstand, represents the Jewish community; the corresponding symbol of the Christian community is the cross.

In the apocalyptic writings of the Bible—the books of Ezekiel, Daniel, and Revelation—frequently appearing symbols such as animals, colors, and numbers were used as a form of code by the authors, and readers were expected to understand their significance. See also SIGN.

Synagogue

Jesus answered, "I have spoken openly to the world; I have always taught in synagogues and in the temple . . . ."–John 18:20

Synagogue is derived from the Greek word *synagoge*, meaning "gathering" or "assembly." The synagogue was a house of worship where Jews gathered on the sabbath; it also served as a school, courtroom, meeting hall, place of shelter for travelers, and home for synagogue leaders. Though the origin of the synagogue is uncertain—the word was not used until the first century AD—many scholars speculate that synagogues arose during the exile in Babylon and after the destruction of the TEMPLE. Inscriptions in Egypt speak of Jewish "places of prayer" as early as the third century BC.

In contrast to the temple, synagogues were not run by priests and were not places to conduct sacrifices. Local elders often appointed a "leader of the synagogue" (Mt 9:18) to care for the building and direct the sabbath services. Typically, a service included readings from the law of Moses and the prophets, prayers, a sermon, and a benediction. Visitors from out of town were often invited to read selected passages and address the group. According to Acts of the Apostles, Jewish-Christian missionaries, such as Paul, took advantage of this custom to talk about Jesus. In the Gospels, Jesus is often described as teaching in the synagogues of Galilee.

Excavations of ancient synagogues show that many had a raised platform on which people stood when reading from scrolls. Worshipers apparently sat on the floor. Benches along the remaining walls were likely reserved for elders and respected guests. Jesus once criticized Pharisees and scribes for taking "the best seats in the synagogues" (Mt 23:6).

Above are the remains of the synagogue at Gamala in the lower Golan. In a bloody battle in AD 67, the Romans sacked the synagogue and slaughtered the inhabitants of the city.

Carved in Hebrew on the modern-day tablets at right, the TEN COMMANDMENTS, *God's laws handed down to Moses, are displayed on a wall of Rachel's tomb, located on the road between Jerusalem and Bethlehem.*

TABERNACLE

THEY MINISTERED WITH SONG BEFORE THE TABERNACLE . . . UNTIL SOLOMON HAD BUILT THE HOUSE OF THE LORD IN JERUSALEM . . . . –1 CHRONICLES 6:32

When the Israelites reached Sinai on their trek to the Promised Land, they built a portable worship center that is sometimes called the tent of meeting. Here they offered sacrifices and stored the ark of the covenant, a chest containing the ten commandments. Telling Moses to gather the construction material from the people, God said, "And have them make me a sanctuary, so that I may dwell among them" (Ex 25:8). The people responded with contributions of gold, silver, bronze, hardwood, gems, linen, and animal hides.

Volunteers crafted a wall of linen and hung it from a frame of poles mounted in bronze bases. This wall, about 7 feet high, enclosed a courtyard 150 feet long by 75 feet wide. Inside, a few yards from the entrance, stood a bronze-plated altar topped with grating on which priests burned sacrifices. Nearby sat a bronze basin, filled with water that priests used to purify themselves (Ex 40:30–32).

Dominating the courtyard was the tent sanctuary, which was 45 feet long and 15 feet wide and high. It was made of four layers of fabric and animal hides draped over a frame of gold-plated pillars, which were set in silver bases. The inner layer, which became the ceiling and walls, was of fine linen swaths held together by golden clasps and decorated with cherubim. There were two rooms in the tent, separated by a linen hanging. The first room, the holy place, contained a menorah, an incense altar, and a table for holy bread. The inner room, the Holy of Holies, held the ark, which represented the presence of God. Only the high priest could enter this sanctuary once a year, on the Day of Atonement.

The Israelites worshiped at the tabernacle for several centuries until Solomon built the temple in Jerusalem.

TABLE

MEPHIBOSHETH ATE AT DAVID'S TABLE, LIKE ONE OF THE KING'S SONS.–2 SAMUEL 9:11

In the ancient Near East, many homes had tables made of wood or metal, which were close to the ground so that guests could recline on rugs or cushions while eating. By the time of the New Testament, table legs had been lengthened, and diners probably reclined on couches. Eating at a king's table, as Mephibosheth did at David's, was considered a great honor. Malachi 1:7 refers to an altar as "the LORD'S table." The Gospel of Matthew relates that Jesus entered the temple and "overturned the tables of the money changers" (Mt 21:12); here the word *table* probably means small trays set on stands. In the apocryphal book Ecclesiasticus, its author devotes an entire section to proper table etiquette at a banquet (Sir 31:12–24).

TAMARISK TREE

THEN THEY TOOK THEIR BONES AND BURIED THEM UNDER THE TAMARISK TREE IN JABESH, AND FASTED SEVEN DAYS.–1 SAMUEL 31:13

The tamarisk is an small, shrub-like evergreen with gray-green, feathery needles and pink and white flowers, which flourishes in dry climates. The tree was valued for the shade it provided; it also served as a burial place. Saul, the first king of Israel, and three of his sons died in battle with the Philistines, who mutilated their bodies and hung them on the walls of Beth-shan. In the passage above, the people of Jabesh-gilead later recovered their remains and buried them under a tamarisk tree. The story is repeated in 1 Chronicles 10, in which the tree is an oak. Abraham is said to have planted a tamarisk in Beer-sheba (Gen 21:33).

Tanner

". . . he is lodging with Simon, a tanner, whose house is by the seaside."
–Acts of the Apostles 10:6

The tanner was a craftsman who transformed animal skins into soft, usable leather. The tanner cleaned the skins and then treated them in a solution that was probably made from a combination of plant extracts, lime, and tree bark or leaves. In Exodus, the ram's skin that covered the tabernacle during the exodus is described as tanned (Ex 26:14), presumably because of its reddish hue. Since tanners worked with animals that were ceremonially unclean and the tanning process itself produced a foul odor, tanning was considered an undesirable occupation among the ancient Jews. According to the passage above, while in Joppa, the apostle Peter stayed in the home of a tanner named Simon. See also box for LEATHER.

Tax Collector

Even tax collectors came to be baptized . . . . He said to them, "Collect no more than the amount prescribed for you."
–Luke 3:12–13

In the New Testament era, the Roman Empire collected taxes and customs fees through private contractors. Those hired were often not native to the provincial areas for which they were responsible; thus, they subcontracted work to local collectors. Tax collectors padded the amount owed to ensure profits for themselves, a corrupt practice that made tax collectors despised figures. A Greek poet referred to them as "birds of prey." Apparently Zacchaeus, who was called "chief tax collector" (Lk 19:2), amassed a huge fortune.

In the King James Bible, tax collectors are called publicans and exactors—the latter term meaning a stern taskmaster. Many Jews had disdain for tax collectors, who were considered ritually unclean because they mixed with Gentiles and worked on the sabbath. Castigated by the Pharisees for eating with "tax collectors and sinners" (Mt 9:11), Jesus defended their faith: "Truly I tell you, the tax collectors . . . are going into the kingdom of God ahead of you. For John came to you . . . and you did not believe him, but the tax collectors and the prostitutes believed him" (Mt 21:31–32).

Taxes

All the leaders and all the people rejoiced and brought their tax . . . .
–2 Chronicles 24:10

The Scriptures do not contain a complete explanation of Israel's tax system, but numerous details affirm that taxes were a constant and often onerous fact of life. In Israel's early history, only worship taxes are mentioned, dedicated to

Like all residents in the Roman Empire, Mary and Joseph had to register for taxation (Lk 2:1–5), as seen in this Byzantine mosaic.

supporting the priestly caste and the maintenance of the tabernacle. After the monarchy was established in Israel, the basic form of direct taxation for centuries was a share of all crops. During the Roman occupation this share was reportedly 12.5 percent. Apparently, censuses mentioned in the Bible were usually undertaken for the purpose of collecting a tax on individuals (Ex 38:26), which may have been one denarius in the time of Jesus (Mt 22:19).

Other taxes levied by government and religious leaders to raise revenue included tolls or customs duties as steep as 25 percent at boundaries, port fees, and market taxes. To support the great building programs of Solomon and Herod, taxation included FORCED LABOR. In addition, the temple imposed an annual tax of half a shekel on all males, and the Levites were allotted 10 percent—or a tithe—of all produce from the ground.

In New Testament times, Roman bureaucrats in Israel taxed income, land, and personal property, with an additional house tax for the citizens of Jerusalem. Local tax collectors were especially hated because evidently they were given free rein to make huge profits from their fellow Jews. Even so, Jesus surprised the Pharisees when he refused to dispute Caesar's right to collect taxes, declaring: "Give to the emperor the things that are the emperor's" (Mk 12:17). Paul reiterated this idea in Romans when he urged Christians to submit to the governmental officials by paying taxes, "for the authorities are God's servants . . . . Pay to all what is due them—taxes to whom taxes are due" (Rom 13:6–7).

This 20th-century statue depicts two great rabbinic teachers of the first century AD. Hillel, seated, ponders the Torah, and Shammai, standing, fervidly addresses a point of law.

TEACHER

SO THEY SENT THEIR DISCIPLES TO HIM . . . SAYING, "TEACHER, WE KNOW THAT YOU ARE SINCERE, AND TEACH THE WAY OF GOD IN ACCORDANCE WITH TRUTH . . . ." –MATTHEW 22:16

Parents were the first teachers in the ancient Near East. Biblical and Jewish law required parents to educate their children in religion and in practical skills, such as a trade for boys and housekeeping for girls. Children learned the precepts of their faith by listening to stories of their heritage and by watching their parents honor the sabbath, celebrate festivals, and observe other Mosaic laws. During the first century BC, some Jewish boys started formal classes in the synagogue and were taught by an assistant to the head of the synagogue. Older boys could pursue advanced classes under the guidance of a respected rabbi. Scribes were considered both scholars and teachers of the Torah and gained considerable power over the people as members of the Sanhedrin, the Jews' highest court.

In the New Testament, Jesus is repeatedly addressed as Teacher, particularly when being asked his opinion on a religious or legal point: "Teacher, which commandment in the law is the greatest?" (Mt 22:36). Jesus was regarded as a teacher by his disciples and even by his opponents. He taught publicly in synagogues and in the temple. See also EDUCATION.

TEETH

O GOD, BREAK THE TEETH IN THEIR MOUTHS; TEAR OUT THE FANGS OF THE YOUNG LIONS, O LORD!–PSALM 58:6

In the Bible, teeth often symbolize destruction caused by humans, animals, mythical creatures, or even insects, such as when a swarm of locusts wreaks havoc in Joel 1:4. Many vivid expressions refer to teeth, most notably in the legal concept mandating that punishment match the crime "tooth for tooth" (Ex 21:24). In the book of Amos, the phrase "cleanness of teeth" (Am 4:6) denotes famine or starvation. Contesting a proverb that blames ancestors for one's problems—"The parents have eaten sour grapes, and the children's teeth are set on edge" (Ezek 18:2)—the prophet Ezekiel argues that each generation will be punished only for its own sins. See also GNASHING OF TEETH.

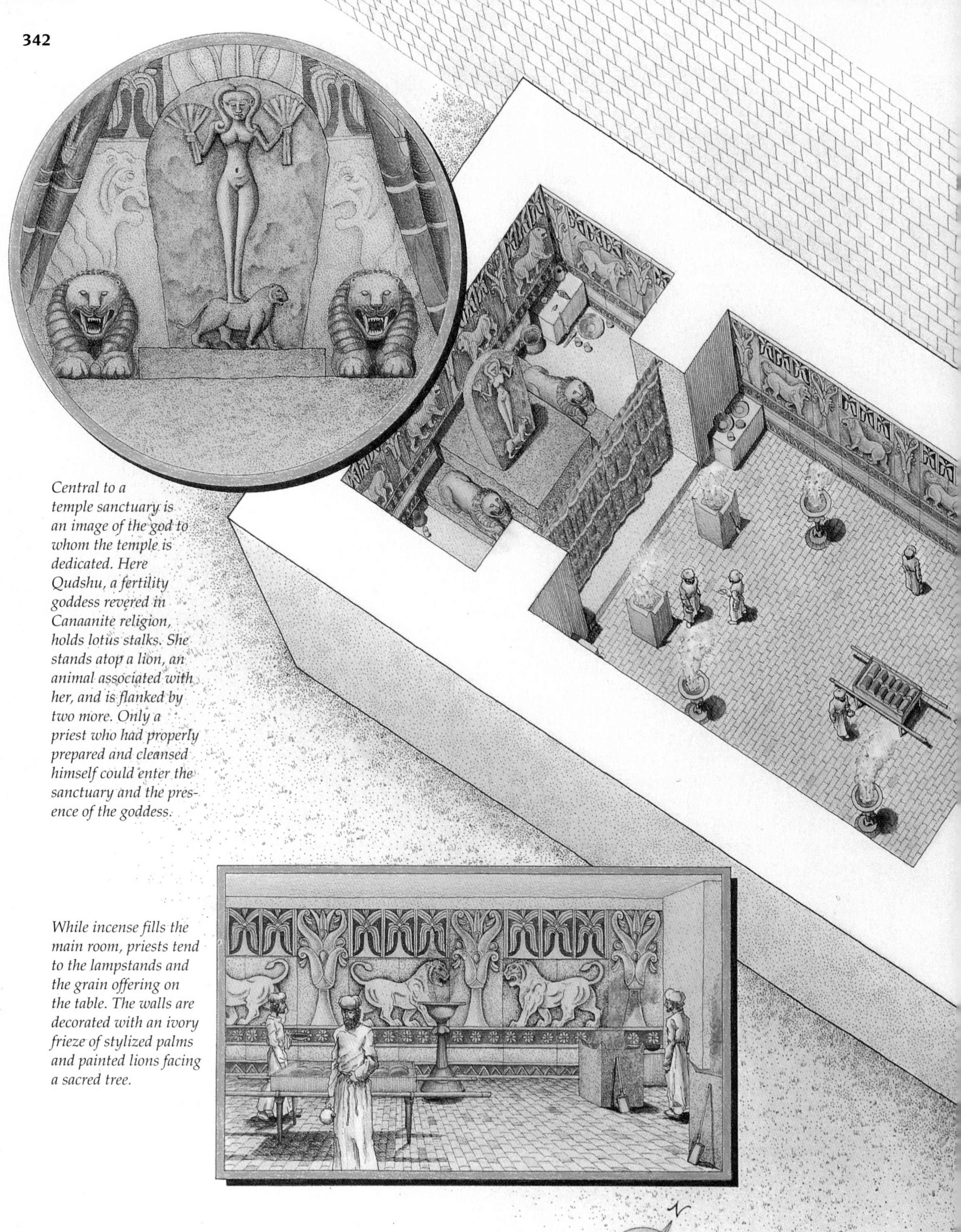

Central to a temple sanctuary is an image of the god to whom the temple is dedicated. Here Qudshu, a fertility goddess revered in Canaanite religion, holds lotus stalks. She stands atop a lion, an animal associated with her, and is flanked by two more. Only a priest who had properly prepared and cleansed himself could enter the sanctuary and the presence of the goddess.

While incense fills the main room, priests tend to the lampstands and the grain offering on the table. The walls are decorated with an ivory frieze of stylized palms and painted lions facing a sacred tree.

Temples served as a depository for temple offerings. Over a period of years a temple treasury could amass an abundance of objects, such as these gold and silver bowls, kept in the main room.

A SYRIAN TEMPLE

". . .FOR THE TEMPLE WILL NOT BE FOR MORTALS BUT FOR THE LORD GOD."–1 CHRONICLES 29:1

Although there is no archaeological record of Solomon's temple, a temple found at Tel Tainat in Syria, built slightly later in the ninth or eighth century BC, closely resembles the biblical description of Solomon's temple in 1 Kings and 2 Chronicles. Both temples were oriented with their doors facing east, as had been the practice in Syria since 2400 BC. In a typical temple a single long room was divided into two or three adjoining areas—a porch, a main room, and a small sanctuary, in this case. Excavations have revealed buildings throughout Canaan and Syria, including those at Tel Munbaqa, Ebla, Emar, Hazor, Shechem, and Lachish, that follow this plan and have been identified as temples. The interior of Solomon's temple is described in the Bible as being lavishly decorated with gold, ivory, and rare woods using motifs such as cherubim, palms, and lotus flowers. Examples of these motifs have been found in Phoenician and Syrian art and architecture of the period, and it can be assumed that temples contemporary with Solomon's were similarly decorated.

A pair of stone lions serve as the base for each column on the porch. The two columns are reminiscent of the columns fronting Solomon's temple as described in the Bible. The columns illustrated here, however, probably supported a roof, a debatable feature in the temple of Solomon.

TEMPLE

. . . HE SHALL BUILD THE TEMPLE OF THE LORD.
–ZECHARIAH 6:12

During the 1,000 years from the time of Solomon to that of Jesus, the Israelites worshiped at a succession of three temples built on a Jerusalem hilltop. Biblical law permitted them to offer sacrifices only at the Jerusalem temple, where pilgrims also came to celebrate three annual religious festivals.

The first temple, built by Solomon, lasted about 400 years until Babylonian soldiers looted and destroyed it. The second, built by Jews returning from Babylonian exile, survived nearly 500 years. The third and grandest temple was King Herod's work. Though it took some 80 years to complete, this structure lasted only about seven years. Roman soldiers demolished it when they crushed a Jewish rebellion in AD 70.

Solomon's temple was the nation's first permanent worship center, replacing the mobile TABERNACLE. The king insisted on an elegant building, worthy of God's presence. Beginning about 960 BC, Solomon imported rot-resistant cedars of Lebanon, hired the finest craftsmen in neighboring nations, and employed nearly 200,000 Israelite workers. Seven years later, he dedicated a temple that rivaled the finest pagan temples in the Near East (see reconstruction, pp. 342–343). It consisted of three areas. The vestibule, with its two large pillars, led into the nave, which only priests could enter. It in turn led into the Holy of Holies, which housed the ark of the covenant. The entire interior, overlaid with gold, was about 90 feet long, 30 feet wide, and 45 feet high. Outside, in the courtyard, sat the sacrificial altar and a 30-ton bronze basin filled with 11,000 gallons of water that priests used to purify themselves. At the dedication ceremony, according to 1 Kings 8:10–11, a cloud entered the sanctuary as "the glory of the LORD filled the house of the LORD."

Israel's second temple was a disappointment to older Jews, who remembered the majesty of Solomon's temple. As the younger ones sang for joy during its construction, the elders "wept with a loud voice" (Ezra 3:12).

King Herod, an unpopular ruler, apparently decided to ingratiate himself with the people by erecting a temple even more wondrous than Solomon's. In 20 BC, he began to dismantle the existing temple to build the new one. He expanded the temple courtyard into a 30-acre, walled enclosure maintained by a corps of temple servants.

Throughout the millennium, each temple served as a symbol of Israel's unity. Romans leveled the third and final temple because they knew it could become a rallying point for renewed rebellion. Other than a few ruins, all that remains of Herod's marvel is a stretch of foundation blocks along the perimeter of the temple courtyard. Part of this is the Western Wall, the most sacred site in modern Judaism. Above it, on the temple mount, sits a 1,300-year-old Muslim shrine, the Dome of the Rock.

TEMPTATION

BLESSED IS ANYONE WHO ENDURES TEMPTATION.
–JAMES 1:12

The main tempter in the Bible is the devil, or Satan. The synoptic Gospels recount that after being baptized, Jesus went into the wilderness to pray and fast. There he was tempted by Satan, who, noting his hunger, taunted him: "If you are the Son of God, command this stone to become a loaf of bread" (Lk 4:3). Jesus resisted this temptation, among others. Probably referring to Deuteronomy 6:16, he answered the devil, "It is said, 'Do not put the Lord your God to the test'" (Lk 4:12).

Jesus rejects the temptation of Satan, as seen in this 15th-century illumination.

The Old Testament frequently speaks of God testing—or tempting, according to some

translations—individuals. God tests Abraham when he commands him to sacrifice his son Isaac. Job is also tested, as is the entire nation of Israel during the wandering in the desert. In these situations, God is not enticing people to do wrong; rather, he is seeing "whether they will follow my instruction or not" (Ex 16:4). In the Lord's Prayer, Jesus beseeches his Father, "Do not bring us to the time of trial" (Mt 6:13).

Ten Commandments

And he wrote on the tablets the words of the covenant, the ten commandments.
–Exodus 34:28

The ten commandments, sometimes called the Decalogue (meaning "ten words" in Greek), are a series of rules that God established for the Israelites. In their familiar form, they appear twice in the Bible: in Exodus 20:1–17, when God proclaims them from Mount Sinai, and slightly differently in Deuteronomy 5:6–21, as part of Moses' remembrance of the Israelites' wanderings.

Many interpreters have compared the ten commandments with the stipulations of a treaty, a type of ancient Near Eastern contract made between sovereign and vassal. The ten commandments were an integral part of God's covenant with Israel, which he inscribed on two pieces of stone—"tablets of the covenant"—and presented to Moses (Ex 31:18). On returning to his people, Moses discovered them worshiping a golden calf, and he smashed the tablets in disgust (Ex 32:19). He then had to persuade an angry God to reinstate his covenant with the Israelites. Moses "was there with the LORD forty days and forty nights; he neither ate bread nor drank water" (Ex 34:28). He then inscribed "the words of the covenant, the ten commandments" on new tablets, which were later placed in the ark of the covenant (Ex 34:28; 40:20).

Phrased as brief, mostly negative directives, the commandments were easily memorized and were probably recited on ceremonial occasions. They are broad principles of conduct rather than specific instructions. Many are helpful in preserving the life of the community. The commandment to honor one's parents, for example, ensures that the dignity of elderly people will be respected, and the prohibition against adultery protects stability in families.

In the Near East, the nomadic Bedouins live in tents much like those of the patriarchs. The tents shown above were pitched in the vast Negeb Desert, south of Beer-sheba.

Tent

My dwelling is plucked up and removed from me like a shepherd's tent . . . .
–Isaiah 38:12

In biblical times, tents were the typical living quarters for shepherds, nomads, and armies. They were made either of animal hides or rugs of woven goat hair that had shrunk, making them waterproof. A SKIN or rug was stretched over poles and tent cords and fixed to the ground with pegs. To enter the tent, the side or a flap covering an opening was raised.

Abraham and the other patriarchs lived in tents. An entire household often occupied only one tent, with an interior curtain dividing the space. One area was usually reserved for the female members of the household, and it was likely to contain the cooking equipment. Having separate tents for individual family members and servants was a sign of wealth.

During their wilderness wanderings, the Israelites lived in tents. They worshiped at a portable tabernacle that was also called the tent of meeting. It was protected by a tent of goat-hair curtains joined together with bronze clasps; additional coverings were made of animal skins. The entrance was marked by an ornate screen of "blue, purple, and crimson yarns, and fine twisted linen, embroidered with needlework" (Ex 36:37).

Although the Israelites moved into permanent housing when they occupied Canaan, the tentmakers' trade flourished. In some communities, people abandoned their houses in the summer and moved into tents in the cooler climate of the hills. A nomadic lifestyle was practiced by the Rechabite religious sect, which continued to dwell in tents (Jer 35:8–10).

In New Testament times, Paul was a tentmaker (Acts 18:3). Writing to the Corinthians, he used the image of a temporary "earthly tent" (2 Cor 5:1) in contrast to an eternal home in heaven.

Terebinth

They . . . make offerings upon the hills, under oak, poplar, and terebinth, because their shade is good.—Hosea 4:13

The terebinth, a tree found in the hills of the Holy Land, has large, spreading branches. During biblical times, people took advantage of the cool area beneath the tree to conduct various rites of worship, including idolatry. The tree's bark was also of value, and its sap was used to make turpentine. The image of a terebinth is used by the prophet Isaiah in speaking of those who initially escape God's judgment but eventually are destroyed—"burned again, like a terebinth or an oak whose stump remains standing when it is felled"(Isa 6:13).

The terebinth provides welcome shade in the heat of the Sinai peninsula.

Testimony

For many gave false testimony against him, and their testimony did not agree.—Mark 14:56

The term *testimony* refers to oral or written evidence given in a legal proceeding. Biblical law stipulated that at least two witnesses had to testify against a wrongdoer to prove guilt. A WITNESS who refused to give testimony, however, could be punished. The Gospels relate that Jesus' accusers had difficulty finding corroborating testimony against him. John proclaims that Jesus' followers "testify that the Father has sent his Son as the Savior of the world" (1 Jn 4:14).

Testimony also signifies an agreement with God. Thus, the tablets bearing the ten commandments are referred to as "the testimony" in some translations of the Bible.

Thanksgiving

Let us come into his presence with thanksgiving; let us make a joyful noise to him with songs of praise! —Psalm 95:2

In biblical times, thanksgiving was reserved almost exclusively for God, to whom people expressed gratitude through words and songs. They also made special sacrifices, called thank offerings, of animals and grain (Lev 7:12; 22:29). The Israelites gave thanks to God for his many blessings, ranging from his faithfulness to the covenant he made with them to his healing power, forgiveness of sin, and protection from harm.

Thanksgiving was central to worship, especially during Passover and other pilgrimage feasts that drew thousands of the faithful to Jerusalem. A psalmist recalled his part in these events: "I went with the throng, and led them in procession to the house of God, with glad shouts and songs of thanksgiving, a multitude keeping festival" (Ps 42:4).

It was a Jewish custom to begin meals by giving thanks over a loaf of bread before distributing it. Jesus did this at the Last Supper. Christians continued the tradition of expressing thanks both during meals and during the ritual of the LORD'S SUPPER, later called the Eucharist, a Greek word meaning "thanksgiving."

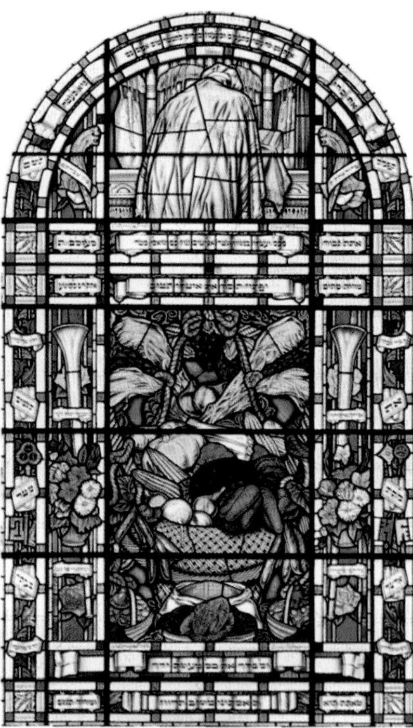

Titled "Harvest Thanksgiving," a modern London synagogue window features the fruits of field and vineyard.

In the late first century BC, *King Herod built this grand theater in the Judean port city of Caesarea, which he named in honor of the Roman emperor Caesar Augustus. The impressive structure was part of Herod's ambitious municipal building program.*

THEATER

THE CITY WAS FILLED WITH THE CONFUSION; AND PEOPLE RUSHED TOGETHER TO THE THEATER . . . .
–ACTS OF THE APOSTLES 19:29

The theater, from a Greek word meaning "a place for seeing," was an integral part of Greco-Roman life. Theaters were generally carved out of hillsides, with the audience rising up in a semicircle above the orchestra, where the action took place. The Greeks performed plays, but the Romans introduced spectacles such as gladiator shows. Theater evolved from ancient religious rituals, and performances sometimes began with a sacrifice to a god. Because of this custom, when rulers built theaters in the Holy Land, the Jews were outraged.

Theaters also served as sites for public assembly. During a riot in Ephesus, a mob dragged Paul's companions into the theater, where the town clerk was able to reason with the crowd (Acts 19:23–41).

THESSALONIANS, 1 & 2

FOR YOU YOURSELVES KNOW . . . THE DAY OF THE LORD WILL COME LIKE A THIEF IN THE NIGHT.
–1 THESSALONIANS 5:2

Paul's first of two letters to Christian converts in Thessalonica, the capital of the Roman province of Macedonia, is perhaps the oldest book in the New Testament. The apostle wrote it about AD 51, soon after opponents forced him to flee the city, where he had preached for only a few weeks. Paul had enough time there to start a congregation, but he left the members confused about several important issues—especially about the second coming of Christ.

The first letter to the Thessalonians is affectionate from beginning to end. Paul thanks the believers for their warm reception, then gently admonishes them to pursue holiness and to abstain from meddling, sexual immorality, and other transgressions. Some Thessalonians evidently feared that believers who died before Jesus' return would miss entering the kingdom of heaven. Paul replied that when the Lord descends, "the dead in Christ will rise first" (1 Thess 4:16).

The second letter, probably written shortly after the first, addressed further confusion about the DAY OF THE LORD. Apparently some believers were so certain Jesus would return immediately that they quit working simply to wait. To them Paul said: "Anyone unwilling to work should not eat" (2 Thess 3:10).

THIGH

". . . AFTER I WAS DISCOVERED, I STRUCK MY THIGH . . . ."
–JEREMIAH 31:19

The human thigh held powerful associations in the biblical world. Deep feelings such as remorse and sorrow might be expressed by slapping the thigh, as in the passage above. The basic personal weapon, the sword, was worn there; "gird your sword on your thigh," says Psalm 45:3. The proximity of the reproductive organs caused the thigh ("loins" in some translations) to be figuratively linked to children and future generations. Thus, when swearing an oath, a man might put a hand under another's thigh (Gen 24:9; 47:29), suggesting that the latter man's progeny were being called upon as witnesses. By Mosaic law, the right thigh of a sacrificial animal was given to the priests (Lev 7:33–34).

THORN

THEREFORE, TO KEEP ME FROM BEING TOO ELATED, A THORN WAS GIVEN ME IN THE FLESH . . . .
–2 CORINTHIANS 12:7

Thorns are sharp spines found on the branches of thornbushes. In the Bible, thorny desert plants are referred to as brambles, briers, or thistles, and land covered with such plants was considered worthless. In addition, the metaphorical use of *thorn* indicates a bad, desolate, or hopeless situation. Thus, anticipating the time when the Israelites would be freed from captivity, Isaiah proclaims: "Instead of the thorn shall come up the cypress" (Isa 55:13).

Thorns did have some value. Thickets of thornbushes or piles of the cut plants were an effective enclosure for animals and a barrier against strangers Dried thorny plants could be burned as fuel.

Thorns can pierce the skin of an animal or human, causing pain. Roman soldiers placed a CROWN OF THORNS on Jesus' head and called him "King of the Jews" (Jn 19:2–3). Paul spoke of a "thorn" in his flesh, possibly meaning a chronic disease, given to him by "a messenger of Satan to torment me" (2 Cor 12:7).

THOUSAND

HE IS MINDFUL OF HIS COVENANT FOREVER . . . FOR A THOUSAND GENERATIONS . . . .
–PSALM 105:8

In the Bible, *thousand* is often an imprecise word that simply designates a large number. Indeed, the Hebrew term for a thousand can also be translated as "family," "clan," or "tribe." Military units of "a thousand," as in 1 Samuel 18:13, may have actually been smaller. The word is sometimes used metaphorically to indicate a long period of time, as when humans are described as short-lived compared with God: "For a thousand years in your sight are like yesterday" (Ps 90:4). The eschatological vision in Revelation makes similar use of the term: "He seized . . . that ancient serpent, who is the Devil and Satan, and bound him for a thousand years" (Rev 20:2).

THRESHING

YOUR THRESHING SHALL OVERTAKE THE VINTAGE, AND THE VINTAGE SHALL OVERTAKE THE SOWING . . . .
–LEVITICUS 26:5

The edible seeds of wheat and barley are enclosed in coarse husks, or chaff. After the grain is harvested, the threshing process separates the seeds, or kernels, from the chaff and stalks. In biblical times, threshing was performed on a threshing floor, which might be a large, flat rock or an area of earth leveled off, wetted down, and stamped smooth and hard. The threshing floor was usually located in an open public place away from houses.

Threshing could be done in several ways. One method was to beat the grain with a jointed stick, called a flail. Another was to drive hoofed animals back and forth over the grain. A third technique

Threshing was one of several steps taken to refine grain for consumption. As seen in this illustration, a boy arrives from the fields with wheat, at left, as oxen drag a threshing sledge, at right, to break up the grain that has already been spread on the threshing floor. In the background, farmers use winnowing forks to toss the grain into the air, allowing the wind to carry away the chaff as the heavier seeds fall back to the threshing floor. The women standing next to them use sieves for the final refining step, which involves feeding the grain through the sieves to remove more of the chaff. The grain is placed temporarily in baskets, and the next day it will be put in storage jars or into a silo to keep it dry.

involved the use of a threshing sledge, which had sharp stones or iron teeth set on its underside. Oxen pulled the sledge across the threshing floor until the job was completed. After threshing, WINNOWING took place to separate out the loosened chaff and straw (see illustration).

THRESHOLD

ONE WHO LOVES TRANSGRESSION LOVES STRIFE; ONE WHO BUILDS A HIGH THRESHOLD INVITES BROKEN BONES.
–PROVERBS 17:19

The threshold is the bottom piece of a DOOR frame that supports the doorposts. In the ancient Holy Land, it was often a stone slab cut to size, although sometimes a row of smaller stones sufficed. To keep out rainwater and dirt, the threshold stood a little higher than the level of the street outside. People had to step over it to enter the house; thus "one who builds a high threshold invites broken bones" (Prov 17:19). In Zephaniah 1:9, God says he will punish those who "leap over the threshold"—a probable reference to a Philistine ritual introduced into the temple. The "keeper of the threshold" was a temple official.

THRONE

. . . I WILL ESTABLISH THE THRONE OF HIS KINGDOM FOREVER.
–2 SAMUEL 7:13

A throne was a seat for a ruler, either human or divine. The throne was elevated to stress the superiority of the person occupying it; thus, Isaiah had a vision of "the Lord sitting on a throne, high and lofty" (Isa 6:1). Solomon's throne was made of ivory and covered with "the finest gold" (1 Kings 10:18). As the instrument of God on earth, Solomon sat upon "the throne of the kingdom of the LORD over Israel" (1 Chr 28:5). Being seated next to the royal throne was a mark of respect and power. Solomon's mother sat on her own throne to his right (1 Kings 2:19). The letter to the Hebrews speaks of the resurrected Jesus as "seated at the right hand of the throne of the Majesty in the heavens" (Heb 8:1).

The ultimate monarch, God proclaims that "heaven is my throne and the earth is my footstool" (Isa 66:1). God is portrayed as dispensing justice from his heavenly throne, just as kings, judges, and governors often hand down decisions from their thrones on earth. Jeremiah predicts that after the exile, "Jerusalem shall be called the throne of the LORD" (Jer 3:17).

Thunder

"Enough of God's thunder and hail!"–Exodus 9:28

In the Holy Land, most rainstorms, which produce thunder, occur in the winter months. Thus, when Samuel prevails on God to send thunder and rain during the summer harvest, the unlikely event is viewed as a miracle (1 Sam 12:17). Many of the Bible's references to thunder invoke the power and presence of God, such as Psalm 29:3, which likens God's voice to a violent thunderstorm moving inland from the Mediterranean Sea. According to the book of Job, God, in his role as creator, made "a way for the thunderbolt" (Job 28:26). In the book of Revelation, the voice of the great multitude praising God's reign is described as being like "the sound of mighty thunderpeals" (Rev 19:6).

Time

Whether it was two days, or a month, or a longer time . . . the Israelites would remain in camp . . . . –Numbers 9:22

The ancient Israelites measured time in a different way from that used by most people today. Without mechanical timepieces, the measurement of time was of necessity imprecise. The Israelites tracked time by the height of the sun in the sky and the temperature variations of the day, such as "the heat of the day" (Gen 18:1), as well as by the passing of the seasons.

The Bible uses a variety of words for units of time, including *hour, day, month,* and *year.* A day was either the period of sunlight or the time between sunsets on two consecutive days. By the time of Jesus, it was customary to break this period into 12 hours. The hour was not fixed as it is today but rather was 1/12 of the period between sunrise and sunset, which varied in length depending on the season. At night, time was measured by the three watches that sentinels stood—a watch being roughly four hours long.

Like the Western calendar, the biblical calendar had a week of seven days and a year of 12 months. By Jesus' time, the Roman Empire had adopted the Julian calendar. Named for Julius Caesar, it used a 365-day solar year, with every fourth year having 366 days.

In the Scriptures, the word *time* frequently expresses a point in time, whether an instant or a longer span, such as a lifetime. It also denotes the period allotted to a task (Gen 24:11). Festivals were celebrated and offerings were made at their "appointed time" (Ex 23:15; Num 28:2). Just as the Greeks used the date of the first Olympic Games and the Romans the founding of Rome as a base point, so the Israelites used epochal events as markers of time that had passed. The exodus, the Babylonian exile, and the building of Solomon's temple were such markers.

Time is often expressed in the Bible in symbolic rather than in literal ways. Thus, the 40 days and 40 nights that the flood is said to have lasted and the incredible longevities of patriarchs such as Abraham are not to be taken literally.

Using a device such as this Bronze Age Egyptian shadow clock, people calculated the approximate time of day by the length of the shadow cast by the sun on its steps.

Timothy appears with his mother, Eunice, in an 18th-century stained-glass window.

Timothy, 1&2

Do not be ashamed, then, of the testimony about our Lord . . . but join with me in suffering for the gospel . . . . –2 Timothy 1:8

Combined with his letter to Titus, Paul's two letters to Timothy are called the Pastoral Letters because they deal with leadership in the Christian community. Mentioned as close associates of Paul elsewhere in the New Testament, Titus ministered on the island of Crete and Timothy in Ephesus. In the first letter to Timothy, Paul gives advice about how to lead the church, describes the qualifications that bishops and deacons should have, offers instruction about prayer and public worship, and warns against heretical teachers.

The second letter is more concerned about Timothy than about church administration. Writing from prison, Paul says he expects to die soon. In what may have been his last words to a dear friend, he encourages Timothy to face persecution with courage and to "hold to the standard of sound teaching that you have heard from me" (2 Tim 1:13). The style and content of the letters differ from the apostle Paul's other letters, and many scholars have concluded that Paul himself did not write them. Rather, it is thought, they were written by an author who used Paul's name to give his letters greater authority.

TITHE

SET APART A TITHE OF ALL THE YIELD OF YOUR SEED THAT IS BROUGHT IN YEARLY FROM THE FIELD.
–DEUTERONOMY 14:22

A tithe was tribute paid to rulers or an offering made to fund religious practices. Ten percent of the year's harvest, livestock, or other goods were to be paid, the word *tithe* meaning "tenth." It is not known where or when 10 percent became the accustomed rate for tithing, for the practice existed throughout the ancient world from Babylon, Persia, and Egypt to China. The patriarchs were familiar with tithing: Abraham gave "one tenth of everything" (Gen 14:20) to the Canaanite priest-king Melchizedek. God promised Jacob land and countless progeny; Jacob, in turn, promised God a 10 percent tithe (Gen 28:13–22).

Complicated laws governing annual tithes evolved in Israel, but the primary objective remained the same: to support the Levites and priests in charge of temple worship. Every third year a tithe was levied on the Israelites for the benefit of the "Levites . . . the resident aliens, the orphans, and the widows in your towns" (Deut 14:29). Under Roman rule, some Pharisees tithed even herbs (Lk 11:42).

TITUS, LETTER OF PAUL TO

I LEFT YOU BEHIND IN CRETE FOR THIS REASON, SO THAT YOU SHOULD . . . APPOINT ELDERS IN EVERY TOWN, AS I DIRECTED YOU . . . .
–TITUS 1:5

The last of the three Pastoral Letters, which begin with 1 and 2 Timothy, Paul's letter to Titus continues the theme of leading the CHURCH. Titus was a Gentile who often traveled with Paul (Gal 2:1) and occasionally served as his emissary to individual churches. The letter advises Titus on the moral qualifications for church leaders and suggests what to teach various groups of believers. Because it uses words not found in Paul's other letters and the church offices that it mentions seem more developed than in Paul's time, many scholars think that the letter to Titus, like those to Timothy, was not written by Paul himself.

TOBIT, BOOK OF

I, TOBIT . . . PERFORMED MANY ACTS OF CHARITY FOR . . . MY PEOPLE WHO HAD GONE WITH ME IN EXILE TO NINEVEH . . . .
–TOBIT 1:3

The apocryphal book Tobit is a story about a pious Israelite who was exiled in Nineveh after Assyria conquered the northern kingdom of Israel. Though Tobit lived among Gentiles, he refused to abandon his Jewish traditions. When the king prohibited burial for people executed by the empire, Tobit ignored the order and buried executed Jews. The state confiscated his property. One night after a burial, he observed the law of ritual cleanliness by sleeping outdoors. Sparrow droppings fell into his eyes, blinding him. Through the intervention of his son, Tobias, who was aided by an angel in human disguise, Tobit was healed and his wealth restored.

TOMB

THEN JOSEPH . . . TAKING DOWN THE BODY, WRAPPED IT IN THE LINEN CLOTH, AND LAID IT IN A TOMB THAT HAD BEEN HEWN OUT OF THE ROCK.–MARK 15:46

In the Holy Land, the dead were buried in tombs, which were usually natural caves or chambers dug out of rock specifically for that purpose. Niches, called sepulchers, were carved out of the rock to hold the individual bodies of deceased family members. Out of this custom arose various biblical idioms for the dead, who were "gathered to" (Gen 25:8) or "slept with" (1 Kings 2:10) their ancestors. When decay reduced the body to bones, the remains were placed elsewhere in the cave to make room for new bodies.

As instructed by the angel Raphael, Tobias applies a salve made from "the gall of the fish" to Tobit's eyes, and his blindness is healed (Tob 11:7–14), as depicted in this 17th-century painting.

TONGUE

A GENTLE TONGUE IS A TREE OF LIFE . . . .—PROVERBS 15:4

In the Bible, the word *tongue* is used infrequently in a purely anatomical sense. More often, the tongue is used to portray the diverse characteristics of human speech. A tongue is capable of praising the Lord, creating strife, or generating wickedness. Above all, the tongue reveals one's true nature. In Proverbs, "To watch over mouth and tongue is to keep out of trouble" (Prov 21:23).

From a 16th-century panel, the tower of Babel is a symbol of the origin of different languages, or tongues (Gen 11:1–9).

Languages are considered to be separate tongues, and Isaiah refers to foreign speech as an "alien tongue" (Isa 28:11). At the Pentecost described in Acts of the Apostles, "divided tongues, as of fire" (Acts 2:3) rested on the assembled apostles, miraculously enabling them to speak in actual foreign languages. The practice of glossolalia, or "speaking in tongues" that are incomprehensible by ordinary means, was common in some early churches. The apostle Paul discussed the problem in 1 Corinthians 13 and gave a number of directives about the use of glossolalia, including that it was to be done in a nonthreatening fashion and be accompanied by interpretation.

TOOLS

. . . [HEZEKIAH] TUNNELED THE ROCK WITH IRON TOOLS, AND BUILT CISTERNS FOR THE WATER. —ECCLESIASTICUS 48:17

Though the word *tool* appears only a few times in the Bible, various tools used in crafts, industry, and agriculture are referred to by name. Stone tools, often made of flint, are the earliest known tools. Later, copper and bronze implements were also used. Iron, an extremely hard metal, was found to be the most desirable material. Tools made with iron cutting surfaces began to be used in Canaan about 1200 BC, roughly the same time that the Israelites settled there. The Hebrew word for axhead means "iron," indicating that axes were routinely made from that metal. Wood, leather, bone, or ivory were often used for handles and other tool parts.

Though the use of tools in construction was widespread, Moses was directed by God not to make an altar of "hewn stones; for if you use a chisel upon it you profane it" (Ex 20:25). In conformity with this commandment, Solomon's temple was "built with stone finished at the quarry, so that neither hammer nor ax nor any tool of iron was heard in the temple" (1 Kings 6:7). See also ARMS.

The primitive stone agricultural tools pictured here include, from left to right, an ax, a sickle, and an adz, which were refurbished with wooden handles.

TORCH

SO JUDAS BROUGHT A DETACHMENT OF SOLDIERS TOGETHER WITH POLICE . . . AND THEY CAME WITH LANTERNS AND TORCHES AND WEAPONS. —JOHN 18:3

Torches, consisting of oil-soaked cloths wrapped around one end of a pole and ignited, provided fire and light. Gideon and 300 Israelite soldiers terrified the vast Midian army by descending on it at night, "holding in their left hands the torches, and in their right hands the trumpets to blow" (Judg 7:20). Fields were set alight with torches after harvest to eliminate mildew and pests. Samson tied torches to the tails of foxes, which ran into the fields of the Philistines and destroyed their grain (Judg 15:4–5). In Daniel, the eyes of an angelic figure were said to be like "flaming torches" (Dan 10:6).

TOWER

IN JEZREEL, THE SENTINEL STANDING ON THE TOWER SPIED THE COMPANY OF JEHU ARRIVING . . . . —2 KINGS 9:17

From Canaanite times until the Roman occupation and beyond, the Holy Land suffered from almost constant warfare, and every city had one or more towers for defensive purposes. From the tower the sentinel spied approaching enemies, archers shot arrows, and defenders might hurl rocks and boiling oil on attackers who were in close range. Some towers were apparently large enough to offer refuge to as many as 1,000 people (Judg 9:49). Towers far beyond the city walls served as military outposts.

Farmers also built watchtowers (Isa 5:2) to guard their fields against depredations by birds, animals, and raiders.

Town

Some wandered in desert wastes, finding no way to an inhabited town . . . .
–Psalm 107:4

Towns were centers of population that were larger than a village but smaller than a CITY. Many of the early Israelites lived in towns in the hills of the Holy Land. Though generally less well fortified than cities, towns were often walled and gated (1 Sam 23:7). Some large towns had satellite villages in the countryside (Num 21:25). These villages probably supplied the town with food; in return the town provided protection from enemy attacks.

During the Greek and Roman eras, the town clerk, or *grammateus*, meaning "scribe," was an important local official responsible for the decrees presented to the public. In Acts of the Apostles, the town clerk of Ephesus, who was the highest government authority in town, defused a riot provoked by the followers of the apostle Paul. He skillfully argued that the mob should resort to the legal system to redress their grievances rather than risk the wrath of Roman intervention (Acts 19:35–41).

Trade

The ships of Tarshish traveled for you in your trade. So you were filled and heavily laden in the heart of the seas.–Ezekiel 27:25

International trade, either by sea or by overland CARAVAN, existed from the earliest biblical times. Strategically located between Mesopotamia and Egypt, the Holy Land became a natural corridor through which traders moved. Egyptian tomb paintings from the second millennium BC portray Semitic traders and their families conveying merchandise on donkeys. A passing caravan of Arabian traders "carrying gum, balm, and resin, on their way to . . . Egypt" (Gen 37:25) bought Jacob's son Joseph for 20 pieces of silver. Tradesmen and farmers earned their living supplying the caravans with needed supplies and were also exposed to other cultures.

During the era of the united monarchy in Israel—particularly under the rule of Solomon—international trade flourished. Exotic goods were imported into ancient Israel: incense, spices, gold, horses, chariots, ivory, and peacocks from Africa and across the Near East. In return, Israel exported agricultural products and iron. Ezekiel 27:17 lists the products being sent to Tyre as "wheat from Minnith, millet, honey, oil, and balm." There were no deep-water ports on Israel's coast, so sea commerce was carried out for them by coastal peoples such as the Phoenicians. Ezekiel referred to the Phoenician city of Tyre as the "merchant of the peoples on many coastlands" (Ezek 27:3), a place that commanded "abundant wealth and merchandise" (Ezek 27:33). Yet Ezekiel predicted the destruction of Tyre because its success had bred arro-

Pictured above are the ancient remains of the port of Caesarea. Built in the first century BC by Herod in honor of Caesar Augustus, Caesarea was a major trading port.

gance and corruption: "By your great wisdom in trade you have increased your wealth, and your heart has become proud in your wealth" (Ezek 28:5). Trade was an integral part of domestic life as well. Hamor, the Hivite, told Jacob and his sons that "the land shall be open to you; live and trade in it" (Gen 34:10).

The word *trade* also refers to an occupation. When Paul went to Corinth, he and his host had the same profession, for "by trade they were tentmakers" (Acts 18:3). Other tradesmen included carpenters, weavers, metalworkers, tanners, potters, jewelers, plasterers, and glassworkers. Such occupations required expertise that was often acquired through apprenticeship to a skilled tradesman. Merchants bought and sold their goods or wares for a profit, and abuses by them were frequently condemned in the Bible: "A merchant can hardly keep from wrongdoing, nor is a tradesman innocent of sin" (Sir 26:29). See also SHIP.

TRADITION

. . . STAND FIRM AND HOLD FAST TO THE TRADITIONS THAT YOU WERE TAUGHT BY US . . . .
–2 THESSALONIANS 2:15

Traditions are the stories, beliefs, and customs that comprise the cultural and religious teachings handed down from one generation to the next. Much of the Bible is derived from oral tradition. Many Old Testament narratives had a long oral history, having originally been told around campfires or used in religious ceremonies before being written down. The Gospels, which recount the life and teachings of Jesus, were written years after Jesus' death. They relied on firsthand accounts of his ministry that were passed on initially by word of mouth.

Jewish tradition and beliefs were based on God's commandments in the Torah. Some traditions that were passed down orally by rabbis were to be considered legally binding, even though they were not written in the Scriptures. Jesus respected Jewish tradition and recognized Pharisees and scribes as legitimate teachers of the Torah. Yet he criticized them for not practicing what they preached. This criticism grew more severe as Jesus began to distinguish the commandments in the Scriptures from the dictates of the elders and denounced them for "teaching human precepts as doctrines" (Mt 15:9; Mk 7:7). See also TEACHER.

TRANCE

. . . WHEN I HEARD THE SOUND OF HIS WORDS, I FELL INTO A TRANCE, FACE TO THE GROUND.
–DANIEL 10:9

A trance is a dreamlike or hypnotic state in which a person is detached from physical reality. To people of biblical times, however, it signified a mental state in which a person received visions and revelations from God while awake. Daniel went into a trance when he had a vision portending the destruction and the triumph of various empires. While praying, Peter fell into a trance and received a VISION assuring him that it was permitted to eat food previously considered unclean (Acts 11:5–9).

TRANSFIGURE

. . . HE WAS TRANSFIGURED BEFORE THEM, AND HIS CLOTHES BECAME DAZZLING WHITE . . . .
–MARK 9:2–3

In the Gospels of Matthew and Mark, Jesus leads Peter, James, and John up a mountain, where he is transfigured, or transformed, from the man they knew into a brilliant figure (Mt 17:2; Mk 9:2–3). The parallel passage from Luke does not use the word *transfigured* but rather relates that "the appearance of his face changed" (Lk 9:29). Moses and Elijah appear and talk to Jesus, and a voice from a radiant cloud proclaims, "This is my Son, the Beloved; with him I am well pleased" (Mt 17:5). The disciples fall to the ground with fear, and when they look up, only Jesus is there. The event is considered a revelation of Jesus' true identity.

Apostles Peter, James, and John witness the transfiguration of Christ in this 13th-century French illuminated manuscript.

TRAVEL

. . . HE HAS ALSO BEEN APPOINTED BY THE CHURCHES TO TRAVEL WITH US . . . .
–2 CORINTHIANS 8:19

Throughout biblical times travel was difficult and slow—a full day's journey being only about 20 miles. The Israelites traveled in order to trade, to attend religious festivals, and to emigrate or procure food in times of famine. Offering hospitality to strangers was considered a sacred obligation, and people frequently opened their homes to weary travelers.

Because the Holy Land served as a land bridge between Egypt and Mesopotamia, important trade and military routes ran through it. These routes included a portion of the Great Trunk Highway, a ROAD that proceeded along the Mediterranean coast, and the King's Highway, east of the Jordan River. Local paths connected these major north–south routes. The Israelites traveled only infrequently by sea, in part because they lacked a good natural port.

The usual mode of transport was walking, and human porters bearing cargo were a common sight. After animals were domesticated, the sure-footed donkey became indispensable, especially in hilly areas; heavy loads were moved by means of ox carts. Camels, which had wide hooves suited for level surfaces and an ability to travel for days without water, were ideal animals for the trade caravans that traversed the desert. Horses and chariots were employed primarily by the military, the wealthy, and couriers delivering royal messages.

In New Testament times, overland travel was somewhat eased by Roman rulers, who built a network of new roads and paved preexisting ones. By far the greatest recorded traveler among early Christians, on land or sea, was Paul. The hazards accompanying sea travel were well illustrated by Paul's harrowing final voyage to Rome, marked by storms, shipwreck, and delays (Acts 27:1–28:14).

Treasure

"The kingdom of heaven is like treasure hidden in a field . . . ."
–Matthew 13:44

In the Bible, *treasure* usually refers generally to hoards of precious metal, whether gold or silver. The book of Proverbs cautions, however, that wisdom is the true treasure for humans (Prov 8:11), for material treasures do not endure.

In ancient Israel, there were storehouses of treasure in the temple and in the royal palace. Accumulated from taxes or offerings, trade, contributions from rich men seeking favors, and the spoils of war, these treasures were used to build and maintain public structures and to support the priests and court. Sometimes they were drawn upon to pay the military, bribe potential conquerors, or buy the support of allies. Under King Nebuchadnezzar, the Babylonians carried off the temple treasure and stored it in the treasury of the gods (Ezra 1:7), but it was released later into the care of the Judean treasurer and sent back to Jerusalem (Ezra 1:8).

In the Apocrypha, the "treasure of all nations" refers to God's promise to Israel of gold and silver to adorn the new temple in Jerusalem (Hag 2:7). The treasury was again plundered in the second century BC by the Seleucid king Antiochus IV.

In the New Testament, references to the temple treasury (Mk 12:41; Lk 21:1) specifically meant the 13 receptacles, each shaped like an inverted trumpet, located in the temple's court of the women in order to receive offerings. When Jesus spoke of treasure, he usually drew a distinction between the material treasures of this world and the spiritual treasures of heaven. By relinquishing one's material goods, Jesus preached, one could turn wordly treasures into spiritual ones (Lk 18:22) and gain everlasting "treasure in heaven." In 2 Corinthians, the apostle Paul describes Jesus' message of salvation as treasure (2 Cor 4:6–7).

A cart drawn by a team of sturdy oxen was a mode of travel in biblical times. In this detail from an eighth century BC relief, women and children are shown fleeing a Babylonian city, which is being ravaged by the Assyrians.

TREE

. . . THE LORD GOD MADE TO GROW EVERY TREE THAT IS PLEASANT TO THE SIGHT AND GOOD FOR FOOD . . . .–GENESIS 2:9

The importance of trees is established early on in the book of Genesis, when God supplies the garden of Eden with fruit-bearing trees, as well as two trees of special significance: The tree of life provides access to immortality. The tree of the knowledge of good and evil tests the obedience of Adam and Eve, who are forbidden by God to eat its fruit. When they do so despite this injunction, they are separated from the tree of life and from Eden. They then use leaves from the trees to cover their nakedness.

Forests originally covered much of the Holy Land. However, as civilization developed and populations increased, extensive deforestation occurred. Trees that still grew in the area were prized as sources of food, shade, fuel, and building materials. Fig trees and mulberry trees provided both shade and fruit. Dates, olives, pomegranates, almonds, pistachios, and walnuts were important foods that came from trees. Cedars and cypresses from Lebanon provided excellent timber for building. Although myrtles are called trees in the Bible, they are actually shrubs that were used to build temporary shelters during the Festival of Booths.

Birds perch on Eden's tree of life in a basilica mosaic from the fourth century AD.

In scriptural writings, trees that survive in the hot desert symbolize stamina and life, and large trees represent strength. Well-watered trees with abundant leaves, as contrasted with trees that have withered leaves or none at all, indicate respectively God's blessing or curse.

TRIBE

A MAN FROM EACH TRIBE SHALL BE WITH YOU, EACH MAN THE HEAD OF HIS ANCESTRAL HOUSE.–NUMBERS 1:4

A tribe was a territorial group made up of people who claimed descent from a common ancestor. Jacob was the original PATRIARCH, fathering a total of 12 sons with his wives, Leah and Rachel, and his concubines, Zilpah and Bilhah. God changed Jacob's name to *Israel,* and his sons and their descendants made up the 12 tribes of Israel.

On his deathbed, Jacob told the Judah, his fourth son with Leah, that "your father's sons shall bow down before you" (Gen 49:8). This was a surprising prediction, since Reuben, as the firstborn son, should have assumed leadership of the brothers. But Reuben lost that position when he had sexual relations with Bilhah, causing Jacob to call him "unstable as water . . . because you went up onto your father's bed" (Gen 49:4).

When the tribes came to Canaan, each was assigned its own land. As Jacob's blessing indicates, the tribe of Judah became the most prominent of the 12. The tribe of Simeon, the second son, was so weak that rather than having its own land, "its inheritance lay within the inheritance of the tribe of Judah" (Josh 19:1). Similarly, the tribe of Levi was not given land. Instead, said Moses, "the LORD God of Israel is their inheritance" (Josh 13:33), and the Levites were assigned special religious functions. The tribe of Joseph eventually split into those of his two sons, Ephraim and Manasseh.

Tribes were made up of a number of clans, which in turn contained groups of extended families. Clan members typically lived near one another, occupying entire villages or areas of a city. Although they all worshiped God, each tribe had a different identity, based on its history of conquest, what its migration pattern had been, and how its members used the land to provide for themselves.

From about 1200 to 1000 BC, tribes were the primary unit of social organization. Each tribe had its own militia, religious leaders, and legal powers. Once the monarchy was established, government became centralized and the authority of the tribes weakened. Yet even in the New Testament, long after the tribal period had ended, people sometimes identified themselves by their tribe. Paul said that he was "a member of the tribe of Benjamin" (Rom 11:1), and Barnabas was identified as a Levite (Acts 4:36).

TRIBUNAL

. . . THE JEWS MADE A UNITED ATTACK ON PAUL AND BROUGHT HIM BEFORE THE TRIBUNAL. –ACTS OF THE APOSTLES 18:12

The tribunal was a public platform for officials of the Roman Empire who decided civil cases. Its bench, or sometimes the entire tribunal, was called the JUDGMENT SEAT. In Corinth, Paul was brought before the Roman proconsul Gallio by Jews who were offended by the

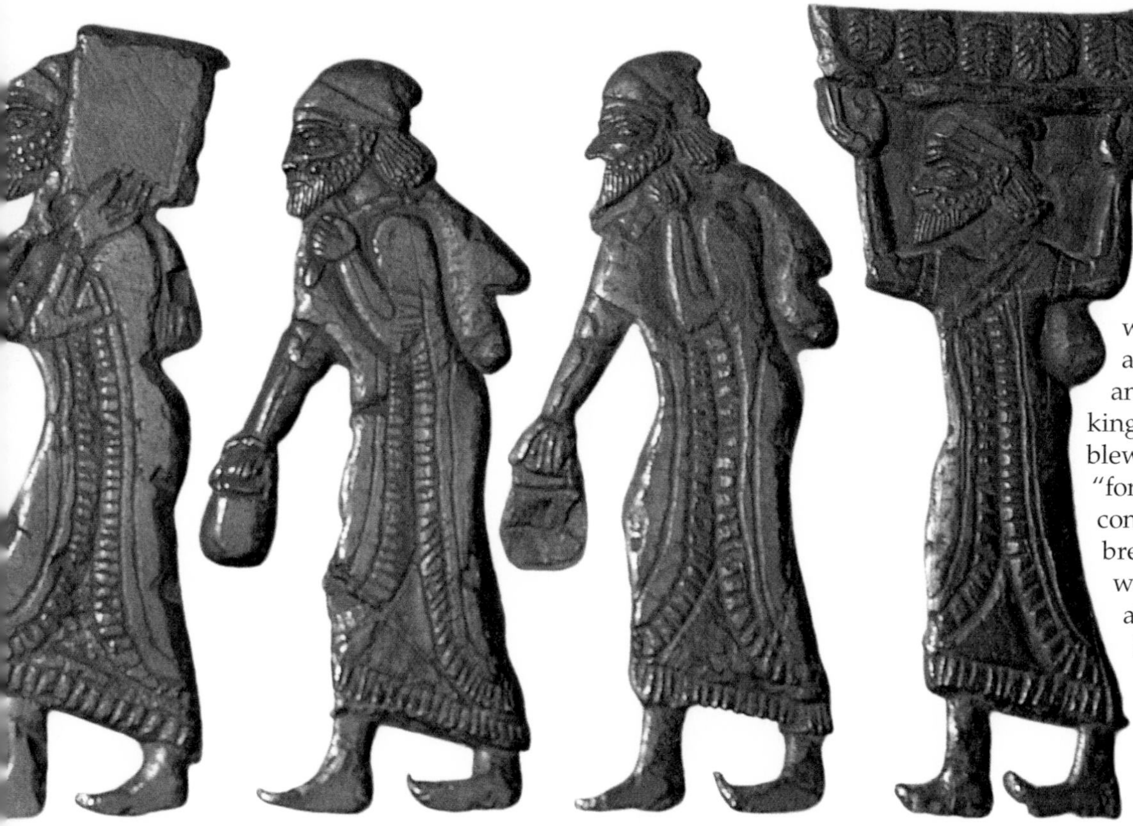

The ninth-century BC *Black Obelisk includes this scene of Israelite porters bearing tribute to the Assyrian king Shalmaneser III.*

apostle's teachings in the synagogue. Because Gallio saw the matter as one pertaining specifically to Jewish law, "he dismissed them from the tribunal" (Acts 18:16). Excavations have uncovered an ornate platform in or near the marketplace that is believed to be this tribunal. At the request of the Jews, Paul was also called before the governor, Festus. At the tribunal in Caesarea, the official could find no crime but only "points of disagreement . . . about a certain Jesus" (Acts 25:19), as he told King Agrippa. Agrippa would have set Paul free if the apostle had not already appealed to the emperor (Acts 26:32).

TRIBUTE

KING AHASUERUS LAID TRIBUTE ON THE LAND AND ON THE ISLANDS OF THE SEA.–ESTHER 10:1

By at least 2000 BC, tribute was a form of payment from a defeated nation or weak ally to a foreign conqueror that was usually made once a year. Delegations bringing gold, silver, or other commodities were a frequent theme of wall carvings in the palaces of the ancient Near East. Tribute obligations could financially weaken a community, but failure to pay was likely to provoke swift military retaliation. Israel was rarely strong enough to demand tribute from other nations, except during the reigns of David, Solomon, and Ahab. However, it was often forced to pay tribute to a larger, more powerful state, such as Assyria, Babylon, Persia, or Rome.

TRUMPET

AND SAUL BLEW THE TRUMPET THROUGHOUT ALL THE LAND, SAYING, "LET THE HEBREWS HEAR!" –1 SAMUEL 13:3

Trumpets existed in the Near East as early as the second millennium BC. Examples of these instruments, made of copper and bronze, have been recovered from the tomb of the Egyptian king Tutankhamen.

Trumpet and HORN blasts were signals used to call people to battle, warn of danger, and announce festivals and the accession of kings. Israelite priests blew silver trumpets "for summoning the congregation, and for breaking camp," as well as to "blow an alarm" (Num 10:2, 5). Two priests usually sounded trumpets during religious ceremonies, but to celebrate the installation of the ark of the covenant in Solomon's temple, 120 priests served as trumpeters (2 Chr 5:12). The term *trumpet* can mean the ram's horn, or shofar, which was blown on great national and religious occasions.

TURBAN

SO THEY PUT A CLEAN TURBAN ON HIS HEAD AND CLOTHED HIM WITH THE APPAREL . . . . –ZECHARIAH 3:5

Turbans were formed by winding strips of cloth around the head. They included both the ceremonial turban worn by the high priest and the regular headdress worn by men—and sometimes by women (Isa 3:23)—as protection from the sun and rain. The high priest's linen turban, or miter, was a symbol of majestic splendor since the time of Aaron's investiture. A gold rosette engraved with the phrase "Holy to the LORD" (Ex 28:36) was attached to it with a blue cord.

Removing one's turban could indicate a state of mourning or shame. See also VEIL.

Mesha, a ninth-century BC *king of Moab, had this black basalt stele inscribed to celebrate his* VICTORY *"over all my enemies," referring to his rebellion against Israel after King Ahab died (2 Kings 3:5). The stele was restored in the 1870s after having been shattered by people in the region who believed it held treasure.*

UNBELIEVER

AND WHOEVER DOES NOT PROVIDE FOR RELATIVES . . . HAS DENIED THE FAITH AND IS WORSE THAN AN UNBELIEVER.
–1 TIMOTHY 5:8

In the Bible, an unbeliever is a person who rejects God. The term signifies more than doubt in God's existence; indeed, unbelievers are seen as disobedient and rebellious, failing to keep God's law. Hebrews 3:12 warns Christians: "Take care, brothers and sisters, that none of you may have an evil, unbelieving heart that turns away from the living God."

The word *unbeliever* is found almost exclusively in the New Testament, and especially in the letters of Paul, who uses it as a general term for non-Christians. Paul advises believers, or Christians, not to forge close relationships with those who do not believe in Jesus as the Messiah: "Do not be mismatched with unbelievers. For what partnership is there between righteousness and lawlessness? Or what fellowship is there between light and darkness?" (2 Cor 6:14). Yet Paul does not advise married people to divorce their non-Christian spouses, "for the unbelieving husband is made holy through his wife, and the unbelieving wife is made holy through her husband" (1 Cor 7:14).

UNITY

FINALLY, ALL OF YOU, HAVE UNITY OF SPIRIT, SYMPATHY, LOVE FOR ONE ANOTHER, A TENDER HEART, AND A HUMBLE MIND.
–1 PETER 3:8

Unity, or oneness, is a central concept in both the Old and New Testaments. The Israelites were joined together by their belief in one God. This unity was reflected in their obligations to one another: avengers sought retribution for murdered kin, redeemers delivered people from hardship, and men married their childless, widowed sisters-in-law to provide their brothers with progeny. Psalm 133:1 notes, in praise of familial harmony, "how very good and pleasant it is when kindred live together in unity!"

In the New Testament, Christians shared the belief in Jesus as the Messiah and were therefore united in the BODY OF CHRIST. They possessed spiritual gifts that were to be used for the common good and were called upon to live in harmony so that they might glorify God "with one voice"(Rom 15:5–6).

A Yemenite woman displays flat, unleavened bread, called mazzah *in Hebrew, fresh from the oven.*

UNLEAVENED BREAD

FOR SEVEN DAYS YOU SHALL EAT UNLEAVENED BREAD WITH IT— THE BREAD OF AFFLICTION . . . .
–DEUTERONOMY 16:3

When God led the Israelites out of Egypt, he told Moses that the deliverance from slavery should be commemorated each year by a seven-day festival. During this Festival of Unleavened Bread, only bread made without yeast would be eaten. This practice was meant to remind the people and their descendants of the haste with which the Israelites departed from Egypt, for there was no time to let the bread dough rise. The "bread of affliction" also became a symbol of the bondage from which the Israelites were rescued. The Festival of Unleavened Bread eventually merged with the Passover festival.

When presented as a sacrificial offering in the temple, bread, which was sometimes in the form of cakes, had to be unleavened if it was to be offered on the altar. Leaven may have been seen as a corrupting agent because it caused fermentation and thus was associated with decomposition.

As ordinary food, unleavened bread was eaten at any time of the year and might be served to guests (1 Sam 28:24–25).

UPPER ROOM

. . . HE CONTINUED TO GO TO HIS HOUSE, WHICH HAD WINDOWS IN ITS UPPER ROOM OPEN TOWARD JERUSALEM . . . . –DANIEL 6:10

The upper room could be either the second story of a house or a tent or other structure set up on a flat roof. It was often where guests lodged. The Last Supper took place in an upper room in Jerusalem large enough to accommodate Jesus and his 12 apostles; in Mark 14:15, Jesus calls it "a large room upstairs." Tradition identifies this same room as the site of an appearance by Jesus after his resurrection (Lk 24:36) and of the descent of the Holy Spirit on Pentecost (Acts 2:1–4). Nehemiah 3:31 speaks of repairs being made to the Jerusalem wall and to "the upper room of the corner."

URIM AND THUMMIM

IN THE BREASTPIECE OF JUDGMENT YOU SHALL PUT THE URIM AND THE THUMMIM . . . . –EXODUS 28:30

The Urim and Thummim were two sacred objects, which were probably stones, used by the high priest to determine God's will. They were kept in a pouch called the breastpiece, which was worn on the priest's ephod, or sacred garment.

Their precise use remains a mystery, but apparently the high priest cast LOTS with them to receive God's answer to a direct, yes-or-no question. When Saul wanted to find out who had broken his vow that all his troops would fast until he had defeated the Philistines, he said to God, "If this guilt is in me or in my son Jonathan . . . give Urim; but if this guilt is in your people Israel, give Thummim" (1 Sam 14:41). The sacred objects indicated that Saul or Jonathan was at fault, and when the lots were cast again, Jonathan was singled out as the offender.

The Urim and Thummim seem to have disappeared from use by the time the monarchy was established in Israel. They were replaced, at least in part, by the words of the prophets.

VALLEY

. . . HE SAID TO ME, RISE UP, GO OUT INTO THE VALLEY, AND THERE I WILL SPEAK WITH YOU. –EZEKIEL 3:22

The Hebrew language has five words for valley, or vale, because the topography of the Holy Land contains so many different types and sizes of valleys. Deep canyons and rocky gorges are prevalent near the Jordan Valley; broad and fertile valleys, well watered by springs and a few flowing rivers, characterize the northern and western parts of the country. Throughout the land, many narrow streambeds, called wadis, are dry except in the rainy season.

The prophet Ezekiel's vision of dry bones coming to life took place in a valley (Ezek 37). Other scriptural writers have used valleys to symbolize the trials of life. In the well-known Psalm 23:4, for example, the author says to God, "Even though I walk through the darkest valley, I fear no evil; for you are with me."

VANITY

VANITY OF VANITIES, SAYS THE TEACHER; ALL IS VANITY. –ECCLESIASTES 12:8

The word *vanity* appears more than 30 times in the book of Ecclesiastes. It is the translation of a Hebrew word that literally means

Yellow chrysanthemums dot the upper Jordan Valley, also known as the Hula Valley, in the springtime, after winter rains have caused vegetation to flourish.

"vapor" or "breath," thus signifying something that is insubstantial or an effort that is useless.

Noting that "there is nothing new under the sun" (Eccl 1:9), the author of Ecclesiastes speaks of everything in life as being vanity, "and a chasing after wind" (Eccl 1:14). He suggests that it is foolish for human beings to attempt to solve life's mysteries. Searching for meaning on earth is a futile act, or vanity, for only God knows his plan for humankind.

VEGETABLE

. . ."GIVE ME YOUR VINEYARD, SO THAT I MAY HAVE IT FOR A VEGETABLE GARDEN . . . ."
–1 KINGS 21:2

According to Genesis, soon after God created the earth, it "brought forth vegetation: plants yielding seed of every kind" (Gen 1:12). Many plants provided edible seeds and other parts. In biblical times, the common vegetables were BEANS, lentils, cucumbers, chickpeas, onions, leeks, and garlic. All were normally bought in the marketplace, where vendors sat on the ground surrounded by their produce. Some grew their wares in gardens, but farmers also cultivated vegetables such as leeks and onions in fields. These plants, as well as cucumbers and garlic, were foods that the Israelites had enjoyed in Egypt and sorely missed during their wilderness sojourn (Num 11:5). Genesis 9:2–3 indicates that humankind had a vegetarian diet until after the flood, although Paul appears to have held a negative view of vegetarians (Rom 14:2). Vegetables play a role in some biblical stories, such as when the hungry Esau sold his birthright to Jacob for lentil stew (Gen 25:34) and Daniel prevailed upon Nebuchadnezzar's guard to put him and other Judean youths on vegetarian rations (Dan 1:12).

VEIL

SO SHE TOOK HER VEIL AND COVERED HERSELF.
–GENESIS 24:65

Unlike the women of some cultures in biblical lands, Israelite women were probably not required to hide their faces behind a veil. However, they often placed a large shawl-like covering over their head and shoulders to guard against the sun. Some veils, drawing attention to the face, might indicate availability for marriage: Rebekah put on a veil when she saw Isaac approaching (Gen 24:65). Women in the upper strata of society sometimes wore long, flowing veils.

Scriptural language is not always precise about the nature of head and face coverings, but lepers were obliged by Mosaic law to wear some kind of veil over their upper lips (Lev 13:45). To conceal the awesome radiance emanating from his face after his direct encounter with God, Moses put on a veil (Ex 34:33). Writing to the Corinthians, Paul referred to the veil of Moses, saying that "in Christ" the veil would be removed so that "the glory of the Lord" could be seen (2 Cor 3:13–18). Paul directed women in the early Christian church to veil their heads during prayer (1 Cor 11:6–10).

Veils are still an integral part of the clothing of Bedouin women in the Sinai.

Ennion, a Phoenician glassblower, made and signed this delicate vessel, probably in the early first century AD.

VESSEL

THE VESSEL HE WAS MAKING OF CLAY WAS SPOILED IN THE POTTER'S HAND, AND HE REWORKED IT INTO ANOTHER VESSEL . . . .
–JEREMIAH 18:4

A vessel was a container used mostly for liquids and food. Most vessels were made of pottery, which was inexpensive and easy to obtain. These included bowls, cups, jars, flasks, decanters, and goblets. Excavations of graves from the biblical period have uncovered pottery vessels that held food for the deceased. Despite the reference to a glaze covering in Proverbs 26:23, pottery decorated with a glazed finish had to be imported from Egypt and was rare in the Holy Land.

Vessels could also be made of stone, wood, animal skins, or baskets woven from reeds. Stone containers were sometimes preferred because they were not considered subject to ritual impurity. Alabaster and other types of soft stone were carved and polished to make cups, large jars, and delicate containers for perfumes and ointments. Skins sewn together were used to carry water, wine, and other liquids. Goblets of ivory, glass, and precious metals could be found in the homes of the rich, and fine vessels of gold and silver were used for offerings in the temple. See also box for POTTER.

VICTORY

THE LORD GAVE VICTORY TO DAVID WHEREVER HE WENT. –1 CHRONICLES 18:6

Military and spiritual victories are linked throughout the Bible, and the same Hebrew word is translated both "victory" and "salvation." The ancient Israelites believed that God controlled events on the battlefield, rewarding his people when they were righteous. New Testament writers portrayed Jesus as the victor over sin and death. His joyful procession into Jerusalem was seen as a fulfillment of prophecy, establishing him as a king, much as crowds in the Old Testament celebrated war heroes with chants and dancing. Throughout the Bible, belief in God and reliance upon him led to the triumph, whether earthly or spiritual, of his followers: "This is the victory that conquers the world, our faith" (1 Jn 5:4).

VILLAGE

JESUS WENT THROUGH ONE TOWN AND VILLAGE AFTER ANOTHER, TEACHING AS HE MADE HIS WAY TO JERUSALEM.–LUKE 13:22

Villages were generally unfortified communities consisting of a small number of simple dwellings. Frequently associated with nearby cities, villages had little in the way of formal government. The Bible often mentions a city "and its villages," as, for example, in Joshua 17:11. Villages depended on the larger, walled urban centers for trade and protection. The houses in a village of the Holy Land, numbering perhaps 20 to 30, were sometimes built around a central open space where livestock was kept. Agriculture was the main occupation of villagers, and pastureland surrounding the village was considered part of the community's property. See also TOWN.

The Gospels mention Bethany, shown above, several times as a place that Jesus visited. Near Jerusalem, the village was the home of Lazarus and his sisters Mary and Martha.

VINE

. . . THEY SHALL BLOSSOM LIKE THE VINE, THEIR FRAGRANCE SHALL BE LIKE THE WINE OF LEBANON.–HOSEA 14:7

Although various fruits and vegetables, such as gourds and cucumbers, grow on vines, in the Bible *vine* almost always refers to the grapevine. Figuratively, the plant can symbolize fertility, prosperity, and peace. In the Old Testament, the vine stands for the chosen people, whom God rescued from captivity in Eygpt and planted in the soil of Israel. This vine is sometimes described as unproductive by the prophets: in Jeremiah 2:21, God says, "I planted you as a choice vine, from the purest stock. How then did you turn degenerate and become a wild vine?"

In the New Testament, Jesus presents himself as the true vine and God the Father as the vinedresser, who removes branches that yield no fruit and prunes the others so that they will bear more fruit. Jesus says that disciples who do not abide in him will be like the discarded branches of the VINEYARD (Jn 5:1–6).

When Moses sent spies into Canaan, they returned with a cluster of grapes so large that "they carried it on a pole between two of them" (Num 13:23). Plump, succulent grapes, like the ones pictured above, are still plentiful in the vineyards of the Holy Land.

Vinegar

They gave me poison for food, and for my thirst they gave me vinegar to drink.
–Psalm 69:21

In biblical times vinegar was used as a seasoning for food. Since pure vinegar is undrinkable, the Hebrew-word for vinegar is sometimes translated as sour wine, which was a common drink among the poor and was part of the rations of a Roman soldier. Offering sour wine to Jesus on the cross may have been a merciful gesture to dull the pain; however, in a possible allusion to the persecution described by the psalmist in the passage above, Luke 23:36 implies that the drink offered Jesus at his crucifixion was part of the torture.

Vineyard

"There was a landowner who planted a vineyard, put a fence around it, dug a wine press in it, and built a watchtower."
–Matthew 21:33

Planting and caring for a vineyard were exacting tasks. As described in Isaiah 5:1–6, the hillside land had to be cleared of stones and planted with young vines in rows. When the branches began to bear grapes, forked sticks were placed under them to keep the fruit off the ground. Constant pruning of the vines was necessary to ensure healthy grapes and to keep the plants from growing wild. The vineyard was guarded from a watchtower. The tower, as well as spine-tipped stone walls and thorny hedges, secured the vineyard from animal and human scavengers. Most grapes were pressed for juice to make WINE, though some were eaten.

Virgin

He shall marry only a woman who is a virgin.
–Leviticus 21:13

In the Bible, virginity was considered a highly desirable virtue. Rebekah, the future wife of Isaac, was first described as a girl who "was very fair to look upon, a virgin, whom no man had known" (Gen 24:16). Women who were promised in MARRIAGE were expected to be virgins, and the parents of the bride were sometimes required to offer evidence of her virginity (Deut 22:15), such as by displaying the bed sheet after her wedding night. If the parents were unable to provide such evidence, the young woman could be put to death.

The prophets occasionally refer to the nation of Israel as a virgin. In Jeremiah 14:17, God laments the ultimate destruction of the Hebrew nation, "the virgin daughter—my people." Idolatry would turn virgin Israel into a harlot. In Ezekiel, God reminds Israel that its loss of purity began when "they played the whore in Egypt . . . their virgin bosoms were fondled" (Ezek 23:3).

The New Testament relates that the Messiah, God's own son, was born to a virgin named Mary. The doctrine of the virgin birth is set out in the book of Matthew: "Mary had been engaged to Joseph, but before they lived together, she was found to be with child from the Holy Spirit" (Mt 1:18).

Vision

In a dream, in a vision of the night, when deep sleep falls on mortals . . . he opens their ears and terrifies them with warnings . . . . –Job 33:15–16

A vision is an experience in which a person believes that he or she is visited by a god, guardian spirit, or other supernatural being. The appearance of God or his messenger was typically received with dread. Visions could contain warnings from God against continued transgressions, prophecies, or promises of an ideal future. The vision was one of the primary means by which God communicated with the prophets.

Visions at night came in dreams, which were often long and detailed, such as Daniel's vision of the four beasts (Dan 7:2–14). Visions by day came in trances, as when Paul saw a vision of a "large sheet coming down from heaven" (Acts 11:5). Trances were often self-induced by means of fasting, prayer, or music. See also DREAM.

Vow

Then Israel made a vow to the LORD and said, "If you will indeed give this people into our hands, then we will utterly destroy their towns."
–Numbers 21:2

In biblical times, a vow was a solemn promise or commitment made to God. Like the majority of vows found in the Old Testament, Israel's vow in the passage above was conditional. Many vows were promises to perform or abstain from an action in return for God's favor. Jacob, for example promised to worship God and give him one-tenth of his income in return for protection (Gen 28:18–22). Other vows were unconditional acts of devotion to God. The nazirites, who devoted their lives to worship, vowed to live apart from normal society, abstain from wine, and not cut their hair.

Once a vow was made, it had to be fulfilled. As Moses noted, "When a man makes a vow to the LORD . . . he shall not break his word" (Num 30:2). The fulfillment of a vow often involved making a sacrifice to God. One of only three vows mentioned in the New Testament is that of Paul cutting his hair, "for he was under a vow" (Acts 18:18), which was probably a reference to a temporary nazirite vow. See also OATH.

Voyage

. . . "Sirs, I can see that the voyage will be with danger and much heavy loss . . . ."
–Acts of the Apostles 27:10

The word *voyage* appears only twice in the New Testament (Acts 21:7; 27:10)—both times in the context of Paul's far-flung missionary activities in Asia Minor and Europe. Despite their proximity to the sea, the Israelites were not great sailors, and they rarely controlled the small harbor cities along the Mediterranean coast (see illustration). One of the most notable voyages in the Bible is that of Jonah, whose attempt to flee the Lord by boarding a "ship going to Tarshish" (Jon 1:3) ends in his spending three days and nights in the belly of a large fish (Jon 1:1–17).

A Phoenician boat sails on a trading voyage in the Mediterranean Sea about 700 BC, as seen in this illustration. As the ship leaves the Phoenician city of Byblos, it travels close to the shore so that it can easily reach land again at night. A single, white linen sail unfurls to catch a light wind, as two banks of oarsmen work to keep the vessel, loaded with cargo, moving swiftly toward its destination.

The pottery fragment pictured here, inscribed with the Aramaic alphabet, probably dates from the first century AD and is thought to have been a student's WRITING tablet. It was found at Herodium, near Bethlehem.

Wafer

FROM THE BASKET OF UNLEAVENED BREAD THAT WAS BEFORE THE LORD, HE TOOK ONE CAKE OF UNLEAVENED BREAD, ONE CAKE OF BREAD WITH OIL, AND ONE WAFER . . . .
—LEVITICUS 8:26

The wafer, a flat, thin bread, was used for food and for SACRIFICE. Made with fine wheat flour, wafers were prepared by beating unleavened dough into round shapes. They were baked on a clay or iron griddle over a fire. Sometimes sweetened with honey, wafers were compared with manna (Ex 16:31). For religious use, they were simply spread with olive oil: "When you present a grain offering baked in the oven, it shall be of choice flour: unleavened cakes mixed with oil, or unleavened wafers spread with oil" (Lev 2:4).

Wafers were required for the nazirite ordination offering and could also be offered independently as a grain offering to thank God for a bountiful harvest. During the offering, a piece of the wafer was burned on the altar. The part burned memorialized the worshiper; the part that remained, referred to as the "most holy part," was eaten by the priest.

Wages

YOU SHALL PAY THEM THEIR WAGES DAILY BEFORE SUNSET . . . .
—DEUTERONOMY 24:15

The agricultural worker in ancient Israel was usually a day LABORER paid by law at the end of each day, but some employees were hired for year-long or three-year periods. Because family members cared for their own herds and fields, paid labor was uncommon. Unskilled laborers probably earned only a share of the harvest as food, but Jacob, an expert shepherd, was paid in sheep that became the basis of his own flock (Gen 30:27–33).

The Scriptures mention several instances in which individuals were paid specific amounts for their work (2 Chr 25:6; Mt 25:15), but no standardized rates for wages are given. Though Deuteronomy clearly states, "You shall not withhold the wages of poor and needy laborers" (Deut 24:14), Jeremiah and other prophets were concerned that workers were being exploited by not being paid a fair wage or not being paid at all (Jer 22:13). Skilled craftsmen and mercenary soldiers were paid handsomely by royalty, and prophets, elders, and priests earned fees of silver or gold for their specialized talents. The "wages," or just recompense, of the Lord could be either a reward given to the righteous or the appropriately negative consequence for sinners. Indeed, according to the book of Romans, "the wages of sin is death" (Rom 6:23).

Wall

[UZZIAH] WENT OUT AND MADE WAR AGAINST THE PHILISTINES, AND BROKE DOWN THE WALL OF GATH AND THE WALL OF JABNEH AND THE WALL OF ASHDOD . . . .
—2 CHRONICLES 26:6

Cities of the ancient Near East were often protected by massive defensive walls. The oldest walls found are those at Jericho, which date about 7000 BC. Walls of this kind did not appear regularly until some 4,000 years later.

City walls up to 35 feet high and 25 feet thick were constructed of stone, mud brick, or brick erected on a stone FOUNDATION, and enclosed an average area of 5 to 10 acres, though some cities were much larger. By the 10th century BC, double-wall systems, known as casemates, were used. Two thin parallel walls were connected at regular intervals by short transverse ones, creating inner spaces used for living or storage.

Walls for simple homes were made of sun-baked mud bricks, usually waterproofed with a plaster coating. Wealthier homes were constructed with walls of stone or fired brick. Low walls were often built from unhewn stones, which were stacked atop one another or set in mud or mortar, to define field boundaries.

War

Joshua made war a long time with all those kings.—Joshua 11:18

In ancient times, as today, wars were waged for political, economic, and religious reasons. War was a part of life since before the age of the patriarchs. Tribal unity during times of war waged under Moses and Joshua helped the Israelites to conquer Canaan. Because of its central location, the Holy Land was constantly attacked by other nations, such as the Egyptians and the Assyrians. To defend themselves from these invaders, the Israelites built massive walls around their cities.

Throughout ancient times, the basic armory of Near Eastern armies changed little, except in the gradual development of stronger, longer swords, spearpoints, and arrowheads and the substitution of iron for bronze. Swords, javelins, and spears were the individual soldier's most important weapons in hand-to-hand combat, which was the principal mode of fighting. Groups of archers and slingers were essential assets in full-scale charges across open plains. Battering rams often brought down entire cities in SIEGE warfare.

Old Testament accounts mention a variety of battlefield tactics, including the surprise attack, flank movement, ambush, feint, deployment of specialized forces, and raids. David and Solomon are credited with forming the first Israelite chariot squadrons, which revolutionized the Israelite army. Occasionally, during battle, the two opposing sides lined up against each other but sent champions forward to fight in single combat, as in the encounter between David and Goliath (1 Sam 17). Defeat was devastating not only for the army but for the entire city or nation. Victorious soldiers stripped corpses and ransacked houses for spoils.

To the Israelites, defeat was often a sign of God's wrath. Many of Israel's wars were undertaken as part of the Lord's plan for the future of his chosen people. Priests, the only large class of males exempt from military service, accompanied troops into battle, marking the beginning and conclusion of all military actions with sacrifices. Victory was celebrated with music and dancing in praise of the Lord.

During periods of subservience to Persia and other foreign powers, Israel had no independent national army, but its citizens served as mercenaries or as middle-ranking soldiers. The gifted military strategist Judas Maccabeus was able to raise a guerrilla army by about 167 BC that achieved remarkable successes. Palestinian Jews did not serve in the Roman army, which was a professional, well-armed force.

Images of war are often used in the Scriptures to describe the struggle of righteous believers against supernatural forces of evil (Rev 13:1–7). Although most biblical writers seem to regard war as a natural part of human life and peace as a temporary interlude, Jesus cautions his disciples at Gethsemane that "all who take the sword will perish by the sword" (Mt 26:52).

Two bodyguards of the Assyrian king Sennacherib (705–681 BC) are depicted armed for war, above, in a relief from Nineveh.

Washing

. . . they noticed that some of his disciples were eating with defiled hands, that is, without washing them. —Mark 7:2

Washing appears throughout the Bible as a ritual of purification. Aaron and his sons, like others who were about to take part in religious services, washed before donning priestly robes and being anointed with oil (Ex 30:19–21). A person who was ritually unclean had to wash according to a strict code of rules, which were dictated by Mosaic law. In Christian tradition, BAPTISM is a kind of symbolic washing—perhaps derived from a form of ritual immersion practiced by some Jewish groups—signifying a cleansing of individual sin (Acts 22:16), repentance, and participation in Christ's death and resurrection (Col 2:12).

This stone watchtower is akin to those used in ancient times to safeguard crops.

WATCHTOWER

FOR OUR OWN MIND SOMETIMES KEEPS US BETTER INFORMED THAN SEVEN SENTINELS SITTING HIGH ON A WATCHTOWER. –ECCLESIASTICUS 37:14

Stone watchtowers were common in ancient times, as evidenced by the great number that have been excavated throughout the Near East. A watchtower defending a community probably was built right into the city walls and had its own entryway (Judg 9:52). Watchmen stood guard atop city walls or in fortified towers; if an enemy approached, an alarm was sounded. Though the word *watchman* is not used in the Bible, references are made to the people who stood watch. The spot designated for the sentry was the watchpost: "I will stand at my watchpost, and station myself on the rampart" (Hab 2:1).

Watchtowers were also built in the fields to protect livestock from the depredations of other animals and thieves: "He built towers in the wilderness . . . for he had large herds" (2 Chr 26:10). Watchmen—often the farmer himself—stood watch from towers that overlooked vegetable fields and vineyards Agricultural implements could be stored in the watchtower's lower portion, while the upper story was used as a lookout and for sleeping.

WATER

YOU HAVE GIVEN NO WATER TO THE WEARY TO DRINK, AND YOU HAVE WITHHELD BREAD FROM THE HUNGRY.–JOB 22:7

Water was a vital resource in ancient Israel, whose inhabitants relied almost entirely on rainfall and subterranean springs to grow crops. The use of cisterns—underground reservoirs—made it possible to survive in areas with marginal rainfall, yet a few years of drought in such regions drove people out in search of water. Because people tended to seek permanent water supplies, water influenced settlement in the ancient Near East. People eventually learned to harness sources of water by building tunnels (see illustration), as during Hezekiah's reign (2 Kings 20:20), or aqueducts, as Herod did, to carry water inside city walls.

In the Bible, water was considered a source of life as well as refreshment. The Israelites also used water for purification, a practice prescribed by law for people who had become ritually unclean (Lev 15:1–33). Before they entered the tent of meeting, priests washed with water from a bronze basin set apart for that purpose (Ex 30:18–21). Mixed with dust from the floor of the tabernacle, this fluid became "water of bitterness" (Num 5:18), the drink given to a woman accused of adultery. If the concoction caused illness and sterility, the woman was deemed guilty (Num 5:11–31).

Abundant water was frequently a sign of God's favor, although God could also send excess water—as in the great flood—as a punishment. A watercourse was a dry streambed, or wadi, which God, in his mercy, would fill with run-off from RAIN (Ps 126:4). In Jeremiah 2:13, God refers to himself as the fountain of "living water," a translation of the Hebrew term meaning "running water." In the New Testament, the expression "living water" is connected with Jesus, who is identified as the source of eternal life (Jn 4:10–14).

WATER JAR

NOW STANDING THERE WERE SIX STONE WATER JARS FOR THE JEWISH RITES OF PURIFICATION . . . . –JOHN 2:6

In biblical times, women filled clay water jars at community wells or cisterns and carried them home balanced on their head or shoulders. In Genesis 24:17, Rebekah poured water from a jar for Abraham's servant to drink. These jars typically had one or two handles. Larger water jars made of pottery or stone might hold up to 30 gallons and were used for ceremonial purification and for household use. The water that Jesus miraculously changed into wine at the Cana wedding feast was held in such jars (Jn 2:1–11).

WAY

. . . KEEP THE COMMANDMENTS OF THE LORD YOUR GOD, BY WALKING IN HIS WAYS . . . . –DEUTERONOMY 8:6

The word *way* literally means "path" or "road." Sometimes a specific route is meant, as in "by way of the land of the Philistines" (Ex 13:17). More often the word is used metaphorically to describe both human and divine conduct. The wicked "walk in the way of darkness (Prov 2:13–14), and the "way of the righteous" is watched over by the Lord (Ps 1:6). God's ways include his teachings to Israel (Isa 2:3). Similar to other religious movements throughout history, the early Christians called their faith "the Way" (Acts 9:2). Jesus also identifies himself as "the way, and the truth, and the life" (Jn 14:6).

The underground water tunnel illustrated here is located in the ancient city of Hazor. This marvel of engineering is among several Israelite water systems from the 10th through the 8th centuries BC *that have been discovered in fortified cities in the Holy Land. Wells such as this one sustained life in biblical times, especially during times of siege. Here, in daylight hours, women descend five flights of stairs, hewn from solid rock, 100 feet below ground to draw water for cooking, washing, and drinking (see inset). This daily chore is a time for socializing. Men also draw water for themselves and their livestock from this subterranean chamber.*

WEALTH

. . . "How hard it will be for those who have wealth to enter the kingdom of God!"
–Mark 10:23

Wealth in the agricultural Near East generally took the form of material goods, which could include livestock, precious metals, and slaves. In the Old Testament, wealth was considered a blessing conferred upon the righteous. The patriarchs, Job, and King Solomon, for example, owned substantial possessions, which were understood to be a gift from God. However, a certain responsibility accompanied such good fortune: the Scriptures instruct the wealthy to share their riches with the poor, as did Job (Job 29:12–16), rather than to accumulate a fortune for its own sake.

Although wealth was often viewed as a sign of God's favor, never does the Bible suggest that poverty is a sign of his displeasure. New Testament writers, perhaps responding to the high levels of poverty around them and the relative poverty of many early Christians, were more likely to view wealth, or mammon, as a dangerous excess rather than as a reward from God. They believed that God's true blessings consisted of "treasures in heaven," as Jesus explained in Matthew 6:20.

Many of Jesus' other teachings reinforce this theme, emphasizing that an obsession with material riches can be morally and spiritually hazardous, distracting the believer from the faith. Jesus warned, "No slave can serve two masters . . . . You cannot serve God and wealth" (Lk 16:13).

Although affluent people played a prominent role in the early church, many of them sold their goods and land to support poorer members. Such prosperous believers were encouraged to devote their riches to spreading the gospel and strengthening the church. The New Testament repeatedly warns against the lure of wealth, most famously in Paul's first letter to Timothy: "For the love of money is a root of all kinds of evil" (1 Tim 6:10).

Flocks of sheep and other property were signs of wealth in biblical times. In a Vatican fresco by Raphael, Jacob and his family take their possessions and travel to Canaan.

WEANING

But I have calmed and quieted my soul, like a weaned child with its mother . . . .
–Psalm 131:2

In ancient times, CHILDREN usually were not weaned away from their mothers' milk and introduced to other food until the age of two or three. Weaning of offspring was sometimes celebrated with a banquet or sacrifice: Abraham "made a feast" to mark the weaning of his son Isaac (Gen 21:8). In some cases, a child left the mother's care when he or she was no longer dependent on her for nourishment. Samuel's mother vowed that she would deliver her son for training as a nazirite, a special servant of God, "as soon as the child is weaned" (1 Sam 1:22). After weaning one child, the mother could bear and feed the next one, as did Gomer, the prophet Hosea's wife: "When she had weaned Lo-ruhamah, she conceived and bore a son" (Hos 1:8).

WEAVER

My days are swifter than a weaver's shuttle . . . .
–Job 7:6

Weavers create cloth by interlacing at right angles one set of threads, called the warp, with another set, called the weft or woof. A wooden frame, the loom, is used for this process.

A typical loom in the Holy Land had two vertical beams topped by a horizontal beam. Warp threads were hung from the upper beam and held straight and taut by weights of stone or clay. Alternate warp threads were attached by string loops to the heddle rod, the "weaver's beam" with which the shaft of Goliath's sword was compared (1 Sam 17:7). While raising or lowering the heddle rod to separate a set of warp threads, the weaver used a shuttle to draw the horizontal woof threads through the opening created in the warp. The weaver then beat the intertwined threads with a stick, or "pin," to make a tight web.

While Samson slept, Delilah, intending to sap his strength, wove "the seven locks of his head" on a loom and "made them tight with the pin." However, when the still-powerful Samson awoke, he "pulled away the pin, the loom, and the web" (Judg 16:14).

Though spinning was considered women's work, weaving was done by both sexes. Some weavers belonged to a guild. The textile industry was critical to Egypt's economy: when predicting that country's collapse, Isaiah said, "The carders and those at the loom will grow pale. Its weavers will be dismayed" (Isa 19:9–10). Isaiah compared the end of a person's life with the weaver's removal of a finished piece of cloth—"like a weaver I have rolled up my life; he cuts me off from the loom" (Isa 38:12). See also box for SPINDLE.

WEEK

"HE SHALL MAKE A STRONG COVENANT WITH MANY FOR ONE WEEK, AND FOR HALF OF THE WEEK HE SHALL MAKE SACRIFICE AND OFFERING CEASE . . . ."–DANIEL 9:27

The seven-day week may have been an invention of the ancient Israelites. It is slightly less than one quarter of the time span between two consecutive new moons, the lunar cycle being 29½ days. Although the use of seven days corresponds with the book of Genesis' account of creation, the first appearance of the word *week* in the Bible occurs later, in the story of Jacob (Gen 29:27). Here it may refer to the duration of the wedding festivities or to a "week" of—or seven—years.

Though many cultures named the days of the week after deities, the Israelites called them simply first day, second day, and so on until the seventh day, which was called the sabbath, meaning "rest day" or "stop-work day." The earliest Christians, who were Jews, continued to observe the seventh day as the sabbath. Many also celebrated Jesus' resurrection on the FIRST DAY OF THE WEEK, which was Sunday, and later Christians shifted their sabbath to that day.

WEIGHTS

DIFFERING WEIGHTS ARE AN ABOMINATION TO THE LORD, AND FALSE SCALES ARE NOT GOOD. –PROVERBS 20:23

The basic unit of weight in the ancient Holy Land—the shekel—was the same as that used in the Babylonian and Canaanite systems. The shekel was equivalent to about one third of an ounce, yet its precise weight varied from place to place and sometimes changed according to the type of goods being sold.

The Hebrew root for *shekel* means "to weigh," which was synonymous with "to pay." The widespread use of coins and the establishment of an economy based on money did not take place in the Holy Land until after the Persians came to power, about 500 BC. Before that time, precious metals were carefully measured out and weighed on balance scales for commercial transactions. Carved stones, often marked with their specific weights, were used as a counterbalance to ascertain the amount of silver or gold needed. For example, when buying a burial place for his wife, Sarah, Abraham "weighed out . . . four hundred shekels of silver, according to the weights current among the merchants" (Gen 23:16). Other important weights included the talent, the mina, and the pound (see chart, p. 370).

Buyers going to the marketplace might carry their own weights to compare them with those being used by the merchants. Weights were sometimes chiseled out on the bottom to alter their real weight; it was probably from this practice that *chisel* came to mean "cheat." Warning against fraudulent weights, Deuteronomy 25:13 says that "you shall not have in your bag two kinds of weights, large and small." In the book of Leviticus, God

The seven-day week is associated with the story of creation according to Genesis 1:1–24, in which God created the world in six days and rested on the seventh. An illumination from a 17th-century Armenian Bible depicts the six days in which God executed his grand design.

Ancient Weights

As the Israelites moved among the peoples of the ancient Near East, they adopted the weight standards of the surrounding cultures. At times the values of a weight, such as the shekel, changed also. In the chart below, the weights and their equivalences listed as Old Testament were those in use prior to 700 BC. The weights pictured below were placed in one pan of a balance to determine the weight of the object in the other pan.

The stone relief above appears on a Mesopotamian funeral stele from about the eighth century BC. The figure, a merchant, holds a balance, or pair of scales, for weighing metals.

OLD TESTAMENT

UNIT	BIBLICAL EQUIVALENT	APPROXIMATE EQUIVALENCE METRIC SYSTEM	US SYSTEM
talent	3,000 shekels	30 kg	66 lb
mina	50 shekels	500 g (or 0.5 kg)	1 lb
shekel		10 g	1/3 oz
pim	2/3 shekel	7 g	1/4 oz
beka	1/2 shekel	5 g	1/6 oz
gerah	1/20 shekel	0.5 g	1/60 oz

Stone weights in the shape of a duck were common in ancient Mesopotamia. The example above, inscribed with its weight of five minas, dates from 2090 BC.

This eighth-century BC bronze weight, perhaps from Egypt, is decorated with a gold beetle.

These round Israelite stone weights from the seventh century BC are marked with shekels on their tops.

The inscription on a mina from the time of Nebuchadnezzar II, king of Babylon (605–562 BC), states that it adheres to the standard weight established in the city of Ur about 2000 BC.

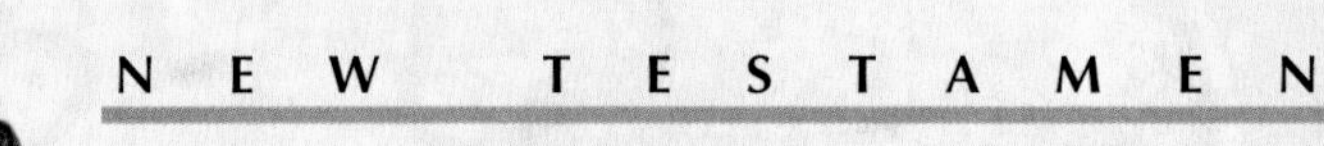

This small stone pim *weight was used in ancient Israel.*

NEW TESTAMENT

UNIT	BIBLICAL EQUIVALENT	APPROXIMATE EQUIVALENCE METRIC SYSTEM	US SYSTEM
talent	125 libra	41 kg	90 lb
pound (*litra*)	(Latin *libra*)	327 g	12 oz

The bronze lions below are from a set of weights in minas made for Assyrian king Shalmaneser V (727–722 BC).

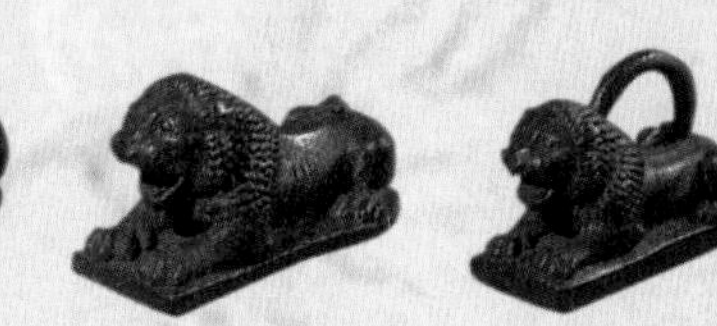

commands the Israelites: "You shall not cheat in measuring length, weight, or quantity. You shall have honest balances, honest weights" (Lev 19:35–36). The prophet Ezekiel calls for adherence to a standard system of weights and measures in the restored Jerusalem (Ezek 45:10–12).

Well

Jacob's well was there, and Jesus, tired out by his journey, was sitting by the well.
–John 4:6

Because rain fell only in the winter months, water was a scarce and precious commodity in the Holy Land. Wells were dug to reach underground sources of water, which might be in the wilderness (Gen 16:7, 14), in fields (Gen 29:2), or in settlements (2 Sam 23:15). City wells, which were generally near the gates, were central meeting places, particularly for women drawing water for their households. Abraham's servant found a wife for Isaac—Rebekah—at the well of the city of Nahor; this happened "toward evening, the time when women go out to draw water" (Gen 24:11). Jesus asked a Samaritan woman for water from "Jacob's well" in the city of Sychar (Jn 4:5–7).

Digging a well was an occasion for joy and song: "Spring up, O well!—Sing to it!" (Num 21:17). But conflicts also arose over wells. Moses came to the defense of some women who were driven away by shepherds as they watered their flock at a well (Ex 2:16–17). Some wells were covered by a large stone, perhaps to prevent accidents or unauthorized use (Gen 29:2–3). Wells were considered property that could be inherited. After Abraham's death, the Philistines filled his wells with dirt, but his son Isaac dug them out again (Gen 26:15, 18).

Wheat

Be dismayed, you farmers . . . over the wheat and the barley; for the crops of the field are ruined.–Joel 1:11

Wheat was generally used for baking bread because it made a tastier loaf than any other grain. Varieties included einkorn, emmer, and perhaps spelt. Wheat was so important to the Israelites that it symbolized God's goodness and was brought to the temple as an offering. According to the Gospel of Matthew, John the Baptist used wheat as a metaphor for those who heard God's message, and chaff, which was separated out during the process of threshing and sometimes burned, for those who did not (Mt 3:12). Wheat was parched, or dried, to preserve it. The Festival of Weeks, also called Pentecost, celebrated the spring wheat HARVEST.

A sunset silhouettes stalks of wheat in a field in the hills of Samaria.

Wheel

The crack of whip and rumble of wheel, galloping horse and bounding chariot!
–Nahum 3:2

Archaeological evidence suggests that the wheel was invented in Mesopotamia before 3000 BC. The earliest wheels were solid wood, and they turned with the axle that connected them. After the horse-drawn CHARIOT was introduced about 2000 BC, wheels became lighter, had spokes and hubs, and could spin independently of the axle, increasing the maneuverability of vehicles. The common people of biblical times used two- and four-wheeled carts pulled by oxen, whereas kings and warriors rode in swift chariots pulled by horses.

Aside from its role in transportation, the wheel facilitated tasks such as making pottery and, as part of a pulley, drawing water from a cistern (Eccl 12:6). In Solomon's temple, the 10 washing basins rested on stands that were each fitted with four wheels, like those of a chariot (1 Kings 7:30–33).

In the Bible, wheels can represent crushing power. The book of Proverbs says that a wise king "drives the wheel" over the wicked (Pr 20:26). Wheels are also a striking element in Ezekiel's vision of God: the prophet sees four cherubim with four gleaming wheels filled with eyes, forming a structure he calls a "wheelwork" (Ezek 10:2–19). The mysterious wheels may support the throne of God or belong to his chariot.

Whirlwind

For they sow the wind, and they shall reap the whirlwind.
–Hosea 8:7

Biblical whirlwinds are usually fierce windstorms, which are frequent in the Holy Land's rainy season, rather than tornadoes, which are rare and appear only in early winter on the coast. In the Negeb region, the desert heat clashes with Mediterranean breezes to produce winds so violent that they were used in the Bible as metaphors for conquering armies, terrible misfortunes, and divine visitations. God spoke to Job "out of the whirlwind" (Job 38:1; 40:6), and Elijah was miraculously lifted into the heavens by a windstorm (2 Kings 2:11). In Psalm 77:18, based upon an ancient hymn, the Hebrew word that is translated "whirlwind" suggests a circular, tornado-like motion.

WHITE

". . . THEY WILL WALK WITH ME, DRESSED IN WHITE, FOR THEY ARE WORTHY."–REVELATION 3:4

In the Bible, white usually connotes purity or is a sign of glorification. When Jesus is transfigured, his clothes become "dazzling white, such as no one on earth could bleach them" (Mk 9:3). The angel at Jesus' empty tomb wears "clothing white as snow" (Mt 28:3). In Revelation, the Messiah, atop a white horse that signifies victory, leads an army of angels clad in white linen and riding white horses (Rev 19:11–14). However, physical ailments are also described as being white. A leprous hand is "white as snow" (Ex 4:6), and in the apocryphal book of Tobit, blindness is brought about by "white films" on the eyes (Tob 2:10).

WICKEDNESS

FOR YOU ARE NOT A GOD WHO DELIGHTS IN WICKEDNESS; EVIL WILL NOT SOJOURN WITH YOU.–PSALM 5:4

Wickedness, or evil, is ever present in the Bible and is set in contrast with RIGHTEOUSNESS, or good. In Genesis, God decided to destroy what he had made because he "saw that the wickedness of humankind was great in the earth" (Gen 6:5). But he spared the family of Noah, who "walked with God" (Gen 6:9). In the Gospel of Mark, Jesus told his followers that wickedness

In this 13th-century fresco, God punishes the Philistines for their wickedness by causing an idol to fall and break.

comes "from within, from the human heart" (Mk 7:21–23). Warning that the deeds of the wicked condemned them to eternal damnation, Jesus said that at the end of the world, "the angels will come out and separate the evil from the righteous and throw them into the furnace of fire" (Mt 13:49–50).

WIDOW

THE KING ASKED HER, "WHAT IS YOUR TROUBLE?" SHE ANSWERED, "ALAS, I AM A WIDOW; MY HUSBAND IS DEAD."–2 SAMUEL 14:5

Widows were a vulnerable group in ancient Israel. They had no inheritance rights, and the status of widowhood during childbearing years was seen as a divine reproach, as having children was considered to be a blessing from God. The law offered some protection: the practice of levirate marriage obligated a childless widow's BROTHER-IN-LAW to marry her in order to produce an heir for the dead husband. High priests, however, were forbidden to marry "a widow, or a divorced woman, or a woman who has been defiled" (Lev 21:14). Widows of kings became the property, and sometimes the wives, of the new king.

The Bible notes God's concern for the plight of widows. God warns anyone who would abuse them: "My wrath will burn, and I will kill you with the sword" (Ex 22:24). Because widows were often forced to beg for sustenance, the early church distributed food to them. Paul recommended that older widows who had raised children and carried out their religious duties be put on an official list for assistance (1 Tim 5:9–10).

WIFE

ENJOY LIFE WITH THE WIFE WHOM YOU LOVE . . . .–ECCLESIASTES 9:9

The role of wife was treasured in biblical times. A woman was considered a wife even before the wedding ceremony, at the time of betrothal. Though polygamy was allowed, monogamy was the usual practice in Israel. The author of the book of Ecclesiastes believed that having many concubines was VANITY but that having a wife was a sane and rewarding approach to a happy life (Eccl 2:8, 11; 9:9). The book of Proverbs presents a portrait of the ideal Israelite wife, who is "far more precious than jewels" (Prov 31:10). Wise, kind, and hard-working, she manages the household and provides for her family's welfare.

Carved about 2600 BC, a gypsum statue from Nippur portrays the unity of husband and wife.

Wilderness

. . . "In the wilderness
prepare the way of the LORD,
make straight in the desert a
highway for our God."
–Isaiah 40:3

For the ancient Israelites, the term *wilderness* meant a sparsely populated region beyond the boundaries of civilization. To the east and south of the Holy Land lay the vast wildernesses of the Transjordan, the Negeb, and the Sinai Peninsula, and there were smaller such areas within the land as well. Although DESERT comprised much of these regions, a wilderness was not necessarily barren and sandy. It might support enough vegetation to pasture sheep and goats.

In the Old Testament, *wilderness* has mostly negative connotations: it invokes the years of wandering that the Israelites endured before reaching the Promised Land—years spent in "the great and terrible wilderness, an arid wasteland with poisonous snakes and scorpions" (Deut 8:15). In the book of 1 Samuel, David took refuge from Saul in "the Wilderness of Ziph" (1 Sam 26:2), the same region in which, according to some scholars, Jesus was later tempted by the devil. In the New Testament, the "wilderness" (Mk 1:4) of John's ministry of baptism—a mission interpreted as the fulfillment of Isaiah 40:3—was probably located where the Jordan River empties into the Dead Sea.

Wind

Awake, O north wind,
and come, O south wind!
Blow upon my garden . . . .
–Song of Solomon 4:16

Air movements strongly influence the climate of the Holy Land, and references to the wind—both as a natural force and as a manifestation of God—are frequent in the Bible. The Israelites believed that God sent the four winds "from the four quarters of heaven" (Jer 49:36). In the arid summer, the moisture-laden west wind blew in from the Mediterranean, lowering the scorching midday temperatures and depositing dew on the crops at night. During the winter, the west wind brought thunderstorms and much-needed rain. The cold north wind of winter also produced rain, and Proverbs compared this wind with "a backbiting tongue" producing "angry looks" (Prov 25:23).

Between the seasons, the dusty and oppressive sirocco blew from the south; it was "a hot wind . . . out of the bare heights in the desert" (Jer 4:11). From the east came a similar wind, such as the one that God sent to part the Red Sea and save the fleeing Israelites from Pharoah's army (Ex 14:21).

Wind has many symbolic meanings in the Bible. It can stand for transience and for useless effort, as in "a chasing after wind" (Eccles 4:6). More often, it heralds God's presence or awesome power. The very act of creation begins when "a wind from God" stirs the face of the waters (Gen 1:2). Only God can control the wind, which he "brings out . . . from his storehouses" (Jer 10:13). The Gospels record that the apostles were amazed when Jesus "rebuked the wind" and it ceased (Mk 4:39). The coming of the Holy Spirit to the disciples on Pentecost is likened to "the rush of a violent wind" (Acts 2:2).

*The Hebrew word for wilderness—*midbar*—is the same as that for desert. Here camels are seen crossing the Judean Desert, one of the wilderness areas in the Holy Land.*

WINDOW

... BUT I WAS LET DOWN IN A BASKET THROUGH A WINDOW IN THE WALL, AND ESCAPED FROM HIS HANDS.
—2 CORINTHIANS 11:33

Windows let in light and air and let out smoke from cooking. However, to stay cool in summer and warm in winter, houses in the ancient Near East were built with few windows. To keep intruders out, windows were small and placed high up the wall, particularly if they were on the first floor. Cities often had large windows in their outer walls, such as the window through which Rahab lowered two Israelite spies (Josh 2:15), so that they could escape unseen. Windows were closed with a lattice or shutters, as window GLASS was not in use until after the biblical period.

WINE

GO, EAT YOUR BREAD WITH ENJOYMENT, AND DRINK YOUR WINE WITH A MERRY HEART; FOR GOD HAS LONG AGO APPROVED WHAT YOU DO.
—ECCLESIASTES 9:7

The climate and terrain of the Holy Land are perfectly suited to the cultivation of grape vines, and the wine produced from its vineyards was prized in biblical times throughout the Near East. Both the positive and negative qualities of fermented grape juice were well known. Wine was typically enjoyed at most meals, but the Israelites disapproved of drinking too much. As Eli said to Hannah, "How long will you make a drunken spectacle of yourself? Put away your wine" (1 Sam 1:14). In his letter to the Ephesians, Paul urged that his readers "not get drunk with wine ... but be filled with the Spirit" (Eph 5:18), a condition that might resemble drunkenness.

Wine was stored in large jars often kept underground in cisterns

1. The harvest has begun at an ancient Israelite vineyard. Since late June, when the grapes began to ripen, a guard posted at a watchtower has protected them from scavengers and thieves. Now gatherers use small sickle knives to cut clusters of grapes from the vines and place them in baskets. The laden baskets are then taken by donkey and ox cart to the winery.

Wine Making

The grape harvest was a time of joyful celebration in the Holy Land. Men, women and children took to the vineyard, often accompanied by the sound of music and song, from late August to September to bring in the grapes. Vineyards usually were situated on hillsides, which were terraced, because the flatlands were reserved for growing grains and legumes. Stones removed from the rocky soil were used to build up the terraces. The vines were staked above the ground on forked sticks in rows about four to six feet apart. At harvest time, some of the ripe grapes were eaten fresh from the vine, and some were sprinkled with olive oil and dried in the sun on rooftops to make raisins. Most of the gathered grapes, however, were taken to the winery and made into wine.

2. The grapes are poured in the winepress, a shallow, plastered vat made of stone. Several men tread the grapes to extract their juice, helped in their task by musical accompaniment. As the grapes are trampled, the juice they produce flows through a channel into a collecting vat set slightly below. Men fill storage jars with the juice. These jars are then sealed with a linen stopper, put aside, and allowed to ferment.

3. When fermentation is complete, in about six weeks, the wine is filtered into large storage jars and sealed with clay stoppers. Some of the jars are sold at this point; others are stored in a cool, dark place, such as the cistern pictured at left. The men above gently lower the sealed jars to the men inside the cistern. The jars are carefully placed on the floor of the cistern, and another layer of jars will be stacked on top of them. The wine can be stored like this for about three years.

cut out of the rock; these jars could hold as much as 10 gallons of liquid.

Wine was sometimes carried in a portable, flexible sack called a wineskin, which was made from goatskin with the hair on the outside. When wineskins became old, the leather was considered unfit to hold new wine. Jesus used this image to illustrate the incompatibility between new and traditional beliefs in his parable about the danger of putting new wine into old wineskins (Lk 5:36–39).

New wine (Acts 2:13)—wine made from the grapes of the most recent harvest—was said to cause drunkenness quickly. In the book of Psalms, wine is used figuratively to describe God's judgment: "For in the hand of the LORD there is a cup with foaming wine . . . he will pour a draught from it, and all the wicked of the earth shall drain it down to the dregs"(Ps 75:8).

WINEPRESS

. . . HE THREW IT INTO THE GREAT WINE PRESS OF THE WRATH OF GOD. . . . AND BLOOD FLOWED . . . .
–REVELATION 14:19–20

The winepress was a large stone vat or container into which GRAPES were poured and their juice was pressed out by the feet of wine makers as they trod the grapes (see box, pp. 374–375). The grape juice was drained through a small hole at the bottom of the winepress into a smaller vat below, where the fermentation process began. The liquid was then transferred to jars or other containers. The Festival of Booths took place after the pressing of grapes to celebrate a successful harvest (Deut 16:13–14).

Kings supported a large retinue and entertained constantly, so they often had their own winepresses. Archaeologists found a winery at Gibeon from about 700 BC, equipped with presses, fermentation tanks, and cellars large enough to store 25,000 gallons of wine. In the passage cited from Revelation, the winepress is used as an image of God's judgment, which will fall on those who do not believe and will be as uncompromising as squeezing blood-red juice from grapes.

WINNOWING FORK

"HIS WINNOWING FORK IS IN HIS HAND, AND HE WILL CLEAR HIS THRESHING FLOOR AND WILL GATHER HIS WHEAT INTO THE GRANARY . . . ."
–MATTHEW 3:12

After grain had been threshed, the kernels were further separated from the chaff and straw by a process called winnowing. Farmers used a winnowing fork, similar to a pitchfork with broad-bladed tines, to fan the grain and chaff mixture into the air. A slight breeze was sufficient to carry away the lightweight chaff and straw, while the heavier kernels fell to the threshing floor. The grain was then raked into heaps with the fork and tossed into the air again with a shovel. Lastly, the grain was sifted through a sieve to remove pebbles and the last remnants of chaff.

A winnowing fork and shovel, at left, are reconstructed from wood to resemble those used in biblical times.

Wisdom, personified in Proverbs 8, sits upon a cloud in a painting by Titian.

WISDOM

FOR THE LORD GIVES WISDOM; FROM HIS MOUTH COME KNOWLEDGE AND UNDERSTANDING . . . .
–PROVERBS 2:6

In the ancient Near East, wisdom was both religious and intensely practical. To govern others successfully, one had to have "a wise and discerning mind" (1 Kings 3:12), able to distinguish good from evil (1 Kings 3:9). Individuals also needed wisdom in order to lead a successful and happy life. Possessing technical expertise was a sign of wisdom; the "wise woman" referred to in 2 Samuel 20:16 was a skillful negotiator. According to Proverbs, wisdom is a necessity for leading an ethical life, in which one understands "righteousness and justice and equity" (Prov 2:9).

Wisdom is personified in the book of Proverbs as a woman, who is perhaps a teacher, crying out in the street to urge humankind to turn its back on waywardness and embrace the security provided by her counsel. The ultimate source of wisdom, however, is God, and creation itself is a product of his wisdom: "O LORD, how manifold are your works! In wisdom you have made them all" (Ps 104:24). It is those who discover wisdom who find true WEALTH, for wisdom's "income is better than silver, and her revenue better than gold" (Prov 3:14).

Wisdom of Solomon

But I perceived that I would not possess wisdom unless God gave her to me . . . .
–Wisdom of Solomon 8:21

A JEW residing in ancient Alexandria is thought to have written the apocryphal book called Wisdom of Solomon. The book encourages fellow Jews to take pride in their religion, perhaps in the face of Caligula's persecution of Egyptian Jews from AD 38 to 41. The anonymous author writes as though he were King Solomon himself. In the spirit of Solomon, who sought wisdom, he praises godly wisdom and warns that the ungodly who trust in their reasoning skills will face punishment. The author also addresses the emerging Jewish doctrine of immortality and seems to provide the first known Jewish teaching that the soul exists even before God gives it a human body (Wis 8:19).

Wise Men

Then Pharaoh summoned the wise men and the sorcerers . . . .
–Exodus 7:11

Every ancient culture developed its own elite group of educated wise men, or sages, whose advice was sought after by kings, as well as by common citizens. Moses commanded that every tribe choose leaders who were wise (Deut 1:13). A professional class of wise men evolved, joining priests and prophets as key figures in Israelite society. They provided guidance at the royal court and established wisdom schools. In the Gospel of Matthew, "wise men from the East" (Mt 2:1), or the Magi, were the first to pay homage to the newborn Jesus, whom Paul later identifed as "the wisdom of God" (1 Cor 1:24).

The three wise men draw close to Mary and the baby Jesus to offer precious gifts, as depicted in the 15th-century painting Adoration of the Magi *by Andrea Mantegna.*

Witness

"Take this book of the law and put it beside the ark of the covenant of the LORD your God; let it remain there as a witness against you."–Deuteronomy 31:26

In the Bible, *witness* is a legal term for a person who provides personal knowledge about an event that has occurred. A witness can even be an inanimate object: the tablets bearing the ten commandments serve as "witness" or "testimony" to God's covenant with the Israelites. God himself is often called upon to act as a witness (Gen 31:50; 1 Sam 12:5; Rom 1:9).

Old Testament law required people providing evidence to be both responsible and truthful. In a trial, at least two accusers were needed to convict someone of a capital offense, and these witnesses were required to take a role in the execution (Deut 17:6–7), perhaps to demonstrate the veracity of the charge. To bear false witness—to commit PERJURY—was specifically prohibited in the Decalogue (Ex 20:16; Deut 5:20). If a person was proved a false witness, he was subject to the same punishment that was to be inflicted on the accused.

The New Testament also uses the word *witness* in a legal sense. During the trial of Jesus, "false witnesses" come forward to provide trumped-up evidence of Jesus' blasphemy (Mt 26:60). Jesus, however, expands the concept of *witness* to include one who proclaims God's message. In John, Jesus states that he is one of two witnesses who will testify on his own behalf, the other being "the Father who sent me" (Jn 8:18). After his resurrection, Jesus twice calls on the apostles to act as his witnesses to spread the message of his suffering and resurrection throughout the world (Lk 24:48; Acts 1:8, 22). Revelation characterizes Jesus as the "faithful witness"

(Rev 1:5). Indeed, because "witnessing" for Christ could result in persecution and death (Rev 2:13), the Greek word for witness took on the connotation of "martyr."

WOLF

"THE HIRED HAND, WHO IS NOT THE SHEPHERD AND DOES NOT OWN THE SHEEP, SEES THE WOLF COMING AND LEAVES THE SHEEP AND RUNS AWAY . . . ."–JOHN 10:12

Carnivorous animals known for their fierce attacks, wolves hunt at night singly or in pairs. About three feet long with drooping tails, they are larger than most breeds of dogs. Wolves hunted in packs in ancient Israel and were considered a shepherd's worst enemy.

Biblical references to the animal are mostly metaphorical. In Genesis, the tribe of Benjamin is compared with a wolf (Gen 49:27) because of its fearlessness. The wolf is frequently contrasted with the innocent, defenseless SHEEP, such as when Jesus describes false prophets as ravenous wolves disguised in sheep's clothing (Mt 7:15). Isaiah 11:6 foresees a time of peace when "the wolf shall live with the lamb," a theme echoed in Isaiah 65:25.

WOMAN

. . . THE RIB THAT THE LORD GOD HAD TAKEN FROM THE MAN HE MADE INTO A WOMAN. –GENESIS 2:22

According to Genesis 1:27, both man and woman were made in God's image, perhaps implying that they were created equal. The subsequent subordination of women was divine punishment for the first woman's disobedience to God (Gen 3:16).

In Israel's patriarchal society, a woman's primary role was that of wife and mother. The laws governing marriage and divorce were more restrictive for women than for men. A young women who was found not to be a VIRGIN when she married could be stoned to death, and only a husband could obtain a divorce. Women were also subject to religious and economic restrictions: their vows could be nullified by their fathers or husbands (Num 30:1–15), and they could not inherit family property unless there were no sons. Additionally, circumcision, which symbolized God's covenant with his people, was exclusively for males; no similar rite existed for women.

Though male leadership was presumed in ancient Israel, female leaders periodically emerged. The Bible tells of several instances when women wielded great influence. The book of Micah names Miriam, along with Moses and Aaron, as a leader of the exodus (Mic 6:4). Deborah was a judge and national hero who led the Israelites (Judg 4:4). Jezebel and Athaliah were powerful queens.

In the New Testament, Jesus often referred to women in his parables and included them among his disciples. In the early church, women spread the gospel and prophesied, and at least one woman was an apostle (Rom 16:7). Paul declared, "There is no longer male and female; for all of you are one in Christ Jesus" (Gal 3:28).

Carved of wood, a Nubian servant girl balances a water jar on her hip. This Egyptian statue dates from the 14th century BC.

WOOD

FACING THE THRESHOLD THE TEMPLE WAS PANELED WITH WOOD ALL AROUND, FROM THE FLOOR UP TO THE WINDOWS . . . . –EZEKIEL 41:16

In the ancient Near East, wood was used for construction, shipbuilding, weapons, musical instruments, ox yokes, and fuel. Pine, oak, cypress, and sycamore were popular materials; costly cedar was reserved for fine buildings and furniture. According to the Old Testament, Noah was commanded by God to build his ark of cypress (Gen 6:14), and the tabernacle was made of acacia wood (Ex 26:15). To build the tabernacle, God appointed artisans who were skilled "in carving wood, in every kind of craft" (Ex 31:5).

Timber was often shipped as logs or trunks with the limbs removed. In a parable, Jesus used the great difference in size between a log and a speck of wood to expose the human tendency to find a small fault in another person while ignoring a bigger flaw in oneself (Mt 7:3). The book of Isaiah satirizes the carpenter's use of wood for the making of idols: "Half of it he burns in the fire; over this half he roasts meat . . . . The rest of it he makes into a god, his idol" (Isa 44:16–17).

WORD OF GOD

EVERY WORD OF GOD PROVES TRUE; HE IS A SHIELD TO THOSE WHO TAKE REFUGE IN HIM. –PROVERBS 30:5

At the heart of the Bible is the word of God. In creating the world, God said, "'Let there be light'; and there was light" (Gen 1:3). It is through his word that God revealed his will and purpose to humankind. God often chose a specific person, such as a prophet, to hear and convey his word. To deliver his covenant laws, God spoke directly to Moses, who "wrote on the tablets the words of the covenant, the ten commandments" (Ex 34:28). In the book of Isaiah, the prophet refers to God's promise of salvation to Israel as his "word" (Isa 55:10–11).

In the New Testament, the phrase "the word of God" often signifies the Christian message preached by the apostles and others. In some instances, the phrase "the word of the Lord" is used to convey the same idea. In the prologue to the fourth Gospel, the Greek word *logos*, which means "word," has the special meaning of the eternal word of God—"and the Word was with God and the Word was God" (Jn 1:1). It "became flesh and lived among us" (Jn 1:14) in the person of Jesus Christ.

WORKS

". . . LET YOUR LIGHT SHINE BEFORE OTHERS, SO THAT THEY MAY SEE YOUR GOOD WORKS AND GIVE GLORY TO YOUR FATHER IN HEAVEN." –MATTHEW 5:16

Throughout the Bible, an individual's works demonstrate his or her FAITH. Those without faith illustrate their wickedness by their evil works; believers show their closeness to God by good deeds. The Old Testament frequently cites the works of God as proof of his power and divinity. With a cry of wonder —"what God in heaven or on earth can perform deeds and mighty acts like yours!"(Deut 3:24)—Moses bears witness to God's miraculous works in the wilderness. Job is warned to "consider the wondrous works of God" (Job 37:14).

In this mosaic from the sixth-century church of San Vitale in Ravenna, Italy, the prophet Jeremiah holds a scroll containing the word of God.

Works take on increased importance in the New Testament. The mark of a good person, claims James, is one who both has a strong faith and does good works (Jas 2:24). Neither alone will guarantee salvation. John addresses the interconnection between the works of God and the works of Jesus. It is through Jesus that God's works are manifest on earth, and Jesus reveals himself to be the Son of God by his works (Jn 5:36). Indeed, Jesus often points to his works to prove he is the Messiah (Jn 14:11).

WORLD

EVEN IF YOU ARE EXILED TO THE ENDS OF THE WORLD, FROM THERE THE LORD YOUR GOD WILL GATHER YOU . . . .–DEUTERONOMY 30:4

World has a variety of meanings in the Bible. Sometimes the term appears to include both the heavens and the earth, which comprised the universe as it was understood by ancient peoples (Gen 1:1). *World* can also mean simply the EARTH (Ps 24:1).

The Bible proclaims God to be the creator of the world. Paul refers to "the God who made the world and everything in it, he who is Lord of heaven and earth" (Acts 17:24). Applying the term to humankind, the Gospel of John claims that Jesus "takes away the sin of the world!" (Jn 1:29). *World* can also refer to the realm of the material, as opposed to the spiritual (Mt 13:22).

WORM

BUT I AM A WORM, AND NOT HUMAN; SCORNED BY OTHERS, AND DESPISED BY THE PEOPLE. –PSALM 22:6

The word *worm* refers to the larval stage of various insects, including flies, beetles, butterflies, and moths. The insect at this stage of the life cycle is also called a maggot. A small, legless, soft-bodied creature, the worm symbolizes lowliness. In the passage above, the psalmist emphasizes his humiliation by likening himself to a worm.

During the exodus, uneaten manna was spoiled by worms, which were probably fly larvae: "But they did not listen to Moses; some left part of it until morning, and it bred worms and became foul" (Ex 16:20).

Wormwood

... but in the end she is bitter as wormwood, sharp as a two-edged sword.
–Proverbs 5:4

Many species of wormwood, a plant with an extremely bitter taste, are found in the Near East. Goats and camels feed on this heavily branched shrub, and Bedouins make a strong, aromatic tea from its gray leaves. Wormwood is a folk remedy for curing intestinal worms, which may explain its name. It also may have been used as a purgative. In the Bible it appears as a metaphor for acrimony or sorrow, as in Lamentations 3:15.

Artemisia judaica *is a species of wormwood that grows in the Sinai peninsula.*

Worship

All the ends of the earth shall remember and turn to the LORD; and all the families of the nations shall worship before him.
–Psalm 22:27

The word *worship* is from the Hebrew, meaning to "bow down" or to "prostrate oneself." To show reverence to God in such a way was the cornerstone of scriptural religious life. Indeed, worship was of such importance in the biblical world that God spoke of it in the first of his commandments, decreeing: "I am the LORD your God ... you shall have no other gods before me. ... You shall not bow down to [idols] or worship them" (Deut 5:6–9).

Numerous types of worship appear throughout the Bible, from the intensely private forms, such as personal prayer and confession, to public worship, which sometimes included singing and dancing. In Old Testament times, strict rituals were followed for daily worship in the temple, the weekly sabbath, and annual religious celebrations, such as Passover and the Day of Atonement. Prayer and sacrifice were at the center of this worship, although sacrifice ended with the destruction of the temple in AD 70. Early Christian worship services consisted of singing, community prayer, the reading of the Scriptures, and the celebration of the Lord's supper.

Wrath

Much more surely then, now that we have been justified by his blood, will we be saved through him from the wrath of God.
–Romans 5:9

The Bible distinguishes between the wrath of God, which is a divine reaction to sin, and the wrath of human beings, which is discouraged. Concerning human anger, the book of Proverbs advises that "a soft answer turns away wrath" (Prov 15:1). The letter to the Colossians counsels that "you must get rid of ... anger, wrath, malice" (Col 3:8).

Although God's wrath is serious and can have severe consequences, such as the destruction of Sodom and Gomorrah (Deut 29:23), the Lord is nonetheless a righteous God, who is "slow to anger" (Ps 86:15). The New Testament puts more emphasis on God's love than on his wrath. Even so, Jesus displays some of the force of divine wrath when he drives the money changers from the temple (Jn 2:14–16). According to the apostle Paul, humanity's disobedience toward God will bring on the "day of wrath," when "there will be anguish and distress for everyone who does evil" (Rom 2:5, 9). However, because Jesus has taken God's wrath upon himself, those who believe in him have no reason to fear the judgment day.

God's wrath descends on Sodom as angels lead Lot and his family away.

Wrestling

Jacob was left alone; and a man wrestled with him until daybreak.–Genesis 32:24

Wrestling contests were enjoyed throughout antiquity. The sport was often conducted hand to hand, but belt wrestling, in which one ATHLETE grabbed hold of the other's tightly cinched belt, was also popular in the Near East. A famous biblical wrestling match was Jacob's night-long struggle with a man, later identified as God or an angel. Jacob was victorious but his hip "was put out of joint" (Gen 32:25).

Wrestling could also refer to emotional or spiritual struggles. Speaking of her rivalry with Leah, Rachel said, "With mighty wrestlings I have wrestled with my sister, and have prevailed" (Gen 30:8). In the letter to the Colossians, the author describes the faithful Epaphras as "always wrestling in his prayers on your behalf" (Col 4:12).

WRITING

. . . AND THE WRITING WAS THE WRITING OF GOD, ENGRAVED UPON THE TABLETS.–EXODUS 32:16

Writing—the capacity to transcribe spoken language accurately into visual symbols—evolved over a very long period. An early method of writing, which developed by the fourth millennium BC, involved pictographs, which were images of the objects being referred to. The Sumerians refined this practice into a cuneiform system that included images representing words or ideas, along with symbols for syllables. For example, to communicate the word for live, which was pronounced "til," a Sumerian SCRIBE drew an arrow, which was pronounced "ti"—an adequate approximation. The Assyrians, Babylonians, and other Near Eastern peoples adopted this cuneiform system. The Egyptians used hieroglyphics, which were pictorial, but their system also included symbols denoting consonant sounds.

By 1500 BC, the Canaanites had developed an alphabet that, for the most part, represented consonant sounds. The Phoenician form of this alphabet had a profound influence on the ancient world. The Israelites developed their alphabetic system from the Phoenician system. The Greeks learned this system through commerce and, in a great leap forward, devised an alphabet with signs also for vowels.

Different mediums were used for writing. Cuneiform was incised on clay tablets. Important political and religious texts were often inscribed in stone, although some were written in ink on walls coated with plaster. Scribes also wrote upon leather, papyrus, parchment, and strips of wood or soft metal. As a mark of their profession, scribes often carried writing cases attached to their belts containing ink, brushes, styluses, and pens.

A marble relief from about 510 BC portrays two men engaged in a wrestling match. The relief appears on a statue base found in the Dipylon cemetery in Athens.

XANTHICUS

". . . THOSE WHO GO HOME BY THE THIRTIETH OF XANTHICUS WILL HAVE OUR PLEDGE OF FRIENDSHIP . . . ." –2 MACCABEES 11:30

Xanthicus, a word that appears in the Bible only in chapter 11 of 2 Maccabees, is the name of a MONTH in the Syrian-Macedonian calendar. This calendar was decreed by Seleucus Nicator, a general of Alexander the Great who made himself master of much of the Near East beginning in 312 BC. Greek became the common language of this huge realm, and the Jews adopted Seleucus' calendar for secular use until the Romans reformed the calendar. Xanthicus corresponded to the Jewish month of Nisan (March–April). In 2 Maccabees, it is mentioned in official letters of the Seleucid king and the Romans concerning the Jews.

YEAR

ADD YEAR TO YEAR; LET THE FESTIVALS RUN THEIR ROUND.–ISAIAH 29:1

The ancient civilizations of the Near East based the year on the agricultural cycle. The new year began in the spring for the Babylonians, when new life burgeoned, but scholars are divided as to when the Israelites started their year. Many believe that, like their Canaanite neighbors, the Israelites originally chose the fall, when the harvest cycle was completed, but eventually began to celebrate the new year in the spring. This change may have occurred after the exile, under the influence of the Babylonians, which would explain why the Babylonian names of months became part of the Jewish calendar.

The new year fell close to the equinox, whether autumnal or vernal. It did not exactly match, however, because the new year began on the first of the month, or the new moon, and the moon's cycles are not the same as those of the sun. The 354-day lunar year was composed of 12 months, each averaging 29½ days. The Israelites were able to make their calendar correspond to the solar year of 365¼ days by adding another month every two or three years. See also chart for FESTIVAL.

Calendars charted the passage of years. Inscribed on clay, this first-millennium BC calendar is Babylonian.

YELLOW

. . . THE PRIEST SHALL EXAMINE THE DISEASE. IF IT APPEARS DEEPER THAN THE SKIN AND THE HAIR IN IT IS YELLOW AND THIN, THE PRIEST SHALL PRONOUNCE HIM UNCLEAN . . . .
–LEVITICUS 13:30

The word *yellow* appears only in the book of Leviticus. It refers to the color of hair in a patch of skin, occurring on the head or in the beard, that was believed to be leprous. (Yellowing hair can signal a fungal disease called favus, which at the time was considered a manifestation of LEPROSY.) Because leprosy made a person ritually unclean, priests were required to diagnose the disease by checking for the telltale yellow hair.

Yellow was also a decorative color used for yarn. Extractions from plants, such as saffron, turmeric, and pomegranate rind, produced the yellow dye.

YOKE

"FOR MY YOKE IS EASY, AND MY BURDEN IS LIGHT."
–MATTHEW 11:30

The yoke is a wooden device that harnesses oxen to a plow or wagon. The word can also refer to a pair of yoked oxen or to the amount of land such a team could plow in one day. Egyptian tomb paintings show that paired oxen were originally harnessed by ropes tied to their horns. The first improvement on this method, which placed great stress on the animals' necks, was to tie a beam across the oxen's horns and hitch the plow or wagon to that. Later, a second beam was added under the animals' necks and fastened to the upper beam by stout pegs, enabling the oxen to handle the load with ease. Yokes were also used on donkeys and horses, but they could press against the animals' windpipes and choke them. Mosaic law forbade plowing with an OX and a donkey yoked together (Deut 22:10).

Biblical writers often presented the yoke as a symbol of slavery or oppression. Jeremiah, for example, speaks repeatedly of "the yoke of the king of Babylon." The device can also symbolize submission to God's law. In the passage above, Jesus says that following his teachings is an easy burden.

Yoked oxen in the Golan Heights tread on grain as part of the threshing process.

ZEALOT

HE DARED TO DESIGNATE AS A PLOTTER AGAINST THE GOVERNMENT . . . A ZEALOT FOR THE LAWS.
–2 MACCABEES 4:2

In biblical times, a zealot was a person who was so devoted to religious laws and customs that he was ready to die in their defense. He might even go so far as to kill someone else who had defiled the law. Such was the case of the priest Phinehas, who slew his fellow Israelite Zimri because of a sexual and idolatrous transgression (Num 25:1–15). In the first century AD, Jewish guerrillas who called themselves Zealots banded together to fight against the Roman occupation of the Holy Land. The apostle Simon the Zealot may have belonged to this group, or his name may simply be a general reference to his religious fervor.

ZECHARIAH, BOOK OF

. . . THUS SAYS THE LORD, I HAVE RETURNED TO JERUSALEM WITH COMPASSION; MY HOUSE SHALL BE BUILT IN IT . . . .
–ZECHARIAH 1:16

Like his contemporary Haggai, the prophet Zechariah, active from 520 to 518 BC, encouraged the returned Jewish exiles to rebuild the temple in Jerusalem. In the book bearing his name, Zechariah promised that if the Jews did so, a ruler would come to lead Israel into a glorious future. The first eight chapters report Zechariah's highly symbolic visions of Israel's restoration. The remaining six chapters contain warnings that were probably written by other authors two or three centuries after Zechariah. This closing section speaks of war but describes the coming of a victorious king, "humble and riding on a donkey" (Zech 9:9), who will establish a universal rule of peace.

Zephaniah, Book of

I will utterly sweep away everything from the face of the earth, says the LORD. –Zephaniah 1:2

Zephaniah announced the catastrophic day of the Lord, when God would punish Judah and, eventually, all other nations for their pride and immorality. Except for a faithful REMNANT, warned the prophet, God would "cut off humanity from the face of the earth" (Zeph 1:3).

This jarring, three-chapter prophecy, delivered in King Josiah's reign (640–609 BC), may have sparked the short-lived religious reform movement that Josiah launched. The movement crumbled after Josiah died while fighting the Egyptians. Not long after, the Babylonians defeated Judah and exiled many of the survivors.

Zion

Then I looked, and there was the Lamb, standing on Mount Zion! –Revelation 14:1

Zion is a Hebrew word that may have originally meant "citadel" or "fortress." It came to refer to the fortified section of Jerusalem, an area also called the City of David. Eventually, *Zion* was used for the temple mount and then for the entire city of Jerusalem.

The word took on special significance for the Jews after they were exiled from their holy city in the sixth century BC. To them, *Zion* indicated both the homeland they had lost and their former sovereignty. It was in Jerusalem that God had dwelt in the temple and that they had fulfilled their role as his chosen people. A psalm laments their loss: "By the rivers of Babylon—there we sat down and there we wept when we remembered Zion" (Ps 137:1). The restoration of Jerusalem provided hope for the future. The prophet Zechariah predicted that "the LORD will again comfort Zion" (Zech 1:17). In this verse, the term *Zion* may represent the people of God; it could also refer to "the heavenly Jerusalem" (Heb 12:22), or God's abode. The Lord's throne was on "his holy mountain . . . Mount Zion" (Ps 48:1–2).

In a 19th-century painting by Edward Lear, two people sit on the Mount of Olives to take in the splendor of Jerusalem at sunrise. Biblical writers often called the city Zion, a term that evokes its unique importance and wondrous holiness.

GLOSSARY

As a supplement to the word entries appearing in the main body of the book, this glossary contains words found in the Scriptures that require a less detailed definition than those in the dictionary section. Each glossary entry is followed by a chapter and verse citation from the Bible to place the word in context.

accursed ones
People who are not in fellowship with God because they do not follow his laws. ◆ *You rebuke the insolent, accursed ones, who wander from your commandments . . . . –Psalm 119:21*

accuser
A legal adversary; a synonym for Satan. ◆ *"Though I am innocent, I cannot answer him; I must appeal for mercy to my accuser." –Job 9:15*

acre
A translation of the Hebrew word meaning "yoke," referring to the area of land a pair of oxen could plow in a day. ◆ *In that first slaughter Jonathan and his armor-bearer killed about twenty men within an area about half a furrow long in an acre of land.–1 Samuel 14:14*

Adar
The 12th month in the Jewish calendar, equivalent to parts of February and March, which was adapted from the Babylonian calendar. ◆ *This was on the thirteenth day of the month of Adar, and on the fourteenth day they rested and made that a day of feasting and gladness.–Esther 9:17*

adder
In the Bible, any of several snakes, both poisonous and nonpoisonous ◆ *You will tread on the lion and the adder, the young lion and the serpent you will trample under foot.–Psalm 91:13*

administrator
A mid-level functionary working for a government. ◆ *Such should be those who are administrators of the law, shielding it with their own blood and noble sweat in sufferings even to death.–4 Maccabees 7:8*

adornment
Something that beautifies the body or spirit. ◆ *. . . keep sound wisdom and prudence, and they will be life for your soul and adornment for your neck.–Proverbs 3:21–22*

aftergrowth
The second growth of a crop after the harvest. ◆ *You shall not reap the aftergrowth of your harvest or gather the grapes of your unpruned vine.–Leviticus 25:5*

altar of incense
An altar on which incense was burned, often carved from a single block of stone. ◆ *He made the altar of incense of acacia wood, one cubit long, and one cubit wide; it was square, and was two cubits high; its horns were of one piece with it.–Exodus 37:25*

anklet
A band worn around the ankle as an adornment. ◆ *She put sandals on her feet, and put on her anklets . . . .–Judith 10:4*

ant
In the Bible, a symbol of industry and foresight. ◆ *Go to the ant, you lazybones; consider its ways, and be wise. –Proverbs 6:6*

anvil
A heavy block on which a smith hammers and shapes metal. ◆ *So too is the smith, sitting by the anvil, intent on his iron-work . . . .–Ecclesiasticus 38:28*

apartment
Living quarters within a large building. ◆ *Now the king was sitting in his winter apartment (it was the ninth month), and there was a fire burning in the brazier before him.–Jeremiah 36:22*

aroma
Fragrance, especially that rising to God from burning incense or an offering. ◆ *For we are the aroma of Christ to God among those who are being saved and among those who are perishing . . . . –2 Corinthians 2:15*

asp
In the Bible, any of several venomous snakes, especially the cobra, a snake that lives in holes. An asp can symbolize treachery or the unrighteous. ◆ *The nursing child shall play over the hole of the asp.–Isaiah 11:8*

assailant
Someone who attacks, especially in battle. ◆ *For you girded me with strength for the battle; you made my assailants sink under me.–Psalm 18:39*

assessment
The value assigned an offering, such as an animal or land, at the tabernacle or temple. ◆ *The priest shall assess it: whether good or bad, according to the assessment of the priest, so it shall be.–Leviticus 27:12*

attendant
A helper or a servant; a member of a king's entourage. ◆ *These words pleased Holofernes and all his attendants . . . . –Judith 7:16*

author
In the Bible, a reference to God as the creator. ◆ *If through delight in the beauty of these things people assumed them to be gods, let them know how much better than these is their Lord, for the author of beauty created them.–Wisdom of Solomon 13:3*

autumn
The season of the year following summer and before winter; however, not a very distinct season in the Holy Land. Some harvests took place in autumn. ◆ *They are waterless clouds carried along by the winds; autumn trees without fruit, twice dead, uprooted . . . .–Jude 12*

awning
A woven cloth spread as a covering to conceal something or someone or to give shade. ◆ *Of fine embroidered linen from Egypt was your sail, serving as your ensign; blue and purple from the coasts of Elishah was your awning.–Ezekiel 27:7*

backbone
The spinal column; in the Bible, referred to in an explanation of the ritual sacrifice of a sheep. ◆ *You shall present its fat from the sacrifice of well-being, as an offering by fire to the LORD: the whole broad tail, which shall be removed close to the backbone . . . . –Leviticus 3:9*

bandit
An outlaw; used mainly in the New Testament, where Barabbas is called a bandit, as are the men crucified on either side of Jesus. ◆ *And with him they crucified two bandits, one on his right and one on his left.–Mark 15:27*

banishment
A condemnation in which one must leave his or her land or people. ◆ *"All who will not obey the law of your God and the law of the king, let judgment be strictly executed on them, whether for death or for banishment or for confiscation of their goods or for imprisonment."–Ezra 7:26*

bazaar
An area in a town in which merchants sell goods. ◆ *Ben-hadad said to him, ". . . you may establish bazaars for yourself in Damascus, as my father did in Samaria." –1 Kings 20:34*

bdellium
A word of unknown meaning; in the Bible, probably a yellow resin obtained from trees of the genus *Commiphora*. It may also refer to a stone or pearl. Bdellium is associated with the land of Havilah, an area in Arabia. ◆ *. . . and the gold of that land is good; bdellium and onyx stone are there. –Genesis 2:12.*

beka
A weight equal to one-half shekel; the tax in silver that was required of male Israelites 20 years of age and older for construction of the tabernacle. ◆ *The silver from those of the congregation who were counted was . . . a beka a head (that is, half a shekel, measured by the sanctuary shekel) . . . .–Exodus 38:25–26*

Beliar
A name for Satan or an evil power; a variant form of *Belial*, which derives from the Hebrew for worthlessness. ◆ *What agreement does Christ have with Beliar? Or what does a believer share wih an unbeliever?–2 Corinthians 6:15*

believer
In the New Testament, someone who believes that Jesus is the Messiah. ◆ *Now as Peter went here and there among all the believers, he came down also to the saints living in Lydda.–Acts of the Apostles 9:32*

berries
Small fruits; in the Bible, olives. ◆ *Gleanings will be left in it, as when an olive tree is beaten—two or three berries in the top of the highest bough . . . .–Isaiah 17:6*

birthday
In biblical times, an anniversary sometimes celebrated by kings and pharaohs with feasts ◆ *But an opportunity came when Herod on his birthday gave a banquet for his courtiers and officers and for the leaders of Galilee.–Mark 6:21*

blood of the covenant
Blood that establishes or attests to a covenant between God and humankind. ◆ *Then he took a cup, and after giving thanks he gave it to them, saying, "Drink from it, all of you; for this is my blood of the covenant . . . ."–Matthew 26:27–28*

boar
The male wild pig, abundant in parts of the Holy Land, especially near bodies of water. It threatened farmers' crops and so was used to symbolize destruction by enemies of the nation of Israel. ◆ *The boar from the forest ravages it, and all that move in the field feed on it.–Psalm 80:13*

bowshot
A linear measure equal to the distance that an arrow can travel when shot from a bow. ◆ *Then she went and sat down opposite him a good way off, about the distance of a bowshot . . . .–Genesis 21:16*

box
A container, such as a flask, often used for perfume. ◆ *In that day the Lord will take away . . . the headdresses, the armlets, the sashes, the perfume boxes, and the amulets . . . .–Isaiah 3:18, 20*

brawler
A noisy, quarrelsome person; used figuratively in the book of Proverbs in a warning against excessive drinking. ◆ *Wine is a mocker, strong drink a brawler, and whoever is led astray by it is not wise. –Proverbs 20:1*

breaking of bread
The tearing of bread so that it may be shared with others; in the New Testament, participating in the Lord's supper, a Christian practice in which sacramental bread is eaten. ◆ *They devoted themselves to the apostles' teaching and fellowship, to the breaking of bread and the prayers.–Acts of the Apostles 2:42*

broom
As used metaphorically in the book of Isaiah, a hand broom made from twigs. ◆ *. . . I will sweep it with the broom of destruction, says the LORD of hosts.–Isaiah 14:23*

broth
Water in which meat has been boiled, served as a food. ◆ *. . . the meat he put in a basket, and the broth he put in a pot, and brought them to him under the oak and presented them.–Judges 6:19*

Bul
The eighth month in the calendar used by the Israelites before the exile, corresponding to parts of October and November. ◆ *In the eleventh year, in the month of Bul, which is the eighth month, the house was finished in all its parts, and according to all its specifications. –1 Kings 6:38*

bulwark
A wall or rampart built as a defense or fortification; used figuratively, someone or something that gives strength or protection. ◆ *. . . I am writing these instructions to you so that, if I am delayed, you may know how one ought to behave in the household of God, which is the church of the living God, the pillar and bulwark of the truth. –1 Timothy 3:14–15*

burial mound
A raised pile of stones or earth over a grave. ◆ *Whoever builds his house with other people's money is like one who gathers stones for his burial mound. –Ecclesiasticus 21:8*

bushel basket
A container that was used in the Greco-Roman world to measure capacity. ◆ *He said to them, "Is a lamp brought in to be put under the bushel basket, or under the bed, and not on the lampstand?"–Mark 4:21*

busybody
A person who is overly inquisitive to no productive end; said of some early Christians in New Testament letters. ◆ *For we hear that some of you are living in idleness, mere busybodies, not doing any work.–2 Thessalonians 3:11*

buzzard
A bird of prey, listed as unclean. The identification of the bird is uncertain. ◆ *But these are the ones that you shall not eat: the eagle, the vulture, the osprey, the buzzard . . . .–Deuteronomy 14:12–13*

byword
An object of derision; usually applied to the nation of Israel or an individual who has incurred the wrath of God. ◆ *Let them say, "Spare your people, O LORD, and do not make your heritage a mockery, a byword among the nations."–Joel 2:17*

cage
An enclosure, sometimes portable and usually barred, for the trapping and confinement of animals or birds; possibly used also for prisoners of war. ◆ *Like a cage full of birds, their houses are full of treachery; therefore they have become great and rich, they have grown fat and sleek. –Jeremiah 5:27–28*

cake
A small loaf of bread; also dried, pressed fruit, such as a cake of figs or raisins. ◆ *She took dough, kneaded it, made cakes in his sight, and baked the cakes. –2 Samuel 13:8*

caldron
Any of several types of cooking pots used by the Israelites and made of ceramic or metal. ◆ *The king fell into a rage, and gave orders to have pans and caldrons heated.–2 Maccabees 7:3*

camel's thorn
A small, thorny bush whose roots were used to make a fragrant ointment. ◆ *"Like cassia and camel's thorn I gave forth perfume, and like choice myrrh I spread my fragrance . . . ."–Ecclesiasticus 24:15*

canal
A natural or artificial water channel, especially of the Nile River, flowing through its delta. ◆ *"Say to Aaron, 'Take your staff and stretch out your hand over the waters of Egypt—over its rivers, its canals, and its ponds, and all its pools of water—so that they may become blood . . . .'" –Exodus 7:19*

capital
The topmost section of a column, often ornamented with carvings. ◆ *In front of the house he made two pillars thirty-five cubits high, with a capital of five cubits on the top of each.–2 Chronicles 3:15*

carder
Someone who combs such fibers as wool, linen, and cotton to align the fibers and rid them of impurities, in preparation for spinning. ◆ *The workers in flax will be in despair, and the carders and those at the loom will grow pale.–Isaiah 19:9*

carnelian
A gemstone having a clear, deep red color; one of the stones set in the high priest's breastpiece. ◆ *You were in Eden, the garden of God; every precious stone was your covering, carnelian, chrysolite, and moonstone . . . .–Ezekiel 28:13*

carpet
A textile used as a floor covering. In the Bible, however, the meaning is unclear. ◆ *"Tell of it, you who ride on white donkeys, you who sit on rich carpets and you who walk by the way."–Judges 5:10*

carrion
The spoiling flesh of a dead animal, especially one that died from disease or animal attack. Eating or even touching it was considered ritually unclean. ◆ *All the kings of the nations lie in glory, each in his own tomb; but you are cast out, away from your grave, like loathsome carrion . . . . –Isaiah 14:18–19*

castanets
In the Bible, a musical instrument consisting of disks or beads loosely strung on short rods across a U shape, held by a short handle and shaken to produce a rattling sound; also called a sistrum or noisemaker. ◆ *David and all the house of Israel were dancing before the LORD with all their might, with songs and lyres and harps and tambourines and castanets and cymbals.–2 Samuel 6:5*

castle
A stronghold or citadel; possibly a palace. ◆ *When a strong man, fully armed, guards his castle, his property is safe. –Luke 11:21*

cat
A domesticated animal revered in Egypt, though not mentioned by Old or New Testament writers. The apocryphal letter of Jeremiah does refer to the animal. ◆ *Bats, swallows, and birds alight on their bodies and heads; and so do cats. –Letter of Jeremiah 22*

caulker
A worker who applies a compound to the seams of a ship to make it watertight. ◆ *. . . your caulkers, your dealers in merchandise, and all your warriors within you sink into the heart of the seas on the day of your ruin.–Ezekiel 27:27*

cemetery
An area for the burial of the dead. ◆ *. . . the holy city, which he was hurrying to level to the ground and to make a cemetery, he was now declaring to be free . . . . –2 Maccabees 9:14*

chaff
Husks of grain after being separated from the edible seeds by threshing or winnowing. ◆ *"How often are they like straw before the wind, and like chaff that the storm carries away?"–Job 21:18*

chalkstone
A type of limestone found in the Holy Land that is soft and fragile and produces an infertile soil. ◆ *. . . when he makes all the stones of the altars like chalkstones crushed to pieces, no sacred poles or incense altars will remain standing.–Isaiah 27:9*

chamberlain
An official who oversees the private rooms of a king or noble. ◆ *Now Herod was angry with the people of Tyre and Sidon. So they came to him in a body; and after winning over Blastus, the king's chamberlain, they asked for a reconciliation . . . . –Acts of the Apostles 12:20*

chameleon
A small, tree-dwelling reptile resembling a lizard and noted for its ability to

change its skin color. Although the chameleon does live in the Holy Land, the identity of the animal that the Bible refers to by this name is uncertain. ◆ *These are unclean for you among the creatures that swarm upon the earth . . . the gecko, the land crocodile, the lizard, the sand lizard, and the chameleon.* –Leviticus 11:29–30

champion
A mighty warrior or defender; in 1 Samuel 17, a man who steps into the space between two warring camps to fight a single opponent. ◆ *And there came out from the camp of the Philistines a champion named Goliath, of Gath, whose height was six cubits and a span.*–1 Samuel 17:4

chaos
A void; untracked space. ◆ *For thus says the LORD . . . who formed the earth and made it (he established it; he did not create it a chaos, he formed it to be inhabited!): I am the LORD, and there is no other.*–Isaiah 45:18

charmer
Someone who uses charms or incantations, especially to control snakes. ◆ *If the snake bites before it is charmed, there is no advantage in a charmer.* –Ecclesiastes 10:11

checker work
A crisscrossed design on the capitals of the two pillars on the porch of the temple built by Solomon. ◆ *There were nets of checker work with wreaths of chain work for the capitals on the tops of the pillars; seven for the one capital, and seven for the other capital.*–1 Kings 7:17

cheek
Part of the face. Hitting someone on the cheek was considered a humiliating insult; thus the act could be referred to figuratively to mean imparting any grave insult. Jesus preached a peaceable reaction to such offenses. ◆ *"But I say to you, Do not resist an evildoer. But if anyone strikes you on the right cheek, turn the other also . . . ."*–Matthew 5:39

Chislev
The name of the ninth month in the calendar used by the Jews after the Babylonian exile, corresponding to parts of November and December. ◆ *In the fourth year of King Darius, the word of the LORD came to Zechariah on the fourth day of the ninth month, which is Chislev.* –Zechariah 7:1

chorus
In Greek theater, a group of dancers that moved in a line and spoke together. ◆ *. . . so these youths, forming a chorus, encircled the sevenfold fear of tortures and dissolved it.*–4 Maccabees 14:8

chrysolite
A green precious stone; in some Bible translations, equated with beryl. Job speaks of chysolite to emphasize the value of wisdom. ◆ *"The chrysolite of Ethiopia cannot compare with it, nor can it be valued in pure gold."*–Job 28:19

chrysoprase
A gemstone having a light green color; in Revelation, one of the jewels in the wall foundations of the new Jerusalem. ◆ *The foundations of the wall of the city are adorned with every jewel; the first was jasper . . . the tenth chrysoprase . . . .*–Revelation 21:19–20

clapping
A gesture that could express either joy or derision in biblical times. ◆ *All who pass along the way clap their hands at you; they hiss and wag their heads at daughter Jerusalem . . . .*–Lamentations 2:15

club
A blunt type of weapon, used to strike an opponent. ◆ *Like a war club, a sword, or a sharp arrow is one who bears false witness against a neighbor.*–Proverbs 25:18

coastland
In the Bible, the inhabited islands along the coasts of the Mediterranean Sea. The plural of the word, as used by some of the prophets, can mean distant nations. ◆ *So I took the cup from the LORD'S hand, and made all the nations to whom the LORD sent me drink it . . . all the kings of Tyre, all the kings of Sidon, and the kings of the coastland across the sea . . . .* –Jeremiah 25:17, 22

coat of mail
Armor sometimes made with bronze scales, probably attached to two leather pieces that went from neck to waist, and joined under the arms. ◆ *He had a helmet of bronze on his head, and he was armed with a coat of mail; the weight of the coat was five thousand shekels of bronze.*–1 Samuel 17:5

colonnade
A series of columns set at regular intervals. In the Bible, the meaning is at times uncertain. ◆ *On the east there were six Levites each day . . . and for the colonnade on the west there were four at the road and two at the colonnade.*–1 Chronicles 26:17–18

commissioner
An official assigned a particular task or duty by a government. ◆ *"And let the king appoint commissioners in all the provinces of his kingdom to gather all the beautiful young virgins to the harem in the citadel of Susa . . . ."*–Esther 2:3

common people
People of lower socioeconomic classes, who could not afford private rock-hewn tombs. ◆ *. . . and they took Uriah from Egypt and brought him to King Jehoiakim, who struck him down with the sword and threw his dead body into the burial place of the common people.*–Jeremiah 26:23

consolers
People who give comfort to the bereaved or take part in mourning with the bereaved. ◆ *. . . the officials of the Ammonites said to Hanun, "Do you think, because David has sent consolers to you, that he is honoring your father?"* –1 Chronicles 19:3

cor
A unit of dry and liquid measure that was adapted from the Babylonians by the Israelites. It may have contained between 3.8 and 6.5 bushels, or between 35.5 and 60.75 gallons. ◆ *This is the offering that you shall make . . . as the fixed portion of oil, one-tenth of a bath from each cor (the cor, like the homer, contains ten baths) . . . .* –Ezekiel 45:13–14

coriander seed
The seed of an annual plant (*Coriandrum sativum*) used to flavor food. ◆ *Now the manna was like coriander seed, and its color was like the color of gum resin.*–Numbers 11:7

cormorant
Any of various sea birds belonging to the family Phalacrocoracidae. Some species winter around the Sea of Galilee. ◆ *But these are the ones that you shall not eat . . . the desert owl, the carrion vulture and the cormorant . . . .*–Deuteronomy 14:12, 17

cotton
The fibers surrounding the seeds of the plant *Gossypium herbaceum*; yarn or fabric made from this fiber. Cotton was grown in Persia, one of the countries where Jews lived in exile. ◆ *This was held for six*

days in the courtyard of the royal palace, which was adorned with curtains of fine linen and cotton . . . . –Additions to Esther 1:5–6

courtiers
The members of a king's court. ◆ *"He will take the best of your fields and vineyards and olive orchards and give them to his courtiers."–1 Samuel 8:14*

crane
Any of various tall wading birds with long legs and necks belonging to the family Gruidae. Cranes come to the Holy Land while migrating in the spring, but their identification in the Bible is uncertain. ◆ *Like a swallow or a crane I clamor, I moan like a dove.–Isaiah 38:14*

crescent
A piece of jewelry or an amulet in the shape of the crescent moon. ◆ *So Gideon proceeded to kill Zebah and Zalmunna; and he took the crescents that were on the necks of their camels.–Judges 8:21*

cricket
A translation of a Hebrew word that may instead mean "grasshopper" or "locust." ◆ *Of them you may eat: the locust according to its kind . . . the cricket according to its kind, and the grasshopper according to its kind. –Leviticus 11:22*

crossing over
Passing over or through a boundary, such as a river. ◆ *For I am going to die in this land without crossing over the Jordan, but you are going to cross over to take possession of that good land. –Deuteronomy 4:22*

crow
The call of a rooster; used in the time of Jesus to designate certain times of night. ◆ *Jesus answered, "Will you lay down your life for me? Very truly, I tell you, before the cock crows, you will have denied me three times."–John 13:38*

crucible
A pot, usually ceramic, in which metal is melted and refined. ◆ *The crucible is for silver, and the furnace is for gold, but the LORD tests the heart. –Proverbs 17:3*

cushion
A support for the head, back, or buttocks; a pillow. ◆ *But he was in the stern, asleep on the cushion; and they woke him up and said to him, "Teacher, do you not care that we are perishing?"–Mark 4:38*

dart
A type of weapon with a sharpened point and a short shaft, used for thrusting or throwing. ◆ *"Though the sword reaches it, it does not avail, nor does the spear, the dart, or the javelin."–Job 41:26*

daughter-towns
Small towns or villages subject to political and economic influence from a larger city or metropolis. ◆ *Your daughter-towns in the country he shall put to the sword. –Ezekiel 26:8*

delegation
A group of people chosen to act for an individual, such as a king, or for another group. ◆ *If he cannot, then, while the other is still far away, he sends a delegation and asks for the terms of peace.–Luke 14:32*

delusion
Something that cannot fulfil what it promises, such as the false religion of the Canaanites. ◆ *"Truly the hills are a delusion, the orgies on the mountains. Truly in the LORD our God is the salvation of Israel." –Jeremiah 3:23*

dependencies
Villages or towns that are governed by another, more powerful town. ◆ *The towns belonging to the tribe of the people of Judah in the extreme South, toward the boundary of Edom, were . . . Ekron, with its dependencies and its villages . . . . –Joshua 15:21, 45*

deputy
Someone appointed to act for another. ◆ *Rehum the royal deputy and Shimshai the scribe wrote a letter against Jerusalem to King Artaxerxes . . . .–Ezra 4:8*

detestable thing
An idol or other object of worship that was abhorrent to God and forbidden to the Israelites. ◆ *When they come there, they will remove from it all its detestable things and all its abominations.–Ezekiel 11:18*

double-minded
Wavering in thought; having doubts; having divided convictions or loyalties. ◆ *Cleanse your hands, you sinners, and purify your hearts, you double-minded.–James 4:8*

double-tongued
In the original Greek, to repeat oneself; in 1 Timothy, to speak insincerely or inconsistently, such as to different listeners, or to be hypocritical. ◆ *Deacons likewise must be serious, not double-tongued, not indulging in much wine, not greedy for money . . . .–1 Timothy 3:8*

dromedary
A camel with one hump; used for riding, for transport of goods, and also for food. ◆ *They shall bring all your kindred from all the nations as an offering to the LORD, on horses, and in chariots, and in litters, and on mules, and on dromedaries, to my holy mountain Jerusalem . . . .–Isaiah 66:20*

drum
A percussive instrument consisting of a hollow chamber or cylinder made of animal skin, played by striking the sides with the hands, sticks, mallets, or the like. ◆ *And Darius sent with them a thousand cavalry to take them back to Jerusalem in safety, with the music of drums and flutes . . . .–1 Esdras 5:2*

Elul
The name of the sixth month of the calendar used by the Israelites after the Babylonian exile, corresponding to parts of August and September. ◆ *So the wall was finished on the twenty-fifth day of the month Elul, in fifty-two days.–Nehemiah 6:15*

emerald
A brilliant green type of beryl mined in Egypt. Although it is listed as one of the stones in the high priest's breastpiece, identification is uncertain, with some scholars believing the breastpiece stone instead to be the green feldspar. ◆ *And the one seated there looks like jasper and carnelian, and around the throne is a rainbow that looks like an emerald.– Revelation 4:3*

emission
In the Bible, a discharge of semen mentioned in terms of ritual cleanliness. ◆ *If a man has an emission of semen, he shall bathe his whole body in water, and be unclean until the evening.–Leviticus 15:16*

enchanter
One who uses spells and charms to practice magic or divination. ◆ *Then the magicians, the enchanters, the Chaldeans, and the diviners came in, and I told them the dream, but they could not tell me its interpretation. –Daniel 4:7*

end of the age
The day when God puts an end to the world and judges each human being. ◆ *Just as the weeds are collected and burned up with fire, so will it be at the end of the age.–Matthew 13:40*

ends of the earth
The entire world; most distant reaches of the world; all the people of the world. ◆ *May God continue to bless us; let all the ends of the earth revere him.–Psalm 67:7*

ensign
A banner or standard, probably attached to a pole, raised to signal or identify an army, nation, or tribe. ◆ *. . . build up the highway, clear it of stones, lift up an ensign over the peoples.–Isaiah 62:10*

entrails
The intestines, or viscera; in the Bible, mentioned mainly concerning the ritual sacrifice of rams and other animals. ◆ *He washed the entrails and the legs and, with the burnt offering, turned them into smoke on the altar.–Leviticus 9:14*

ephah
A dry measure equal to a bath, a liquid measure, and to one-tenth of a homer; equivalent to three-fifths of a bushel; used to measure flour and cereals. ◆ *For a ram, you shall offer a grain offering, two-tenths of an ephah of choice flour mixed with one-third of a hin of oil . . . .–Numbers 15:6*

Ethanim
The seventh month in the calendar used by the Israelites before the Babylonian exile, corresponding to parts of September and October and the post-exilic month of Tishri. ◆ *All the people of Israel assembled to King Solomon at the festival in the month Ethanim, which is the seventh month.–1 Kings 8:2*

ewe
A female sheep. ◆ *He said, "These seven ewe lambs you shall accept from my hand, in order that you may be a witness for me that I dug this well."–Genesis 21:30*

fathom
A translation of the Greek linear measure for the distance from fingertip to fingertip of outstretched arms, equivalent to about six feet. ◆ *So they took soundings and found twenty fathoms; a little farther on they took soundings again and found fifteen fathoms.–Acts of the Apostles 27:28*

fee
Payment for the use of something, such as a beast of burden, or for a service. ◆ *So the elders of Moab and the elders of Midian departed with the fees for divination in their hand . . . .–Numbers 22:7*

fever
A general term for any of several diseases accompanied by fever, very likely including malaria, undulant fever, and dysentery. ◆ *He came and took her by the hand and lifted her up. Then the fever left her, and she began to serve them.–Mark 1:31*

figured stone
A carved or painted stone that was revered in Canaanite religion and forbidden to the Israelites. ◆ *. . . When you cross over the Jordan into the land of Canaan, you shall drive out all the inhabitants of the land from before you, destroy all their figured stones, destroy all their cast images, and demolish all their high places. –Numbers 33:51–52*

finger
A digit of the hand; a linear measure equal to three-fourths of an inch. ◆ *. . . the height of the one pillar was eighteen cubits, its circumference was twelve cubits; it was hollow and its thickness was four fingers.–Jeremiah 52:21*

first day of the month
The first day of the new moon, observed with rest and special sacrifices. ◆ *. . . In the first month, on the first day of the month, you shall take a young bull without blemish, and purify the sanctuary.–Ezekiel 45:18*

flagon
A large vessel of ceramic or metal with a handle and spout, used for wine. ◆ *Drinking was by flagons, without restraint; for the king had given orders to all the officials of his palace to do as each one desired.–Esther 1:8*

flay
To slice the flesh from the body, done to slaughtered animals as part of some sacrificial rituals and to human beings as a form of torture. ◆ *Should you not know justice?—you . . . who eat the flesh of my people, flay their skin off them . . . . –Micah 3:1–3*

flea
A small, wingless insect with strong legs for leaping that feeds on the blood of mammals; a metaphor for something small or insignificant. ◆ *"Against whom has the king of Israel come out? Whom do you pursue? A dead dog? A single flea?" –1 Samuel 24:14*

fleece
Wool shorn from a sheep ◆ *". . . I am going to lay a fleece of wool on the threshing floor; if there is dew on the fleece alone, and it is dry on all the ground, then I shall know that you will deliver Israel by my hand, as you have said."–Judges 6:37*

fleshpot
A cooking pot, probably made of clay or bronze, for meat. ◆ *The Israelites said to them, "If only we had died by the hand of the LORD in the land of Egypt, when we sat by the fleshpots and ate our fill of bread . . . ." –Exodus 16:3*

fodder
Food for livestock. ◆ *"Does the wild ass bray over its grass, or the ox low over its fodder?"–Job 6:5*

foot soldier
In biblical times, member of an army who fought from the ground and was usually equipped with a shield and a spear. ◆ *. . . the Israelites killed one hundred thousand Aramean foot soldiers in one day. –1 Kings 20:29*

foresail
On a Roman ship, a small, square sail attached to the foremast. ◆ *. . . they loosened the ropes that tied the steering-oars; then hoisting the foresail to the wind, they made for the beach.–Acts of the Apostles 27:40*

furrow
A narrow trench left in the earth by a plow. ◆ *In that first slaughter Jonathan and his armor-bearer killed about twenty men within an area about half a furrow long in an acre of land.–1 Samuel 14:14*

gadfly
A fly that bites, such as a horsefly or botfly; used in the Bible to symbolize Nebuchadnezzar, who invaded Egypt. ◆ *A beautiful heifer is Egypt—a gadfly from the north lights upon her.–Jeremiah 46:20*

gallon
A unit of liquid measure equal to four quarts. ◆ *Now standing there were six stone water jars for the Jewish rites of purification, each holding twenty or thirty gallons. –John 2:6*

gangrene
A type of spreading sore that kills the soft tissue of the body. ◆ *Avoid profane chatter, for it will lead people into more and more impiety, and their talk will spread like gangrene.–2 Timothy 2:16–17*

garments of gauze
In the Bible, items of finery owned by Jerusalem women. The exact meaning of the original Hebrew is uncertain, but it perhaps refers to clothing of a lightweight, transparent woven fabric. ◆ *In that day the Lord will take away the finery of . . . the garments of gauze, the linen garments, the turbans, and the veils.–Isaiah 3:18, 23*

gash
A cut in the skin, inflicted as a sign of mourning or during ecstatic pagan rites. ◆ *You shall not make any gashes in your flesh for the dead or tattoo any marks upon you: I am the LORD.–Leviticus 19:28*

gauntlets
Heavy gloves that cover the wrist and forearm. In the book of 4 Maccabees, iron gauntlets are instruments of torture. ◆ *. . . the guards brought in the next eldest, and after fitting themselves with iron gauntlets having sharp hooks, they bound him to the torture machine and catapult. –4 Maccabees 9:26*

general
A leader of an army; someone of high rank. ◆ *It was reported to Holofernes, the general of the Assyrian army, that the people of Israel had prepared for war . . . . –Judith 5:1*

gerah
A unit of weight equal to $1/20$ of a shekel; the smallest biblical weight. ◆ *All assessments shall be by the sanctuary shekel: twenty gerahs shall make a shekel. –Leviticus 27:25*

goat-demon
A pagan god that was part goat. ◆ *Jeroboam and his sons had prevented them from serving as priests of the LORD, and had appointed his own priests for the high places, and for the goat-demons . . . . –2 Chronicles 11:14–15*

governor's headquarters
Residence of Roman governor Pontius Pilate while he was in Jerusalem, probably Herod's palace. ◆ *Then the soldiers of the governor took Jesus into the governor's headquarters, and they gathered the whole cohort around him.–Matthew 27:27*

grape-gatherer
A laborer who harvests grapes, gathering the ripe fruit into baskets. ◆ *. . . Glean thoroughly as a vine the remnant of Israel; like a grape-gatherer, pass your hand again over its branches.–Jeremiah 6:9*

grating
A bronze network attached to the sides of the altar of burnt offering in the tabernacle. There were rings through which poles were inserted at the corners. ◆ *He made for the altar a grating, a network of bronze, under its ledge, extending halfway down.–Exodus 38:4*

gravel
Tiny stones. Biblical references to gravel may indicate its occasional presence in bread, perhaps as fragments of mill stones used to make flour or as rocks mixed in with the original grain. ◆ *Bread gained by deceit is sweet, but afterward the mouth will be full of gravel. –Proverbs 20:17*

greaves
Armor for the shins or lower legs. ◆ *He had greaves of bronze on his legs and a javelin of bronze slung between his shoulders. –1 Samuel 17:6*

guardroom
A room in a palace or fortification that is reserved for the guards. ◆ *As often as the king went into the house of the LORD, the guard carried them and brought them back to the guardroom.–1 Kings 14:28*

"half of my kingdom"
A customary, though exaggerated, promise by a king to offer half of his dominion to another. ◆ *And he solemnly swore to her, "Whatever you ask me, I will give you, even half of my kingdom." –Mark 6:23*

handbreadth
A linear measure based on the width of the hand at the base of the fingers, equal to about three inches, originating in Egypt. ◆ *You shall make around it a rim a handbreadth wide, and a molding of gold around the rim.–Exodus 25:25*

handkerchief
A cloth, perhaps similar to a napkin or towel. ◆ *. . . when the handkerchiefs or aprons that had touched his skin were brought to the sick, their diseases left them . . . . –Acts of the Apostles 19:12*

harbor
A sheltered area within a body of water, suitable for use as a port or for anchorage. ◆ *Since the harbor was not suitable for spending the winter, the majority was in favor of putting to sea from there, on the chance that somehow they could reach Phoenix, where they could spend the winter. It was a harbor of Crete, facing southwest and northwest. –Acts of the Apostles 27:12*

harrow
To smooth or break up soil after plowing, perhaps by dragging branches over it. The exact procedure is unclear. ◆ *. . . I will make Ephraim break the ground; Judah must plow; Jacob must harrow for himself.–Hosea 10:11*

haven
A protected, calm harbor. ◆ *Then they were glad because they had quiet, and he brought them to their desired haven. –Psalm 107:30*

headband
A strip of metal, such as gold or silver, worn as an ornament on the head. ◆ *In that day the Lord will take away the finery of the anklets, the headbands, and the crescents . . . .–Isaiah 3:18*

headdress
An ornamental covering worn on the head, such as a priest's hat or a woman's turban. ◆ *For Aaron's sons you shall make tunics and sashes and headdresses; you shall make them for their glorious adornment. –Exodus 28:40*

hedgehog
A small mammal of the subfamily Erinaceinae. Having both hair and spines, it protects itself by rolling into the shape of a ball with its spines stuck outward. Several species live in the Holy Land; in the Bible, Isaiah mentions it as one of the wild creatures that would take over a devastated city. ◆ *But the hawk and the hedgehog shall possess it; the owl and the raven shall live in it. –Isaiah 34:11*

hin
A unit of liquid measure equal to ⅙ of a bath, or approximately one gallon. ◆ *And you shall drink water by measure, one-sixth of a hin; at fixed times you shall drink.–Ezekiel 4:11*

hippodrome
In ancient Greek culture, an oval shaped stadium used for chariot and horse races. ◆ *Just as Eleazar was ending his prayer, the king arrived at the hippodrome with the animals and all the arrogance of his forces.–3 Maccabees 6:16*

hoarfrost
A synonym for frost and an example of the genius of God as nature's creator. ◆ *From whose womb did the ice come forth, and who has given birth to the hoarfrost of heaven?–Job 38:29*

holm tree
Possibly the holm oak *(Quercus ilex)*, a small evergreen that grows in southern Europe, or the cypress *(Cupressus sempervirens)*. ◆ *He cuts down cedars or chooses a holm tree or an oak and lets it grow strong among the trees of the forest.–Isaiah 44:14*

holy mountain
A mountain claimed by God where he reveals himself to worshipers; also Mount Zion in Jerusalem. ◆ *Extol the LORD our God, and worship at his holy mountain; for the LORD our God is holy. –Psalm 99:9*

homer
A unit of dry measure equal to 10 ephahs and to the liquid measure of 10 baths; the same volume as the *cor*. ◆ *The ephah and the bath shall be of the same measure, the bath containing one-tenth of a homer, and the ephah one-tenth of a homer; the homer shall be the standard measure. –Ezekiel 45:11*

hoopoe
A bird with a plumed crest and a long, curved bill. Although this translation of the original Hebrew word is not certain, it is likely: the bird would have been considered unclean because it foraged for insects in dunghills. ◆ *But these are the ones that you shall not eat . . . the stork, the heron, of any kind; the hoopoe and the bat.–Deuteronomy 14:12, 18*

horns of the altar
The projections at the corners of an altar, especially a sacrificial altar. ◆ *On the day I punish Israel for its transgressions, I will punish the altars of Bethel, and the horns of the altar shall be cut off and fall to the ground.–Amos 3:14*

ibex
A wild mountain goat characterized by large, backward curving horns. It is a ritually clean animal. ◆ *These are the animals you may eat . . . the deer, the gazelle, the roebuck, the wild goat, the ibex . . . . –Deuteronomy 14:5*

image
A physical representation of a human or divine form; in the Bible, an idol, or representation of a deity used in worship. ◆ *They exchanged the glory of God for the image of an ox that eats grass.–Psalm 106:20*

image of jealousy
Probably the image of the deity Asherah, a goddess of love. The original Hebrew word can mean "ardor "or "zeal" as well as "jealousy." ◆ *. . . and there, north of the altar gate, in the entrance, was this image of jealousy.–Ezekiel 8:5*

impale
To drive a sharpened stake through the body; in the ancient Near East, practiced especially by the Assyrians to display prisoners of war. Some scholars believe biblical references are to hanging for display rather than impalement. ◆ *. . . he gave them into the hands of the Gibeonites, and they impaled them on the mountain before the LORD.–2 Samuel 21:9*

imperishability
The state of being incorruptible; not subject to defilement, disease, or deterioration. Used in the New Testament, it refers to the resurrected body. ◆ *For this perishable body must put on imperishability, and this mortal body must put on immortality.–1 Corinthians 15:53*

insurrection
A rebellion against a political authority. During New Testament times, many such uprisings took place in Judea. ◆ *Now a man called Barabbas was in prison with the rebels who had committed murder during the insurrection.–Mark 15:7*

ivy
A climbing or creeping evergreen vine *(Hedera helix)*, native to Europe and Asia and sacred to Dionysus, the Greek god of wine. ◆ *. . . when a festival of Dionysus was celebrated, they were compelled to wear wreaths of ivy and to walk in the procession in honor of Dionysus.–2 Maccabees 6:7*

jacinth
A red-orange semiprecious stone; one of the gems in the high priest's breastpiece. In the book of Revelation, it is among the jewels adorning the foundations of the wall of the new Jerusalem. ◆ *They set in it four rows of stones. A row of carnelian, chrysolite, and emerald was the first row . . . and the third row, a jacinth, an agate, and an amethyst . . . . –Exodus 39:10, 12*

jasper
An opaque quartz of several colors, especially green chalcedon; part of the high priest's breastpiece. In Revelation, it is the material of the wall of the new Jerusalem and the first gemstone in its foundations. ◆ *The wall is built of jasper, while the city is pure gold, clear as glass. –Revelation 21:18*

kab
A measure of capacity used by the Israelites, slightly larger than a quart. ◆ *As the siege continued, famine in Samaria became so great that a donkey's head was sold for eighty shekels of silver, and one-fourth of a kab of dove's dung for five shekels of silver. –2 Kings 6:25*

kidnaping
In biblical times, a frequent practice in which the person captured was sold into slavery. According to Israelite law, it was a crime punishable by death. ◆ *If someone is caught kidnaping another Israelite, enslaving or selling the Israelite, then that kidnaper shall die.–Deuteronomy 24:7*

landholding
Land that is owned. ◆ *If a person consecrates to the LORD any inherited landholding, its assessment shall be in accordance with its seed requirements: fifty shekels of silver to a homer of barley seed.–Leviticus 27:16*

lane
A narrow street; a city alley. ◆ *"Then the master said to the slave, 'Go out into the roads and lanes, and compel people to come in, so that my house may be filled.'"–Luke 14:23*

Latin
The official language of the Roman Empire, thus one of the official languages of the rulers of the Holy Land in the time of Jesus. It was also used in military matters. ◆ *Many of the Jews read this inscription, because the place where Jesus was crucified was near the city; and it was written in Hebrew, in Latin, and in Greek. –John 19:20*

latter days
A subsequent time or period. ◆ *Afterward the Israelites shall return and seek the LORD their God . . . they shall come in awe to the LORD and to his goodness in the latter days. –Hosea 3:5*

latticework
A crisscrossed or perhaps mesh decoration used on the two enormous pillars at the entrance of Solomon's temple. ◆ *. . . latticework and pomegranates, all of bronze, were on the capital all around. –2 Kings 25:17*

lawyer
A person trained in law; in the Gospels, probably the same as a teacher of the law of Moses. Its usage in Titus 3:13 may refer instead to a person knowledgeable in the laws of a political state. ◆ *Just then a lawyer stood up to test Jesus. "Teacher," he said, "what must I do to inherit eternal life?"–Luke 10:25*

league
A pact or agreement. ◆ *"No one discloses to me when my son makes a league with the son of Jesse, none of you is sorry for me or discloses to me that my son has stirred up my servant against me . . . ."–1 Samuel 22:8*

lift the heel
An idiom meaning to act treacherously, deceitfully. ◆ *Even my bosom friend in whom I trusted, who ate of my bread, has lifted the heel against me.–Psalm 41:9*

lime
A caustic, white solid containing calcium oxide, produced by heating shells and limestone. It was used in mortar and plaster or mixed with soil to improve crops. ◆ *"And the peoples will be as if burned to lime, like thorns cut down, that are burned in the fire."–Isaiah 33:12*

linen wrappings
Strips of linen cloth used to wrap a dead body before burial. ◆ *He bent down to look in and saw the linen wrappings lying there, but he did not go in. –John 20:5*

litter
An enclosed seat, couch, or bed in which a person rides while it is borne by poles on the shoulders of men. ◆ *Look, it is the litter of Solomon! Around it are sixty mighty men of the mighty men of Israel . . . . –Song of Solomon 3:7*

log
Wood, usually for contruction, such as a beam; a unit of liquid measure used by the Israelites, equal to 1/72 of a bath, mentioned in the Bible concerning purification rites for lepers. ◆ *The priest shall take one of the lambs, and offer it as a guilt offering, along with the log of oil, and raise them as an elevation offering before the LORD. –Leviticus 14:12*

lotus
A common name for many plants in the Holy Land, including a low thorny tree (*Zizyphus lotus*) and the water lily of Egypt (*Nymphaea lotus*). ◆ *"Under the lotus plants it lies, in the covert of the reeds and in the marsh."–Job 40:21*

lute
A musical instrument, perhaps with three strings, a triangular body, and a long neck. ◆ *Praise him with trumpet sound; praise him with lute and harp! –Psalm 150:3*

lye
A strong alkaline solution containing potassium carbonate, produced from wood ash, used in soap and for washing. ◆ *Though you wash yourself with lye and use much soap, the stain of your guilt is still before me, says the Lord GOD. –Jeremiah 2:22*

manacles
Shackles used to restrain the hands of a prisoner, made of bronze, wood, or iron. To increase the manacles' effectiveness, the prisoner's shackled hands could be fastened to a rope around his neck. ◆ *Therefore the LORD brought against them the commanders of the army of the king of Assyria, who took Manasseh captive in manacles, bound him with fetters, and brought him to Babylon.–2 Chronicles 33:11*

mantelet
A portable shelter used to protect soldiers, during the siege of a city, from attacks by the city's defenders. The word is used in Nahum in a description of an attack on Nineveh. ◆ *He calls his officers; they stumble as they come forward; they hasten to the wall, and the mantelet is set up. –Nahum 2:5*

mastic tree
A shrublike tree that provides a resin used in medicine and as chewing gum, found throughout the Mediterranean. ◆ *"Now then, if you really saw this woman,*

tell me this: Under what tree did you see them being intimate with each other?" He answered, "Under a mastic tree."–Susanna 54

mattock
A tool similar to a modern hoe that was used to break up soil, typically made of iron, with a wooden handle. ◆ *. . . so all the Israelites went down to the Philistines to sharpen their plowshare, mattocks, axes, or sickles; The charge was two-thirds of a shekel for the plowshares and for the mattocks . . . .* –1 Samuel 13:20–21

mile
A Roman mile, which is equal to 4,854 feet, or roughly $^{11}/_{12}$ of an English mile. ◆ *Now Bethany was near Jerusalem, some two miles away, and many of the Jews had come to Martha and Mary to console them about their brother.*–John 11:18–19

mina
A unit of measurement equal to roughly one pound, or about 20 ounces. ◆ *He made three hundred shields of beaten gold; three minas of gold went into each shield; and the king put them in the House of the Forest of Lebanon.*–1 Kings 10:17

mist
Vapor; in a biblical context, a flood or swell of water. ◆ *When he utters his voice, there is a tumult of waters in the heavens, and he makes the mist rise from the ends of the earth.*–Jeremiah 10:13

mixed people
Those of foreign descent. ◆ *So I took the cup from the LORD's hand, and made all the nations to whom the LORD sent me drink it . . . Pharaoh, king of Eygpt, his servants, his officials, and all his people; all the mixed people . . . .*–Jeremiah 25:17-20

mole
An animal mentioned in the book of Isaiah. The true mole, of the genus *Talpa*, has not been observed in the Holy Land. The biblical reference may mean instead the mole rat (*Spalax typhlus*), a rodent that lives underground. ◆ *On that day people will throw away to the moles and to the bats their idols of silver and their idols of gold . . . .*–Isaiah 2:20

moonstone
A translucent feldspar mineral with a luster similar to that of an opal, mentioned as one of the stones on the high priest's breastpiece. ◆ *You shall set in it four rows of stones. A row of carnelian, chrysolite, and emerald shall be the first row; and the second row a turquoise, a sapphire and a moonstone . . . .*–Exodus 28:17–18

most holy place
The innermost room of tabernacle or temple. The word is also used in Ezekiel for land put aside for the Zadokite priests to live on. ◆ *Then the priests brought the ark of the covenant of the LORD to its place, in the inner sanctuary of the house, in the most holy place, underneath the wings of the cherubim.*–1 Kings 8:6

muster
An account, inventory, or registry of soldiers. ◆ *Moreover Uzziah had an army of soldiers, fit for war, in divisions according to the numbers in the muster made by the secretary Jeiel and the officer Maaseiah . . . .* –2 Chronicles 26:11

muzzle
A covering for an animal's mouth, which prevented the animal from eating or biting. Mosaic law explicitly prohibited the muzzling of working oxen. ◆ *You shall not muzzle an ox while it is treading out the grain.* –Deuteronomy 25:4

myrtle
A leafy evergreen shrub used to cover booths during the Festival of Booths. ◆ *Instead of the thorn shall come up the cypress; instead of the brier shall come up the myrtle . . . .*–Isaiah 55:13

network
A bronze grating, or screen, on the tabernacle's altar of burnt offerings. Four bronze rings attached to it held the poles for transporting the altar. ◆ *You shall also make for it a grating, a network of bronze; and on the net you shall make four bronze rings at its four corners.*–Exodus 27:4

nighthawk
A bird referred to in the Bible that may be a barn owl or another type of owl. ◆ *These you shall regard as detestable among the birds. They shall not be eaten; they are an abomination . . . the ostrich, the nighthawk, the sea gull, the hawk of any kind . . . .* –Leviticus 11:13, 16

Nisan
The first month of the Jewish calendar, corresponding to parts of March and April. Before the Babylonian exile, it was called Abib. In the book of Esther, lots were cast in the month of Nisan to determine the future. ◆ *In the first month, which is the month of Nisan, in the twelfth year of King Ahasuerus, they cast Pur—which means "the lot" . . . .*–Esther 3:7

obelisk
A tall, four-sided stone pillar, tapering toward the top and capped by a small pyramid, built in Egypt to honor the sun god, Re. ◆ *He shall break the obelisks of Heliopolis, which is in the land of Egypt; and the temples of the gods of Egypt he shall burn with fire.*–Jeremiah 43:13

object of horror
A people or territory punished by God, resulting in such grave devastation as to horrify observers. ◆ *You shall become an object of horror, a proverb, and a byword among all the peoples where the LORD will lead you.*–Deuteronomy 28:37

oblation
A sacrifice or offering. ◆ *As midday passed, they raved on until the time of the offering of the oblation, but there was no voice, no answer, and no response.* –1 Kings 18:29

omer
A dry measurement equal to $^{1}/_{10}$ of an ephah, or about two quarts. ◆ *And Moses said to Aaron, "Take a jar, and put an omer of manna in it, and place it before the Lord, to be kept throughout your generations."* –Exodus 16:33

onycha
A plant, or perhaps a mollusk. In the Bible, it was an ingredient in the incense burned at the altar of incense. ◆ *The LORD said to Moses: Take sweet spices, stacte, and onycha, and galbanum, sweet spices with pure frankincense (an equal part of each) and make an incense blended as by the perfumer . . . .* –Exodus 30:34–5

osprey
A large hawk (*Pandion haliaetus*) that feeds on fish. The reference in the Bible may be instead to the short-toed eagle or a variety of vulture, birds more common in the Holy Land. ◆ *You may eat any clean birds. But these are the ones that you shall not eat: the eagle, the vulture, the osprey . . . . –Deuteronomy 14:11–12*

palanquin
A canopied throne or couch carried, by means of poles, on men's shoulders. ◆ *King Solomon made himself a palanquin from the wood of Lebanon. –Song of Solomon 3:9*

pattern
In the Bible, usually instructions given by the Lord detailing how the tabernacle and other sacred objects were to be built. ◆ *In accordance with all that I show you concerning the pattern of the tabernacle and of all its furniture, so you shall make it. –Exodus 25:9*

peacock
A species of peafowl not native to the Holy Land, imported from India. The Bible names the birds in the list of treasure brought to Israel by Solomon's merchant vessels. However, it may be a mistranslation of the word for monkey. ◆ *For the king's ships went to Tarshish with the servants of Huram; once every three years the ships of Tarshish used to come bringing gold, silver, ivory, apes, and peacocks. –2 Chronicles 9:21*

pearl
A lustrous, valuable gem, originating as a deposit that some mollusks create around invasive foreign matter. In biblical times, pearls were worn by the wealthy and used for trade. ◆ *"Again, the kingdom of heaven is like a merchant in search of fine pearls; on finding one pearl of great value, he went and sold all that he had and bought it."–Matthew 13:45–46*

peasantry
Small landowners or farmworkers; people living in a rural, rather than in an urban, setting. ◆ *The peasantry prospered in Israel, they grew fat on plunder, because you arose, Deborah, arose as a mother in Israel. –Judges 5:7*

peddler
A seller of merchandise who travels from place to place or door to door; in the Bible, a pejorative term for one who adulterates or sells the word of God. ◆ *For we are not peddlers of God's word like so many; but in Christ we speak as persons of sincerity, as persons sent from God and standing in his presence.–2 Corinthians 2:17*

pediment
In the Bible, the stone base upon which the molten sea was placed. It was a substitute for the bronze oxen, which were removed to pay tribute to the king of Assyria. ◆ *Then King Ahaz cut off the frames of the stands, and removed the laver from them; he removed the sea from the bronze oxen that were under it, and put it on a pediment of stone.–2 Kings 16:17*

penknife
A knife used to make, sharpen, and repair reed writing instruments. It was also useful for cutting papyrus. ◆ *As Jehudi read three or four columns, the king would cut them off with a penknife and throw them into the fire in the brazier, until the entire scroll was consumed in the fire that was in the brazier. –Jeremiah 36:23*

perishable
Something subject to deterioration or ruin. ◆ *So it is with the resurrection of the dead. What is sown is perishable, what is raised is imperishable.–1 Corinthians 15:42*

phalanx
Armed infantry in close formation. ◆ *Then Simon brought forward his force and engaged the phalanx in battle (for the cavalry was exhausted); they were overwhelmed by him and fled . . . .–1 Maccabees 10:82*

phantom
An apparition; something that appears to be real, but is not. ◆ *They are like a dream when one awakes; on awaking you despise their phantoms.–Psalm 73:20*

pharmacist
One who prepares and dispenses drugs. In Ecclesiasticus, the pharmacist is said to use God's works to make his mixture, or medicine. ◆ *The Lord created medicines out of the earth . . . the pharmacist makes a mixture from them. God's works will never be finished; and from him health spreads over all the earth. –Ecclesiasticus 38:4–8*

phoenix
In the Bible, the mythical bird who rose from its own ashes to live again; also a harbor in Crete. ◆ *"Then I thought, 'I shall die in my nest, and I shall multiply my days like the phoenix . . . .'"–Job 29:18*

pick
An iron tool, with a wooden handle, sharpened at one or both ends. King David is said to have put the defeated Ammonites to work with iron picks. ◆ *He brought out the people who were in it, and set them to work with saws and iron picks and iron axes, or sent them to the brickworks. Thus he did to all the cities of the Ammonites.–2 Samuel 12:31*

piece of money
Currency of unknown worth, though as used in the Bible, perhaps having significant value. ◆ *. . . they showed him sympathy and comforted him for all the evil that the LORD had brought upon him; and each of them gave him a piece of money and a gold ring. –Job 42:11*

pilot
The captain or other person who steers a ship. ◆ *Or look at ships: though they are so large that it takes strong winds to drive them, yet they are guided by a very small rudder wherever the will of the pilot directs. –James 3:4*

pistachio nut
A greenish, edible seed, encased in a shell. It is considered a delicacy in the Near East and was one of the foods Jacob gave his sons to take back to Egypt as a gift for Pharaoh. ◆ *"Take some of the choice fruits of the land in your bags, and carry them down as a present to the man—a little balm and a little honey, gum, resin, pistachio nuts, and almonds."–Genesis 43:11*

pitch
A sticky substance derived from plant resin or from natural asphalt, used for mortar, waterproofing, and as an adhesive or sealant. The distinction between pitch and bitumen is sometimes unclear. ◆ *When she could hide him no longer she got a papyrus basket for him, and plastered it with bitumen and pitch . . . .–Exodus 2:3*

plane tree
A deciduous tree *(Plantanus orientalis)* characterized by a height as tall as 60 feet and the annual shedding of its bark. ◆ *The cedars in the garden of God could not rival it, nor the fir trees equal its boughs; the plane trees were as nothing compared with its branches; no tree in the garden of God was like it in beauty. –Ezekiel 31:8*

plate
A kitchen utensil or, more commonly in the Bible, a vessel used for offerings. Typically it was made of hammered metal. ◆ *. . . his offering was one silver plate weighing one hundred thirty shekels, one silver basin weighing seventy shekels, according to the shekel of the sanctuary, both of them full of choice flour mixed with oil for a grain offering . . . .–Numbers 7:13*

poplar
A tree that flourished in the Holy Land, along with oaks and terebinths. According to scholars, the biblical poplar may be one of two varieties: the Storax (*Styrax officinalis*) or the white poplar *(Populus alba)*. ◆ *They sacrifice on the tops of the mountains, and make offerings upon the hills, under oak, poplar, and terebinth, because their shade is good. –Hosea 4:13*

porphyry
A purple rock with feldspar crystals; in Esther, part of the decorative floor in the king's palace at Susa. ◆ *. . . There were couches of gold and silver on a mosaic pavement of porphyry, marble, mother-of-pearl, and colored stones.–Esther 1:6*

poultice
A mixture of herbs and medicines, typically heated and applied to a wound or sore. ◆ *For neither herb nor poultice cured them, but it was your word, O Lord, that heals all people.–Wisdom of Solomon 16:12*

pound
A weight equal to about 3/4 of a U.S. pound; in the Gospel of Luke, a monetary unit. ◆ *"He summoned ten of his slaves, and gave them ten pounds, and said to them, 'Do business with these until I come back.'" –Luke 19:13*

prefect
An official who ruled over a city or province. ◆ *Then the king promoted Daniel, gave him many great gifts, and made him ruler over the whole province of Babylon and chief prefect over all the wise men of Babylon.–Daniel 2:48*

president
A governor under the Persian ruler. Daniel was appointed president by King Darius above many satraps, whose envy resulted in Daniel being thrown in the den of lions. ◆ *Soon Daniel distinguished himself above all the other presidents and satraps because an excellent spirit was in him, and the king planned to appoint him over the whole kingdom. –Daniel 6:3*

princess
The daughter of a king. According to 1 Kings 11:3, Solomon's wives numbered 700 princesses and 300 concubines. ◆ *The princess is decked in her chamber with gold-woven robes . . . .–Psalm 45:13*

prize
As used in the book of Jeremiah, booty or spoil for the victors. In Philippians 3:14, the term refers to a higher calling. ◆ *For I will surely save you, and you shall not fall by the sword; but you shall have your life as a prize of war, because you have trusted in me, says the LORD. –Jeremiah 39:18*

proconsul
An official representing the Roman government in the provinces. He held power in military and judicial matters. ◆ *He was with the proconsul, Sergius Paulus, an intelligent man, who summoned Barnabas and Saul and wanted to hear the word of God.–Acts of the Apostles 13:7*

propitiation
An act of atonement to secure pardon for a deed offensive to God. ◆ *For a blameless man was quick to act as their champion; he brought forward the shield of his ministry, prayer and propitiation by incense . . . . –Wisdom of Solomon 18:21*

proselyte
A new convert. In the Bible, the term specifically refers to a convert to Judaism. ◆ *What they said pleased the whole community, and they chose Stephen, a man full of faith and the Holy Spirit, together with Philip, Prochorus, Nicanor, Timon, Parmenas, and Nicolaus, a proselyte of Antioch.–Acts of the Apostles 6:5*

pyre
A pile of wood, intended for the burning of human bodies. In the book of Isaiah, it may mean a place for human sacrifice. ◆ *For his burning place has long been prepared; truly it is made ready for the king, its pyre made deep and wide, with fire and wood in abundance; the breath of the LORD, like a stream of sulfur, kindles it.–Isaiah 30:33*

quartermaster
An officer in the army, responsible for the distribution of rations and supplies. ◆ *The word that the prophet Jeremiah commanded Seraiah son of Neriah son of Mahseiah, when he went with King Zedekiah of Judah to Babylon, in the fourth year of his reign. Seraiah was the quartermaster. –Jeremiah 51:59*

quiver
A bag, often made of leather, designed to hold arrows. Typically a quiver was worn over the shoulder. ◆ *"Now then, take your weapons, your quiver and your bow, and go out to the field, and hunt game for me . . . . –Genesis 27:3*

rabble
A disorderly crowd. In Numbers, the word may refer to non-Israelites who came out of Egypt with the Israelites. ◆ *The rabble among them had a strong craving; and the Israelites also wept again, and said, "If only we had meat to eat!" –Numbers 11:4*

Rabmag
The title of an official in the court of the Babylonian king Nebuchadnezzar. In Jeremiah, he was present at the fall of Jerusalem. ◆ *So Nebuzaradan the captain of the guard, Nebushazban the Rabsaris, Nergal-sharezer the Rabmag, and all the chief officers of the king of Babylon sent and took Jeremiah from the court of the guard . . . . –Jeremiah 39:13–14*

Rabshakeh
A high–ranking Assyrian official. ◆ *The king of Assyria sent the Rabshakeh from Lachish to King Hezekiah at Jerusalem, with a great army. He stood by the conduit of the upper pool on the highway to the Fuller's Field.–Isaiah 36:2*

rack
An instrument of torture, referred to especially in 2 and 4 Maccabees. It was usually a frame on which a body was stretched. ◆ *"Will you not consider this, that if you disobey, nothing remains for you but to die on the rack?"–4 Maccabees 8:11*

Rahab
A mythical monster, possibly the same as Leviathan, or the dragon destroyed by God; used metaphorically as a derogatory name for Egypt. It was also the name of the prostitute who helped Joshua's men. ◆ *You crushed Rahab like a carcass; you scattered your enemies with your mighty arm.–Psalm 89:10*

raft
A collection of reeds or logs bound together to form a water vehicle either floated by itself or towed by a boat. Hiram of Tyre transported timber for the temple by making it into rafts. ◆ *"We will cut whatever timber you need from Lebanon, and bring it to you as rafts by sea to Joppa . . . ."–2 Chronicles 2:16*

raid
In the Bible, an attack or invasion either of a military or criminal nature. ◆ *While he was still speaking, another came and said, "The Chaldeans formed three columns, made a raid on the camels and carried them off, and killed the servants with the edge of the sword; I alone have escaped to tell you."–Job 1:17*

rampart
A steep earthen embankment that strengthened the walls of a city.
◆ *Joab's forces came and besieged him in Abel of Beth-maacah; they threw up a siege ramp against the city, and it stood against the rampart. Joab's forces were battering the wall to break it down.–2 Samuel 20:15*

ram's horn
A trumpet, also called a shofar, used for signaling. It was blown to summon the Israelites to battle and to prayer. ◆ *"When they make a long blast with the ram's horn, as soon as you hear the sound of the trumpet, then all the people shall shout with a great shout; and the wall of the city will fall down flat, and all the people shall charge straight ahead."–Joshua 6:5*

Rechabites
An Israelite sect that followed the precepts of Jehonadab, perhaps an ancestor of the members, who abstained from wine and lived a nomadic life. ◆ *Go to the house of the Rechabites, and speak with them, and bring them to the house of the* LORD *. . . .–Jeremiah 35:2*

recorder
One of the highest–ranking officials in Israel's royal court. His duties included advising the king and representing him in negotiations. ◆ *Then Eliakim son of Hilkiah, who was in charge of the palace, and Shebna the secretary, and Joah son of Asaph, the recorder, came to Hezekiah with their clothes torn and told him the words of the Rabshakeh.–2 Kings 18:37*

regiment
A division in the Israelite army, organized by tribal group. ◆ *The Israelites shall camp each in their respective regiments, under ensigns by their ancestral houses; they shall camp facing the tent of meeting on every side. –Numbers 2:2*

resin
Yellowish to brownish substance produced from a variety of plants of a brittle or gummy texture. Resins were an important product of trade in the Near East. ◆ *Now the manna was like coriander seed, and its color was like the color of gum resin.–Numbers 11:7*

retinue
Attendants and courtiers who followed a king, queen, or other official. ◆ *She came to Jerusalem with a very great retinue, with camels bearing spices, and very much gold, and precious stones; and when she came to Solomon, she told him all that was on her mind.–1 Kings 10:2*

revelry
Merrymaking or carousing. As used in the Bible, the term has negative connotations and is associated with drunkenness, gluttony, and sexual indulgence.
◆ *Therefore they shall now be the first to go into exile, and the revelry of the loungers shall pass away.–Amos 6:7*

reviler
Someone who slanders or insults another human being or God. ◆ *Do you not know that wrongdoers will not inherit the kingdom of God? Do not be deceived! Fornicators, idolaters, adulterers, male prostitutes, sodomites, thieves, the greedy, drunkards, revilers, robbers—none of these will inherit the kingdom of God.–1 Corinthians 6:9–10*

rooster
A male fowl. Used only once in the Bible, the Hebrew word is usually translated "cock." ◆ *Three things are stately in their stride; four are stately in their gait: the lion, which is mightiest among wild animals and does not turn back before any; the strutting rooster, the he-goat, and a king striding before his people.–Proverbs 30:29–31*

rue
An herb (possibly *Ruta latifolia Salisb* or *Ruta graveolens*) used as a condiment or a medicine. Rue grows as a shrub and has gray-green leaves and clusters of yellow flowers. ◆ *"But woe to you Pharisees! For you tithe mint and rue and herbs of all kinds, and neglect justice and the love of God; it is these you ought to have practiced, without neglecting the others."–Luke 11:42*

rug
Fabric floor covering; in the Bible, either a cloak or a carpet. ◆ *Jael came out to meet Sisera, and said to him, "Turn aside, my lord, turn aside to me; have no fear." So he turned aside to her into the tent, and she covered him with a rug.–Judges 4:18*

runner
A guard who accompanied the royal chariot. A runner might also bring news of war from the front to the king. In 1 Corinthians 9:24, the word refers to a competitor in a race. ◆ *One runner runs to meet another, and one messenger to meet another, to tell the king of Babylon that his city is taken from end to end . . . . –Jeremiah 51:31*

S

sacrilege
A religiously offensive image or action. In Matthew, the word may refer to the statue of himself that Caligula wanted to erect in the temple. ◆ *"So when you see the desolating sacrilege standing in the holy place,*

as was spoken of by the prophet Daniel (let the reader understand) then those in Judea must flee to the mountains . . . .
–Matthew 24:15–16

saffron
A spice derived from crocus flowers (*Crocus sativus*), used to dye clothing and to flavor food. ◆ *Your channel is an orchard of . . . nard and saffron, calamus and cinnamon, with all trees of frankincense, myrrh and aloes, with all chief spices . . . .*
–Song of Solomon 4:13–14

sages
Wise men; often officials of the royal court. ◆ *Then the king consulted the sages who knew the laws (for this was the king's procedure toward all who were versed in law and custom . . . .)–Esther 1:13*

salve
A medicinal ointment. ◆ *Therefore I counsel you to buy from me gold refined by fire so that you may be rich; and white robes to clothe you and to keep the shame of your nakedness from being seen; and salve to anoint your eyes so that you may see.*
–Revelation 3:18

sapphire
A gem that is a variety of corundum, often of a transparent blue. The biblical translation is uncertain, however, and is sometimes rendered lapis lazuli. ◆ *Under his feet there was something like a pavement of sapphire stone, like the very heaven for clearness.–Exodus 24:10*

satrap
Official who governed provinces in the Persian Empire. Satraps were often members of the Persian nobility. ◆ *He wrote in behalf of all the Jews who were going up from his kingdom to Judea, in the interest of their freedom, that no officer or satrap or governor or treasurer should forcibly enter their doors . . . .–1 Esdras 4:49*

scale armor
A heavy metal tunic, made of small scales or interlocking rings, worn to protect the body during warfare. ◆ *But a certain man drew his bow and unknowingly struck the king of Israel between the scale armor and the breastplate; so he said to the driver of his chariot, "Turn around, and carry me out of the battle, for I am wounded."*
–1 Kings 22:34

scarf
A gauze veil, worn by women, which covered the head and face. ◆ *In that day the LORD will take away the finery of the anklets, the headbands, and the crescents; the pendants, the bracelets, and the scarfs . . . .*
–Isaiah 3:18–19

scented wood
Possibly a type of cypress. The wood was valued both for its aroma and its beautiful grain. The Romans often polished this wood to a high gloss and used it to make tabletops. ◆ *And the merchants of the earth weep and mourn for her, since no one buys their cargo anymore, cargo of gold, silver, jewels and pearls, fine linen, purple, silk and scarlet, all kinds of scented wood . . . .*
–Revelation 18:11–12

scorpion
An arachnid. In the Holy Land, the most common is the *Buthus quinquestriatus*, with two pinchers and an elongated, segmented body and tail. The tip of the tail carries a sting, which, though painful, is rarely fatal. ◆ *See, I have given you authority to tread on snakes and scorpions, and over all the power of the enemy; and nothing will hurt you.–Luke 10:19*

scurvy
A fungal disease characterized by flakes or scales on the scalp and by intense itching. It is not related to the disease of the same name caused by a deficiency of vitamin C. ◆ *The LORD will afflict you with the boils of Egypt, with ulcers, scurvy, and itch, of which you cannot be healed.*
–Deuteronomy 28:27

scythe
A curved, sharpened blade; in the Bible, attached to a war chariot. It kept the infantry at a distance and was a popular weapon among the Persians and the Greeks. ◆ *Each of them had a Greek force of one hundred ten thousand infantry, five thousand three hundred cavalry, twenty-two elephants, and three hundred chariots armed with scythes.–2 Maccabees 13:2*

sea gull
An aquatic web-footed, long-winged bird of the family Laridae. Several types of gulls live along the Mediterranean and the Sea of Galilee: the common gull, the black-headed gull, the herring gull, and the lesser black-backed gull. ◆ *These you shall regard as detestable among the birds. They shall not be eaten; they are an abomination . . . the ostrich, the nighthawk, the sea gull, the hawk of any kind . . . .*
–Leviticus 11:13–16

secretary
In the Bible, a scribe or a state official. ◆ *Then Shaphan the secretary came to the king, and reported to the king, "Your servants have emptied out the money that was found in the house, and have delivered it into the hand of the workers who have oversight of the house of the LORD."–2 Kings 22:9*

sect
A group with clearly defined religious or philosophical principles, as in a school of thought. ◆ *But some believers who belonged to the sect of the Pharisees stood up and said, "It is necessary for them to be circumcised and ordered to keep the law of Moses."*
–Acts of the Apostles 15:5

second death
The death of the soul, manifested by eternal suffering in a fiery lake. ◆ *"But as for the cowardly, the faithless, the polluted, the murderers, the fornicators, the sorcerers, the idolaters, and all liars, their place will be in the lake that burns with fire and sulfur, which is the second death."–Revelation 21:8*

seer
A prophet; one who receives messages from God. In some biblical passages, it refers to someone who offers advice to the king when he is faced with a difficult decision. ◆ *When David rose in the morning, the word of the LORD came to the prophet Gad, David's seer, saying, "Go and say to David: Thus says the LORD: Three things I offer you; choose one of them, and I will do it to you."–2 Samuel 24:11–12*

senate
A governing body. In the Bible, it was either a Jewish legislative and judicial body made up of elders and headed by the high priest or a legislative, administrative, and judiciary body in Rome. ◆ *So they went to Rome and entered the senate chamber and said, "The high priest Jonathan and the Jewish nation have sent us to renew the former friendship and alliance with them."–1 Maccabees 12:3*

sentinel
A watchman, often posted at gates or on city walls, who guarded against enemy attack. He also kept a lookout for runners

arriving with messages for the king. ◆ *Then the sentinel saw another man running; and the sentinel called to the gatekeeper and said, "See, another man running alone!" The king said, "He also is bringing tidings."* *–2 Samuel 18:26*

sentry
A soldier who stands guard. ◆ *From a distance Judith called out to the sentries at the gates, "Open, open the gate! God, our God, is with us, still showing his power in Israel and his strength against our enemies, as he has done today!"–Judith 13:11*

shackles
Rings or bands made of wood, iron, or bronze and joined together with chains. They encircled a prisoner's wrists or ankles, making movement difficult. ◆ *So the Philistines seized him and gouged out his eyes. They brought him down to Gaza and bound him with bronze shackles; and he ground at the mill in the prison.–Judges 16:21*

shades
The world inhabited by the dead. ◆ *"The shades below tremble, the waters and their inhabitants."–Job 26:5*

sheaf
Stalks of wheat or barley tied into a bundle. According to Mosaic law, forgotten sheaves were to be left for gleaners. ◆ *When you reap your harvest in your field and forget a sheaf in the field, you shall not go back to get it; it shall be left for the alien, the orphan, and the widow, so that the LORD your God may bless you in all your undertakings.* *–Deuteronomy 24:19*

Shebat
The 11th month in the Jewish calendar, corresponding to parts of January and February. ◆ *On the twenty-fourth day of the eleventh month, the month of Shebat, in the second year of Darius, the word of the LORD came to the prophet Zechariah son of Berechiah son of Iddo; and Zechariah said, In the night I saw a man riding on a red horse . . . .–Zechariah 1:7–8*

sheepfold
Often a space within a circular stone wall roofed with branches of thorny bushes. Sheep were herded into the protected area at night to keep them safe from predators. The shepherd would then make his bed in front of the entrance and sleep by his flock. ◆ *"Very truly, I tell you, anyone who does not enter the sheepfold by the gate but climbs in by another way is a thief and a bandit."–John 10.1*

sheet
As seen in a vision by Peter, possibly a ship's sail. In Isaiah 25:7, the word may mean either "shroud" or "veil." ◆ *He saw the heaven opened and something like a large sheet coming down, being lowered to the ground by its four corners.* *–Acts of the Apostles 10:11*

sherd
Potsherd, a piece of broken pottery. It was often used for writing on, or for carrying water or hot coals. Its edges were also used to scrape boils, as in Job 2:8. ◆ *. . . its breaking is like that of a potter's vessel that is smashed so ruthlessly that among its fragments not a sherd is found for taking fire from the hearth, or dipping water out of the cistern.–Isaiah 30:14*

shoes
Foot covering. Working people wore simple sandals consisting of a wooden, leather, or woven rush sole strapped onto the foot. The rich wore many different types of foot covering. Some were sandals with straps elaborately crisscrossed over the foot and ankle. Others were shoes like a low boot. Some had upturned toes. ◆ *As shoes for your feet put on whatever will make you ready to proclaim the gospel of peace. –Ephesians 6:15*

shoulder-pieces
Straps attached to the priest's ephod. ◆ *You shall set the two stones on the shoulder-pieces of the ephod, as stones of remembrance for the sons of Israel; and Aaron shall bear their names before the LORD on his two shoulders for remembrance. –Exodus 28:12*

shovel
A small bronze tool used to clear away the ashes from the altar; as used in Isaiah, a large, shallow shovel used to winnow grain. ◆ *. . . and they shall put on it all the utensils of the altar, which are used for the service there, the firepans, the forks, the shovels, and the basins, all the utensils of the altar . . . . –Numbers 4:14*

shroud
Fabric that literally means "covering"; in Isaiah, it probably means fine linen garments worn by mourners. ◆ *And he will destroy on this mountain the shroud that is cast over all peoples, the sheet that is spread over all nations . . . .–Isaiah 25:7*

sickle
A tool made from a curved piece of sharpened metal, affixed to a wooden handle, used to harvest wheat or barley. The earliest sickles were made of flint embedded in wood. ◆ *If you go into your neighbor's standing grain, you may pluck the ears with your hand, but you shall not put a sickle to your neighbor's standing grain.* *–Deuteronomy 23:25*

silage
Feed made for livestock. ◆ *On that day your cattle will graze in broad pastures; and the oxen and donkeys that till the ground will eat silage, which has been winnowed with shovel and fork.–Isaiah 30:23–24*

sinew
Tendons, probably used in the phrase "iron sinew" in the passage from Isaiah to mean "stiff-necked." ◆ *. . . I know that you are obstinate, and your neck is an iron sinew and your forehead brass . . . .* *–Isaiah 48:4*

Sivan
The third month in the Jewish calendar, corresponding to parts of May and June. ◆ *The king's secretaries were summoned at that time, in the third month, which is the month of Sivan, on the twenty-third day; and an edict was written . . . .–Esther 8:9*

sky
The upper atmosphere; in the Bible, also called dome, firmament, or heaven. ◆ *God called the dome Sky. And there was evening and there was morning, the second day.–Genesis 1:8*

snail
A mollusk; in Psalms, possibly a slug. ◆ *Let them be like the snail that dissolves into slime; like the untimely birth that never sees the sun.–Psalm 58:8*

soap
A cleansing agent made in biblical times by combining oil, probably from olives, with alkali, a salt taken from the ashes of certain plants. The reference to fuller's soap in Malachi 3:2 suggests it was also

used to clean clothes. ♦ *I shall be condemned; why then do I labor in vain? If I wash myself with soap and cleanse my hands with lye, yet you will plunge me into filth, and my own clothes will abhor me.–Job 9:29–31*

solstice
Longest day of the year (first day of summer) and shortest day of the year (first day of winter). ♦ *For it is he who gave me unerring knowledge of what exists . . . the beginning and end and middle of times, the alternations of the solstices and the changes of the seasons . . . .–Wisdom of Solomon 7:17–18*

songs of swans
According to myth, sorrowful songs uttered by swans before they die. ♦ *Neither the melodies of sirens nor the songs of swans attract the attention of their hearers as did the voices of the children in torture calling to their mother. –4 Maccabees 15:21*

sorcery
Use of magic or witchcraft, prohibited by biblical law. ♦ *". . . and the light of a lamp will shine in you no more; and the voice of bridegroom and bride will be heard in you no more; for your merchants were the magnates of the earth, and all nations were deceived by your sorcery."–Revelation 18:23*

sorcerer
Someone knowledgeable in witchcraft, reviled by biblical writers but apparently widely practiced. ♦ *Then I will draw near to you for judgment; I will be swift to bear witness against the sorcerers, against the adulterers, against those who swear falsely . . . against those who thrust aside the alien, and do not fear me, says the LORD of hosts. –Malachi 3:5*

span
A linear measure based on the distance between the ends of the extended thumb and little finger. A span is equal to about nine inches. ♦ *And there came out from the camp of the Philistines a champion named Goliath, of Gath, whose height was six cubits and a span.–1 Samuel 17:4*

specter
A ghost or apparition. ♦ *. . . they all . . . were driven by monstrous specters, and now were paralyzed by their souls' surrender; for sudden and unexpected fear overwhelmed them . . . .–Wisdom of Solomon 17:14–15*

spelt
An inferior-quality wheat (perhaps *Triticum spelta*). It is able to grow in areas of barren soil where a regular crop of wheat cannot grow. In Ezekiel 4:9, it is combined with other grains and legumes to make a coarse bread. ♦ *When they have leveled its surface, do they not scatter dill, sow cummin, and plant wheat in rows and barley in its proper place, and spelt as the border? –Isaiah 28:25*

spider
An arachnid. There are hundreds of varieties in the Holy Land. In Isaiah, the plans of the wicked are likened to a spider's web. ♦ *They hatch adders' eggs, and weave the spider's web; whoever eats their eggs dies, and the crushed egg hatches out a viper.–Isaiah 59:5*

sponge
The porous skeleton of a type of marine animal. It is commonly found along the shores of the Mediterranean Sea. In the Gospel of Mark, a sponge soaked with wine was offered to Jesus on the cross. ♦ *And someone ran, filled a sponge with sour wine, put it on a stick, and gave it to him to drink, saying, "Wait, let us see whether Elijah will come to take him down."–Mark 15:36*

sport
To make fun of or to ridicule, or to entertain oneself. ♦ *"But now they make sport of me, those who are younger than I, whose fathers I would have disdained to set with the dogs of my flock."–Job 30:1*

spot
A condition that marks a skin disease, feared to be leprosy. ♦ *When a person has on the skin of his body a swelling or an eruption or a spot, and it turns into a leprous disease on the skin of his body, he shall be brought to Aaron the priest or to one of his sons the priests.–Leviticus 13:2*

squad
A group of four soldiers who took charge of one of the four watches of the night. The watches lasted three or four hours each. In Acts of the Apostles, Peter was guarded by four squads, equaling 16 soldiers. ♦ *When he had seized him, he put him in prison and handed him over to four squads of soldiers to guard him, intending to bring him out to the people after the Passover. –Acts of the Apostles 12:4*

stacte
An ingredient in the holy incense burned in the tent of meeting that was probably gum. It was perhaps extracted from the storax tree (*Styrax officinalis*). ♦ *The LORD said to Moses: Take sweet spices, stacte, and onycha, and galbanum, sweet spices with pure frankincense (an equal part of each), and make an incense blended as by the perfumer, seasoned with salt, pure and holy . . . .–Exodus 30:34–5*

stag
A male deer, perhaps the small fallow deer (*Dama dama*) or the red deer (*Cervus elaphus*). In the Bible, the word may refer to a mountain goat. ♦ *Make haste, my beloved, and be like a gazelle or a young stag upon the mountains of spices! –Song of Solomon 8:14*

stake
Several uses in the Bible: a peg used to secure a tent to the ground; something at issue or in question; or a reassurance of God's presence. ♦ *Look on Zion, the city of our appointed festivals! Your eyes will see Jerusalem, a quiet habitation, an immovable tent, whose stakes will never be pulled up, and none of whose ropes will be broken. –Isaiah 33:20*

stall
A place to feed and shelter individual livestock. Israelite houses often had stalls for their animals in their houses. In 1 Kings 4:26, Solomon was said to have 40,000 stalls for his horses. ♦ *Alas for those who lie on beds of ivory, and lounge on their couches, and eat lambs from the flock, and calves from the stall . . . .–Amos 6:4*

standard
In the Bible, either an identifying flag or emblem for troops to rally under or rules set by tradition or authority. ♦ *The standard of the camp of Judah set out first, company by company, and over the whole company was Nahshon son of Amminadab. –Numbers 10:14*

statute
A law pertaining either to a ritual or to a civil matter. ♦ *This shall be a statute to you forever: In the seventh month, on the tenth day of the month, you shall deny yourselves, and shall do no work, neither the citizen nor the alien who resides among you. –Leviticus 16:29*

steppe
The wide region between fertile agricultural land and the desert, which supports minimal vegetation, such as grass and shrubs. The same Hebrew word is often translated elsewhere as "desert" or "wilderness." ◆ *. . . To the rest of the Merarites [were given] on the east side of the Jordan, out of the tribe of Reuben: Bezer in the steppe with its pasture lands, Jahzah with its pasture lands . . . .–1 Chronicles 6:77–78*

stork
A bird renowned for its fidelity and attentive care of its young. The stork referred to in the Bible may be the white stork (*Ciconia ciconia*) or the black stork (*Ciconia nigra*). ◆ *The trees of the LORD are watered abundantly, the cedars of Lebanon that he planted. In them the birds build their nests; the stork has its home in the fir trees. –Psalm 104:16–17*

strong drink
An alcoholic drink, probably barley beer or a fermented drink made from another grain or fruit. Nazirites were forbidden to drink it. ◆*". . . but he said to me, 'You shall conceive and bear a son. So then drink no wine or strong drink, and eat nothing unclean, for the boy shall be a nazirite to God from birth to the day of his death.'" –Judges 13:7*

stronghold
A fortress. In the Bible, the word is also used to refer to God as a refuge for the righteous. ◆ *Then the prophet Gad said to David, "Do not remain in the stronghold; leave, and go into the land of Judah." So David left, and went into the forest of Hereth.–1 Samuel 22:5*

stubble
Remains of stalks of grain left after harvesting. In the Bible, it is often used to mean something that is worthless.
◆ *Scarcely are they planted, scarcely sown, scarcely has their stem taken root in the earth, when he blows upon them, and they wither, and the tempest carries them off like stubble. –Isaiah 40:24*

stucco
Plaster used on the interior walls of buildings. ◆ *A mind settled on an intelligent thought is like stucco decoration that makes a wall smooth.–Ecclesiasticus 22:17*

stylus
A sharp-pointed tool for marking or engraving. ◆ *The carpenter stretches a line, marks it out with a stylus, fashions it with planes, and marks it with a compass . . . . –Isaiah 44:13*

suburb
In the Bible, probably smaller villages dependent on a city. ◆ *From there he went to Gaza . . . and burned its suburbs with fire and plundered them.–1 Maccabees 11:61*

suet
The fat found around the kidneys and loins of cattle and sheep. ◆ *Aaron's sons the priests shall arrange the parts, with the head and the suet, on the wood that is on the fire on the altar . . . .–Leviticus 1:8*

swaddling band
Strips of cloth used to wrap a newborn infant in biblical times. ◆ *"Or who shut in the sea with doors when it burst out of the womb?—when I made the clouds its garment, and thick darkness its swaddling band . . . ."–Job 38:8–9*

swallow
A songbird from the family Hirundinedae. Swallows spend much of their time in the air hunting for insects.
◆ *Like a sparrow in its flitting, like a swallow in its flying, an undeserved curse goes nowhere.–Proverb 26:2*

tableland
Part of the Transjordanian plateau between the Arnon river valley and Heshbon. ◆ *So at that time we took . . . all the towns of the tableland, the whole of Gilead, and all of Bashan, as far as Salecah and Edrei, towns of Og's kingdom in Bashan. –Deuteronomy 3:8, 10*

talent
A measure of weight. It varied from Old Testament to New Testament times and was equal to about 66 to 90 pounds. In the New Testament, a talent was also a unit of currency. ◆ *It, and all these utensils, shall be made from a talent of pure gold. –Exodus 25:39*

tambourine
Percussion instrument used in celebrations; also called a timbrel. ◆ *Then the prophet Miriam, Aaron's sister, took a tambourine in her hand; and all the women went out after her with tambourines and with dancing. –Exodus 15:20*

Tartan
Title of an Assyrian army official. This position ranked second to the king.
◆ *The king of Assyria sent the Tartan, the Rabsaris, and the Rabshakeh with a great army from Lachish to King Hezekiah at Jerusalem . . . .–2 Kings 18:17*

taskmaster
An overseer in charge of a group or groups of laborers. The word is most frequently used in Exodus to refer to those who pressed the Israelites into forced labor at Pharaoh's bidding.
◆ *When King Rehoboam sent Adoram, who was taskmaster over the forced labor, all Israel stoned him to death. King Rehoboam then hurriedly mounted his chariot to flee to Jerusalem.–1 Kings 12:18*

taunt-song
A song of mockery. ◆ *I have become the laughingstock of all my people, the object of their taunt-songs all day long. –Lamentations 3:14*

Tebeth
The 10th month in the Jewish calendar, corresponding to parts of December and January. ◆ *When Esther was taken to King Ahasuerus in his royal palace in the tenth month, which is the month of Tebeth, he set the royal crown on her head and made her queen instead of Vashti.–Esther 2:16–17*

temple police
Probably the temple's watchmen, sentries, and guards of the treasures in the temple, presided over by the captain of the temple. ◆ *Then the captain went with the temple police and brought them, but without violence, for they were afraid of being stoned by the people.–Acts of the Apostles 5:26*

terrace
A raised level space; in the Bible, probably a row of olive trees. ◆ *". . . between their terraces they press out oil; they tread the wine presses, but suffer thirst."–Job 24:11*

thong
A strip of leather used to tie prisoners; a strap for sandals. ◆ *He proclaimed, "The one who is more powerful than I is coming after me; I am not worthy to stoop down and untie the thong of his sandals." –Mark 1:7*

thumbscrews
A torture instrument used to compress the thumbs. ◆ *When the guards had placed before them . . . braziers and thumbscrews and iron claws and wedges and bellows, the tyrant resumed speaking . . . .*–4 Maccabees 8:13

tiara
A decorative headdress. ◆ *. . . she fastened her hair with a tiara and put on a linen gown to beguile him.*–Judith 16:8

timbrel
A percussion instrument made of a round wooden frame, about 10 inches in diameter, covered with a stretched animal skin. It was often used by women to accompany singing and dancing. ◆ *Then Jephthah came to his home at Mizpah; and there was his daughter coming out to meet him with timbrels and with dancing.* –Judges 11:34

token portion
Part of a holy offering. ◆ *The priest shall remove from the grain offering its token portion and turn this into smoke on the altar, an offering by fire of pleasing odor to the* LORD. –Leviticus 2:9

tongs
A grasping tool made of gold for use in Solomon's temple, possibly to remove and replace the wicks in the lampstands. ◆ *So Solomon made all the things that were in the house of God . . . the flowers, the lamps, and the tongs, of purest gold . . . .* –2 Chronicles 4:19, 21

topaz
A mineral used as a gem. It usually appears in a yellow, red, blue, or green translucent or transparent quartz form. ◆ *The foundations of the wall of the city are adorned with every jewel; the first was jasper . . . the ninth topaz . . . .*–Revelation 21:19–20

torrent-bed
A wadi, or dry riverbed, which could become dangerous after a storm, when it might act as a sluice for rainwater. ◆ *"My companions are treacherous like a torrent-bed, like freshets that pass away . . . ."* –Job 6:15

tow
The highly flammable short fibers extracted from flax. ◆ *An assembly of the wicked is like a bundle of tow, and their end is a blazing fire.*–Ecclesiasticus 21:9

train
A procession; the hem of a garment; as a verb, to instuct or educate. ◆ *You ascended the high mount, leading captives in your train and receiving gifts from people . . . .* –Psalm 68:18

travail
Hard or painful work; in some translations, the labor pains of childbirth. ◆ *"Why then was I born? Or why did not my mother's womb become my grave, so that I would not see the travail of Jacob and the exhaustion of the people of Israel?"* –2 Esdras 5:35

treaty
An agreement or alliance between two nations; a type of covenant. ◆ *And Joshua made peace with them, guaranteeing their lives by a treaty . . . .*–Joshua 9:15

trellis
Lattice frame; in the Bible, probably carved woodwork around the entrance of the temple. ◆ *At the upper entrance they hacked the wooden trellis with axes.* –Psalm 74:5

trench
A long, narrow ditch dug in the ground. ◆ *Then he made a trench around the altar, large enough to contain two measures of seed.* –1 Kings 18:32

tribune
A high-ranking Roman military officer in charge of a unit of soldiers called a cohort. ◆ *When they saw the tribune and the soldiers, they stopped beating Paul.* –Acts of the Apostles 21:32

trigon
A type of lyre. ◆ *" . . . when you hear the sound of the horn, pipe, lyre, trigon, harp, drum, and entire musical ensemble, you are to fall down and worship the golden statue . . . ."*–Daniel 3:5

trireme
Ancient Greek galley ship that had three rows of oars. ◆ *So this money was intended by the sender for the sacrifice to Hercules, but by the decision of its carriers it was applied to the construction of triremes.* –2 Maccabees 4:20

trough
A long, shallow container for animal feed or water. ◆ *So she quickly emptied her jar into the trough and ran again to the well to draw, and she drew for all his camels.* –Genesis 24:20

trousers
In the book of Daniel, an article of clothing worn by the three Jews thrown into the furnace. The meaning of the original Aramaic is uncertain. ◆ *So the men were bound, still wearing their tunics, their trousers, their hats, and their other garments, and they were thrown into the furnace of blazing fire.*–Daniel 3:21

trowel
A small hand tool used for digging or for smoothing a wet material, such as plaster or mortar. ◆ *With your utensils you shall have a trowel; when you relieve yourself outside, you shall dig a hole with it and then cover up your excrement.*–Deuteronomy 23:13

tumors
Painful swellings, possibly associated with bubonic plague. ◆ *The hand of the* LORD *was heavy upon the people of Ashdod, and he terrified and struck them with tumors, both in Ashdod and in its territory.* –1 Samuel 5:6

turquoise
An opaque stone having a blue-green color; one of the stones in the high priest's breastpiece. ◆ *Edom did business with you because of your abundant goods; they exchanged for your wares turquoise . . . .* –Ezekiel 27:16

twilight
The period after sunset and before the full darkness of night; dusk. ◆ *In the first month, on the fourteenth day of the month, at twilight, there shall be a passover offering to the* LORD *. . . .*–Leviticus 23:5

ulcers
In the Bible, sores associated with one of the plagues of Egypt. ◆ *The* LORD *will afflict you with the boils of Egypt, with ulcers, scurvy, and itch, of which you cannot be healed.*–Deuteronomy 28:27

umpire
An impartial third party who acts as a mediator. ◆ *There is no umpire between us, who might lay his hand on us both.*–Job 9:33

undefiled
Uncorrupted or pure. ◆ *For it was fitting that we should have such a high priest, holy, blameless, undefiled, separated from sinners, and exalted above the heavens. –Hebrews 7:26*

undergird
To strengthen by passing a rope or chain underneath. ◆ *After hoisting it up they took measures to undergird the ship; then, fearing that they would run on the Syrtis, they lowered the sea anchor and so were driven. –Acts of the Apostles 27:17*

ungodliness
The quality of not following religious or moral laws; sinfulness. ◆ *And so all Israel will be saved; as it is written, "Out of Zion will come the Deliverer; he will banish ungodliness from Jacob."–Romans 11:26*

unknown god
An expression common in pagan inscriptions, often in the plural, used to express gratitude when a person had been favored by a god but did not know which one. ◆ *"For as I went through the city and looked carefully at the objects of your worship, I found among them an altar with the inscription, 'To an unknown god.'" –Acts of the Apostles 17:23*

untimely birth
A miscarriage or spontaneous abortion. In 1 Corinthians 15:8, Paul speaks of himself as being "untimely born" in a religious sense, perhaps referring to his sudden conversion. ◆ *Let them be like the snail that dissolves into slime; like the untimely birth that never sees the sun. –Psalm 58:8*

upbuilding
In the New Testament, a term used in letters to the early Christians, referring to the bolstering of a person's sense of self. ◆ *On the other hand, those who prophesy speak to other people for their upbuilding and encouragement and consolation. –1 Corinthians 14:3*

upper gate
A gate built by King Jotham of Judah, who reigned from 740 to 736 BC, for the temple at Jerusalem. ◆ *He built the upper gate of the house of the Lord, and did extensive building on the wall of Ophel. –2 Chronicles 27:3*

valet
A manservant who attends to the personal needs and the clothing of his employer; in the Bible, mentioned as an indication of King Solomon's prosperity. ◆ *When the queen of Sheba had observed all the wisdom of Solomon . . . and the attendance of his servants, their clothing, his valets, and his burnt offerings . . . there was no more spirit in her. –1 Kings 10:4–5*

vanguard
A military unit at the front of an advancing army. ◆ *"Although the LORD your God has given you this land to occupy, all your troops shall cross over armed as the vanguard of your Israelite kin."–Deuteronomy 3:18*

vapor
Water in the form of gas; a mist; used figuratively in Proverbs to indicate the evanescent quality of riches procured by deception. ◆ *The getting of treasures by a lying tongue is a fleeting vapor and a snare of death.–Proverbs 21:6*

vassal
A ruler subject to the authority of one more powerful; often a king who has been defeated but is still allowed to rule over his own people. ◆ *King Shalmaneser of Assyria came up against him; Hoshea became his vassal, and paid him tribute. –2 Kings 17:3*

vault
Arched ceiling; in the Bible, used figuratively for the apparent domelike shape of the sky or heavens. ◆ *The new moon, as its name suggests, renews itself; how marvelous it is in this change, a beacon to the hosts on high, shining in the vault of the heavens! –Ecclesiasticus 43:8*

vermilion
A bright red-orange pigment obtained from red ocher. It was used for painting palace walls and bas reliefs. ◆ *Woe to him who builds his house by unrighteousness, and his upper rooms by injustice . . . who says, "I will build myself a spacious house with large upper rooms," and who cuts out windows for it, paneling it with cedar, and painting it with vermilion.–Jeremiah 22:13–14*

vestibule
The first room of Solomon's temple, also called the porch or portico. ◆ *The vestibule in front of the nave of the house was twenty cubits wide, across the width of the house.–1 Kings 6:3*

vestments
Special items of clothing, particularly those worn by a priest. ◆ *You shall make sacred vestments for the glorious adornment of your brother Aaron.–Exodus 28:2*

vial
A small vessel used to hold oil or perfume. ◆ *Samuel took a vial of oil and poured it on his head, and kissed him; he said, "The LORD has anointed you ruler over his people Israel."–1 Samuel 10:1*

violet
A reddish-purple color obtained from mollusks. ◆ *And he encircled him . . . with the sacred vestment, of gold and violet and purple, the work of an embroiderer . . . . –Ecclesiasticus 45:9–10*

virtue
A quality considered desirable in a person, such as courage, justice, self-control, and balanced judgment, as defined by Platonism and Stoicism. ◆ *For reason is the guide of the virtues, but over the emotions it is sovereign. –4 Maccabees 1:30*

visitation
A time when God is present on earth. ◆ *Lo, heaven and the highest heaven, the abyss and the earth, tremble at his visitation! –Ecclesiasticus 16:18*

votive offering
A sacrifice associated with keeping a vow. ◆ *But if the sacrifice you offer is a votive offering or a freewill offering, it shall be eaten on the day that you offer your sacrifice, and what is left of it shall be eaten the next day . . . .–Leviticus 7:16*

vulture
Any of various large carrion-eating birds belonging to the families Accipitridae and Cathartidae; considered unclean by the Israelites. ◆ *"Wherever the corpse is, there the vultures will gather." –Matthew 24:28*

wagon
A wheeled vehicle drawn by one or more animals. It is also called a cart. ◆ *They brought their offerings before the LORD, six covered wagons and twelve oxen, a wagon for every two of the leaders, and for each one an ox; they presented them before the tabernacle.–Numbers 7:3*

waistcloth
An undergarment made of cloth and worn around the loins. ◆ *"He looses the sash of kings, and binds a waistcloth on their loins."–Job 12:18*

walk
In the Bible, a word often used figuratively to mean "live." ◆ *For all the peoples walk, each in the name of its god, but we will walk in the name of the LORD our God forever and ever.–Micah 4:5*

wand
A lightweight, slender rod or staff that was carried in the hand. Ivy-wreathed wands were often carried during processions for the Greek god Dionysus; in the books of Judith and 2 Maccabees, Jews used them to celebrate and offer thanks to their God. ◆ *She took ivy-wreathed wands in her hands and distributed them to the women who were with her . . . . –Judith 15:12*

watch
One of the divisions of the night. The Israelites divided the night into three watches, and the Greco-Roman world divided it into four. ◆ *At the morning watch the LORD in the pillar of fire and cloud looked down upon the Egyptian army, and threw the Egyptian army into panic. –Exodus 14:24*

water hen
In the Bible, perhaps a bird belonging to the rail family. Such birds frequent marshes and lakes. ◆ *But these are the ones that you shall not eat . . . the little owl and the great owl, the water hen and the desert owl . . . .–Deuteronomy 14:12, 16–17*

water of rebirth
The rite of baptism. ◆ *. . . he saved us, not because of any works of righteousness that we had done, but according to his mercy, through the water of rebirth and renewal by the Holy Spirit.–Titus 3:5*

waterskins
Animal skins used to hold water. ◆ *"Who has the wisdom to number the clouds? Or who can tilt the waterskins of the heavens?" –Job 38:37*

wayfarer
A traveler, especially one on foot. Wayfarers were often dependent on the hospitality of strangers. ◆ *When the old man looked up and saw the wayfarer in the open square of the city, he said, "Where are you going and where do you come from?" –Judges 19:17*

weasel
A small, carnivorous mammal belonging to the family Mustelidae and the genus *Mustela*; considered unclean by the Israelites. ◆ *These are unclean for you among the creatures that swarm upon the earth: the weasel, the mouse, the great lizard according to its kind . . . .–Leviticus 11:29*

web
A spider's web; also the woven portion of a cloth while it is on a loom. ◆ *So while he slept, Delilah took the seven locks of his head and wove them into the web, and made them tight with the pin.–Judges 16:14*

whale
A sea mammal. Several species live in the Mediterranean and Red seas, including the humpback and fin whales. Dolphins, their close relatives, are also native to these waters. ◆ *Bless the LORD, you whales and all that swim in the waters; sing praise to him and highly exalt him forever.–Prayer of Azariah 57*

whitewash
A soluble liquid coating made with lime and used to whiten a surface. ◆ *I will break down the wall that you have smeared with whitewash . . . . –Ezekiel 13:14*

whoredom
Immorality, especially of a sexual nature. ◆ *For the spirit of whoredom is within them, and they do not know the LORD.–Hosea 5:4*

willow
A tree belonging to the genus *Salicaceae* that usually grows close to water. It is also called a poplar. ◆ *The lotus trees cover it for shade; the willows of the wadi surround it. –Job 40:22*

wily
Full of guile or trickery. ◆ *He takes the wise in their own craftiness; and the schemes of the wily are brought to a quick end. –Job 5:13*

winebibbers
People who drink wine, especially to excess. ◆ *Do not be among winebibbers, or among gluttonous eaters of meat . . . . –Proverbs 23:20*

wreath
A circular ornament; a circular crown formed from the vines, flowers, leaves, or branches of a plant. ◆ *Athletes exercise self-control in all things; they do it to receive a perishable wreath, but we an imperishable one. –1 Corinthians 9:25*

yeast
A small fungus used to leaven bread or to ferment beverages. ◆ *He told them another parable: "The kingdom of heaven is like yeast that a woman took and mixed in with three measures of flour until all of it was leavened."–Matthew 13:33*

Ziv
The second month in the Jewish calendar, corresponding to parts of April and May. After the Babylonian exile, it was known as Iyyar. ◆ *In the fourth year the foundation of the house of the LORD was laid, in the month of Ziv.–1 Kings 6:37*

Credits

Illustrations, Maps, and Charts

Gary Aagaard 86, 277
Patrizia Bove 80, 312
Bill Farnsworth 307, 334–335, 367
Howard Friedman 14, 20, 64, 81, 208, 289
H. Tom Hall 262–263
Joe Le Monnier 15, 107, 125, 207, 241, 302
Albert Lorenz 26–27, 180–181, 342–343
Christopher Magadini 34–35, 57, 116–117, 146–147, 211, 232–233, 256–257, 282, 331, 374–375
Jose Miralles 16, 62–63, 93, 164, 224–225, 318–319
Gabriel Picart 97, 190–191
Ray Skibinski 226
Dahl Taylor 128, 171, 363
Richard Williams 66–67, 136–137, 198–199, 294–295, 348–349

Photographs

ABBREVIATIONS

Al	Alinari, Rome
AR	Art Resource, New York
BAL	The Bridgeman Art Library, London
BM	Copyright British Museum
ETA	E.T. Archive, London
DH	David Harris, Jerusalem
EL	Photography by Erich Lessing
GC	The Granger Collection, New York
Gi	Giraudon, Paris
IAA	Israel Antiquities Authority
IDAM	Israel Department of Antiquities and Museums
IMJ	Israel Museum, Jerusalem
Lo	Musée du Louvre, Paris
MMA	All Rights Reserved, The Metropolitan Museum of Art, New York
NGS	National Geographic Society
PML	Pierpont Morgan Library, New York
REHM	Reuben and Edith Hecht Museum, University of Haifa
RN	Richard T. Nowitz
Sc	Scala, Rome
SH	Sonia Halliday Photographs
SH & LL	Sonia Halliday and Laura Lushington
SS	Superstock, Inc.
ZR	Zev Radovan, Jerusalem

Pages: 2 Illustration by Tom McNeely © NGS. **6** *Left-center* Dr. Richard Cleave/Pictorial Archive. *Bottom-right* Statue by Tito Sarrochi; Cappella Pozzesi, Siena, Italy; Al/AR. *Center* PML, *(detail)* M.619, recto/AR. *Top-right* Dave G. Houser. *Top-center* Reed Holmes/Holmes Photography. *Bottom-left (detail)* Armenian Patriarchate, Jerusalem © DH. **7** *Top* Museo Archaeologico Nazionale, Naples; Sc/AR. *Bottom-right* PML, M.639, f.294/AR. *Center-left* Bibliothèque Mazarine, Paris/Dennise Bourbonnais. **8** *Top-center* Collection of the IAA; Exhibited IMJ/Photo: ZR. *Bottom* Detail of a painting by Josef Molar; National Gallery Budapest; ETA/SS. **9** *Top-right* Dr. David Darom. **10** *Top-left* SS. **11** *Bottom* PML, M.730, f.109v/AR. **12** *Bottom-right* National Museum, Aleppo, Syria; EL/AR. *Bottom-left* IMJ. **13** *Bottom-right* DH. *Top* IMJ (IDAM); EL/AR. **14** *Bottom-center* Rendering from a photo by Adam Woolfitt/Woodfin Camp & Associates, Inc. *Top* Detail of a painting by Thomas Matthews Rooke; Tate Gallery, London/AR. **17** *Top-right* IMJ © DH. *Left* Detail of painting by Fra Bartolemeo; Pinacoteca, Lucca, Italy; Sc/AR. **18** *Bottom-left* BM. **19** *Top right* PML, M.43, f.27v/AR. *Bottom-left* The Bible Lands Museum, Jerusalem © DH. **20** *Bottom-right* PML, M.700, f.1v/AR. *Inset* Nahsholim Museum, Kibutz Nahsholim © DH. **21** *Top-center* Detail of an engraving by Julius Schnorr von Carolsfeld; Foto Marburg/AR. **22** *Top-center* Collection of the IAA/Photo: the Estate of Yigael Yadin. **23** *Top-left* Painting by Eugene Burnand, Musée d'Orsay, Paris, Gi/AR. *Center* Litchfield Cathedral, England/SH & LL. **24** *Center* REHM; EL/AR. *Bottom-center* IMJ. *Bottom-left* Collection of the IAA; Exhibited IMJ/ZR. **25** *Top* Paolo Matthaie/Missione Archeologica Italiana A Ebla, Syria. **28** *Bottom-left (detail)* BM; EL/AR. **29** *Top-left* Photo by Joseph Parnell, Jewish Museum, New York/AR. **30** *Bottom-right* Hebrew Union College; Jewish Institute of Religion/ZR. *Top-center* Pskov School, Museum of History, Russia/SS. **31** *Bottom-right* Musée Antoine Vivenel, Compiègne, France, EL/AR. **32** *Top-left* Detail of a painting by James J. Tissot, Jewish Museum, New York/SS. **33** *Bottom-right* ZR. *Top-center* IMJ. **34** *Top-center* BM; EL/AR. **36** *Top-center* BM/Michael Holford. **37** *Bottom-right* RN. **38** *Bottom-center* Garo Nalbandian. *Bottom-center* Detail of painting by Domenico Ghirlandajo; Lo; EL/AR. **39** *Top-right* BM. **40** *Center* IMJ; EL/AR. **41** *Top-left* Collection of IAA; Exhibited and photographed IMJ. *Bottom-right* Collection of the IAA; Exhibited and photographed IMJ. **42** *Top-center* Iraq Museum, Baghdad; EL/AR. *Bottom-left* BM. **43** *Bottom-left* PML/AR. **44** *Left* ZR. *Bottom-right* Painting by Tom Lovell © NGS. **45** *Top-center* Museo Ostiense, Ostia, Italy; EL/AR. **46** *Bottom-center* IMJ. **47** *Top-left* Nik Wheeler. **48** *Top-left* Detail of a painting by Frank W.W.

Topham/Mary Evans Picture Library. **49** *Bottom-right* Gil Yarom. *Inset* Beth Yigal Allon. **50** *Top* Museum of Navarra, Pamplona, Spain; MMA. **53** *Top-center* IMJ. *Bottom-center* Museum Ha'aretz, Tel Aviv/Daniel Blatt. **54** *Bottom-left* BM. *Bottom-center* DH/IMJ. **55** *Top-left (detail)* Yoram Lehmann/IMJ. *Bottom-right* Painting by Antoine Coypel; Lo; EL/AR. **56** *Left* Museum of Antiquities of the University and Society of Antiquaries of Newcastle Upon Tyne. **58** *Left* IMJ (IDAM); EL/AR. *Top* Hubertus Kanus/Photo Researchers, Inc. **59** *Bottom-right* National Museum, Aleppo, Syria; EL/AR. **60** *Center* REHM; EL/AR. **61** *Top-right (detail)* GC. *Bottom-left* Garo Nalbandian. **62** *Top-center* Collection of IAA; Exhibited and photographed IMJ. **64** *Top-right* DH. **65** *Bottom* Robert Frerck/Woodfin Camp & Associates, Inc. **68** *Bottom-right* ZR. *Center (detail)* Victor Boswell, Jr. © NGS. **69** *Top-center* RN. *Bottom-right* DH/IMJ. **70** *Bottom-center* BM. **71** *Top-left* Lo; EL/AR. **72** *Top-left (detail)* Lo; EL/AR. **73** *Right* Courtesy of Hunt Institute for Botanical Documentation, Carnegie Mellon University, Pittsburgh. *Bottom-left* EL/AR. **74** *Center* The National Gallery, London. **75** *Top-left* Duby Tal; Moni Haramati/Albatross Aerial Photography. **76** *Center-left* Duby Tal; Moni Haramati/Albatross Aerial Photography. **77** *Top-left* PML, M.644, f.115v/AR. *Bottom-center* IAA. *Bottom-right* DH. **78** *Left* IAA © Israel Exploration Society. *Bottom-center* IAA. **79** *Top-right* The Bible Lands Museum, Jerusalem/DH. *Left-center* Egyptian Museum, Cairo/ETA. **80** *Center-left* ZR. **81** *Top* Donna Carroll/Travel Stock. **82** *Top-right* Kunsthistorisches Museum, Vienna; EL/AR. **83** *Center* SH. **84** *Bottom-right* Painting by Hildesheim, Niedersachsisches Museum/ETA. **85** *Top-center* SH. *Bottom-right* Collection of IAA; Exhibited & photographed IMJ. **87** *Top-right* Lo/BAL. **88** *Top-left* F.H.C. Birch/SH. **89** *Bottom-right* Detail of a painting by Giambattista Tiepolo; Archbishopric, Udine, Venetia, Italy; M. Magliani/SS. **90** *Bottom-center* PML, M.302, f.1/AR. **91** *Left* Kunsthistorisches Museum, Vienna; EL/AR. *Top-left* Kunsthistorisches Museum, Vienna; EL/AR. **92** *Bottom-left* IMJ/IDAM © DH. *Top-right* PML, M.50, f.30/AR. **94** *Top-right* Garo Nalbandian. *Inset* RN. *Left-center* IAA. **95** *Bottom-right* IMJ (IDAM); EL/AR. **96** *Top-left* University of Pennsylvania Museum (neg. # T4-625c.2). **98** *Top-left* Detail of a painting by Simeon Solomon/BAL. **99** *Center-right* "The Last Judgment" window by Hans Acker/SH. **100** *Bottom-center* Nachum Slapak/IMJ. **102** *Bottom-right* Shai Ginott. **103** *Top-left* Sc/AR. **104** *Top-right* DH. *Bottom-center* Ashmolean Museum, Oxford. **105** *Right* Mike Newton/Robert Harding Picture Library. **106** *Top* Sheffield City Art Galleries/BAL. **108** *Center* BM/Ronald Sheridan, Ancient Art & Architecture Collection. *Top* IAA. **109** *Bottom* BM/ETA. **110** *Top* Nik Wheeler/Black Star. **111** *Bottom-center (detail)* Bibliothèque Nationale, Paris; BAL/SS. **112** *Top-left* Painting by Menabuoi, Baptistry of the Cathedral, Padua, Italy/SS. *Bottom-right* Garo Nalbandian. **113** *Top* Cathedral, Monreale, Italy; Sc/AR. **114** *Top-center* PML, M.338, f.160V/AR. **115** *Top-left* Adam Woolfitt/Woodfin Camp & Associates, Inc. **118** *Top-center* IMJ. *Right* IMJ (IDAM); EL/AR. **119** *Top-center* ZR. **120** *Bottom-left* IMJ. **121** *Top-right* Egyptian Museum, Cairo; Victor R. Boswell, Jr. © NGS. *Right-center* SH. *Bottom-left* Detail of a Gustave Doré engraving; GC. **122** *Top-center* Kunsthistorisches Museum, Vienna; EL/AR. **123** *Bottom-center* ZR. **124** *Top-center* Detail of a painting by Theodore Chasseriau; Musée du Petit Palais, Paris; Gi/AR. **126** *Bottom-right* Detail from Beno Elkan menorah; ZR. **127** *Top* Wolfson Museum of Jewish Art/DH. **129** *Top* Lo; EL/AR. **130** *Left* RN. **131** *Top-left* Trinity window, Litchfield Cathedral, England/SH & LL. **133** *Left* Tel Miqne-Ekron Excavations; Photographer I. Sztulman. **134** *Top-right* F.H.C. Birch/SH. **135** *Center* ZR. **138** *Bottom-left* Collection of IAA; Exhibited and photographed IMJ. *Top* ZR. **139** *Bottom-center* SH. **140** *Top-left* Museo Egizio, Turin, Italy; SEF/AR. *Bottom* Dom St. Mauritius und Catharina, Magdeburg, Germany; Foto Marburg/AR. *Left-center* ZR. **141** *Center* BM/ZR. **142** *Bottom-right* Detail of a painting by Sir Edward Poynter; BAL/AR. **143** *Top-right* Dudu Netah; Moni Haramati/Albatross Aerial Photography. **144** *Top-right* ZR. **145** *Bottom-left* Dr. David Darom. **148** *Top-center* Gift of Mr. T. Kollek, Photo: DH/IMJ. **149** *Bottom-right* Russ Busby. *Center* Collection of IAA, Photo: DH/IMJ. *Right* Collection of IAA, Photo: DH/IMJ. **150** *Center* Detail of a painting by Emile Semenowsky; Whitford & Hughes, London/BAL. **151** *Bottom-right* Robert Frerck/Woodfin Camp & Associates, Inc. **152** *Bottom-center* Musée des Beaux-Arts, Lyon, France; Kavaler/AR. *Top-left* Rod Williams/Bruce Coleman Inc. **153** *Bottom-right* The Rockefeller Museum, Jerusalem/ZR. **154** *Bottom-right* Painting by Andrea del Castagno, "The Youthful David," Widener Collection, © 1996 Board of Trustees, National Gallery of Art, Washington. **155** *Top-center* REHM/ZR. *Top-right* ZR. **156** *Left* The Anastasis; Kariye Camii, Istanbul/SH. **157** *Bottom-left* The Shelby White and Leon Levy Collection. Photograph by Sheldan Comfert Collins; MMA. **158** *Left* ZR. *Bottom-left* REHM; EL/AR. **159** *Left* Iraq Museum, Baghdad; EL/AR. **160** *Left* Illuminaton by Jean Fouquet; Bibliothèque Nationale de France. **161** *Bottom-left* Werner Braun. *Bottom-right* Collection of IAA, Photo: DH/IMJ. **162** *Top-center* Gift of Mr. T. Kollek; Photo: DH/IMJ. **163** *Bottom-left* ZR. **165** *Top* DH. **166** *Bottom* Bibliothèque Municipale, Dijon, France; Ms132,f.2v; Gi/AR. *Top-center* The Shrine of the Book, IMJ/DH. **167** *Center* DH/IMJ. **168** *Center* Collection of the IAA, IMJ/ZR. **169** *Top* Jewish Museum, NY/SS. *Bottom-left* BM. **170** *Left* Yossi Eshbol. **172** *Bottom* IMJ/IDAM ©DH. **173** *Center-right* IMJ. *Top-left* PML; M.945, f.168v/AR. **174** *Left* ZR. **175** *Top* RN. **176** *Top-left* Detail of a painting by Edward Steinle/SS. **177** *Top-center* MS Ashmole 1511 fol.75 Verso; Bodleian Library, University of Oxford. *Bottom-right* ZR. **178** *Bottom* REHM;

EL/AR. **179** *Top-center* Detail of a painting by Francesco Brizio; Al/SEAT/AR. **182** *Center* Relief by Andrea Pisano; Museo dell'Opera del Duomo, Florence; Sc/AR. **183** *Top* BM. **184** *Bottom-left* ZR. *Right* Botanical by Haynes/ETA. **185** *Top-left* Collection of IAA; Exhibited and photographed IMJ. **186** *Top-right* Tretyakov Gallery, Moscow; Beniaminson/AR. **187** *Right* By Nicholas of Verdun; Sammlungen Stiftes, Klosterneuburg, Austria; EL/AR. *Bottom-left* BM/Michael Holford. **188** *Bottom-left* Lo; EL/AR. *Center-left* The Schoyen Collection MS 1655/2. **189** *Top-left* IAA. *Bottom-left* Dr. David Darom. **192** *Top-center* SH & LL. *Bottom-right* MMA, Rogers Fund, 1960. (60.145.11). **193** *Center* Yossi Eshbol. **194** *Top-center* Detail of a painting by Gregorio Pagani; Kunsthistoriches Museum, Vienna; EL/AR. *Right* Collection of IDAM, Rockefeller Museum, Jerusalem; EL/AR. **195** *Bottom-right* British Library, London; Bridgeman Art Library/AR. **196** *Bottom* Cathedral, Ravello, Italy; Sc/AR. **200** *Bottom-right* Detail of a painting by Cristofano Allori; Galleria Palatina, Florence; Al/AR. *Top-left* GC. **201** *Inset* ZR. *Center* ZR. **202** CL PML, M.619 f.1v/AR. **203** *Bottom (detail)* MMA, Gift of J.P. Morgan, 1916. (16.32.288). **204** *Top-center* BM/ZR. *Right* Lo; EL/AR. *Bottom-left* Dagon Museum, Haifa, Israel; EL/AR. **205** *Top-center* DH. *Bottom-right* Darmstadt Museum/SH & LL. **206** *Top-left* Detail of a window by Joshua Price, Great Whitley Church, England/SH & LL. **207** *Bottom* ZR. **209** *Bottom-right* ZR. **210** *Left* Musée Condé, Chantilly, France; Gi/BAL. **212** *Top-right* ZR. **213** *Top* Collection of the IAA; The Shrine of the Book, D. Samuel and Jeane H. Gottesman Center for Biblical Manuscripts/IMJ. *Top-center* ZR. **214** *Right* SH. *Top* Sc/AR. **215** *Bottom-center* IAA © DH. **216** *Top* Museo Archeologico Nazionale, Naples; EL/AR. **217** *Bottom* ZR. **218** *Center* Detail of a painting by Joseph-Marie Vien; Musée des Beaux-Arts de Nantes, Nantes, France; Gi/AR. **219** *Right* Detail of a watercolor by William Blake; GC. *Top-center* BM. **220** *Left-center* BM. **221** *Top-right* BAL. *Bottom* Painting by Evelyn de Morgan, The De Morgan Foundation, London/BAL. **222** *Top* Painting by Thomas Matthews Rooke; Russell-Cotes Art Gallery and Museum, Bournemouth, England/BAL. **223** *Bottom-left* "Cain" by Domenico Trentacoste; Galleria Nazionale d'Arte Moderna, Rome; Al/AR. *Top-center* GC. **227** *Bottom-center* Museum Ha'aretz, Tel Aviv/Daniel Blatt. *Top-center* Nik Wheeler/Black Star. **228** *Top-right* ZR. **229** *Bottom* Masada Excavations/ZR. **230** *Left* Musée de la Civilisation, Paris; Gi/BAL. *Top-right* Wadsworth Atheneum, Hartford. Bequest of Mrs. Clara Hinton Gould. **231** *Bottom-right* Painting by Ferdinand Hodler; Christies, London/BAL. **234** *Center* Relief by Andrea Pisano; Baptistry, Florence; Sc/AR. **235** *Top-right* Museo Egizio, Turin, Italy; Werner Forman Archive/AR. **236** *Top-right* Logge, Vatican Palace, Vatican State; Sc/AR. **237** *Bottom* Bijbels Museum, Amsterdam. *Right* IMJ; EL/AR. **238** *Top-left* IMJ; EL/AR. *Center-right* IMJ. *Bottom-left* IMJ. *Left-center* IMJ. *Center-left* IMJ. *Top-right* DH/IMJ. *Left-center* IMJ. *Center-right* DH/IMJ. *Bottom-right* IMJ. *Bottom-left* Photo: DH/IMJ. *Bottom-right* DH/IMJ. **239** *Center-right* Aleppo Museum, Syria/ETA. *Top-left* Scrovegni Chapel, Padua, Italy/BAL. **240** *Right* Window by Edward Burne-Jones/SH & LL. *Bottom-left* Collection of IAA; Exhibited IMJ © DH. **242** *Bottom-center* Lo; EL/AR. **243** *Center-left* Musée Romain de Vidy, Lausanne, Switzerland/Photothèque André Held. *Top-center* EL/AR. **244** *Center-left* Courtesy of Hunt Institute for Botanical Documentation, Carnegie Mellon University, Pittsburgh. **245** *Top-left (detail)* M. Caine/The Shrine of the Book, IMJ. *Bottom-right (detail)* "Commentary on the Apocalypse" by Beatus de Liebana; M.644, f.4v; PML, NY/AR. **246** *Top* Painting by Luca Signorelli; Lo; EL/AR. **247** *Bottom-left* Armenian Patriarchate, Jerusalem; Julba Bible, MS. 973 © DH. *Center-right* GC. **248** *Bottom-left* Detail from Beno Elkan menorah/ZR. **249** *Bottom-center* Dr. David Darom. *Top* Laura Zito/Photo Researchers, Inc. **250** *Top* ZR. **251** *Top-right* Detail of a Gustave Doré engraving; GC. *Bottom-center* IMJ. **252** *Center-right* Collection of IAA; Photo: Avraham Hay/IMJ. **253** *Top-right* Detail of a painting by Andrea Celesti; Palazzo Ducale, Venice; Cameraphoto/AR. *Bottom-center* Collection of IAA; Photo: Yoram Lehmann/IMJ. **254** *Bottom-left* Rijksmuseum van Oudheden, Leiden, Netherlands; EL/AR. **255** *Top-left* DH/IMJ. **256** *Left* Painting by John Metropolitos; Gallery of Art, Skopje, Macedonia; Gi/AR. *Bottom-right* SH. **258** *Bottom-left* Eitan Simanor/ASAP, Ltd. **259** *Bottom* REHM; EL/AR. *Top-right* Daniel Blatt. **260** *Bottom* ETA. **261** *Top* Garo Nalbandian/ASAP, Ltd. *Top-center (detail)* IAA. **264** *Top-center* Window by Burlinson & Gryles; St. Nicholas' Church, Buckinghamshire, England/SH & LL. *Bottom* Rockefeller Museum, Collection of IAA; Photo: Yoram Lehmann/IMJ. **266** *Center-left* GC. **267** *Top-left* ZR. *Bottom-center* ZR. **268** *Top-right* The Pontifical of Winchester, Ms. 369, fol.20 v; Bibliothèque Municipale, Rouen, France; Gi/AR. **269** *Bottom-center* Collection of IAA; Photo: DH/IMJ. **270** *Center* IMJ. **271** *Bottom-right* Museo del Duomo, Siena, Italy; Photo Nimatallah/AR. **272** *Top* Tony Gervis F.R.P.S./Robert Harding Picture Library. *Bottom-center* IAA. **273** *Top-left* ZR. *Bottom-right* ZR. **274** *Top* N.A. Callow/Robert Harding Picture Library. **275** *Center* BM/ZR. *Bottom-right* Detail from Sarajevo Haggadah/ZR. **276** *Bottom-center* Lo; EL/AR. **278** *Top-left* BM/ZR. *Right* IMJ. **279** *Top-left* Max Richardson. **280** *Top-center* ZR. *Bottom* DH. **281** *Top-right* Scrovegni Chapel, Padua, Italy/ETA. **283** *Top-center* Detail from San Zeno Altarpiece; Musée des Beaux-Arts, Tours, France; Gi/AR. **284** *Left* Painting by Pietro Perugino; Galleria Nazionale dell'Umbria, Perugia, Italy; Sc/AR. **285** *Bottom-left* BLMJ Borowski Collection/ZR. *Top-right* SH. **286** *Bottom* Painting by Antonio Balestra; Civicche Racc Verona Castellvecchio/ETA. **287** *Center* Arnstein Bible,

Harley 2799 fol. 57v., By permission of The British Library. **288** *Top* Duby Tal; Moni Haramati/Albatross Aerial Photography. **289** *Top-left* DH/IMJ. **290** *Bottom* Doug Armand/Tony Stone Images. **292** *Top-center* The Moussaieff Collection, London. **293** *Center-left* Window by Gabriel Loire, Coignieres Church, France/SH&LL. *Bottom* Doron Horowitz/Nature Reserve Authority, Israel. **296** *Bottom-left* PML, M. 709, f.1v/AR. *Top* Daniel Blatt. **297** *Bottom* BM/BAL. **298** *Top-center* RN. **299** *Bottom-right* PML, M.644, f.87/AR. **300** *Top-center* Winchester Bible, folio 270v./BAL. *Bottom-right* Lo; EL/AR. *Bottom-center* Lo; EL/AR. **301** *Top-right* EL/AR. **303** *Bottom-center* Werner Braun. **304** *Top-left* IMJ. *Right* Collection of IAA/ Exhibited and photographed IMJ. **305** *Top-left* Gil Yarom. *Bottom-center* The Moussaieff Collection, London. **306** *Top (detail)* IAA. **308** *Top-center* Benaki Museum, Athens/AR. *Bottom* Garo Nalbandian. **310** *Center* Courtesy of the REHM/ZR. **311** *Top* ZR. **312** *Top-left* Collection of IAA/Exhibited and photographed IMJ. *Bottom-right* Lo; Photo: H. Lewandowski; © Réunion des Musées Nationaux Agence Photographique, Paris. **313** *Center* Itsik Marom. **314** *Left* Garo Nalbandian. **315** *Right* DH. *Top-center (detail)* PML, M.250, f.62v/AR. **316** *Top* Arquivo Nacional da Torre do Tombo; Gi/AR. **317** *Bottom-left* Garo Nalbandian/ ASAP, Ltd. **319** *Bottom* Collection of IAA; Photo: Avi Hay/ IMJ. **320** *Top-right* RN. **321** *Center* Detail of cover to the Lorsca Gospels, Mus. no. 138-1868; Courtesy of the Trustess of the Victoria & Albert Museum. **322** *Center* The Bible Lands Museum, Jerusalem © DH. **323** *Top-left* Museo dell'Opera del Duomo, Florence; Sc/AR. *Bottom-right* IMJ, The Shrine of the Book, D. Samuel and Jeane H. Gottesman Center for Biblical Manuscripts. **324** *Center* Lo/BAL. **325** *Top-left (detail)* ETA. *Bottom-right* EL/AR. **326** *Top-left* Gil Yarom. *Bottom-center* BM. **327** *Bottom* Lo; Gi/AR. **328** *Top-left* By permission of the estate of Zeev Raban Shir Ha'shirim/IMJ. **329** *Top* Tom Till. **330** *Top-right* Shai Ginott. *Bottom-center* DH. *Top-left* Itsik Marom. **332** *Bottom* Sc/AR. **333** *Top-left* RN. *Bottom-center* The Egyptian Museum, Cairo; photo courtesy of Kodansha Ltd. **335** *Bottom-center* Museo Egizio, Turin, Italy; EL/AR. **336** *Top* SS. *Bottom-right* Victor R. Boswell, Jr., © NGS. **337** *Bottom-center* National Museum, Damascus; EL/AR. **338** *Bottom-right* Duby Tal; Moni Haramati/Albatross Aerial Photography **339** *Top-center* © The Jerusalem Publishing House; photo Moshe Caine. **340** *Bottom* C. M. Dixon. **341** *Top-center* Sculpture by Jules Butansky; Courtesy of the Library of The Jewish Theological Seminary of America. **344** *Top-right* Musée Condé, Chantilly, France, Ms.139, ex.1363, f.14v; Gi/AR. *Bottom* DH. **346** *Top-center* Itamar Grinberg/Visual Photo Library, Tel Aviv. *Bottom-right* Central Synagogue, London/SH & LL. **347** *Top* SH & LL. **350** *Bottom-left* Museum Ha'aretz/Daniel Blatt. *Top-right* Detail of Vyner Memorial Window by Edward Burne-Jones; Christ Church, Oxford/SH & LL. **351** *Bottom-right* Painting by Bernardo Strozzi; Hermitage, St. Petersburg/BAL. **352** *Bottom-center* IMJ/IDAM © DH. *Center-left* Detail of a painting by Hendrick van Cleve; Galerie de Jonckheere, Paris/BAL. **353** *Top-right* Werner Braun. **354** *Top-right* Psalter of Ingeburg of Denmark; Musée Condé, Chantilly, France/BAL. **355** *Bottom* ZR. **356** *Top* BM/ZR. *Left* Basilica Aquileia, Italy/ETA. **358** *Bottom* ZR. *Top-center* Lo; EL/AR. **359** *Bottom-right* RN. **360** *Bottom-center* RN. *Top-right* SH. **361** *Top-right* Russ Busby. **362** *Top-left* Gil Yarom. **364** *Top-center* Studium Biblicum Franciscanum, Jerusalem; EL/AR. **365** *Bottom-center* BM/AR. **366** *Top-left* ZR. **368** *Center (detail)* Sc/AR. **369** *Bottom-left* Armenian Patriarchate, Jerusalem; Istanbul Bible © DH. **370** *Bottom* BM. *Right-center* BM. *Bottom-left* Iraq Museum, Baghdad; EL/AR. *Left/right* Lo; EL/AR. *Center-left* BM. *Center* ZR. *Right* DH. **371** *Top-right* Duby Tal; Moni Haramati/Albatross Aerial Photography. *Center* RN. **372** *Top-center* Anagni Cathederal, Italy/ETA. *Bottom* Iraq Museum, Baghdad; Sc/AR. **376** *Bottom-center* Museum Ha'aretz, Tel Aviv/Daniel Blatt. *Top-right* Biblioteca Marciana, Venice/BAL. **377** *Top-right (detail)* The Collection of the J. Paul Getty Museum, Malibu, CA/BAL. **378** *Bottom* Photo: Mike Smith, The Oriental Museum, Durham University, England. **379** *Top-center* Sc/AR. **380** *Left* Courtesy of Hunt Institute for Botanical Documentation, Carnegie Mellon University, Pittsburgh. *Bottom* National Archaeological Museum, Athens/BAL. *Top-right* Detail of a painting by Louis de Caullery; Rafael Valls Gallery, London/BAL. **382** *Top-right* The Bible Lands Society. *Center-left* Museum of Oriental Antiquities, Istanbul; EL/AR. **383** *Bottom* The Fine Art Society, London/BAL.

Acknowledgments

Staff of Art Resource, New York. Photo Department of Biblical Archaeology Review, Washington, DC. David Harris, Jerusalem. Staff of Photographic Archives of the Israel Antiquities Authority. Staff of Photographic Services, The Israel Museum, Jerusalem. Jerry L. Kearns. Irene Lewitt, Photo Research Consultant, Jerusalem.

INDEX

A

B

Page numbers in **bold** type refer to illustrations, and page numbers in *italic* refer to cross-references within other entries.

D

E

F

Page numbers in **bold** type refer to illustrations, and page numbers in *italic* refer to cross-references within other entries.

G

H

Page numbers in **bold** type refer to illustrations, and page numbers in *italic* refer to cross-references within other entries.

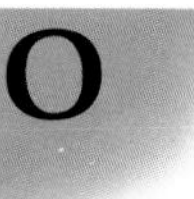

Page numbers in **bold** type refer to illustrations, and page numbers in *italic* refer to cross-references within other entries.

Page numbers in **bold** type refer to illustrations, and page numbers in *italic* refer to cross-references within other entries.